Bishop

Present and Future

Martin Davie

GILEAD
B O O K S
PUBLISHING

To Sarah, who loves books.

This one is for you for when you are older.

GileadBooksPublishing.com

First published in Great Britain, August 2022
2 4 6 8 10 9 7 5 3 1

Copyright ©Martin Davie 2022
British Library Cataloguing-in-Publication Data:
A catalogue record for this book is available from the British Library.

ISBN: 978-1-8381828-3-0

Indexer: Wendy Baskett
Cover design: Nathan Ward

Contents

Introduction

It is a little-known fact, but the farewell advice of the Reformer John Knox to the Church of Scotland was that what the Kirk needed was more and better bishops. The lesson I take from Knox's farewell words is that bishops matter and that is also the big overall conclusion of this study. It matters that churches should have bishops and it matters that those bishops perform their episcopal calling in a proper manner and to the best of their ability.

This study is the fruit of over twenty years study of episcopacy in general, and episcopacy in the Church of England in particular, undertaken first as the Theological Secretary to the Church of England's Council for Christian Unity and Theological Consultant to its House of Bishops and latterly as a Latimer Trust Fellow and Theological Consultant to the Church of England Evangelical Council.

In the course of my work on this this subject it has become ever clearer to me that majority of people in the Church of England, including many people who are otherwise theologically well-informed, are confused about the answers to three key questions: 'Why should the Church of England have bishops?' 'What is the proper role of bishops?' and 'How should bishops respond to the challenges facing the Church of England and the Church in the West in general today?'

The purpose of this study is to provide answers to these three questions. It is an exercise in following the Reformation principle that theological wisdom can be achieved by a return *'ad fontes'* ('to the sources'), that is, by a return to the basic sources of theological knowledge. For a Church of England theologian such as myself these basic sources are the Scriptures, the teaching and practice of the orthodox Fathers, Councils and Creeds of the early centuries of the Church, and the teaching and practice of the Church of England theologians of the sixteen and seventeenth centuries summarised in the three 'historic formularies' of the Church of England, the *Thirty-Nine Articles*, the *Book of Common Prayer* and the 1662 *Ordinal*.

The contention of this study is that careful attention to these sources provides the answers we need to the three questions listed above. They tell us why the Church of England should have bishops and what the proper role of bishops is, and they set out the principles that tell us how bishops should approach the challenges facing the Church today. Furthermore, by acting in accordance with what we learn in these sources, bishops of the Church of England will be acting in a way that is faithful to what is required of bishops by the current Canons of the Church of England.

This study has three parts.

Part I, 'Why should the Church of England have bishops?' (Chapters 1-6) traces the history of episcopacy from New Testament times to the present day, and argues that the reason why the Church of England should have bishops is that the threefold ministry of bishops, priests and deacons was instituted by the apostles themselves in the earliest days of the Church and for this reason has divine authority.

Part II, 'The role and character of bishops' (Chapters 7-11) traces the understanding of the episcopal role and the character required of those called to exercise it from New Testament times to the present day and argues that the official teaching of the Church of England about the matter remains in line with the teaching of the New Testament, the Fathers, and the Church of England theologians of the sixteenth and seventeenth centuries.

Chapter 9 also argues that the claims made for the universal authority of the Pope in Roman Catholic teaching should not be accepted as they are not supported by the evidence of the New Testament or the Patristic period.

Part III, 'The nature and exercise of jurisdiction' (Chapters 12-16) first outlines what is meant by episcopal jurisdiction, arguing that it is a limitation of the exercise of episcopal ministry instituted by the Church, for the well-being of Church, and as a result such limitation may be exceeded in situations where the well-being of the Church demands it. It then goes on to argue that the distinction that exists between episcopal orders and episcopal jurisdiction helps us to make sense of the proper role of suffragan bishops, who differ from diocesan bishops not in regard to their episcopal orders, but in regard to the nature of the jurisdiction they are given. After that the following two chapters explain that while no bishop will ever be perfect, a bishop can be 'good-enough' and explore what it means for bishops to exercise their jurisdictions in a 'good-enough' and 'not good-enough fashion.'

The final chapter summarises what has been learned in the study as a whole and applies this to the issue of how Church of England bishops should respond to the challenges facing the Western Church today, looking at the lessons bishops need to learn for the present situation from the triumph of the Early Church, at why bishops the bishops need to uphold the Church's traditional teaching on human sexuality in the wake of the *Living in Love and Faith* process, and at what doing so would mean in practice.

The study also has two appendices. The first looks at the process that led to the appointment of women bishops in the Church of England. It notes that the process focused on the how the appointment of women bishops could be achieved and never explained why women bishops would be a theologically permissible development. The second explains why objections to the fact that Church of England bishops are appointed by the Queen are unfounded.

Because bishops have historically been male the historical parts of this study have used the male pronoun to refer to them. When bishops of the Church of England today are referred to, however, male, female and plural pronouns are used to reflect that fact that since 2015 the Church of England has had female bishops.

I should like to thank my Trustees, Stephen Hofmeyr, Wallace Benn, and Mark Burkill for their support and prayers for my work and for their patience over the fact that other urgent writing projects have delayed the completion of this study.

I should also like to thank my former boss at the Council for Christian Unity, Paul Avis (from whom I have borrowed the idea of a 'good-enough bishop) for teaching me that ecclesiology is a serious theological discipline. Although I know he will disagree with much that is in this study, I hope he will be able to recognise it as a fruit of our shared commitment to the belief that that the Church of England's practice cannot be driven simply by pragmatism but needs to have a solid theological foundation.

Part I

Why should the Church of England have bishops?

Chapter 1
Ministry in the New Testament I - Apostles, deacons and elders

The claim made by the Church of England for the apostolic origin of episcopacy

The first stage in thinking about the ministry of bishops is to ask why we have bishops in the first place. The answer to this question is that the Church of England has had, and continues to have, bishops because the Christian Church as a whole has had bishops since the time of the apostles.

At the time of the Reformation, Bishop John Jewel declared in his 1562 *Apology of the Church of England* that one of the things that showed the continuity of the Church of England with the Church of the apostles was that although it did not accept the claims made for the authority of the Pope, like the apostolic Church it did:

...believe that there be divers degrees of ministers in the Church; whereof some be deacons, some priests, some bishops; to whom is committed the office to instruct the people, and the whole charge and setting forth of religion.[1]

While Jewel's claim that the office of bishops goes back to apostolic times is implicit, the Preface to the 1662 Ordinal claims explicitly that:

It is evident unto all men diligently reading holy Scripture and ancient Authors, that from the Apostles' times there have been these Orders of Ministers in Christ's Church; Bishops, Priests and Deacons.

In line with the position taken by Jewel and the Preface to the Ordinal, Canon C1 of *The Canons of the Church of England*, 'Of Holy Orders in the Church of England,' likewise states:

---

[1] John Jewel 'An apology of the Church of England' in J. Ayre (ed.) *The Works of John Jewel* Vol 1 (Cambridge: CUP/Parker Society 1848), p.59.

The Church of England holds and teaches that from the Apostles' time there have been these orders in Christ's Church: bishops, priests and deacons.

It is important to note at this point that in English the word priest has to 'do duty for two distinct and very different ideas; (1) as the equivalent of the Hebrew sacrificing priest (Heb. Cohen); (2) as the equivalent of the Greek word 'presbyter' or 'elder.''[2] Because the Temple in Jerusalem no longer exists, and because the sacrifices offered under the Old Covenant have been superseded by the once for all sacrifice of Christ (Hebrews 10:1-18), it follows that the term 'priest' when used in the quotations above does not refer to a sacrificing priest in the Old Testament sense, but someone who has the role of an 'elder' or 'presbyter' in the New Testament sense that we shall look at below.

When the term priest is understood in this sense, the historical evidence we have supports the claim made in these quotations. In the remainder of this chapter and in the five that follow we shall look at the how the Church of England's threefold ministry of bishops, priests and deacons can be traced back to the time of the apostles and explain why this fact shows not only why the Church of England does have bishops, but also why it *should* have them.

The New Testament contains a single basic pattern of ministry
In his 1644 work *The Original of Bishops and Metropolitans,* James Ussher notes that the ministry of the New Testament is a continuation in a new form of the ministry exercised by the Priests and Levites in the Old Testament:

The government of the Church of the Old Testament was committed to the priests and Levites, unto whom the ministers of the New do now succeed, in like sort as our Lord's Day hath done unto their Sabbath, that it might be fulfilled which was spoken by the prophet, touching

---

[2] W H Griffith Thomas, *The Catholic Faith* (London: Church Book Room Press, 1960), p.142.

the vocation of the Gentiles, 'I will take of them for priests, and for Levites, saith the Lord' [Isaiah 66:21].[3]

What we learn from the New Testament itself, from an early Christian document known as the *Didache* which tells us what the Church in Syria was like in about 70 AD, and from a letter known as *1 Clement* written by Clement of Rome at the end of the New Testament period, is that in New Testament times the form of ministry which first succeeded the ministry of priests and Levites was a threefold ministry of apostles, elders and deacons. Prophets and evangelists also played an important role in the life of the New Testament Church, but they did not constitute additional orders of ministry.

a. Apostles

The Gospels and Acts

According to the Gospels and Acts,[4] the first leaders of the Church were the twelve, that is to say the eleven original apostles appointed by Our Lord Himself (Matthew 10:1-4, Mark 3:13-19; Luke 6:12-16) plus Matthias, who was appointed to take the place left vacant by the death of Judas Iscariot (Acts 1:15-26). It is the twelve who receive the power of the Holy Spirit on the day of Pentecost (Acts 1:8, 2:1-4), and who are appointed by Christ to be his witnesses 'in Jerusalem and in all Judea and Samaria and to the end of the earth' (Acts 1:8), and the Church comes into being as they are faithful to this commission. In Acts 2:42 the first Christians are said to have been 'devoted

---

[3] James Ussher, *The Original of Bishops and Metropolitans* in Richard Snoddy (ed.), *James Ussher and A Reformed Episcopal Church* (Lincoln: The Davenant Press, 2018), p. 118.

[4] In what is said here and later in the chapter it is assumed that the Gospels and Acts give us historically reliable information about the ministry of Jesus and the early history of the Church. For the reasons behind this position see Richard Bauckham, *Jesus and the Eyewitnesses: The Gospels as Eyewitness* Testimony, 2ed (Grand Rapids: Eerdmans, 2017), Peter Williams, *Can we trust the Gospels?* (Wheaton: Crossway, 2018), Colin Hemer, *The Book of Acts in the setting of Hellenistic History* (Tubingen: Mohr, 1989), I H Marshall, (Luke: Historian and Theologian, Exeter: Paternoster Press, 1970).

themselves' to the 'apostles' teaching' and it is the teaching of the twelve that is meant.

As many commentators have pointed out, the number twelve has important symbolic significance. The Church is the renewed Israel and the twelve are its Patriarchs. They are the leaders of the renewed Israel just as the Patriarchs were the first leaders of the original Israel. When Jesus declares in Matthew 19:28 and Luke 22:30 that the apostles will sit 'on twelve thrones, judging the twelve tribes of Israel' it is this leadership role that is meant, with 'judging' being used in the sense of 'governing.' [5]

A similar point about the significance of the twelve apostles is made in Revelation 21:14 where we are told that wall surrounding the New Jerusalem 'had twelve foundations, and on them the twelve names of the twelve apostles of the Lamb.' What this verse is saying is that the ministry of the twelve apostles is the foundation for the eschatological community of God's people that exists now, but will be fully revealed at the end of time.

As Acts continues, however, we find two more figures joining the original twelve apostles in exercising apostolic leadership in the Church. The first of these is Paul, who from Acts 9 onwards becomes the major figure in Luke's narrative and who is the leader of the mission to the Gentiles and the second is James, the Lord's brother, who in Acts 12:17, 15: 1-21 and 21:17-26 is seen as exercising a leadership role in the church in Jerusalem and who is referred to as an apostle in 1 Corinthians 15:7 and Galatians 1:19.

---

[5] 'St Mark's setting for the solemn calling of the of the Twelve – the great company from all over Palestine (3:7f), the confession of Christ's Sonship by the unclean spirits, the high mountain – makes it clear that a New Israel is being formed on a new Sinai, a truth which is further underlined by the choice of *twelve*. The apostles are, as it were, the twelve patriarchs of the new people of God. 'Ye shall sit upon twelve thrones judging the twelve tribes of Israel (Matt 10:28; cf. Luke 22:30).' (Alan Richardson, *An Introduction to the Theology of the New Testament* (London: SCM, 1982), pp.313-314).

The Epistles

The evidence of Acts is reinforced by the Epistles, which refer in various places to the leadership role of the twelve, Paul, and James (see for example Galatians 1:18-2:10, 1 Corinthians 15:1-11) and which show some of them exercising that leadership in the form of letters written to give authoritative guidance to particular churches, or groups of churches. As Thomas Bilson writes, what we learn from the Epistles is that the apostles:

...had in the church of Christ right to require and command, power to rebuke and revenge,[6] authority to dispose and ordain in all such cases as touched the soundness of faith, seemliness of life, or seemliness of order among the faithful; and that in so doing they did not usurp upon their brethren, nor tyrannize over them, but were guided by God's Spirit, and obeyed as Christ's messengers and legates in every place where the truth was admitted. [7]

The most basic form of ministry in the New Testament is thus the Spirit inspired apostolic ministry exercised by the twelve plus St. Paul and St. James.

Besides these fourteen, there are other people are also described as 'apostles' in the New Testament. These include Barnabas (Acts 14:4), Andronicus and Junia (Romans 16:7), the 'apostles of the churches' (2 Corinthians 8:23) and Epaphroditus (Philippians 2:25). The distinction between these people and the fourteen is that they are 'apostles,' that is to say commissioned delegates, appointed by particular churches to act on their behalf whereas the fourteen are the 'apostles of Christ' (1 Thessalonians 2:6), those appointed to a leadership role in the Church as a whole by the risen Christ himself.

---

[6] 'Revenge' in this context means to inflict judgement in response to wrongdoing.
[7] Thomas Bilson, *The Perpetual Government of Christ's Church* (Oxford: OUP, 1842), p.89.

b.   Deacons

The appointment of the first deacons in Acts 6

As Joseph Lightfoot notes in his essay on 'The Christian Ministry' in his commentary on Philippians, Acts tells us that the apostles originally saw to all the affairs of the Church themselves:

St Luke's narrative represents the Twelve Apostles in the earliest days as the sole directors and administrators of the Church. For the financial business of the infant community, not less than for its spiritual guidance, they alone are responsible.[8]

However, as he goes on to say:

This state of affairs could not last long. By the rapid accession of numbers, and still more by the admission of heterogeneous classes into the Church, the work became too vast and too various for them to discharge unaided. To relieve them from the increasing pressure, the inferior and less important functions passed successively into other hands: and thus each grade of the ministry, beginning from the lowest was created in order. [9]

The 'lowest grade' to which Lightfoot refers is the diaconate. The traditional view of its origins, going back to the early Patristic period, is set out as follows by Richard Hooker in *The Laws of Ecclesiastical Polity*. Commenting on Acts 6:1-7 he declares:

The ancient custom of the Church was to yield the poor much relief especially widows. But as poor people are always querulous and apt to think themselves less respected than they should be, we see that when the Apostles did what they could without hindrance to their weightier business yet there were which grudged that others had too much and they too little, the Grecian widows shorter commons than the Hebrews. By means whereof the Apostles saw it meet to obtain

[8] J B Lightfoot, *St Paul's Epistle to the Philippians*, 4ed (London & New York: Macmillan, 1891), p. 187.
[9] Lightfoot p. 187.

deacons. Now tract of time having clean worn out those first occasions for which the deaconship was then most necessary, it might the better be afterwards extended to other services, and so remain as at this present day a degree in the clergy of God which the Apostles of Christ did institute.[10]

To put it simply, the diaconate was established by the Apostles sometime around 31 or 32 AD as a response to the specific problem described in Acts 6. However, with the passing of time, the diaconate was no longer required as a means of tackling this specific problem and so it was possible for it to develop into the more general ministry of assistance to the leadership of the Church, which it became by the early Patristic period and has remained ever since. [11]

This traditional view of the origins of the diaconate has been challenged in two ways.

First, it has been questioned whether the reading of Acts 6 that sees the problem in Jerusalem to which the appointment of the seven was the solution as Greek speaking widows getting less poor relief than those widows whose native language was Hebrew is correct.

The Australian scholar John Collins has suggested that the Greek noun *diakonia* used in Acts 6:1 and 4 and the Greek verb *diakoneo* used in Acts 6: 2 have one meaning, which is the proclamation of the word. In Collins' view the linking of diakonia with the spreading of the word is so strong that any ancient reader would interpret this passage to refer to the spreading of the word not to the distribution of food. This means that what the Greek speaking widows were missing out on was hearing the word of God spoken about at tables (which would either be where people sat to eat, or the place where financial assistance was passed out).

[10] Richard Hooker, *The Laws of Ecclesiastical Polity*, V: lxxviii.5 (Oxford: OUP, 1841), vol.2, p.182.
[11] The service for the 'Ordering of Deacons' in the 1662 Ordinal reflects the traditional view of the matter by setting Acts 6:1-7 as one of the readings for the service alongside 1 Timothy 3:8-13.

Collins therefore argues that Acts 6:1-4 should be understood as follows:

Now during those days, when the disciples were increasing in number, the Hellenists complained against the Hebrews because their widows were being neglected in the daily ministry (i.e. the day by day ministry of the word). And the twelve called together the whole community of the disciples and said, 'It is not right that we should neglect the word of God (i.e. the public proclamation of the word before large crowds) in order to minister at table (i.e. in a more local, domestic context) ...we, for our part will dedicate ourselves to prayer and to ministering to the word (i.e. the public proclamation of the word).' [12]

However, as Paula Gooder has commented, this is not a natural reading of these verses given that there is an explicit contrast drawn in verse two between 'the preaching of the word of God' and 'serving tables.' In her view:

A more natural reading of this passage would be that the *daikon* - words be understood to refer to carrying out a commissioned task: focused at the table in verse 2 and focused on public proclamation of the word in verse 4. Thus the crucial meaning here would be that it is not right for the twelve to neglect their commissioned task with respect to the word for the sake of undertaking a commissioned task at tables (which might mean waiting at tables, or helping financially). Therefore the seven are given the task at tables while the twelve continue to spread the word of the Lord publicly – both however would be undertaking the spread of the word each in their own commissioned way.[13]

[12] John Collins, *Deacons and the Church: Making Connections between Old and New*, (Harrisburg: Morehouse Publishing, 2003), p. 52.
[13] Paula Gooder, *Diakonia in the New Testament: A Dialogue with John Collins*, p.10 at
https://www.researchgate.net/publication/233653611_Diakonia_in_the_New_Testament_A_Dialogue_with_John_N_Collins

Gooder's traditional reading of Acts 6:1-4 is supported by the link between the account of the appointment of the seven in Acts 6:1-7 and the story of the healing of the lame man at the Beautiful Gate of the Temple in Acts 3.

As David Gooding points out in his commentary on Acts:

Both stories show the early Christians taking seriously their social responsibility, the one to the world around (as with the cripple) and the other to the members of the church (the daily distribution of food to the Christian widows). And both stories remind us of the all-important need to keep our social duties in their proper place and proportion, and never to allow them to usurp or eclipse the pre-eminent place and importance of the preaching of the gospel and the teaching of the Word of God. [14]

In the case of the story of the healing of the lame man at the Beautiful Gate, he notes, Luke records that the people at large were:

...quite ready to take the church's charity to relieve their poor, and the apostles ready to give not only money (if they had it) but much more besides. But when the crowd gathered to hear Peter's explanation of the miracle, he did not allow them to go away with the impression that charity to the poor and healing to the sick were the main things Christianity was about. Quite the reverse. The main and all important thing for Peter was the preaching of the gospel.[15]

In a similar fashion, Luke tells us in Acts 6 that 'the early Christians had a very vigorous and active concern for the social needs of its members' and when it was discovered that some widows were missing out 'the apostles advised the church to appoint efficient and spiritual men to administer the common resources in a fair and systematic way.' However, the apostles were not prepared to neglect the ministry of the word 'to administer that social relief themselves'

[14] David Gooding, *True to the Faith: A Fresh Commentary on the Acts of the Apostles* (London: Hodder and Stoughton 1990), p. 103.
[15] Gooding, p.103.

and because they stuck to their appointed task 'the word of God increased; and the number of the disciples multiplied greatly in Jerusalem, and a great many of the priests were obedient to the faith' (Acts 6:7).[16]

In Acts 3 and Acts 6 we are shown that the Church needs both to meet people's physical needs and to preach the gospel. However, the latter has a higher priority than the former, and that is why the care for the distribution of relief to those in need was delegated to the seven in order free up the apostles to pray and to preach the word.

Secondly, it has also been questioned whether Luke's account of the appointment of the seven is meant to describe the origins of the diaconate. John Kelly writes, for example:

The origin of a specific order of deacons in the primitive Church has been much discussed, but remains wrapped in obscurity. The traditional explanation, viz. that it is to be sought in the appointment of the Seven (they are nowhere actually termed 'deacons') in Acts 6, is almost certainly wrong. Stephen and his companions were not strictly ministers in any sense analogous to the deacons of the later apostolic and post apostolic ages. They were *ad hoc* representatives of the Hellenist with the Twelve, and are depicted as evangelists disputing, teaching and baptizing alongside them. [17]

However, there are good reasons for following the traditional view that it was Luke's intention to describe the origin of the diaconate in Acts 6. To quote Lightfoot again:

If the word deacon does not occur in the passage, yet the corresponding verb and substantive διακονειν and διακονία, are repeated more than once. The functions moreover are precisely those which devolved on the deacons of the earliest ages, and which still in theory, though not altogether in practice, form the primary duties of the office. Again, it seems clear from the emphasis with which St Luke

[16] Gooding p,104.
[17] John Kelly, *The Pastoral Epistles* (London: A&C Black, 1986), pp.80-81.

dwells on the new institution that he looks on the establishment of this office, not as isolated incident, but as the initiation of a new order of things in the Church. It is in short one of those representative facts, of which the earlier part of his narrative is almost wholly made up. Lastly, the tradition of the identity of the two offices has been unanimous from the earliest times. Irenaeus, the first writer who alludes to the appointment of the Seven, distinctly holds them to have been deacons. The Roman Church some centuries later, though the presbytery had largely increased meanwhile, still restricted the number of deacons to seven, thus preserving the memory of the first institution of this office. And in like manner a canon of the Council of Neo- Caesarea (AD 315) enacted that there should be no more than seven deacons in any city however great, alleging the apostolic model. This rule, it is true, was only partially observed; but the tradition was at all events so far respected, that the creation of an order of subdeacons was found necessary in order to remedy the inconvenience arising from the limitation.[18]

It should also be noted that the fact that Stephen and Philip (nothing further is said about the other five of the seven) are subsequently described in Acts 6:8-8:40 and 21:8 as evangelists engaged in disputing, teaching and baptizing does not mean that they were not originally called to serve God as deacons in a ministry focussed on meeting the needs of the poor. This part of Kelly's argument ignores the fact that God can call those who been appointed to one ministry to later serve him in another way. Indeed, this is precisely what Acts describes. Stephen and Philip are set aside by prayer and the laying on of hands to be deacons Acts 6:6, but then they also serve God as evangelists.

[18] Lightfoot, p.189. The references in Irenaeus are *Adversus Haereses* I.26.3, III.12.10, IV.15.1.

Deacons in the rest of the New Testament

In the rest of the New Testament there are clear references to the diaconate as a separate order of ministry in Philippians 1:1,[19] 1 Timothy 3:8-13 and Romans 16:1 and possible references to deacons in what Paul says about those whose gift is 'service' in Romans 12:7 and about God's appointment of 'helpers' in the Church in 1 Corinthians 12:28.

As Roger Beckwith argues in his book *Elders in Every City*, just as the original role of the seven was to assist the apostles in their ministry in Jerusalem, so the subsequent role of deacons seems to have been to support the elders in providing leadership in each local church, particularly in matters to do with providing material support to those in need. Seeing the New Testament deacons as assistants to the elders makes sense of what is said by Luke about the origins of the diaconate in Acts 6, the way in which the deacons are listed after elders and bishops in 1 Timothy 3:1-13, Philippians 1:1 and other early texts such as *1 Clement* 42, *Didache* 15:1 and *The Epistle of Polycarp* 5, and the way in which deacons are universally seen as those who assist the bishop and the presbyters in the Christian literature of the immediate post New Testament period and then in the subsequent tradition of the Church.

It has also been noted that the list of the characteristics for deacons in 1 Timothy 3:8, 'sobriety, straightforwardness, freedom from excess and greed, probity' are those that 'would be particularly appropriate for those with responsibilities in finance and administration.' [20]

---

[19] Some commentators have argued that Philippians 1:1 should be seen as referring not to two classes of people, bishops, and deacons, but to one class of people exercising both oversight and diaconal service. However, the traditional interpretation still seems to make most sense in context.

[20] Andrew Walls, 'Deacon,' in J D Douglas (ed), *The New Bible Dictionary* (Leicester: Inter-Varsity Press, 1962), p.297.

Beckwith suggests that the term 'ministerial assistant' best expresses the deacon's role.[21] This term both reflects the assistant role of the deacons and the fact emphasised by Collins that the Greek term *diakonia* of which the term *diakonos* or 'deacon' is a cognate implies ministry undertaken on behalf of God. [22] Deacons have a God given ministry, but it is a ministry of assistance.

Beckwith further notes that in 1 Timothy 3 the qualifications for elders and deacons are very similar:

'They cover character, ability and reputation, and extend even to qualifications for the exercise of a measure of oversight by deacons (verse 12, cp. verse 4f).' In the light of this similarity, it is, he says:

...no doubt a significant exception that aptitude to teach is not required of candidates for the diaconate, though not of course excluded. Their essential spiritual gift would be that of *antilempseis*, helps or helpful deeds (1 Corinthians 12:28; cp. Romans 16:2). Helping other ministers is a most honourable task, not a degrading one, which is why candidates are ordained to perform it. The way deacons are singled out in Philippians 1:1 and 1 Timothy 3 implies, likewise, that their office is a very distinguished one, as 1 Timothy 3:13 indeed states. [23]

Women deacons
In 1 Timothy 3:11, in the middle of his account of the qualifications required for deacons, Paul[24] refers to 'women' (In Greek *gunaikas*).

---

[21] Roger Beckwith, *Elders in Every City* (Carlisle: Paternoster Press, 2003), pp. 64-65.
[22] John Collins, *Diakonia: Re- interpreting the Ancient Sources,* (Oxford: OUP, 1990).
[23] Beckwith, p.65. The biblical concept of a deacon as someone ordained to a ministry of assistance with a particular focus on providing care for those in need continues to be reflected in the description of the deacon's role in the 1662 Ordinal.
[24] For reasons for accepting the Pauline authorship of 1 and 2 Timothy and Titus, see E Ellis, 'Pastoral Letters' in Gerald Hawthorne, Ralph Martin and Daniel Reid

As Kelly notes, there is general agreement amongst commentators 'that Paul cannot, in a passage concerned with special groups, be interjecting a reference to the women of the congregation in general.'[25] Many Commentators have suggested that Paul is referring to the women of the male deacons previously mentioned (i.e. their wives). However, as Kelly goes on to observe, there are three problems with this suggestion.

First, if this was what was meant 'we should have expected the definite article before 'Women,' or at least the genitive pronoun after it, or some other term bringing out that they were 'their wives.'[26]

Secondly, 'it is very strange that that only deacon's wives are singled out for mention,' since Paul says nothing in Timothy 3:1-7 about the wives of bishops, who would have 'occupied an even more influential position.'[27]

Thirdly, the use of the term 'likewise' when describing the qualities these women should possess 'leads us to expect a fresh category of officials, as does the list of parallel, if not identical qualities.'[28]

For these three reasons, says Kelly:

...the translation **Women deacons** is likely to be the correct one. The absence of the article is, if anything, a point in its favour, **Women** being used almost adjectivally – 'deacons who are women.'[29]

Another reference to women deacons is in Romans 16:1 where Phoebe is referred to as the *diakonos* of the Church at Cenchreae (a seaport of Corinth). The word here is the same word that is used in

(eds), *Dictionary of Paul and his Letters* (Downers Grove & Leicester: Inter-Varsity Press, 1993), pp.659-666, Kelly, pp.1-36 and Donald Guthrie, *New Testament Introduction*, (Leicester, Inter Varsity Press, 1970), pp.584-622.
[25] Kelly, p. 83.
[26] Kelly p.83.
[27] Kelly, p.83.
[28] Kelly, p.83.
[29] Kelly, p.83 (bold in the original).

Philippians 1:1 and 1 Timothy 3:8-11 and 13 to refer to male deacons and there seems no reason to translate it differently in this verse. Phoebe had an official ministry as a deacon of the Church of Cenchreae.

External confirmation of the existence of women deacons in the Early Church Is provided by a letter written by the Roman writer Pliny the younger to the Emperor Trajan in 112 in which he refers to them by the Latin term 'ministrae' [30] and, as Lightfoot suggests, the appointment of women deacons makes good historical sense as a response to the challenge facing the Church in providing pastoral care for women in first century society:

'The strict seclusion of the female sex in Greece and in some Oriental countries necessarily debarred them from the ministrations of men: and to meet the want thus felt, it was found necessary at an early date to admit women to the diaconate.'[31]

c. Elders

The origins of the eldership
The diaconate seems to have been an invention by the apostles since it does not seem to correspond to any existing office within Judaism. This is not the case with the eldership, the third main form of ministry in the Church during New Testament times.

Jewish synagogues in the first century were led by 'elders' (in Greek *presbuteroi* - hence the alternative English term 'presbyters'), such as the 'elders of the Jews' referred to in Luke 7:3, [32] and the earliest Christian churches in Palestine, which were made up of Jews, seem to have simply followed their example. As Lightfoot says:

As soon as the expansion of the Church rendered some organization necessary, it would form a 'synagogue' of its own. The Christian

---

[30] Pliny, *Letters*, X.96.
[31] Lightfoot, p.191.
[32] For details see Beckwith, Ch.5.

congregations in Palestine long continued to be designated by this name, though the term 'ecclesia' took its place from the first in heathen countries. With the synagogue itself they would naturally, if not necessarily, adopt the normal government of a synagogue, and a body of elders or presbyters would be chosen to direct the religious worship and partly also to watch over the temporal well-being of the society.[33]

The first reference to Christian elders is in Acts 11:30. This tells us that in about 46 AD the church at Antioch provides relief to the Christians in Judea who are facing famine by 'sending it to the elders by the hands of Barnabas and Saul.' In this reference it appears that the 'elders' are those who have governing authority in the churches in Judea.

It is sometimes suggested that the fact that the collection for famine relief was sent to the elders indicates that they were the people who had succeeded the seven deacons in Acts 6 in having responsibility for the administration of the church's finances and the distribution of aid to those in need. F. F. Bruce, for example, comments 'The elders were now responsible for those matters which were earlier superintended by the seven Hellenistic almoners.'[34]

However, neither in the rest of the New Testament, nor in the immediate post New Testament literature, do we find any evidence for elders exercising a 'diaconal' function. A better suggestion is that made by John Calvin in his commentary on Acts. He writes that it is to the elders:

---

[33] Lightfoot, p.192. The origins of the eldership in the church in Judaea is further indicated by the fact that the term *presbuteros* was a term that does not seem to have been used in diaspora Judaism until the end of the second century. Jews outside Judaea referred to elders as *archontes* or *gerontes* instead (Richardson p.326)
[34] F. F. Bruce, *The Acts of Apostles*, 3ed (Grand Rapids and Leicester: Eerdmans/Apollos, 1990), p. 277.

...that the Antioch church submit the money that they have dedicated and appointed for the poor. If anyone objects that these were responsibilities imposed on the deacons, when the apostles said that they were not able to cope with the service of tables and the labour of teaching at the same time, the answer is easy, that the deacons were in charge of tables, but in such a way that they were still under the elders and did nothing without their authority.[35]

Following this suggestion, we can envisage the money from Antioch being given to the elders as those with overall responsibility for the Church in Judaea and the elders then passing it on to the deacons for subsequent disbursement. We cannot prove that this was the case, but it is a plausible scenario in the light of the available evidence.

Later on in Acts we find the elders acting with the apostles in settling the dispute between Jewish and Gentile Christians at the Council of Jerusalem in Acts 15 and Paul meeting with James and the elders when he pays his final visit to Jerusalem in Acts 21:1-26.

It also seems likely that the 'brethren' referred to in Acts 12:17 are elders since the term 'brethren' is also used of elders in Acts 15:23. If the 'brethren' in this verse are elders this makes sense of the specific reference to James ('tell this to James and to the brethren'). He is singled out for mention because he together with the elders constitute the leadership of the church. If this is the case, then Acts 12:17 is further evidence that the leadership the church in Jerusalem consisted of James plus the elders. 'Tell this to James and to the brethren' means St. Peter's release is to be reported to the church leadership.

Taken together, these references indicate that the government of the churches in Judea and Jerusalem was in the hands of the apostles and the elders, with the former possessing the ultimate authority, but exercising it in conjunction with the latter.

---

[35] John Calvin, *The Acts of the Apostles 1-13* (Edinburgh and London; Oliver & Boyd, 1965), p.335.

We are not told when or how these elders were introduced into the life of the Church. They simply appear without comment in Acts 11.30. One suggestion is that the church in Jerusalem and Judea was originally governed directly by the apostles and that elders on the existing Jewish synagogue model were introduced to assist James in its government when the persecution mentioned in Acts 12 resulted in the dispersion of the twelve around the Mediterranean world in 42 AD. 'Since Jerusalem would no longer be their home as hitherto, it became necessary to provide for the permanent direction of the Church there; and for this purpose the usual government of the synagogue would be adopted.'[36] This suggestion is plausible, and explains why the elders first appear in Acts 11:30, but in the absence of any direct evidence we cannot be certain about the matter.[37]

What we can be certain about, however, is that given the church was originally governed by the apostles they would have been responsible for this new development and would have appointed the first elders. This is what the later Church believed to have happened (see *1*

---

[36] Lightfoot, p.193.

[37] As Lightfoot notes in his commentary on Galatians, this reconstruction of events in Jerusalem sees St Luke's account in Acts 11 and 12 as being thematic rather than strictly chronological. He writes:

> The order of events in St. Luke's narrative is as follows: (1) the notice of St. Paul's setting out from Antioch for Jerusalem 11:30; (2) the persecution of Herod, the death of James, and the imprisonment and death of Peter, 12:1-19; (3) the death of Herod, and the spread of the word, 12:20-24; St Paul's business at Jerusalem and his departure thence, 12:25. The narrative itself suggests the motive of this order, which is not directly chronological. Having mentioned in (1) St. Paul's mission to Jerusalem, the writer is led in (2) to describe the condition of the Church there *kat' ekeinon ton kairon*. This obliges him to pass to (3) in order to show that God defeated the purposes of man, the persecutor dying ignominiously, and the persecuted church continuing to flourish. He then resumes the subject of (1) in (4). Thus it may be assumed, I think, that the Church was suffering from Herod's persecutions when St. Paul arrived, but not that Herod was already dead. In other words, the chronological order was probably (2), (1), (4), (3). (Joseph Lightfoot, *The Epistle of St. Paul to the Galatians* (Grand Rapids: Zondervan, 1966), p.124).

Clement 42 below) and it is supported by the fact that when elders are appointed for the churches in Asia Minor it is Paul and Barnabas, acting with apostolic authority, who do the appointing (Acts 14:23).

In Acts 14:23 we are told that elders were 'appointed...with prayer and fasting,' but we are not told that Paul and Barnabas laid hands on them. However, in Acts 6:6 the first deacons are specifically said to have been ordained to their office by prayer and the laying on of hands and 1 Timothy 4: 14 and 5:22 and 2 Timothy 1:6 indicate that this was true for elders as well.

The appointment of elders in Acts 14 is also significant because it indicates that, although the role of elders may have originated with the Jewish Christian churches in Judea, it was seen as a form of church government that was exportable to the churches of the Gentile mission. In these Gentile churches, however, the term 'bishop' (*episkopos*) came to be used as a synonym for elder. The Greek word *episkopos* refers to someone who exercises some form of oversight[38] and it would seem to have been used as an alternative to elder in situations where people were not familiar with the governmental structure of the Jewish synagogue.

Bishop and elder as synonymous terms

The evidence for the terms bishop and elder being used as synonyms in the New Testament has been generally accepted since the Patristic period.[39] It is set out as follows by Lightfoot in his commentary on Philippians (he uses 'presbyter' for 'elder'):

- In the opening of this epistle [i.e. Philippians 1:1] St Paul salutes the 'bishops' and 'deacons.' Now it is incredible that he should recognise only the first and third order and pass over

[38] See the entry for επίσκοπος in W. Bauer, F. W. Gingrich and F. Danker, *A Greek-English Lexicon of the New Testament and other Early Christian Literature* (Chicago & London: Chicago UP 1979) p. 299.
[39] See, for example, St Jerome, 'Letter CXLVI to Evangelus,' in *The Nicene and Post Nicene Fathers*, Second Series, vol.vi, Edinburgh & London, T&T Clark/Eerdmans, 1996), pp.288-289.

the second, though the second was absolutely essential to the existence of a church and formed the staple of its ministry. It seems therefore to follow of necessity that the 'bishops' are identical with the 'presbyters.'

- In the Acts (20:17) Paul is represented as summoning to Miletus the 'elders' or 'presbyters' of the Church of Ephesus. Yet in addressing them immediately after he appeals to them as 'bishops' or 'overseers' of the church (20:28).

- Similarly Peter, appealing to the 'presbyters' of the churches addressed by him, in the same breath urges them to 'fulfil the office of bishops'...with disinterested zeal (1 Peter 5:2).

- Again in the First Epistle to Timothy Paul, after describing the qualifications for the office of a 'bishop' (3:1-7), goes on at once to say what is required of 'deacons' (3:8-13). He makes no mention of presbyters. The term 'presbyter' however is not unknown to him; for having occasion in a later passage to speak of Christian ministers he calls these officers no longer 'bishops' but 'presbyters' (5:7-19).

- The same identification appears still more plainly from the Apostle's directions to Titus (1:3-7): 'That thou shouldst set in order the things that are wanting and ordain *elders* in every city, as I appointed thee; if anyone be *blameless*, the husband of one wife, having believing children who are not charged with riotousness or unruly; for a *bishop*...must be *blameless* etc. [40]

In the 1980s, however, a number of New Testament scholars such as Kevin Giles, Bengt Holmberg, and Gerd Theissen [41] challenged the idea

[40] Lightfoot, *Philippians*, pp.96-97.
[41] Kevin Giles, *Patterns of Ministry among the First Christians* (Melbourne, Collins, Dove, 1980), Bengt Holmberg, *Paul and Power: The Structure of Authority in the Primitive Church as reflected in the Pauline Epistles* (Philadelphia: Fortress Press, 1980), Gerd Theissen, *The Social Setting of Early Christianity* (Edinburgh: T&T Clark, 1982).

that elders and bishops were two names for the same office. They argued instead that the elders were community leaders while the bishops were the leaders of house churches. In the words of Colin Kruse, they suggested that:

...the heads of households came to have supervisory responsibilities for the churches which met in their house, and that these were the bishops of the early church... Further, it has been suggested that as elders in the Jewish Community were not synagogue officials but community leaders, so too Christian elders were community leaders not church officials. Thus elders are to be distinguished from bishops in the NT. Bishops were the hosts of the house churches and they exercised a supervisory role over the church meeting in their houses. Elders were leaders in the Christian community, but were not necessarily hosts of house churches as well. There is the possibility that one person was both an elder (community leader) and a bishop (host of house church) which accounts for the overlapping of the descriptions of the tasks of elders and bishops in the Pastoral Letters.... If this suggestion could be shown to be correct it would throw light upon the references to elders who rule only (community leaders only), and elders who also labour in teaching (hosts of house churches as well as community leaders). [42]

This suggestion is implausible for three reasons:

First, the way that the terms presbyter and bishop are used as synonyms in the New Testament indicates that there was one office with two names rather than two offices that might be exercised by one person.

Secondly, there are four references to people hosting churches in their houses in the New Testament (Romans 16:5, 1 Corinthians 16:19, Colossians 4:15 and Philemon 2) and none of these references says

---

[42] Colin Kruse, 'Ministry,' in Gerald Hawthorne, Ralph Martin and Daniel Reid (eds), *Dictionary of Paul and his Letters* (Downers Grove & Leicester: Inter-Varsity Press, 1993, pp.603-604.

anything about the host of the church being called a bishop. Furthermore, this connection is never made anywhere else in the New Testament and nothing is ever said about hosts of house churches being responsible for teaching.

Thirdly, the Patristic tradition is likewise silent about the idea that bishops were originally house church leaders. There is nothing in the Patristic literature that supports this idea.

The older notion that presbyters and bishops were identical in the New Testament period makes more sense of the New Testament evidence and also explains the silence of the Patristic tradition about bishops having originally been the leaders of house churches. We should therefore still accept it.

In addition to using the terms elder and bishop, the New Testament also refers to the same form of ministry by the use of the term 'leader' (*hegoumenos*) in Hebrews 13:17 and 24 and the term 'pastor' (*poimen*) in Ephesians 4:11. As Beckwith notes, in Galatians 6:6 and 1 Thessalonians 5:12 'none of the standard names are used (for whatever reason), but the activities that the presbyter-bishops perform are merely described, namely ruling, teaching and admonishing.'[43] As he goes on to say, all these different references show:

...how widespread the institution of presbyter-bishop was in the apostolic church. Corinth is the is the sole church where there is reason to doubt its existence, and this may only be because the enthusiastic Corinthians disregarded the presbyter- bishops, not because they did not exist there.[44]

He suggests that 1 Corinthians 16:15-16 may indicate that the role of elders and deacons were filled by members of the household of Stephanas, but that they were being disregarded by the Corinthians

---

[43] Beckwith, p.48.
[44] Beckwith, p.48.

just as a generation later *1 Clement* declares that they were disregarding their presbyters at that time. [45]

In 1 Peter 5:1 Peter describes himself as a 'fellow elder' and in 2 John 1:1 and 3 John 1:1 John likewise describes himself as 'the elder.' In 1 Peter 5:1 Peter is making the point that he is exhorting the elders as someone who shares with them the responsibility to care for the sheep of God's flock. In 2 John 1:1 and 3 John 1:1 the term can be seen as an appropriate title for John in his old age. In the words of John Stott:

He was only '*an* apostle,' as Paul and Peter also styled themselves (e.g. Romans 1:1, 1 Peter 1:1). But he could be called '*the* elder' *par excellence*. There were other elders in Ephesus, but he was unique among them because he was an apostle as well, and a venerable patriarch in old age. [46]

The duties of elders
If we ask what precise role or roles the elders performed, a good summary of the New Testament evidence is once again provided by Lightfoot:

The duties of the presbyters were twofold. They were both rulers and instructors of the congregation. This double function appears in St Paul's expression 'pastors and teachers' [Ephesians 4:11], where, as the form of the original seems to show, the two words describe the same office under different aspects. Though government was probably the first conception of the office, yet the work of teaching must have fallen to the presbyters from the very first and have assumed greater prominence as time went on. With the growth of the Church, the visits of the apostles and evangelists to any individual community must have become less and less frequent, so that the burden of instruction would gradually be transferred from these missionary preachers to the local

---

[45] Beckwith, p.48.
[46] John Stott, *The Epistles of John* (Leicester and Grand Rapids: IVP/Eerdmans, 1988), pp. 43-44.

officers of the congregation. Hence St. Paul in two passages, where he gives direction relating to bishops or presbyters, insists specially on the faculty of teaching as a qualification for this position. Yet even here this work seems to be regarded rather as incidental to than as inherent in the office. In the one epistle he directs that double honour shall be paid to those presbyters who have ruled well, but especially to such as 'labour in word and doctrine' [1 Timothy 5:17] as though one holding this office might decline the work of instruction. In the other, he closes the list of qualifications with the requirement that the bishop (or presbyter) hold fast the faithful word in accordance with the apostolic teaching 'that he may be able both to exhort in the healthy doctrine and to confute gainsayers,' [Titus 1:9] alleging as the reason the pernicious activity and growing numbers of the false teachers. Nevertheless, there is no ground for supposing that the work of teaching and the work of governing pertained to separate members of the presbyteral college. As each had his special gift, so would he devote himself more or less exclusively to the one or the other of these sacred functions.[47]

At the Reformation, those in the Presbyterian tradition came to see the New Testament as distinguishing between two types of elders, 'ministers of word and sacrament who serve as teaching and ruling elders and lay elders who share in the oversight of the church.'[48] However, as Lightfoot says, the New Testament does not distinguish between different types of elder, but between different roles which belong to the one office. Furthermore, the writers of the Patristic period make no mention of lay elders either existing, or ever having existed, in the Church. As Bilson puts it, there are 'no such elders expressed or testified in any father or writer of the primitive church.'[49]

[47] Lightfoot, *Philippians*, p.195.
[48] T. Harvey 'Presbyterianism' in Martin Davie, Tim Grass et al, *New Dictionary of Theology Historical and Systematic* (London & Downers Grove: Inter Varsity Press, 2016), p.703.
[49] Bilson, p.215.

In addition to the two basic functions of governing and teaching identified by Lightfoot, James 5:13-15 describes the involvement of elders, as leaders of the local church, in the ministry of healing and in Acts 20: 28-29 and in 1 Peter 5:1-5 we also have the idea, drawn from Old Testament imagery (see for example Ezekiel 34:11-31), of the elders as God's under shepherds taking care of God's flock on behalf of Christ the chief shepherd.

In the same way as in Titus 1:9, in Acts 20:28-31 the role of elders as shepherds is linked to the provision of sound teaching and the protection of the Church from those who would lead it astray.

In Acts 20:28 the Greek verb *poimainein* (translated 'care for' in the RSV) means 'to lead a flock to pasture, and so feed the sheep.'[50] In the context in Acts what such feeding involves is following Paul's example by testifying faithfully to 'the gospel of the grace of God' (Acts 20:24). It is this gospel that gives Christ's sheep the spiritual food they need.

In Acts 29-30 Paul goes on to warn the Ephesian elders that 'after my departure fierce wolves will come in among you, not sparing the flock; and from among your own selves will arise men speaking perverse things, to draw away the disciples after them.' The reference here is to heretical teachers coming both from outside and inside the Ephesian church and in response to these teachers the Ephesian elders are called to 'be alert' (Acts 20:31) guarding the flock by challenging such teaching.

Discipline and the Sacraments
We know from passages such as 1 Corinthians 5:1-13, 2 Thessalonians 3:6-15, Titus 3:10-11 and 2 John 10-11 that discipline was exercised in the Church of New Testament times for both moral and doctrinal offences. Although the New Testament does not say that the elders were involved in administering such discipline, it seems likely that this was the case (as with elders in the Jewish synagogues) as part of their

---

[50] John Stott, 'The New Testament Concept of Episkope,' in R.P. Johnston (ed.), *Bishops in the Church* (London: Church Book Room Press, 1966), p.14.

calling to govern the churches and protect them from the wolves who would threaten the flock.

The New Testament is also silent about the role of elders in conducting baptisms and celebrating Holy Communion. However, it seems *prima facie* likely that as those with overall responsibility for the governance of the churches they would have been responsible for seeing that the sacraments ordained by Christ were duly ministered, or would have performed this task themselves.

Furthermore, as we shall see below, evidence from the *Didache* and *I Clement* indicates both that the elders and deacons were responsible for ensuring that Holy Communion took place and that the elders themselves presided at it.

d.   Prophets, Evangelists and Teachers

Alongside the Apostles, deacons and elders there are three other forms of ministry mentioned in the New Testament that need to be considered. These are the ministries of prophets, evangelists and teachers mentioned by St Paul in Ephesians 4:11 and 1 Corinthians 12:28.

If we take the ministry of prophets first of all, we find this mentioned in Acts 11:27-28, 13:1, 15:32, 21:9-10 and Romans 12:6. It was clearly an important part of the life of the Church in New Testament times and was part of the fulfilment of the prophecy in Joel 2:28-32 about the pouring out of God's Spirit upon His people in the latter days to which Peter refers on the day of Pentecost (Acts 2:14-21). What we do not find, however, is the idea that the prophets formed a regular organised order of ministry alongside the elders and deacons.

This last point is well made by Hooker:

Touching Prophets, they were such men as having otherwise learned the gospel had from above bestowed upon them a special gift of expounding Scriptures and of foreshadowing things to come. Of this sort Agabus was and beside him in Jerusalem sundry others, who notwithstanding are not therefore to be reckoned with the clergy, because no man's gifts or qualities can make him a minister of holy things, unless ordination do give him power. And we nowhere find Prophets to have been made by ordination, but all whom the church did ordain were either to serve as presbyters and deacons.[51]

Moving on to evangelists, we find two references outside the ones previously mentioned. These are Acts 21:8 where we read of 'Philip the evangelist' and 2 Timothy 4:5 where Timothy is exhorted to 'do the work of an evangelist.' Neither these references, nor the passages from 1 Corinthians and Ephesians previously mentioned, point to the idea that the term 'evangelist' refers to membership of a recognised order of ministry as opposed to the exercise of a particular function within the life of the Church. Just as what made a prophet was the exercise of the prophetic gift, so what made someone an evangelist was their exercise of a particular gift of evangelism, that is to say, the proclamation of the good news of Jesus Christ to those who do not yet know or believe it, as in the case of Philip's proclamation of the gospel to the Samaritans and to the Ethiopian eunuch in Acts 8:4-40.

In Acts 13:1, 1 Corinthians 12:28 and Ephesians 4:11 we also find references to those who are 'teachers'. In Ephesians 4:11 'teachers' seems to be a reference, together with the preceding mention of 'pastors,' to the ministry of elders. Elders are pastors and teachers. This leaves the other two verses, and in these 'teachers' appears to mean those who teach, just as the prophets, who are mentioned immediately before the teachers in both verses, are those who prophesy.

In his influential book *The Church and the Ministry,* Charles Gore argues that prophets, evangelists and teachers constituted a class of 'apostolic men' who had 'imparted to them by the laying-on of apostolic hands what was essentially apostolic authority to guard the faith, to found and rule churches, to ordain and discipline the clergy.'[52]

---

[51] Hooker Bk V.lxxviii.6, p.183.
[52] Charles Gore, *The Church and the Ministry*, revd. ed (London: SPCK, 1936), p.239.

However, there is no indication in the New Testament itself that this was the case. In the New Testament, prophets, evangelists and teachers are those called by God to exercise particular roles, not those who belong to a particular class of 'apostolic' ministers with authority over the elders and deacons.

To sum up, the evidence we have looked at so far in this chapter shows us that in New Testament times there were in existence the three orders of apostles, elders and deacons. The apostles were directly appointed by Christ and the elders and deacons were originally appointed by the apostles acting under Christ's authority.

As we shall now go on to see, the earliest external evidence we possess, that provided by the *Didache* and *First Clement,* further supports this reading of the internal New Testament evidence.

The Didache

The *Didache* (the full title of which is *The Teaching* [Gk. *didache*] *of the Lord to the Gentiles through the Twelve Apostles*) is a two-part document. The first part, running from 1.1-6.2, is a basic summary of the Christian way of life which was probably intended for those preparing for baptism. The second part, running from 6.3-16.8, contains instructions about fasting, prayer, the celebration of the Eucharist, the welcome to be extended to travelling 'apostles' 'prophets,' and 'teachers,' the appointment of ministers in the local church, and the need to be prepared for the Lord's return.

The date of the *Didache* has been much debated. However, it seems likely that it was put into its present form in about 150, but on the basis of material which reflects the state of the Church in Syria in about A.D. 70.[53]

What the *Didache* tells us about Christian ministry at that time is that there were itinerant charismatic ministers (which is what the terms 'apostles,' 'prophets' and 'teachers' means – the three terms referring

---

[53] J P Audet, *La Didache: Instructions des Apotres* (Paris: Gabalda, 1958), pp. 187-206.

to the same people) who are to be welcomed if their teaching 'contributes to righteousness and knowledge of the Lord.'[54] However, if what they teach is contrary to the Christian faith as set out in the first part of the *Didache* then they should not be listened to, and if they stay for more than two or three days, ask for money, or are unwilling to work for a living, then their ministry is bogus. [55]

However, alongside these itinerant ministers, local churches are also to choose for themselves 'bishops and deacons worthy of the Lord, men who are humble and not avaricious and true and approved.' It is these people who constitute the regular local ministry of the church and who enable the community to meet together on the Lord's Day to 'break bread and give thanks.' [56] The *Didache* warns its readers not to 'despise' these bishops and deacons 'for they are your honoured men, along with the prophets and teachers.' [57]

As in the New Testament, the presence of charismatic forms of ministry is recognised and affirmed (although with appropriate caution), but the regular form of local ministry is that of 'bishops and deacons' which, as in Philippians 1:1, means elders and deacons. As the full title of the *Didache* also makes clear, the basis for having this kind of local ministry is the teaching of the Lord given through the apostles. This in turn points to the fact that, like the New Testament, the *Didache* regards the ministry of Christ through the apostles as authoritative for the life of the Church.

1 Clement

According to a tradition which there is no good reason to doubt, Clement of Rome was the co-worker of St Paul mentioned in

---

[54] *The Didache,* 11.2 in J B Lightfoot, J R Harmer and Michael Holmes, *The Apostolic Fathers*, 2ed (Leicester: Apollos, 1990), p.155.
[55] *The Didache,* 11:3-13:7, pp. 155-157.
[56] *The Didache,* 5:1, p. 157.
[57] The Didache, 15:2, p.157.

Philippians 4:3: 'they have laboured side by side with me in the gospel together with Clement and the rest of my fellow workers.'[58]

At the end of the first century there had been a division in the church in Corinth ('the detestable and unholy schism, so alien and strange to those chosen by God, which a few reckless and arrogant persons have kindled to such a pitch of insanity that your good name, once so renowned and loved by all, has been greatly reviled'[59]). Clement wrote to the Corinthians on behalf of the Church in Rome in about 96 to urge them to bring this division to an end. One of the causes of division in Corinth had been a revolt against the leadership of the church by some of its younger members[60] and as part of his response to this issue Clement writes as follows about the origins of the orders of ministry in the Church:

The apostles received the gospel for us from the Lord Jesus Christ; Jesus the Christ was sent forth from God. So then Christ is from God and the apostles are from Christ. Both, therefore, came of the will of God in good order. Having therefore received their orders and being fully assured by the resurrection of our Lord Jesus Christ and full of faith in the Word of God, they went forth with the firm assurance that the Holy Spirit gives, preaching the good news that the kingdom of God was about to come. So, preaching both in the country and in the towns, they appointed their first fruits, when they had tested them by the Spirit, to be bishops and deacons for the future believers. And this was no new thing they did, for indeed something had been written about bishops and deacons many years ago; for somewhere thus says the Scripture: 'I will appoint their bishops in righteousness and their deacons in faith.'[61]

---

[58] See Eusebius, *Ecclesiastical History*, III. xv in Eusebius Ecclesiastical History (Cambridge and London: Harvard University Press, 1980), vol.1, pp.233-234.
[59] *1 Clement* 1:1, in Lightfoot, Harmer and Holmes, p. 28.
[60] See *1 Clement* 3:3, 44:6, 47:6.
[61] *1 Clement* 42:1-5, in Lightfoot, Harmer and Holmes, p.51. The quotation at the end is Clement's rendering of the LXX version of Isaiah 60:17.

In addition, elsewhere in *1 Clement* there are also references to 'elders' and the context in both cases indicates that 'elders' is being used as a synonym for 'bishops.' [62]

In agreement with the New Testament and with the *Didache*, *1 Clement* thus teaches that Christ appointed the apostles and the apostles in turn appointed bishops/elders and deacons. There is a threefold ministry of apostles, bishops/elders and deacons and this threefold ministry has divine authority.

In 1 Clement 44:4 Clement warns the Corinthians: '...it will be no small sin for us, if we depose from the bishop's office those who have offered the gifts blamelessly and in holiness.' Some translators see these words as a general reference to the performance of the duties of a bishop. Maxwell Staniforth, for example, translates the passage as warning against taking the bishopric away 'from men who have been performing its duties with this impeccable devotion.'[63] However what the text literally says is that these men 'presented the offerings proper to the episcopate' (*ta dora tes episkopes apobalomen*) and this is most probably a reference to offering the bread and wine to God for consecration at Holy Communion. As previously noted, this would provide evidence that it was the elders who presided when Holy Communion took place.

Conclusion

In this chapter we have seen why the Preface to the Ordinal is right to say that 'holy Scripture and Ancient Authors' show that the offices of elder and deacon have existed in the Church since the time of apostles. The evidence that we have looked at from the New Testament, the *Didache* and *1 Clement* clearly shows this to have been the case.

What we have not seen in this chapter, however, is evidence that the Preface is right to say that a separate office of bishop, distinct from,

[62] *1 Clement* 44:4, and 47:6, pp.53 and 55,
[63] Maxwell Staniforth, *Early Christian Writings* (Harmondsworth: Penguin, 1978), p.46.

and superior to, the office of elder, also goes back to apostolic times. In the texts we have looked at in this chapter 'bishop' (*episkopos*) is simply an alternative word for elder.

Nevertheless, there is evidence that a separate office of bishop, distinct from that of elder did exist in New Testament times. In the next two chapters we shall examine this evidence, starting in the next chapter with the evidence from the New Testament, the *Didache* and *1 Clement*.

Chapter 2
Ministry in the New Testament II - Bishops in the New Testament

The apostles as the first bishops

In this chapter we are going to begin by examining the evidence in the New Testament for the existence of an office of bishop which is distinct from the office of elder.

Before we begin this examination, we first of all need to define more precisely what we mean by the term 'bishop' in this connection. The definition which we shall use is that given by Richard Hooker in *The Laws of Ecclesiastical Polity*. He defines a bishop as:

...a minister of God, unto whom with permanent continuance there is given not only power of administering Word and Sacrament, which power other Presbyters have, but also a further power to ordain ecclesiastical persons, and a power of chiefty in government over Presbyters as well as Layman, a power to be by way of jurisdiction a Pastor even to Pastors themselves.[64]

The word 'chiefty' means the power to exercise the authority of a chief and so what Hooker is saying is that bishops are ministers of God who have power given to them by God:

- To preach the Word and administer the sacraments;

- To ordain other ministers;

- To exercise lawful authority ('jurisdiction') over both elders and all other members of the Church;

- To be a pastor to the other pastors.

---

[64] Hooker Bk. VII.ii.3, p. 334.

As Hooker goes on to say, when the term bishop is understood in this way it is clear from the New Testament that 'The first Bishops in the Church of God were his blessed Apostles.' [65]

The biblical evidence, he says, shows that just as the apostles preached the gospel, so also they governed the Church, and in the exercise of their governmental role they performed the office of bishop.

They which were termed Apostles, as being sent of Christ to publish his gospel throughout the world, and were named likewise Bishops, in that the care of government was also committed unto them, did no less perform the offices of their episcopal authority by governing, than of their apostolical by teaching.[66]

As we saw in the last chapter, the apostles initially exercised their governmental role entirely on their own, but in time they delegated some aspects of it to the deacons and elders. However, as Acts and the Epistles make clear, the apostles nonetheless retained overall governmental responsibility for the Church as a whole and for the various churches that were part of it.

Hooker goes on to explain that originally the apostles were bishops 'at large' but that in time some of them at least became bishops 'with restraint.'[67] What he means by this is that originally the apostles were given by Christ an indefinite commission not restricted to any one place, as we see in passages such as Matthew 28:19-20, John 21:15-17 and Acts 1:8. However, from the New Testament, and from later Church historians, we also learn that the apostles, under the guidance of the Holy Spirit, subsequently put limits or 'restraints' on the exercise of their ministry. To quote Hooker again:

[65] Hooker Bk, VII.iv.1. p.336. In support of this statement, he quotes the words of Cyprian 'But deacons ought to remember that the Lord chose apostles, that is bishops and overseers' (Cyprian, Epistle LXIV in *The Ante-Nicene Fathers*, vol.V, Edinburgh and Grand Rapids: T&T Clark/Eerdmans, 1995, p.366).
[66] Hooker, Bk. VII.iv.1. pp.336-337.
[67] Hooker, Bk. VII.iv.1-2, p.337.

...notwithstanding our Saviour's commandment unto them to go and preach unto all nations; yet some restraint we see there was made, when by agreement between Paul and Peter, moved with those effects of their labours which the providence of God brought forth, the one betook himself to the Gentiles, the other unto the Jews, for the exercise of that office of everywhere preaching. A further restraint of their apostolic labours as yet there was also made, when they divided themselves into several parts of the world; John for his charging taking Asia, and so the residue other quarters to labour in.[68]

What was at first a general episcopal ministry exercised by the apostles thus became over the course of time a specific episcopal ministry relating to particular people and particular places.

James in Jerusalem
A further example of this episcopal restraint can be seen in the ministry of James, the brother of Jesus. As we noted in the previous chapter, James was someone who had the ministry of an apostle. This meant that he possessed episcopal authority, 'chiefly in government' to use Hooker's phrase. However, there seems to have been only one place where he exercised his episcopal authority and that was Jerusalem.

In the New Testament, subsequently to the resurrection, we only ever find James in Jerusalem and there he exercises episcopal ministry over the church.

Acts
We noted in the previous chapter that in Acts 12:17, after his miraculous deliverance from prison, Peter tells the Christians whom he has seen at the house of Mary the mother of Mark to report what has happened to 'James and to the brethren.' Those who are to be told are the leadership of the church in Jerusalem which consists of 'the

---

[68] Hooker, Bk.VII.iv.2, pp.337-338. For the division of labours between Peter and Paul he cites Galatians 2:8 and for John's ministry in Asia Minor he cites Eusebius, *Ecclesiastical History*, Bk.III.16, and Tertullian, *Against Marcion*, Bk.IV.5.

brethren' (i.e. the elders) and James, who is mentioned separately because he is not just an elder, but the person who exercises episcopal authority over them and over the Jerusalem church as a whole.

We next encounter James in Acts 15 in connection with the council which takes place in Jerusalem to consider the question of whether Gentile converts to Christianity need to be circumcised and to keep the law of Moses in its entirety. In the same way that the Jewish Sanhedrin, which made legal decisions for the Jewish nation, consisted of the chief priests and the elders (Matthew 27:1, Luke 22:66, Acts 4:33) and was presided over by the high priest,[69] so in like manner the council at Jerusalem acts as the Christian Sanhedrin, making a decision for the New Israel,[70] and it consists of the apostles and the elders (Acts 15: 3, 6, 22, 23) and, in place of the high priest, James, who gives the final judgement on the matter under discussion that is then accepted by the apostles and elders and communicated by letter to the Gentile Christians in Antioch, Syria and Cilicia (Acts 15: 13-29).

If we ask why it is James who gives the decisive verdict at the council and appears to have also framed the letter that was sent out to communicate its decision,[71] the answer cannot be that it was because he was the most senior apostle present. That was Peter. The answer has to be that it was because he was the person with episcopal authority in the church in Jerusalem and it was the church in Jerusalem, as the centre of Jewish Christianity, which needed to be persuaded about the conditions on which Gentiles should be admitted into the Church.

The final reference to James in Acts is in 21:18. Paul is back in Jerusalem, once again bringing a collection for the assistance of the church in Judaea (Acts 24:17), and Luke tells us, 'Paul went in with us

---

[69] Beckwith p.33.

[70] Alan Richardson, *An Introduction to the Theology of the New Testament* (London: SCM, 1958), p.327.

[71] Lightfoot, *Philippians*, p.197, notes that the letter 'is clearly framed on his recommendations and some indecisive coincidences of style with his epistle have been pointed out.'

to James, and all the elders were present.' As in Acts 12:17, we have here a description of the leadership of the church in Jerusalem and it consists of the elders and James as the person with episcopal authority.

Galatians

If we move on to Galatians we find Paul visiting Jerusalem three years after his conversion. There he sees Peter ('Cephas' as he is referred to, using the Aramaic form of his name) and James (Galatians 1:18-19) both of whom are referred to as 'apostles.'

Then in chapter 2. Paul visits Jerusalem again fourteen years later. There he meets with those reputed to be pillars, 'namely 'James, Cephas and John' (Galatians 2:9) who agree that Paul and Barnabas 'should go to the Gentiles and they to the circumcised.'

As Lightfoot notes, the term 'pillars' was one that was 'commonly used by the Jews in speaking of the great teachers of the law'[72] the idea being that as pillars hold up a building so the teachers of the law uphold the people of God. Its use here indicates that James, Peter and John are regarded as the three great teachers of the Christian faith who by their teaching uphold the Church.

The reason Paul uses the word 'reputed' is because he wants to make the point that they only actually function as pillars if they remain faithful to the gospel and, as he will go on to explain in v11-21, he thinks Peter has failed to do this by caving into pressure from conservative Jewish Christians and withdrawing from fellowship with Gentile Christians in Antioch even though he has previously accepted the admission of Gentiles into the Church.

As Lightfoot further notes, the order in which the three pillars are named in verse 9, with James coming first and then Peter, is significant. In his words:

The relative positions here assigned to Peter and James accord exactly

---

[72] Lightfoot, *Galatians*, p. 109,

with the account in the Acts. When St. Paul is speaking of the missionary office of the Church at large, St. Peter holds the foremost place (ver.7-8); when he refers to a special act of the Church of Jerusalem, St. James is mentioned first (ver.9). [73]

In Jerusalem James is the leading authority and this explains why in Galatians 2:12 those conservative Jewish Christians who have come down from Jerusalem and disrupted the church in Antioch are described as 'certain men' who 'came from James.' This does not mean that what they said actually had James' support. This would be inconsistent with his endorsement of Paul's mission in Galatians 2:9 and Acts 15:24 also says specifically that this was not the case, declaring that they 'troubled you with words, unsettling your minds' although 'we gave them no instructions' ('we' here including James). What seems likely, as Donald Guthrie suggests, is that these people:

...were doing some special mission under the direction of James and had not been sent specifically to spy out the position regarding Jewish-Gentile fellowship. They possibly protested when they saw what had happened and their protests may have been the occasion of Peter's inconsistency, since he wished to avoid a rift. [74]

However, the fact that these people obviously invoked James' support for their position, and that this claim carried sufficient weight to disrupt the church at Antioch, is further testimony to the authority he had as the person with episcopal authority in the church in Jerusalem. Because he has such authority what he said (or even what it was claimed he said) mattered.

The Letter of James
The final piece of New Testament evidence is the Letter of James. If we accept that James was its author,[75] we see him, like the authors of the

---

[73] Lightfoot, *Galatians*, p.109.
[74] Donald Guthrie, *Galatians* (Grand Rapids & London: Eerdmans/Marshall, Morgan & Scott, 1973), p 84.
[75] For the arguments for this position see Guthrie, *New Testament Introduction*, pp. 736-758, F.J.A. Hort, *The Epistle of James* (London: Macmillan, 1909), pp. xi-

other letters in the New Testament, speaking with apostolic authority to those Christians to whom the letter is addressed.

In James 1:1 the letter is addressed to 'the twelve tribes of the dispersion.' This could be a term that refers to Christians in general, but the traditional view that it was addressed to Jewish Christians scattered across the Roman Empire still seems preferable.[76] If this is correct, the letter provides further evidence of the authority that James had among Jewish Christians as the leader of the church in Jerusalem. In the words of Frederick Hort, 'His own position as head of the Jerusalem Church gave him a special right to address Jewish Christians.'[77]

Summary of the New Testament material on James

What the New Testament material we have just looked at tells us is that from a very early date James the Lord's brother became the leader of the church in Jerusalem, a role that distinguishes him from the elders, who are mentioned separately. It is in this role that he is told about St. Peter's deliverance from prison in Acts 12:17, plays a decisive role in the council of Jerusalem in Acts 15:13-29, and receives St. Paul and his companions in Acts 21:18. It is also in this role that he endorses St. Paul's mission to the Gentiles in Galatians 2:9 and sends people to Antioch in Galatians 2:12. Finally, it is in this role that he addresses Jewish Christians across the Roman world in his letter.

The witness of the Early Church

What the New Testament tells us about. James receives additional support from what is said about him by the writers of the Early Church.

Papias, who was Bishop of Hierapolis in Asia Minor, lived from about 60-130 AD and is said to have been a pupil of John. In Fragment X of

---

xxii, Doulas Moo, *James* (Leicester & Grand Rapids: Inter-Varsity Press/Eerdmans, 2000), pp.19-30.

[76] Guthrie, pp.758-761.

[77] Hort, p. xxiii.

his writings, dating from the end of the first or the beginning of the second century, he refers to 'James the bishop and apostle.'[78]

Hegesippus, who lived from about 110-180 AD, was a Jewish convert who wrote a five-volume work entitled *Commentaries on the Acts of the Church*. This has now been lost to us, but two statements concerning James from the fifth volume are preserved by Eusebius of Caesarea and Jerome. The first says that 'The charge of the Church passed to James the brother of the Lord, together with the Apostles.'[79] The second declares 'After the apostles, James the brother of the Lord surnamed the Just was made head of the Church in Jerusalem.'[80]

Clement of Alexandria was a theologian who lived from c150-c215. He recorded in the sixth book of his work called the *Hypotyposes* that 'Peter and James and John after the Ascension of the Saviour did not struggle for glory, because they had previously been given honour by the Saviour, but chose James the Just as bishop of Jerusalem.'[81]

Eusebius of Caesarea, who, lived from c260- c340 AD, was the first major Church historian. As well as quoting from Hegesippus, he writes in Book II of his *Ecclesiastical History* about 'James, the brother of the Lord, to whom the throne of the bishopric in Jerusalem had been allotted by the Apostles.'[82] In Book VII he further writes about 'the throne of James, who was the first to receive from the Saviour and the apostles the episcopate of the church at Jerusalem, who also, as the divine books show, was called a brother of Christ.'[83]

Jerome, who lived from c347-420 AD, was a theologian and biblical scholar. As well as quoting from Hegesippus, he writes in his book

---

[78] Papias, Fragment X, in *The Ante-Nicene Fathers*, vol.I. (Edinburgh and Grand Rapids: T&T Clark/Eerdmans, 1996) p.155.
[79] Eusebius, *Ecclesiastical History,* II: xiii, vol.1, p.171.
[80] Jerome, 'Lives of Illustrious Men,' in *The Nicene and Post Nicene Fathers,* 2nd series, vol.3 (Edinburgh and Grand Rapids: T&T Clark/Eerdmans, 1996) p.361.
[81] Eusebius, *Ecclesiastical History*, II.i, vol.1 p. 105.
[82] Eusebius, *Ecclesiastical History*, II.xiii, vol.1. p.169.
[83] Eusebius, Ecclesiastical History, VII.xix, vol.2, p.177.

Lives of illustrious men that St. James was 'after our Lord's passion at once ordained by the apostles bishop of Jerusalem' and that he 'ruled the church of Jerusalem thirty years.' [84]

The apocryphal letter of Clement to James, which probably dates from the fourth century, and which reflects the very high estimate of James among Jewish Christians, describes James as 'the bishop of bishops, who rules Jerusalem, the holy church of the Hebrews, and the churches everywhere evidently founded by the providence of God.' [85]

What is said in these sources is consistent with, but also supplements, what we are told about James in the New Testament. What we are told in these sources is that:

- James was an apostle and he originally led the Church in Jerusalem alongside the other apostles.

- At some point early on in the history of Church, the leadership of the church in Jerusalem was passed by the other apostles to James, the choice of James originally being made by the three leading apostles, Peter, John and James.

- He then led the church in Jerusalem for many years and achieved a very high reputation among Jewish Christians. 86

The description of James in these later sources as bishop of Jerusalem is strictly speaking an anachronism. There is no evidence that during his own lifetime he was ever referred to as a bishop. In the New Testament the titles given to him are 'apostle,' 'pillar' and 'servant of God and of the Lord Jesus Christ.'[87] However, the use of the title employs later terminology to express the truth that he exercised

[84] Jerome, pp.361-2.
[85] Epistle of Clement to James, Inscription, in *The Ante-Nicene Fathers*, vol.I (Edinburgh and Grand Rapids: T&T Clark/Eerdmans, 1995) p. 218.
[86] For a detailed argument in support of the view of James summarised here see Bruce Chilton and Jacob Neusner, *The Brother of Jesus - James the Just and His Mission* (Louisville: Westminster John Knox Press: 2004).
[87] James 1:1.

individual episcopal oversight in the church in Jerusalem. He was in fact, if not in name, the bishop of the church in Jerusalem.

As we saw in the last chapter, there were also elders and deacons in the church in Jerusalem. This means, in the words of the nineteenth century English writer James Cartwright, that in the earliest days of the church in Jerusalem: 'there were the three orders of bishop, presbyter or priest and deacon.'[88] The evidence we have tells us that:

There was a superior pastor, not occasionally or temporarily, but permanently presiding, and whom we now call a bishop; there were 'elders' or presbyters dispensing the Word of Life under the chief pastor, and whom we now usually call 'priests;' and there were other ministers specially ordained to take care of the poor, and who yet united ministerial labours with this charge, whom the Church has called deacons.[89]

As Cartwright goes on to explain, it also appears the early church in Jerusalem constituted what we would now call a 'diocese.' That is to say, James was the bishop not just of a single congregation but of multiple congregations meeting in different places. In the words of Cartwright, the church in Jerusalem is referred to as one church, a 'particular body.' However:

The members of this particular body had their assemblies for Christian worship and spiritual edification, and from their numbers must have formed into many separate congregations. No one room could have accommodated the three thousand persons converted on the day of Pentecost, much less the many thousands added within a few weeks of that time. We have, therefore, from the very

---

[88] James Cartwright, *The Church of St James. The primitive Hebrew Christian Church of Jerusalem: its history, character and constitution* (Miami: Hard Press, 2017), Kindle edition, Loc. 726.
[89] Cartwright, Loc. 726.

commencement of the Church, an instance of one bishop presiding over many congregations.[90]

The episcopal succession in Jerusalem after James

Even though the evidence for the episcopal ministry of James in Jerusalem is incontrovertible, the possibility exists that this was a purely personal ministry which ended when he was martyred in about 62 AD and was then replaced by a different form of church government. The New Testament is silent on this issue, but the evidence from the Early Church is not.

Hegesippus tells us that:

After James the Just had suffered martyrdom for the same reason as the Lord, Symeon, his cousin the son of Clopas was appointed bishop, whom they all proposed because he was another cousin of the Lord. [91]

Eusebius gives his own, slightly expanded version of the same story:

After the martyrdom of James and the capture of Jerusalem which immediately followed, the story goes that those of the Apostles and of the disciples of the Lord who were still alive came together from every place with those who were, humanly speaking, of the family of the Lord, for many of them were then still alive, and they all took counsel together as to whom they ought to adjudge worthy to succeed James, and all unanimously decided that Simeon the son of Clopas, whom the Scripture of the Gospel also mentions [Luke 24:18, John 19:25] was worthy of the throne of the diocese there. [92]

Eusebius also records a list of Jewish bishops who ruled over the church in Jerusalem until the expulsion of Jews from Jerusalem after the Bar Kokhba rebellion of 132-136 AD. He writes:

---

[90] Cartwright, Loc. 737.
[91] Eusebius, *Ecclesiastical History*, IV.xxii, p.375.
[92] Eusebius, *Ecclesiastical History*, III.xi, p. 233.

I have not found any written statement of the dates of the bishops in Jerusalem, for tradition says that they were extremely short-lived, but I have gathered from documents this much – that up to the siege of the Jews by Hadrian the successions of the bishops were fifteen in number. It is said that they were all Hebrews by origin who had nobly accepted the knowledge of Christ, so that they were counted worthy of episcopal ministry by those who had the power to judge such questions. For their whole church at that time consisted of Hebrews who continued Christian from the Apostles down to the siege at the time when the Jews rebelled against the Romans and were beaten in a great war. Since the Jewish bishops then ceased, it is now necessary to give their names from the beginning. The first then was James who was called the Lord's brother, and after him Simeon was second. The third was Justus, Zacchaeus was the fourth. Tobias the fifth, the sixth Benjamin, the seventh John, the eighth Matthias, the ninth Philip, the tenth Seneca, the eleventh Justus, the twelfth Levi, the thirteenth Ephres, the fourteenth Joseph and last of all the fifteenth Judas. Such were the bishops in the city of Jerusalem, from the Apostles down to the time mentioned, and they were all Jews. [93]

Later on in his *Ecclesiastical History* he further notes that after Jerusalem ceased to be a Jewish city following the Bar Kokhba rebellion:

...the church in that city was composed of Gentiles, in succession to the Jewish Christians, and that the first of the Gentile bishops was Marcus. After him the local successions record that Cassian was bishop, and after him was Publius, then Maximus, in addition to them Julian, then Gaius, after him Symmachus and Gaius the second, and then another Julian, and Capito, and in addition to them Valens and Dolichianus, and after them all Narcissus, the thirtieth from the apostles according to the regular succession.[94]

[93] Eusebius, *Ecclesiastical History*, IV.v, pp.309-311.
[94] Eusebius, *Ecclesiastical History,* V.xii, pp.465-467. In this quotation only thirteen names are listed. Comparison with another of Eusebius' works called the

The fact that the list of Jewish bishops contains thirteen names covering a period of less than thirty years has led to the accuracy of this list being questioned. However, Eusebius' own words indicates that the short length of the episcopates of the early Jewish bishops was something that was recognised and accepted as true in the sources he drew upon and we have no better sources of information which indicate that these sources were wrong. Furthermore, as Lightfoot notes, there are parallels in the history of the Papacy, with thirteen Popes listed between 882 and 904 AD and almost as rapid succession in other times of trouble.[95]

There is thus no good reason to question the fact there was an unbroken line of episcopal succession in the mother church of Jerusalem from the time of the apostles onwards. To put the same thing another way, from almost the very beginning of the Church there have been bishops in Jerusalem.

The issue that arises, however, is whether it was *only* in Jerusalem that there were bishops from the time of the apostles. Is there any evidence to indicate that there were bishops in other churches as well in New Testament times? The answer is that there is such evidence, and the first piece of evidence is what we learn about the ministries of Timothy and Titus in the letters sent to them by Paul sometime around 65-67 AD.

Timothy and Titus in Ephesus and Crete

The biblical witness
Timothy was the son of a Greek father and a Jewish mother (Act 16:1) who was converted to Christianity at some point early in his life and who became a companion of Paul during the apostle's second missionary journey (Acts 16:1-3). He then travelled with Paul during his second and third missionary journeys. At some point he was

Chronicon indicates that the names of Maximus the second and Antoninus are missing after Capito.
[95] Lightfoot, p.209.

ordained as an elder by Paul (1 Timothy 4:14, 2 Timothy 1:6) and he represented Paul in special missions to a number of churches including those at Thessalonica (1 Thessalonians 3:1-2) and Corinth (1 Corinthians 4:17).

He was in Rome with Paul at the time of St. Paul's first imprisonment there (Philemon 1, Philippians 1:1, 2:19-24, Colossians 1:1) and at the time 1 and 2 Timothy was written he was in Ephesus where the apostle had asked him to remain in order to tackle the threat of heresy in the Ephesian church. In Paul's words:

As I urged you when I was going to Macedonia, remain at Ephesus that you may charge certain persons not to teach any different doctrine, nor to occupy themselves with myths and endless genealogies which promote speculations rather than the divine training that is in faith (1 Timothy 1:3-4).

Titus was a Gentile who accompanied Paul and Barnabas to Jerusalem in the visit recorded in Galatians 2:1-10. He acted as Paul's representative to the church at Corinth (2 Corinthians 5:6-7, 13-15, 8:6, 16-17, 23, 12:18) and at the time Titus was written he had been left in Crete by Paul 'that you might amend what was defective, and appoint elders in every town as I directed you' (Titus 1:5).

As Bilson observes, the background to the ministries of Timothy in Ephesus and Titus in Crete was the need to counteract the divisions that were opening up in both churches as the result of the activities of false teachers.

In Bilson's words:

To prevent these deceivers and repress these perverse teachers, Paul was forced, whiles he lived and laboured in other places, to send special substitutes to the churches most endangered; and by their pains and oversight to cure the sores and heal the wounds, which these pestilent and unquiet spirits had made. [96]

At Ephesus, Bilson writes, this meant that:

....when the teachers and doctors began to 'affirm they knew not what, even profane and doting fables, whose word did fret as a canker, and crept into houses leading captive simple women laden with sins and led with divers lusts; and other having itching ears gat them teachers after their own lusts, and turned their ears from the truth to fables;'[97] Paul sent Timothy thither to 'stay these profane and vain babblings,' to 'commend that they taught no strange doctrine,' ' to 'impose hands' on such as were fit, to 'receive accusations against' sinful and ungodly presbyters, and to 'rebuke them openly' according to their deserts, to 'reject' young and wanton 'widows' and to see true 'labourers in the word' honoured and cherished and finally to oversee the whole house of God and every part thereof, as well teachers and presbyters, as deacons, widows and hearers.[98] And not only instructed him how he should 'behave himself' as governor in the church, but 'charged him before the living God and his elect angels, that he observed these things without respecting persons or any inclining to parts.'[99]

In Crete, likewise, when:

...many vain talkers and deceivers of minds, subverted whole houses,' and loaded the church 'with Jewish fables and commandments of men;' Paul left Titus there to 'redress' things amiss, to 'stop their mouths that taught things which they ought not for filthy lucre's sake,' to 'stay foolish questions and contentions about the law,' to 'reject heretics after one of two admonitions,' and 'sharply to rebuke with all authority, not suffering any man to despise him;' as also to 'ordain' good and religious 'presbyters and bishops in every city,' that should

[96] Bilson, p.299.
[97] 1 Timothy 1:7, 4:7, 2 Timothy 2:17, 3:6, 4:3-4.
[98] 2 Timothy 2:16, 1 Timothy 1:3, 5:22, 5:19, 5:20, 5:11, 5:17.
[99] 1 Timothy 3:15, 5:21. Text in Bilson pp.299-300.

be 'able to exhort with wholesome doctrine' and 'improve gainsayers'.[100]

In giving Timothy and Titus the authority to act in these ways, Paul was giving them what later Christian terminology would call episcopal authority over the churches in Ephesus and Crete.

If we look at the letters to Timothy and Titus, we find that in order to carry out the ministry summarised by Bilson Timothy and Titus have the authority to teach, to ordain, and to exercise godly discipline over all members of the church, whether ordained or lay. Furthermore, as in the case of James in Jerusalem, this authority is one that has been given to them as individuals. It is not one that is shared with other elders, but one that belongs to them and to them alone.

The witness of the Early Church

Recognising their possession of episcopal authority, the writers of the Early Church subsequently declared that Timothy and Titus had been bishops in Ephesus and Crete in the same way that James had been the bishop in Jerusalem.

Eusebius, for example, declares that 'Timothy is related to have been the first appointed bishop of the diocese of Ephesus, as Titus of the churches in Crete.'[101]

As Bilson notes, Eusebius' testimony has the support of numerous other writers from the Early Church. For example:

- Jerome:

'Timothy was ordained bishop of Ephesus by blessed Paul; and Titus bishop of Crete preached the gospel there and in the islands round about.'

- Ambrose (c339-397 AD, bishop and theologian):

---

[100] Titus 1:10, 11, 3:9-10, 2:13, 1:5,9. Text in Bilson p.300.
[101] Eusebius of Caesarea, III. iii, pp.195-197.

'(Paul) by his epistle instructeth Timothy, now created a bishop, how he ought to order the church.'

'The apostle had consecrated Titus to be a bishop, and therefore warned him to be careful in ecclesiastical ordination.'

- John Chrysostom (c 347-407 AD, bishop and theologian):

'Paul saith in his epistle to Timothy, 'Fulfil thy ministry,' when he was now a bishop; for that (Timothy) was a bishop, (Paul) declareth by his writing thus unto him. 'Lay hands hastily on no man''

'Why doth Paul write only to Timothy and Titus, whereas Silas and Luke were (also his disciples and) endued with marvellous virtues? Because he had delivered to them the government and charge of the church; the others as yet he did carry about with him.'

- Epiphanius of Salamis (c 315-403 AD, bishop and writer against heresy):

'The divine speech of the apostle teacheth who is a bishop, and who a presbyter; in saying to Timothy, a bishop, 'Rebuke not a presbyter, but exhort him as a Father.' How could a bishop rebuke a presbyter, if he had no power over a presbyter? As also 'Receive not an accusation against a presbyter, but under two or three witnesses.'

- Theodoret of Cyrus (c393-c466 AD, bishop, theologian and church historian):

'Titus was a notable disciple of Paul, and ordained by Paul a bishop of Crete, and authorised to make the bishops that were under him.' [102]

As the reference in Eusebius to Timothy and Titus as the *first* Bishops of Ephesus and Crete indicates, it was also held in the Early Church that, as in the case of James in Jerusalem, Timothy and Titus had successors. They were but the first in a continuous line of bishops in Ephesus and Crete. It was noted at the Council of Chalcedon in 451, for

[102] Bilson p.p.302-303.

example, that there had been twenty-seven bishops ordained at Ephesus in succession to Timothy.[103]

Objections to the idea that Timothy and Titus were bishops

The view expressed by the writers we have just looked at that Timothy and Titus were bishops was generally accepted throughout the Church for most of its history. However, since the nineteenth century it has come to be widely challenged and generally discounted. Four examples will serve to illustrate why this has been the case.

First, Lightfoot writes in his essay on 'The Christian Ministry' in 1868 that Timothy and Titus were not bishops, but 'apostolic delegates' with temporary commissions whose ministries formed a bridge between the role of the apostles and the role of bishops of the second century:

It is the conception of a later age which represents Timothy as bishop of Ephesus and Titus as bishop Crete. St Paul's own language implies that the position they held was temporary. In both cases their term of office is drawing to a close, when the Apostle writes. But the conception is not altogether without foundation. With less permanence but perhaps greater authority, the position occupied by these apostolic delegates fairly represents the functions of the bishop early in the second century. They were in fact the link between the Apostles whose superintendence was occasional and general and the bishop who exercised a permanent supervision over an individual congregation.[104]

Secondly, Gore declares in his book *The Church and the Ministry* in 1919 that Timothy and Titus were 'apostolic legates' with a ministry that was permanent, but was not localised in the same way as the ministry of later bishops, and which does not seem to have involved the appointment of successors:

[103] Richard Price and Michael Gaddis, *The Acts of the Council of Chalcedon* (Liverpool: Liverpool University Press, 2007), 3:16.
[104] Lightfoot, *Philippians*, p.199.

As apostolic legates, then, Timothy and Titus exercise what is essentially the later episcopal office, but it would not appear that their authority, though essentially permanent, was localized like that of the later diocesan bishop. Timothy indeed had been left at Ephesus by St. Paul to represent himself in view of that church's needs, and St. Paul certainly contemplates his continuing his ministry after his own death, and presumably in the same church of Ephesus, in which again it would appear that he had been solemnly ordained to his office. Nor perhaps can we argue against his localization from the fact of St. Paul summoning him to Rome, or from the fact of his having gone there. But there is a close analogy between the office of Timothy and that of Titus, and Titus certainly appears to have left Crete to join St. Paul, to have been his companion in Rome, and to have left again not for Crete but for Dalmatia. Again we do not gather from these Epistles any clear intimation that Timothy and Titus, though they were to prepare for a succession of sound teachers, were to ordain men to succeed them in their apostolic office in the local churches. All that we can fairly conclude is that St. Paul after ordaining, or with a view to ordaining, the local ministers, bishops and deacons, appointed delegates to exercise the apostolic office of supervision in his place, both before and after his death: and the needs which required this extension of the apostolic ministry were not transitory ones. They were the needs of 'the last times' – the constant phenomena of moral failure and doctrinal and moral instability and disorder. [105]

Thirdly, Gordon Fee argues in his commentary on 1 and 2 Timothy and Titus in 1988 that the temporary nature of the assignment given to Timothy and Titus means that their role was very different from the role of the bishops in Antioch and Smyrna at the beginning of the second century:

It is a mistaken notion to view Timothy or Titus as model pastors for a local church. The letters simply have no such intent. Although it is true that Timothy and Titus carry full apostolic authority, in both cases

---

[105] Gore, pp. 222-223.

they are itinerants on special assignment, there as Paul's apostolic delegates, not as permanent resident pastors. It is a far cry from Timothy's role in Ephesus and Titus' in the churches of Crete to that of Ignatius in Antioch or Polycarp in Smyrna fifty years later.[106]

Fourthly, Dick France explains in his commentary on Timothy, Titus and Hebrews in 2001 that in the Pastoral Letters 'bishop' is the name given to those appointed and overseen by Timothy and Titus rather than what they themselves are called:

''Bishops' (the Greek word might also be translated 'overseers' or 'superintendents') and 'elders' are apparently different names for the same people. They feature always as a group within a given church: there is no single 'bishop' or 'elder' who holds office on his own. If anyone in the Pastoral Letters is in such a position, it is Timothy and Titus, who are individuals brought in from outside to act under Paul's authority in their respective churches. But they are not called bishops; rather, the 'bishops' are those they appoint and oversee within the church, and those bishops (elders) are local people from within the church, not imports like Timothy and Titus. [107]

Why these objections are not persuasive
What are we to make of these objections to the traditional view?

First, it has to be acknowledged that, as in the case of James, the use of the term 'bishop' to refer to Timothy and Titus is anachronistic. That is not how their role would have been described in the first century. However, this does not mean that they were not in fact bishops in the sense that they performed the role to which the term bishop later came to be applied. As we have noted, they exercised an episcopal role in Ephesus and Crete and therefore it is not inaccurate to say that they were bishops in fact if not in name.

---

[106] Gordon Fee, *1 and 2 Timothy, Titus* (Exeter and Peabody: Paternoster Press/ Hendrickson), 1988), p.21.
[107] Dick France, *Timothy, Titus and Hebrews* (Oxford: BRF, 2001), p.15.

Secondly, there is nothing in the letters to Timothy and Titus that suggests that they were itinerant ministers who were only given a local ministry in Ephesus and Crete on a temporary basis. It is true that elsewhere in the New Testament we find them ministering in a variety of places. However, as we have noted above, in the letters to Timothy and Titus they have been appointed to exercise a localised ministry in Ephesus and Crete and no time limit on the exercise of this localised ministry is either stated or implied.

It is true that in 2 Timothy 4:9-13 and Titus 3:12 St. Paul asks Timothy and Titus to come to him and that in 2 Timothy 4:9 Titus is said to be in Dalmatia. However, there is no suggestion that this means that their ministry in Ephesus and Crete is drawing to a close or has drawn to a close.

Later tradition tells us that after spending time with Paul and ministering in Dalmatia they returned to resume their ministries in Ephesus and Crete and that they continued to exercise these ministries until their deaths at the end of the first century. The Pastoral Epistles do not provide evidence for this later ministry, but on the other hand they say nothing that rules it out. Indeed, it can be argued that what is said in the Pastoral Epistles supports the tradition in that, as Gore writes, they suggest that Paul appointed Timothy and Titus 'to exercise the apostolic office of supervision in his place, both before and after his death.' All that the later tradition tells us is that they faithfully fulfilled this apostolic commission after Paul's death in the places that he had specified.

It is likewise true that nothing is said in these letters about Timothy and Titus appointing anyone to succeed them. However, this does not mean that the tradition that they had successors is mistaken. If, at the end of the first century, the remaining apostles and the churches in Ephesus and Crete knew that the ministry that had been exercised by Timothy and Titus was of apostolic appointment, and if they saw that the need for this ministry still remained, then it is entirely likely that they would take steps to ensure that this ministry continued by appointing people to exercise it, in the same way that Simeon had been appointed to continue the ministry of James in Jerusalem.

To summarise, the internal evidence of the letters to Timothy and Titus and the external evidence of later tradition combine to tell us that Timothy and Titus exercised an episcopal ministry in Ephesus and Crete from the middle 60s onwards. They exercised this ministry, which had been given to them by Paul, until the end of the century and after their deaths their ministry was continued by a line of episcopal successors.

Taken with the evidence for elders and deacons in these letters, what this means is that we know there was a threefold ministry of bishops, elders and deacons not only in Jerusalem, but also elsewhere, from early on in the history of the Church.

It should also be noted, that like the ministry of James in Jerusalem, the episcopal ministry of Timothy and Titus seems to have involved the oversight of multiple congregations. To use later terminology, they were responsible for dioceses in Ephesus and Crete. In Titus 1:5 we are specifically told that Titus was charged by Paul with appointing elders 'in every town' in the island, which presumably means that there were congregations in those towns, and if the church in Ephesus followed the pattern we see elsewhere in the New Testament it would have consisted of a number of congregations meeting in people's homes.

The angels of the churches in Revelation 1-3
A final piece of New Testament evidence for the existence of bishops is what is said about the angels of the seven churches in Asia in Revelation 1-3.

In Revelation 1:16 Christ holds 'seven stars' in his right hand and in 1:20 John is told that 'the seven stars are the angels of the seven churches.' Then in Revelation 2:1-3:22 John is told to write to these angels, the angels of the churches of Ephesus, Smyrna, Pergamum, Thyratira, Sardis, Philadelphia and Laodicea.

Revelation is conventionally dated to between 90 and 95 AD and there seems to be no good tradition to challenge this dating.[108] The issue with regard to the letters to seven churches is what (if anything) these tell us about the form of ministry in these churches at this date.

The traditional view that the angels were the leaders of the churches

As Bilson notes, the traditional view, held both in the Early Church and at the time of the Reformation, was that the angels of the churches were the presiding pastors or bishops of the churches. He writes:

I take it to be a matter out of question, confirmed by the scriptures, and confessed by the old and new writers, that the Son of God willed St John the apostle in his Revelation to write to the seven chief pastors of the seven churches of Asia, calling them by the name of angels. 'By the divine voice,' saith Austin[109] ,'the ruler of the church (of Ephesus) is praised under the name of an angel. 'Angels he calleth bishops,' saith Ambrose, 'as we learn in the Revelation of John.' 'Angels he calleth those that be rulers of the churches,' saith Jerome, 'even as Malachi the prophet doth witness the priest to be an angel.' And Gregory[110]: 'The preachers in in the scripture are sometimes called angels, as the prophet saith, 'The lips of the priest should keep knowledge, and they should ask of the law at his mouth; for he is the angel (or messenger) of the Lord of Hosts." The new writers with one consent acknowledge the same. 'The angels,' saith Bullinger[111], 'are the ambassadors of God, even the pastors of the churches.' 'The heavenly letter is directed to the church of Smyrna, that is, to the pastor. Now the stories witness that angel and pastor of the church of Smyrna to have been Polycarp, ordained bishop (there) by the apostles themselves, I mean by St. John. He was made bishop of Smyrna thirteen years before the

---

[108] See the discussion in Guthrie, pp. 949-961 and Ian Paul, *Revelation* (London/Downers Grove: Inter-Varsity Press, 2018), pp. 19-22.
[109] Austin is an old name for Augustine of Hippo, 354-430, bishop and theologian.
[110] Gregory the Great, c540- 604, Pope and theologian.
[111] Heinrich Bullinger, 1504-1575, Swiss Reformer and theologian.

Revelation (of John) was written.' Marlorat[112]: 'John beginneth with the church of Ephesus for the celebrity of the place; and speaketh not to the people, but to the prince (or chief) of the clergy, even the bishop.' Seb Meyer[113]: "To the angel of the church of Sardis.' Among the bishops of this church, Melito was renowned, a man both learned and godly; but what predecessors or successors he had in the ministry of the church is not recorded.' Beza[114] saith: 'To the angel, that is to the chief president, who should have the first warning of these things, and from him the rest of his colleagues and the whole church.' [115]

Other pre-modern writers who held this view include the early English historian and biblical scholar the Venerable Bede (c 673-735) [116] and the Mediaeval biblical scholar Nicholas of Lyra (c1270-1340)[117]

The rejection of this traditional view

Like the view that Timothy and Titus were the bishops of Ephesus and Crete, the view that the angels of the churches were the presiding ministers of the seven churches of Asia has come to be generally rejected since the nineteenth century. In its place it has been held either that the angels of the churches are angelic beings who represent the seven churches before God, or that language about a church's angel is simply a way of personifying that prevailing characteristics of that church.

The four extracts below illustrate these two approaches.

First, in his essay on 'The Christian ministry,' Lightfoot declares that the idea that the angels of the churches are bishops is not suggested by the word angel itself and is not in keeping with 'the highly figurative

---

[112] Augustin Marlorat, 1506-1562, French Reformer and biblical commentator.
[113] Sebastian Meyer, a former Franciscan who helped to lead the Reformation in Berne.
[114] Theodore Beza, 1519-1565, Swiss Reformer and theologian.
[115] Bilson pp.373-375.
[116] Bede, *The Exposition of the Apocalypse* (Downers Grove: IVP, 2011), p.118.
[117] Philip Krey, *Nicholas of Lyra's Apocalypse Commentary* (Kalamazoo: Western Michigan University Press, 1997), pp.40-41,

style' of Revelation. He argues that the angels should be seen instead as either the guardian angels who represent the seven churches or as the personifications of these churches:

St John's own language gives the true key to the symbolism. 'The seven stars,' so it is explained, 'are the seven angels of the seven churches, and the seven candlesticks are the seven churches.' This contrast between the heavenly and the earthly fires – the star shining brightly by its own inherent eternal light, and the lamp flickering and uncertain, requiring to be fed with fuel and tended with care – cannot be devoid of meaning. The star is the supersensual counterpart, the heavenly representative; the lamp, the earthly realisation, the outward embodiment. Whether the angel is here conceived as an actual person, the celestial guardian, or only as a personification, the idea or spirit of the church, it is unnecessary for my present purpose to consider. But whatever may be the exact conception, he is identified with it and made responsible for it to a degree wholly unsuited to any human officer. Nothing is predicated of him, which may not be predicated of it. To him are imputed all its hopes, its fears, its graces, its shortcomings. He is punished with it and he is rewarded with it. [118]

Secondly, in his 1984 commentary on Revelation, George Caird maintains that the angels of the churches are spiritual beings who are the heavenly counterparts of the churches on earth:

The angels are not to be identified with bishops or pastors. The Jews had long since become accustomed to the idea that each nation had its angelic representative in heaven, who presided over its fortunes and was held accountable for its misdeeds, and John is simply adapting this familiar notion to a new situation. We must not confuse John's apocalyptic way of thinking with Platonic idealism, and suppose that the angel symbolizes the perfect heavenly pattern of which the earthly church is only a shadowy and imperfect reproduction. For John addresses his letters not to the earthly churches but to the angels, and holds them responsible for the faults of the communities they

[118] Lightfoot, pp.199-200.

represent. If we are to understand John's mind, we must rid our minds of the presupposition that earth is the place of faults and failings and heaven the place of perfection. In John's world heaven and earth are equally parts of the physical universe which God created, they belong inseparably together, and everything on earth, including its evil equivalent in heaven. When the old order is finally destroyed, John sees a new heaven as well as a new earth, for the former heaven and earth together, along with their contaminating evil, have been removed. The angels, then, are the 'spiritual counterparts of human individuals or communities, dwelling in heaven, but subject to changes depending on the good or evil behaviour of their complementary beings on earth.' [119]

Thirdly, in his 1998 commentary on Revelation, Robert Mounce writes that while the angels of the churches could be guardian angels it is better to see them as personifications of the spirit that prevails in each of the seven churches:

Many explanations have been proposed for the angels. If they are human beings (Matt 11:10 and other verses would allow this), they could be prominent officials of the local congregations or delegates sent to Patmos to be entrusted with the letters. The use of 'angel' in the book of Revelation (it occurs some 60 times) favors identifying the angels as heavenly beings. They could be guardian angels (cf. Dan 10:13, 20-21; Matt 18:10; Acts 12:15) or perhaps heavenly counterparts that came to be identified with the church. The most satisfactory answer, however, is that the angel of the church was a way of personifying the prevailing spirit of the church. This interpretation is strengthened by the fact that all seven letters are addressed to separate angels, a strange phenomenon if they refer to

---

[119] George Caird, *The Revelation of St John the Divine* (London: A&C Black, 2ed, 1984), pp. 24-25, quoting J H Moulton, 'It is his Angel,' *Journal of Theological Studies* III, p.514.

anything but the church since the contents are obviously intended for the congregation as a whole. [120]

Finally, in his 2018 commentary on Revelation, Ian Paul follows Caird in suggesting that the angels of the churches are angelic beings who represent the earthly reality of the seven churches in heaven:

The *angels* of the churches are unlikely to be human messengers, despite their role in receiving the messages that follow, since angels are so prominent in Revelation and are consistently heavenly. Neither should they be taken as standing for the 'spirit' of the churches in terms of their character. The most likely background is that of Daniel, where angels represent the earthly reality of nations and peoples in the heavenly realms (Dan. 10:12, 12:1) so Jesus holding the star/angel signifies his hold on the church communities themselves.[121]

What are we to make of the alternatives to the traditional view?
If we start with the view that the angels of the churches are simply the personifications of those churches, we find that it faces three major problems:

- One of the key objections to the traditional view is that it involves the word 'angel' having a different meaning to that which it has elsewhere in Revelation. However, this objection applies just as much to the personification idea. Angels elsewhere in Revelation are not bishops, but they are equally certainly not just personifications, but really existent spiritual beings.

- The use of the term angel as a personification is without parallel anywhere else in the Bible (unlike the use of the term *angelos* to refer to a human being which does occur – see Haggai 1:13, Malachi 2:7, 3:1, Matthew 11:10, Mark 1:2, Luke 7:27).

[120] Robert Mounce, *The Book of Revelation* (Grand Rapids/Cambridge: Eerdmans revd.ed, 1998),p.63.
[121] Paul, p.55.

- Proponents of this view have never explained why in the theology of Revelation the risen Christ asks John to write to a personification. If the message is really addressed to the church concerned why isn't John simply asked to write to that church? What is the point of writing to the angel of that church instead?

For these three reasons, and particularly for the last two, the personification approach is unconvincing.

If we turn to the view that the angels of the churches are not simply personifications, but actual angels in the sense of created spiritual beings we find that there are major difficulties with this view as well. As Peter Leithart argues in his recent commentary on Revelation, the view that the angels are human beings is far more plausible.

Leithart notes first of all that because the word *angelos* can be used for both a spiritual being and a human messenger of God: 'The word cannot decide the issue for us, and we are left to rely on the context.'[122]

One clue provided by the context is:

The fact that John has been associated with the stars, touched with the star hand of Jesus... If John is touched by the angel hand and joins the angels as a messenger to the churches, then it seems plausible that the other stars in Jesus' hands are also human beings.[123]

Furthermore, the fact that Jesus dictates messages to be sent to the angels by a human being also suggests that these angels are not angelic beings:

The widespread conclusion that these are angel-spirits rests on an abstract, ahistorical conception of what Jesus tells John to do. If Jesus *actually* appeared to John, dictated the *actual* words we read in the

[122] Peter Leithart, *Revelation 1-11* (London/New York: T&T Clark, 2018), Kindle Edition, Loc. 3040.
[123] Leithart, Loc.3040.

text, and expected John to *actually* send the messages to the churches, then the notion that the recipients are angel-spirits makes little sense. Why could not Jesus simply speak directly to his angelic messengers (as he appears to do in other places in Revelation)? Angels presumably have access to heaven, so Jesus can address them without the bother of sending off a circuit rider. Why send the letters off to the *churches* of Asia, if the messages themselves are addressed to angel-spirits? What interest would the churches of Asia have in Jesus' instructions to heavenly hosts? To put it provocatively, or snarkily: *Where do the angels receive their mail?* And, *how does John know the addresses?* The more we imagine a set of letters sent to angel-spirits, the more implausible it becomes. And then we are left with the unhappy (perhaps unfair) suspicion that commentators do not think Jesus *really* intended John to write to the angels at all. [124]

In addition, writes Leithart, the contents of the letters dictated to John also indicates that the recipients are human beings rather than angelic spirits:

Modern English translations distract us because they do not distinguish between the singular and plural of the second person, but in Greek most of the exhortations of the messages are explicitly addressed to a single person – the angel. Jesus charges the *angel* of Ephesus with leaving his first love (τὴν ἀγάπην σου τὴν πρώτην ἀφῆκες, 2:4). Jesus tells the *angel* of the church at Pergamum to repent, because Jesus is coming quickly (ἔρχομαί σοι ταχύ, 2:16). The *angel* of the church at Laodicea is lukewarm (χλιαρὸς εἶ, 3:16). Now, as difficult as it might be to imagine that Jesus holds the human leader of a city church responsible for the condition of his flock, it is far *more* difficult to determine what these charges and exhortations mean when addressed to an angel-spirit. Do angels suffer spiritual lethargy? Do they have dry spells and dark nights of the soul? Do they experience acedia? How does an angel *repent*? [125]

---

[124] Leithart, Loc. 3040-3053, italics in the original.
[125] Leithart, Loc. 3053-3065, italics in the original.

The view that angel-spirits are addressed makes the welfare of the members of the church apparently dependent on the spiritual state of the angels concerned:

...Jesus threatens to remove the lampstand (the church, 1:20) from Ephesus if the angel fails to repent. That leaves the future of the Ephesian church dependent *not* on the repentance of the community or its leader, but on the repentance of its spiritual guardian, over which the community can exert *no* influence. The leaves the church at the mercy of angels (who seem subject to volatile mood swings) the very sort of enslavement to principalities and powers from which Jesus delivers us.[126]

By contrast, what Revelation tells us, declares Leithart, is that under the new covenant the only supernatural angel that now mediates between God and his people:

...is Jesus' own angel, the Angel that is his Spirit (Revelation 1:1). The message of Jesus comes through a Spirit-filled man, through the slave John to the human messengers of the churches.[127]

The angels and the heavenly temple
As Leithart points out, the fact that these human messengers are described as angels fits in with what Revelation teaches about the participation by Christians in the worship of the heavenly temple:

That the church is led by 'angels' fits neatly with John's 'temple ecclesiology.' Priests in the tabernacle and temple were servants of God's house, which was an intrusion of heaven into earth. With their winged robes, they served among the cherubim around the throne of Yahweh. They were angels of the holy house. In the new covenant, all the baptized are made priests, hands filled to draw near to God in service round his throne. All are saints (ἅγιοι) and dwell in heaven (Rev, 12:12; 13:6) in contrast to others who are earth-bound land-dwellers (11:10, 14;6). If they live and serve God in heaven, they form

[126] Leithart, Loc. 3065-3075, italics in the original.
[127] Leithart Loc.3075.

a company of human angels, and their leaders are chief angels. The head angel over the churches of a city is the angel of that church, as the chief Angel of all the angels of the churches is the Angel of Jesus, the Spirit.[128]

Leithart says that the angels were the leaders of the churches (plural) in each city because of the New Testament evidence, to which we have already referred, that in New Testament times Christians met together in small assemblies in people's houses. The angel of each church had overall responsibility for all these assemblies which together constituted 'the church' in a particular place such as Ephesus or Smyrna.

The angels as bishops

The same evidence from the letters that points to the angels of the churches being human beings rather than angelic spirits also points to those humans being the bishops of the churches concerned, in the same way that James was the bishop in Jerusalem and Timothy and James were the bishops In Ephesus and Crete. This point is well made by Richard Trench in his *Commentary on the Epistles to the Seven Churches in Asia*. He notes that the way that the angels are held to account for the state of their churches only make sense if they were possessed of episcopal power and responsibility in those churches:

But if some human person in the Church, who but the chief shepherd, in other words, the bishop? To whom else would all which we here in these Epistles find ascribed to the Angel apply? For myself, I cannot but think that the argument for the existence of the episcopate in the later apostolic times, and that as a divinely recognized institution, which may be drawn from the position of the Angels in the several Churches, and from the language in which they are addressed, is exceedingly strong. The Angel in each Church is one; but surely none can suppose for an instant that there was only one presbyter, or other minister serving in holy things, for the whole flourishing Church of Ephesus, or of Smyrna; and that we are in this way to account for the

---

[128] Leithart, Loc.3088.

single Angel of the several Churches. Thirty years before this time St. Paul had uttered his parting words at Miletus to the elders of the Ephesian Church (Acts xx. 17), and certainly addressed them even then as many (ver. 25). Taking into account what we know of the spread of the Christian faith in these parts during the intermediate time, it is probable that their number was at this time largely increased. And yet now, with this large number of presbyters, there is only one Angel in each of these Churches. What can he be but a bishop? —a bishop too with the prerogatives which we ascribe to one. His pre-eminence cannot be explained away, as though he had been merely a ruling elder, a primus inter pares, with only such authority and jurisdiction as the others, his peers, may have lent him. For the great Bishop of souls who is here on his spiritual visitation, everywhere holds the Angel responsible for the spiritual condition of his Church; for the false teaching which he has not put down, for the false teachers whom he has not separated from the communion of the faithful, —in short, for every disorder in doctrine or discipline which has remained unrepressed. But Christ could not so deal with them, could not charge them personally with these negligences and omissions, unless upon the ground that they had been clothed with power and authority sufficient to have prevented them, so that these evils could only have existed through their neglect and allowance.[129]

The same point was previously made by Bilson, who writes that we need to ask:

...how the Son of God could write precisely to one angel in every of those seven churches, if there were many or none? And what reason to charge him above the rest; if he had no pastoral power besides the rest? It is therefore evident the churches of Christ before that time were guided by certain chief pastors, that moderated as well the presbyters as the rest of the flock; and those the Son of God acknowledgeth for stars and angels, that is for messengers and

---

[129] Richard Trench, *Commentary on the Epistles to the Seven Churches in Asia* (New York: Charles Scribner, 1863), pp. 78-80.

stewards of the Lord of Hosts; at whose mouth the rest should ask and receive the knowledge of God's divine will and pleasure. [130]

It is true that Revelation itself does not give the title 'bishop' to the angels of the churches. However, as in the case of James in Jerusalem or Timothy and Titus in Ephesus and Crete, the evidence indicates that the office existed before the name bishop was given to it. In the words of Hooker:

This one president or governor among the rest had his known authority established a long time before that settled difference of name and title took place, whereby such alone were named bishops. And therefore in the book of St. John's Revelation we find that they are entitled angels.[131]

This internal evidence that the angels were indeed bishops is supported by the fact that we know that there was a bishop in one of these churches, the church in Ephesus, from the mid-60s. It is also supported by letters written by Ignatius of Antioch in about 110, which we shall look at in more detail in the next chapter, which show that there were bishops in three of the seven churches of Asia at that date, the churches concerned being those in Ephesus, Philadelphia and Smyrna.[132] In addition, they also show that there were bishops in two other churches in the same area, the churches in Magnesia and Tralles.[133]

This evidence for the existence of episcopacy in at least some of the churches to which John writes, and in other churches in the same area, thirty years before he wrote and fifteen to twenty years afterwards,

---

[130] Bilson, p.376.

[131] Hooker, Bk VII.v.2, p.340.

[132] See the letters of Ignatius 'To the Ephesians,' 'To the Philadelphians,' 'To the Smyrnaeans,' and 'To Polycarp' In Lightfoot, Harmer and Holmes, pp. 86-93 and 106-118.

[133] See the letters 'To the Magnesians' and 'To the Trallians' in Lightfoot Harmer and Holmes, pp. 93-101.

supports the belief that there were also bishops in the church in Asia at the time he was writing.

The God given authority of the angels of the churches

Nothing is said in Revelation about the angels having been appointed by the apostles. However, as Bilson points out, what Revelation does tell us is that the ministry of the angels carries the authority of God himself. He writes that when Christ himself calls them angels:

The name that he giveth them sheweth their power and charge to be authorized and delivered to them by God: for an angel is God's messenger; and consequently those seven, each in his own several charge and city, are willed to reform the errors and abuses of the churches, that it both presbyters and people. They are warned at whose hands it shall be required; and by him that shall sit judge to take account of their doings. Hence I infer, first their pre-eminence above their helpers and coadjutors in the same churches, is warranted to be God's ordinance. Next, they are God's messengers to reprove and redress things amiss in their churches, be they presbyters or people that be offenders. Which of these two can you refuse? Shall they be angels, and not allowed of God? Can they be his messengers, and not sent by him? He would never reward them, if he did not send them. [134]

Furthermore, John never asks who the angels are, or why he should write to them. The apostle is clearly familiar with who the angels are and why they are regarded as accountable to God for the state of their churches. This suggests that at the time he is writing the episcopal ministry of the bishops is not a new or contested phenomenon (at least in the case of the churches concerned).

In addition, as in the case of the ministry given to Timothy and Titus in the Pastoral Epistles, there is nothing said in Revelation that suggests that the ministry given to the angels is of temporary duration, or that it is one that cannot be passed on to someone else. God has sent these angels. There is nothing to say that he cannot, or will not, send other

---

[134] Bilson, p.375.

angels in their place.

The Didache and 1 Clement

It has sometimes been argued that the *Didache* and *1 Clement* suggest the existence of an alternative pattern of Christian ministry in which the ministry of the local simply consists of elders/bishops and deacons, but without one individual having episcopal oversight. In some churches, the argument goes, there may have been single bishops, but the *Didache* and *1 Clement* show that in other places there was a more plural pattern of oversight. There were thus two patterns of ministry co-existing in the Early Church.

What are we to make of this argument?

In the case of the *Didache*, what the evidence tells us, as we saw in the last chapter, is that in the Church in Syria in around 70 there was a regular ministry of elders and deacons and also an itinerant ministry of charismatic apostles, prophets and teachers. What the evidence does not tell us, however, is that the twofold ministry of elders and deacons, is regarded as an alternative to a threefold ministry of bishops, elders and deacons. No such idea is found in the *Didache*.

If we place this evidence contained in the *Didache* in the wider context of the evidence provided by the New Testament and the writers of the Early Church what makes best sense is to say that in about 70 the Church in Syria was still adhering to the primitive pattern of ministry in which the Church was governed by elders and deacons under the overall episcopal supervision of the apostles. It had not (yet) been seen to be necessary to appoint bishops in Syria, just as it had not yet been seen as necessary to appoint a bishop in Ephesus when Paul spoke to the Ephesian elders at Miletus (Acts 20:17-38) or in Philippi when Paul wrote his letter to the church there (Philippians 1:1).

As we have seen, the evidence of the New Testament, supported by the evidence of the writers of the Early Church, is that the appointment of bishops was a development that gradually took place during the course of the first century. All that the *Didache* tells us is that at the time it was written this development had not taken place in Syria.

In the case of *1 Clement* the evidence likewise tells us that at the end of the first century there were elders and deacons in the church in Corinth. However, it also indicates that in addition to the threefold ministry of apostles, bishops/elders and deacons another form of ministry also existed in Corinth as well.

In chapters 1:3 and 21:6 a distinction is made between the 'leaders' and the 'elders'[135] with the implication that the two groups of people are different, with the latter exercising a distinctive leadership role in the life of the Church to which those in Corinth are called to 'submit' and 'respect.' Similarly, in chapter 44:2-3 reference is made to 'reputable men' who are distinct from the bishops and deacons and who have been given authority by the apostles to appoint them in future. [136]

The two roles given in these chapters to these 'leaders' and 'reputable men,' namely leadership and the appointment of other ministers, are exactly the same episcopal roles first exercised by the apostles and then delegated to James in Jerusalem, to Timothy and Titus in Ephesus and Crete and to the angels of the seven churches in Revelation. This being the case it makes sense to see them as being bishops in the later sense of a class of people distinct from the elders and called to exercise a distinctive episcopal ministry.

The reason reference is made to leaders and 'reputable men' in the plural is because the texts concerned are referring to a series of people holding the office in question. The texts do not imply that the office itself could be held by more than one person at a time.

Further evidence for the existence of what would subsequently be called a threefold order of bishops, elders and deacons is provided in chapter 40. In this chapter Clement writes that Christians 'ought to do, in order, everything that the Master (which in context means Christ)

---

[135] Lightfoot, Harmer and Holmes, pp. 28 and 41.
[136] Lightfoot, Harmer and Holmes, pp.53-53.

has commanded us to perform at the appointed times.' He then goes on to say that:

Those, therefore who make their offerings at the appointed times are acceptable and blessed: for those who follow the instructions of the Master cannot go wrong. For to the high priest the proper services have been given, and to the priests the proper office has been assigned, and upon the Levites the proper ministries have been imposed. The layman is bound by the layman's rules.[137]

As in the reference to the 'making of offerings' by the bishops in *1 Clement* 44:4, Clement seems to be writing here about Holy Communion, and what he is saying is that Christ's will for his Church is that three orders of ministry should be involved in the celebration of the sacrament. There should be a high priest, priests and Levites.

Clement is not referring here to the threefold hierarchy of ministry found in the Old Testament. He is referring to the threefold hierarchy of ministry to be found in the Church and the most plausible interpretation of his words is that the Levites are the deacons, the priests are the elders and the high priest is what would subsequently be called a bishop. As we saw in the previous chapter, *1 Clement* 44:4 tells us that the priests who 'make their offerings' at Holy Communion are the elders. The Levites are then the deacons, who assist the elders as the Levites in the Old Testament assisted the priests. This leaves the 'high priest,' an individual who is an elder and yet has an office which is above that of the other elders, which is precisely what the later Christian tradition meant when it called someone a bishop.

The American scholar Bart Ehrman writes that *1 Clement* contains:

...no indication that the hierarchical structures later so important to proto-orthodox Christians - in which there was a solitary bishop over a group of presbyters and deacons - was yet in place.[138]

---

[137] 1 Clement 40:1 and 4-5 in Lightfoot, Harmer and Holmes, p.50.
[138] Bart Ehrman, *The Apostolic Fathers,* Volume I (Cambridge: Harvard University. 2003), pp. 24-25.

The reference to the Christian high priest in *1 Clement* 40, like the references to the 'leaders' and 'reputable men' elsewhere in the letter, show that he is wrong. What is said in *1 Clement* clearly points to the existence of a structure of ministry in which one person (who would later be called a bishop) enjoys episcopal authority over a number of elders and deacons.

As a letter written from the Rome to Corinth, the letter also makes clear that this was a structure of ministry that existed in the Church both places and was traditional in both places. The argument of 1 Clement is based on the idea that there is an accepted threefold structure of ministry in both Rome and Corinth and that the problem in Corinth is that some of the younger members of the church have rebelled against it. *1 Clement* is not arguing for the acceptance of a new structure of ministry. It is arguing for submission to a structure of ministry that already exists.

Furthermore, this structure of ministry has the authority of both the apostles and of Christ himself. As we have seen both in this chapter and the previous one, according to *1 Clement* it was the apostles who appointed elders and deacons and who laid down that reputable men should appoint them in future. In addition, as we have seen in this chapter, it is Christ who has instituted the worship of the Church should be led by a threefold hierarchy of a high priest, priests and Levites (i.e. bishops, elders and deacons).

Conclusion
What we have seen in this chapter is that the New Testament tells us that episcopal authority, that is to say authority over elders, deacons and the laity, was originally exercised by the apostles.

However, it was then subsequently exercised, with the assent of the apostles and of God himself, by

- James in Jerusalem

- Timothy in Ephesus

- Titus in Crete

- The angels of the seven churches in Asia

- Those in Rome in Corinth who *1 Clement* refers to as leaders, reputable men and the high priest.

None of these references specifically refer to those who exercise episcopal authority as 'bishops.' However, the role they exercise is that which the Church later came to call the office of bishop. The office of bishop is present even though the name is absent.

We have also seen that later tradition also tells us that there was a succession of subsequent bishops in Jerusalem, Ephesus and Crete. There is nothing in the New Testament (or *1 Clement*) that contradicts this tradition and if, as it says, the office of bishop was first instituted by the apostles, it makes sense that when the first bishops died others would be appointed to take their place so that the office might continue.

The *Didache* is silent about both the office of bishop, but all this tells us is that the office of bishop had not yet emerged in Syria at the time the *Didache* was written.

In the next chapter we shall look in detail at what the writers of the second century have to say about bishops. What we shall find is that their evidence coheres with evidence from the first century that we have looked at in this chapter.

Chapter 3
The witness of the second century

Ignatius of Antioch

The earliest second century witness to episcopacy is Ignatius, who was Bishop of Antioch at the end of the first and the beginning of the second century.

After being arrested by the Roman authorities he was transported to Rome where he was martyred for the faith in about 110. In the course of his journey to Rome he wrote seven letters which have survived. These letters are addressed to the churches in Ephesus, Magnesia, Tralles, Rome, Philadelphia and Smyrna and to Polycarp. Bishop of Smyrna.

The witness of Ignatius on the existence and importance of bishops.

One of the key features of these seven letters is that in them, for the first time, the Greek word *episkopos* (in English 'bishop') is used to refer to a single individual who has ministerial oversight over the elders, deacons and lay people of a particular church.

For Ignatius the God given ministry in the local church is not a twofold ministry of bishops/elders and deacons, but a threefold ministry of bishops, elders and deacons. For there to be a church these three orders of ministry must be present and anyone, whether ordained or lay, who wishes to be united to God must be in unity with their bishop.

Four extracts from the letters will serve to illustrate these points.

First, in his letter to the church in Ephesus Ignatius writes:

...Jesus Christ, our inseparable life, is the mind of the Father as the bishops appointed throughout the world are the mind of Christ.

Thus it is proper for you to act together in harmony with the mind of the bishop, as you are in fact doing. For your presbytery, which is worthy of its name and worthy of God, is attuned to the bishop as strings to a lyre. Therefore in your unanimity and harmonious love Jesus Christ is sung. You must join this chorus, every one of you, so that by being harmonious in unanimity and taking your pitch from God you may sing in unison with one voice through Jesus Christ to the Father, in order that he may both hear you and, on the basis of what you do well, acknowledge that you are members of his Son.[139]

Secondly, in his letter to the church in Tralles he writes:

...let everyone respect the deacons as Jesus Christ, just as they should respect the bishop, who is a model of the Father, and the presbyters as God's council and as the band of the apostles. Without these no group can be called a church. [140]

Thirdly, in his letter to the church in Philadelphia he writes:

For all those who belong to God and Jesus Christ are with the bishop, and all those who repent and enter into the unity of the church will belong to God, that they may be living in accordance with Jesus Christ. Do not be misled by brothers: if anyone follows a schismatic, he will not inherit the kingdom of God. If anyone holds to alien views, he disassociates himself from the Passion.

Take care, therefore, to participate in one Eucharist (for there is one flesh of our Lord Jesus Christ, and one cup which leads to unity with his blood; there is one altar, just as there is one bishop, together with the presbytery and deacons, my fellow servants), in order that whatever you do, you do in accordance with God. [141]

Fourthly, in his letter to the church in Smyrna he writes:

---

[139] Ignatius of Antioch, *To the Ephesians* 4:3-4, in Lightfoot, Harmer and Holmes, p. 87.
[140] Ignatius of Antioch, *To the Trallians* 3:1, in Lightfoot, Harmer and Holmes, p.98.
[141] Ignatius of Antioch, *To the Philadelphians*, 3:2-4 in Lightfoot, Harmer and Holmes, p.107.

Flee from divisions, as the beginning of evils. You must all follow the bishop, as Jesus Christ followed the Father, and follow the presbytery as you would the apostles, respect the deacons as the commandment of God. Let no one do anything that has to do with the church without the bishop. Only that Eucharist which is under the authority of the bishop (or whomever he himself designates) is to be considered valid. Wherever the bishop appears, there let the congregation be; just as wherever Jesus Christ is, there is the catholic church. It is not permissible either to baptize or hold a love feast without the bishop. But whatever he approves is also pleasing to God, in order that everything you do may be trustworthy and valid. [142]

Furthermore, in these letters Ignatius does not just refer to bishops in the abstract. He also refers to a number of bishops he knows. He refers to Onesimus, Bishop of Ephesus, Damas, Bishop of Magnesia, Polybius, Bishop of Tralles, and Polycarp, Bishop of Smyrna.[143]

What these letters establish beyond doubt is that by the time they were written mono-episcopacy, the existence of a single bishop in each Church distinct from, and with authority over, the elders, was a reality in the churches of Asia Minor. Ignatius' letters make no sense if this was not the case. You do not greet by name bishops who do not exist and likewise there is no point in urging Christians to respect, and be in unity with, their bishop if there is no bishop for them to respect and be in unity with.

Why bishops were not a new idea in the time of Ignatius.
However, the suggestion has been made that the existence of bishops in Asia Minor was a recent innovation at the time Ignatius was writing.

---

[142] Ignatius of Antioch, To the Symrnaeans, 8:1-2, in Lightfoot, Harmer and Holmes, pp. 112-113.
[143] Ignatius of Antioch, *To the Ephesians* 1:3, *To the Magnesians* 2, *To the Trallians* 1:1, *To Polycarp*, Salutation, in in Lightfoot, Harmer and Holmes, pp. 86, 93, 97 and 115,

In the words of Thomas Manson 'Ignatius is championing a new idea.'[144]

A recent variation of this suggestion is contained in the book *Ignatius of Antioch: A Martyr Bishop and the Origins of Episcopacy* by the Patristic scholar Allen Brent. He argues that mono-episcopacy was not only a new development, but something that Ignatius actually invented. In Brent's words, when Ignatius refers to a threefold hierarchy of a bishop, a body of presbyters and a number of deacons in each church, he is 'not describing an established church order in an existing historical situation' but is instead 'creating a new social reality.'[145]

According to Brent, the church at Antioch was divided between those who favoured an egalitarian and charismatic authority structure and those who favoured a hierarchical twofold ministry of bishops (i.e. elders) and deacons (with the latter group not being able to agree among themselves). Ignatius, who was himself a charismatic, sought to resolve this division by promoting himself as the sole bishop of the Church in Antioch with the elders and deacons subordinate to him.

Ignatius' actions led to further division and eventually violence in Antioch and it was because of this violence that the Roman authorities arrested him and sent him to Rome for execution. However, he was able to use this state of affairs to further his ecclesiastical agenda. During the course of his journey to Rome he managed to persuade Onesimus, Damas, Polybius and Polycarp to take on the new role of bishop in their churches. In addition, his successful depiction of himself as a scapegoat and a martyr led those in Antioch to feel 'collective guilt' for what had happened and to 'accept his particular vision of ecclesial unity.'[146] It was on this basis that mono-episcopacy

---

[144] Thomas Manson, *The Church's Ministry* (London: Hodder and Stoughton, 1948), pp.68-69.
[145] Allen Brent, *Ignatius of Antioch; A Martyr Bishop and the Origins of Episcopacy* (London: T&T Clark, 2009), p.151.
[146] Brent, p. 56.

became established in Antioch and Asia Minor, and eventually in the rest of the Church.

There are a number of reasons why Brent's reconstruction of events in Antioch and Asia Minor is unconvincing.

First, as we have seen, the evidence of the New Testament and of *1 Clement* indicates that the office (if not the name) of bishop was established in the Church, including in Asia Minor, well before the time Ignatius journeyed to Rome. He therefore cannot have invented the office of bishop because it already existed. In addition, Brent ignores the Patristic tradition found in Eusebius and other sources that declares that Ignatius was not the first, but the third Bishop of Antioch, having been preceded in that role by the apostle Peter and by Evodius.[147]

Secondly, although there is evidence in Ignatius' letters for division in the church in Antioch and for this division having come to an end,[148] there is no evidence either from the letters or from any other source for Brent's account of the nature of this division and its resolution. What he writes about this is pure imagination.

Thirdly, there is no evidence at all, either in the letters or in other sources, to suggest that Onesimus, Damas, Polybius, or Polycarp were appointed as bishops by Ignatius. This again is pure imagination on Brent's part.

Fourthly, if mono-episcopacy was a new invention by Ignatius, as Brent, Manson, and others have suggested, we would expect to find material in his letters explaining the nature of this new office and why it should be accepted, and defending it against supporters of the previously existing pattern of ministry. We find none of this in his letters. The letters are addressed to people who know about the threefold ministry of bishops, elders and deacons and accept it in

[147] Eusebius of Caesarea, *Ecclesiastical History* III.xxii, p. 281.
[148] Ignatius of Antioch, *To the Smyrnaeans*, 11, *To Polycarp,* 7, in Lightfoot, Harmer and Holmes, pp. 114 and 117.

principle, but who need encouragement to live out this acceptance in the way that they behave.

If we set aside the approach taken by Brent and Manson for these reasons, we are left with solid evidence that just as there were angels in the churches in Asia Minor when John wrote Revelation so also there were bishops in Asia Minor at the time when Ignatius wrote his letters. Furthermore, the reference in the letter to the Ephesians to 'the bishops appointed throughout the world' provides evidence that there were bishops elsewhere as well. Lightfoot comments that 'Ignatius would be contemplating regions as distant as Gaul on the one hand and Mesopotamia on the other.'[149]

Ignatius and the presence of a bishop in Rome.

It is also sometimes suggested that the fact that in his letter to the church in Rome Ignatius does not mention the name of the bishop there, or urge the Christians there to be in unity with their bishop, means that there was no bishop in Rome at the time the letter was written. Thus, Raymond Brown and John Meier write 'No single-bishop is mentioned in Rome, probably because the church still had the twofold structure of presbyter-bishops and deacons.' [150]

 This suggestion is unconvincing for three reasons.

First, Ignatius does not mention the name of the bishop in his letters to the churches in Philadelphia and Smyrna even though it is clear from these letters that there was a bishop in both of these churches. Ignatius only mentions the name of the bishop when he has met them (as in the letters to Ephesus, Magnesia and Tralles), or when he is writing to them (as in the letter to Polycarp). In the case of the letter to the church in Rome neither of these factors apply and so the absence of the bishop's name is not surprising.

[149] Cited in Gore, p. 267.
[150] Raymond Brown and John Meier, *Antioch and Rome – New Testament Cradles of Catholic Christianity* (New York and Mahwah: Paulist Press, 1983), p.202.

Secondly, the subject matter of the letter to the church in Rome makes the absence of any mention of a bishop in Rome likewise unsurprising. In all the other letters Ignatius' aim is to encourage the growth in godliness of the church concerned and his references to bishops fit into this context. In the letter to the Romans, by contrast, he has the specific aim of dissuading the Christians in Rome from trying to save him from martyrdom. In this context a reference to how the Roman Christians should relate to their own bishop would be out of place because it is irrelevant to his argument.

Thirdly, however, in his letter to the church in Rome Ignatius does in fact make two references to the existence of mono-episcopacy. In section 2:2 he writes that 'God has judged the bishop from Syria worthy to be found in the West, having summoned him from the East.'[151] The bishop here is Ignatius himself who has come from Antioch In Syria and is going to Rome. Then in section 9:1 he asks the Christians in Rome to 'Remember in your prayers the church in Syria, which has God for its shepherd in my place. Jesus Christ alone will be its bishop – as will your love.'[152] In this passage Syria again means Antioch and, as Gregory Vall notes, the passage: 'expresses Ignatius's conviction that Jesus Christ is, in the truest sense, the church's one bishop, while at the same time reflecting his well-formed ecclesiological understanding that each local community of Christians ought to have also a 'visible' bishop (Magn 3.2), a 'bishop in the flesh' to represent Christ on earth (Eph 1:3).' [153]

What is significant about these two references is that Ignatius feels no need to explain what a bishop is or what the bishop's role involves. He is confident that the office of bishop and the role of the bishop as the

---

[151] Ignatius of Antioch, *To the Romans*, 2:2, in Lightfoot, Harmer and Holmes, p.103.
[152] Ignatius of Antioch, *To the Romans*, 9:1, in Lightfoot, Harmer and Holmes, p.105.
[153] Gregory Vall, *Learning Christ – Ignatius of Antioch and the Mystery of Redemption* (Washington DC: The Catholic University of America Press, 2013), p.345.

visible shepherd of the local church are things that the Christians in Rome already know and accept,

What the letter actually shows, therefore, is that the office of bishop was known and accepted in the church of Rome, and the nature of the letter makes the absence of any reference to the Bishop of Rome unsurprising and does not constitute evidence that Rome did not have a bishop when the letter was written.

Ignatius and the apostolic origin of episcopacy.

A final point that needs to be noted is that as well as viewing the office of bishop as one that is spread throughout the world, Ignatius also sees it as something that is apostolic in origin. This is made clear in the letter to the church in Tralles. In section 7:1 Ignatius declares that the Trallians need to 'cling inseparably to Jesus Christ and to the bishop and to the commandments of the apostles.'[154] The point here is that clinging to the 'commandment of the apostles' means clinging to their teaching concerning Jesus Christ as God incarnate and to the office of bishop which they instituted.

In similar fashion, Ignatius writes in section 12:2 of the same letter '...it is right for each one of you, and especially the presbyters, to encourage the bishop, to the honour of the Father, and to the honour of Jesus and to the honour of the apostles.' [155] Because the office of bishop has been instituted by God the Father and Jesus his Son through the apostles, to encourage a bishop in his ministry is to honour all three.

Both of these references only make sense if bishops were instituted by the apostles and Ignatius was someone who was in a position to know at first hand whether or not they had done so. In his letter to Polycarp Ignatius speaks as an older man to someone who is many years his junior. The account we have of Polycarp's martyrdom indicates that he

[154] Ignatius of Antioch, *To the Trallians*, 7:1, in Lightfoot, Harmer and Holmes p. 99.
[155] Ignatius of Antioch, *To the Trallians*, 7:1, in Lightfoot, Harmer and Holmes p. 100.

was forty in 110[156] and so for Ignatius to be markedly older than him he must have been born in the middle years of the first century and have grown to adulthood when the apostles were in the midst of their ministries.

As Gore puts it:

Here then we have a very notable witness. He is a man who, though he loves to describe himself as 'only now beginning to be a disciple' is probably old in years. He would have been a boy when St. Paul wrote his great Epistles; he would have been in full manhood when the last days came upon Jerusalem.[157]

This chronology fits the tradition previously noted that Ignatius was the third Bishop of Antioch after Peter and Evodius and, as Gore further says, it means that Ignatius 'can bear unexceptionable witness to apostolic intentions.' [158] He was someone who was in a position to know what the apostles had done and his testimony is that they had, in accordance with the will of God, instituted episcopacy.

Polycarp of Smyrna
As noted in the previous section, one of the people to whom Ignatius wrote was Polycarp, Bishop of Smyrna. Additional information about Polycarp and how he became Bishop of Smyrna is provided by a number of writers from the late second century onwards.

Irenaeus, Bishop of Lyons, who came from Smyrna, testifies in his work *Against Heresies* (written sometime between 180-and 188) that he had seen Polycarp when he was a young man and further writes that Polycarp had been appointed bishop by the apostles themselves:

But Polycarp also was not only instructed by apostles, and conversed with many who had seen Christ, but was also, by apostles in Asia, appointed bishop of the Church in Smyrna, whom I also saw in my

[156] His martyrdom took place about 156 and the account tells us that he was 86 at that time.
[157] Gore pp.260-261.
[158] Gore, p.261.

early youth, for he tarried [on earth] a very long time, and, when a very old man, gloriously and most nobly suffering martyrdom, departed this life, having always taught the things which he had learned from the apostles, and which the Church has handed down, and which alone are true. To these things all the Asiatic Churches testify, as do also those men who have succeeded Polycarp down to the present time — a man who was of much greater weight, and a more steadfast witness of truth, than Valentinus, and Marcion, and the rest of the heretics.[159]

In his work *On the Prescription of Heretics*, written at the end of the second or the beginning of the third century, the North African theologian Tertullian declares that the church in Smyrna 'records that Polycarp was placed therein by John.'[160] In context 'placed therein' means appointed as bishop of the place in question, in this case Smyrna.

Writing at the beginning of the fourth century, Eusebius of Caesarea describes Polycarp in Book III of his *Ecclesiastical History* as 'the companion of the Apostles, who had been appointed to the bishopric of the church in Smyrna by the eyewitnesses and ministers of the Lord.'[161] 'Eyewitnesses and ministers of the Lord' is a reference back to Luke 1:2 and means apostles.

Writing at the end of the fourth century in his *Lives of Illustrious Men* Jerome records that 'Polycarp disciple of the apostle John and by him ordained bishop of Smyrna, was chief of all Asia where he saw and had as teachers some of the apostles and of those who had seen the Lord.'[162] 'Chief of all Asia' means that Polycarp was the senior bishop in what we would now all Asia Minor.

[159] Irenaeus of Lyons, *Against Heresies* III.4, in *The Ante-Nicene Fathers*, vol. I (Edinburgh and Grand Rapids: T&T Clark/Eerdmans, 1995) p. 416.
[160] Tertullian, *On Prescription Against Heretics*, XXXII, in in *The Ante-Nicene Fathers*, vol. III (Edinburgh and Grand Rapids: T&T Clark/Eerdmans, 1997) p.258.
[161] Eusebius of Caesarea, *Ecclesiastical History*, III xxxvi, p.281.
[162] Jerome, *Lives of illustrious Men*, XXVI in *The Nicene and Post Nicene Fathers*, vol. III (Edinburgh and Grand Rapids: T&T Clark/Eerdmans, 1996) p.367.

What these references all tell us is that there was a tradition stretching back to those who knew Polycarp personally which said that he had known and been taught by the apostles. Given that, as we have said, he was forty in 110 and was therefore born in 70, there is nothing that renders this tradition implausible.

At first sight there would seem to be a contradiction between the testimony of Irenaeus and Eusebius who state that Polycarp was appointed bishop by a number of the apostles and the testimony of Tertullian and Jerome that he was appointed by John. However, this apparent contradiction can be satisfactorily resolved if the reality was that John appointed Polycarp, but that he acted on behalf of his fellow apostles. We cannot prove that this was the case, but it would account for the existence of both strands of tradition.

The significance of this tradition for the question of the origin of the episcopate is that, together with evidence from other sources which we shall look at below, it shows that the existence in Asia Minor of bishops like Ignatius and Polycarp can be traced back to the actions of John and others of the apostles.

The letter of Polycarp and episcopacy in Philippi.
While Polycarp thus provides evidence for the existence of the episcopate in Asia Minor, he has also been cited as evidence for the non-existence of the episcopate in Macedonia at the beginning of the second century. This is because in a letter he wrote to the church in Philippi in about 110 he refers to the deacons and the presbyters,[163] but does not refer to a bishop. The inference that is commonly drawn from this fact is that at that time mono-episcopacy did not exist in Philippi in the way that it did in Asia Minor.

Lightfoot, for example, writes:

---

[163] Polycarp. *The Letter to Polycarp to the Philippians,* 5-6, in Lightfoot, Harmer and Holmes, pp. 125-126.

...we are thus led to the inference that episcopacy did not exist at all among the Philippians at that time, or existed only in an elementary form, so that the bishop was a mere president of the presbyteral council.[164]

There are, however, two pieces of evidence that point in the opposite direction.

First, the salutation at the beginning of the letter is from 'Polycarp and the presbyters with him.'[165] In this salutation Polycarp, as Bishop of Smyrna, makes a distinction between himself as the bishop and the presbyters on whose behalf he is also writing. The fact that Polycarp does not feel the need to explain or justify this distinction between himself and the presbyters indicates that he thinks the Christians in Philippi know and accept this distinction, which means in turn that they know and accept mono-episcopacy.

Secondly, in chapter 13 of the letter Polycarp indicates that things had gone well when Ignatius visited Philippi on his way to Rome, to the extent that they wanted copies of any letters from Ignatius that Polycarp had in his possession:

Both you and Ignatius have written me that if anyone is travelling to Syria, he should take your letter along also. This I will do, if I get a good opportunity, either myself or the one whom I will send as a representative, on your behalf as well as ours. We are sending you the letters of Ignatius that were sent to us by him together with any others that we have in our possession, just as you requested. They are appended to this letter; you will be able to receive great benefit from them, for they deal with faith and patient endurance and every kind of

---

[164] Lightfoot, p.215.
[165] Polycarp. *The Letter to Polycarp to the Philippians,* Salutation, in Lightfoot, Harmer and Holmes, p.123

spiritual growth that has to do with the Lord. As for Ignatius himself and those with him, if you learn anything more definite, let us know.[166]

However, it is impossible to believe that things would have gone well when Ignatius visited them had the Philippians not accepted the belief about the importance of episcopacy which was a central part of Ignatius' theology. As Gore puts it:

We have already seen that Ignatius when he wrote his epistles from Smyrna certainly regarded episcopacy as extended 'to the ends of the earth:' with equal certainty he regarded it as an essential of church organisation - without these [the three orders],' he had written, 'no church has a title to the name.' He moved from Smyrna to Troas and his tone is still the same; there is the same insistence upon episcopacy. He went to Philippi and enjoyed, as we gather, the same cordial intercourse which he had held in other churches. He left behind him when he passed a venerated name. Had he rebuked them or remonstrated with them in any way, we must certainly have caught an echo of it through their correspondence with Polycarp. It is impossible, on the other hand, to believe that Ignatius suddenly dropped the urgent tone about episcopacy which had been one of the two main topics of all that he wrote in Asia.[167]

As Gore goes on to say, the issue we are left with is whether we can 'consistently with Polycarp's letter suppose some such state of things at Philippi as would not have shocked the mind of Ignatius?'[168] There seem to be two possibilities. The first is that Philippi, like Antioch, was for some reason in an episcopal vacancy at the time when Ignatius visited and Polycarp wrote. The second is that Philippi did not have a bishop of its own but came under the episcopal authority of the bishop of a wider area. To use later terminology, it was but part of a wider diocese.

---

[166] Polycarp. *The Letter to Polycarp to the Philippians,* 13 in Lightfoot, Harmer and Holmes, pp.129-130.
[167] Gore, pp.289-290.
[168] Gore p.290.

We lack the evidence to prove either theory, but whatever the true solution, it cannot be that Philippi was a non-episcopal church. The evidence of Polycarp's letter rules this out for the reasons given above.

The Shepherd of Hermas

The *Shepherd of Hermas* is a second century Christian document that was widely regarded as Scripture in the Eastern Church in the second and third centuries, but was eventually excluded from the New Testament canon on the basis that it lacked apostolic provenance.

The *Shepherd* consists of five visions, twelve 'mandates' or statements on Christian behaviour, and ten 'similitudes' or parables. It seems to have been written in Rome and reflects a Jewish Christian theological perspective. Its contents are an attempt by its author:

...to deal with questions and issues, for example, postbaptismal sin and repentance, and the behaviour of the rich and their relationship to the poor within the church – of great significance and concern to him and that part of the Christian community in Rome to which he belonged. [169]

The *Muratorian Canon*, the earliest list of New Testament books and other early Christian writings, which was written at the end of the second century declares:

Hermas wrote the Shepherd very recently, in our times, in the city of Rome, while bishop Pius, his brother, was occupying the [episcopal] chair of the church of the city of Rome.[170]

The Pius referred to is Pius 1 who was Bishop of Rome from 142-157.

In terms of the ministries of the Church, the third vision refers to:

...the apostles and bishops and teachers and deacons who have walked according to the holiness of God and have ministered to the elect of

[169] Lightfoot, Harmer and Holmes, p.189.
[170] *The Muratorian Canon,* 73-76 at http://www.bible-researcher.com/muratorian.html

God as bishops and teachers and deacons with purity and reverence; some have fallen asleep, while others are still living.[171]

Similitude 9 also refers to bishops as 'hospitable men, who were always glad to welcome God's servants into their homes without hypocrisy.' It further adds that;

...the bishops always sheltered the needy and the widows by their ministry without ceasing, and conducted themselves in purity always.[172]

If we accept the dating of the Shepherd given in the *Muratorian Canon* (and there seems no reason not to), 'bishop' would mean bishop in the same sense as in the letters of Ignatius. This would then mean that there was a threefold ministry in Rome in the mid second century consisting of bishops, elders (referred to in Vision 3 as 'teachers') and deacons. This evidence is in line with the evidence we have previously noted for the existence of a threefold ministry in Rome from at least the time of Clement's letter to the Corinthians at the end of the first century.

Hegesippus.

As we saw in the previous chapter, Hegesippus, a Jewish convert to Christianity who lived from about 110 -180, is one of the witnesses to the fact that James was appointed by the apostles as the first Bishop of Jerusalem and that he was succeeded by his brother Symeon.

Eusebius also records that at some point during the episcopate of Anicetus, who was Bishop of Rome from 157-168. Hegesippus travelled to Rome from the Eastern end of the Mediterranean (possibly Palestine). In Eusebius' words:

Hegesippus has left a complete record of his own opinions which have come down to us. In them he explains how when travelling as far as Rome he mingled with many bishops and that he found the same

---

[171] *Shepherd of Hermas*, Vision 3.5, in Lightfoot, Harmer and Holmes, p. 204.
[172] *Shepherd of Hermas,* Similitude 9.27 in Lightfoot, Harmer and Holmes, p282.

doctrine among them all. But it is well to listen to what he said after some remarks about the epistle of Clement to the Corinthians. 'And the Church of the Corinthians remained in the true doctrine until Primus was bishop of Corinth, and I conversed with them on my voyage to Rome, and spent some days with the Corinthians during which we were refreshed by the true word. When I was in Rome I recovered the list of the succession until Anicetus, whose deacon was Eleutherus; Soter succeeded Anicetus, and after him came Eleutherus. In each list and in each city things are as the law, the prophets, and the Lord preach.'[173]

The significance of this brief statement is that it tells us that when Hegesippus journeyed to Rome in the mid second century he found an episcopal succession list for the church in each city he visited and that the succession of bishops was accompanied by the fidelity of the church concerned to the teaching of the Old and New Testaments (as opposed to the teaching of the various Gnostic sects that were prevalent in the second century).

Eusebius' quotation from Hegesippus does not tell us how far back these succession lists went. However, since Hegesippus traced the succession of bishops in Jerusalem back to the appointment of James in the time of the apostles, and since the purpose of his drawing up lists of bishops seems to have been to show continuity of teaching back to apostolic times it seems that he must have traced the succession of bishops in other churches back to apostolic times as well.

It follows that, as Gregory Dix puts it:

Unless we are to believe that Hegesippus deliberately wrote what he knew to be untrue, he had obtained from Churches in Syria, Greece,

---

[173] Eusebius of Caesarea, *Ecclesiastical History*, V xxii, p.375.

and the West material for a number of 'succession lists' of bishops, each professing to stretch back to the apostolic age.[174]

Dix goes on to say:

The modern student may doubt – if he is prepared to do so on other grounds- whether they all did in reality go back so far, whether there was not an unrecognized gap of a generation or so between the time of the apostles and first names in some or all of these lists. But in all events the earlier names were there in local memories for Hegesippus to record them in the third quarter of the second century, barely a century after the close of the apostolic age. They must even be good evidence of what some older members of those churches had *supposed* to be true in the generation before Hegesippus collected his information – when there were other Christians alive besides Polycarp who could personally remember the sub-apostolic age.[175]

What Dix does not tell us is what the grounds would be for thinking that there was in reality a gap of a generation between the time of the apostles and the first bishops of some or all of the churches visited by Hegesippus. As we have seen, the evidence from the New Testament and the early second century does not suggest such a gap. In every church we have looked at the evidence tells us that episcopacy had its origins in apostolic times and there is no good reason to think that it was different elsewhere.

It is also important to note that Dix is wrong when he suggests that the time when Hegesippus undertook his journey was a century after the apostolic age. Tradition tells us that John died in about 100 which would mean that the gap between the end of the apostolic age and the time of Hegesippus was just over half a century. What Polycarp's generation would thus remember would not be just the sub-apostolic age, but the apostolic age itself.

---

[174] Gregory Dix, 'The Ministry in the Early Church' in Kenneth Kirk et al, *The Apostolic Ministry* (London: Hodder and Stoughton 1947), p.208.
[175] Gregory Dix, 'The Ministry in the Early Church' p.208.

Furthermore, there is no reason to think that the gap between the apostolic age and the time of Hegesippus was covered purely by people's memories as Dix seems to suggest. The Early Church was part of a literate society and there were people in the Church who could and did write. We also know that historic documents were preserved and copied (such as the New Testament writings and the letters of Clement, Ignatius and Polycarp). There is therefore no reason to think that the churches did not have written records (including possibly episcopal succession lists) that they could have drawn on alongside people's memories to answer Hegesippus when he enquired who their bishops had been.

All this means that while we cannot check the details of Hegesippus' lists of episcopal succession, since the lists themselves are no longer extant and we are not in a position to check his sources of information, there is no a priori reason to think that he did not discover genuine lists of bishops going back to the apostolic age and every reason to think that he did.

Dionysius of Corinth

Dionysius was Bishop of Corinth in the third quarter of the second century. In his *Chronicle*, or universal history, Eusebius records that Dionysius was bishop in the eleventh year of the Emperor Marcus Aurelius, that is in 171, and in his *Ecclesiastical History* he gives extracts from a letter written by him to Soter, who was Bishop of Rome from c166 to c175 in response to a letter previously written to him by the church in Rome.

In Book IV of his *Ecclesiastical History* Eusebius also mentions a number of other letters written by Dionysius. He tells us that in his letter to the church in Athens Dionysius refers to two recent bishops of that church, Publius who has been martyred and Quadratus who has replaced him, and that he also mentions that 'Dionysius the Areopagite was converted by the Apostle Paul to the faith, according to the narrative in Acts, and was the first to be appointed to the bishopric of the diocese of Athens.'[176]

Eusebius further tells us that Dionysius also wrote to Philip, who was Bishop of Gortyna and other Cretan churches, to Pintyos, Bishop of Knossos in Crete, and to Palmas, Bishop of Amastris in Pontus in what is now Turkey. He also records that in his letter to Soter, Dionysius tells him that the letter written by his predecessor Clement was regularly read out in the church in Corinth.[177]

The evidence of Dionysius recorded by Eusebius confirms the existence of episcopacy in Corinth, Rome, Athens, Crete and Pontus in his day and that the belief in his day was that episcopacy in Athens went back to the time of the apostles. It also tells us that 1 Clement was preserved and read out in Corinth, thus providing evidence for the preservation of historic documents by the second century Church.

Irenaeus of Lyons
Irenaeus of Lyons was born into a Christian family in Smyrna between 120 and 130. As a young man he sat at the feet of Polycarp and absorbed his teaching.[178] At some point before Polycarp's martyrdom in 156 he moved from Smyrna to Rome. He then moved again to Lyons in Southern Gaul where he became bishop in 178 following the death of bishop Pothinus in the persecution that took place the previous year.

Irenaeus' argument about episcopal succession.
As previously noted, Irenaeus wrote his work *Against Heresies,* which was designed to combat the various Gnostic heresies of his day, in about 180. In Book 3 of this work he follows Hegesippus in arguing that the true faith has been handed down through lines of episcopal succession which have their origin in the appointment of the first bishops by the apostles themselves. To put the same thing another

[176] Eusebius of Caesarea, *Ecclesiastical History*, IV xxiii, p.379.
[177] Eusebius of Caesarea, *Ecclesiastical History*, IV xxiii, pp.379-83.
[178] See his letter to Florinus in Eusebius of Caesarea, *Ecclesiastical History*, V xx, pp. 499.

way, for Irenaeus we know that what the Gnostic sects teach is untrue because it is not what was delivered by the apostles to the first bishops and passed on by them and by the bishops who have held office in descent from them.

In Irenaeus' words:

It is within the power of all, therefore, in every Church, who may wish to see the truth, to contemplate clearly the tradition of the apostles manifested throughout the whole world; and we are in a position to reckon up those who were by the apostles instituted bishops in the Churches, and [to demonstrate] the succession of these men to our own times; those who neither taught nor knew of anything like what these [heretics] rave about. For if the apostles had known hidden mysteries, which they were in the habit of imparting to 'the perfect' apart and privily from the rest, they would have delivered them especially to those to whom they were also committing the Churches themselves. For they were desirous that these men should be very perfect and blameless in all things, whom also they were leaving behind as their successors, delivering up their own place of government to these men; which men, if they discharged their functions honestly, would be a great boon [to the Church], but if they should fall away, the direst calamity.[179]

Because, he says, 'it would be very tedious, in such a volume as this, to reckon up the successions of all the Churches,'[180] Irenaeus gives three examples of churches which illustrate how fidelity to the apostolic faith and a continuous line of episcopal descent from the time of the apostles have gone together.

---

[179] Irenaeus of Lyons, *Against Heresies*, Bk.III.3.1 in *The Ante-Nicene Fathers*, vol. I (Edinburgh and Grand Rapids: T&T Clark/Eerdmans, 1996), p.415.
[180] Irenaeus of Lyons, *Against Heresies*, Bk.III.3.2, p.415.

The first is the 'very great, the very ancient, and universally known Church founded and organized at Rome by the two most glorious apostles, Peter and Paul.'[181]

Concerning the church in Rome he writes:

The blessed apostles, then, having founded and built up the Church, committed into the hands of Linus the office of the episcopate. Of this Linus, Paul makes mention in the Epistles to Timothy. To him succeeded Anacletus; and after him, in the third place from the apostles, Clement was allotted the bishopric. This man, as he had seen the blessed apostles, and had been conversant with them, might be said to have the preaching of the apostles still echoing [in his ears], and their traditions before his eyes. Nor was he alone [in this], for there were many still remaining who had received instructions from the apostles. In the time of this Clement, no small dissension having occurred among the brethren at Corinth, the Church in Rome dispatched a most powerful letter to the Corinthians, exhorting them to peace, renewing their faith, and declaring the tradition which it had lately received from the apostles, proclaiming the one God, omnipotent, the Maker of heaven and earth, the Creator of man, who brought on the deluge, and called Abraham, who led the people from the land of Egypt, spoke with Moses, set forth the law, sent the prophets, and who has prepared fire for the devil and his angels. From this document, whosoever chooses to do so, may learn that He, the Father of our Lord Jesus Christ, was preached by the Churches, and may also understand the apostolic tradition of the Church, since this Epistle is of older date than these men who are now propagating falsehood, and who conjure into existence another god beyond the Creator and the Maker of all existing things. To this Clement there succeeded Evaristus. Alexander followed Evaristus; then, sixth from the apostles, Sixtus was appointed; after him, Telephorus, who was gloriously martyred; then Hyginus; after him, Pius; then after him, Anicetus. Soter having succeeded Anicetus, Eleutherius does now, in

---

[181] Irenaeus of Lyons, *Against Heresies*, Bk.III.3.2, p.415.

the twelfth place from the apostles, hold the inheritance of the episcopate. In this order, and by this succession, the ecclesiastical tradition from the apostles, and the preaching of the truth, have come down to us. And this is most abundant proof that there is one and the same vivifying faith, which has been preserved in the Church from the apostles until now, and handed down in truth.[182]

The second is Irenaeus' home church of Smyrna where he focuses on the witness borne by Polycarp as the bishop of that church:

But Polycarp also was not only instructed by apostles, and conversed with many who had seen Christ, but was also, by apostles in Asia, appointed bishop of the Church in Smyrna, whom I also saw in my early youth, for he tarried [on earth] a very long time, and, when a very old man, gloriously and most nobly suffering martyrdom, departed this life, having always taught the things which he had learned from the apostles, and which the Church has handed down, and which alone are true. To these things all the Asiatic Churches testify, as do also those men who have succeeded Polycarp down to the present time — a man who was of much greater weight, and a more steadfast witness of truth, than Valentinus, and Marcion, and the rest of the heretics. He it was who, coming to Rome in the time of Anicetus caused many to turn away from the aforesaid heretics to the Church of God, proclaiming that he had received this one and sole truth from the apostles — that, namely, which is handed down by the Church. There are also those who heard from him that John, the disciple of the Lord, going to bathe at Ephesus, and perceiving Cerinthus within, rushed out of the bath-house without bathing, exclaiming, "Let us fly, lest even the bath-house fall down, because Cerinthus, the enemy of the truth, is within." And Polycarp himself replied to Marcion, who met him on one occasion, and said, "Do you know me?" "I do know you, the first-born of Satan." Such was the horror which the apostles and their disciples had against holding even verbal communication with any corrupters of the truth; as Paul also

---

[182] Irenaeus of Lyons, *Against Heresies*, Bk.III.3.3, p.416.

says, "A man that is an heretic, after the first and second admonition, reject; knowing that he that is such is subverted, and sins, being condemned of himself." Titus 3:10 There is also a very powerful Epistle of Polycarp written to the Philippians, from which those who choose to do so, and are anxious about their salvation, can learn the character of his faith, and the preaching of the truth. [183]

The third is the church in Ephesus, on which he comments:

Then again, the Church in Ephesus founded by Paul, and having John remaining among them permanently until the times of Trajan, is a true witness of the tradition of the apostles.[184]

Although he does not say so explicitly, the implication of Irenaeus' comments is that in Ephesus as in Smyrna and Rome there was an episcopal succession going back to the time of the apostles through which the 'true witness of the tradition of the apostles' had been maintained.

In Book 4 Irenaeus draws the moral that because the apostolic faith has been passed on to faithful bishops who are in descent from the apostles, it is to these bishops and their teaching that we should look if we wish to know theological truth. As he puts it:

Where, therefore, the gifts of the Lord have been placed, there it behoves us to learn the truth, [namely,] from those who possess that succession of the Church which is from the apostles, and among whom exists that which is sound and blameless in conduct, as well as that which is unadulterated and incorrupt in speech. For these also preserve this faith of ours in one God who created all things; and they increase that love [which we have] for the Son of God, who accomplished such marvellous dispensations for our sake: and they expound the Scriptures to us without danger, neither blaspheming God, nor dishonouring the patriarchs, nor despising the prophets.[185]

[183] Irenaeus of Lyons, *Against Heresies*, Bk.III.3.2, p.416.
[184] Irenaeus of Lyons, *Against Heresies*, Bk.III.3.2, p.416.
[185] Irenaeus of Lyons, *Against Heresies,* Bk IV.26.5, p. 498.

Like Ignatius before him, Irenaeus declares that this means that is incumbent on faithful Christians to obey their bishops and to regard those who depart from such obedience with suspicion:

Wherefore it is incumbent to obey the presbyters who are in the Church—those who, as I have shown, possess the succession from the apostles; those who, together with the succession of the episcopate, have received the certain gift of truth, according to the good pleasure of the Father. But [it is also incumbent] to hold in suspicion others who depart from the primitive succession, and assemble themselves together in any place whatsoever, [looking upon them] either as heretics of perverse minds, or as schismatics puffed up and self-pleasing, or again as hypocrites, acting thus for the sake of lucre and vainglory. For all these have fallen from the truth.[186]

'Presbyter' here means bishop as a comparison of the two halves of the first sentence makes clear. As Lightfoot notes, while Irenaeus never calls presbyters bishops, he does call bishops presbyters.[187] This is because in his writings 'the venerable title of 'presbyter,' the 'ancient' or 'elder' is still used in an inclusive sense for the Church's rulers.'[188] The bishops are therefore called presbyters because they are the senior rulers of the Church.

Assessing Irenaeus' three examples of episcopal succession.
If we look at the three examples of churches with episcopal succession cited by Irenaeus there is no reason to doubt the existence in both Smyrna and Ephesus of an episcopate going back to apostolic times.

We saw in chapter 2 that there was a bishop/angel in Smyrna at the time when John wrote Revelation at the end of the first century (Revelation 2:8-11) and we saw earlier in this chapter that the letters of Ignatius and Polycarp himself tell us that Polycarp was Bishop of Smyrna in 110. We have also seen that Irenaeus had been brought up

---

[186] Irenaeus of Lyons, *Against Heresies,* Bk IV.26.2, p. 497.
[187] Lightfoot. p.228.
[188] Gore, p.102.

in a Christian home in Smyrna and knew Polycarp personally. He was thus someone with personal knowledge that Polycarp had been appointed bishop by the apostles and he was also someone who would have known the entire history of the church in Smyrna from the time of Polycarp to the time he was writing. This means that Irenaeus is a primary witness to an unbroken chain of episcopal succession in Smyrna from the time of the apostles to the time when he wrote. The evidence for episcopal succession in Smyrna going back to apostolic times is thus solid.

Turning to Ephesus, we saw in chapter 2 that the witness of 1 and 2 Timothy and the united testimony of later Patristic tradition tells us that having founded the church in Ephesus (Acts 18:19-21) Paul appointed Timothy to act as the bishop there at some point in the mid-60s and that Timothy continued this ministry after Paul's death. We also saw in chapter 2 that there was a bishop/angel in Ephesus at the time John wrote Revelation (Revelation 2:1-7) and in this chapter that Onesimus was Bishop of Ephesus at the time when Ignatius wrote to the church there in 110. This means that there is clear evidence of a continuity of episcopal ministry in Ephesus from the second half of the first century to the first decade of the second. The gap between that point and the time Irenaeus was writing would be covered by the knowledge of Irenaeus himself and the knowledge of those in Asia Minor he had known as a young man before moving to Rome and then Lyons. As in the case of Smyrna, the evidence for episcopal succession in Ephesus going back to apostolic times is solid.

If we move on to what Irenaeus has to say about the succession in the church in Rome, we have to acknowledge that many scholars today would continue to agree with the claim by Manson that '....there is strong evidence that the Roman Church was ruled not by a bishop but by a college of presbyters until well into the second century'[189] This, for example, is the view taken by the distinguished Roman Catholic

[189] Manson, p.63.

historian Eamon Duffy who argues in his history of the Papacy that mono-episcopacy was only introduced in Rome in about 150.[190]

There are two main problems with this argument.

First it means that Irenaeus was involved in a deliberate act of deception which somehow no one spotted.

If mono-episcopacy had been introduced in Rome in about 150 it was introduced either when he was living there or very shortly before. Irenaeus would therefore have known for certain that there was no line of bishops in Rome going back to the apostles. It follows that in giving Rome as his prime example of episcopal succession he would have been engaged in deliberate deception. He would have been basing his argument on something he knew to be untrue.

Furthermore, if this was the case then it is not clear why this deception was not spotted either at the time or in the decades and centuries that followed. As far as we know, no one at the time or subsequently ever challenged his argument by pointing out that bishops in Rome only went back to the mid second century. Why was this the case? Why did knowledge of what had really been the case suddenly and totally vanish from the Church's memory?

It is far more plausible to hold that there was no deception and that the reason no one challenged Irenaeus' argument was that it was historically unchallengeable.

Secondly, it goes against the evidence of *I Clement*. As we saw in chapter 2, the evidence of *1 Clement* tells us that a that a threefold ministry existed in Rome at the end of the first century and that it was believed to have been instituted by the apostles. This supports the claim of Irenaeus (and Hegesippus before him) that there was a list of Bishops of Rome stretching back to apostolic times, but it renders

---

[190] Eamon Duffy, *Saints and Sinners: A History of the Popes* (New Haven and London, Yale University Press, 2014), Part I. ii.

impossible the idea that there were no bishops in Rome until the mid-second century.

It is sometimes suggested that the fact that *1 Clement* was sent in the name of the 'church of God which sojourns in Rome'[191] rather than in the name of Clement himself tells against the idea that he was the Bishop of Rome as Irenaeus says he was.[192] However, this suggestion is unconvincing since it assumes we know that there was a protocol in place at the end of the first century that said a bishop had to write in his own name rather than in the name of his church. This assumption is unwarranted. It makes perfectly good sense to hold the view of Jerome that Clement wrote on behalf of the church of Rome.[193]

It is also sometimes suggested that the reference to Clement in the second vision of the *Shepherd of Hermas* suggests that Clement was the 'corresponding secretary' of the church in Rome rather than its bishop.[194] It is true that in the vision Hermas is told to write a book which 'Clement will send…to the cities abroad, because that is his job.'[195] However, if we accept the evidence of the Muratorian Canon that the *Shepherd* was written in the mid second century then there is no reason to identify this Clement with the Clement who was Bishop of Rome at the end of the first century. It makes more sense to see him as someone in the writer's church in his own day.

If we set aside these objections, there is no good reason to think that Clement was not Bishop of Rome and there is likewise no good reason to think that the others listed by Irenaeus were not Bishops of Rome either. In the cases of Pius, Soter, Anicetus and Eleutherius we have independent early confirmation from Hegesippus, Dionysius of Corinth and the Muratorian Canon that they were Bishops of Rome as Irenaeus claims. Similar independent early confirmation is lacking for

[191] *I Clement,* superscription, in Lightfoot, Harmer and Holmes, p,28.
[192] See, for example, Lightfoot, p.218.
[193] Jerome, *Lives of illustrious Men*, XV, in *The Nicene and Post Nicene Fathers*, vol.3 p.367.
[194] Lightfoot, Harmer and Holmes, p.24.
[195] *Shepherd of Hermas*, Vision 2.4, in Lightfoot, Harmer and Holmes, p.199.

the earlier names on the list, but this does not mean that these names are incorrect.

There is also no good reason to question the claim that the first bishop on the list, Linus, was appointed by 'the apostles,' by whom Irenaeus means Peter and Paul. The universal view of the Early Church, which is still accepted by most scholars today, is that Peter and Paul ministered in Rome where they were martyred under Nero in the mid-60s. As we have previously seen, the evidence we have tells us that Peter, together with the other apostles, had appointed James as Bishop of Jerusalem, that Peter had appointed Evodius Bishop of Antioch, and that Paul had appointed Timothy to be Bishop of Ephesus and Titus to be Bishop of Crete. In the light of this earlier activity it would make sense for them to have also jointly appointed Linus to provide continuing episcopal ministry in Rome since the need for such ministry would be as great in Rome as it was in Jerusalem, Antioch, Ephesus and Crete.

Once episcopacy had been established in Rome by Peter and Paul in this way it would then have continued as we know it did elsewhere with the result being the list of Roman bishops recorded by Irenaeus.

Polycrates of Ephesus
In Book V of his *Ecclesiastical History* Eusebius quotes from a letter sent in about 190 by Polycrates, Bishop of Ephesus, to bishop Victor of Rome. Victor had tried to insist that Easter should always be celebrated on a Sunday. Polycrates, however, having held a council of local bishops in Ephesus, decided to continue to observe the tradition of the church in Asia Minor, which was to celebrate Easter on the 14th day of Nisan (the day of the Jewish Passover) whatever day of the week that fell on.

According to Eusebius, he wrote to Victor as follows:

Therefore we keep the day undeviatingly, neither adding nor taking away, for in Asia great luminaries sleep, and they will rise on the day of the coming of the Lord, when he shall come with glory from heaven and seek out all the Saints. Such were Philip of the twelve apostles, and two of his daughters who grew old as virgins, who sleep in Hierapolis, and another daughter of his, who lived in the Holy Spirit rests at Ephesus. Moreover, there is also John, who lay on the Lord's breast, who was a priest wearing the breastplate, and a martyr, and teacher. He sleeps at Ephesus and there is also Polycarp at Smyrna both bishop and martyr, and Thraseas, both bishop and martyr from Eumenaea, who sleeps in Smyrna. And why should I speak of Sagaris, bishop and martyr, who sleeps at Laodicea, and Papirius, too, the blessed, and Melito the eunuch, who lived entirely in the Holy Spirit, who lies at Sardis, waiting for the visitation from heaven when he will rise from the dead? All these kept the fourteenth day of the Passover according to the gospel, never swerving, but following according to the rule of the faith. And I also, Polycrates, the least of you all, live according to the tradition of my kinsmen, and some of them I have followed. For seven of my family were bishops and I am the eighth, and my kinsmen ever kept the day when the people put away the leaven. Therefore, brethren, I who have lived sixty-five years in the Lord and conversed with brethren from every country, and have studied all holy Scripture, am not afraid of threats, for they have said who were greater than I, 'It is better to obey God rather than men.'[196]

Eusebius further tells us that:

He continues about the bishops who when he wrote were with him and shared his opinion, and says thus: 'And I could mention the bishops who are present whom you required me to summon. And I did so. If I should write their names they would be many multitudes; and they knowing my feeble humanity, agreed with the letter, knowing that not in vain is my head grey, but that I have ever lived In Christ Jesus.' [197]

The importance of this material for our concerns is that it confirms that episcopacy was very widespread in Asia Minor by the end of the first century, that there had been a long succession of bishops in Asia

---

[196] Eusebius of Caesarea, *Ecclesiastical History*, V xxiv, pp.505-507.
[197] Eusebius of Caesarea, *Ecclesiastical History*, V xxiv, pp.507-509.

Minor by that time and that the Apostles Philip and John had lived in Asia Minor at the end of their lives.

As Lightfoot notes, the statement by Polycrates that he has lived 'sixty five years in the Lord' may refer to his baptism rather than his baptism or conversion,[198] but even if it does this would mean that he was born in about 125, only a quarter of a century after the death of the Apostle John and like Irenaeus he would have known people who were first hand witnesses of the apostolic era. This observation reinforces the point already made that it is unlikely that the idea that the apostles appointed the first bishops would have been plausible during the second century unless it was true. Even at the end of the second century there would have been too many people like Polycrates around who knew people who had lived during the apostolic era for a fabricated claim for the apostolic origin of episcopacy to have been accepted. People would have said, as Polycrates says about the Roman date for Easter, 'this is not the tradition we have been taught and therefore not something we can accept.'

Clement of Alexandria

Clement of Alexandria was a convert from classical paganism to Christianity who lived. from c 150 to c 215. He was a presbyter and a theologian who taught at the Catechetical School in Alexandria, an institution designed to teach Christians to understand and defend the Christian faith, particularly in relation to the teachings of Greek philosophy.

Clement takes as a given that there are three grades of ordained ministry, of which the episcopate is the highest, and he argues that these different grades of ministry are intended to point us towards the advance 'from one degree of glory to another' (2 Corinthians 3:18) that awaits Christians in the life of the world to come.

In his work *Stromata* or *Miscellanies* he writes:

---

[198] Lightfoot, pp.213-214.

...according to my opinion, the grades here in the Church of, bishops, presbyters and deacons, are imitations of the angelic glory, and of that economy which, the Scriptures say, awaits those who, following in the footsteps of the apostles, have lived in perfection of righteousness according to the Gospel. For those taken up in the clouds, the apostle writes, will first minister [as deacons], then be classed in the presbyterate, by promotion in glory (for glory differs from glory) till they grow into 'a perfect man. [199]

Clement also holds that these three grades of ministry are found in the Bible. In his work *Paedogogus* (*The Instructor*) he lists a wide variety of biblical instructions concerning godly behaviour and then comments:

Innumerable commands such as these are written in the holy Bible appertaining to chosen persons, some to presbyters, some to bishops, some to deacons, others to widows, of whom we shall have another opportunity of speaking.[200]

In his book *Quis Dives Salvetur* (*How shall the rich man be saved?*) which explores the implications of the story in the gospels about Jesus' meeting with a rich young ruler in Matthew 10:16-30, Clement of Alexandria also bears witness to the apostolic origin of episcopacy in Asia Minor. He writes of:

...a legend, which is no legend but very history, which has been handed down and preserved about John the Apostle. When on the death of the tyrant [i.e. Domitian] he returned from the isle of Patmos to Ephesus, he used to go away when he was summoned to the neighbouring districts as well, in some places to establish bishops, in

---

[199] Clement of Alexandria, *The Stromata, or Miscellanies,* Bk VI.XIII, in *The Ante-Nicene Fathers*, vol. II, (Edinburgh and Grand Rapids: T&T Clark/Eerdmans, 2001), p.505.
[200] Clement of Alexandria, *The Instructor,* Bk III.XII in *The Ante-Nicene Fathers*, vol. II, p.295.

others to organise whole churches, on others to ordain to the clergy one of those indicated by the Spirit.[201]

In the last line of this quotation 'clergy' refers to bishops. We know this because the story then goes on to tell is about someone who was made a bishop by John.

What we learn from these quotations from Clement is that when he was writing at the end of the second or the start of the third century the church in Alexandria accepted the threefold order of ministry as a given and believed, like the other writers we have looked at, that the episcopate was apostolic in origin.

Tertullian

Tertullian was a Christian writer from Carthage in North Africa who lived from c160-c225. He was the first Christian writer to write extensively in Latin and he wrote a large number of works on Christian apologetics, theology and spirituality.

Like Clement, he wrote at the end of the second and the beginning of the third century and like Clement he accepts the threefold order of bishops, priests and deacons as a given part of the life of the Church. We can see this, for example, in his work *On Baptism*, written at the end of the second century, in which he writes about the roles of the three orders of ordained ministry and of the laity in performing baptism:

For concluding our brief subject, it remains to put you in mind also of the due observance of giving and receiving baptism. Of giving it, the chief priest (who is the bishop) has the right: in the next place, the presbyters and deacons, yet not without the bishop's authority, on account of the honour of the Church, which being preserved, peace is preserved. Beside these, even laymen have the right; for what is equally received can be equally given. Unless bishops, or priests, or deacons, be on the spot, other disciples are called i.e. to the work. The

---

[201] Clement of Alexandria, *Quis Dives Salvetur* 42 cited in Gore op. cit. p.256.

word of the Lord ought not to be hidden by any: in like manner, too, baptism, which is equally God's property, can be administered by all. But how much more is the rule of reverence and modesty incumbent on laymen— seeing that these powers belong to their superiors—lest they assume to themselves the specific function of the bishop![202]

Tertullian also follows Hegesippus and Irenaeus in linking a succession of bishops stretching back to the apostles with the maintenance of the apostolic faith. Like Irenaeus, Tertullian holds that heresy is a novelty and that this can be shown to be the case because the teaching of the heretics can be tested against the faith of those churches which have a line of bishops going back to the apostles through which the apostolic faith has been handed down.

Tertullian makes this point in his work *The Prescription Against Heretics*, to which we have referred previously in this chapter with reference to Polycarp, in which he appeals to the example of the churches in Smyrna, Rome and other unnamed places:

But if there be any (heresies) which are bold enough to plant themselves in the midst of the apostolic age, that they may thereby seem to have been handed down by the apostles, because they existed in the time of the apostles, we can say: Let them produce the original records of their churches; let them unfold the roll of their bishops, running down in due succession from the beginning in such a manner that [that first bishop of theirs] bishop shall be able to show for his ordainer and predecessor some one of the apostles or of apostolic men,-a man, moreover, who continued steadfast with the apostles. For this is the manner in which the apostolic churches transmit their registers: as the church of Smyrna, which records that Polycarp was placed therein by John; as also the church of Rome, which makes Clement to have been ordained in like manner by Peter. In exactly the same way the other churches likewise exhibit (their several worthies),

---

[202] Tertullian, *On Baptism,* XVII, in *The Ante-Nicene Fathers*, vol. III (Edinburgh and Grand Rapids: T&T Clark/Eerdmans, 1997), p.677.

whom, as having been appointed to their episcopal places by apostles, they regard as transmitters of the apostolic seed. [203]

In similar fashion, Tertullian writes in his work *Against Marcion,* that Marcion's version of the Christian faith, which involved a rejection of the God of the Old Testament, can be shown to be a heretical novelty if it is compared with the rule of faith preserved in the churches founded by the apostles. In the course of this argument he appeals to the example of seven churches mentioned in the Book of Revelation which, he says, have line of bishops going back to bishops appointed by the apostle John:

We have also St John's foster churches. For although Marcion rejects his Apocalypse the order of the bishops thereof when traced up to their origin will yet rest on John as their author. [204]

What Tertullian says in these last two quotations about the origins of the episcopate in Smyrna and in Asia Minor more generally fits in with the evidence we have looked at earlier in this chapter and in chapter 2. The same is also true of what he says about the apostolic origin of episcopacy in Rome.

Where there is an apparent discrepancy is that Tertullian appears to suggest that Clement was the first Bishop of Rome and was appointed by Peter whereas Irenaeus, as we saw above, states that Linus was the first Bishop of Rome and was appointed by Peter and Paul jointly.

The discrepancy of tradition about where Clement came in the Roman line on succession is noted by Jerome in his comments on Clement in his *Lives of Illustrious Men* in which he writes that Clement was:

...the fourth bishop of Rome after Peter, if indeed the second was Linus and the third Anacletus, although most of the Latins think that Clement was second after the apostle. [205]

---

[203] Tertullian, *On Prescription Against Heretics*, XXXII, in *The Ante-Nicene Fathers*, vol. III, p.258.
[204] Tertullian, *Against Marcion*, Bk IV.5, in *The Ante-Nicene Fathers*, vol. III, p. 350.

We do not now have the evidence that would enable us to conclusively resolve either who appointed Clement or where he came in the line of succession. However, with regard to the first point, a possible solution is that Peter ordained Clement with the agreement of Paul. With regard to the second, a possible solution is provided by Epiphanius who, apparently drawing on the *Memoirs* of Hegesippus suggests that Clement was ordained by Peter and declined to be bishop, but twenty-four years later exercised the office for nine years.[206]

What would be unjustified would be to suggest that the discrepancy casts doubt on the whole idea that there was episcopacy in Rome in the first century and that either Linus or Clement (or both) were appointed to be Bishops with the agreement of Peter and Paul.

Conclusion

What we have seen in this chapter is that from the very start of the second century until its end the threefold order of bishops, presbyters and deacons was in existence across the Christian world. There is no church we know of where it does not seem to have existed.

We have also seen that during the second century the term bishop (*episkopos*) was used exclusively to refer to a single individual who had ministerial oversight over the elders, deacons and lay people of a particular church. Furthermore, all the writers who comment on the subject see episcopacy as apostolic in origin with writers such as Hegesippus, Irenaeus and Tertullian testifying to unbroken lists of bishops in the churches going back to apostolic times.

Hegesippus, Irenaeus and Tertullian also link the existence of lines of episcopal descent with the preservation of orthodox apostolic teaching in the churches concerned. They see the apostolic teaching handed down to the first bishops having then been handed down the episcopal line. For them this unbroken line of teaching, alongside the

---

[205] Jerome, *Lives of illustrious Men*, XXVI in *The Nicene and Post Nicene Fathers*, vol. III p.366
[206] Epiphanius, *Adversus Haereses.*, xxvii, 6.

teaching of Scripture, serves to prove the antiquity of orthodoxy by contrast with the novelty of heresy.

The historical question that arises is how to account for the universal existence of the threefold ministry and the universal belief in the apostolic origin of the episcopate throughout the second century.

As we have seen, there are scholars who hold that episcopacy was invented during the second century rather than the apostolic era and only gradually spread across the Christian world, with an episcopal form of ministry not being found in the church of Rome until the middle of the century.

However, there is no evidence of anyone inventing episcopacy during the second century or any church adopting it. Episcopacy exists in all the churches we know of from the start of the second century until its end.

Furthermore, the idea that someone successfully persuaded people that a newly invented episcopal form of church government was apostolic in origin when in fact it was not, is difficult to maintain given that not only were there in all probability written records about the histories of the churches which have since been lost, but also that that there was a living chain of historical memory linking the apostolic age and the entire second century.

A distinction is often made between the Church of the apostolic age and the Church of the second century. What we have seen in this chapter, however, calls this distinction into question. First, John and possibly others of the apostles seem to have lived on in Asia Minor until the start of the second century. Secondly, early second century figures such as Ignatius of Antioch and Polycarp of Smyrna seem to have been born and grown to adulthood during the latter years of the first century. Thirdly, even in the second half of the second century there were those such as Hegesippus and Irenaeus who were born towards the beginning of the second century and who would know those who had lived during the apostolic era. Fourthly, even those born in the second half of the second century, such as Clement of

Alexandria and Tertullian, would have known people who had known people with first-hand knowledge of the practice of the apostolic Church. They were only two generations away from the apostolic age.

All this being so, the best explanation for the second century belief that the apostles had appointed the first apostles is that this was the case.

Furthermore, this explanation coheres with the evidence from the New Testament and other sources that we looked at in chapter two which points to the existence of bishops appointed by the apostles in the churches of the first century from the time of the appointment of James as the first Bishop of Jerusalem. The evidence we have for the second century follows on seamlessly from this evidence we have for the first century.

Chapter 4
From the third century onwards

In the previous chapter we found that in the second century a threefold order of bishops, presbyters and deacons was accepted in all the churches of which we have knowledge. This universal acceptance of the threefold order is also what we find from the third century onwards. Two examples, the *Apostolic Tradition* of Hippolytus and the Canons of the First Council of Nicaea, will serve to illustrate this

The Apostolic Tradition of Hippolytus

The *Apostolic Tradition* is treatise concerned with matters to do with liturgy, church order and Christian moral conduct. It was re-discovered in the 19th century and subsequently attributed to Hippolytus, a presbyter, theologian and martyr of the church of Rome who lived from c 170 to c 236. The attribution of this treatise to Hippolytus has been widely questioned in recent years, but it still seems 'safe...to use this document as evidence for early third century Rome.'[207]

Among the liturgical material in the treatise are instructions for the ordination of a bishop, a presbyter ('elder') and a deacon.

The instructions for the ordination of a bishop run as follows:

He who is ordained as a bishop, being chosen by all the people, must be irreproachable. When his name is announced and approved, the people will gather on the Lord's from day with the council of elders and the bishops who are present. With the assent of all, the bishops will place their hands upon him, with the council of elders standing by, quietly. Everyone will keep silent, praying in their hearts for the descent of the Spirit. After this, one of the bishops present, at the

---

[207] Cheslyn Jones, Geoffrey Wainwright and Edward Yarnold (eds), *The Study of Liturgy* (London: SPCK, 1985), p.59.

request of all, shall lay his hand upon him who is being ordained bishop, and pray, saying

God and Father of our Lord Jesus Christ, Father of mercies and God of all consolation, you who live in the highest, but regard the lowest, you who know all things before they are, you who gave the rules of the Church through the word of your grace, who predestined from the beginning the race of the righteous through Abraham, who instituted princes and priests, and did not leave your sanctuary without a minister; who from the beginning of the world has been pleased to be glorified by those whom you have chosen, pour out upon him the power which is from you, the princely Spirit, which you gave to your beloved Son Jesus Christ, which he gave to your holy apostles, who founded the Church in every place as your sanctuary, for the glory and endless praise of your name. Grant, Father who knows the heart, to your servant whom you chose for the episcopate, that he will feed your holy flock, that he will wear your high priesthood without reproach, serving night and day, incessantly making your face favourable, and offering the gifts of your holy church; in the spirit of high priesthood having the power to forgive sins according to your command; to assign lots according to your command; to loose any bond according to the authority which you gave to the apostles; to please you in mildness and a pure heart ,offering to you a sweet scent, through your son Jesus Christ, through whom to you be glory, power, and honor, Father and Son, with the Holy Spirit, in the Holy Church, now and throughout the ages of the ages. Amen.[208]

The instructions for the ordination of an elder are as follows:

When an elder is ordained, the bishop places his hand upon his head, along with the other elders, and says according to that which was said above for the bishop, praying and saying: God and Father of our Lord Jesus Christ, look upon your servant here, and impart the spirit of grace and the wisdom of elders, that he may help and guide your

---

[208] *The Apostolic Tradition of Hippolytus of Rome*, 2-3 at
www.bombaxo.com/hippolytus.html

people with a pure heart, just as you looked upon your chosen people, and commanded Moses to choose elders, whom you filled with your spirit which you gave to your attendant. Now, Lord, unceasingly preserving in us the spirit of your grace, make us worthy, so that being filled we may minister to you in singleness of heart, praising you, through your son Christ Jesus, through whom to you be glory and might, Father and Son with the Holy Spirit, in your Holy Church, now and throughout the ages of the ages. Amen.[209]

The instructions for the ordination of a deacon are as follows:

When one ordains a deacon, he is chosen according to what has been said above, with only the bishop laying on his hand in the same manner. In the ordination of a deacon, only the bishop lays on his hand, because the deacon is not ordained to the priesthood, but to the service of the bishop, to do that which he commands. For he is not part of the council of the clergy, but acts as a manager, and reports to the bishop what is necessary. He does not receive the spirit common to the elders, which the elders share, but that which is entrusted to him under the bishop's authority. his is why only the bishop makes a deacon. Upon the elders, the other elders place their hands because of a common spirit and similar duty. Indeed, the elder has only the authority to receive this, but he has no authority to give it. Therefore he does not ordain to the clergy. Upon the ordination of the elder he seals; the bishop ordains. The bishop says this over the deacon: O God, you who have created all and put it in order by your Word, Father of our Lord Jesus Christ, whom you sent to serve by your will, and to manifest to us your desire, give the Holy Spirit of grace and earnestness and diligence to this your servant, whom you have chosen to serve your church and to offer up in holiness in your sanctuary that which is offered from the inheritance of your high priests, so that serving without reproach and in purity, he may obtain a higher degree ,and that he may praise you and glorify you, through your son Jesus Christ our Lord, through whom to you be glory, and power, and praise,

---

[209] *The Apostolic Tradition of Hippolytus of Rome*, 7.

with the Holy Spirit, now and always, and throughout the ages of the ages. Amen.[210]

As well as specifying how bishops, presbyters and deacons are to be ordained, the treatise also gives instructions about the role they are to play in other services. We can see this for example in what the treatise says about how baptisms are to be conducted, instructions which lay down the particular roles to be played by the bishops, the elders and the deacons.

At the time determined for baptism, the bishop shall give thanks over some oil, which he puts in a vessel. It is called the Oil of Thanksgiving. He shall take some more oil and exorcise it. It is called the Oil of Exorcism. A deacon shall hold the Oil of Exorcism and stand on the left. Another deacon shall hold the Oil of Thanksgiving and stand on the right.

When the elder takes hold of each of them who are to receive baptism, he shall tell each of them to renounce, saying, 'I renounce you Satan, all your service, and all your works.' After he has said this, he shall anoint each with the Oil of Exorcism, saying, 'Let every evil spirit depart from you.' Then, after these things, the bishop passes each of them on nude to the elder who stands at the water. They shall stand in the water naked. A deacon, likewise, will go down with them into the water. When each of them to be baptized has gone down into the water, the one baptizing shall lay hands on each of them, asking, 'Do you believe in God the Father Almighty?' And the one being baptized shall answer, 'I believe.' He shall then baptize each of them once, laying his hand upon each of their heads. Then he shall ask, 'Do you believe in Jesus Christ, the Son of God, who was born of the Holy Spirit and the Virgin Mary, who was crucified under Pontius Pilate, and died, and rose on the third day living from the dead, and ascended into heaven, and sat down at the right hand of the Father, the one coming to judge the living and the dead?' When each has answered, 'I believe,' he shall baptize a second time. Then he shall ask, 'Do you believe in the Holy

[210] *The Apostolic Tradition of Hippolytus of Rome*, 8.

Spirit and the Holy Church and the resurrection of the flesh?' Then each being baptized shall answer, 'I believe.' And thus let him baptize the third time.

Afterward, when they have come up out of the water, they shall be anointed by the elder with the Oil of Thanksgiving, saying, 'I anoint you with holy oil in the name of Jesus Christ.' Then, drying themselves, they shall dress and afterwards gather in the church.

The bishop will then lay his hand upon them, invoking, saying, 'Lord God, you who have made these worthy of the removal of sins through the bath of regeneration, make them worthy to be filled with your Holy Spirit, grant to them your grace, that they might serve you according to your will, for to you is the glory, Father and Son with the Holy Spirit in the Holy Church, now and throughout the ages of the ages. Amen. After this he pours the oil into his hand, and laying his hand on each of their heads, says, 'I anoint you with holy oil in God the Father Almighty, and Christ Jesus, and the Holy Spirit.'

Then, after sealing each of them on the forehead, he shall give them the kiss of peace and say, 'The Lord be with you.' And the one who has been baptized shall say, 'And with your spirit.' So shall he do to each one.

From then on they will pray together will all the people. Prior to this they may not pray with the faithful until they have completed all. After they pray, let them give the kiss of peace.

Then the deacons shall immediately bring the oblation. The bishop shall bless the bread, which is the symbol of the Body of Christ; and the bowl of mixed wine, which is the symbol of the Blood which has been shed for all who believe in him; and the milk and honey mixed together, in fulfilment of the promise made to the fathers, in which he said, 'a land flowing with milk and honey,' which Christ indeed gave, his Flesh, through which those who believe are nourished like little children, by the sweetness of his Word, softening the bitter heart; and water also for an oblation, as a sign of the baptism, so that the inner person, which is psychic, may also receive the same as the body. The bishop shall give an explanation of all these things to those who are receiving.

Breaking the bread, distributing a piece to each, he shall say, 'The Bread of Heaven in Jesus Christ.' And the one who receives shall answer, 'Amen.'

The elders, and the deacons if there are not enough, shall hold the cups and stand together in good order and with reverence: first the one who holds the water, second the one who holds the milk, and third the one who holds the wine. They who partake shall taste of each three times. And he who gives shall say, 'In God the Father Almighty.' The one who receives shall respond, 'Amen.' The one giving shall say, 'And in the Lord Jesus Christ.' The one who receives shall respond, 'Amen.' The one giving shall say, 'And in the Holy Spirit, and in the Holy Church.' And the one who receives shall respond, 'Amen.' It shall be done so for each.

When these things are done, they shall be zealous to do good works, and to please God, living honourably, devoting themselves to the church, doing the things which they were taught, and advancing in piety.[211]

What we see in these extracts was that the church in Rome in the early third century was a church in which there was a threefold ministry of bishops, elders/presbyters and deacons, each of whom had their own particular role to play in the life and worship of the Church. Following a tradition which goes back at least as far as *1 Clement* at the end of the first century, this threefold ministry is seen as a Christian version of the forms of ministry found in the Old Testament.

The Canons of the First Council of Nicaea
Just over a century later, the First Council of Nicaea took place in 325. This council, the first of the seven great 'ecumenical councils' was summoned by the Emperor Constantine as a means of addressing the

---

[211] *The Apostolic Tradition of Hippolytus of Rome*, 21.

Arian controversy. It was intended to be a council representative of the whole Church and several hundred bishops and other clergy attended from churches across the whole Roman Empire (including Britain). There were also representatives from the churches in the Sassanid (Persian) Empire.

The Council is best remembered for its production of the Creed of Nicaea, the anti-Arian statement of Trinitarian faith which was the forerunner of the Nicene Creed used today. However, the Council also issued twenty Canons, or Church laws, a number of which have to do with the ordering of the Church's ministry. Four examples are given below.

Canon 2 declares that someone who has only recently been baptised should not be made a bishop or presbyter.

Forasmuch as, either from necessity, or through the urgency of individuals, many things have been done contrary to the Ecclesiastical canon, so that men just converted from heathenism to the faith, and who have been instructed but a little while, are straightway brought to the spiritual laver, and as soon as they have been baptized, are advanced to the episcopate or the presbyterate, it has seemed right to us that for the time to come no such thing shall be done. For to the catechumen himself there is need of time and of a longer trial after baptism. For the apostolic saying is clear, 'Not a novice; lest, being lifted up with pride, he fall into condemnation and the snare of the devil.' But if, as time goes on, any sensual sin should be found out about the person, and he should be convicted by two or three witnesses, let him cease from the clerical office. And whoever shall transgress these [enactments] will imperil his own clerical position, as a person who presumes to disobey the great Synod.[212]

[212] The Canons of the Council of Nicaea, Canon 2, in *The Nicene and Post-Nicene Fathers*, 2nd series, vol. XIV (Edinburgh and Grand Rapids: T&T Clark/Eerdmans, 1997) p.10.

Canon 3 lays down that no bishop, presbyter or deacon should have a woman ('subintroducta') living with him who is not a female relative or some other person beyond suspicion.

The great Synod has stringently forbidden any bishop, presbyter, deacon, or any one of the clergy whatever, to have a subintroducta dwelling with him, except only a mother, or sister, or aunt, or such persons only as are beyond all suspicion.[213]

Canon 15 forbids bishops, presbyters or deacons from moving from city to city. They are to remain in the church into which they were ordained.

On account of the great disturbance and discords that occur, it is decreed that the custom prevailing in certain places contrary to the Canon, must wholly be done away; so that neither bishop, presbyter, nor deacon shall pass from city to city. And if anyone, after this decree of the holy and great Synod, shall attempt any such thing, or continue in any such course, his proceedings shall be utterly void, and he shall be restored to the Church for which he was ordained bishop or presbyter.[214]

Canon 18 sets down rules for how deacons should behave at the Eucharist in relation to bishops and presbyters.

It has come to the knowledge of the holy and great Synod that, in some districts and cities, the deacons administer the Eucharist to the presbyters, whereas neither canon nor custom permits that they who have no right to offer should give the Body of Christ to them that do offer. And this also has been made known, that certain deacons now touch the Eucharist even before the bishops. Let all such practices be utterly done away, and let the deacons remain within their own bounds, knowing that they are the ministers of the bishop and the

---

[213] The Canons of the Council of Nicaea, Canon 3, in *The Nicene and Post-Nicene Fathers*, 2nd series, vol. XIV, p. 11.
[214] The Canons of the Council of Nicaea, Canon 15, in *The Nicene and Post-Nicene Fathers*, 2nd series, vol. XIV, p. 32.

inferiors of the presbyters. Let them receive the Eucharist according to their order, after the presbyters, and let either the bishop or the presbyter administer to them. Furthermore, let not the deacons sit among the presbyters, for that is contrary to canon and order. And if, after this decree, anyone shall refuse to obey, let him be deposed from the diaconate.[215]

What these Canons show is that at the beginning of the fourth century there appears to have been no question about whether churches should have a threefold ministry of bishops, presbyters and deacons. This seems to have been absolutely taken for granted. What was at question was who ought to be ordained and how bishops, presbyters and deacons should behave.

Material which seems to identify bishops and presbyters

The material that we have looked at in the first three chapters of this study, and in the first section of this chapter, is that there is clear evidence for the existence of a threefold ministry of bishops, presbyters and deacons from very early in the history of the Church. However, there is also material from the early centuries of the Church that appears, either implicitly or explicitly, to identify bishops and presbyters.

This latter material can be divided into three categories.

First, there are places in the writings of Irenaeus and Clement of Alexandria from the second century in which bishops are referred to as presbyters.

As we saw in the previous chapter, Irenaeus (like Hegesippus and Tertullian) declares in his work *Adversus Haereses* that there has been a succession of bishops, stretching back to the time of the apostles, through which orthodox teaching has been maintained in the Church.

---

[215] The Canons of the Council of Nicaea, Canon, 3 in *The Nicene and Post-Nicene Fathers*, 2nd series, vol. 14, p. 39.

However, in a number of passages in the *Adversus Haereses* he uses the term presbyter to refer to these bishops.

In Book III, for example, he writes that when heretics are referred to:

...that tradition which originates from the apostles, [and] which is preserved by means of the successions of presbyters in the Churches, they object to tradition, saying that they themselves are wiser not merely than the presbyters, but even than the apostles, because they have discovered the unadulterated truth.[216]

In Book IV he further writes that

...it is incumbent to obey the presbyters who are in the Church, those who, as I have shown, possess the succession from the apostles; those who, together with the succession of the episcopate, have received the certain gift of truth according to the good pleasure of the Father.[217]

As the mention of the 'succession of the episcopate 'in the second passage makes clear, when he talks about 'presbyters' in these two passages Irenaeus is referring to those he also calls 'bishops.'

In Book IV Irenaeus also mentions those:

...who are believed to be presbyters by many, but serve their own lusts, and do not place the fear of God supreme in their hearts, but conduct themselves with contempt towards others, and are puffed up with the pride of holding the chief seat, and work evil deeds in secret, saying 'No man sees us,' shall be convicted by the Word, who does not judge after outward appearance (*secundum gloriam*), nor looks upon the countenance, but the heart... From all such persons, therefore, it behoves us to keep aloof, but to adhere to those who, as I have already observed, do hold the doctrine of the apostles, and who, together with

---

[216] Irenaeus, *Against Heresies*, Bk III.2.2, p.415.
[217] Irenaeus, *Against Heresies*, Bk IV.26.2, p.497.

the order of priesthood (*presbyterii ordine*) display sound speech and blameless conduct for the confirmation and correction of others. [218]

As the references to 'the pride of holding the chief seat' [i.e. the bishop's throne] and holding 'the doctrine of the apostles' indicate, Irenaeus is talking here about those who are either believed to be bishops, or who actually are bishops, and yet he refers to them as presbyters.

Irenaeus goes on to cite the examples of Moses, Samuel and Paul as godly leaders of God's people and declares:

Such presbyters does the Church nourish, of whom also the prophet says: 'I shall give thy rulers in peace, and thy bishops in righteousness.' (Isaiah 60:17) ...Where, therefore the gifts of the Lord have been placed, there it behoves us to learn the truth, [namely,] from those who possess that succession of the Church which is from the apostles, and among whom exists that which is sound and blameless in conduct, as well as that which is unadulterated and incorrupt in speech. [219]

Here again the 'bishops' prophesied in Isaiah are bishops in the sense of sole leaders after the pattern of Moses, Samuel and Paul, but they are referred to as 'presbyters.'

The final passage from Irenaeus is found in a letter quoted by Eusebius in Book V of his *Ecclesiastical History*. In this letter Irenaeus writes to Pope Victor on behalf of the church in Gaul urging him to take a tolerant approach to the Eastern tradition of observing Easter on 14 Nissan. He cites as examples of those who have previously taken such an approach 'the presbyters before Soter who presided over the church of which you are now the leader. I mean Anicetus, and Pius and Telesphorus and Xystus' and adds that 'the presbyters before you who did not observe it sent the Eucharist to those from other dioceses who did.' [220]

---

[218] Irenaeus, *Against Heresies,* Bk IV.26 3-.4, p.497.
[219] Irenaeus, *Against Heresies*, Bk IV.26.5, p.498.
[220] Eusebius *Ecclesiastical History,* V. xxiv, p.511.

In this letter 'presbyters' has to mean 'bishops' since the people whom he lists were bishops of Rome and Irenaeus is urging Pope Victor as the current bishop to follow their good example.

If we turn to the writings of Clement of Alexandria we find, as we saw in chapter 3, that he refers to a threefold ecclesiastical hierarchy of bishops, presbyters and deacons. However, in other passages he refers to a twofold hierarchy consisting only of presbyters and deacons.

We can see this in the following two passages from Books VI and VII of the *Stromata.*

In Book VI he declares that those who are lay may be regarded as spiritually ordained as presbyters and deacons:

Those...who have exercised themselves in the Lord's commandments, and lived perfectly and gnostically [i.e. in accordance with true knowledge] according to the Gospel, may be enrolled in the chosen body of the apostles. Such a one is in reality a presbyter of the church, and a true minister (deacon) of the will of God, if he do teach what is the Lord's; not as being ordained by men, nor regarded as righteous because a presbyter, but enrolled in the presbyterate because righteous. And although here on earth he be not honoured with the chief seat, he will sit down on the four-and-twenty thrones, judging the people, as John says in the Apocalypse. [221]

In Book VII he contrasts two kinds of service, that which involves improvement and that which is ministerial, assigning the first kind to the presbyters and the second to the deacons.

...of the service bestowed on men, one kind is that whose aim is improvement, the other ministerial. The improvement of body is the object of the medical art, of the soul of philosophy. Ministerial service is rendered to parents by children, to rulers by children. Similarly, also, in the Church, the elders [presbyters] attend to the department

[221] Clement of Alexandria, *The Stromata,* Bk VI.XIII, p.504.

which has improvement for its object; and the deacons to the ministerial.[222]

The only way to make sense of both these passages and his references elsewhere to bishops is to think that Clement regards those who are bishops as also being part of the presbyterate, a supposition which is supported by the way that the same person is referred to in his work *Quis Dives Salvertur* as both a bishop and a presbyter.[223]

Secondly, there are references in the letters of Cyprian of Carthage and Augustine which suggest a custom of bishops referring to presbyters as their 'fellow' or 'co' presbyters.

As we shall see in a subsequent chapter, Cyprian was a bishop who placed a very strong emphasis on the distinctive ministry of the bishops as necessary for the unity of the Church. However, in a series of letters he writes to 'our fellow- presbyters, Donatus and Fortunatus, Novatus and Gordius,' [224] to Primitivus our co-presbyter,' [225] to Lucian, our co-presbyter [226] and to 'Nemesianus, Felix, Lucius, another Felix, Litteus, Polianus, Victor, Jader and Dativus his fellow-bishops, also to his fellow-presbyters and deacons [227]

In addition, when he writes to Pope Cornelius he refers to the letters he has received from the Roman presbyter Novatian (Cornelius' rival for the see of Rome) as 'the letters of your co-presbyter sitting with you.' [228]

[222]Clement of Alexandria, *The Stromata,* Bk VII, I, p.523.
[223] Clement of Alexandria, *Who is the rich man that shall be saved?* XLII, in *The Ante-Nicene Fathers*, vol. II, (Edinburgh and Grand Rapids: T&T Clark/Eerdmans, 2001), p.603.
[224] Cyprian Epistle, V, in *The Ante-Nicene Fathers*, Vol. V (Edinburgh and Grand Rapids: Eerdmans, 1995), p283.
[225] Cyprian Epistle, XL, p. 319.
[226] Cyprian Epistle LXX, p.377.
[227] Cyprian Epistle, LXXVI, p.402.
[228] Cyprian Epistle XLI, p.320.

Moving on to the fifth century we find Augustine, the Bishop of Hippo, referring to the presbyter Jerome as 'My holy brother and fellow-presbyter' [229]

What is implicit in these greetings, as in the material from Irenaeus and Clement of Alexandria, is the idea that a bishop is a presbyter even though he is a bishop.

Thirdly, if we move on to the fourth century, we find a series of people who are explicit about the identity of bishops and presbyters and who ground this identity in the references to bishops and presbyters in the New Testament.

The first of these people is Aerius of Sebaste. We learn about Aerius from a work by Epiphanius called the *Panarion*, or 'medicine chest,' which he wrote to provide antidotes to various kinds of heresy.

In Book III of the *Panarion* Epiphanius tells us that Aerius was a presbyter who fell out with his bishop Eustathius at some point after 355 and left the hospice which Eustathius had appointed him to run. According to Epiphanius he then began to teach that there was no difference between bishops and presbyters:

...when he left the hospice, he took a large body of men and women with him. With his fellowship he was driven from the churches, and from cultivated lands and villages, and the other towns. He often lived out in the snow with his numerous band of followers, and lodged in the open air and caves, and took refuge in the woods. But his teaching was more insane than is humanly possible, and he says, 'What is a bishop compared with a presbyter? The one is no different from the other. There is one order,' he said, 'and one honour and one rank. A bishop lays on hands,' he said, 'but so does a presbyter. The bishop administers baptism, and the presbyter does too. The bishop performs the eucharistic liturgy, the presbyter likewise. A bishop occupies the

[229] Augustine Letter LXXXII, *The Nicene and Post-Nicene Fathers,* Vol I, (Edinburgh and Grand Rapids: T&T Clark/Eerdmans, 194), p. 349.

throne, and the presbyter also occupies one.' With this he misled many, who regarded him as their leader.[230]

The second is the anonymous writer known as Ambrosiaster (so called because his work was attributed to Ambrose of Milan) who wrote a commentary on the letters of Paul during the papacy of Pope Damasus (366-384).

In his comments on Ephesians 4:11-12 Ambrosiaster writes:

...our present system does not correspond in all respects with the writings of the apostle, because these were written at the beginning of things. Thus he even calls Timothy a presbyter, though he had made him a bishop, because the first presbyters were entitled bishops, in such wise that when Timothy withdrew, the next in rank should succeed him. (In actual fact presbyters still give confirmation in Egypt, if the bishop is not present.) But because the presbyters next in rank began to seem unworthy to hold the first places, a change of system was introduced, the purpose of which was to secure that not rank but merit should make a man a bishop, who should be appointed by the vote of many priests, lest an unfit person should acquire the office without qualification and be the cause of offence to many.[231]

In his comments on 1 Timothy 3:10 he further writes:

But after the episcopate he [Paul] goes on to mention the order of the diaconate. What possible explanation can there be of this, if not that the orders of bishops and presbyters are the same? For each is a priest, but the bishop is the head, so that although every bishop is a presbyter, not every presbyter is a bishop. For the bishop is simply the chief among the presbyters. The apostle too shows that Timothy had

[230] Epiphanius of Salamis, *Panarion*, Bk III: 75, text in Frank Wilson, *The Panarion of Epiphanius of Salamis, Books II and III* (Leiden and Boston: Brill, 2013), p. 505.
[231] Ambrosiastet, *Comm. In Eph.* Iv.11 in Kenneth Kirk et al. *The Apostolic Ministry* (London: Hodder and Stoughton, 1947), pp.322-323.

been appointed presbyter, but because there is no one higher in rank than he, he was in fact a bishop. [232]

The third is Jerome. In his commentary on Titus Jerome comments on Titus 1:7:

So you see that presbyter is the same as bishop. For until by the inspiration of the devil there arose factions in our religion and people were saying 'I am Paul's man, etc.' (1 Cor 1:12) ...the churches were ruled by a corporate body of presbyters. But when everyone began to regard those whom he had baptised as his own rather than Christ's, it was decreed throughout the world, that one chosen from the presbyters should be set over the others, to whom entire responsibility for the (local) Church should belong, and thus the seeds of schism be removed. But if anyone supposes that in so writing I am voicing my own opinion and not the teaching of the Scriptures, namely that bishop and presbyter are in fact the same, and that the latter term denotes age, while the former denotes office, let him read again the words of the apostle saying to the Philippians; (Phil 1:1) ...now Philippi is a city of Macedonia and assuredly there could not have been several bishops (as they are described there) in a single city. But because at that time they used to call the same persons bishops and presbyters therefore he spoke indifferently of bishops meaning presbyters... (quotes Acts 20:28). Note rather carefully here how in summoning their presbyters of the single city of Ephesus he afterwards addresses them as 'bishops.' And if anyone accepts the letter which was written under the name of Paul to the Hebrews there too responsibility for the (local) church is divided equally among several people (Hebrews 13:17). Peter too, who received his name on account of the stability of his faith, speaks in his letter saying: (1 Pet 5:1f). We have mentioned the foregoing examples to show that among those of old times presbyters were the same as bishops and that to root out the seedlings of dissension the entire responsibility was handed over to one man. Therefore while presbyters realise that they

---

[232] Ambrosiaster, *Comm. In 1 Tim.*iii.10, in Kirk, p. 321.

have been subjected to him who is set over them by the custom of the Church, let bishops remember that they are superior to presbyters only by custom and not by the fact of our Lord's appointment and that they ought to rule the Church in the common interest, imitating Moses, who though possessing authority to preside alone over the people of Israel, yet chose seventy to assist him in the judgement of the people (Numbers 11:16f). [233]

Jerome later repeats and develops the same points in a letter to man called Evangelus in which he writes as follows:

We read in Isaiah the words, 'the fool will speak folly,' and I am told that someone has been mad enough to put deacons before presbyters, that is, before bishops. For when the apostle clearly teaches that presbyters are the same as bishops, must not a mere server of tables and of widows Acts 6:1-2 be insane to set himself up arrogantly over men through whose prayers the body and blood of Christ are produced? Do you ask for proof of what I say? Listen to this passage: 'Paul and Timotheus, the servants of Jesus Christ, to all the saints in Christ Jesus which are at Philippi with the bishops and deacons.' Do you wish for another instance? In the Acts of the Apostles Paul thus speaks to the priests of a single church: 'Take heed unto yourselves and to all the flock, in the which the Holy Ghost has made you bishops, to feed the church of God which He purchased with His own blood.' And lest any should in a spirit of contention argue that there must then have been more bishops than one in a single church, there is the following passage which clearly proves a bishop and a presbyter to be the same. Writing to Titus the apostle says: 'For this cause left I you in Crete, that you should set in order the things that are wanting, and ordain presbyters in every city, as I had appointed you: if any be blameless, the husband of one wife, having faithful children not accused of riot or unruly. For a bishop must be blameless as the steward of God.' Titus 1:5-7 And to Timothy he says: 'Neglect not the gift that is in you, which was given you by prophecy, with the laying on

[233] Jerome, *Comm. in Tit.* I 6-7, in Kirk, ppp.326-327.

of the hands of the presbytery.' 1 Timothy 4:14 Peter also says in his first epistle: 'The presbyters which are among you I exhort, who am your fellow presbyter and a witness of the sufferings of Christ and also a partaker of the glory that shall be revealed: feed the flock of Christ...taking the oversight thereof not by constraint but willingly, according unto God.' In the Greek the meaning is still plainer, for the word used is ἐπισκοποῦντες, that is to say, overseeing, and this is the origin of the name overseer or bishop. But perhaps the testimony of these great men seems to you insufficient. If so, then listen to the blast of the gospel trumpet, that son of thunder, Mark 3:17 the disciple whom Jesus loved John 13:23 and who reclining on the Saviour's breast drank in the waters of sound doctrine. One of his letters begins thus: 'The presbyter unto the elect lady and her children whom I love in the truth;' and another thus: 'The presbyter unto the well-beloved Gaius whom I love in the truth.' When subsequently one presbyter was chosen to preside over the rest, this was done to remedy schism and to prevent each individual from rending the church of Christ by drawing it to himself. For even at Alexandria from the time of Mark the Evangelist until the episcopates of Heraclas and Dionysius the presbyters always named as bishop one of their own number chosen by themselves and set in a more exalted position, just as an army elects a general, or as deacons appoint one of themselves whom they know to be diligent and call him archdeacon. For what function, excepting ordination, belongs to a bishop that does not also belong to a presbyter? It is not the case that there is one church at Rome and another in all the world beside. Gaul and Britain, Africa and Persia, India and the East worship one Christ and observe one rule of truth. If you ask for authority, the world outweighs its capital. Wherever there is a bishop, whether it be at Rome or at Engubium, whether it be at Constantinople or at Rhegium, whether it be at Alexandria or at Zoan, his dignity is one and his priesthood is one. Neither the command of wealth nor the lowliness of poverty makes him more a bishop or less a bishop. All alike are successors of the apostles.

But you will say, how comes it then that at Rome a presbyter is only ordained on the recommendation of a deacon? To which I reply as follows. Why do you bring forward a custom which exists in one city only? Why do you oppose to the laws of the Church a paltry exception which has given rise to arrogance and pride? The rarer anything is the more it is sought after. In India pennyroyal is more costly than pepper. Their fewness makes deacons persons of consequence while presbyters are less thought of owing to their great numbers. But even in the church of Rome the deacons stand while the presbyters seat themselves, although bad habits have by degrees so far crept in that I have seen a deacon, in the absence of the bishop, seat himself among the presbyters and at social gatherings give his blessing to them. Those who act thus must learn that they are wrong and must give heed to the apostle's words: 'it is not reason that we should leave the word of God and serve tables.' Acts 6:2 They must consider the reasons which led to the appointment of deacons at the beginning. They must read the Acts of the Apostles and bear in mind their true position.

Of the names presbyter and bishop the first denotes age, the second rank. In writing both to Titus and to Timothy the apostle speaks of the ordination of bishops and of deacons, but says not a word of the ordination of presbyters; for the fact is that the word bishops includes presbyters also. Again, when a man is promoted it is from a lower place to a higher. Either then a presbyter should be ordained a deacon, from the lesser office, that is, to the more important, to prove that a presbyter is inferior to a deacon; or if on the other hand it is the deacon that is ordained presbyter, this latter should recognize that, although he may be less highly paid than a deacon, he is superior to him in virtue of his priesthood. In fact as if to tell us that the traditions handed down by the apostles were taken by them from the Old Testament, bishops, presbyters and deacons occupy in the church the same positions as those which were occupied by Aaron, his sons, and the Levites in the temple.[234]

The fourth person is John Chrysostom.

---

[234] Jerome, 'Letter CXLVI to Evangelus,' in *The Nicene and Post-Nicene Fathers*, 2nd series, vol. VI (Edinburgh and Grand Rapids: T&T Clark/Eerdmans, 1996), pp. 288-289.

In his homily on 1 Timothy he writes that the reason Paul omitted to mention presbyters alongside bishops and deacons in 1 Timothy 3 is because:

...there is not much difference between them (sc. presbyters) and bishops. For they too have been entrusted with teaching and the presidency of churches. Moreover that which he (sc. St. Paul) says about bishops, he applies also to presbyters. For they (sc. bishops) are superior to them only in the power of ordination, and in this respect alone have they advantage over presbyters.[235]

In his homily on Philippians he further notes that in the New Testament the terms 'bishop' and 'presbyter' refer to the same office:

So, as I have already pointed out, while old time presbyters were called bishops and deacons of Christ, bishops were also called presbyters; just as even today many bishops write 'to a fellow-presbyter' or 'to a fellow-deacon.' But later the distinctive titles of 'bishop' and 'presbyter' were assigned to each.[236]

The fifth and final person is Theodore of Mopsuestia (c350-428), who was a bishop, a biblical commentator and a theologian. Commenting on 1 Timothy 3:8 he writes:

Anyone who is unfamiliar with the sacred Scriptures might suppose the blessed Paul had ignored presbyters. Yet this is not so. For all that he has said about the bishop applies also to presbyters. Formerly presbyters were designated by both these titles, as we pointed out in commenting on the Epistle to the Philippians, where he writes: 'to fellow-bishops and deacons.' For obviously it is impossible that there could have been several bishops of a single city...so although he ought to have said 'presbyter' he actually calls the same person 'bishop' and 'presbyter.'

---

[235] John Chrysostom, *Hom. In Tim.* iii.8 in Kirk, p. 332.
[236] John Chrysostom, *Hom. In Phil. i.1* in Kirk pp.332-333.

At first there were presbyters everywhere after the Jewish fashion who were known as *episcopi* from the nature of their duties. But those presbyters who had the privilege of ordaining ruled over whole provinces like Timothy in Asia or Titus in Crete. Later, as the number of Christians increased, the successors of the apostles were multiplied. These men, not presuming to call themselves apostles, differentiated the titles by deciding to be called *episcopi* exclusively, thus reserving the title to one who had authority to ordain and applying it to one entrusted with a general responsibility.[237]

The material in this third category makes four basic points:

- In the New Testament the terms presbyter and bishop mean the same thing and therefore bishops are presbyters;

- It was only gradually that the Church came to single out one individual from among the presbyters as the chief presbyter and to use the term bishop as the title for that individual;

- Bishops differ from other presbyters chiefly in the fact that they alone have the power to ordain;

- Because a bishop is a presbyter a deacon ought not to think that he is superior to a presbyter because he acts on behalf of the bishop (it is this last point that particularly exercises Jerome).

These four points have continued to be influential in the subsequent history of the Western Church. They underly the teaching of the Roman Catholic Church that there is one order of priesthood in which both bishops and presbyters participate to different degrees.[238] They

---

[237] Theodore of Mopsuestia, Exp. In 1 Tim.iii.8, in Kirk, pp.333-334.
[238] *The Catechism of the Council of Trent*, 'The Degrees of the Priesthood,' at http://catholicapologetics.info/thechurc/catechism/Holy7Sacraments-Orders.shtml and *Catechism of the Catholic Church*, Chapter 3.6.3 (London: Geoffrey Chapman, 1994).

also underly the teaching of Reformed,[239] Lutheran[240] and Anglican[241] theologians that presbyters and bishops were originally identical with bishops only gradually emerging from the ranks of the presbyters from the end of the first century onwards.

Assessing the material which seems to identify bishops and presbyters

How are we to assess the material we have just noted which seems to identify bishops and presbyters?

First, we have to acknowledge that there was an early and persistent tradition which included bishops within the larger category of the presbyterate. The fact that Irenaeus switches between using bishop and presbyter without feeling any need to explain why he is doing so indicates that there was a widely shared tradition in the second century that the terms bishop and presbyter to one and the same ministerial office.

However, we also have to note that this does not mean that Irenaeus regarded all presbyters as bishops. He reserves the term 'bishop' for those individuals who are in line of succession from the apostles and are the leaders of the churches. The best explanation as to why he and the other people in the first two categories we looked at above also use the term 'presbyter' for these individuals is because this term was used in an inclusive sense for all the senior leaders of the Church. This means that all bishops were presbyters (hence the language of Cyprian and Augustine about 'co' and 'fellow' presbyters), but not all presbyters were bishops.

[239] See John Calvin, *Institutes of the Christian Religion*, Bk IV.4,1-10 and Michael Kruger, 'Were Early Churches Ruled by Elders or a Single Bishop?', July 13, 2015 at https://www.michaeljkruger.com/were-early-churches-ruled-by-elders-or-a-single-bishop/.
[240] See Luther 'Preface to Jerome Letter 146' in *Works Vol.60* (St. Louis: Concordia, 2011) and *The Book of Concord*, 'A Treatise on the Power and Primacy of the Pope' at http://bookofconcord.org/treatise.php.
[241] See Beckwith Ch.7, Arthur Headlam, *The Doctrine of the Church and Reunion*, (London: John Murray, 1920), pp.93-99 and Lightfoot, pp 227-234.

Secondly, there are a number of problems with the material in the third category which identifies bishops and presbyters as a single form of ministry.

1. The statement of Aerius that bishops are 'no different' to presbyters falls foul of the evidence we have looked at in this study. This evidence tells us that from very early on in the history of the Church there were a series of individuals, such as James, Timothy, Titus and the 'angels of the churches' who followed the apostles in exercising pastoral oversight over the presbyters, deacons, and laity of a church, or group of churches, and that from the early second century their successors in this role came to be called bishops. Because these bishops exercised pastoral oversight over the presbyters it follows that to say with Aerius that bishops are no different from presbyters is simply wrong.

2. The argument that because the terms 'bishop' and 'presbyter' are synonymous in the New Testament it therefore follows that these terms mean (or should mean) the same thing in the later history of the Church is likewise mistaken. The meanings of words develop over time and, as we have just noted, from the early second century the word 'bishop' came to be used in the specific sense of the individual who exercised general pastoral oversight over the presbyters, deacons and laity of a church or groups of churches. The role of these later bishops was not the same as that exercised by the bishops/presbyters in the New Testament and is a mistake to ignore this difference.

3. It is also a mistake to focus in on the right to ordain as if this was the chief thing that distinguished bishops from their fellow presbyters. It is true that the evidence of the Pastoral Epistles (1 Timothy 3:1-13, 5:22, Timothy 2:1-2, Titus 1:5-9) indicates that what later came to be called ordination was part of the bishop's role from New Testament times, but this was only part of a more general calling to exercise pastoral

oversight over a church or group of churches and it is this more general calling to exercise pastoral oversight over presbyters, deacons and laity that makes the bishop's role distinctive.

4. Jerome (and following him Severus of Antioch in the early sixth century [242]) may have been correct to say that in the early history of the church in Alexandria the bishop was appointed by the Presbyters. Whether the evidence supports their claim remains a matter of dispute. [243] However, even if they are correct, this does not mean that bishops and presbyters are identical. All that it shows is that in the particular case of Alexandria presbyters chose someone from their own ranks to be the successor of Mark as the Patriarch of Alexandria. It does not mean that thereafter there was no difference between this individual and the presbyters by who he had been appointed (any more than, to use Jerome's example, a general chosen by an army simply retains his previous rank and duties).

5. There does not seem to be any evidence either from the New Testament, or from other early sources, to support the statement by Ambrosiaster that in the earliest days of the Church a bishop was automatically succeeded by the next most senior presbyter. As Bilson notes, the evidence we have from the New Testament is that ministers were chosen by reason of merit rather than seniority and there is nothing to suggest that this replaced an earlier pattern of appointment by seniority. [244]

6. There is also no evidence either from the New Testament, or from other early sources, to support the claim by Jerome that the move from government by a corporate body of presbyters

[242] See Gore, pp.122-124.
[243] See William Telfer, 'Episcopal succession in Egypt,' *Journal of Ecclesiastical History*, Vol. 1 Issue 3, January 1952, pp.1-13 and the response from Eric Kemp in 'Bishops and Presbyters at Alexandria,' *Journal of Ecclesiastical History*, Vol 6, Issue 2, October 1955, pp.125-142.
[244] Bilson, pp. 312-313.

to government by an individual bishop was simply in order 'to remedy schism.' As 1 Corinthians indicates, schism caused by individuals attracting groups of followers to themselves was a real problem in in the earliest days of the Church. However, when we look at the New Testament evidence concerning James, Timothy, Titus and the angels of the churches we do not find that their sole or only role is to prevent churches from fragmenting. Rather their role is to exercise general pastoral oversight and to ensure, as far as possible, that the apostolic faith is upheld, that Christians live in a godly fashion, and that godly people are appointed as presbyters and deacons. As we shall see in more detail in chapter 7, even in the letters of Ignatius of Antioch, in which there is a great stress on the necessity for Christians to be in unity with their bishops, this is not simply to avoid schism, but also to ensure that Christians continue to adhere to orthodox doctrine and maintain godly standards of behaviour.

Furthermore, there is no evidence that the first bishops were all chosen out of the ranks of the presbyters as Jerome suggests. There is nothing in the New Testament that says James, Titus or the angels of the churches were originally presbyters, and we have no evidence that tells us that anyone else (apart from Timothy) appointed by the apostles to be the first bishops had previously been presbyters. Some of the first bishops, other than Timothy, may first have been presbyters, but we have no means of knowing if this was the case.

Jerome's comment that bishops 'are superior to presbyters only by custom and not by the fact of our Lord's appointment' can be misleading if it is understood to mean that the distinction between bishops and presbyters is simply a human invention. As we have seen, for Jerome the existence of a threefold ministry of bishops, presbyters and deacons is something 'handed down by the apostles' and as such carries divine rather than merely human authority. Why then does he contrast 'custom' and 'our Lord's appointment'? As Bilson notes, the answer is provided by what he then says about the importance of bishops 'imitating Moses.' Bilson expounds Jerome's argument as follows:

Let the bishops know, that (according to the truth of the Lord's disposition, however the custom of the church be now to the contrary) they should rule the church in common (with the presbyters) after the example of Moses, who when it lay in his power to be ruler alone over the people of Israel, he chose seventy to help him judge the people. What they ought to do, that was the truth of the Lord's disposition: now they ought to do as Moses did. What, to have all governors equal? No; but when they might rule alone, to join with them others in the fellowship of their power and honour, as Moses did. Moses did not abrogate his superiority above others; but took seventy elders into part of his charge. This saith Jerome was the truth of the Lord's ordinance, although by the customer of the church, as it then was (which grew paulatim,[245] not when bishops were first ordained, but by degrees in decurse [246] of time) they had the whole charge of the church without advising or conferring with the presbyters. [247]

In summary, what we learn from the material that appears to identify bishops and presbyters is that in the early church bishops were regarded as being presbyters in the sense of being part of the senior leadership of the Church, but they were always recognised as having a distinctive ministry of oversight, in descent from the oversight first exercised by the apostles, which other presbyters did not possess.

What we do not learn is that bishops and presbyters were identical, that the first bishops emerged out of the presbyterate to prevent schism, that having bishops is simply a human custom, or that bishops differ from presbyters chiefly in having the right to ordain.

[245] Little by little.
[246] The flow of.
[247] Bilson, pp.308-309).

The origins and operation of the provincial system

It is often suggested that the bishops of the early church were, like

traditional Church of England parish priests, responsible for one church meeting together in one place. However, this idea is misleading.

As we have seen, it seems to have been the case that the first bishops we know of, James, Timothy Titus and the angels of the churches had responsibility for multiple churches in Jerusalem, Ephesus Crete and the seven cities referred to in Revelation. It has also been suggested that the as the bishops of the leading cities in Roman Asia the angels in Revelation may have had responsibility not only for the church in those cities, but also for the churches in the areas surrounding those cities.

In the words of James Ussher:

So that in all reason we are to suppose, these seven churches, comprising all the rest within them, were not bare parochial ones, or so many particular congregations as we used to call them, if not metropolitical rather. For that in Laodicea, Sardis, Smyrna, Ephesus, and Pergamum, the Roman governors held their courts of justice to which all the cities and towns about had recourse for the ending of their suits, is noted by Pliny. And besides these, which were the greatest, Thyatira is also by Ptolemy expressly named a metropolis, as Philadelphia also is, in the Greek acts of the council of Constantinople held under Menas. Which gives us good ground to conceive, that the seven cities, in which these seven churches had their seat, were all of them metropolitical and so had relation unto the rest of the towns and cities of Asia, as under daughters rising under them.[248]

In using the term 'metropolitical' Ussher is using the vocabulary that developed from the second century onwards.

[248] James Ussher, 'The Original of Bishops and Metropolitans' in Richard Snoddy (ed), *James Ussher and a Reformed Episcopal Church*, (Lincoln: The Davenant Press, 2018), pp. 136-137.

In the early church the area under the immediate oversight of a particular bishop (which might include several churches) was called a parish (Greek *parochia*) The term diocese did not come to be generally used for this until the ninth century.

In the second century we find formal ecclesiastical provinces being formed on the basis of the civil provinces of the Roman Empire. By the second half of the century the custom developed for the bishops of those civil provinces to meet together in provincial synods to take counsel together on important matters.

From the end of the century the summons to attend such synods was normally sent out by the bishop of the capital city (or 'metropolis') of the province concerned and, especially in the Eastern Church, he also presided over the synod itself. Important communications between churches in the different parts of the Roman Empire were sent to the same bishops to be brought to the notice of the other bishops of the province.

We can see this for example, in the case of the synod of the bishops of Asia held in about 190 to consider the question of when Easter should be observed to which we referred in chapter 3. Bishop Victor of Rome asked Polycrates of Ephesus, as the senior bishop in Asia, to convene a synod of the other Asian bishops to consider the matter and after the synod was held Polycrates then wrote back to Victor reporting on what had been decided. Eusebius also tells us that similar synods to consider the matter were held in places such as Palestine, Pontus, Gaul and Osrhoene.[249]

These developments meant that during the third century the bishop of the metropolis came to be accepted as having a position of superiority over the other bishops of the province and he was given the title of 'metropolitan' to mark his position as the bishop of the metropolis and referred to as the 'arch' or chief bishop to mark his consequent superiority.

[249] Eusebius of Caesarea, *Ecclesiastical History,* V xxiv, pp.503-509.

If we ask why it was felt necessary to develop this kind of provincial organisation with the metropolitan bishop being recognised as having superiority over the other bishops in the province, the answer is helpfully given by Richard Hooker in *The Laws of Ecclesiastical Polity*. He writes:

The ground therefore of their pre-eminence above bishops is the necessity of the often concurrency of many bishops about the affairs of the Church, as consecration of bishops, consultations of remedy of general disorders, audience judicial when the actions of any bishop should be called in question, or appeals are made from his sentence by such as think themselves wronged. These and like affairs usually requiring that many bishops should assemble, begin, and conclude somewhat; it hath seemed in the eyes of reverend antiquity a thing most requisite, that the Church should not only have bishops, but even among bishops some to be in authority chiefest.[250]

The reason, he says, why bishops acting together in this way required one bishop to have authority over the rest was because of the danger of confusion and disorder that exists when a group of people try to work together, but no one person is in charge:

...the wisdom of both God and man hath evermore approved it as most requisite, that where many governors must of necessity concur for the ordering of the same affairs, of what nature soever they be, one should have some kind of sway or stroke more than all the residue. For where number is there must be order, or else of force there will be confusion. Let there be diverse agents, of whom each hath his private inducements with resolute purpose to follow them (as each may have); unless in this case some had pre-eminence above the rest, a chance it were if anything should be either begun, proceeded in, or brought to any conclusion by them, deliberations and counsels would seldom go forward, their meetings would always be in danger to break up with jars and contradictions. In an army a number of captains, all of

---

[250] Richard Hooker, *The Laws of Ecclesiastical Polity*, Vol II (Oxford: OUP, 1841), Bk VII.8.6, p.368.

equal power, without some higher to over sway them; what good would they do? In all nations where a number are to draw any one way, there must be some one principal mover. [251]

Hooker explains that the existence of the capital cities of the Roman provinces was not the cause of the distinction between bishops, but simply something that the Church made use of in order to determine which bishops should have preeminence over the others:

...other causes having made it necessary even amongst bishops to have in some degree higher above the rest, the civil dignity of place was considered only as a reason wherefore this bishop should be preferred before that: which deliberation had been likely enough to have raised no small trouble, but that such was the circumstance of place, as being followed in that choice, besides the manifest conveniency thereof, took away all show of partiality, prevented secret emulations, and gave no man occasion to think his person disgraced in that another was preferred before him.[252]

Hooker then further explains that over the course of time the need for order in the Church meant that a distinction emerged between the metropolitans, as it had previously emerged between the bishops, with the bishops of the most important metropolitan cities being given the titles of primates and patriarchs:

...there being oftentimes within some one more large territory divers and sundry mother churches, the metropolitans whereof were archbishops; as for orders sake it grew hereupon expedient there should be some difference also amongst them, so no way seemed in those times more fit than to give preeminence unto them whose metropolitan sees were of special desert or dignity: for which cause these as bishops in the chiefest mother churches were named primates, and at the length by way of excellency, patriarchs. [253]

[251] Hooker, p.367.
[252] Hooker, p.370.
[253] Hooker, p.371.

The developments which have been described above are reflected in the Canons which were produced by the Ecumenical Councils of the Church in the fourth century, canons which were accepted as authoritative by the later Church.

At the Council of Nicaea in 325 these developments were reflected in Canons 4, 5 and 6.

Canon 4 declared that the appointment of a new bishop requires either the participation, or at least the assent, of all the existing bishops in a province and needs to also be ratified by the metropolitan bishop:

It is by all means proper that a bishop should be appointed by all the bishops in the province; but should this be difficult, either on account of urgent necessity or because of distance, three at least should meet together, and the suffrages of the absent [bishops] also being given and communicated in writing, then the ordination should take place. But in every province the ratification of what is done should be left to the Metropolitan.[254]

Canon 5 laid down that provincial synods should be held twice a year for the bishops to consider the cases of those who have been excommunicated:

Concerning those, whether of the clergy or of the laity, who have been excommunicated in the several provinces, let the provision of the canon be observed by the bishops which provides that persons cast out by some be not readmitted by others. Nevertheless, inquiry should be made whether they have been excommunicated through captiousness, or contentiousness, or any such like ungracious disposition in the bishop. And, that this matter may have due investigation, it is decreed that in every province synods shall be held twice a year, in order that when all the bishops of the province are assembled together, such questions may by them be thoroughly

[254] Synod of Nicaea, Canon 4, in *The Nicene and Post Nicene Fathers*, 2nd series vol. XIV (Edinburgh & Grand Rapids: T&T Clark/Eerdmans, 1997), p.11.

examined, that so those who have confessedly offended against their bishop, may be seen by all to be for just cause excommunicated, until it shall seem fit to a general meeting of the bishops to pronounce a milder sentence upon them. And let these synods be held, the one before Lent, (that the pure Gift may be offered to God after all bitterness has been put away), and let the second be held about autumn.[255]

Canon 6 re-affirmed the precedence which had come to be given to certain metropolitan bishops and set out what should happen in a province where there was a dispute about the appointment of a new bishop:

Let the ancient customs in Egypt, Libya and Pentapolis prevail, that the Bishop of Alexandria have jurisdiction in all these, since the like is customary for the Bishop of Rome also. Likewise in Antioch and the other provinces, let the Churches retain their privileges. And this is to be universally understood, that if anyone be made bishop without the consent of the Metropolitan, the great Synod has declared that such a man ought not to be a bishop. If, however, two or three bishops shall from natural love of contradiction, oppose the common suffrage of the rest, it being reasonable and in accordance with the ecclesiastical law, then let the choice of the majority prevail.[256]

The situation referred to in the first half of this canon is one in which the Bishop of Alexandria has Patriarchal authority over the churches of Egypt and Libya, the Bishop of Rome has Patriarchal authority over the churches of Southern Italy and the Bishop of Antioch has Patriarchal authority over the churches of the Roman civil diocese of Oriens, which covered the area from the Mediterranean to Mesopotamia. We also know that the Bishop of Carthage had similar Patriarchal authority over the churches of the Roman provinces in Africa (what we now call Tunisia, Algeria and Morocco).

[255] Synod of Nicaea, Canon 5, p. 13
[256] Synod of Nicaea, Canon 6, p. 15

Canon IX of the Council of Antioch in 341 further emphasised the importance of the role of the metropolitan bishops and their authority over the other diocesan bishops. Using the term 'parishes' to refer to what we would call dioceses, it stated:

It behoves the bishops in every province to acknowledge the bishop who presides in the metropolis, and who has to take thought for the whole province; because all men of business come together from every quarter to the metropolis. Wherefore it is decreed that he have precedence in rank, and that the other bishops do nothing extraordinary without him (according to the ancient canon which prevailed from [the times of] our Fathers), or such things only as pertain to their own particular parishes and the districts subject to them. For each bishop has authority over his own parish, both to manage it with the piety which is incumbent on everyone, and to make provision for the whole district which is dependent on his city; to ordain presbyters and deacons; and to settle everything with judgement. But let him undertake nothing further without the bishop of the metropolis; neither the latter without the consent of the others. [257]

In 381 a further Patriarch was added to those mentioned by the Council of Nicaea when Canon III of the First Council of Constantinople declared that 'The Bishop of Constantinople, however, shall have the prerogative of honour after the Bishop of Rome; because Constantinople is New Rome.' [258] This canon reflects the way in which the civil prestige of a city was reflected in the ecclesiastical standing of its bishop. Because Constantinople had been established by the Emperor Constantine as the new Rome, the new capital of the Christian Empire, its Bishop is seen as having status within the Church second only to the Bishop of the old Rome.

[257] Council of Antioch, Canon IX, in *Nicene and Post Nicene Fathers* 2nd series vol XIV, p.112.
[258] First Council of Constantinople, Canon III, in *Nicene and Post Nicene Fathers* 2nd series vol XIV, p.178.

After the collapse of the Roman Empire in the West from the early fifth century onwards the provincial system described above continued to be maintained, but was adapted to fit the political structures of the new states that emerged after the Empire's demise. A new set of churches emerged in Western Europe, each with their own provincial system, but all acknowledging the overall authority of the Bishop of Rome as not only the Patriarch of the Western Church, but the senior bishop of the Church as whole.

What we have seen in the first four chapters of this study is when and how a threefold order of ministry consisting of bishops, presbyters and deacons emerged in the early church and how from the second century onwards a provincial and patriarchal system emerged in which some bishops had seniority over others.

This situation forms the background to the history of episcopacy in the Church of England which we shall go on to consider in the next chapter.

Chapter 5
Episcopacy in the Church of England

The beginnings of Christianity in Britain

Like the roots of Christianity itself, the roots of the Church of England go back to the time of the Roman Empire when a Christian church came into existence in the British Isles.

The earliest evidence we have for the existence of this church is found in a treatise called *An Answer to the Jews* which was written by Tertullian sometime between 198 and 208. In this treatise he refers to 'the haunts of the Britons – inaccessible to the Romans but subjugated to Christ.'[259]

In his *Fourth Homily on Ezekiel, written* in 240, Origen likewise declares that Christianity is present not only in those parts of Britain subject to Rome, but even in those parts of Britain outside the borders of the Roman Empire: 'The power of God our Saviour is even with them which in Britain are apart from our world.' [260]

Tertullian's work pushes the existence of the Church in Britain back into the second century and further evidence for a second century British church is provided by the tradition concerning the British King Lucius. The earliest form of this tradition is found in the *Catalogus Felicianus*, a list of Papal biographies dating from 530. This tells us that Eleutherius, who was Bishop of Rome from 177-192, 'received a letter from Lucius, King of Britain, asking him to appoint a way by which Lucius might become a Christian.'[261]

---

[259] Tertullian, *An Answer to the Jews*, Ch. VII, in *The Ante Nicene Fathers,* Vol. III. (Edinburgh/Grand Rapids: T&T Clark/Eerdmans, 1997), p.158.
[260] Text in David J Knight, *King Lucius of Britain* (Stroud: The History Press, 2012), Kindle Edition, Loc. 483.
[261] Text in Knight op.cit., Loc. 170.

This tradition was universally accepted by later writers on the early history of British Christianity.[262] The Venerable Bede, for example, tells us in his *History of the English Church and People,* which was completed in 731:

In the year of our Lord's Incarnation 156, Marcus Antoninus Verus, fourteenth from Augustus, became emperor jointly with his brother Aurelius Commodus. During their reign, and while the holy Eleutherus ruled the Roman Church, Lucius, a British king, sent him a letter asking to be made a Christian by his direction. This pious request was quickly granted, and the Britons received the Faith and held it peacefully in all its purity and fullness until the time of the Emperor Diocletian.[263]

The tradition continued to be accepted until the nineteenth century, but in 1904 the famous German church historian Adolph von Harnack wrote an influential article arguing that the tradition was based on a scribal error and that the letter to Pope Eleutherius recorded in the *Catalogus Felicianus* was in fact written by Abgar VIII of Edessa, who also had the Latin name Lucius, with an unknown scribe substituting 'Britannio' (Britain) for the word 'Britio,' a Latin form of the name given to the citadel at Edessa.[264] Harnack's argument has been generally accepted by modern writers, but as David Knight shows in his recent book on King Lucius, it is not convincing.

There is no evidence that Abgar VIII was ever referred to as King Lucius, or that he was ever referred to as king of the citadel at Edessa, and the citadel itself was not built until 205, after the time of Pope Eleutherius.

---

[262] For the evidence for this see Knight op.cit. throughout.
[263] Bede, *A History of the English Church and People*, Bk 1.4 (Harmondsworth: Penguin, 1968), p. 42.
[264] Adolph von Harnack, *Der Brief des britischen Konigs Lucius an den Papst Eleutherus* (Sitzungsberichte der Koniglich Preussichen Akademie der Wissenschaften, 1904), pp. 909-916.

In fact, as Knight shows, a study of the relevant evidence points us towards taking the basic tradition about King Lucius at face value, namely that:

...a king of Britannia in the year 177 requested of the Bishop of Rome, Elueutherius, instruction in the Christian religion. Bishops were sent to Britannia and the king was baptised Lucius, the 'Great Light.' His involvement in establishing Christian churches in various locations throughout the island was extensive. He lived and ruled long. He died and was presumed buried in Britain.[265]

This would mean that there was a British church from at least 177 onwards. However, there is also evidence that Christianity was present in Britain even earlier than that. Thus, Eusebius writes in his *Demonstration of the Gospel* in 311 that the apostles 'crossed the Ocean and reached the Isles of Britain'[266] and Hilary of Poitiers writing later on in the fourth century also notes that early apostolic missions had reached Britain. [267]

In the sixth century the British monk Gildas gives a more detailed account of the arrival of Christianity in Britain in apostolic times. In his work *Of the Fall and Conquest of Britain*, which explains the Saxon invasion of Britain as God's judgement on the sins of the British, he declares:

Meanwhile these islands, stiff with cold and frost, and in a distant region of the world, remote from the visible sun, received the beams of light, that is, the holy precepts of Christ, the true Sun, showing to the whole world his splendour, not only from the temporal firmament, but from the height of heaven, which surpasses everything temporal, at the latter part, as we know of the reign of Tiberius Caesar, by whom

---

[265] Knight, op.cit, Loc 2883. In context 'king of Britannia' does not mean that Lucius was king of Britain, but that he was a Roman client king in the Roman province of Britannia, in the same way that there were Indian princes in India when it formed part of the Britain Empire.
[266] Eusebius of Caeseara, *Demonstratio Evangelica* 3.5.
[267] Hilary of Poitiers, *Tract XIV*, Ps 8.

his religion was propagated without impediment, and death threatened to those who interfered with its professors.

These rays of light were received with lukewarm minds by the inhabitants, but they nevertheless took root among some of them in a greater or lesser degree, until the nine years' persecution of the tyrant Diocletian, when the churches throughout the whole world were overthrown, all the copies of the Holy Scriptures which could be found were burned in the streets, and the chosen pastors of God's flock butchered together with their innocent sheep, in order that not a vestige, if possible, might remain in some provinces of Christ's religion.[268]

This passage can be read as saying that the first coming of Christianity to Britain took place at the end of Tiberius' reign (i.e. in 37 AD), but a more likely reading is it was during the reign of Tiberius that the light of Christ began to shine upon the world 'from the height of heaven' (i.e. after his ascension into heaven) and that this light reached Britain during the period identified by the 'meanwhile' at the start of the passage, which is the early years of the Roman occupation of Britain in the latter half of the first century.

None of the writers just mentioned give any details about who took part in the apostolic mission to Britain. The well-known tradition that the mission was led by Joseph of Arimathea is first found in the thirteenth century in a later interpolation into the work *Of the Antiquity of Glastonbury* by the historian William of Malmesbury.[269]

The early tradition about the matter, which has now been largely forgotten, is that the mission was led by Aristobulus, a Jewish Christian who is said to have been one of the seventy disciples of

---

[268] Gildas, *Liber Querulus de excidio Britanniae. English* (A Public Domain Book: Kindle), Ch.2.8-9, Loc 119.
[269] See J Armitage Robinson, *William of Malmesbury 'On the Antiquity of Glastonbury,'* at https://en.wikisource.org/wiki/Somerset_Historical_Essays/William_of_Malmesbury_%27On_the_Antiquity_of_Glastonbury%27

Christ mentioned by Luke in Luke 10:1 and who is also identified with the Aristobulus whose family is greeted by Paul in Romans 16:10.

An early list of the seventy known as *Pseudo-Hippolytus* tells us that Aristobulus was 'bishop of Britain'[270] and a list of the seventy apostles going back to Bishop Dorotheus of Tyre (255-362) also refers to Aristobulus as 'Bishop of Britannia.'[271] The use of the title 'bishop' in these lists is an anachronism. As we have noted in the previous chapters of this study, the use of the term bishop for the person with overall responsibility for the leadership of a particular church only developed after the time of Aristobulus. What the use of the title means is that Aristobulus was the person with responsibility for leading the new church in Britain and was in that sense its bishop in the same way that James was Bishop of Jerusalem and Mark was Bishop of Alexandria.

Barring some unexpected archaeological discovery, we have no way of independently verifying what these early lists say about the role of Aristobulus. However, there is equally nothing intrinsically impossible either about the first Christian missionary activity in Roman Britain taking place in the second half of the first century, or about a Jewish Christian called Aristobulus leading it. If the Apostle Thomas could use the existing transport and trade routes to take the gospel to South India in the first century, then there is no reason why Aristobulus and others could not have travelled to Britain to preach the gospel in the same period and so no reason to doubt what these lists tell us.

Episcopacy in the early church in Britain
We do not have many details about how the ministry of the Church in Britain was structured during the earliest centuries of its existence. However, what we do know suggests that in common with other early churches there was a single individual who had overall responsibility

---

[270] 'The same Hippolytus on the Seventy Apostles' in *The Ante Nicene Fathers*, Vol. V. Edinburgh/Grand Rapids: T&T Clark/Eerdmans, 1995, p.256.
[271] http://www.orthodox.net/saints/70apostles.html

for it when it was first founded and that it was subsequently led by bishops in the later sense of the term.

As we have seen, tradition tells that Aristobulus initially had overall responsibility for the Church in Britain. There is then a gap in our knowledge until the last quarter of the second century when we are told that bishops were sent from Rome to lead the British church that was founded by King Lucius.

There is then a further gap in our knowledge until the early years of the fourth century when the records of the Council of Arles in 314 list a number of bishops from Britain as having attended that council. The records tell us that those present from Britain were:

Eborius, Bishop of the City of York in the province of Britain.

Restitutus, Bishop of the City of London in the province above written.

Adelfius, Bishop of the City Colonia Londinensium.

Sacerdos, Priest; Arminius Deacon.[272]

We are not sure exactly where Colonia Londinensium was. Both Colchester and Lincoln have been suggested, with the latter being the more likely. As David Petts notes in his book *Christianity in Roman Britain*, what is interesting about this list is that it suggests that by this date the Church in Britain not only had bishops, but had a system of metropolitan bishops along the lines that we looked at in chapter four:

...the three bishops appear to have come from not merely Roman towns, but the capitals of three of the four provinces of Britain: London was the capital of Maxima Caesariensis, York was probably the capital of Flavia Caesariensis and Lincoln was the capital of Britannia Secunda. This leaves one province, Britannia Prima, without a representative bishop. It is possible that for some reason this province

---

[272] Text in H Gee and W R Hardy (eds) *Documents illustrative of the History of the English Church* (London: Macmillan, 1896), p. 1.

may have been temporarily without a bishop, and that Arminius and Secerdus represented its interests. The capital of Britannia Prima is most likely to have been Cirencester, as the governor is recorded on a dedication inscription from the town. It is unlikely that the representatives of the church from the four provinces were the only bishops in Britain. They were probably Metropolitan bishops representing the bishops from the other *civitates* [cities]within their provinces.[273]

Later on in the fourth century we also find bishops from Britain attending the Council of Nicaea in 325, the Council of Serdica in 343 and the Council of Ariminium in 359. Athanasius records that the British bishops supported the rejection of Arianism at the Council of Nicaea and Hilary of Poitiers also mentions the support that he received from the British bishops in his later struggle against Arianism.

Petts also notes that in addition to this literary evidence there is possible inscriptional evidence for bishops in Roman Britain on a silver serving dish from Ripley in Derbyshire, on a salt pan from Shavington in Cheshire and on a pewter bowl from Ely in Cambridgeshire.[274]

In 410, the year that the city of Rome fell to the army of Alaric the Goth, the Roman Emperor Honorius wrote to the civic authorities in Britain 'telling them to look to their own defence.' [275] In other words, they were on their own. Rome no longer had money or men to spare for the defence of Britain from the Saxons, the Picts and the Irish. The British would henceforth have to look after themselves.

As John Morris explains, the letter from Honorius did not mean that Roman Britain ceased to exist:

[273] David Petts, *Christianity in Roman Britain* (Stroud: Tempus publishing, 2003), p.38.
[274] Petts, pp. 38-39.
[275] Zosimus, *Historia Nova* 6.10 quoted in John Morris, *The Age of Arthur* (London: Phoenix, 1973), p.29.

The internal machinery of government was not changed, and the Roman civilisation of Britain lasted some thirty years more, its towns and villas, its agriculture, trade and industry little affected by political independence. [276]

By the beginning of the fifth century the Church was an integral part of Roman civilisation and it too survived the political separation from Rome. The evidence we have tells us that the major threat it faced was the fact that it had become infected by the Pelagian heresy (the belief that human beings can take the initial steps towards God by their own efforts, choosing the good by virtue of their created natures[277]). In the face of this threat to the orthodoxy of the British church, three bishops, Germanus of Auxerre, Lupus of Troyes, and Severus of Trier, were sent to Britain from the continent to root out Pelagianism.

According to Bede's account they successfully achieved this aim,[278] but the fact that a visitation by these external bishops was needed suggests that there was a problem with the British bishops who were apparently either unable or unwilling to take on this heresy themselves. In the fourth century the British bishops had been steadfast against Arianism. In the fifth century it appears that they were not equally steadfast against Pelagianism.

In about 442 there was major revolt by the Saxons led by Hengest and Horsa that resulted in the establishment of Saxon control in Kent, Norfolk, and the Cambridge - Newmarket area. From about 460-495 there was successful resistance by the British, led first by Ambrosius, and then by Arthur, that resulted in the Saxons being restricted to Kent, Sussex, East Anglia and parts of Lincolnshire, Nottinghamshire and South East Yorkshire and the expulsion of the Irish from Wales. [279]

---

[276] Morris, p.30.
[277] Nicholas Adams, 'Pelagianism: Can people be saved by their own efforts?' in Ben Quash and Michael Ward (eds), *Heresies and How to Avoid Them* (London: SPCK, 2007), p. 91.
[278] Bede, Bk. 1.17-21, pp. 58-65.
[279] Morris, chs. 5-7.

However, this success was to prove only temporary. In the words of Morris: 'A second Saxon revolt won decisive victories in the 570s, and by the early 7th century had permanently mastered most of what is now England.'[280]

In the areas that remained in British control between 495 and 570 the Church seems to have continued to be an integral part of society. Thus, Gildas writes about the existence of an ordered Christian society in which: 'kings, public magistrates, and private persons, with priests and clergymen, did all and every one of them live orderly according to their several vocations.'[281]

Alongside the evidence from the attendance list at the Council of Arles that the metropolitan bishops of the Church in Britain were based in the big cities, other evidence suggests that in Britain, unlike in Gaul: 'it is in the countryside and the small towns in particular that Christianity appears to have been strongest.'[282] As Petts explains:

It is the integration of Christianity into the rural world that allowed the Church to weather the disruptive effects of the warfare and political conflict of the fifth century. Although life in towns changed radically in this period, this did not trouble the Church, which was already developing a semi-rural rather than semi-urban infrastructure.[283]

In particular, it appears that the many of the Church's dioceses were based in small towns and that much of this this diocesan structure was sufficiently robust for it to survive the transition from British to Anglo-Saxon control and become the basis for later Anglo-Saxon dioceses and Minister churches.[284]

---

[280] Morris, p.43.
[281] Gildas, Loc. 280.
[282] Petts, p.170.
[283] Petts, p.271.
[284] See Steven Bassett, 'Church and diocese in the West Midlands; the transition from Romano-British to Anglo-Saxon control' in John Blair and Richard Sharpe (eds), *Pastoral Care Before the Parish* (Leicester: Continuum, 1992), pp.13-40.

The mission to the Saxons

However, although the British church thus survived the crises of the fifth century, it had one great weakness, noted by Bede, which is that it: 'never preached the Faith to the Saxons or Angles who dwelt with them in Britain.' [285] We do not know whether this was because of fear, or because of animosity towards the foreign invaders. What we do know was that this was a failure to obey the great commission (Matthew 28:16-20), and it seems likely that this failure may well have contributed to the final downfall of Roman-British society in England during the second half of the sixth century.

If the British church, led by its bishops, had been willing to evangelise the Saxons and this had resulted in their conversion, this could have opened up the possibility of some form of peaceful co-existence between Britons and Saxons. As it was, the Saxons remained the pagan enemy and the conflict with this enemy led to British society being overthrown.

Having noted the failure of the British to preach the gospel to the Saxons or Angles, Bede then goes on to note that this was not the end of the matter:

God in his goodness did not utterly abandon the people he had chosen; for he remembered them, and sent this nation more worthy preachers of truth to bring them to the faith. [286]

The evidence we have from Bede and other sources is that these 'more worthy preachers of truth' were primarily bishops. The evangelisation of the Saxon kingdoms that had come into existence either in the fifth century, or as a result of the second Saxon revolt from 570 onwards, was spearheaded by a series of missionary bishops. With one exception, these bishops came either from the churches of continental

---

[285] Bede, Bk. 1.22. p. 66. In distinguishing between the Saxons and the Angles Bede is referring to two different ethnic groups within the Saxons, the Saxons proper who came from the area West of the Elbe River and the Angles who came from the area now known as Schleswig Holstein.
[286] Bede, Bk 1.22, p.66.

Europe that adhered to the customs of the church in Rome, or from the Church in what is now Scotland that adhered to the customs of what has come to be known as the Celtic Christian tradition.

This 'Celtic' tradition had its origins in the form of Christianity which developed in Ireland as a result of the missionary activity of a British missionary (and later bishop) called Patrick in the fifth century. This form of Christianity then came to what is now Scotland following the foundation of the monastery at Iona by Columba in 563.

Christians in the Celtic tradition accepted the same theology as the other Western churches of the time and like those churches they acknowledged the Bishop of Rome as the senior Patriarch of the Church as a whole. They differed from these churches over matters such as the correct date for the celebration of Easter, the rites to be used at baptism, and the correct form of the monastic tonsure, and also in the way that churches were organised. Celtic Christianity was organised on a tribal and monastic rather than a diocesan basis. The key institution was the monastery, with the abbot exercising ecclesiastical jurisdiction over the surrounding area. Like all the other churches, Celtic churches had bishops who exercised specific functions such as ordination, but unless the abbot was himself a bishop, the bishop was subject to the authority of the abbot.[287]

The way in which missionary bishops from Europe and from the Scottish Celtic tradition spearheaded the evangelisation of the Saxon kingdoms in what is now England can be set out in tabular form as follows.

- Kent: evangelised by Augustine who was sent from Rome by Pope Gregory the Great in 595 and consecrated bishop in Arles. Pope Gregory appointed Augustine as archbishop over the whole of Britain in 597, but by the time of Augustine's

---

[287] See Morris, pp.397-400. As Morris notes, the great esteem in which abbots were held is reflected in the Irish tradition of referring to the Pope as the 'abbot of Rome' and Christ as the 'abbot of heaven.'

death in 604 his authority only extended over Kent (divided into the two dioceses of Canterbury and Rochester) and Essex.

Bede records that Augustine met with seven bishops from the British church, but, put off by his perceived arrogance, they refused to accept his authority as archbishop, or to join with him in evangelising the Saxons.[288]

- Essex: evangelised by Mellitus, sent from Rome and consecrated bishop by Augustine.

- Northumbria: evangelised by Paulinus, sent from Rome and consecrated bishop by Augustine's successor, Justus, and by Aidan, a bishop consecrated in Iona and sent out from there. Aidan was succeeded as Bishop of Northumbria by Finan who was also from Iona.

- East Anglia: evangelised by Felix, a bishop from Burgundy, and Cedd, a bishop in the Celtic tradition, who was consecrated by Finan. Important evangelistic activity was also undertaken by an Irish monk called Fursey.

- Wessex: evangelised by Birinius who was sent from Rome by Pope Honorius and consecrated bishop in Genoa.

- Mercia: evangelised by four presbyters in the Celtic tradition, Cedd, Adda, Betti and Diuma, a Scot who was subsequently consecrated bishop by Finan.

- Sussex: evangelised by Wilfrid, who came from Northumbria and was initially a monk in the Celtic tradition, but who became an enthusiastic advocate of Roman customs after a visit to Rome. He was consecrated by the church in Gaul as Bishop of Northumbria, but after being exiled from Northumbria he went to Sussex where he established a bishopric at Selsey.

[288] Bede, Bk 2.2, pp. 101-104.

A good example of what this episcopal missionary activity involved in practice is provided by Bede's account of the ministry of Paulinus in Northumbria. Bede tells us that Paulinus was determined:

...to bring the nation to which he was sent the knowledge of the Christian truth, and to fulfil the Apostle's saying, 'to espouse her to one husband, that he might present her as a chaste virgin to Christ'. Therefore, directly he entered the province he began to toil unceasingly not only by God's help to maintain the faith of his companions unimpaired, but if possible to bring some of the heathen to grace and faith by his preaching. [289]

Paulinus' missionary efforts were initially unfruitful, but after the baptism of the Northumbrian king, Edwin, his people began to turn to Christianity as well:

Indeed, so great was the fervour of faith and the desire for baptism among the Northumbrian people that Paulinus is said to have accompanied the king and the queen to the royal residence at Ad-Gefrin and remained there thirty-six days constantly occupied in instructing and baptizing. During this period, he did nothing from dawn to dusk but proclaim Christ's saving message to the people, who gathered from all the surrounding villages and countryside; and when he had instructed them, he washed them in the cleansing waters of baptism in the nearby River Glen.[290]

The result of this sort of evangelistic activity was that an episcopally led church was established not only in Northumbria, but in each of the seven kingdoms listed above.

At the Council of Whitby in 664 the Church in Northumbria agreed to follow Roman rather than Celtic customs and in 668 a monk called Theodore, who came from Tarsus in Cilicia, was sent from Rome by Pope Vitalius to be the new bishop of Canterbury and the archbishop over all the new churches that had now been formed. Bede records

[289] Bede Bk 2.9 p.115.
[290] Bede Bk 2.14, 14 p.129

that soon after he arrived Theodore 'visited every part of the island occupied by the English peoples[291] and received a ready welcome and hearing everywhere.' [292]

Bede adds that 'Theodore was the first archbishop whom the entire Church of the English obeyed[293] When he arrived the country had been afflicted by plague, and the Church was disorganised and lacking bishops. To counteract this state of affairs 'Theodore consecrated bishops in suitable places, and with their assistance he corrected abuses wherever he found them.'[294] He also held synods of bishops at Hertford in 672 and Hatfield in 680 at which rules were laid down to ensure order and uniformity in the Church across England as a whole and its adherence to orthodox teaching with regard to the Trinity and the Person of Christ. [295]

The early organisation of the Church of England
By the time Theodore died in 690 the Church of England (the *Ecclesia Anglicana* or Church of the English) was a single, unified, episcopally led, church that covered most of what is now England. Some forty years later Bede describes as follows how this church was organised in his own day:

At the present day Tatwin and Aldwulf preside over the churches in Kent; Ingwald is Bishop of the East Saxons; Aldbert and Hadulac are Bishops of the East Angles; Daniel and Forthere are Bishops of the West Saxons; and Aldwin is Bishop of the Mercians. Walchstod is Bishop of the folk who live in the West, beyond the River Severn; Wilfrid is Bishop of the Hwiccas; Cynibert is Bishop of the province of Lindsey. The bishopric of the Isle of Wight belongs to Daniel, Bishop of Winchester. The province of the South Saxons has now been without a

---

[291] The word 'English' is here is used as a way of referring to all the people who were Saxon rather than British regardless of whether they were originally Saxons, Angles or Jutes.
[292] Bede, Bk 4.2, p. 206.
[293] Bede Bk 4.2, p.206.
[294] Bede Bk 4.2, p.207.
[295] Bede Bk 4.5 pp.214-217 and Bk 4.17, pp. 234-236.

bishop for some years, and seeks the offices of a bishop from the prelate of the West Saxons All these provinces, together with the others South of the River Humber and their kings, are subject to Ethelbald King of the Mercians.

In the province of the Northumbrians, ruled by Ceolwulf, four bishops hold office: Wilfrid in the church of York, Ethelwald at Lindisfarne, Acca at Hexham and Pecthelmn in the see known as the White House, where the number of believers has so increased that it has recently become an episcopal see with Pecthelm as its first Bishop.[296]

Translated into modern terms, what this tells us is that when Bede wrote in 731 the Church of England was organised on a diocesan basis and had seventeen dioceses. In Kent: Canterbury and Rochester. In Essex: London. In East Anglia: Dunwich and Elmham. In Wessex: Winchester and Sherborne. In Mercia: Lichfield, Worcester, Hereford, Dorchester and Lindsey. In Sussex: Selsey. In Northumbria: York, Lindisfarne, Hexham and Whithorn.

The Church of England as it exists today is directly descended from the church described by Bede. All the current bishops of the Church of England have their episcopal line of descent from one or more of the bishops listed by Bede, and, with the exception of the Diocese of Sodor and Man (which was originally a Norwegian diocese), all of the current dioceses of the Church of England have developed from the dioceses to which he refers.

In 735 the Bishop of York became an archbishop and the metropolitan for the North of England, the position retained by the Archbishops of York to this day. After lengthy disputes about whether the Archbishop of Canterbury should have precedence over the Archbishop of York, the matter was finally settled in 1352 when Pope Innocent VI confirmed an existing arrangement that the existence of two primates (metropolitan bishops) in England should be acknowledged, with the precedence of the Archbishop of Canterbury being reflected in his

---

[296] Bede Bk 5.23, p. 331.

having the title Primate of All England while the Archbishop of York had the title Primate of England.

In 787 the archdiocese of Canterbury was divided, with Bishop Higbert of Lichfield being raised to the rank of archbishop and given authority over the dioceses of Worcester, Leicester, Lincoln, Hereford, Elmham and Dunwich. This arrangement was instigated by King Offa of Mercia who wanted an archbishop of his own to rival the Archbishop of Canterbury. However, after Offa's death in 796 the Pope decided to abolish the new archbishopric and restore the dioceses to Canterbury. This decision was then accepted by the Council of Clovesho in 803 and the Church of England has remained divided into the two archdioceses of Canterbury and York ever since.

The four Welsh dioceses of Llandaff, Bangor, St David's and St Asaph came under English jurisdiction in 982, 1081, 1115 and 1141 respectively as part of the growth of English political and ecclesiastical authority over Wales, and their bishops were bishops of the Church of England until the formation of the Church in Wales in 1920.

Episcopacy in the Middle Ages
The Church of England survived intact the turmoil of the Viking raids and invasions from the end of the eighth century onwards and the Norman Conquest in 1066. The church that entered the Middle Ages was still the same church that had been created by Theodore of Tarsus in the seventh century.

That church continued to exist during the Middle Ages and like all the churches during that period it continued to be episcopally led. There were continuing disputes during the Middle Ages about the roles that should be played by cathedral chapters, the Pope and the monarch in the appointment of bishops,[297] but no one doubted that there should be bishops. In the Middle Ages the question of whether there should be bishops was simply not a matter for discussion. Even the Lollards, the radical movement which developed out of the teaching of the fourteenth century Oxford theologian John Wycliffe, and which questioned many areas of medieval theology and church practice, do not seem to have called for the abolition of the bishops. [298]

The major change that did take place in the Church of England during the Middle Ages concerned what bishops actually did. As we have seen, in the earliest days of the English church the role of the bishops was primarily that of leaders in mission. The bishops pioneered the conversion of the Saxon kingdoms and the creation of churches within them. After these churches had become established the role of the bishops changed to that of the chief pastor, visiting, teaching, and disciplining the faithful lest they succumb to the attacks of the world and the devil.

We can see this latter view of the bishop's role set out, for example, in the decrees from the Pope set forth by the Papal legates (representatives) at the Synods held at Chelsea and Mercia in 787. The third decree states:

And let every bishop go round his diocese once every year, carefully appointing places of meeting at convenient distances; that all may meet to hear the word of God, lest any, through the neglect of the shepherd, ignorantly going astray, be victims to the bite of the roaring lion. Let him with watchful care preach to and confirm the flock committed to his charge; let him separate the incestuous, coerce soothsayers, fortune-tellers, enchanters, diviners, wizards, and sacrilegious ones, and suppress all vices. And let no man affect to feed

[297] See Colin Podmore, 'The choosing of bishops in the Early Church and the Church of England' in *Working with the Spirit: choosing diocesan bishops* (London: Church House Publishing 2001), pp. 116-120.
[298] See, for example, the *Lollard Conclusions* of 1394 in Gee and Hardy pp.126-132.

the flock committed to him for filthy lucre's sake, but in hope of an eternal reward; and what he has freely received let him freely give to all, as the apostle protests (2 Timothy 1:1), and as the prophet says (Isaiah 40:9), that so he may excel in merit as he does in dignity. And that he may not be cramped by fear whilst he is teaching, let him hearken (Isaiah 40:9). Jeremiah also says (Jeremiah 1:17). Alas for this lamentable lukewarmness. As many thoughtful men say: why will ye be involved in the love of secular things, or be dismayed by crime and confounded in opening the word of truth? If the prelates of the Church are silent through fear, or worldly friendship, and do not reprove sinners, or run away like false shepherds who care not for the sheep, when they see the world coming, why are they not more afraid of the King of Kings, and Lord of Lords? who reprehends shepherds by the prophets saying (Ezekiel. 13: 5). Lastly, as the watchful shepherd guards the sheep against the wild beasts, so the priest of God ought to be solicitous for the flock, lest the enemy spoil, the persecutor annoy; lest the ravening of the powerful disturb the life of the poor; since the prophet says (Ezekiel 3: 18); for 'The good shepherd layeth down his life for the sheep.' Endeavour, my fathers and brethren, that ye bear these things in mind, lest it be said to you, as to the shepherds of Israel, 'Ye feed yourselves,' &c., but that ye may deserve to hear, 'Well done, good and faithful servant' &c.[299]

During the Middle Ages this understanding of the bishop's role continued to be affirmed in principle and there were godly bishops such as Hugh of Lincoln (1140-1200), Edmund of Abingdon (c1174-1240) and Richard of Chichester (1197-1253) who sought to put it into practice. However, as T M Parker explains, there were two factors which 'pressed in upon the medieval bishop and made him less and less a pastor of souls and more and more a temporal magnate.' [300]

On the one hand, he writes:

---

[299] Gee and Hardy pp.33-34.
[300] T M Parker, 'Feudal Episcopacy' in Kirk, p. 377.

...he was by virtue of his position a feudal lord, with similar privileges and immunities to those of his lay peers. He, like them, possessed not only broad lands and their revenues in money and kind, but also rights of private jurisdiction and even his own private army. (The bishops knights were a feature of every Episcopal estate and household). However much he delegated the administration of all this responsibility to underlings he himself was ultimately the controller, and no small part of his time had to be given up to it.[301]

On the other hand:

...the Bishop, both by virtue of his local importance and through the dependence of the central government upon his learning had duties towards the State as a whole. He was expected to be an adviser of the Crown: In England his membership of the Great Council and, when Parliament was developed, of the House of Lords, was the visible sign of this. In a number of cases to his duties in the central administration were more direct and immediate: he was likely to hold the office of Chancellor or Treasurer or some other ministry of state. Even if not in permanent royal service he was quite likely from time to time to be called upon to undertake specific missions for the State: the medieval embassy was commonly ecclesiastical in composition, wholly or in part.[302]

Combined with the large size of medieval English dioceses and the difficulties of travel in medieval times, these factors restricted the amount of time the bishop could spend in his diocese and the amount of time he had to carry out his spiritual responsibilities when he was there.

As Parker further explains, at the end of the Middle Ages there was a general tendency for bishops to get around this problem by delegating their episcopal duties to others:

[301] Parker, in Kirk, p.377.
[302] Parker in Kirk, p.378.

All acts requiring the possession of episcopal orders could be farmed out to suffragans under formal contract at a fixed rate of payment, whilst administration and discipline could be left in the hands pf archdeacons, vicars-general, and officials -principal of the consistory court. This was no doubt to some extent satisfactory, but it was a poor substitute for the New Testament conception of *episcope*, or even the ideals set out in St. John Chrysostom's *De Sacerdotio* and St. Gregory's *Regula Pastoralis*. [303]

A final problem was the way in which the office of bishop came to be seen in primarily legal terms. To quote A H Thompson:

To the medieval mind a bishop was not so much a father in God as a *iudex ordinarius*, the 'ordinary' whose court was the natural tribunal for the punishment of spiritual offences and the resort for litigants in spiritual causes within the area under his jurisdiction.[304] When he went out on visitation,[305] it was as a judge. In the churches and monasteries which he visited he sat 'judicially as a tribunal;' the injunctions which he issued after visitation were decrees to be inviolably observed. In this way his register is a collection of legal documents and instruments entered by clerks whose education and attitude to the business of their offices was entirely legal.[306]

In summary, during the Middle Ages the episcopal system inherited from the earliest days of the English Church remained in place. However, the character of episcopacy changed in practice. Although

---

[303] Parker in Kirk, p.379. The two texts mentioned are two classic patristic texts on presbyteral and episcopal ministry, which we shall look at in chapter 8 of this study. The suffragan bishops mentioned in this quotation would be bishops who had titular sees in places in the Middle East under Muslim rule, or Irish bishops whose sees lay beyond the pale of English settlement in Ireland. There were at this stage no English suffragan bishops.

[304] 'Spiritual causes' include what we would now call moral offences and matters of family law as well as matters to do with theology and the administration of the Church.

[305] A visitation was formal inspection of a diocese by the bishop.

[306] A H Thompson, 'Ecclesiastical History,' in Kenneth Kirk (ed), *The Study of Theology* (London: Hodder and Stoughton, 1939) p. 357.

the role of the bishop as the pastor of the clergy and people committed to his charge continued to be accepted in theory, in reality most bishops spent most of their time as acting as feudal magnates, senior officers of state, and judges of those who offended against church law.

Episcopacy at the Reformation
One of the central features of the English Reformation was the rejection of the authority of the Pope.

Prior to the English Reformation it was accepted by the Church of England that the Pope was the chief bishop of the universal Church. What followed from this in practical terms was not only that he had authority in theological matters, but that he had a role to play in the appointment of people to bishoprics and other church offices, that he should receive payment in relation to such appointments, and that the Papal court in Rome should serve as the final court of appeal in spiritual causes.

In the 1530s, during the reign of Henry VIII these links between the Church of England and the Papacy were all cut,

Between 1532 and 1534 a series of Acts of Parliament abolished all legal appeals from England to Rome, any role for the Papacy in making church appointments in England and any payments to the Papacy relating to such appointments. Then in March and May 1534 the Convocations of Canterbury and York (the meetings of the bishops and representative clergy of the two provinces) passed resolutions denying that 'the Roman pontiff has any greater jurisdiction bestowed on him by God in the Holy Scriptures than any other foreign bishop.' This meant in effect that the Pope had no jurisdiction in England. This conclusion was accepted by the Universities of Oxford and Cambridge and the abolition of Papal supremacy in England was approved by Parliament and passed into statute in November of that year. This Henrician legislation was rescinded during the reign of Queen Mary, but it was then restored by Elizabeth I's Act of Supremacy of 1559 and remained in force thereafter.[307]

Underlying the cutting of the ties between the Church of England and the Papacy were two fundamental theological convictions.

The first conviction was that the claim to exercise worldwide jurisdiction made by the Pope involved an encroachment on the authority given to monarchs by God. For the English Reformers there could only be one source of authority in a state, the monarch, and not two, the monarch and the Pope.

We can see this conviction expressed, for instance, in the homily 'Concerning good order and obedience' which is contained in the *First Book of Homilies*, the book of model sermons issued by the Church of England in 1547. The homily quotes 1 Peter 2:13-15 on the need for Christians to submit political authorities of the Roman Empire:

Be subject for the Lord's sake to every human institution, whether it be to the emperor as supreme, or to governors as sent by him to punish those who do wrong and to praise those who do right. For it is God's will that by doing right you should put to silence the ignorance of foolish men.

It then contrasts these words of Peter, and similar words of Paul, with the unwarranted demands for submission made by the Papacy:

St Peter doth not say, Submit yourselves unto me, as supreme head of the Church: neither saith he, Submit your selves from time to time to my successors in Rome: but he saith, Submit your selves unto your king, your supreme head, and unto those that he appointeth in authority under him, for that you shall so show your obedience, it is the will of God, God's will that you be in subjection to your head and king. This is God's ordinance, God's commandment, and God's holy will, that the whole body of every realm, and all the members and

---

[307] For this Henrician legislation see Gerald Bray, *Documents of the English Reformation* (Cambridge: James Clarke, 1994), pp.72-110.

parts of the same, shall be subject to their head, their king, and that, as St. Peter writeth, for the Lord's sake (1 Peter 2.13), and, as St. Paul writeth, for conscience sake, and not for fear only (Romans 13.5).[308]

The second conviction was that the claim made by the Pope to have authority over all other bishops was contrary to the teaching of Scripture and the Early Church.

We find this conviction expressed by, among others, the Bishop of Salisbury, John Jewel, in his 1562 *Apology of the Church of England* from which we quoted at the start of chapter one. Describing the Church of England's understanding of the nature of the Church Jewel writes:

We believe that there is one church of God, and that the same is not up (as in times past among the Jews) into some one corner or kingdom. but that it is catholic and universal, and dispersed throughout the whole world; so that there is now no nation which can truly complain that they be shut forth, and may not be one of the church and people of God; and that this church is the kingdom, the body, and the spouse of Christ: and that Christ alone is the prince of this kingdom; that Christ alone is the head of this body and that Christ alone is the bridegroom of this spouse.

Furthermore, that there be divers degrees of ministers in the church; Whereof some be deacons, some priests, some bishops: to whom is committed the office to instruct the people, and the whole charge and setting forth of religion. [309]

He then goes on to explain that the Church of England does not accept the claims for universal episcopal authority made by and for the Bishop of Rome because episcopal authority has been given equally to all bishops, and not to one bishop above all the rest.

---

[308] 'Concerning good order and obedience' in Ian Robinson (ed.). *The Homilies* (Bishopstone: Brynmill/Preservation Press, 2006), p.86.
[309] Jewel, p.59.

Yet notwithstanding we say that there neither is, nor can be any one man, which may have the whole superiority in this universal state: for that Christ is ever present to assist his church, and needeth not any man to supply his room, as his only heir to all his substance; and that there can be no one mortal creature, which is able to comprehend or conceive in his mind the universal church, that is to wit, all the parts of the world, much less able to put them in order and to govern them rightly and duly. For all the apostles, as Cyprian saith, were of like power among themselves, and the rest were the same that Peter was and that it was said indifferently to them all, 'Feed ye;' indifferently to them all, 'Go into the whole world;' indifferently to them all, 'Teach ye the gospel.' And, as Hierome[310] saith, 'all bishops wheresoever they be, be they at Rome, be they at Eugubium, be they at Constantinople, be they at Rhegium, be all of like pre-eminence and of like priesthood.' And, as Cyprian saith, 'there is but one bishoprick, and that a piece thereof is perfitly[311] and wholly holden of every particular bishop,' And, according to the judgment of the Nicene council, we say that the bishop of Rome hath no more jurisdiction over the church of God, than the rest of the patriarchs, either of Alexandria or Antiochia, have. And as for the bishop of Rome, who now calleth all matters before himself alone, except he do his duty as he ought to do, except he administer the sacraments, except he instruct the people, except he warn them and teach, we say that he ought not of right once to be called a bishop, or so much as an elder. For a bishop, as saith Augustine, 'is a name of labour, and not of honour;' because he would have that man understand himself to be no bishop, which will seek to have pre-eminence, and not to profit others. And that neither the pope, nor any other worldly creature, can no more be head of the whole church, or a bishop over all, than he can be the bridegroom, the light, the salvation, and life of the church: for these privileges and names belong only to Christ, and be properly and only fit for him alone. [312]

[310] Jerome.
[311] Perfectly.
[312] Jewel, pp.59-60.

As we noted in chapter one, what we see in these quotations from Jewel is that the Anglican Reformers, while rejecting the claims made for the Pope, nevertheless continued to hold that bishops were an integral part of the life of the Church alongside deacons and presbyters. As we also noted in chapter one, this was because they believed that bishops had been a part of the life of the Church since the time of the apostles and therefore being in continuity with apostles and the subsequent practice of the universal Church meant having bishops. As we have seen, this argument is put forward in the Preface to the 1662 Ordinal, and it was the standard argument for the retention of bishops throughout the sixteenth and seventeenth centuries.

A classic version of this argument is put forward by Richard Hooker who, appealing to the historical evidence that we have looked at in this chapter and in the previous chapters of this study, argues for the continuous history of episcopacy both in the Church in general and in the Church of England in particular:

A thousand five hundred years and upward the Church of Christ hath now continued under the sacred regiment of bishops. Neither for so long have Christianity ever been planted in any Kingdom throughout the world but with this kind of government alone; which to have been ordained of God, I am for my own part even as resolutely persuaded, as that any other kind of government in the world whatsoever is of God. In this realm of England, before Normans yea before Saxons, there being Christians, the chief pastors of their souls were bishops. This order from about the first establishment of Christian religion first, which was publicly begun through the virtuous disposition of King Lucie not fully two hundred years after Christ, continued till the coming in of the Saxons; by whom Paganism being everywhere else replanted, only one part of the island, whereinto the ancient natural inhabitants the Britons were driven, retained constantly the faith of Christ, together with the same form of spiritual regiment, which their fathers had before received. Wherefore in the histories of the Church we find very ancient mention made of our own bishops. At the council of Ariminum, about the year three hundred and fifty-nine, Britain had three of her bishops present. At the arrival of Augustine the monk, whom Gregory sent Heather to reclaim the Saxons from Gentility[313] about six hundred years after Christ, the Britons he found observers still of the selfsame government by bishops over the rest of this clergy; under this form Christianity took root again, where it had been exiled. Under the selfsame format remained till the days of the Norman conqueror. By him and his successors thereunto sworn, it has from that time till now by the space of five hundred years more been upheld.

O nation utterly without knowledge, without sense! We are not through error of mind deceived, but some wicked thing hath undoubtedly bewitched us, if we foresake that government, the use whereof universal experience hath for so many years approved, and betake ourselves into a regiment neither appointed of God himself, as they who favour it pretend, nor till yesterday ever heard of among men. [314]

The importance attached by the Church of England to the maintenance of episcopal continuity was clearly demonstrated after Elizabeth I came to the throne in 1558 and re-instituted the Reformation settlement of religion introduced by Henry VIII and Edward VI.

Queen Elizabeth was faced with an acute shortage of bishops. Queen Mary's Archbishop of Canterbury, Reginald Pole, died a few hours after she did, and all the other serving bishops, with the sole exception of the Bishop of Llandaff, Anthony Kitchin, refused to acknowledge Elizabeth, rather than the Pope as 'supreme governor' of the Church of England and were therefore deposed from office. To fill the gaps thus created Matthew Parker was consecrated as Archbishop of Canterbury on 17 December 1559 and the consecration of other diocesan bishops then followed.

As Stephen Neill explains, when Parker was consecrated:

[313] i.e. paganism rather than gentility in the modern sense.
[314] Hooker Bk. VII.1.4, pp.329-330.

...the greatest care was taken to maintain continuity with the past, and above all to ensure that the succession of episcopal consecration was unbroken. Four bishops performed the consecration according to the form in the Edwardian Ordinal, and of these, two had been consecrated in the reign of Henry VIII under the old order.[315]

What this said liturgically was that the same episcopal government that had always existed in the Church of England was continuing in spite of the breach with Rome. The Church of England was no longer under the Pope, but it remained episcopal just as it always had been.

During the English Reformation steps were also taken to try to ensure that episcopal ministry would be exercised more effectively, and in a manner that was more in line with the teaching of the Bible and the Fathers.

In the reign of Henry VIII six new English dioceses were created between 1540 and 1542 (Westminster[316], Bristol, Chester, Gloucester, Oxford and Peterborough). The *Suffragan Bishops Act* of 1534 also made provision for the first time for the appointment of English suffragan bishoprics [317] and during the sixteenth century suffragan sees were established at Ipswich, Thetford, Colchester, Berwick, Penrith, Shrewsbury, Malborough, Dover, Bedford, Bristol, Taunton, Hull, Shaftesbury and Nottingham. Both of these developments were attempts to deal with the large size of the medieval English dioceses and so allow episcopacy in the Church of England to operate more effectively.

As we shall see in more detail in chapter 10, Cranmer's proposed revision of the Church of England's Canon law (the *Reformatio Legum*

---

[315] Stephen Neill, *Anglicanism,* 4ed (London: Mowbray, 1977) pp.103-104. The four consecrating bishops were William Bancroft, formerly Bishop of Bath and Wells, Miles Coverdale, formerly Bishop of Exeter, John Scory, formerly Bishop of Chichester, and Thomas Hodgkin, suffragan Bishop of Bedford.
[316] This only existed from 1540-1550.
[317] The Suffragan Bishops Act 1534 at https://www.legislation.gov.uk/aep/Hen8/26/14/contents

Ecclesiasticarum) and the reformed Church of England Ordinal (originally issued in 1550 and then revised in 1552 and 1662) stipulate that bishops are to instruct their people from the Scriptures and take action to protect them from heresy. They are also to exercise pastoral discipline, ordain and appoint clergy, confirm, and provide help to the poor and needy. These stipulations mark a deliberate return to a biblical and patristic view of the bishop's role. Bishops are not to be primarily feudal magnates or judges, but teachers and pastors.

In practice, Tudor bishops found that the many demands on their time from the state as well as the Church meant that they were not always able to focus on providing teaching and pastoral care, but the Reformation vision of a what a bishop should be doing was clear.

The Puritans and episcopacy

As the *Oxford Dictionary of the Christian Church* tells us, the term Puritan refers to

The more extreme English Protestants who, dissatisfied with the religious settlement of Elizabeth I, sought a further purification of the Church from supposedly unscriptural and corrupt forms. [318]

By the 1570s those on the radical wing of the Puritan movement, influenced by the Genevan theologian Theodore Beza, had come to believe that episcopacy need to be abolished in the Church of England and replaced by a Presbyterian system of church government like that practiced in Geneva.[319]

---

[318] 'Puritans' in Elizabeth Livingstone (ed), *The Concise Oxford Dictionary of the Christian Church* (Oxford: OUP, 1980), p.423.

[319] It is worth noting that there is evidence that Beza's predecessor as the leader of the Church in Geneva, John Calvin, was not only unopposed to episcopacy, but actually sought episcopacy from the Church of England during the reign of Edward VI. In his life of Archbishop Parker, the historian John Strype (1643-1737) gives the evidence as follows: And how Calvin stood affected in the said point of episcopacy, and how readily and gladly he and other heads of the Reformed Churches would have received it, is evident enough from his writings and

In 1570, for example, the leading Puritan theologian Thomas Cartwright, who, it is said, 'infected the minds of the scholars of the younger sort with mighty prejudices against the episcopal government

epistles. In his book Of the Necessity of reforming the Church, he hath these words: *Talem nobis hierarchiam exhibeant*, &c. 'Let them give us such an hierarchy, in which Bishops may be so above the rest, as they refuse not to be under Christ, and depend upon him as their only Head; that they maintain a brotherly society, &c. If there be any that do not behave themselves with all reverence and obedience towards them, there is no anathema, but I confess them worthy of it.'

But especially his opinion of episcopacy is manifest from a letter he and Bullinger, and others, learned men of that sort, wrote anno 1549 to King Edward VI. offering to make him their Defender, and to have Bishops in their Churches for better unity and concord among them: as may be seen in - Archbishop Cranmer's Memorials; and likewise by a writing of Archbishop Abbot, found among the MSS. of Archbishop Usher: which, for the remarkableness of it, and the mention of Archbishop Parker's papers, I shall here set down.

Archbishop Parker's account thereof found in his papers by Archbishop Abbot

'Perusing some papers of our predecessor Matthew Parker, we find that John Calvin, and others of the Protestant churches of Germany and elsewhere, would have had episcopacy, if permitted: but could not upon several accounts, partly fearing the other princes of the Roman Catholic faith would have joined with the Emperor and the rest of the Popish Bishops, to have depressed the same; partly being newly reformed, and not settled, they had not sufficient wealth to support episcopacy, by reason of their daily persecutions. Another, and a main cause was, they would not have any Popish hands laid over their Clergy. And whereas John Calvin had sent a letter in King Edward the VIth's reign, to have conferred with the Clergy of England about some things to this effect, two Bishops, viz. Gardiner and Boner, intercepted the same: whereby Mr. Calvin's offerture perished. And he received an answer, as if it had been from the reformed Divines of those times; wherein they checked him, and slighted his proposals: from which time John Calvin and the Church of England were at variance in several points; which otherwise through God's mercy had been qualified, if those papers of his proposals had been discovered unto the Queen's Majesty during John Calvin's life. But being not discovered until or about the sixth year of her Majesty's reign, her Majesty much lamented they were not found sooner: which she expressed before her Council at the same time, in the presence of her great friends, Sir Henry Sidney, and Sir William Cecil.' (John Strype, *The Life and Acts of Matthew Parker*, vol.1, Oxford: Clarendon Press, 1821, pp.139-140).

and liturgy established in the reformation of the Church,' gave a series of lectures on Acts in Cambridge in which he argued that:

The certain and unchangeable form of Church government commanded in the Scriptures was...the Presbyterian system. Thus the names and functions of Archbishops and Bishops should be suppressed; the Church should rid itself of ecclesiastical chancellors and other such officials; ministers should be in charge of one congregation, and no more, and they should reside there; ministers should be elected by the congregation, not created by the Bishop.[320]

The attempts by the Puritan radicals to achieve bring in a Presbyterian system took two forms.

First, they attempted to achieve change by Parliamentary action.

- In 1572 and 1573 the *First and Second Admonitions to Parliament* were published. These criticised the ministry and liturgy of the English Church and calling for their replacement with a pattern of ministry and liturgy on the Genevan model.[321]

- In 1584-5 Peter Turner introduced a bill into Parliament which would have replaced the Prayer Book with an adaptation of John Knox's Genevan liturgy known as the *Waldergrave Liturgy* after its printer Robert Waldergrave, and 'further proposed to erect Presbyterianism, committing the government of the Church to pastors and elders, acting through congregational consistories and assemblies of the ministers and elders of each shire.'[322]

---

[320] John Strype, *The Life and Acts of John Whitgift DD*, Vol. 1 (Oxford: Clarendon Press, 1822), p. 38.
[321] For the *Admonitions* see W H Frere and C E Douglas eds, *Protestant Manifestoes* (London: SPCK, 1907).
[322] Patrick.Collinson, *The Elizabethan Puritan Movement* (Oxford: OUP, 1998), p. 286.

- Finally, in 1587 Sir Anthony Cope presented a two clause bill to Parliament. The preamble declared that 'Christ had committed the guidance of his Church to pastors, teachers and elders, and had ordained synods and councils, national and provincial.' [323] The first clause provided that the Middleburg Liturgy, a revised version of the *Waldergrave Liturgy*, should 'be authorized, put in use and practised' and the second clause abolished all existing laws touching on Ecclesiastical Government (with the idea being that a Presbyterian system would be introduced in their place). [324]

Secondly, from 1572 onwards they also established an underground presbyteral system. This functioned as a parallel church alongside the official structures of the Church of England and was organized on the Genevan Presbyterian model as expounded by the Puritan theologian Walter Travers in his Full and *Plain Declaration of Ecclesiastical Discipline* of 1574, and in his *Book of Discipline* of 1586. [325]

These efforts to introduce the Genevan discipline into the Church of England came to nothing. The Parliamentary bills were either voted down or quashed by Elizabeth I, and the Archbishop of Canterbury, John Whitgift, took strong and effective disciplinary action against those Puritan ministers who were seeking to subvert the exiting ecclesiastical order: 'using the Court of High Commission he insisted that law and order should be preserved and the Prayer Book obeyed.'[326]

During the reign of James I the episcopal system continued to be upheld with Canon VII of the *Constitutions and Canons Ecclesiastical* of 1604 laying down that:

---

[323] Collinson, p.307.
[324] Collinson, p.308.
[325] For details see Collinson. pp. 131-159 and 272-371.
[326] John Moorman, *A History of the Church in England* (Harrisburg: Morehouse Publishing, 1980), p .214.

Whosoever shall hereafter affirm, that the Government of the Church of *England*, under his Majesty, by Archbishops, Bishops, Deans, Archdeacons, and the rest that bear Office in the same, is Antichristian, or repugnant to the Word of God: Let him be Excommunicated *ipso facto*, and so continue until he repent, and publickly revoke such his wicked Errors.[327]

However, during the reign of Charles I episcopacy became associated with unpopular policies of the king and his Archbishop of Canterbury, William Laud, and in 1640 a petition calling for its abolition signed by 15,000 Londoners was presented to Parliament. This petition, known as the *Root and Branch Petition*, declared that:

...the government of archbishops and lord bishops, deans, and archdeacons, &c., with their courts and ministrations in them, have proved prejudicial and very dangerous both to the Church and Commonwealth.[328]

It therefore asked

...that the said government with all its dependencies, roots and branches, may be abolished, and all laws in their behalf made void, and the government according to God's word may be rightly placed amongst us.[329]

The petition became the basis of the Root and Branch Bill, which was introduced in Parliament by Henry Vane and Oliver Cromwell in May 1641. Although this bill was defeated in August that year, and although the Archbishop of Armagh, James Ussher, produced a proposal for a system of Church government that would combine episcopacy and Presbyterianism,[330] in 1646 Parliament eventually abolished episcopacy altogether under the *Ordinance for the*

---

[327] *Constitutions and Canons Ecclesiastical 1604,* Canon VII, text at https://www.anglican.net/doctrines/1604-canon-law/.
[328] 'The Root and Branch Petition (1640)' in Gee and Hardy, p. 537.
[329] Gee and Hardy, p.538.
[330] James Ussher, 'The Reduction of Episcopacy' in Snoddy, pp. 148-154.

abolishing of Archbishops and Bishops in England and Wales and for settling their lands and possessions upon Trustees for the use of the Commonwealth.[331]

Following on from the Westminster Assembly, which met from 1643-1649 to reform the Church of England and to try to bring about a united church in England (which then included Wales), Scotland and Ireland, episcopacy was then officially replaced by *The Form of Presbyterial Church Government,* a Presbyterian polity in line with that in place in Scotland.[332]

However, many on the victorious Parliamentary side in the Civil War were as opposed to a Presbyterian form of Church government as they were to episcopacy, and so during the Commonwealth period from 1649-1660, although episcopacy was abolished, no one form of church government took its place. Instead there was what Judith Maltby has called 'an experiment with privatization and free market Christianity'[333] in which a variety of different forms of non-episcopal Protestantism were permitted to exist side by side.

Those who had been on the losing Royalist side in the Civil War, however, tended to associate loyalty to episcopacy with loyalty to the monarchy and when the monarchy was re-instituted in 1660 they made sure that the Church of England's traditional three-fold order of ministry was restored as well, with those Puritan ministers who could not accept it being expelled from their livings in the Great Ejectment of St Bartholomew's day 1662.

The Church of England was able to be maintain episcopal continuity, just as it did at the Reformation, because at the restoration of the

---

[331] *Ordinance for the abolishing of Archbishops and Bishops* at https://www.british-history.ac.uk/no-series/acts-ordinances-interregnum/pp879-883.

[332] The text of the *Form of Presbyterial Church Government* can be found at www.reformed.org/documents/wcf_standards/index.html?mainframe=/docume nts/wcf_standards/p395-form_presby_gov.html.

[333] Judith Maltby, *Prayer Book and People* (Cambridge: CUP, 1998), p. 234.

monarchy there were nine English and Welsh bishops still living and these bishops were able to pass on episcopal orders to a new generation of bishops.

Episcopacy after the Restoration

Even after the restoration of the episcopate, the bishops of the Church of England faced two further crises before the end of the seventeenth century.

The first was in 1687-1688 when King James II, who was a convert to Roman Catholicism, issued a Declaration of Indulgence suspending the penal laws against Roman Catholics and Protestant dissenters from the Church of England and ordered the bishops to ensure that it was read out in every church.

The Archbishop of Canterbury, William Sancroft, and six other bishops,[334] who doubted whether the Declaration of Indulgence was legal, and who feared that James II was aiming to turn England back into a Roman Catholic country, signed a petition asking the king to withdraw his declaration and refused to order it to be read.

In response the seven bishops were imprisoned in the Tower of London and put on trial for the crime of seditious libel. Upon their acquittal, they became popular heroes and the affair was one of the key factors that precipitated the overthrow of James II in the Glorious Revolution in November 1688 and the eventual replacement by Parliament of James by William and Mary the following April. [335]

However, the replacement of James by William and Mary caused its own problems for the bishops of the Church of England. Nine bishops, including Archbishop Sancroft, and four other bishops who had been

---

[334] The six other bishops were Thomas Ken, Bishop of Bath and Wells, John Lake, Bishop of Chichester, William Lloyd, Bishop of St. Asaph, Jonathan Trelawny, Bishop of Bristol, Francis Turner, Bishop of Ely and Thomas White, Bishop of Peterborough. Other bishops supported the action but did not sign the petition.
[335] For an account of the trial of the seven bishops see William Gibson, *James II and the Trial of the Seven Bishops* (Basingstoke: Palgrave Macmillan, 2009).

on trial with him,[336] refused to take the oath of allegiance to William and Mary. They had previously taken the oath of allegiance to James, and, as he had neither abdicated nor died, in their view he was still the king. Around four hundred members of the clergy followed their example.

In Scotland, where all the bishops of the Church of Scotland refused to take the oath of allegiance, they were replaced by a Presbyterian system of church government, In the Church of England, however, the bishops and other clergy involved were eventually deprived of their posts and others were then appointed to replace them. A number of the so-called Non-Jurors (i.e. those who would not swear a new oath of allegiance) then formed their own church with its own episcopal succession that lasted until 1805.[337]

Episcopacy in the eighteenth century

The eighteenth century saw the continuation in the Church of England of the episcopal form of church government that had been re-established in 1660 and that had survived the political turbulence of the reign of James II and the Glorious Revolution.

Although there are well known cases of eighteenth-century bishops who failed to ordain clergy, perform confirmations, consecrate churches, or undertake visitations of their dioceses, there are many counter examples of eighteenth century bishops who were diligent in the performance of their duties.

As Beatrice Hamilton Thompson notes:

They held annual ordinations in their cathedrals; they made triennial visitations, preceded by letters addressed to the clergy asking for

---

[336] The other bishops apart from William Sancroft were Thomas Ken, John Lake, Francis Turner, Thomas White, Thomas Cartwright, Bishop of Chester, Robert Frampton, Bishop of Gloucester, William Lloyd, Bishop of Norwich and William Thomas, Bishop of Worcester.
[337] For details on the Non-Jurors see J W C Wand, *The High Church Schism* (London: Faith Press, 1951).

them to reply to specific questions with regard to the conditions prevailing in their parishes; in the course of their visitation journeys they confirmed in the chief centres of the diocese. Contemporaries commented on the diligence of Bishop Gibson, who held confirmations in London almost every year and did 'even more than he is obliged to do by Canon.' Another shining example among bishops was Porteous of London, who endeavoured to revive the long-neglected observance of Lent by preaching a course of sermons in St. James's, Piccadilly, during four successive Lents and was, like Gibson, an active supporter of the Sunday School movement.[338]

The twin problems facing those bishops who did want to perform their diocesan duties properly were time and the difficulty of travel. Bishops were appointed by the Government acting through the monarch and the Government expected them to attend the House of Lords when it was in session in order to speak and vote on its behalf. This meant that bishops had to live in London for nine months of the year and had only a few weeks in the summer when Parliament was not in session in which to visit their dioceses. The size of the dioceses combined the continuing difficulties of travel in the eighteenth century further meant that it was difficult for bishops to get around their dioceses when they did visit them.

To quote, Hamilton Thompson again, the end result was that bishops:

...did not preside over diocesan committees, they seldom appeared at public meetings, intercourse with their clergy was formal, and they played little or no part in the spiritual life of the parishes.[339]

A good illustration of this detachment of the bishops from the day to day life of their dioceses is provided by a letter written by the Evangelical clergyman John Newton in 1784. In this letter he explains to the minister of an Independent chapel that he has no difficulty in operating under the authority of a bishop because in practice the

---

[338] Beatrice Hamilton Thompson in Kirk, pp.445-446.
[339] Hamilton Thompson in Kirk, p.446.

authority exercised by both his archdeacon and his bishop is purely formal and imposes no constraints on his ministry.

Nor am I under any disagreeable constraint from my superiors in the church. The Archdeacon in his district, and the Bishop in his diocese, hold their respective visitations; the former annually, the latter once in three years. At these visitations the clergy (especially in the country) are expected to attend. On these occasions we answer to our names, hear a sermon or a charge, and usually dine together. There is nothing painful to me in paying these tokens of respect to my acknowledged superiors, and receiving marks of civility from them. At all other times, while we keep within the limits which I have already told you, I subscribed and consented to *ex animo,* we scarcely know, at least we do not feel, that we have any superiors. So far as I am concerned, I have reason to acknowledge that the administration of our church-government is gentle and liberal. I have from the first preached my sentiments with the greatest freedom. I have always acted in the parishes which I have served according to my own judgment: and I have done some things which have not the sanction of general custom, but I never met with the slightest check, interference or mark of displeasure from any of my superiors in the church, to this hour. Such are my restraints, and such is my liberty. I am bound by no regulations but what I myself approve, no man constraining or controlling me. [340]

The beginnings of the overseas episcopate
One significant development that took place at the end of the eighteenth century was that the Church of England began to consecrate bishops for service overseas. A combination of colonisation and missionary activity meant that by the end of the eighteenth century there were a growing number of overseas churches in places as far apart as America, Australia and India that were part of the Church of England. As parts of the Church of England these churches were technically episcopal, but they had no local bishops of their own.

[340] John Newton, *The Works of the Rev. John Newton* (Edinburgh: Peter Brown & Thomas Nelson ,1827), p.890.

This situation created a serious problem for the churches in in the newly independent United States after the end of the American War of Independence in 1783.

Prior to the war the Church of England churches in the American colonies had come under the episcopal jurisdiction of the Bishop of London and all their clergy had to take an oath of obedience not only to him, but also to the British monarch. As William Jacob notes, the problem they therefore faced was

How could they continue to be an episcopal Church if their bishops were citizens of a foreign country, and, to be ordained, their clergy had to swear an oath of allegiance to a foreign ruler, thus making them traitors to their own country?[341]

In the face of this situation the churches in Connecticut elected Samuel Seabury as their bishop in 1783 and sent him to England for consecration by the Archbishop of Canterbury in order that he could then begin to ordain clergy in America who would be free of the link to the British Crown. However, the Archbishop of Canterbury, John Moore, found that he was unable to create new bishops without parliamentary legislation or dispense with the Oath of Allegiance to the British Crown as part of the consecration rite.

Seabury then turned to the Scottish Episcopal Church (the church formed by those who continued to remain loyal to episcopacy after the Church of Scotland became Presbyterian in 1690), which was not bound by the same legal restrictions as the Church of England. The bishops of that church agreed to help and on 14 November 1784 Seabury was consecrated in Aberdeen by three Scottish bishops, Robert Kilgour, the Primus (senior bishop) of the Scottish Episcopal Church, Arthur Petrie and John Skinner.

In order to remove the legal difficulties that had prevented the Archbishop of Canterbury consecrating Seabury, the British

[341] William Jacob, *The Making of the Anglican Church Worldwide* (London: SPCK, 1997), p.62.

Parliament passed the 'Consecration of Bishops Abroad Act' in 1786. This Act was 'to empower the Archbishop of Canterbury, or the Archbishop of York, for the time being, to consecrate to the Office of a Bishop, persons being Subjects or Citizens of countries out of His Majesty's Dominions.' A royal licence was still required for this to happen, but the consecration could happen without requiring those being consecrated 'to take the oaths of allegiance and supremacy, and the oath of obedience to the Archbishop for the time being.'

Under the provisions of this Act, the Archbishops of Canterbury and York consecrated William White as Bishop of Pennsylvania and Samuel Provoost as Bishop of New York in 1787 and the Archbishop of Canterbury consecrated James Madison as Bishop of Virginia in 1790. This gave the American church four bishops, one in the Scottish and three in the English lines of episcopal succession, and from then on it was able to consecrate and ordain all its own bishops and clergy.

The precedent of consecrating bishops for ministry overseas having been set, Charles Inglis was consecrated Bishop of Nova Scotia with jurisdiction over all the remaining British possessions in North America on August 12, 1787 and Jacob Mountain was then consecrated as Bishop of Quebec in 1793. Unlike their counterparts in the United States, these two bishops were still part of the Church of England. They were consecrated in England and were regarded as extra-territorial suffragan bishops of the Archbishop of Canterbury.

Episcopacy in the nineteenth century
As part of the political union of Great Britain and Ireland under the Act of Union of 1800, the Church of England and the Church of Ireland combined to form the United Church of England and Ireland with the Archbishop of Canterbury as its senior Metropolitan. This united church remained in existence until 1871 when the union was dissolved and an independent Church of Ireland, which was no longer the established church in Ireland, came into existence.

In the Church of England the nineteenth century saw bishops becoming far more actively involved in the life of their dioceses than had been the case in the previous century. To quote Hamilton Thompson again:

Bishops withdrew more and more from political life, taking part in debates in the House of Lords only when the interests of religion or morals were at stake. They ceased to have houses in London, and devoted the major part of their time to their dioceses. Experiments were made in the revival of synods of the clergy; diocesan conferences became general; organisations, presided over by the bishop, for the furtherance of the work of the church in religious education, home and foreign missions, and the like, grew apace. The bishop no longer stood outside the religious life of the diocese but at its centre.[342]

A classic example of this new approach to episcopal ministry is the ministry of Samuel Wilberforce as Bishop of Oxford from 1845-1870:

'It is the Bishop who must be the main instrument in encouraging the zealous,' he wrote to Lord Shaftesbury, 'in steering up the fainthearted, in animating the despondent.' He made ordinations intensely devotional occasions; he used horses or the railways to be all over his diocese for confirmations over inspections of the six hundred parishes; he consecrated more than a hundred new churches and approved of more than seventy new parsonages and more than two hundred and seventy church restorations; he received regular reports on the parish priests from the rural deans, and wrote many letters of praise or blame in his own hands; he addressed the clergy in spiritual retreats and the laity in parochial missions; he founded a college to train priests and another for schoolmasters.[343]

Admirers of Wilberforce's episcopal ministry have argued that he pioneered this new approach. John Burgon declared, for example, that he was 'the remodeller of the episcopate'[344] while Sabine Baring-Gould wrote that he was 'the first of the Bishops of the Victorian Age

---

[342] Hamilton Thompson in Kirk, p. 452.

[343] David Edwards, *Christian England* (London: Fount, 1989), Vol.3, p.210.

[344] John Burgon, *Lives of Twelve Good Men* (London: John Murray, 1891), Chap V.

to show what the duties of a Bishop were.' [345] However, a series of studies of Victorian bishops since the 1950s have called into question this view of the matter. What these studies have shown is that Wilberforce was in fact part of a larger group of reforming bishops, who developed a much more activist approach to episcopal ministry from the 1830s onwards.[346]

If we ask why this new approach to episcopal ministry developed, there are a number of answers. First, as Hamilton Thompson notes, bishops were less involved in the work of the House of Lords and this gave them more time to undertake work in their dioceses. Secondly, improvements in communications, and particularly the coming of the railways meant that bishops were able to travel around their dioceses and travel between London and their dioceses much more easily than had previously been the case. Thirdly, there was a general feeling in the Victorian era that members of the professions, including the members of the clerical profession, ought to be more assiduous in the performance of their duties. However, the most important reason was theological conviction. Bishops and others in the Church came to believe that only the sort of activist episcopal ministry developed by Wilberforce and others did justice to the teaching about the nature of episcopal ministry found in the Bible, the Fathers and the 1662 Ordinal.

In order to enable bishops to perform their office more effectively in the face of a vastly increased population a series of new dioceses were created. The first was Manchester in 1847 and this was followed by Truro (1876), St Albans (1877), Liverpool (1880), Newcastle (1882), Southwell (1884) and Wakefield (1888). In 1897 the diocese of Bristol, which had been divided between Salisbury and Gloucester in 1836, was also revived in a new form.

---

[345] Sabine Baring-Gould, *The Church Revival* (London: Methuen, 1914), p. 175.
[346] For this point see Arthur Burns, *The Diocesan Revival in the Church of England, c.1800-1870* (Oxford: Clarendon Press, 1999), pp. 10-13.

In addition, suffragan bishops were appointed for the first time since the end of the sixteenth century. The last Tudor suffragan bishop, John Sterne, Bishop of Colchester, was appointed in 1592 and no new suffragan bishops were appointed thereafter. Immediately before the restoration of the monarchy the future Charles II declared:

Because the dioceses, especially some of them, are thought to be of too large an extent, we will appoint such number of suffragan bishops in every diocese as shall be sufficient for the due performance of their work.[347]

However, this never happened. In the second half of the nineteenth century diocesan bishops were being assisted by retired colonial bishops, but this was felt to be an unsatisfactory expedient and pressure grew for the office of suffragan bishop to be revived. In response to this pressure two of the suffragan sees listed by the Suffragan Bishops Act of 1534 were revived in 1870 with Edward Parry appointed as Bishop of Dover to assist the Archbishop of Canterbury and Henry Mackenzie appointed as Bishop of Nottingham to assist the Bishop of Lincoln. This was then followed by the revival of the suffragan sees of Guildford (1874), Bedford (1879) and Colchester (1882). In 1888 the *Suffragans Nomination Act* allowed the monarch to create additional suffragan sees alongside those specified under the 1534 Act and a number of new suffragan sees such as Barrow in Furness, Burnley and Beverley were subsequently created. [348]

Another important nineteenth century development was the revival of structures for joint consultation and decision making between the bishops, the clergy, and the laity at both the diocesan and the national level.

At the diocesan level, diocesan synods, which had existed during the Middle Ages, but which had died out after the Reformation, were re-

[347] Text in The Archbishops' Group on the Episcopate, *Episcopal Ministry* (London: Church House Publishing, 1980), p.186.
[348] The Suffragan Nominations Act at
http://www.legislation.gov.uk/ukpga/Vict/51-52/56

established from 1866 onwards as diocesan conferences in which bishops could consult with representatives of the clergy and the laity about the life and work of the diocese.[349]

At the national level, the Convocations of Canterbury and York, which had only had brief formal meetings at the start of each new Parliament since 1717, were reactivated in 1851 and 1860 respectively. In order to provide a lay voice at the national level in a context in which members of Parliament were no longer necessarily members of the Church of England, a House of Laity was added to Convocation in the Province of Canterbury in 1886 and in the Province of York in 1890.

The establishment of the diocesan conferences and the re-activation of the Convocations, together with the re-emergence of suffragan bishops and the re-invigoration of the offices of archdeacon and rural dean, meant that bishops had to operate in a new way. Even in the case of diocesan bishop, episcopal ministry could no longer mean acting in isolation as the absolute monarch within a particular diocese. It meant instead working together with other bishops and members of the clergy and consulting and making decisions with other bishops and with the representatives of the clergy and the laity at both the national and the diocesan level.

A final development in the nineteenth century was the continuing development of overseas Anglican churches, involving both the development of entirely new churches and existing churches such as those in Canada, New Zealand and South Africa joining the Episcopal Church in the United States in becoming self-governing churches with their own Metropolitan bishops independent of the Archbishop of Canterbury.

From 1867 onwards the practice developed of the bishops of these overseas churches meeting together with the bishops of the Church of England roughly every ten years at what came to be known as the Lambeth Conferences. These meetings helped to foster the idea that

[349] For the establishment of diocesan conferences see Burns pp.215-219.

Church of England bishops were not simply bishops of the Church in England, but were also bishops of a global communion of episcopally led churches. [350]

Episcopacy in the twentieth and twenty first centuries

In many ways the developments that took place in the nineteenth century have set the pattern for episcopacy in the Church of England in the twentieth and twenty first centuries.

- The activist approach to the exercise of episcopal ministry that developed from the 1830s onwards has continued to be regarded as the norm during the twentieth and twenty first centuries.

- New dioceses (such as Chelmsford, Derby and Leicester) and suffragan sees (such as Jarrow, Loughborough and Tonbridge) have continued to be created.

- The practice of bishops working together with other bishops and members of the clergy and consulting and making decisions with other bishops, other members of the clergy and with members of the laity at both the diocesan and national levels has continued. From 1919 onwards the diocesan conferences and the Convocations were supplemented by a national Church Assembly consisting of the bishops and clergy of the Convocations and laity from the Provinces of Canterbury and York. This system was then replaced in 1970 with the present system in which bishops, clergy and laity participate in diocesan synods and in the national General Synod.

- Church of England bishops have continued to see themselves as bishops of a global communion of episcopal churches.

---

[350] For the developments in these two paragraphs see Stephen Neill, *Anglicanism* (London: Mowbray, 1977), Chs.11-13 and William Jacob, *The Making of the Anglican Church Worldwide* (London: SPCK, 1997), Ch.4-7.

However, there have been two significant developments involving episcopacy which have taken place since the nineteenth century.

The first is the involvement of the Church of England in the ecumenical movement.

The twentieth century saw widespread efforts by churches of different traditions to overcome the divisions of the past and to create ever greater forms of visible unity between them and this effort has continued, albeit with less intensity in the twenty first century. The Church of England has been deeply involved in this search for ever greater unity, but like the other Anglican churches it has emphasised that the visible unity of the Church of Christ must include bishops.

This emphasis can be seen in the 'Appeal to All Christian People' which was issued by the Lambeth Conference of 1920 and which has been the foundation for Anglican ecumenical endeavour ever since. This appeal for churches to engage in the quest for unity declares that one of the key components of visible unity needs to be:

...a ministry acknowledged by every part of the Church as possessing not only the inward call of the Spirit, but also the commission of Christ and the authority of the whole body.[351]

It then goes on to say:

May we not reasonably claim that the episcopate is the one means of providing such a ministry? It is not that we call in question for a moment the spiritual reality of the ministries of those Communions which do not possess the episcopate. On the contrary we thankfully acknowledge that these ministries have been manifestly blessed and owned by the Holy Spirit as effective means of grace. But we submit that considerations alike of history and of present experience justify the claim which we make on behalf of the episcopate. Moreover, we

---

[351] Lambeth Conference 1920, Resolution 9 in Roger Coleman (ed), *Resolutions of the twelve Lambeth Conferences, 1867 -1988* (Toronto: Anglican Book Centre, 1992), p.47.

would urge that it is now and will prove to be in the future the best instrument for maintaining the unity and continuity of the Church.

In line with what is said in the 'Appeal to All Christian People,' the Church of England has continued to affirm subsequently that visible unity needs to involve having bishops in historic succession, that is to say, in some form of historic descent from the bishops of the Early Church.

For example, the report *An Anglican-Methodist Covenant* agreed by the Church of England and the Methodist Church of Great Britain in 2001 notes that the ecumenical agreements that the Church of England has entered into with non-episcopal churches shows that:

...the Church of England is able to acknowledge a non-episcopal church as a church belonging to the one, holy, catholic and apostolic Church. However, the fact that the agreements mentioned above are not agreements for full visible unity but bring about a stage on the way towards that goal, shows that the Church of England holds (as the Anglican Communion has formally held since the Lambeth Quadrilateral in 1888) that ordained ministry within the historic episcopate belongs to the full unity of the Church. The reasons for this lie in the Anglican understanding of the Episcopal office and its representative nature in focusing the *koinonia* [communion] of the Church in time in space. Anglicans must remain committed on this point, in discussion with non-episcopally ordered churches, if they are to be consistent with what they have said over many decades to the Roman Catholic, Orthodox and Old Catholic churches.[352]

The Church of England has also maintained the discipline which it adopted at the Restoration, and which is expressed in the Preface to the 1662 Ordinal, that no one can serve as a bishop, priest of deacon in

---

[352] *An Anglican-Methodist Covenant* (Peterborough and London: Methodist Publishing House/Church House Publishing, 2001), pp.52-53.

the Church of England unless they have been episcopally ordained.[353] This means that although ecumenical progress means that ordained ministers from non-episcopal churches can help lead services in, and provide pastoral care for, Church of England churches they can only become ministers of the Church of England by receiving episcopal ordination.

The second development is the appointment of women as bishops.

Women were ordained as deaconesses in the Church of England from 1924, as deacons from 1987 and as priests from 1994. After a long period of debate beginning in 2000, the legislation to allow women to become bishops received final approval from the General Synod in November 2014 and the first woman bishop, the suffragan Bishop of Stockport, Libby Lane, was consecrated bishop the following January. The first female diocesan bishop, Rachel Treweek, Bishop of Gloucester, was consecrated in July 2015.

There are currently five female diocesan bishops and thirteen female suffragan bishops in post and two female suffragans who have been appointed, but who have not yet been consecrated. What is important to note is that as far as the Church of England is concerned women bishops do not belong to a new category of ordained ministry. A female bishop holds exactly the same office as her male counterpart. The continuity of the historic episcopate has thus been maintained.

There are, however, those in the Church of England who hold that a woman either cannot, or should not, be a bishop, just as there are those who hold that a woman either cannot, or should not, be a priest. The Church of England has appointed four male suffragan bishops (known as Provincial Episcopal Visitors or PEVs), the Bishops of Beverley, Ebbsfleet, Maidstone and Richborough, to cater for the needs of those who are unable to receive the ministry women bishops

---

[353] See *The Canons of the Church of England,* 6ed (London: Church House Publishing, 2000), Canon C.1.

or priests for these reasons. The Bishop of Fulham performs a similar role within the Diocese of London.

The significance of the history surveyed in this chapter

What the history we have looked at in this chapter shows us is that, just as the episcopate had a continuous history in the early church from the time of the apostles, so also from the time of the early church until now the episcopate has had a continuous history in the Church of England.

As we saw earlier in this chapter, at the end of the sixteenth century Hooker argued that that the Church of England had been an episcopal church from the beginning of its history. The evidence we have looked at in this chapter shows that he was right.

Although, as we have seen, bishops have operated in a variety of different ways in a variety of different circumstances, what has been constant is that bishops in historic succession (that is, in actual and intentional succession from the bishops of the early church) have always been present in the Church of England as part of the threefold ministry of bishops, priests and deacons. The only exception was during the Commonwealth period when episcopacy was officially abolished. However, in the context of the overall history of the Church of England this period has to be regarded as a temporary deviation from Church's the normal pattern.

The reason that Hooker draws attention to the fact that the Church of England has always had bishops is not just to make a historical point, but also a theological one. For him, as for other Church of England writers of his era, the historic origins and subsequent continuity of the episcopate showed that it was a form of ministry which carried the authority of God himself. In the next chapter we shall go on to look at this argument in more detail.

Chapter 6
The theological case for episcopacy

Sixteenth and Seventeenth century Anglican arguments for episcopacy

Prior to the sixteenth century we do not find theologians from the Church of England making a theological case for the existence of the episcopal form of church government. This is because it was not necessary for them to do so.

As was noted in the previous chapter, the question of whether there should be bishops was simply not a matter for discussion. No one doubted there should be bishops any more than they doubted that there should be priests.

As we also saw in the previous chapter, the situation changed radically from the 1570s onwards, with continual calls from the more radical Puritans for episcopacy to be abolished in the Church of England and for some version of government by elders to be put in its place. These Puritan calls for its abolition led Church of England theologians who supported episcopacy to make the case for its retention and what we find is that they defended it on the basis that it was the form of Church government, testified to by Scripture and the Fathers, that was instituted by the apostles and as such carried divine authority.

In the first part of this chapter we will establish this point by looking at the defence of episcopacy mounted by six representative Church of England theologians during the course of the sixteenth and seventeenth centuries. These theologians are John Whitgift, Thomas Bilson, Richard Hooker, John Overall, Joseph Hall and James Ussher.

John Whitgift, The Defence of the answer to the Admonition

As we noted in the last chapter, the *First Admonition to Parliament* was published by the Puritans in 1572. It contained a 'review of Popish abuses,' that is to say, abuses introduced into the Church of England by the Papacy and retained by the Church of England even after the official breach with Rome.

In this review, the writers of the *Admonition* claim that what they call the 'pontifical' (what we would call the 1550 ordinal) is Papal in origin and contains a form of government which is contrary to Scripture. In their words:

Their pontifical (which is annexed to the Book of Common Prayer, and whereunto subscribing to the Articles we must subscribe also) whereby they consecrate bishops, make ministers and deacons, is nothing else but a thing word for word drawn out of the Pope's pontifical, wherein he showeth himself to be Antichrist most lively. And as the name of Archbishops, Archdeacons, Lord Bishops, Chancellors etc, are drawn out of the Pope's shop together with their offices, so the government which they use, by the life of the Pope which is the Canon law, is anti-Christian and devilish and contrary to the Scriptures. And as safely may we by the warrant of God's word subscribe to allow the dominion of the Pope universally to reign over the Church of God, as of an Archbishop over an whole province, or a Lord Bishop over a diocese which contains many shires and parishes. For the dominion that they exercise, the Archbishop above them, and they above the rest of their brethren, is unlawful and expressly forbidden by the word of God. [354]

The writers go on to criticise the government over the Church exercised by diocesan bishops, together with their suffragan bishops, archdeacons, and sundry legal officers, as contrary to the form of government established by Christ and used by the early Church. To quote the admonition again:

In that the Lorde Bishops, their suffragans, Archdeacons, Chancellors, officials, proctors, Doctors, summoners and such ravening rabblers take upon them, which is most horrible, the rule of God's Church, spoiling the pastor of his lawful jurisdiction over his own flock given by the word, thrusting away most sacrilegiously that order which Christ has left to his church & which the primitive church hath used,

---

[354] *An Admonition to the Parliament*, para 14 in Frere and Douglas, p.30, spelling modernised.

they shew they hold the doctrine with us, but in unrighteousness, with an outward show of Godliness, but having denied the power thereof, entering not in by Christ, but by a Popish and unlawful vocation.[355]

The future Archbishop of Canterbury, John Whitgift, who was then Master of Trinity College, Cambridge, responded to the manifesto in his *Answer to the Admonition* which was first published in 1572 and then in an enlarged edition in 1573. In the same year Thomas Cartwright replied to Whitgift in his *A Reply to an Answer Made of M. Doctor Whitgift against the Admonition to the Parliament,* to which Whitgift in turn replied in his *Defence of the answer to the Admonition,* which was published in 1574.

In the *Defence* Whitgift accepts the Puritan claim that there is an equality between the ministers of the word:

It is not to be denied but that there is an equality of all ministers of God's word *quoad ministerium*: 'touching the ministry;' 'for they all have like power to preach the word, to minister the sacraments: that is to say, the word preached, or the sacraments ministered, is as effectual in one (in respect of the ministry) as it is in another.[356]

However, he says:

...*quoad ordinem et politiam*: 'touching order and government,' there always hath been and must be degrees and superiority among them. For the church of God is not a confused congregation, but ruled and directed as well by discipline and polity in matters of regiment, as by the word of God in matters of faith.[357]

Whitgift further argues that those who uphold the Church of England's existing order do not make the office of archbishop 'necessary to salvation.' However, they do hold that this office is:

---

[355] *An Admonition to the Parliament*, para 16 in Frere and Douglas, p.30.
[356] Text in John Ayre (ed), *The Works of John Whitgift D.D. – The second portion* (Cambridge: CUP, 1842), p.265.
[357] Whitgift, *Works*, p.265.

...profitable to the government of the church, and therefore consonant to the word of God; as shall be declared. We know the Church of Christ is not builded upon any man, either as upon foundations, or 'pillars,' if we speak properly, but on Christ himself and his word, which remain unmovable: we know also that the same church may stand without the external help of man. But yet hath God appointed functions in his church both ecclesiastical and civil, as a means to keep it in external peace, discipline, and order; and, though he had not expressed the names, yet he has allowed the offices.[358]

According to Whitgift, Paul's reference to 'pastors' in Ephesians 4:11 (a favourite Puritan text) is general reference that 'doth comprehend both archbishops and bishops.'[359] This is because the term pastor 'doth but signify an order of government convenient for the state of the church in the external policy of it'[360] and archbishops and bishops are simply two forms of this general order of government instituted by God.

As Whitgift sees it, within the general pattern of the government of the Church which God has put in place, the two terms 'archbishop' and 'bishop' both refer to one form of ministry, namely the ministry exercised by someone who has the oversight of a church and its pastors in a particular area. When the terms are understood in this way, we can correctly say that the roles of archbishop and bishop were first exercised by the apostles and it is this same role that is exercised by bishops today:

Although the apostles had not this name of Archbishop among them, yet they had the same authority and office. For they had the government and direction of divers churches, Both in matters of doctrine and discipline: they ended controversies, repressed errors, kept them in quietness, ordained them bishops, and visited them; as appeareth, Acts 14, 15, 18; 1 Cor 3, 4, 5, 11 and in the epistles to

[358] Whitgift, *Works,* p.91.
[359] Whitgift, *Works,* p.99.
[360] Whitgift, *Works,* p.99.

Timothy and Titus. Eusebius, declareth of John the evangelist, that, after he returned from Patmos, he visited and governed sundry churches, and ordained their ministers. The like Epiphanius report of Peter in Pontus and Bithynia, And what other office than those hath the Archbishop? Therefore, though the name of Archbishop was not among the apostles, yet was his office and function. And, notwithstanding that part of the office of the apostles is ceased which consisted in planting and founding of churches throughout the world, yet this part of government and direction of churches remaineth still, and is committed to bishops. Therefore, saith Ambrose *Apostoli episcopi sunt:* 'Apostles are bishops because bishops do succeed them in preaching the word, and governing the church.' [361]

The reason we can say that this part of the apostolic role is committed to bishops, argues Whitgift, is because the witness of Scripture and Church history tells us that the apostles, guided by the Spirit, appointed bishops to exercise this role:

It is not unknown to such as be willing to learn, that, where the apostles could not be present themselves, there they appointed some other to govern the churches for them; as the apostle Paul did Titus at Crete. Therefore, this reason of yours is soon answered. And, in that the apostles did appoint bishops in churches which they planted, and gave unto them such authority, it is evident that therein they made them their successors; which they did not do without sufficient testimony and warrant of the Spirit of God.[362]

In addition to the example of Titus given in this quotation, Whitgift further mentions James and Simeon, the first two Bishops of Jerusalem, Linus, Bishop of Rome, Timothy, Bishop of Ephesus, and Dionysius, Bishop of Athens, as examples of bishops appointed by the apostles. He comments that the appointment of the first bishops by the apostles 'is so manifest and so well known to all that read

---

[361] Whitgift, *Works,* pp.229-230.
[362] Whitgift, *Works,* pp.252-253.

ecclesiastical histories, that I am sure they will marvel at your gross oversight in denying the same.' [363]

Thomas Bilson, The Perpetual Government of Christ's Church
Thomas Bilson was Bishop of Worcester and then Winchester during the reigns of Elizabeth I and James I. *The Perpetual Government of Christ's Church*, which was first published in 1593 when he was the Warden of Winchester College, is his most famous theological work.

As its title suggests, the issue which Bilson addresses in this work is whether God has established a perpetual form of government for the Church and, if so, what this form is. At the time he was writing, the Presbyterian Puritans contended that God had instituted a Presbyterian form of government in which ordained and lay elders met together in Synods. Bilson argues that there is no support from either Scripture or the Fathers for any such form of government. Instead, Scripture and the Fathers show that the true form of government God has instituted is episcopacy.

Bilson argues that there were four functions delegated by Christ to the apostles that 'must have their permanence and perpetuity in the church of Christ.' [364] These are 'the dispensing the word, administering the sacraments, imposing of hands, and guiding the keys to shut or open the Kingdom of heaven.'[365]

As he sees it, the first two of these functions:

...by reason they be the ordinary means and instruments by which the Spirit of God worketh each man's salvation, must be general to all pastors and *presbyters* of Christ's church.[366]
However, the other two functions:

---

[363] Whitgift, Works, pp. 252-253.
[364] Thomas Bilson, *The Perpetual Government of Christ's Church* (Oxford: OUP, 1842), p.12.
[365] Bilson, p.12.
[366] Bilson, p.12.

...by which meet men are called to the ministry of the word, and obstinate persons not only repelled from the society of the Saints, but also from the promise and hope of eternal life, respect rather the cleansing and governing of Christ's church, and therefore no cause they should be committed to the power of every presbyter, as the word and sacraments are: for as there can be no order, but confusion, in the Commonwealth where every man ruleth, so would there be no peace, but a pestilent perturbation of all things in the Church of Christ, if every presbyter might impose hands, and use the keys at his pleasure. [367]

If we turn the New Testament, what we find, writes Bilson, is that these latter two functions were exercised either by the apostles themselves or by those appointed by them to be their successors in this regard:

...though the *presbyters* of each church had charge of the word and sacraments even in the apostles times, yet might they not impose hands, nor use the keys, without the apostles, or such as the apostles departing or dying left to be their substitute and successors in the churches which they had planted. At Samaria, Philip 'preached' and 'baptised;' (Acts 8:5,12) and albeit he dispensed the words and sacraments, yet could he not impose hands on them, but Peter and John came from Jerusalem and 'laid their hands on them, and (so) they received the Holy Ghost' (Acts 8:17). The churches of Lystra, Iconium, and Antioch, were planted before, yet were Paul and Barnabas at their return (Acts 14:21) forced to increase the number of presbyters in each of these places, by imposition of their hands (Acts 14:23): for so the word χειροτονήσαντες signifies with all Greek divines and stories, as I have sufficiently proved, and not to ordain by election of the people, as some men of late had new framed the text. The churches of Ephesus and Crete were erected by Paul and had their *presbyteries*, yet could they not create others, but Timothy and Titus were left there to

---

[367] Bilson, p.12.

'impose hands,' and 'ordain elders' in every city as occasion required (1 Timothy 5:22, Titus 1:5.' [368]

What the evidence we have further shows, contends Bilson, is that the successors of the apostles were not all the presbyters universally, but certain individuals (who came to be called bishops). In his words:

...who succeeded the apostles, whether all presbyters equally, or certain chief and chosen men, one in every church and city trusted with the government both of people and presbyters, I have largely debated, and made it plain, as well by the scriptures as by other ancient writers, past all exception, that from the apostles to the first Nicene council, and so along to this our age, there have always been selected some of greater gifts than the residue to succeed in the apostles' places, to whom it belonged both to moderate the presbyters of each church, and to take the special charge of imposition of hands; and this their singularity in succeeding, and superiority in ordaining, have been observed from the apostles times, as the peculiar and substantial marks of the episcopal power and calling.[369]

Bilson acknowledges that there are those in his day who 'vehemently spurn' this reading of the evidence and who 'hardly endure any difference between bishops and presbyters, unless it be by custom and consent of men, but in no case by any order or institution of the apostles.'[370] However, he declares, those who argue this cannot:

...rebate the full and sound evidence that is for the contrary: for what more pregnant probation[371] can be required than that the same power and precepts which Paul gave to Timothy when he had the charge of Ephesus, remained in all the churches throughout the world, to certain special and tried persons authorized by the apostles themselves, and from them derived to their after-comers by a general and perpetual succession in every church and city without conference to enlarge it,

[368] Bilson, pp.12-13. Italics in the original.
[369] Bilson, p.13.
[370] Bilson, p.13.
[371] Proof.

or council to decree it; the continuing whereof for three descents the apostles saw with their eyes, confirmed with their hands, and St. John amongst others witnessed with his pen, as an order of ruling the church approved by the express voice of the Son of God. when the original preceded from the apostles' mouth, and was observed in all the famous places and churches of Christendom, where apostles taught and whiles they lived, can any man doubt whether that course of governing the church were apostolic? [372]

Richard Hooker, The Laws of Ecclesiastical Polity

As was noted in the last chapter, Hooker's comments on bishops in Book VII of *The Laws of Ecclesiastical Polity* were written at the end of the sixteenth century, a few years after the work of Bilson.

As we saw in chapter 2, Hooker holds that episcopal authority was first exercised by the apostles and he further holds that it was then passed on them to the bishops as their successors. As he puts it:

The Apostles therefore were the first which had such authority, and all others who have it after them in orderly sort are their lawful successors, whether they succeed in any particular church, where before them some Apostle hath been seated, as Simon succeeded James in Jerusalem; or else be otherwise endued with the same kind of bishoply power, although it be not where any Apostle before hath been. For to succeed them, is after them to have that episcopal kind of power which was first given to them. 'All bishops are,' saith Jerome 'the Apostles' successors.' In like sort Cyprian doth term bishops, '*Præpositos qui Apostolis vicaria ordinatione succedunt.*'[373] From hence it may haply seem to have grown, that they whom we now call Bishops were usually termed at first Apostles, and so did carry their very names in whose rooms of spiritual authority they succeeded.[374]

---

[372] Bilson, p.14.
[373] Elders who succeed in the place of the Apostles through ordination.
[374] Hooker Bk.VII.4,3, pp. 338-339.

Having declared that the bishops are the successors of the apostles he then explains precisely what this does (and does not) mean:

In some things every presbyter, in some things only bishops, in some things neither the one nor the other are the Apostles' successors. The Apostles were sent as special chosen eyewitnesses of Jesus Christ (Acts 1:21, 22; 1 John 1:3; Gal. 1:1; Revelation 21:14; Matt. 18: 19.), from whom immediately they received their whole embassage,[375] and their commission to be the principal first founders of an house of God, consisting as well of Gentiles as of Jews. In this there are not after them any other like unto them; and yet the Apostles have now their successors upon earth, their true successors, if not in the largeness, surely in the kind of that episcopal function, whereby they had power to sit as spiritual ordinary judges, both over laity and over clergy, where churches Christian were established.[376]

Hooker's account of how the bishops became the successors of the apostles in this regard runs as follows.

First, he says:

The Apostles of our Lord did according unto those directions which were given them from above, erect churches in all such cities as received the word of truth, the gospel of God. All churches by them erected received from them the same faith, the same sacraments, the same form of public regiment.[377]

The form of government ('regiment') they established for these churches consisted of a college of presbyters/bishops:

The form of regiment by them established at first was, that the laity or people should be subject. unto a college of ecclesiastical persons, which were in every such city appointed for that purpose. These in their writings they term sometime presbyters, sometime bishops. To

---

[375] Embassy
[376] Hooker Bk. VII.4.4, p.339.
[377] Hooker Bk. VII. 5.1 p. 339.

take one church out of a number for a pattern what the rest were; the presbyters of Ephesus, as it is in the history (Acts 20: 36-37) of their departure from the Apostle Paul at Miletum, are said to have wept abundantly all, which speech doth shew them to have been many. And by the Apostle's exhortation it may appear that they had not each his several flock to feed, but were in common appointed to feed that one flock, the church of Ephesus; for which cause the phrase of his speech is this *Attendite gregi,* 'Look all to that one flock over which the Holy Ghost hath made you bishops' (Acts 20:28). These persons ecclesiastical being termed as then, presbyters and bishops both, were all subject unto Paul as to an higher governor appointed of God to be over them (Acts 20:30). [378]

Secondly, however, in time it became necessary for the apostles to appoint one individual in each church to exercise episcopal authority over the rest of the presbyters. This was because the apostles:

...could not themselves be present in all churches, and as the Apostle St. Paul foretold the presbyters of the Ephesians that there would 'rise up from amongst their own selves, men speaking perverse things to draw disciples after them' (Acts 20:30) there did grow in short time amongst the governors of each church those emulations, strifes, and contentions, whereof there could be no sufficient remedy provided, except according unto the order of Jerusalem already begun, someone were endued with episcopal authority over the rest, which one being resident might keep them in order, and have pre-eminence or principality in those things wherein the equality of many agents was the cause of disorder and trouble.[379]

According to Hooker, the appointment by the apostles of this 'one president or governor amongst the rest' took place:

...a long time before that settled difference of name and title took place, whereby such alone were named bishops. And therefore in the

---

[378] Hooker, Bk.VII.5.1, p.340.
[379] Hooker, Bk VII.5.2. p.340.

book of St. John's Revelation we find that they are entitled angels (Revelation 2). [380]

Furthermore, this form of church government was not 'peculiar unto some few churches.' Rather, the whole Christian world:

...universally became subject thereunto; insomuch as they did not account it to be a church which was not subject unto a bishop. It was the general received persuasion of the ancient Christian world, that *Ecclesia est in Episcopo*, 'the outward being of a church consisteth in the having of a bishop.'[381]

As Hooker sees it, the fact that the episcopal form of church government was established by the apostles in the way just described means that it carries the authority of God himself:

...whether the Apostles alone did conclude of such a regiment, or else they together with the whole Church judging it a fit and a needful policy did agree to receive it for a custom; no doubt but being established by them on whom the Holy Ghost was poured in so abundant measure for the ordering of Christ's Church, it had either divine appointment beforehand, or divine approbation afterwards, and is in that respect to be acknowledged the ordinance of God, no less than the ancient Jewish regiment, whereof though Jethro were the deviser (Exodus 18: 19), yet after that God had allowed it, all men were subject unto it, as to the polity of God, and not of Jethro.[382]

John Overall, The Convocation Book

John Overall was Dean of St. Paul's, Bishop of Coventry and Lichfield and finally Bishop of Norwich. His work *Concerning the Government of God's Catholick Church, and the Kingdoms of the Whole World*, which was written in 1606, is known as *The Convocation Book* because it was

---

[380] Hooker, Bk. VII.5.2. p.340.
[381] Hooker, Bk. VII.5.2. p.341.
[382] Hooker, Bk. VII.5.2. p.341.

approved by the Convocation of Canterbury in 1610, although it was not actually published until 1690.

Like Hooker, Overall holds that the apostles initially committed the government of the churches they founded to a college of presbyters/bishops who were given authority to preach and administer the sacraments. However, experience of the quarrels that broke out between the presbyters in the absence of the apostles, and the divisions within the churches that resulted from these quarrels. then led the led the apostles to give those who worked with them (their 'coadjutors') the two prerogatives that they had retained in their own hands, namely ordination and the exercise of the 'power of the keys' (i.e. excommunication), and to appoint them to rule over the churches in their place.

In his words:

...whereas before, the Apostles held it convenient, when they first planted Ministers in every City, to detain still in their own hand the Power of Ordination, and the authority of the Keys of Ecclesiastical Government (because they themselves, for that time, with the Evangelists and others their Coadjutors, were sufficient to oversee and rule them:) Now for the Reasons above-mentioned they did commit those their said two Prerogatives, containing in them all Episcopal Power and Authority, unto such of their said Coadjutors, as upon sufficient trial of their Abilities and Diligence, they knew to be meet Men; both, whilst they themselves lived, to be their Substitutes, and after their deaths to be their Successors, both for the Continuance of the work of Christ, for the further building of his Church, and likewise for the perpetual Government of it. And in this manner, the Ministers of the Word and Sacraments, who had the charge but of one particular Church or Congregation, and were of an inferior Degree, were distinguished from the first and superior sort of Ministers, termed (most of them) before, The Apostles Coadjutors; and now and from thenceforth called Bishops.[383]

To these bishops, writes Overall,

...the Apostles did commit the charge and oversight of all the particular Congregations, Ministers and Christian people that dwelt in one City, and in the Towns and Villages thereunto appertaining. And such were the Angels of the seven Churches in Asia, who were then the Bishops of those Cities, with their several Territories; and so in all times and ages that since have succeeded, have ever been reputed.[384]

Furthermore, some of these bishops were given a wider jurisdiction:

And unto some others the most principal and chief men of the said Number, the Apostles did likewise give Authority, not only over the particular Congregations, Ministers and People in one City, and in the Towns that did belong unto it; but likewise over all the Churches in certain whole Provinces and Countries, as unto Timothy all that were in Asia the less, and unto Titus all that were planted throughout the Island of Crete. And this sort of Bishops who had so large Jurisdictions over the Bishops themselves in particular Cities, were afterward called Archbishops.[385]

According to Overall, this pattern of Church government can be seen to follow the pattern of government established by God himself amongst the Jewish people in Old Testament times. As he puts it:

And thus we see, how by degrees the Apostles did settle the Government of the Church amongst the Gentiles converted to Christ, most suitable and agreeing with the Platform ordain'd by God himself amongst the Jews. Ministers are placed in particular Congregations, as

[383] John Overall, *Convocation Book*, Bk II, Ch VII, text at
https://www.anglican.net/
works/john-overall-convocation-book-1606-government-of-catholic-church-kingdoms-of-the-world/#p3-15
[384] Overall, Bk.II, Ch.VII.
[385] Overall, Bk.II, Ch.VII.

Priests or Levites were in their Synagogues. Four and twenty Priests termed *Principes Sacerdotum*, had in that Kingdom the charge over the rest of the Priests: and amongst Christians, one sort of Priests named Bishops or Arch-Bishops (as their Jurisdictions were extended) had the oversight of the rest of the Ministry or Priesthood. Lastly, as over all the Priests, of what sort soever, and over the rest of all the Jews, Aaron had the chief pre-eminence; so had the Apostles over all the Bishops and Priests, and over the rest of all Christians. [386]

Overall then goes on to note that the evidence from the subsequent history of the Church is that all the churches that were founded by the apostles or their co-workers shared the conviction that the that the episcopal form of church government established by the apostles under the guidance of the Holy Spirit was to remain in the Church forever after:

...it is apparent by the testimonies of all Antiquity, Fathers, and Ecclesiastical Histories, that all the Churches in Christendom, that were planted and govern'd by the Apostles, and by such their Coadjutors, Apostolical Persons, as unto whom the Apostles had to that end fully communicated their Apostolical Authority; did think, that after the Death, either of any of the Apostles, which ruled amongst them, or of any other the said Bishops ordained by them, it was the meaning of the Holy Ghost, testified sufficiently by the practice of the Apostles, that the same Order and Form of Ecclesiastical Government should continue in the Church for ever. And therefore upon the death of any of them, either Apostles or Bishops, they (the said Churches) did always supply their places with others the most worthy and eminent Persons amongst them: who with the like Power and Authority, that their Predecessors had, did ever succeed them. Insomuch as in every City and Episcopal See, where there were divers Priests and Ministers of the Word and Sacraments, and but one Bishop only; the Catalogues of the Names, not of their Priests but of their Bishops, were very carefully kept from time to time, together with the

---

[386] Overall, Bk.II, Ch. VII.

Names of the Apostles, or Apostolical Persons, the Bishops their Predecessors, from whom they derived their Succession. [387]

In addition, Overall argues that the distinction between different forms of ministry was instituted by Christ himself when he differentiated the apostles from the rest of his disciples, and that reason tells us that he intended this distinction to continue after the time of the apostles:

Again, forasmuch as it was thought by our Saviour Christ, the best means for the building and continuing of his Church in the Apostles times, to ordain sundry degrees of Ministers in Dignity and Authority one over another, when such a kind of pre-eminence might have been thought not so necessary, because the Apostles by working of Miracles, might otherwise (as it is probable) have procured to themselves sufficient Authority: How can it with any reason be imagined, but that Christ much more did mean to have the same still to be continued after the Apostles days, when the gifts of doing Miracles were to cease, and when Men's zeal was like to grow more cold, than it was at the first? [388]

It makes no sense, Overall says, to think:

...that Form of Church-Government to be unfit for our times, that was held necessary for the Apostles times; or that Order, so much commended amongst all Men...should be necessary to build the Church, but unfit to preserve it; or, that the same Artisans, that are most meet to build this or that House, are not the fittest both to keep the same in good Reparations, and likewise to build other Houses when there is cause. [389]

Joseph Hall, Episcopacy by divine right asserted
Joseph Hall was Bishop of Exeter and then Bishop of Norwich. As he explains in his 'Epistle dedicatory' to Charles I, his book *Episcopacy by*

[387] Overall, Bk.II, Ch.VIII.
[388] Overall, Bk.II, Ch.VIII.
[389] Overall, Bk. II, Ch.VIII.

divine right asserted, which was published in 1640, was a response to the action of the Bishop of Orkney in the Church of Scotland. At a meeting of the Church's General Assembly the bishop had 'renounced his episcopal function, and craved pardon for having accepted it, as if thereby he had committed some heinous offence.' [390] The purpose of his book is to show that there were no grounds for the bishop to renounce his episcopal office because episcopacy was instituted by God himself.

The starting point for Hall's defence of this position is the argument that the form of church government instituted by Christ and the apostles was instituted by God:

That government, whose ground being laid by our Saviour himself, was afterwards raised by the hands of his Apostles, cannot be denied to be of divine institution. A proposition so clear, that it were an injury to go about to prove it. He cannot be a Christian, who will not grant, that, as in Christ, the Son of God, the deity dwelt bodily; so, in his servants also and agents under him; the Apostles, the Spirit of the same God dwelt; so as all their actions were Gods' by them. Like as it is the same spring water that is derived to us, by the conduit pipes; and the same sunbeams, which pass to us through our windows.[391]

Hall then argues that that:

...not only the government which was directly commanded, and enacted; but that which was practiced and recommended by the Apostles, is justly to be held for an Apostolical institution.[392]

Furthermore, he writes, this form of government must be regarded as possessing universal and perpetual authority:

...It is no less evident, that the form which the Apostles set and ordained for the governing of the Church, was not intended by them

---

[390] Joseph Hall, *Episcopacy by divine right asserted* (London: 1640), The Epistle dedicatory (spelling updated).
[391] Hall, pp.28-29.
[392] Hall, p.30.

for that present time, or place only; but for continuance and succession for ever. For no man, I suppose, can be so weak, as to think, that the rules of the apostles were personal, local, temporary; as some dials or almanacs that are made for some special meridians: but as their office and charge, so their rules were universal to the whole world; as far, and as long as the world lasteth.[393]

According to Hall, what the evidence shows is that the form of church government instituted by Christ and the apostles was episcopal, but that this form of government developed gradually in response to the need to prevent division between presbyters dividing the Church.

As he sees it, what the New Testament tells us is that the apostles:

...comprehended in themselves whole the hierarchy: they were Christians, Presbyters, Bishops, Apostles. So it was, they were Apostles immediately called, miraculously gifted, infallibly guided, universally charged. Thus, they had not, they could not, have any successors; they were (withal) Church governors appointed by Christ to order and settle the affairs of his Spiritual Kingdom; And therein (besides the preaching of the gospel and baptising, come into them, with other ministers) to ordain a succession of the meet administrators of his church. Thus they were, would be, must be succeeded: neither could the church otherwise have subsisted.[394]

At first, he declares:

...wherever they came, they found a necessity to ordain meet assistants to them, and they promiscuously imparted unto them their own style (but Apostolical) naming them Bishops and Deacons according to the familiarity and indifferency of their former usage therein: but when they, having divided themselves into several parts of the world, found that the number of Christians (especially in the greater cities) so multiplied, that they must needs be divided in to many congregations, and those congregations must necessarily have

[393] Hall, p.33.
[394] Hall. p.99.

217

many presbyters, and those many presbyters, in the absence of the apostles, began to emulate each other, and to make parties for their own advantage, then (as St Jerome truly notes) began the manifest and constant distinction betwixt the office of Bishops and Presbyters to be both known and observed. For now, the Apostles, by the direction of the Spirit of God found it requisite and necessary for the avoiding of schism and disorder that some eminent persons should be everywhere lifted up above the rest, and ordained to succeed them in the overseeing and ordering both the Church and their many presbyters under them, who, by an eminence, were called their Bishops. [395]

These bishops, he says:

...were the men whom they furnished with their own ordinary power, as Church-governors, for this purpose; now the offices grew fully distinct, even in the Apostles days, and under their hands, although sometimes the names, after the former use were confounded. [396]

Finally, Hall contends that the fact that the development of a distinct episcopal office took place in the apostles' time points to this development having more than merely human authority:

Had there been any sensible gap of time betwixt the days of the Apostles and the ordination of Bishops in the Christian Church, we might have had some reason to suspect this institution to have been merely human; but now, since it shall appear that this work of erecting episcopacy passed both under the eyes and hands of those sacred ambassadors of Christ, who lived to see their Episcopal successors planted in the several regions of the world, what reason can any man pretend but this institution should be any other than apostolical, had it been otherwise, they lived to have countermanded it.[397]

[395] Hall, p.102.
[396] Hall, pp.102-103.
[397] Hall, p.132.

James Ussher, The Original of Bishops and Metropolitans

James Ussher was the Archbishop of Armagh in the Church of Ireland. His best known work on the subject of episcopacy was his 1641 work *The Reduction of Episcopacy* which sought to give presbyters a proper place in governing the Church alongside the bishops through the creation of a system of deanery, diocesan and national synods in which bishops and presbyters would work together.

However, he also wrote another work, published in 1644, which explained the grounds on which held that it was right for there to be bishops in the Church given the demand by many Puritans that episcopacy should be abolished. This work is *The Original of Bishops and Metropolitans.*

Ussher begins this work by declaring that the basis of episcopacy is found in both the Old and the New Testaments:

The ground of episcopacy is derived partly from the pattern prescribed by God in the Old Testament and partly from the imitation thereof brought in by the apostles, and confirmed by Christ himself in the time of the New.[398]

On the Old Testament, Ussher notes that there was no parity among priests and Levites, but rather a hierarchy, with both orders of ministry being ruled by heads and governors who are referred to as 'bishops' (*episkopoi*) in the Septuagint version of Nehemiah 11:14 and 22. The ministers of the gospel are the successors of the priests and Levites, not as those who serve the altar in the Temple (this role ceased with the once for all sacrifice of Christ), but as the teachers of the people 1 Timothy 3:2 cf. Deuteronomy 33:10) who are supported by the Church to perform this duty (1 Corinthians 9:13-14).

Given that the principle of ministerial hierarchy is thus taught in the Old Testament, on what basis, he asks, should it now be rejected?

[398] Ussher, p.118.

With what show of reason then can any man imagine, that what was instituted by God in the Law, for mere matter of government and preservation of good order, without all respect of type or ceremony, should now be rejected in the Gospel, as a device of Antichrist? That what was by the Lord once 'planted a noble vine, wholly a right seed' should now be so 'turned into the degenerate plant of a strange vine;' that no purging or pruning of it will serve the term, but it must be cut down root and branch, as 'a plant which our heavenly Father had never planted?'[399]

However, because people are so willing to describe as the work of the Antichrist 'whatsoever in church matters we do not find to suit with our own humours' we need, he says, not just to rely on Old Testament precedent, but 'to consult with Christ himself herein, and here what he delivers on the cause.' [400]

In order to 'consult with Christ' Ussher turns to the letters to the seven churches in Revelation 1:4-3:22 where Christ addresses the 'angels' of these churches. Ussher argues that the testimony of Patristic writers such as Leontius of Magnesia, Ignatius of Antioch, Irenaeus, Polycrates and Tertullian shows that these angels 'were no other, but such as in the next age were by the fathers termed bishops.'[401] He further argues that the testimony of Irenaeus and other Patristic orders such as Hegesippus and Clement of Alexandria shows that from apostolic times onwards there was a succession of bishops not only in these churches but also in the churches in Rome, Corinth, Jerusalem and other parts of Asia Minor. Ussher even goes so far as to suggest that the 'first root' of the episcopal succession of the churches in Britain might go back to missionary work in Britain undertaken by the apostle Peter.

As we have seen in chapter 4, Ussher further holds that the angels in Revelation were not simply bishops, but that they were the

[399] Ussher, p.120 quoting Jeremiah 2:21, Matthew 15:13.
[400] Ussher, p. 120.
[401] Ussher, p.135.

metropolitan bishops of the churches of the Roman province of Asia. He also suggests that the evidence of the letter to Titus shows that Titus had metropolitan authority in Crete and that the letters of Ignatius show that the church in Rome (and therefore its bishop) had metropolitical authority over the surrounding area in Italy and that he himself was the not just the bishop of Antioch, but the metropolitan bishop of Syria. This tradition of the bishop of certain churches having metropolitical authority was also testified to by Cyprian in the third century and confirmed as an 'ancient' custom by the sixth Canon of the Council of Nicaea.

Just as he holds that there is Old Testament precedents for bishops, so also he holds that there is Old Testament precedent for metropolitan bishops. He notes that in Numbers 4:16 the Septuagint calls Eleazar a 'bishop' and that in Numbers 3:32 it is further specified that he was 'the president of the presidents of the Levites' and comments that 'none that without prejudice did take the matter into consideration, would much stick to afford unto him the name of an archbishop.' [402]

A summary of the sixteenth and seventeenth century arguments for episcopacy

The arguments for episcopacy put forward by the sixteenth and seventeenth century writers we have just looked at can be summarised as follows:

- Episcopacy is the form of church government that has been universally accepted by the Church;

- Episcopacy is the Christian version of the hierarchical pattern of ministry found in the Old Testament;

- The evidence of Scripture and Fathers shows that it was instituted by the apostles who acted with the authority of Christ and under the guidance of the Holy Spirit, and this means that it carries the authority of God himself;

[402] Ussher p.145.

- Episcopacy was introduced by the apostles in order to prevent rivalry between presbyters causing trouble and disorder in the life of the Church;

- The form of episcopacy instituted by the apostles involved both bishops and metropolitans;

- The bishops were ministers of word and sacrament who were the successors of the apostles in ordaining ministers, governing the churches and exercising the power of the keys;

- Subsequent bishops were (and are) the successors of the first bishops appointed by the apostles and therefore the successors of the apostles in the ways just described.

New arguments for episcopacy in the nineteenth century

The arguments for episcopacy summarised above continued to be used by Anglican writers in the eighteenth and early nineteenth centuries. In the second half of the nineteenth century, however, Anglican writers developed new arguments for episcopacy in the light of the advent of the historical critical approach to the study of the Bible and the Fathers, an approach which challenged both the traditional reading of the Bible and the Fathers and their historical veracity.

The two classic examples of this new approach are the accounts of the origins of episcopacy given by Joseph Lightfoot in his essay 'The Christian Ministry', which was first published in 1868 as an appendix to his commentary on Philippians and by Charles Gore in his book *The Church and the Ministry*, which was first published in 1886. In the second part of this chapter we shall look at these two works in turn.

Joseph Lightfoot, 'The Christian Ministry'

In his essay on 'The Christian Ministry,' Lightfoot notes the existence of a variety of different opinions about the origin of the threefold ministry pattern of ministry consisting of bishops, presbyters and deacons and declares that the correct way of deciding between them is through historical study and it is this approach that his essay will follow. In his words:

History seems to show decisively that before the middle of the second century each church or organised Christian community had three orders of ministers, its bishops, it's presbyters, and its deacons. On this point there cannot reasonably be two opinions. But at what time and under what circumstances this organisation was matured, and to what extent our allegiance is due to it as an authoritative ordinance, are more difficult questions. Some have recognised in episcopacy an institution of divine origin, absolute and indispensable; others have represented it as destitute of all apostolic sanction and authority. Some again have sought for the archetype of the threefold ministry in the Aaronic priesthood; others in the arrangements of synagogue worship. In this clamour of antagonistic opinions history is obviously the sole upright, impartial referees; and the historical mode of treatment will therefore be strictly adhered to in the following investigation. The doctrine in this instance at all events is involved in the history. [403]

As we saw in chapter two, Lightfoot holds that an episcopal form of ministry developed very early on in the Church of Jerusalem, with James exercising the episcopal role. However, as we also saw he rejects the traditional idea that Timothy, Titus or the angels of the churches in Revelation were bishops. He likewise rejects the traditions that episcopacy was established by the apostles in places such as Athens. Alexandria, Corinth or Rome.

In his view the starting point for the later development of episcopacy was the action of John and the other surviving apostles in appointing bishops in Asia Minor at the end of the first century who would exercise the same sort of leadership role that James had exercised in Jerusalem. During the course of the second century churches elsewhere gradually followed the example of Asia Minor by appointing one of their council of presbyters to be their bishop, although there was no direct apostolic instruction that they should do so. In Lightfoot's words:

---

[403] Lightfoot, p.187.

223

We have seen that the needs of the Church and the ascendancy of his personal character placed St James at the head of the Christian brotherhood in Jerusalem. Though remaining a member of the presbyteral council, he was singled out from the rest and placed in a position of superior responsibility. His exact power it would be impossible, and it is unnecessary to define. When therefore after the fall of the city St john with other surviving Apostles removed to Asia Minor and found there manifold irregularities and threatening symptoms of disruption, he would not unnaturally encourage an approach in these Gentile Churches to the same organization, which had been signally blessed, and proved effectual in holding together the mother Church amid dangers not less serious. The existence of a council or college [of presbyters] necessarily supposes a presidency of some kind, whether this presidency be assumed by each member in turn, or lodged in the hands of a different person It was only necessary therefore for him to give permanence, definiteness, and stability to an office which already existed in germ. There is no reason however for supposing that any direct ordinance was issued to the churches. The evident utility and even pressing need of such an office, sanctioned by the most venerated name in Christendom, would be sufficient to secure its wide though gradual reception. Such a reception, it is true, supposes a substantial harmony and freedom of intercourse among the churches, which remained undisturbed by the troubles of the times; but the silence of history is not at all unfavourable to this supposition. In this way, during the historical blank which extends over half a century after the fall of Jerusalem, episcopacy was matured and the Catholic Church consolidated.[404]

Although Lightfoot's reading of the historical evidence is thus different from that put forward by Anglican writers in the 16th and 17th centuries, he agrees with them that the apostolic origin of the historic three-fold ministry means that it is a pattern of ministry that has divine endorsement. To quote Lightfoot himself:

---

[404] Lightfoot, p.207

If the preceding investigation be substantially correct, the threefold ministry can be traced to Apostolic direction; and short of an express statement we can possess no better assurance of a Divine appointment or at least a divine sanction. If the facts do not allow us to unchurch other Christian communities differently organized, they may at least justify our zealous adhesion to a polity derived from this source. [405]

Charles Gore, The Church and the Ministry

Gore agrees with Lightfoot that historical study shows that the historic threefold ministry is of apostolic origin. However, the route by which he arrives at that conclusion is different from that taken by Lightfoot.

As we saw in chapter 1, Gore holds that in the first century there was a class of prophets, teacher and evangelists who exercised a form of apostolic authority in the life of the Church. As well as James in Jerusalem, he writes, we also encounter in the New Testament:

...side by side with the Apostles...'prophets' and 'teachers' and 'evangelists' - names somewhat indefinitely used - who shared the Apostolic function of teaching. And, though they never appear as clothed with the same primary authority as the Twelve, yet prophets and teachers share also the ministry of worship and the laying- on of hands. We recognise then an extension of the apostolic function in some of its main features (a) to 'prophets' whose authority was guaranteed by the permanent possession of those miraculous powers which in the first age witnessed to the inner presence of the Spirit. Such men would have received either Christ's own commission before or after he left the earth, or, failing this, the recognition, as by the laying-on of hands, of those who were apostles and prophets before them, of that divine mission which their miraculous 'gifts' evidenced: (b) to apostolic men like Timothy and Titus known probably as 'teachers' and 'evangelists,' who without, as far as we know, sharing miraculous power, had yet imparted to them by the laying-on of apostolic hands what was essentially apostolic authority to guard the

[405] Lightfoot, p.267.

faith, to found and rule

As we have just seen, Lightfoot holds that bishops emerged at the end of the first and the start of the second centuries through one of the college of presbyters being appointed as the chief minister of each local church. Gore rejects this idea, holding instead that episcopacy emerged as the prophets, evangelists, teachers or rulers became the local presidents of the churches. In Gore's words:

The conclusion which on the whole we have been led to form is that the supreme power did not, in the West any more than in the East ever devolve upon the presbyters. There was a time when they were in many places (as for instance at Corinth and Philippi) the chief local authorities - the sole ordinary occupants of the chief seat. But over them, not yet localized, were men either of prophetic inspiration or of apostolic authority and known character – 'prophets' or 'teachers' or 'evangelists' or 'rulers' - who in the sub-apostolic age ordained to the sacred ministry and in certain cases would have extended the chief teaching and governing authority. Gradually these men after the pattern set by James in Jerusalem or by John the churches of Asia, became themselves local presidents or instituted others in their place. Thus, a transition was effected to a state of things in which every church had its local president, who ranked among the presbytery - a fellow presbyter like St. Peter - sitting with them on the chief seat, but to whom was assigned exclusively the name of 'bishop.' This transference and limitation of a name can hardly be a difficulty when we remember the vague use of official titles which meets us in early church history. In the organisation as in the theology of the church nomenclature was only gradually fixed. The view here expressed od the developments in the ministry, besides appearing to account for all the phenomena of the documents of the period, has the great advantage of accounting also for the strength of the tradition which gave authority to the episcopal successions when they first come into clear view and for the unquestioned position which they held. There is no trace of elevation in the records of the episcopate. [406]

[406] Gore, pp.296-297.

For Gore the fact that the historical evidence shows that the development of episcopacy in the manner just described took place across all the churches without exception points to this being a development intended by Christ. In support of this claim Gore quotes the words of Vincent Stanton as follows:

It was by a common instinct that this [the threefold or episcopal] organization was everywhere adopted. It was as it were a law of the being of the Church that it should put on this form, which worked as surely as the growth of a particular kind of plant from a particular kind of seed. Everywhere there was a development which made unerringly for the same goal. This seems to speak of divine institution almost as plainly as if our Lord had in so many words prescribed this form of church government. He, the founder, the creator of the Church would seem to have impressed upon it this nature. [407]

The arguments of Lightfoot and Gore

Lightfoot and Gore differ in their accounts of how precisely the office of bishop emerged in the early Church. Lightfoot argues that bishops emerged out of the ranks of the local colleges of presbyters, while Gore thinks that the office of bishop was the localisation of the previously itinerant ministry exercised by the prophets, teachers, evangelists and rulers who ranked between the apostles and the presbyters.

Where they agree, however, is in holding that the development of episcopacy began in the time of the apostles, and under their direction, and that it is what we know historically about how episcopacy developed that still allows us to say theologically that it is form of ministry that carries divine authority. For them the historical argument is still key.

---

[407] Gore, p.303 quoting V Stanton 'Christian Ministry Historically Considered.'

Arguments for episcopacy in the twentieth and twenty first centuries

During the early years of the twentieth century there were still Church of England writers who continued to hold that the origins of episcopacy can be traced back to the time of the apostles.

Frederick Puller, 'The Grace of Orders and Apostolic Succession'

For example, in his essay 'The Grace of Orders and Apostolic Succession,' first published in 1913, the Anglo Catholic theologian Frederick Puller argues that Matthew 28:20 Luke 12:42-44, John 20:21-23 and Acts 1:2-5 point us to 'two fundamental truths on which the doctrine of the apostolic succession rests.' These truths are:

(1)That our Lord selected, trained and commissioned his apostles, imparting to them far reaching powers enabling them to propagate and govern the Church; and (2) that our Lord intended that the ordinary powers of the apostolical office should be transmitted by the Apostles to others who should succeed them, and that the office and the powers belonging to the office, thus transmitted, should continue in the Church until our Lord's return in glory.[408]

According to Puller, chapter 44 of *1 Clement* explains how the apostolical office was able to continue in the Church even after the apostles died.

As we saw in chapter 2 of this book, *1 Clement* 44 refers to 'reputable men' who have been given authority by the apostles to appoint people as deacons and bishops (which in context means presbyters). Puller argues that what this tells us is that:

So long as the apostles were in full vigour, they could, either by personal visits or by giving a commission to apostolic delegates like Titus, establish or keep up, by ordination, the supply of clergy; but the question would arise. What is to be done when the apostles die? With a view to that event they gave directions which would secure that

[408] F W Puller, 'The Grace of Orders and Apostolic Succession' in F W Puller, *Orders and Jurisdiction* (London: Longman, Green and Co., 1925), p.17,

after their death other approved persons should succeed their ministry as ordainers and chief rulers.[409]

He goes on to suggest that originally these successors of the apostles would have been 'apostolic evangelists,' such as Timothy and Titus (and possibly Artemas, Tychicus, Crescens and others), plus 'apostolic presidents of churches,' such as Linus of Rome and Evodius of Antioch.

By the time *1 Clement* was written, the appointment of these successors meant that there were two classes of presbyters, those ordained by the Apostles or under a commission from them, and those ordained by these 'reputable men' who succeeded them. That is why *1 Clement* refers to four classes of persons (1) apostles, (2) presbyters ordained by apostles, (3) the successors of the apostles – the 'reputable men' and (4) the presbyters ordained by these successors.[410]

What all this means, declares Puller, is that:

...the Clementine Epistle bears witness to a state of things in the Church of the first century, which is in complete harmony with our Lord's revelation of His Will that the Apostolical office, which he created and empowered, should be perpetuated in the Church until His return in glory.[411]

He then adds that what we have seen in 1 Clement is also 'in complete harmony with the practice of the Apostolic Church from the first century to the present time.'[412] This is because the successors of apostles came to be called 'bishops' from the beginning of the second century and the ministry of bishops as successors of the apostles has been maintained in the Church ever since.

[409] Puller, p. 43.
[410] Puller, pp.43-44.
[411] Puller, p.46.
[412] Puller, p.46.

The traditional view of the origin of the episcopate put forward by Puller was not, however, the one that most Church of England scholars put forward during the twentieth century. Instead, the mainstream view came to be that the episcopal form of ministry was not instituted by the apostles, but was created by the Church of the first and second centuries in response to the needs of the time.

Three examples will serve to illustrate this point.

Arthur Headlam, The Doctrine of the Church and Christian Reunion

First, in his 1920 book *The Doctrine of the Church and Christian Reunion*, Arthur Headlam, who was then Regius Professor of Divinity at Oxford, writes that:

Episcopacy, like all other Church customs, had its roots in Apostolic time; but Episcopacy, as it existed in later days, was not the direct result of Apostolic action, but was the creation of the Church, which gradually moulded its institutions to fit the altered needs of the times. We have seen what those needs were: they were caused by the destruction of everything which had given coherency and unity to the Church. Time and change had swept away all those links which bound the local societies together. They might, under such circumstances, have developed in many different directions; but the strong sense of unity implanted in them from the beginning, the inevitable result of their origin, prevented any such thing; and the Church, out of the elements left it by the Apostles, forged for itself a strong, elastic form of government which never checked free development, but he enabled it to present to the world a splendid coherent solidarity.[413]

He then goes on to write that this means that episcopacy cannot rightly claim the authority of either Christ or the Apostles:

---

[413] Arthur Headlam, *The Doctrine of the Church and Christian Reunion* (London: John Murray, 1920), p.99.

It had its origins in the Apostolic Church; it represents a continuous development from Apostolic times; but we cannot claim that it has Apostolic authority behind it. We must recognise that we cannot claim such authority for any Christian institution or teaching unless there is the clear and certain evidence of documents coming from the time of the Apostles, and we cannot believe that our Lord could have intended that any institution should be looked upon as essential to the existence of the church without giving explicit and certain directions. He instituted the Eucharist and gave a command about Baptism, but he did not directly institute or command episcopacy. We cannot claim that it is essential to the church. Equally it is clear that there is no Apostolic ordinance to be quoted in its support. There is no adequate or sufficient evidence that it was instituted by apostles. We must recognise that the authority that can be claimed for it is so far limited. [414]

Henry Chadwick, *The Early Church*

Secondly, in his 1967 book *The Early Church,* Henry Chadwick (who was also Regius Professor of Divinity at Oxford), describes how the first bishops arose out of the ranks of the presbyters from the end of the first century onwards as a response to four factors in the life of the Church. He writes:

...among the presbyter-bishops one rose to a position of superiority and acquired the title 'bishop' while his colleagues are called presbyters. Four factors helped to bring this about. The first distinctive right naturally assigned to the senior member of the presbyteral college was the power to ordain. This became his prerogative. Secondly, correspondence between churches was normally carried on by the presiding presbyter-bishop. Thirdly, on the solemn occasion of an ordination, leaders from other communities would come as representatives of their own congregations and would take part in the laying on of hands and prayers which confirmed the power of the Spirit and the authority of the community as the body of

[414] Headlam, p.106.

Christ. Frequent exchanges by correspondence and mutual visiting helped the concrete realisation of the Church's unity and universality. Finally, The crisis of the Gnostic sects showed the manifest necessity of a single man as the focus of unity. [415]

Episcopal Ministry

Thirdly, the report *Episcopal Ministry* from the Archbishops' Group on the Episcopate, which was published in 1990, states:

Because the New Testament material is fragmentary it is all too easy to read back into this picture familiar models of ministry and to see there an episcopacy like our own. The evidence of modern scholarship must make the Church of England now question the Preface to the Ordinal of the Book of Common Prayer which says that it is apparent 'unto all men diligently reading the Holy Scriptures and ancient Authors, from the Apostles' times there have been these Orders of ministers in Christ's church: Bishops Priests and Deacons.' But we can say confidently that a ministry of personal oversight clearly emerged as the young church struggled to be missionary, spreading the good news as well as to be faithful to the gospel and to preserving internal coherence.[416]

As a consequence of this abandonment of the traditional reading of the biblical and Patristic evidence concerning the origin of the episcopate, the traditional Church of England argument for having bishops has also been abandoned. Church of England writers have ceased to say that the Church should have bishops because episcopacy was instituted by apostles acting on behalf of Christ. What they have argued instead is that the Church should have bishops because of the key role that bishops play in the life of the Church.

The following six examples illustrate this new form of argument for episcopacy.

---

[415] Henry Chadwick, *The Early Church* (Harmondsworth: Penguin, 1967), p.49.
[416] The Archbishops' Group on the Episcopate, *Episcopal Ministry* (London: Church House Publishing, 1990), p.20

Michael Ramsey, The Gospel and the Catholic Church

Archbishop Michael Ramsey's book *The Gospel and the Catholic Church* was first published in 1936 when he was Sub-Warden of Lincoln Theological College.

At the start of chapter VI of this book Ramsey argues that to ask whether the historical evidence shows that Christ or the Apostles instituted episcopacy is to ask the wrong question. In his words:

The historical problem is well known. Whereas in the Apostolic age we find 'local' ministries of presbyter- bishops and deacons, and a 'general' ministry of Apostles and prophets, there appears from early in the second century a threefold ministry of Bishops, presbyters and deacons, an order which soon became universal, with great importance attached the succession (in more than one sense of the word) of the bishops from the Apostles. What, now, is the important question to ask about this development? Not, surely, whether our Lord and the apostles laid down by definite commands that such and such order was to be followed, but whether the development speaks of the Gospel and the one Body, so that the Bishop by his place in the one Body bears that essential relation to the gospel which the Apostle bore before him. To burrow in the New Testament for forms of ministry and imitate them is archaeological religion: to seek that form of ministry which the whole New Testament creates is the more evangelical way. And our view of the ministry had better be evangelical than archaeological. [417]

Ramsey then goes on to argue that the importance of bishops is that they succeeded the apostles in three ways:

1. ...the succession of Bishop to Bishop in office secured a continuity of Christian tradition and teaching in every See. Each followed the teachings of his predecessor, and so the succession of Bishops was a guarantee that everywhere the

---

[417] Michael Ramsey, *The Gospel and the Catholic Church,* 2ed (London: SPCK, 1990), pp.68-69

Christians were taught the true Gospel of Jesus Christ in the flesh. [418]

2. The Bishops also succeeded the Apostles in the sense that they performed those functions of preaching and ruling and ordaining, which the Apostles had performed. [419]

3. The phrase 'Apostolic succession' is also used to signify that grace is handed down from the Apostles through each generation of Bishops by the laying on of hands...the succession of Bishops is not an isolated channel of grace, since from the first Christ bestows grace through every sacramental act of His Body. But certain actions in this work of grace are confined to the Bishops; and thereby the truth is taught that every local group or Church depends on the life of the one Body and that the Church in any generation shares in the one historic society which is not dead and past but alive in the present.[420]

By succeeding the apostles in these three ways, says Ramsey, 'the Bishop sets forth the Gospel of God'[421] and that is why having bishops matters.

Doctrine in the Church of England

The 1938 report of the Archbishops' Commission on Christian Doctrine, *Doctrine in the Church of England* declares that the case for episcopacy is based on the convergence of five factors. It lists these as follows:

1. The Episcopate symbolises and secures in an abiding form the apostolic mission and authority within the church; historically the Episcopate became the organ of this mission and authority.

---

[418] Ramsey, p.81.
[419] Ramsey, p.82.
[420] Ramsey, pp.82-83.
[421] Ramsey, p.83.

2. In early times the continuous successions of Bishops in tenure of the various Sees were valued because they secured the purity of apostolic teaching as against (for example) the danger of the introduction of novel and erroneous teaching by means of writings or secret traditions falsely ascribed to apostolic authors. No doubt the need for this safeguard became less urgent when authoritative formulations of doctrine were drawn up and the Canon of scripture was finally fixed. But it has remained a function of the Episcopate to guard the church against erroneous teaching.

3. The Bishop in his official capacity represents the whole Church in and to his diocese, and his diocese in and to the Councils of the Church. He is thus a living representative of the unity and universality of the Church.

4. The Bishop in his diocese represents the Good Shepherd; the idea of pastoral care is inherent in his office. Both clergy and laity look to him as Chief Pastor, and he represents in a special degree the paternal quality of pastoral care.

5. Inasmuch as the unity of the Church is in part secured by an orderly method of making new ministers and the Bishop is the proper organ of unity and universality, he is the appropriate agent for carrying on through ordination the authority of the apostolic mission of the Church. [422]

The report comments that:

It is, as has been said, the coalescence of all these elements in a single person that gives to the Episcopate its particular importance. Such coalescence could not effectively take place in a committee or assembly. [423]

[422] *Doctrine in the Church of England* (London: SPCK, 1982), p.122-123.
[423] *Doctrine in the Church of England*, p.123.

Alan Richardson, An Introduction to the Theology of the New Testament

In his well known text book *An Introduction to the Theology of the New Testament* the New Testament scholar and church historian Alan Richardson declares that the question of whether the office of bishop evolved upwards from the ranks of presbyters or devolved downwards from the apostles via the ministry of 'apostolic men' is unimportant. In his view the key point to understand:

...is that monepiscopacy was an urgent practical necessity. Doubtless different presbyters could have taken it in turns to celebrate the Eucharist or to preside at the church meeting; but nothing short of the setting up of one representative man, an ἀρχιποίμην of the flock, who should be the visible, personal guarantee of the unity and continuity of the apostolic fellowship and doctrine, could meet the need of the Church in an age in which schismatics and heretics of every kind threatened the very continuance of the Church and the Church's Gospel. The Bishop became in his person - in what he was as well as what he did - the embodiment of the Gospel of God, by which the Church itself was called into being. The existence of the Church is bound up with the Church's unity and cannot be separated from it: this is the truth which brought the episcopate into being, as distinct from the presbyterate, and which monepiscopacy enshrines and defends.[424]

Episcopal Ministry

The Episcopal ministry report writes about 'three planes' in the life of the Church. The first plane is 'pastoral ministry in the local community,' the second is 'collegial oversight linking the local to the universal Church' and the third is 'the link between the local and universal Church over time.' [425] It then goes on to argue that a consideration of these three planes of the Church's life shows the importance of the existence of the episcopate, not just for the Church of England, but for the unity and mission Church as whole:

[424] Alan Richardson, *An Introduction to the Theology of the New Testament* (London: SCM, 1958), p.328.
[425] *Episcopal Ministry* pp. ch.4.

It demonstrates how, through the office of a bishop, the Church is maintained and strengthened in unity in its service of God and its witness to the world. In the local church the bishop focuses and nurtures the unity of his people; in his sharing in the collegiality of bishops the local church is bound together with other local churches; and through the succession of bishops the local community is related to the Church through the ages. Thus the bishop in his own person in his diocese; and in his collegial relations to the wider church; and through his place in the succession of bishops in their communities in faithfulness to the Gospel, is a sign and focus of the unity of the church.

Insofar as we understand and see the working of the providence of God, we believe it to point to such an episcopate renewed in a future united Church. That is why, we argue, the loss of a common episcopate, the resulting existence of parallel episcopates and diversity diverse forms oversight ministries, diminishes the sign of unity and continuity. Parallel ministries of oversight reflect an imperfect, restricted, or impaired communion. A divided ministry damages the catholicity of the Church and limits eucharistic communion. Our local church which is not related through a ministry of oversight to all other Christians through the world fails to reflect the Catholic fulness of baptismal unity. The seriousness of this is not for the Church's life only but in the impairing of its work in mission, in calling the world the joy of belonging together to the one family of God through Jesus Christ his Son. A single fellowship, served by reconciled ministry, enables the church to interpret and hand on the one Gospel in all its fullness. [426]

Paul Avis, Reshaping Ecumenical Theology

In his book the *Reshaping Ecumenical Theology* the Anglican ecumenist Paul Avis suggests that the importance of bishops lies in the role that they play 'in helping to realise the full visible unity of the Church.' In his view:

---

[426] *Episcopal Ministry*, pp. 160-161.

The episcopal office plays a significant role in the visible unity of the church because episcopal ministry is the most fully representative form of Christian ministry. While all Christians represent Christ and the Church - the Spirit bearing body in head and members - the ordained have a public representative role by virtue of the office to which there are ordained. Even among the clergy, there are degrees of representativeness, culminating in the representative ministry of the Bishop. The tasks of the church - to teach, to sanctify and to govern or lead - which together comprise its mission, appear clearly focused in the ministry of the bishop. Episcopal ministry is also related to the four creedal dimensions of the church. While all Christians are related, as members of the body of Christ, to the unity, holiness, catholicity and apostolicity of the Church, the episcopal office is called to manifest these dimensions in a public representative way in a broad interface with the universal Church and in leading the faithful and their pastors in mission. [427]

J I Packer, Taking God Seriously

In his book *Taking God Seriously*, the veteran Evangelical theologian J I Packer addresses the issue of whether the episcopal system found in Anglican churches is biblical. In his view:

If you mean, is it mandated or exemplified in the Bible, the answer is no, although its ancestry and reflection of the ministry performed by the apostles and their deputies, as we see it in the Pastoral Epistles in particular, is clear.[428]

However, he writes:

...If you mean, does it express New Testament principles and priorities regarding the local church's life, and does it meet the New Testament requirement but everything in the church be geared for edification, then the answer is surely yes, and the incidents of bad bishops from

[427] Paul Avis, *Reshaping Ecumenical Theology* (London and New York, T&T Clark, 2010), p. 130.
[428] J I Packer, *Taking God Seriously* (Wheaton, Crossway, 2013), Kindle edition, Loc. 1291.

time to time does not invalidate that answer. Episcopal ministry in idea, if not always in reality, embodies the connectional link between congregations that our given unity in Christ demands, and can provide unifying leadership for the diocese, just as the consultations of the House of Bishops should do for the province, and the primates' meetings should do for the Anglican Communion as a whole. The demands of Anglican defined Episcopal office, if taken seriously, will doubtless drain the energy of its occupants, but those they lead will be enriched, so that their diocese will have every reason to thank God for them. [429]

Statements about episcopacy in ecumenical agreements

The Church of England has also expressed its understanding of the importance of episcopacy in a number of the ecumenical agreements into which it has entered. In these agreements nothing is said about the historical origins of episcopacy. What is said instead is that having bishops in historic succession is a sign both of God's continuing faithfulness to his people and of their commission and commitment to maintain the characteristics of the Church of the apostles. The following two examples illustrate this.

The Fetter Lane Common Statement

The Fetter Lane Common Statement agreed by the Church of England and the Moravian Church in Great Britain and Ireland explains the significance of the ordination of bishops in historic episcopal succession as follows:

The continuity of the church in apostolic succession is signified in the consecration or ordination of a bishop. In episcopal consecration the laying on of hands with prayer by the ordaining bishops (themselves so consecrated) bears witness to God's faithfulness to his people and to the promised presence of Christ with his Church to the end of time; secondly, it expresses the Church's intention to be faithful to God's initiative and gift by living in the continuity of the apostolic faith and tradition; thirdly, the participation of a group of bishops in the laying

---

[429] Packer, Loc. 1291.

on of hands signifies their churches' acceptance of the new bishop. This expression is the catholicity of the Church. Thus in the act of consecration a bishop receives in faith the sign of divine approval and the commission to lead his particular church in the common faith and apostolic life of all the churches.

We believe that to ordain in historic succession is a sign that the church intends to remain faithful to its apostolic teaching and mission. Neither the sign of ordination nor the sign of an unbroken ministerial succession guarantees the fidelity of any particular church to every aspect of apostolic faith and life; nor does it guarantee the personal faithfulness of those ordained in this way. Nonetheless we believe that to ordain in historic succession is an effective sign of continuity with the characteristics of the Church of the apostles.[430]

The Reuilly Common Statement
The Reuilly Agreement between the Church of England, the other three British and Irish Anglican churches, and the French Lutheran and Reformed churches declares that:

Anglicans believe that the historic episcopate is a sign of the apostolicity of the whole Church. The ordination of a bishop in historic succession (that is, in intended continuity with the apostles themselves) is a sign of God's promise to be with the church, and also the way the church communicates its care for continuity in the whole of its faith, life and mission, and renews its intention and determination to manifest the permanent characteristics of the Church of the apostles. Anglican hold that the full visible unity of the

---

[430] *Anglican Moravian Conversations* (London: Council for Christian Unity, 1996), pp.25-26.

Church includes the historic Episcopal succession. [431]

It goes on to say that Anglicans agree with Lutheran and Reformed Christians:

...that the use of the sign of the historic episcopal succession does not by itself guarantee the fidelity of a church to every aspect of apostolic faith, life and mission. Anglicans increasingly recognise that a continuity in apostolic faith, worship and mission have been preserved in churches which have not retained the historic episcopal succession.

However, Anglicans commend the use of the sign to signify God's promise to be with the Church; God's call to fidelity and unity and a commission to realise more fully the permanent characteristics of the Church of the apostles. [432]

Summary of twentieth and twenty-first century arguments for episcopacy

We have noted that during the twentieth century the argument that the historical evidence shows that the office of bishop was instituted by the apostles has been generally abandoned by Church of England writers. In its place a number of alternative arguments for the importance of episcopacy have been put forward by members of the Church of England in the twentieth and twenty first centuries. These arguments can be summarised as follows:

- Bishops secured the maintenance of apostolic faith and order in the face of heresy and schism and this meant that the bishop became a personal embodiment of the Gospel;

- Bishops continued the apostolic functions of preaching, ruling and ordaining and were thus the means by which the apostolic mission and the apostolic exercise of authority were continued in the Church;

[431] *Called to Witness and Service* (London: Church House Publishing, 1999), p. 3.
[432] *Called to Witness and Service*, pp.31-32.

241

- Bishops represent the pastoral care of Christ the Good Shepherd;

- The existence of bishops in historic succession and the role that bishops play in the life of the Church testify to the Gospel by pointing to the dependence of each local church on the one body of Christ of which they are a part;

- Bishops are a sign and focus of the unity of the Church across space and time;

- Bishops embody the link between congregations and provided unifying leadership for their dioceses;

- Episcopal ministry represents in a focused way the tasks given to the Church as whole and also manifests in a public and representative way the Church's unity, holiness, catholicity and apostolicity.

- Maintaining historic episcopal succession is a sign of God's faithfulness to the Church and of the Church's calling and commitment to maintain the characteristics of the Church of the apostles.

What are to make of the arguments for episcopacy that we have looked at in this chapter?

In the final section of this chapter, I shall assess the strengths and weaknesses of the arguments for having bishops that we have looked at in this chapter.

If we begin with the arguments for episcopacy put forward by Church of England theologians in the twentieth and twenty first centuries, we find that they correctly identify the key practical and symbolic roles which bishops performed in the life of the Early Church and which bishops continue to perform in the life of the Church of England and other Anglican churches today.

For some people the idea that the in early centuries of the Church the bishop was the personal embodiment of the Gospel may be difficult to understand. How can an individual embody the Gospel? The answer to this question is that a key part of the Gospel message is that God has created a community of people who are united in their acceptance of who God is and what he has done for them in Jesus Christ. In the early centuries of the Church's existence the bishops embodied this truth because it was in the churches led by the bishops that this community existed. It was in these churches, and these churches alone, that there was a community of people (the 'Catholic Church') who accepted the truth about God and his saving activity in Jesus Christ. In consequence, accepting the Gospel message and becoming part of the community created by God involved being in relationship with a bishop. The two things necessarily went together.

In similar fashion some people may find it difficult to understand Ramsey's argument that bishops point to the Gospel by pointing to the dependence of each local church on the one body of Christ. How is this dependence part of the Gospel and how do bishops point to it? The answer is that this dependence is part of the Gospel because part of the Gospel is the truth that as Christians we have died to our old existence and been born again to a new life which involves being part of the one body of Christ (see Romans 6:1-11 and 1 Corinthians 12:12-13). The dependence of each local church on the one body of Christ follows from this truth. Each local church only exists because the Church as a whole, the one body of Christ, exists. It exists as a part of this bigger whole.

Having bishops points to this truth because bishops are consecrated as bishops of the Church as a whole.[433] They may be bishops of the Church of England and have particular responsibility for the life of the Church in a specific diocese, but they are first and foremost bishops of the Catholic Church and when they act as bishops they act as such and

---

[433] This is expressed in the service for the consecration of bishops in the 1662 ordinal by the words 'Receive the Holy Ghost for the office and work of a Bishop in the Church of God.' The office and work to which the new bishop is called is not simply to be bishop of this or that place, but to a bishop of the one Church of God.

by so doing they testify to the fact the local church exists as part of the body of Christ as a whole.

The same point explains the idea that bishops are a 'sign and focus' of the unity of the Church across space and time, an idea which, again, some people find difficult. As bishops of the Catholic Church, consecrated as bishops in succession to bishops who have gone before them, bishops of the Church of England signify, and focus in their person and ministry, the truth that local churches belong to the one body of Christ united across space and time.

However, even if we accept the points just made, four major problems remain with these arguments for episcopacy.

First, as we have seen, the premise behind these arguments is that Anglicans can no longer make a case for episcopacy on the basis that episcopacy goes back to the time of the apostles. However, as we saw at the start of chapter 1, the official stance of the Church of England in the Preface to the Ordinal and in Canon C.1 is that episcopacy does go back to the time of apostles. There is thus a basic unresolved contradiction between what the Church of England officially holds and teaches concerning the origins of episcopacy and the premise on which recent Church of England arguments for episcopacy have been based. The question this raises is where the Church of England actually stands on this matter? Does it accept that the apostolic origins of episcopacy can no longer be defended, or does it still stand by what is said in the Preface to the Ordinal and Canon C.1?

Secondly, the Church of England continues to contend that other churches should adopt the historic episcopate and that any future united Church must likewise have bishops in historic succession. This argument makes sense if it is held that the episcopate is a form of ministry instituted by God through the apostles, but if this claim is abandoned it is difficult to sustain. Church of England writers have made out a good case for episcopacy having both practical and symbolic importance, but what they have not shown is that it is preferable to any other way of providing ministerial oversight, or that it is a form of oversight that should be accepted because it carries God's own authority. God is left out of the picture.

Thirdly, Church of England writers who have abandoned the belief that episcopacy goes back to New Testament times have not addressed the theological issue of why the Church of England (and other churches) should not adhere to the form, or forms, of Church government that are found in the New Testament. If, as writers from a range of Protestant traditions have argued, the pattern we find in the New Testament is a twofold ministry of bishops/presbyters and deacons,[434] or if, as some modern scholars have argued, the New Testament contains a diversity of different patterns of ministry,[435] why is it legitimate for Anglicans to insist on a single pattern of ministry involving bishops?

Fourthly, these arguments fail to engage with the evidence that we have looked at in the previous chapters of this book which shows that there has been an unbroken succession of bishops in the Church stretching all the way back to the appointment of James as first Bishop of Jerusalem in the very earliest period of the Church's existence. They fail to reflect the fact that the key argument for having bishops is that the Church has had bishops from the time on and the reason it has had bishops is that the apostles, acting on behalf of Christ, decided that it should have them.

[434] For example. the confession of faith produced by the Particular Baptists in 1677 (the 'Second London Confession') declares that 'the Officers appointed by Christ to be chosen and set apart by the Church (so called and gathered) for the peculiar Administration of Ordinances, and Execution of Power, or Duty, which he entrusts them with, or calls them to. to be continued to the end of the World are Bishops or Elders and Deacons (Acts 20:17, 28, Philippians 1:1).' Text in William Lumpkin, *Baptist Confessions of Faith* (Valley Forge: Judson Press, 1969), p. 287.
[435] See, for example, James Dunn, *Unity and Diversity in the New Testament* (London: SCM, 1977), Ch.VI.

If we turn to the arguments of Lightfoot and Gore, we find that Lightfoot correctly sees that that the key theological issue is in what circumstances episcopacy first came into existence. He rightly sees that the evidence shows that it goes back both to the time of the apostles and to the action of the apostles and that this points to episcopacy having divine authorisation.

The theological point here is that that Jesus Christ did not simply call his Church into being and then leave it to its own devices. Rather, as we learn from the New Testament (Matthew 28:16-20, Acts 1:1-8), he appointed the Apostles to lead it, endowed them with his Spirit, and gave them authority to establish patterns of belief and behaviour that would be in accordance with God's will and would therefore be binding on future generations of believers. It follows that if the apostles did institute episcopacy then the existence this form of ministry was part of God's will for his Church and needs to be accepted as such.

Where Lightfoot's argument is problematic is that he reduces the involvement of the apostles in establishing episcopacy to the appointment of James as the leader of the church in Jerusalem and to the activity of John and the other surviving apostles in Asia Minor at the end of the first century. This reconstruction of what took place fails to do justice to the evidence from the New Testament and Patristic sources that we looked at in chapters 1-3 that indicates that what would later be called bishops were appointed by a range of apostles in a range of places other than Jerusalem and Asia Minor and before the end of the first century.

Like Lightfoot, Gore rightly argues that the case for episcopacy has to have a historical basis. However, the problem is that he argues for a class of ministers, referred to in the New Testament as 'prophets', 'teachers' and 'evangelists' who exercised a form of apostolic authority and who eventually became the first bishops. This argument is problematic because, as we saw in chapter 1, there is no evidence that this class of ministry ever existed. The evidence that we have tells us that there were prophets, evangelists and teachers, but these terms refer to what people did rather than the office they held and there is no evidence to suggests that their exercise of these roles gave them quasi-apostolic authority or that it was those who exercised these roles who eventually became the first bishops.

Furthermore, the theological argument he puts forward for episcopacy on the basis of his reading of the historical evidence is a weak one. As we have seen, his argument is that the fact that the 'common instinct' instinct of the Church eventually led to episcopacy being 'everywhere adopted' points to it being a 'divine institution almost as plainly as if our Lord had in so many words prescribed this form of church government.' This amounts to saying that what the Church as a whole decides to do must be according to God's will, an argument which ignores the possibility noted in Articles XX and XXI of the *Thirty -Nine Articles* that all churches are capable of error. We cannot equate the statement 'all the early churches adopted episcopacy' with the statement 'and this was according to God's will.' The latter statement needs to be argued for on other grounds and this Gore fails to do.

The arguments put forward by the Anglican defenders of episcopacy in the sixteenth and seventeenth century (and by Puller following their example) have the strengths of the arguments put forward by Lightfoot and Gore, but without their weaknesses.

Like Lightfoot and Gore they correctly see that the argument for episcopacy has to be rooted in the historical evidence for the origin of episcopacy, and like Lightfoot they are correct in seeing the evidence as pointing to episcopacy having been instituted by the apostles and in seeing that this fact gives episcopacy divine authorisation.

Where their account of the evidence is better than both Lightfoot and Gore is that they rightly see the evidence of the New Testament and the Patristic sources as seeing bishops having been created by the apostles in a range of places well before the end of the first century.

In regard to the other points made by these writers, the evidence we have indicates that these first bishops were ministers of word and sacrament who were the successors of the apostles in their roles of ordaining new ministers, governing the churches and exercising the power of the keys.

The very early evidence of *1 Clement* 43-44 also suggests that the threat of rivalry and disorder within the Church may have been at least part of the reason that the apostles found it necessary to introduce bishops (although the evidence of the Pastoral Epistles suggests a broader concern for the existence of godly oversight was also involved).

The argument put forward by Ussher that the new covenant hierarchy of bishops, presbyters and deacons is the equivalent of the hierarchy of the chief of the priests, priests and Levites under the old covenant has support from Paul's words in 1 Corinthians 9:13-14 and from the comparison between the two hierarchies in *1 Clement* 40-44.

Finally, the New Testament and Patristic evidence indicates that from the time of James in Jerusalem bishops were responsible for not just one church, but several, and may have had responsibility not just for a particular city but for a wider geographical area (such as Crete or the Roman provinces in Asia). If this is correct it would mean that the origins of the diocesan and metropolitan systems of church government can be traced back to the early years of the Church.

Do the arguments for episcopacy mean that churches have to have bishops?

What we have seen is that the reason for having bishops is that an episcopal system of church government was introduced by the apostles, who were acting with the authority of God. A church which wants to be faithful to the God given apostolic pattern should therefore have bishops and it would make sense for these bishops to be consecrated in historic succession (as happened at the English Reformation) as a visible sign that these bishops are intended to be in continuity with the bishops who were first appointed by the apostles.

What this does not mean, however, is that churches have to have bishops because a body of people lacking a bishop is not really a church at all. The reason for this is explained by Whitgift who gives two reasons why a particular form of government is not needed for a church to be a church.

First, he says:

...I find no one certain and perfect kind of government prescribed or commanded in the scriptures to the Church of Christ, which no doubt should have been done, if it had been a matter necessary unto the Salvation of the church. [436]

As we have seen, Whitgift did believe that Scripture testifies to the existence of bishops in the early Church. The point he is making, however, is that Scripture nowhere explicitly commands that any particular form of church government must be present in order for a church to be a church.

Secondly, he says:

...the essential notes of the church be these only; the true preaching of the word of God, and the right administration of the sacraments: for, as Master Calvin saith in his book against the anabaptists, 'This honour is meet to be given to the word of God and to his sacraments, that, wheresoever we see the word of God truly preached, and God according to the same truly worshipped, and the sacraments without superstition administered, there we may without all controversy conclude the church of God to be;' and a little after: 'So much we must esteem the word of God and his sacraments, that, wheresoever we find them to be, there we may certainly know the church of God to be, although in the common life of men many faults and errors be found." The same is the opinion of other godly and learned writers, and the judgment of the reformed churches, as appeareth by their confessions So that, notwithstanding government, or some kind of government, may be a part of the church, touching the outward form and perfection of it, yet is it not such a part of the essence and being, but that it may be the church of Christ without this or that kind of government; and

[436] Whitgift, p.184.

therefore the 'kind of government' of the church is not 'necessary unto salvation.'[437]

Here Whitgift is saying, in line not only with Calvin, but also with Article XIX of the *Thirty-Nine Articles*, that there are two 'essential' notes of the church, the true preaching of the word and the right administration of the sacraments and from this it follows that a church that has these two notes is a church, regardless of the kind of government it has.

What Whitgift writes in these two quotations was originally a response to the Puritan claim that it was necessary for a church to have Presbyterian form of church government. However, while what he says applies to that original claim. it also applies to the claim that it is necessary for a church to have an episcopal form of church government and this view of the matter was the reason why Anglicans in the sixteenth and seventeenth centuries felt able to acknowledge foreign Lutheran and Reformed church without bishops as being true churches and why Anglicans in more recent times have been able to recognise non-episcopal bodies as true churches in the context of the ecumenical movement.

To summarise, the apostolic origin of episcopacy means that bishops in historic succession are an important part of the 'outward form and perfection' of the Church, but having bishops is not a benchmark by which it can be decided whether or not a particular group of people is a church at all.

---

[437] Whitgift, p.184.

Part II

The role and character of bishops

Chapter 7
What the New Testament tells us about the role and character of bishops

What is in Part II

In the first part of this book, we have seen that the reason why it is right for the Church of England (and other churches) to have bishops is because the evidence tells us that the existence of the episcopal system of church government can be traced back to the fact that the apostles, acting with the authority of God, instituted the first bishops in New Testament times. Having bishops is thus an important way (although not the only way) of maintaining apostolic faith and practice in the life of the Church today.

In the next five chapters of this book we shall go on to examine in more detail at the *role* of bishops (the functions they are called by God to perform within the life of the Church) and the *character* of bishops (what sort of people they need to be to carry out these functions).

In these chapters we shall look in turn at what we learn about this subject from the New Testament, from the writers of the Patristic period, and from Church of England writers in the sixteenth and seventeenth centuries. We shall also look at what the modern Church of England has to say about the bishop's role and character.

In chapter nine we shall look specifically at the teaching of the Patristic period about the specific role of the Bishop of Rome, both in order to give a complete account of the Patristic teaching about the role of bishops, and in order to provide the background to what the English Reformers had to say about this topic and what the Church of England has said about it in more recent times.

The role of bishops in the New Testament

a. Bishop as Christians

As Augustine notes, a bishop is first and foremost a Christian. In his words, in a sermon on the anniversary of his ordination as a bishop: 'For you I am a bishop, with you, after all, I am a Christian.'[438] This means that a bishop shares in the roles of disciple making and witness given to the apostles, as representatives of all other Christians, in Matthew 28:18-20 and Acts 1:8.

In Matthew 28:18-20 we read:

And Jesus came and said to them, 'All authority in heaven and on earth has been given to me. Go therefore and make disciples of all nations, baptizing them in the name of the Father and of the Son and of the Holy Spirit, teaching them to observe all that I have commanded you; and lo, I am with you always, to the close of the age.'

As Peter Leithart observes in his commentary on Matthew, these words are a deliberate echo of the words of the Persian Emperor Cyrus in 2 Chronicles 36:23 which come at the end of the Hebrew Old Testament. In 2 Chronicles 36 Cyrus is given authority by the God of Israel to re-build the house of God – the ruined Temple in Jerusalem. In Matthew Jesus speaks with even greater authority than Cyrus and commands his followers to build a new house for God, a spiritual house consisting of people from all nations.

To quote Leithart:

Israel never existed for herself, but for the sake of the nations. Now that Jesus has risen and issues this command as a new Cyrus, that reality is even more pronounced. Even more than Israel, the church exists for the sake of the world. Jesus did not come to be served but to

---

[438] Augustine, Sermon 340, in Edmund Hill, *Augustine, Sermons III/9 (306-340A) on the Saints* (Hyde Park: New City Press, 1994), p.292.

serve. He came to make disciples, and by his resurrection he gives us the privilege of sharing in making disciples of the nations.

No church exists for the sake of church. We are called together to be sent out, called together so that we can be commissioned to fill our towns with disciples, and to participate in the making of disciples throughout the world. We can have the best worship imaginable, the best teaching, the deepest fellowship. All these are good things, but if we do not go and make disciples, then we are failing to be the church God wants us to be. [439]

As Christians, bishops are called to play their part in the fulfilment of the Church's calling to make disciples, both locally and throughout the world.

In Acts 1:8 we read that Jesus told the apostles:

'But you shall receive power when the Holy Spirit has come upon you; and you shall be my witnesses in Jerusalem and in all Judea and Samaria and to the end of the earth.'

As Tom Wright notes in his commentary on Acts, what this call to witness involves is the worldwide proclamation in word and deed of the fact that Jesus has been exalted to the right hand of the Father to rule as the world's true king to whom all the nations need to submit. In his words:

'My witnesses'? What does that mean? Quite simply this: in the resurrection (and the ascension which is about to happen), Jesus is being enthroned as Israel's Messiah and therefore the king of the whole world. He is the one at whose name every knee shall bow, as Paul puts it in Philippians 2:10. In the word of the first century, when someone was enthroned as king, that new authority would take effect through heralds going off throughout the territory in question with the news, 'We have a king!'...The apostles are to go out as heralds, not

---

[439] Peter Leithart, *The Gospel of Matthew Through New Eyes – Volume Two Jesus as Israel* (West Monroe: Athanasius Press, 2018), Kindle edition, p.300.

of someone who may become king at some point in the future, bit of the one who has *already* been appointed and enthroned. [440]

As Christians, bishops are called to act as the heralds of the universal kingship of Jesus Christ.

b. Bishop as elders

As we saw in chapter 4, since the second century the Christian tradition has felt happy to refer to bishops as elders/presbyters because, while bishops have oversight over other elders, they are nevertheless themselves elders in the sense of being part of the collective senior leadership of the Christian Church. As we saw in chapter 1, the apostles Peter and John also describe themselves as 'elders' for similar reasons. To put it another way, the Church has recognised that while not all elders are bishops, all bishops are elders.

This being the case, it follows that what is said in the New Testament about the role of elders also applies to bishops.

As we saw in chapter 1, in the New Testament the two primary roles of the elders were to rule and instruct the churches, with the latter role becoming more important as time went on and the apostles themselves were not necessarily available to exercise teaching ministry in a particular church. In addition, we know from the letter of James (5:14-15) that elders were involved in prayer for healing and it also seems likely that, as the rulers of the churches they were involved in implementing the pastoral discipline called for in passages such as Matthew 18:15-20 and 1 Corinthians 5:1-12. Finally, while the New Testament itself is silent about the issue of who presided at the Eucharist, the fact that the elders were the leaders of the churches makes it likely that it was the elders who performed this role in New Testament times and the evidence of 1 Clement 44:4 indicates that this was indeed the case.

[440] Tom Wright, *Acts for Everyone, Part1* (London: SPCK, 2008), pp.8-9.

Because bishops are elders, these multiple roles are theirs as well. As elders, bishops are called to be the rulers and instructors of the churches, to be involved in prayer for healing, to implement pastoral discipline and to preside at the Eucharist.

A key image for the basic role of the elders as the rulers and instructors of the churches is that of the elders as shepherds. As was noted in chapter 1, a key passage in this regard is Acts 20:28-31 in which Paul speaks the following words as he says farewell to the Ephesians elders at Miletus:

Take heed to yourselves and to all the flock, in which the Holy Spirit has made you overseers, to care for the church of God which he obtained with the blood of his own Son. I know that after my departure fierce wolves will come in among you, not sparing the flock; and from among your own selves will arise men speaking perverse things, to draw away the disciples after them. Therefore be alert, remembering that for three years I did not cease night or day to admonish every one with tears.

In this passage the word translated 'care for' in the RSV (*'poimainein'*) literally means to tend or shepherd a flock. God has made the Ephesian elders shepherds in his church. What this role involves is helpfully expounded by Stott. He writes that the essence of the ministry of oversight exercised by bishops as well as other presbyters:

...is pastoral not administrative, because it is concerned with sheep (that is, people) not organization. This is not to deny that some organisation is necessary for proper oversight. It is rather to assert that it is an adjunct to it, a framework for it, but not the essence of it.

If the oversight is pastoral not administrative, its characteristic mark will be service, not authority. Jesus said *exousia* belongs to lords, kings or bosses. Shepherds are called to *diakonia;* they give themselves humbly to the service of the sheep.[441]

Stott then further writes that Acts 20 mentions two forms which this service needs to take.

First, presbyters are to feed the sheep:

It is true that the verb *poimainein* (both here and in 1 Peter 5:2) is a general term for doing the work of a shepherd or tending a flock. But it's special meaning is to lead a flock to pasture, and so feed the sheep. A good shepherd will, as his first priority, lead his flock to good and green pastures, where they may lie down and feed themselves. 'Should not shepherds feed the sheep?' (Ezekiel 34:2).

Is it then an exaggeration to say but the essential nature of episcopal ministry, whether by bishops or by presbyters, lies in the realm of teaching? I think not. It is certainly implied in the qualifications of candidates for the ministry which are given to us in 1 Timothy 3 and Titus 1. The presbyter- bishop must be 'an apt teacher' and be 'able to give instructions in sound doctrine.' Oh for bishops and presbyters who will take seriously this fundamental character of oversight in the Church today! We are called to feed the sheep. We are called to teach.[442]

Secondly, presbyters are to protect the sheep from wolves:

Paul warned the elders of the Ephesian Church that after his departure fierce wolves would come in among them not sparing the flock (v.29). He went on to explain that these wolves, who not only devour some of the sheep but divide and scatter the flock, are false teachers 'speaking perverse things, to draw away the disciples after them' (v. 30).

---

[441] John Stott, 'The New Testament Concept of Episkope,' in *Bishops in the Church* (London: Church Book Room Press, 1966, p.14
[442] Stott, p.14.

Sometimes, as Jesus warned in the Sermon on the Mount (Matthew 7:15), they come in sheep's clothing. In this case the sheep themselves do not notice their arrival until it is too late. But the shepherd has no business to be thus deceived. He should be constantly on the lookout for them. 'Be alert,' Paul said (v.31). The shepherd should be keeping watch over his flock by day, and by night as well, like certain privileged shepherds that we often think about at Christmas. If he is a good shepherd, he will protect the sheep from the ravages of wolves even at personal peril.

All this (being interpreted) means that presbyter-bishops will engage not only in the teaching of the truth, but also in the reputation of error...Both our Lord and his apostles did not shrink when necessary from the task of exposing and overthrowing false teaching...If we sit idly by and do nothing, or if we turn tail and flee, we shall earn for ourselves the terrible epithet 'hirelings,' who care nothing for the sheep. Are we to abandon God's flock to the wolves, as defenceless sheep without a shepherd? Is it to be said of the Church of God today: 'so they were scattered because there was no shepherd: and so they became food for all the wild beasts' (Ezekiel 34:5). [443]

Bishops as elders are thus called to be shepherds who feed the sheep by the teaching of truth and protect the sheep by the refutation of error.

Further teaching about the role of elders as shepherds is given in John 21: 15-17 which reads as follows:

When they had finished breakfast, Jesus said to Simon Peter, 'Simon, son of John, do you love me more than these?' He said to him, 'Yes, Lord; you know that I love you.' He said to him, 'Feed my lambs.' A second time he said to him, 'Simon, son of John, do you love me?' He said to him, 'Yes, Lord; you know that I love you.' He said to him, 'Tend my sheep.' He said to him the third time, 'Simon, son of John, do you love me?' Peter was grieved because he said to him the third time, 'Do

[443] Stott, p.15.

258

you love me?' And he said to him, 'Lord, you know everything; you know that I love you.' Jesus said to him, 'Feed my sheep.'

As the passage makes clear, these words were originally addressed by Jesus to the apostle Peter. However, as Peter himself explain in 1 Peter 5:1-4, elders (and therefore bishops as elders) share his role of being a shepherd of Christ's flock and therefore these words apply to bishops as well.

What we learn from these words is that caring for Christ's flock involves three different types of activity. In the words of William Temple:

...the commissions follow an ascending scale: *Feed my lambs - Tend my sheep - Feed my sheep*. The change of expression shows that some change of meaning is intended. *Feed my lambs*: the first charges to supply the needs of the young of the flock - a task of infinite responsibility, but not as spiritual work is reckoned, conspicuously difficult, for the lambs are ready to accept the sustenance offered to them. *Tend my sheep*: the second charge is to exercise general guidance of the flock, including its mature members, a task for one of greater experience than the first. *Feed my sheep*: the third charge is the hardest to supply the needs of the mature members of the flock; for it is less easy to discern their needs than those the 'lambs,' and they often have no knowledge of what their needs are or, still worse, suppose that they know when in fact they do not.[444]

Bishops as elders are thus called to a shepherding role that involves not only providing general spiritual guidance for the flock of Christ as a whole, but also providing teaching that meets the specific spiritual needs of both young Christians, and also those who have been Christians for some time. To use a familiar image they need to provide milk for those who are babes in Christ and solid food for those who are more mature.

[444] William Temple, *Readings in St. John's Gospel* (London: Macmillan, 1947), p.407.

It is as they perform this role that bishops acting as 'pastors and teachers' build up the body of Christ in the way described by Paul in Ephesians 4:11-16:

And his [God's] gifts were that some should be apostles, some prophets, some evangelists, some pastors and teachers, to equip the saints for the work of ministry, for building up the body of Christ, until we all attain to the unity of the faith and of the knowledge of the Son of God, to mature manhood, to the measure of the stature of the fulness of Christ; so that we may no longer be children, tossed to and fro and carried about with every wind of doctrine, by the cunning of men, by their craftiness in deceitful wiles. Rather, speaking the truth in love, we are to grow up in every way into him who is the head, into Christ, from whom the whole body, joined and knit together by every joint with which it is supplied, when each part is working properly, makes bodily growth and upbuilds itself in love.

If we ask where bishop as shepherds find the spiritual food that the sheep need at the different stages of their spiritual growth and that makes possible the growth of the Church as a whole, the answer is given in Acts 20: 24 where Paul tells the Ephesians elders that the ministry that he received from Jesus was 'to testify to the gospel of the grace of God.' It is the same gospel ('the word of his grace' v.32) that the elders are to use as the basis for their own ministries.

If we ask further about the content of the 'gospel of the grace of God' the answer is that its content is the multi-dimensional good news, to which the New Testament bears inspired witness, that the one true creator God, who is Father, Son and Holy Spirit, has fulfilled his purpose for creation, and his promises to the people of Israel recorded in the Old Testament, by his actions in the person of Jesus Christ.

As I have explained in my previous book *The Gospel and the Anglican Tradition*:

The gospel is about God coming in person in Jesus Christ to put the world to rights by restoring a right relationship between humanity and God.

The gospel is about Jesus, as the promised seed of Eve, reversing the disobedience of Adam through his perfect obedience and overthrowing the dominion of Satan over the world which Adam's sin had introduced.

The gospel is about Jesus, as the promised offspring of Abraham, bringing God's blessing to all nations by creating a new people of God drawn from all races and classes and from both sexes consisting of those who are rightly related to God through faith in Jesus and who have received through their baptism the Spirit of adoption who enables them to call God their Father.

The gospel is about Jesus calling his Church into being to fulfil the vocation to be a holy and priestly nation given to Israel at the Exodus by witnessing to the world about God through word and deed and by offering to God the spiritual sacrifices he desires.

The gospel is about Jesus, as the descendant of David, being the shepherd king who lays down his life for his people and who, being raised to the throne of God in heaven, rules over the nations on behalf of God the Father.

The gospel is about Jesus bringing people from all nations into the new Jerusalem, restoring paradise, establishing universal peace and abolishing death for ever.

The gospel is about Jesus establishing a new covenant through his death by means of which believers are set free from sin and death through the work of Christ and are enabled to fulfil the requirements of God's law in the power of the Spirit.

The gospel is about Jesus, as the suffering servant and the Son of Man, bearing the punishment for human sin in his death on the cross so that his people can be set free from sin and death, and being exalted by God in order to make God's true identity known to all the world.

Finally, the end result of all this, as depicted in Revelation 21 and 22, is the fulfilment of God's original intention for his creation – God's people drawn from all nations, living under God's rule in God's place, the holy city in the new creation which is also Eden restored. [445]

As shepherds, the calling of bishops is to feed the flock by helping people to understand and believe this good news and to live in accordance with it, and to guard the flock by protecting it from the influence of all forms of belief and behaviour that are contrary to it. For example, this means helping people to believe in the world to come and to live now in the light of this belief, and protecting people from the idea that this world is all there is and so what matters is what makes them happy in the here and now.

In addition, the calling of bishops as shepherds, is also to recover those members of the flock who have gone astray (become 'apostate') by adopting forms of belief and behaviour contrary to the gospel. We can see this in Matthew 18:12-14 where Jesus declares:

What do you think? If a man has a hundred sheep, and one of them has gone astray, does he not leave the ninety-nine on the mountains and go in search of the one that went astray? And if he finds it, truly, I say to you, he rejoices over it more than over the ninety-nine that never went astray. So it is not the will of my Father who is in heaven that one of these little ones should perish.

As Joachim Jeremias notes, in Matthew these words are addressed to the leaders of the Church, and relate to the instructions about church discipline that follow in verses 15-17, and their meaning is that church leaders, among them bishops, 'should go after your apostate brother as persistently as the shepherd of the parable seeks the lost sheep.' It is a call 'to exercise faithful pastorship towards apostates.'[446]

[445] Martin Davie, *The Gospel and the Anglican Tradition* (Malton: Gilead Books, 2018), pp.97-98.
[446] Joachim Jeremias, *The Parables of Jesus* (London: SCM, 1994), p.40.

c.   Bishops as bishops

Thus far in this chapter we have looked at what the New Testament has to say about the role of bishops as Christians and as elders. In this next section we shall look at what the New Testament tells us, both positively and negatively, about bishops acting as bishops.

To do this we shall look in turn at what the New Testament has to tell us about the episcopal ministries of James, Timothy, Titus and the bishops of the seven churches in Revelation.

The role of James as the first bishop of Jerusalem

As we saw in chapter 2, what we learn from the New Testament and the witness of later Christian writers such as Papias, Hegesippus, and Eusebius of Caesarea is that James was the first bishop of the church in Jerusalem. We know that in that role he exercised episcopal oversight over the elders of the church and that he also provided episcopal leadership for Jewish Christian communities elsewhere in the Roman Empire.

We are now going to look at in more detail at what his exercise of the episcopal role involved. In order to do this, we shall look in turn at the letter of James, Acts and Galatians.

The letter of James

As David Scaer explains in his book *James the Apostle of Faith*, it seems likely that the letter of James is the earliest of the New Testament writings, having been written 'shortly after the persecution recorded in Acts 8 and before the preaching of Peter to Cornelius in Acts 10 and the council of Jerusalem in Acts 15.' [447] This would give a date for the letter sometime between 34 and 40 AD.

The reason for this dating is twofold. First, in James 1:1 the letter is addressed to 'the twelve tribes of the dispersion' and what makes best

---

[447] David Scaer, *James the Apostle of Faith* (Eugene, Wipf and Stock, 1994), p.29. For a detailed argument for an early date for James see Joseph Mayor, *The Epistle of St. James*, 2ed, London: Macmillan, 1897), Ch. VII.

sense of these words is if they are written to: 'the first refugees of the first persecution of Christians from the city of Jerusalem (Acts 8:1) who have fled from the mother church in Jerusalem to the relative security and safety of the Judaean and Samaritan hill country.'[448] Secondly, there is no indication in the letter: '...that these Jewish Christians, forced to flee from Jerusalem had yet been faced with the Gentile problem. The setting aside of Jewish ritual regulations had not yet surfaced as it would later at the Council of Jerusalem (Acts 15:19-20). Though Hellenized Jews were included in the church, Gentiles were not.' [449]

As well as being addressed generally to these early Jewish Christian refugees the letter is also written specifically to the 'brethren' (1:2, 16, 19, 2:1, 14, 3:1, 4:11, 5.7. 9, 10, 19). In the context in James this term makes most sense if the term is used in the same way as in Acts 12:17 and 15:23, namely as a reference to the elders of the churches formed by the refugees from Jerusalem. These churches developed out of the original church in Jerusalem and so their elders would be regarded as elders of that church for whom James, as the bishop of that church, had continuing episcopal responsibility. To use later terminology, the letter of James is the first example of an *Ad Clerum*, an address from a bishop giving guidance to the clergy.

Working through the letter, we can see that he addresses a range of issues:

- Elders who are facing trials and temptations (1:2-18)

- Elders who engage in judgemental preaching (1:19-21, 3:1-12)

- Elders who are not putting their faith into practice (1:22-27, 2:14-26)

- Elders who are favouring the rich members of the church over those who are poor (2:1-13)

[448] Scaer, p. 28.
[449] Scaer, p. 29.

- Elders who are motivated by jealousy and selfish ambition rather than guided by the wisdom of God (3:13-4:10)

- Elders who speak evil of other elders (4:11-12)

- Elders who have difficulty with patience (5:7-11)

- Elders with depression, euphoria and sickness (5:13-18)

- Elders who have fallen into doctrinal error (5:19-20)

In addition, he is also facing both Elders and other members of the churches who behave in a way that fails to recognise that it is God who is in control of what will take place (4:13-16, 5:12) and people outside the Church who have rejected the Christian faith because of their love for their wealth (5:1-6).

What do we learn about James' role as a bishop from the way he addresses these issues in his letter?

First, James addresses them as one who is 'a servant of God and of the Lord Jesus Christ' (1:1). He does not call himself an apostle or the brother of the Lord, but simply 'servant,' a term which has a double significance. First, it indicates that rather than speaking and acting on his own authority, James is acting under the authority of 'God and of the Lord Jesus Christ.' Secondly, it indicates that James has been called by God not to lord it over the churches, but to serve them. He has been called to serve God by serving God's people.

Secondly, James' role as bishop involves knowing what it going on the churches for which he has responsibility. He is aware of the issues in these churches that need addressing and therefore he is able to address them. He is a shepherd who knows his flock.

Thirdly, as their bishop James has a particular concern for the problems and the conduct of his fellow elders, who are, as we have noted, the people he mostly addresses. If we ask why he has this concern, the answer is that he cares for them, but also because if they fail to perform their role properly this will not only put them in danger of the judgement of God, but will also harm other members of the churches concerned.

Fourthly, James addresses the issues he covers in his letter on the basis of the teaching of the Old Testament and his knowledge of the teaching and actions of Jesus Christ. These are his two sources of theological authority. Although James never specifically quotes the teaching of Jesus, there are numerous parallels between what James teaches and the words of Jesus as recorded in the Synoptic Gospels (particularly the teaching of Jesus in the Sermon on the Mount) and also the key theological ideas found in the fourth Gospel.[450]

Likewise, although James never refers explicitly to the events of Jesus' life and ministry, these form the theological undergirding for what James writes. For example, Scaer notes that underlying what James writes about the exaltation of the lowly and the humiliation of the rich in 1:9-11 is a:

...well-formulated Christology. Jesus was the One who humbled Himself by crucifixion so that God could exalt Him by resurrection. His humiliation becomes model and motivation, especially for the rich in the congregation. The words, 'Let...the rich [boast] in his humiliation' silhouette the humiliation of Jesus. Paul uses the same theme in describing Christ's humiliation: 'Though He [Jesus] was rich, yet for your sake He became poor, so that by His poverty you might become rich (2 Corinthians 8:9). James' urging the poor to boast in his exaltation and the rich in his humiliation takes its formative shape against a Christology made more explicit by Paul, but implicitly present in his own writing.[451]

Fifthly, on the basis of his twin sources of theological authority James has a coherent overall theological message, which is in agreement with the teaching of the Old Testament and the subsequent witness of the other New Testament writings, and which underlies his response

[450] For the evidence for this point see Mayor. pp LXXXIV-LXXXVII.
[451] Scaer, pp.48-49.

to the issues present in the churches to which he is writing. A useful summary of this message is given by Joseph Mayor as follows:

Man was created in the image of God (3:9), the All-Good (1:13, 17); but he has fallen into sin by yielding to his lower impulses against his sense of right (1: 14, 15, 4: 1-3, 17); and the natural consequence of sin is death, bodily and spiritual (1:15, 5: 3, 5, 20). Not only is man liable to sin; but as a matter of fact we all sin, and that frequently (3:2). God of His free bounty has provided a means by which we might conquer sin and rise to a new life, in His word sown in our hearts[452] ...Our salvation depends on the way in which we receive the word (1:21). If we have a steadfast faith in God's goodness as revealed to us through our Lord Jesus Christ (1: 13, 2:1, 5-7); if we read, mark, learn, and inwardly digest the word, so as to make it the guiding principle of our life, the law of liberty by which all our words and actions are regulated (1:25, 2:12), then our souls are saved from death, we are made inheritors of the kingdom promised to those that love God (1:12, 25, 2:5).

But the training by which we are prepared for this crown of life is not pleasant to the natural man. It involves trial and endurance (1: 2-4, 12): it involves constant watchfulness and self-control, and prayer for heavenly wisdom, in order that we may resist the temptations of the world, the flesh and the devil (1:26, 3:2-8, 15, 4:1-5). Thus faith is exercised; we are enabled to see things as God sees them (2: 1, 5); to rise above the temporal to the eternal (1: 9-11); to be not simply patient, but to rejoice in affliction (1:2, 5:7, 8, 10, 11), and exult in the hope set before us (1:9-12); until at last we grow up to the full stature of a Christian (1:4, 3:2), wise with that wisdom which comes from above, the wisdom which is steadfast, unpretending, gentle, considerate, affectionate, full of mercy and good fruits, the parent of righteousness and peace (3:17, 18).

But there are many who choose the friendship of the world instead of the friendship of God, so vexing His Holy Spirit, and yielding

---

[452] The 'word' here means the gospel.

themselves to the power of the devil; yet even then He does not leave them to themselves, but gives more grace. He hedges in their way in the present, and warns them of further judgment to come (4:4-6, 5:1-8). If they humble themselves under His hand and repent truly of their sins, He will lift them up; if they draw nigh to Him, He will draw nigh to them (4.:7-10). Here, too, we may be helpful to one another by mutual confession, and by prayer for one another. Great is the power of prayer prompted by the Spirit of God (5: 15-20). [453]

Acts
Turning to what we learn from Acts, as we noted in chapter 1 and 2, in Acts 12:17, following his miraculous release from prison, Peter tells those present in the house of Mary that they are to report what has happened 'to James and to the brethren.' As we have seen, the 'brethren' here are the elders of the Jerusalem church and James is the person who exercises episcopal authority over them and over the church as a whole.

James is mentioned separately because as the bishop he needs to know about what has happened so he can guide the elders and the church as whole in their response to the new situation. James the brother of John has been killed by kind Herod Agrippa (Acts 12:2) and although Peter has escaped from prison he too is still wanted by Herod and so will need to disappear to 'another place' (probably Rome) [454] and so James will need to take on the mantle of responsibility for leading the church in Jerusalem on his own without Peter's support. The buck stops with him.

We can see him exercising this responsibility at the Council of Jerusalem. As we noted in chapter 2, as the bishop of Jerusalem James gives the decisive verdict ('my judgement' Acts 15:19) on how the

[453] Mayor, pp.CX-CXI. For other helpful studies on James' theology see Scaer, James Anderson, *The Epistle of James* (Grand Rapids: Eerdmans, 1976) and Peter Davids, *Commentary on James* (Grand Rapids: Eerdmans, 1982)
[454] For a defence of the traditional view that Peter went to Rome at this point see George Edmundson, *The Church in Rome in the First Century* (London: Longmans, 1913).

issue of Gentile inclusion into the Church should be resolved and he also seems to have framed the letter which was sent out to communicate the Council's decision.

What is important to note for our purposes is that addresses the issue of Gentile inclusion in the same way that he addresses the issues covered in his earlier letter to the leaders of the dispersed Jewish Christian communities. He looks at this new issue, like those earlier issues, within a theological framework which brings together the Old Testament and the gospel and then draws a practical conclusion with regard to behaviour.

The substantive issue under discussion at the Council of Jerusalem was whether Gentile converts to Christianity needed to be circumcised and keep the law of Moses in its entirety (Acts 15:1-4). To put it another way, the question was whether Gentiles Christians needed to cease to be Gentiles and become Jewish in order to be saved.

According to the account in Acts James' decisive answer to this question was as follows:

After they finished speaking, James replied, 'Brethren, listen to me. Simeon has related how God first visited the Gentiles, to take out of them a people for his name. And with this the words of the prophets agree, as it is written,

'After this I will return, and I will rebuild the dwelling of David, which has fallen; I will rebuild its ruins, and I will set it up, that the rest of men may seek the Lord, and all the Gentiles who are called by my name, says the Lord, who has made these things known from of old.'

Therefore my judgment is that we should not trouble those of the Gentiles who turn to God, but should write to them to abstain from the pollutions of idols and from unchastity and from what is strangled and from blood. For from early generations Moses has had in every city those who preach him, for he is read every sabbath in the synagogues.' (Acts 15:13-21)

This answer consists of three parts. First there is the testimony of Peter ('Simeon'). Then there is the quotation from Amos 9:11-12. Finally. there is a practical conclusion based on interpreting Peter's testimony in the light of the words of Amos.

How does James reach this conclusion on the basis of the first two parts of his answer? The answer lies in the reference in the first part of the quotation from Amos to God rebuilding 'the dwelling of David, which has fallen.' In these words the 'dwelling of David' is a reference to the Davidic dynasty which had come to an end when the kingdom of Judah was destroyed by the Babylonians in the sixth century BC.

What James is saying is that Amos had prophesied that a day would come when:

...vast numbers of Gentiles would turn to the Lord and become 'his people.' 'Gentiles on whom his name was called; 'and that this would take place when David's royal line was restored – that is, by the birth of Jesus the Messiah in David's city, and more particularly by his resurrection from the dead (see also Acts 2:25-31, 2 Timothy 2:8).[455]

The testimony of Peter shows that following on from Jesus' resurrection Gentiles have indeed begun to turn to the Lord in accordance with Amos' prophecy. However, what was prophesied was that they would become God's people precisely as Gentiles and therefore, says James it would not be right to 'trouble' them by insisting that they should become Jews.

The further question then arises about what rules should govern the behaviour of these Gentiles if they were not to be subject to the Mosaic law in its entirety? As we have seen, James' judgement, which is then reflected in the letter sent out from the Council, is that Gentile Christians should be asked to abstain from four things: 'the pollutions of idols and from unchastity and from what is strangled and from blood.' What links these four prohibitions is that they are all things

---

[455] Gooding p.236.

that are forbidden to 'the stranger who sojourns among you' in the Book of Leviticus. (Leviticus 17:8, 10, 13, 15, 18:26). The point James is making is that just as there were forms of behaviour that were off limits for all who dwelt in Old Testament Israel (whether they were Israelites or resident aliens) so, analogously there are forms of behaviour which are still off limits to all who belong to the Church, the new Israel (whether they are Jews or Gentiles). [456]

When understood in this way what James offers is a theologically coherent and biblically based justification for accepting Gentiles into the Church as Gentiles while at the same time placing appropriate limits on their behaviour as part of God's new covenant people.

If we move on to Acts 21:17-26 we find an account of how Paul and his companions went to meet with James as the bishop of the church in Jerusalem together with the other elders of that church. The account is as follows:

When we had come to Jerusalem, the brethren received us gladly. On the following day Paul went in with us to James; and all the elders were present. After greeting them, he related one by one the things that God had done among the Gentiles through his ministry. And when they heard it, they glorified God. And they said to him, 'You see, brother, how many thousands there are among the Jews of those who have believed; they are all zealous for the law, and they have been told about you that you teach all the Jews who are among the Gentiles to forsake Moses, telling them not to circumcise their children or observe the customs. What then is to be done? They will certainly hear that you have come. Do therefore what we tell you. We have four men who are under a vow; take these men and purify yourself along with them and pay their expenses, so that they may shave their heads. Thus all will know that there is nothing in what they have been told about you but that you yourself live in observance of the law. But as for the Gentiles

[456] See Richard Bauckham, 'James and the Gentiles (Acts 15:13-21)' in Ben Witherington III (ed), *History, Literature and Society in the Book of Acts* (Cambridge: CUP, 1996), pp.172-174.

who have believed, we have sent a letter with our judgment that they should abstain from what has been sacrificed to idols and from blood and from what is strangled and from unchastity.' Then Paul took the men, and the next day he purified himself with them and went into the temple, to give notice when the days of purification would be fulfilled and the offering presented for every one of them.

What we see here is the Jerusalem elders, led by James, producing the same sort of coherent theological response to a practical issue that we have previously seen in James' letter and in his contribution to the Council of Jerusalem. Paul has an (undeserved) reputation for urging Christian Jews to abandon the law of Moses, and what they suggest as a solution is that he should undertake an action that would show that this was not the case. They are also clear, however, that the decision of the Council of Jerusalem (to which they refer) should govern the behaviour of Gentile converts.

What is proposed shows that Christians are not antinomians (they have not abandoned the law of God), but, for the reasons previously articulated by James in Acts 15, obedience to God's law means something different for Jewish Christians than it does for Christian who are Gentiles.

What is clear from this account is there were still a large number of Jewish Christians who were suspicious of Paul. However, James' leadership at the Council of Jerusalem meant that the elders of the church in Jerusalem, who had been present at the Council, supported Paul's ministry and accepted the theological principle that Gentile Christians could remain Gentiles, but needed to the observe the Levitical law as it applied to the 'stranger who sojourns among you.'

Galatians
Moving on to Galatians, we are told in Galatians 1:19 that when Paul visited Jerusalem three years after his conversion he met with Peter ('Cephas'), but that he 'saw none of the other apostles except James the Lord's brother.'

If we ask why he met with these two people in particular, the most likely answer is that there was a vetting process going on. Peter, as the leading apostle, was checking that Paul's conversion was genuine and James was doing the same as the head of the church in Jerusalem.

That this was so in the case of James is shown by what follows in verses 22-24. He we read:

And I was still not known by sight to the churches of Christ in Judea; they only heard it said, 'He who once persecuted us is now preaching the faith he once tried to destroy.' And they glorified God because of me.

Someone had let the Jewish churches in Judea know that Paul had undergone a genuine conversion, and the most likely person to have told them this is James. We know from his letter that he was in correspondence with these churches as their bishop and it makes sense to think that having vetted Paul he then sent them news of his conversion, both to reassure them that Paul was no longer a threat and to bear witness to what Jesus had done in Paul's life.

If this reconstruction of what happened is correct then what we see is James the bishop caring for his flock by guarding them against possible predators and by informing them about the good news of Paul's conversion.

In Galatians 2:9-10 we are told that when Paul visited Jerusalem again fourteen years later:

...when they perceived the grace that was given to me, James and Cephas and John, who were reputed to be pillars, gave to me and Barnabas the right hand of fellowship, that we should go to the Gentiles and they to the circumcised; only they would have us remember the poor, which very thing I was eager to do.

As we saw in chapter 2, 'pillar' means leading teacher of the faith and James is mentioned first because he was the leading teacher of the church in Jerusalem where the meeting took place. As in Galatians 1:19, what is described in verse 9 is a vetting process, which then leads to a division of ministerial responsibilities. Paul has explained to them his missionary work, 'the gospel which I preach among the Gentiles' (2:2), and they see the grace of God at work in what he is doing and give their endorsement to it.

In verse 10 'the poor' means the Jewish Christians in Jerusalem and Judea. Paul has brought aid to these Christians in the past (Acts 11:29-30) and they urge him, together with Barnabas, to continue to do so in the future. Here we see James (working together with Peter and John) exercising his episcopal role by ensuring that Paul is still 'on message' before endorsing his further missionary activity and by seeking to ensure that Paul and Barnabas continue to provide material support for the Jewish Christians for whom James is responsible.

Timothy

As we saw in chapter 2, Timothy was appointed by Paul to be the bishop of the churches in Ephesus. We learn what that role involved from 1 and 2 Timothy which are the first set of instructions for a bishop in the same way that the letter of James is the first *Ad Clerum*.

I Timothy

In 1 Timothy Paul sets out eight aspects of Timothy's role as the bishop in Ephesus.

First, Timothy is to 'attend to the public reading of scripture, to preaching, to teaching' (4:13). He is to make sure that when the churches meet for worship the Scriptures (the Old Testament writings plus the writings of the apostles and those associated with them) are read out, expounded, and applied. As Dick France explains 'In the absence of personal pocket Bibles (and the ability to read them), this was the primary source of the 'sound teaching' on which the church's health depended.'[457]

Secondly, Timothy is to take action against those who are teaching heresy:

---

[457] Dick France, *Timothy, Titus and Hebrews* (Oxford: BRF, 2001), p,47.

...remain at Ephesus you may charge certain persons not to teach any different doctrine, not to occupy themselves with myths and endless genealogies which promote speculations rather than the divine training that is in faith; whereas the aim of our charge is love that issues from a pure heart and a good conscience and sincere faith. (1:3-5)

There is a continuing debate about the precise nature of the 'different doctrine' that was being taught in Ephesus, but it seems to have been an early form of Gnosticism that combined Jewish, Christian and pagan ideas in a way that departed from the pattern of belief and behaviour taught by Jesus and the apostles.

Thirdly, Timothy is to ensure that worship is conducted properly, with prayers being made for everyone including 'kings and who are in high positions' (2:1-6), with men praying 'without anger or quarreling' (2:8) and with women dressing 'modestly and sensibly in seemly apparel,' having the opportunity to study and learn, but being forbidden to propagate heretical notions that inverted the story of Adam and Eve as recorded in Genesis 2 and 3 and saw childbearing as inimical to salvation (2:9-15)[458]

Fourthly, Timothy is to ensure that suitable people are appointed as bishops (elders) and deacons. In 3:1-13 Paul sets out the qualities that bishops and deacons ought to possess. This only makes sense if Timothy has the responsibility for the appointment of bishops and deacons. That this so is confirmed by Paul's later exhortation to Timothy 'Do not be hasty in the laying on of hands' (5:22).

Fifthly, Timothy is to develop appropriate pastoral relationships with different members of the church family, older and younger men and older younger women (5:1-2).

Sixthly, Timothy is to exercise responsibility for the behaviour and financial support of widows, and for who should be enrolled on the list

[458] For the nature of the heretical ideas referred to in 1 Timothy 2:11-15 see Richard and Catherine Kroeger, *I suffer not a woman* (Grand Rapids: Baker 1992).

of widows (5:3-15). Likewise, he is to make sure the elders receive proper remuneration, are protected against unfounded accusations, and are publicly rebuked if they persist in sin (5:17-21).

Seventhly, Timothy is to make sure that slaves treat their masters with due respect (especially if those masters are Christians) 'so that the name of God and the teaching may not be defamed' (6:1-2). As Kelly explains, 'Paul is painfully aware of the disastrous come-back which would ensue if Christian slaves abused their new-found liberty in Christ to behave insolently towards their masters.'[459]

Eighthly, Timothy is to warn wealthy Christians not to be haughty, to rely on God rather than their wealth and to be generous and 'rich in good deeds' (6:17-19).

2 Timothy

2 Timothy is probably the last letter written by Paul. Paul is in prison in Rome (2:9 and 1:17) and he is facing the prospect of imminent death: 'For I am already on the point of being sacrificed; the time of my departure has come' (4:6). As Stott writes, in this situation the issue that arose was:

Who, then, would do battle for the truth when Paul had laid down his life? This was the question which dominated and vexed his mind as he lay in chains, and which in this letter he addressed himself. Already in his first letter he had pleaded with Timothy to keep safe the deposit: 'O Timothy guard what has been entrusted to you '(1 Timothy 6:20). But since then the situation had worsened. So the apostle's appeal became more urgent. He reminded Timothy that the precious gospel was now committed to him, and that it was now his turn to assume responsibility for it to preach it and teach it, to defend it against attack and against falsification, and to ensure its accurate transmission to the generations yet to come.[460]

---

[459] Kelly, p. 131.
[460] John Stott, *The Message of 2 Timothy* (Leicester: IVP. 1973), p.21.

As we have just seen, in 1 Timothy Paul gives instructions to Timothy about a range of different aspects of his episcopal role in Ephesus. In 2 Timothy, in the light of his coming martyrdom, Paul focuses on a single issue, the need for Timothy to hold on to the orthodox faith, to preach it, and to pass it on to other faithful people so that they can in turn teach it others. In each chapter of the letter Paul returns to this same basic concern. We can see this if we look at the following five quotations, which come from each of the four chapters of the letter.

Follow the pattern of the sound words which you have heard from me, in the faith and love which are in Christ Jesus; guard the truth that has been entrusted to you by the Holy Spirit who dwells within us. (1:13-14)

You then, my son, be strong in the grace that is in Christ Jesus, and what you have heard from me before many witnesses entrust to faithful men who will be able to teach others also. (2:1-2)

Remember Jesus Christ, risen from the dead, descended from David, as preached in my gospel, the gospel for which I am suffering and wearing fetters like a criminal. (2:8-9)

But as for you, continue in what you have learned and have firmly believed, knowing from whom you learned it and how from childhood you have been acquainted with the sacred writings which are able to instruct you for salvation through faith in Christ Jesus. All scripture is inspired by God and profitable for teaching, for reproof, for correction, and for training in righteousness, that the man of God may be complete, equipped for every good work. (3:14-17)

I charge you in the presence of God and of Christ Jesus who is to judge the living and the dead, and by his appearing and his kingdom: preach the word, be urgent in season and out of season, convince, rebuke, and exhort, be unfailing in patience and in teaching. For the time is coming when people will not endure sound teaching, but having itching ears they will accumulate for themselves teachers to suit their own likings, and will turn away from listening to the truth and wander into myths. (4:1-4)

What we learn from these quotations is that Timothy has been entrusted by Paul with a specific understanding of the Christian message (what Paul refers to as 'the pattern of sound words,' 'the truth' and 'my gospel'). This understanding has authority, both because it is the teaching of an apostle, and because it is also taught by the divinely inspired Scriptures of the Old Testament. Timothy's episcopal responsibility is to 'remember,' 'continue in,' and 'guard' this understanding, to unfailingly preach, teach, and apply it on all possible occasions, and to 'entrust it to faithful men who will be able to teach others also.'

Titus

The letter written by Paul to Titus giving instructions about how he is to conduct his episcopal ministry in Crete is similar to 1 Timothy in that, rather than focussing on a single issue in the way that 2 Timothy does, it covers a range of things that Paul wants Titus to do.

First, Paul tells Titus in general terms that he left him in Crete that he 'might amend what was defective' (1:5) In the words of Thomas Oden: 'His mandate was to set in order whatever required attention, straighten out unfinished business, correct whatever had been left unsettled.' [461]

Secondly, among the defects that Titus needs to correct is a lack of elders. Paul tells him to 'appoint elders in every town as I directed you' (1:5). As France comments 'If Paul's visit had been brief, it may have resulted in the founding of churches but not allowed time to set up the structures needed to maintain them. That is what Titus must now look after.' [462]

These elders are to be people of good character who 'hold firm to the sure word as taught' (in other words, know and believe 'the apostolic

---

[461] Thomas Oden, *First and Second Timothy and Titus* (Louisville: John Knox Press, 1989), p.145.
[462] France, p. 92.

faith both in its theological and ethical dimensions'[463]) in order that 'he may be able to give instruction in sound doctrine and also confute those who contradict it' (1:6-9). In Crete as in Ephesus an early form of Gnosticism had taken root (1:10-16, 3:9) and those who Titus appoints as elders must be able to combat it.

Thirdly, Titus is to 'teach what befits sound doctrine' (2:1). To quote Stott:

This compressed phrase indicates that two strands are to be interwoven in Titus' teaching. On the one hand there is 'the sound doctrine,' the definite article once again implying that an identifiable body of teaching is in mind. On the other hand, there are 'the things which fit it,' namely the ethical duties which the sound doctrine demands.[464]

Paul then gives examples of what these ethical duties are that Titus is to teach, setting out what he is to teach older men, older women, young men and young women and finally slaves about what is involved in living 'sober, upright, and godly lives in this world' in response to the grace of God (2:2-13).

In giving such instruction Titus is to 'exhort and reprove with all authority.' He is to 'let no one disregard you.' As someone appointed by Paul to oversee the Cretan churches, he has spiritual authority, and he needs to exercise it.

Fourthly, as part of his task of ethical instruction, Titus is to remind the members of the Cretan churches in general that as those who have been saved by the 'goodness and loving kindness of God our Saviour' they are 'to be obedient, to be ready for any honest work, to speak evil of no one, to avoid quarrelling, to be gentle, and to show perfect courtesy to all men' (3:2-4).

---

[463] France, p.93.
[464] John Stott, *The Message of 1 Timothy and Titus* (Nottingham: Inter-Varsity Press, 1996), Kindle edition, p.185.

Finally, Paul tells Titus that he is to 'avoid stupid controversies, genealogies, dissensions and quarrels over the law for they are unprofitable and futile' (3:9) What this means is that Titus is avoid getting sucked into interminable arguments with the heretics on Crete about their ideas because such arguments simply will not achieve anything. Calvin makes the point well:

...after having given orders to Titus as to the form of doctrine which he should lay down, he now forbids him from wasting time with heretics, because battle would lead to battle and dispute to dispute.[465]

What Titus is to do instead is to exercise pastoral discipline by formally admonishing up to two times those who are dividing the church because of their heretical ideas and then having nothing further to do with them (3:10). Such people have cut themselves off from the Church by what they have done (they are 'self- condemned' 3:11) and their rejection by Titus (and presumably by the Church as whole - see Romans 16:17-18) is a recognition of this fact. Although no mention is made of the handing over of the individuals concerned to Satan (as in 1 Timothy 1:20) what is envisaged is excommunication because it involves formally cutting someone off from being part of the Christian community (see Matthew 18:17, 1 Corinthians 5:1-12).

Revelation
In Revelation we learn of the role of the bishop from two sources. We learn it from the description of the bishops as 'stars' in Revelation 1:16 and 20 and we learn it from what is said to the bishops of the churches of Ephesus, Pergamum and Thyatira in Revelation 2:2,6, 14-16 and 20-21.

[465] John Calvin, *The Complete Bible Commentary Collection of John Calvin*, Kindle edition, Loc. 501465.

The bishops as stars

In Revelation 1:16, as part of John's vision of the risen Christ we are told that Christ 'held seven stars' in his right hand and in 1:20 Christ explains to John that 'the seven stars are the angels of the seven churches.'

As we saw in chapter 2, the angels of the seven churches are the bishops of the seven churches of Asia to whom John writes at the command of Christ in Revelation 2-3. The description of them as 'stars' points us to the key aspects of the role of these bishops. In the words of Leithart:

The angel bishops are stars who shine light into the churches. They are the eyes of the Lord who keep watch over the church and the world. Lamps bring things out of darkness into public view. Lamps are thus associated with surveillance and watching, acts of authority and rule. Christians rule by shining the light of Christ, the light of the gospel, the light of truth into the darkness of the world. Those who are in the dark, and who love darkness, do not want to be exposed, so they fight back. Lights are also eyes, eyes that search but also eyes that judge and discern. The angels of the churches are called to ensure that the lights are burning in the church, to ensure that sin is being scared from the dark corners, ensure that the truth of God is being spoken so that the light can come. The angels of the churches shine the light of authority in order to maintain the health of the bodies that make up the body of Christ. [466]

In summary, as stars bishops are called to bring the light of God to bear by declaring the truth of God and by exposing and judging sin, in order to maintain the spiritual health of the members of the body of Christ. This view of the bishop's role is in line with the role exercised by James as Bishop of Jerusalem and with the instructions given to by Paul to Timothy and Titus as the Bishops of Ephesus and Crete. It is also in line with Paul's injunction to the Ephesian Elders at Miletus to

---

[466] Leithart, *Revelation 1-11*, Loc.3111.

care for (i.e. feed and guard) God's flock in the face of the coming onslaught by wolves who will seek to destroy it.

Christ's words to the Bishops of Ephesus, Pergamum and Thyatira
It is only in the letters to the Bishops of Ephesus, Pergamum and Thyatira that we get references to specific forms of episcopal activity and what all these references have in common is that the bishops in question are either commended or chastised by the risen Christ on the basis of either their attitude to, and action against, particular forms of sin, or their failure to take such action.

In the letter to the Bishop of Ephesus Christ commends the bishop for two things.

First, 'you cannot bear evil men but have tested those who call themselves apostles but are not and have found them to be false' (2:2) and secondly, 'you hate the works of the Nicolaitans which I also hate' (2:6).

The literary structure of Revelation 2:1-7 indicates that verses 2 and 6 refer to the same group of people. The letter is structured as a chiasm in which the end of the letter deliberately reflects its beginning [467] and this means that that the 'evil men' falsely claiming apostolic authority in verse 2 are the same as the 'Nicolaitans' in verse 6.

Verse 6 does not tell us anything more about who the Nicolaitans were or what they taught, although, as we shall see, we learn this from what is said about them in the subsequent letter to the church in Pergamum. What we learn by a comparison of 2:2 and 2:6, however, is that Christ judges them to be evil and hates the works that they perform, and that he commends the bishop for making the same judgement and having the same attitude.

In the letter to the Bishop of Pergamum Christ declares that the bishop needs to repent because 'although you hold fast my name and you did not deny my faith even in the days of Antipas, my witness, my faithful

[467] Leithart, *Revelation 1-11*, Loc.3609.

one, who was killed among you where Satan dwells' (v13), nevertheless:

...I have a few things against you: you have some there who hold the teaching of Balaam, who taught Balak to put a stumbling block before the sons of Israel, that they might eat food sacrificed to idols and practice immorality. So you also have some who hold the teaching of the Nicola'itans (2:14-16)

At first sight it might appear that those 'who hold the teaching of Balaam' and those 'who hold the teaching of the Nicolaitans' were two different groups. However, as Caird comments, in reality 'there were not two types of error in Pergamum, only one: the teaching of Balaam is merely John's opprobrious name for the teaching of the Nicolaitans.'[468]

The reason that the Nicolaitans are described as holding the teaching of Balaam is that according to Numbers 31;16 and Numbers 25:1-9 the pagan prophet Balaam successfully persuaded a large number of Israelite men to engage in sexual immorality with Midianite women and as a result to worship the gods of Midian. In similar fashion the Nicolaitans taught that it was acceptable for Christians 'to join in the idolatrous feasts of their neighbours, and on those occasions, or at other times, to commit fornication.' [469]

At the Council of Jerusalem it had been clearly laid down that all Christians needed to 'abstain from the pollution of idols and from unchastity' (Acts 2:20), but the Nicolaitans were teaching that Christians could fit in with Greco-Roman society by engaging in both. The fault of the bishop in Pergamum was a failure prevent to prevent this teaching taking root in the church there. As a star in the hand of Christ the bishop's role was to expose and judge sin and this the

---

[468] Caird, pp. 38-39.
[469] Thomas Scott, *Commentary on the whole Bible,* vol.III (London: Jordan and Maxwell, 1803) on Revelation 2:14-15.

bishop had failed to do. To put it another way, the bishop had not guarded the flock against the wolves, and hence he needed to repent.

In the letter to the Bishop of Thyatira, Christ issues a similar rebuke to that given to the Bishop of Pergamum:

But I have this against you: you tolerate that woman Jezebel, who calls herself a prophet and is teaching and beguiling my servants to practice fornication and to eat food sacrificed to idols (Revelation 2:19-20).

The name Jezebel that is used here is not the name of the person concerned. Rather, it describes the consequences of her activity. Just as Queen Jezebel led the people of Israel astray by her promotion of the worship of Baal (1 Kings 16:31-32, 18:4, 13, 19:1-4) so the prophetess in Thyatira was leading Christians there astray in similar fashion. In the words of Michael Wilcock:

The sins in the church at Thyatira, like those at Pergamum, are immorality and compromise with idol worship. Here, as there, we may take them literally, though they also constitute the spiritual adultery of which God's people have often been guilty. The biblical metaphor is that the true God is Israel's husband; the false gods are her lovers (Jeremiah; Ezekiel 16; Hosea 2 etc.). Jezebel, like Balaam, was in the Old Testament story an outsider who seduced God's bride into this kind of unfaithfulness (1 Kings 16:31, 2 Kings 9:22). [470]

Wilcock goes on to note, however, that there were differences between the situation in Thyatira and that in Pergamum:

Against beleaguered Christians like those at Pergamum, Satan uses the pressures of the world to 'squeeze' them 'into its own mould' (Romans 12:2 JBP); but where the church is noted for its growth and vigour (verse 19), he knows that he can do most damage not by pressure without but by poison within. So In Thyatira a particular woman takes on both the evil character of Jezebel and the prophetic role of Balaam,

---

[470] Michael Wilcock, *The Message of Revelation* (Leicester: Inter-Varsity Press, 1975), p.49.

and begins to teach, as if from God, new 'deep things' which some members of this new and lively church are only to willing to explore.[471]

In Revelation 2:24 these deep things are described as 'what some call the deep things of Satan.' As Leon Morris explains, this could be a description by those Christians in Thyatira who remained loyal to orthodox apostolic teaching. If this is the case, then it will mean that:

...the heretics have claimed knowledge of 'the deep things of God' in a way which set them apart from lesser mortals. The orthodox are then saying that this 'deep' teaching is not heavenly. It is satanic, and the *depths* the heretics really know are the depths of Satan.[472]

Alternatively, and more probably, this was a claim made by those who propagated the false teaching in Thyatrira. In the words of Trench, this would mean that they held, like some of the later Gnostics, that:

...it was a small thing for a man to despise pleasure and to show himself superior to it, while at the same time he fled from it. The true, the glorious victory was, to remain superior to it even while tasting it to the full; to give the body to all the lusts of the flesh, and yet with all this to maintain the spirit in a region of its own, uninjured by them; and thus, as it were, to fight against pleasure with the arms of pleasure itself; to mock and defy Satan even in his own kingdom and domain.[473]

Whichever interpretation is correct, what is clear is that according to the verdict of Christ this was a form of teaching that led its followers away from God and which rendered them and their prophetess liable to the punishment of the second death which John describes at the end of Revelation (2:22-23).[474] The fact that the Bishop of Thyatira tolerated the existence of his teaching within the church thus represented a very serious failure to exercise his episcopal role. As a

[471] Wilcock, p.50.
[472] Leon Morris, *Revelation* (Leicester: Inter-Varsity Press, 1983), p. 73.
[473] Trench, pp.153-154.
[474] See Leithart, Loc 4407.

star he should have exposed and judged the sin of Jezebel and her followers, but he did not do so.

What we thus see in these three letters is that the Bishop of Ephesus is praised by Christ for his rejection and hatred of the Nicolaitan heresy. By contrast, the Bishop of Pergamum is rebuked and called to repent for allowing this heresy to exist in his Church and the Bishop of Thyatira is likewise rebuked for tolerating the similarly heretical teaching of the prophetess referred to as Jezebel. In these letters, therefore, rejecting heresy and guarding churches against is seen as a key part of the bishop's role.

Summarising what the New Testament has to say about the role of bishops

What we have seen in this chapter is, first of all, that bishops are Christians. This means that, like all other Christians, they are people called by the risen Christ to make disciples, both locally and throughout the world, and to be the heralds of Christ's universal kingship. To put it another way, they are those called to tell people who their true king is and to help them to learn to live rightly as his subjects.

What we have also seen is that bishops are elders. As elders, bishops are called to be the rulers and instructors of the churches teaching their fellow Christians to believe in, and live in accordance with, the gospel of the saving work of God in Jesus Christ, proclaimed prospectively by the writers of the Old Testament and retrospectively by the apostles and those who passed on their teaching. As elders, they are also to follow the example of the apostles by guarding the churches against the 'wolves' who would mislead and divide the faithful, to be involved in prayer for healing, to implement pastoral discipline, and to preside at the Eucharist.

If we ask how the role of bishops is different from that of other elders, the answer is that according to the witness of the New Testament bishops are elders with enhanced responsibilities. They have the ultimate responsibility for the well-being of a group of congregations and in that role, as well as performing the duties common to all other elders, they are responsible for the appointment of elders and deacons, for presiding at meetings of the elders, for instructing their fellow elders and for disciplining them when it is necessary to do so.

To repeat the quotation from Hooker given at the beginning of chapter 2 of this study, according to the evidence of the New Testament a bishop is thus:

...a minister of God, unto whom with permanent continuance there is given not only power of administering Word and Sacrament, which power other Presbyters have, but also a further power to ordain ecclesiastical persons, and a power of chiefty in government over Presbyters as well as Layman, a power to be by way of jurisdiction a Pastor even to Pastors themselves.[475]

The character of bishops

If we ask what sort of people bishops need to be to able to fulfil their role the first answer is that as Christians they need to be people who have repented of their sins, who believe the gospel and who have been baptised. This is because, according to the New Testament, that is what it means to be a Christian.

The second answer is that as elders they need to fulfil the characteristics for elders set out in 1 Timothy 3:1-7 and Titus 1:5-9 (where the word 'bishop' means elder as we have previously noted).

In the first of these passages Paul tells Timothy:

The saying is sure: If anyone aspires to the office of bishop, he desires a noble task. Now a bishop must be above reproach, the husband of one wife, temperate, sensible, dignified, hospitable, an apt teacher, no drunkard, not violent but gentle, not quarrelsome, and no lover of money. He must manage his own household well, keeping his children submissive and respectful in every way; for if a man does not know how to manage his own household, how can he care for God's church? He must not be a recent convert, or he may be puffed up with conceit

---

[475] Hooker Bk. VII.ii.3, p. 334.

and fall into the condemnation of the devil; moreover he must be well thought of by outsiders, or he may fall into reproach and the snare of the devil.

In the second passage Paul tells Titus

This is why I left you in Crete, that you might amend what was defective, and appoint elders in every town as I directed you, if any man is blameless, the husband of one wife, and his children are believers and not open to the charge of being profligate or insubordinate. For a bishop, as God's steward, must be blameless; he must not be arrogant or quick-tempered or a drunkard or violent or greedy for gain, but hospitable, a lover of goodness, master of himself, upright, holy, and self-controlled; he must hold firm to the sure word as taught, so that he may be able to give instruction in sound doctrine and also to confute those who contradict it.

In both of these passages Paul says that an elder must be 'the husband of one wife.' This does not mean that an elder must be married, or that that an elder cannot have married again if widowed. What it does mean is that if an elder is married then they must model in their own life the fact that 'God's long-term plan, intended from the beginning, was for faithful, lifelong partnerships of one man and one woman.'[476] What is therefore ruled out is polygamy, marital unfaithfulness, and same-sex relationships.

As Stott explains, the 'snare of the devil' in 1 Timothy 3:7 is a 'subjective genitive.'[477] That is to say, it refers to a snare set by the devil who seeks to discredit the gospel in the eyes of those outside the Church by drawing attention to the shortcomings of the Church's leaders.

In Titus 1:9 'the sure word as taught' and 'sound doctrine' both refer to the pattern of teaching given by Paul and the other apostles what

---

[476] Tom Wright, *Paul for Everyone, The Pastoral Epistles 1 and 2 Timothy and Titus* (London: SPCK, 2003), p.30.
[477] Stott, *The Message of 1 Timothy and Titus*, p.99.

Colossians 2:7 calls 'the faith as you have been taught it,' what 1 John 2:24 calls 'what you have heard from the beginning' and what Jude 3 calls 'the faith once delivered to the saints.' Holding firm to this teaching means both having a firm grasp of its content and holding tenaciously to it in the face of heresy.

In addition to what we learn from these two passages, we also learn from James 1:1 that bishops need to see themselves as servants accountable to God for their stewardship, and from both the letter of James and Acts 15 that a bishop needs to be someone who can address the issues that arise in the life of the Church in the light of a coherent understanding of the overall biblical message. In addition, we learn from the accounts of James' activity in Acts that bishops are called to work in concert with their fellow elders. James has the chief oversight over the Church in Jerusalem, but he shares the exercise of that oversight with his fellow elders.

In the Pastoral Epistles, as well as what we learn from the two passages already quoted, we also learn that a bishop should be someone who can 'set the believers an example in speech and conduct, in love, faith and purity' (1 Timothy 4:12) and who aims at 'righteousness, godliness, faith, love, steadfastness, gentleness' (1 Timothy 6:11). A bishop must be prepared to 'share in suffering as a good soldier of Jesus Christ' (Timothy 2:3). Finally, a bishop must be someone who is in 'all respects a model of good deeds' and who in their teaching shows 'integrity, gravity, and sound speech that cannot be censured, so that an opponent may be put to shame, having nothing evil to say of us' (Titus 2:7).

If we turn, lastly, to the letters from Christ to the bishops of the churches in Revelation 2 and 3 we find the following characteristics are identified, either explicitly or implicitly:

In the letter to the Bishop of Ephesus we find that the bishop is chided by Christ because 'you have abandoned the love you had at first (Revelation 2:4). The criticism here is that in his zeal for Christian truth and against heresy the bishop has lost the love without which everything else is worthless (see 1 Corinthians 13:1-3). A bishop, then, is called to be a person of love.

In the letter to the Bishop of Smyrna, Christ declares that the bishop needs to be someone who does not 'fear what you are about to suffer' (Revelation 2:10) and who is to be 'faithful unto death' in order to receive 'the crown of life' (Revelation 2:10).

In the letter to the Bishop of Pergamum the bishop of praised for having stood firm and not denied the faith even in the face of a persecution that led to a Christian being martyred (Revelation 2:13).

In the letter to the Bishop of Thyatira Christ praises the bishop for 'your love, faith, and service and patient endurance, and that your latter works exceed the first' (Revelation 2:19). God wants his people to grow in their service of him and is what the bishop is doing.

In the letter to the Bishop of Sardis the Bishop is warned by Christ 'that I have not found your works perfect in the sign of God' (Revelation 3:2). The word translated 'perfect' in the RSV means completed. The bishop has failed to complete the task given to him by God. He has left it unfinished or half done.

In the letter to the Bishop of Philadelphia the bishop is praised by Christ because in the face of persecution 'you have kept my word and not denied my name' (Revelation 3:8).

In the letter to the Bishop of Laodicea the bishop is warned that he has become lukewarm in his service of God. He thinks he is doing well, 'I am rich, I have prospered, and I need nothing,' when in fact he is 'wretched, pitiable, poor, naked and blind' (Revelation 3:16-17). As Trench puts it:

The Laodicean Angel, and the Church which he was drawing into the same ruin with himself, were walking in a vain show and imagination of their own righteousness, their own advances in spiritual insight and knowledge.[478]

In summary, what we learn from the letters to the bishops in Revelation is that bishops are called to be zealous rather than lukewarm, to be loving, to be faithful to the point of death in the face of persecution, to have patient endurance, to be growing in their service of God, to complete the tasks God has given them to do, and to have a realistic sense of their own spiritual weakness. Finally, in the areas where they fall short they are to be people who repent (Revelation 2:5, 16, 19).

In this chapter we have looked at what the New Testament has to tell us about the role of bishops and what sort of people bishops need to be. In the next chapter we shall go on to look at what the writers of the Patristic period have to say about these matters.

---

[478] Trench, p.210.

Chapter 8
The role and character of bishops in the writings of the Patristic period

In the previous chapter we looked at what the New Testament writings teach us about the role and character of bishops. In this chapter we shall look at what we learn about these matters from the writings of the Patristic period and consider whether what is said about them in these writings is in line with the teaching of the New Testament. We shall begin by looking at 1 Clement at the end of the first century and then work forward chronologically until we reach Gregory the Great's Pastoral Rule, which was written at the end of the sixth century.

1 Clement

As we saw in chapters 1 and 2 of this study, reference is made in *1 Clement* 1:3, 21:6 and 44:2-3 to people referred to as 'leaders' and 'reputable men' who are distinct from the elders and deacons and are best seen as bishops. The roles which these bishops exercise, namely leadership and the appointment of other ministers, are exactly the same episcopal roles first exercised by the apostles and then delegated to James in Jerusalem, to Timothy and Titus in Ephesus and Crete and to the angels of the seven churches in Revelation.

As we also saw, in *1 Clement* 40 the bishop, described in Old Testament terms as 'the high priest' also has a distinctive role in the celebration of Holy Communion. The chapter does not give precise details about what this role was, but the distinction between the bishop as 'high priest' the elders as 'priests' and the deacons as 'the Levites' suggests that the bishop played the leading role in the service. This evidence is important because although the New Testament itself is silent about who led the celebration of Holy Communion the evidence of *1 Clement* 40 suggests that at least by the end of the Apostolic period it was led by the bishop and the elders with the assistance of the deacons.

In terms of their character, as we have seen, they are described as people who are 'reputable.' Like the elders who Paul tells Timothy and Titus to appoint they are to be people with a good reputation and as such worthy successors of the apostles and the first bishops appointed by the apostles.

The Letters of Ignatius of Antioch

The bishop's role

As we saw in chapter 3, the seven letters of Ignatius, Bishop of Antioch, to the churches in Ephesus, Magnesia, Tralles, Rome, Philadelphia and Smyrna and to Polycarp, Bishop of Smyrna, were written right at the beginning of the second century.

In order to understand what Ignatius says in these letters about the role of the bishop, we need to begin by noting that God and Jesus Christ are the primary bishops of the Church. In his letter to the church in Magnesia Ignatius refers to 'the Father of Jesus Christ, the bishop of all'[479] and in the salutation to the letter to Polycarp he refers to Polycarp as he who has 'God the Father and the Lord Jesus Christ as his bishop.'[480] At first sight it might appear that there is a tension between these two quotations in that the first sees God the Father as the bishop, whereas in the second Polycarp has both God the Father and the Lord Jesus Christ as his bishop. However, this tension is more apparent than real. As the singular 'bishop' at the end of the second quotation indicates, what Ignatius holds is that the divine oversight of the Church is exercised by God the Father through his Son Jesus Christ.

We can see this same point being made in his letter to the church in Rome in which he asks them to pray for the church in Syria. This church no longer has an earthly bishop since Ignatius has been arrested and is being transported to Rome. However, this church is not therefore without a bishop since it has 'God for its shepherd. Jesus

---

[479] Ignatius of Antioch, *To the Magnesians,* 3:1, in Lightfoot, Harmer and Holmes p. 94.
[480] Ignatius of Antioch, *To Polycarp*, salutation, in Lightfoot, Harmer and Holmes, p.115.

Christ alone will be its bishop.'[481] The bishop is the shepherd of the church, and what Ignatius is saying is that even in his absence the church in Syria will not be shepherd less because God the Father will act as its shepherd through Jesus Christ. There is one divine shepherding/episcopal role which both God the Father and Jesus Christ exercise together.

As Vall explains, in the ecclesiology of Ignatius earthly bishops are the visible representatives of the invisible episcopate exercised by God. In his words, according to Ignatius:

God is the 'invisible' bishop and the επισκοπος is his visible representative, the local church's 'bishop in the flesh.' The bishop 'presides in the place [τοπος] of God' (Magnesians 6:1) and is even 'a type [τυπος] of the Father' (Trallians 3:1). These statements require careful interpretation. The bishop is God's representative but does not replace God or Jesus in the lives of the laity, as if the latter had no intimacy with God of their own. Thus, Ignatius exhorts a fellow bishop 'Let widows not be neglected. After the Lord you are to be their caretaker [φροντιστης]' (Polycarp 4:1). The bishop's ministry is *one* of the ways in which the Lord's love and providence becomes tangibly present in the lives of Christians.[482]

In the letters of Ignatius the bishop acts as the visible representative of God in three ways.

First, the bishop presides over the worship of the church, either in person or through someone to whom he has delegated this role. Thus, he writes in his letter to the church in Smyrna:

Flee from divisions, as the beginning of evils. You must all follow the bishop, as Jesus Christ followed the Father, and follow the presbytery as you would the apostles; respect the deacons as the commandment of God. Let no one do anything that has to do with the church without

---

[481] Ignatius of Antioch, *To the Romans,* 9:1 in Lightfoot, Harmer and Holmes, p.105.
[482] Vall, pp.245-346, italics in the original.

the bishop. Only that Eucharist which is under the authority of the bishop (or whomever he himself designates) is to be considered valid. Wherever the bishop appears, there let the congregation be; just as wherever Jesus Christ is, there is the catholic church. It is not permissible either to baptize or to hold a love feast[483] without the bishop. But whatever he approves is also pleasing to God, in order that everything you do may be trustworthy and valid. [484]

As Vall notes, the key to understanding this passage is the sentence: 'Wherever the bishop appears, there let the congregation be; just as wherever Jesus Christ is, there is the catholic church.' To quote Vall:

The first part of this sentence employs the Greek third-person imperative (εστω) to express a command, while the second part grounds that command in what is taken to be an established fact (albeit expressed in a new way), namely, that the church exists qua church by virtue of the person and event of Jesus Christ. In this context the comparative conjunction ωσπερ ('just as') serves not merely to indicate a comparison but to suggest that the local community's act of congregating for worship ought to imitate the broader and certainly more basic reality of the catholic church's union with Jesus Christ its head. In other words, the 'multitude'[485] ought to act, not simply as a multitude, but as εκκλησια. They are to gather around their 'one bishop' (Philadelphians 4:1), just as the catholic church, in heaven and earth, is united to the 'one Jesus Christ' (Magnesians 7:2).

To put it another way, just as the church is gathered together invisibly through its union with Jesus Christ (and through him with God the Father), so this union needs to visibly represented in the life of the Church by the local church gathering for worship around the bishop (or the person appointed to represent the bishop).

---

[483] The church's communal meal which included the celebration of Holy Communion (see 1 Corinthians 11:17-34).
[484] Ignatius of Antioch, *To the Smyrnaeans*, 8:1-2 in Lightfoot, Harmer and Holmes, pp.112-113.
[485] Vall's preferred translation of 'congregation.'

If we ask why the bishop has this key liturgical role, the answer given by Ignatius is that it is because the bishop has been appointed by God to have the oversight of a particular part of his Church. In Ignatius' words:

...everyone whom the Master of the house sends to manage his own house we must welcome as we would one who sent him. It is obvious, therefore that we must regard the bishop as the Lord himself.' [486]

In his letter to the church in Smyrna Ignatius further declares:

It is good to acknowledge God and the bishop. The one who honours the bishop has been honoured by God; the one who does anything without the bishop's knowledge serves the devil.[487]

In our present-day ecumenical context, these words seem outrageous to the point of insanity. However, we have to see them in their original second century context. In the words of the Orthodox writer Andrew Damick in his study of Ignatius:

...we are dealing with a different context than Ignatius was. In his time the episcopacy was true everywhere. I am not aware of any heretical bishops in his time, so it was literally the case that only with the bishop could a Christian not be a heretic. One could be with the bishop, with the heretics, or with the Jews or pagans, those were the choices.[488]

To put it another way, in Ignatius' context to reject the bishop was necessarily to reject orthodox Christianity and as such to choose to serve the devil. Acknowledging God and acknowledging the bishop went together.

---

[486] Ignatius of Antioch, *To the Ephesians,* 6:1, in Lightfoot, Harmer and Holmes, p. 88.
[487] Ignatius of Antioch, *To the Smyrnaeans*, 8:9 in Lightfoot, Harmer and Holmes, pp.112-113.
[488] Andrew Damick, *Bearing God* (Chesterton: Ancient Faith Publishing, 2017), Kindle edition Loc. 1131.

Secondly, the bishop is to be someone who communicates what Vall calls God's 'mind-set', that is, God's 'eternal counsel or wise plan'[489] made known in Jesus Christ and witnessed to by Scripture and the orthodox teaching of the Church based on Scripture. This means that a bishop has to be someone who 'speaks truthfully about Jesus Christ'[490] and also someone who acts in accordance with that truth. The bishop cannot act just as he wants but only in accordance with the revealed will of God. As Ignatius writes to Polycarp: 'Let nothing be done without your consent, nor do anything yourself without God's consent, as indeed you do not.'[491]

In his letters Ignatius extols the idea of the 'silent bishop.' In his letter to the church in Philadelphia, for example, he declares that their bishop 'accomplishes more through silence than others do by talking'[492] and in his letter to the church in Ephesus he writes 'the more anyone observes the bishop is silent, the more one should fear him'[493]

As Vall notes, these quotations have been used to support the view that 'the episcopal office did not yet involve teaching as an essential responsibility in the early second century' with most bishops being 'administrators responsible for financial matters and the charitable distribution of goods, but not teachers.'[494] However, as he goes on to say:

The sort of 'silence' Ignatius has in mind is not at all the antithesis of 'teaching' but represents rather the authentically Christ-like mode of teaching, that is, with few words and with actions that verify those

---

[489] Vall, p.179.
[490] Ignatius of Antioch, *To the Ephesians,* 6:1, in Lightfoot, Harmer and Holmes, p. 88.
[491] Ignatius of Antioch, *To Polycarp*, 4:1, in Lightfoot, Harmer and Holmes, p. 116.
[492] Ignatius of Antioch, *To the Philadelphians,* 1:1, in Lightfoot, Harmer and Holmes, p. 106.
[493] Ignatius of Antioch, *To the Ephesians,* 6:1, in Lightfoot, Harmer and Holmes, p. 88.
[494] Vall, p.278.

words. Moreover, it is not the case that Ignatius has nothing at all to say about the bishop's responsibility to teach. In the one letter actually addressed to a bishop, he instructs Polycarp to give a 'homily' or 'public lecture' (ομιλια) on a certain subject (*Polycarp* 5:1), employing a term closely related to the verb προσομιλεω ('address with a discourse') which elsewhere refers to Ignatius own didactic discourse to the churches via letters (*Ephesians* 9:2). More tellingly, Ignatius solemnly charges Polycarp to 'exhort all, in order that they may be saved,' and then immediately adds these words: 'vindicate your office' (*Polycarp* 1:2). Moreover, the verb translated 'exhort' in this passage (παρακαλεω) is the same Pauline technical term that Ignatius frequently uses to describe what he himself is doing his letters, which obviously involves imparting the central doctrines of the faith.[495]

The letters of Ignatius illustrate his understanding of what exercising the bishop's teaching role meant in practice. What we find is that, in line with the instructions given by Paul to Timothy and Titus and the assessment by the risen Christ of the activity of the bishops of the seven churches of Asia, this teaching role involved both instructing people in the Christian faith as taught by the apostles and refuting heretical teaching and practice that is contrary to this.

In his letter to the church in Smyrna, for example, he reminds the members of that church of the apostolic teaching regarding the reality of Christ's incarnation, death and resurrection:

I glorify Jesus Christ, the God who made you so wise, for I observed that you are established in an unshakable faith, having been nailed, as it were, to the cross of the Lord Jesus Christ in both body and spirit, and firmly established in love by the blood of Christ, totally convinced with regard to our Lord that he is truly of the family of David with respect to human descent, Son of God with respect to the divine will and power, truly born of the Virgin, baptised by John in order that all righteousness might be fulfilled by him, truly nailed in the flesh for us under Pontius Pilate and Herod the tetrarch (from its fruit we derive

[495] Vall, p.279.

our existence, that is, from his divinely blessed suffering), in order that he might raise a banner for the ages through his resurrection for his Saints and faithful people, whether among Jews or among Gentiles, in the one body of his church.[496]

In the same letter he then goes on to warn the Smyrnaeans against those who are heretical. Thus, in chapter 5 he warns against those who blaspheme against Christ 'by not confessing that he was clothed in flesh' [497] and in chapter 6 he writes:

...note well those who hold heretical opinions about the grace of Jesus Christ which came to us; note how contrary they are to the mind of God. They have no concern for love, none for the widow, none for the orphan, none for the oppressed, none for the prisoner or the one released, none for the hungry or thirsty. They abstain from the Eucharist and prayer, because they refuse to acknowledge that the Eucharist is the flesh of our Saviour Jesus Christ, which suffered for our sins and which the Father by his goodness raised up. [498]

For Ignatius the antidote to such heresy is to: 'pay attention...to the prophets and especially to the gospel, in which the Passion has been made clear to us and the resurrection has been accomplished.'[499] By 'the prophets' Ignatius means what we would call the Old Testament and by 'the gospel' he means the apostolic teaching contained in the writings which we call the New Testament. Debate continues as to precisely which books of the New Testament Ignatius was aware of, but the evidence of his letters suggests that he knew of the Pauline

---

[496] Ignatius of Antioch, *To the Smyrnaeans*, 1:1-2, in Lightfoot, Harmer and Holmes, pp.110.
[497] Ignatius of Antioch, *To the Smyrnaeans*, 5:2, in Lightfoot, Harmer and Holmes, pp.111.
[498] Ignatius of Antioch, *To the Smyrnaeans*, 6:2, in Lightfoot, Harmer and Holmes, pp.112.
[499] Ignatius of Antioch, *To the Smyrnaeans*, 7:2, in Lightfoot, Harmer and Holmes, pp.112.

Epistles and at least some of the other Epistles as well, and that he was acquainted with the Gospels of Matthew, Luke and John. [500]

It is worth noting that the teaching that Ignatius gives is contained in letters written to churches other than his own church in Antioch. What this indicates is that a bishop's teaching role is not confined to their own church, but that bishops can and should provide teaching for other churches as well if what they have to say is applicable to those churches.

Thirdly, Ignatius' letter to Polycarp makes clear that the role of the bishop extends beyond presiding at services and teaching to a general pastoral oversight of all aspects of the life of the church. Thus, Ignatius tells Polycarp that he needs to foster the unity of the church, to minister to individuals, to bring those who are troublesome to a better mind through gentleness, to make sure the widows are not neglected, to hold church meetings more regularly, to exhort slaves to serve their masters faithfully, to instruct husbands and wives to live appropriately in their marriages, and those who are celibate not to be boastful, and finally to give consent to the marriage of members of the church ('that the marriage may be in accordance with the Lord and not due to lustful passions'). [501]

The characteristics bishops should have
Although, the letters of Ignatius do not contain any extended teaching about the characteristics bishops should have, his views about the matter can be seen in a number of places in these letters.

---

[500] Michael Kruger, *Canon Revisited* (Wheaton: Crossway, 2012), Kindle edition Loc. 6020-6055.
[501] Ignatius of Antioch, *To Polycarp*, 1-5, in Lightfoot, Harmer and Holmes, pp.115-117.

First, Ignatius holds that a bishop should have obtained his office 'not by his own efforts nor through men or out of vanity, but in the love of God the Father and the Lord Jesus Christ.' [502]

Secondly, a bishop should be a person of prayer who Is growing in their Christian faith,[503]someone who is loving[504], forbearing, steadfast and gentle, and someone who is silent in the sense previously described. [505]

Thirdly, a bishop should be willing to be a martyr. This is a particular theme in Ignatius' letter to the church in Rome in which writes:

Neither the ends of the earth nor the kingdoms of this age are of any use to me. It is better to for me to die for Jesus Christ than to rule over the ends of the earth. Him I seek, who died on our behalf; him I long for, who whose again for our sake. The pains of birth are upon me. Bear with me brothers: do not keep me from living, do not desire my death.[506]

The paradox here is that death is the gate to new life, whereas the to go on living by evading God's call to martyrdom would be the path to spiritual death. For Ignatius, martyrdom is seen as the completion of the spiritual journey and is the most perfect witness that a Christian can bear to the truth of Christ's own suffering and death.[507]

[502] Ignatius of Antioch, *To the Philadelphians*, 1:1, in Lightfoot, Harmer and Holmes, pp.106.
[503] Ignatius of Antioch, *To the Ephesians* 3:1 and *To Polycarp*, 1:3, in Lightfoot, Harmer and Holmes, pp.87 and 107.
[504] Ignatius of Antioch, *To the Ephesians*, 1:3, in Lightfoot, Harmer and Holmes, p.86.
[505] Ignatius of Antioch, *To the Philadelphians,* 1:1-2, in Lightfoot, Harmer and Holmes, pp.106.
[506] Ignatius of Antioch, *Letter to the Romans* 6:1-2, in Lightfoot, Harmer and Holmes. p, 104.
[507] For Ignatius' understanding of martyrdom see Damick ch.1 and Vall pp.140-158.

Polycarp of Smyrna

Polycarp as teacher

Like the letters of Ignatius, the letter of Polycarp to the Church in Philippi is addressed to a church other than his own, indicating once again the calling of a bishop to be a teacher to the Church as a whole.

In this letter Polycarp fulfils the bishop's teaching role by explaining in general terms what it means for Christians to live before God 'in a manner which is worthy of his commandment and glory.'[508] He also gives specific instructions about the dangers of money, about the responsibilities of Christian spouses, widows, young men, deacons and presbyters, and warns against false teachers who deny the reality of the incarnation, of the cross, and of the resurrection and the coming judgement.

Again like the letters of Ignatius, Polycarp's teaching is based on Scripture, with references to Psalms, Proverbs, Isaiah, Jeremiah, Ezekiel, Matthew, Luke, Acts, Romans, 1 and 2 Corinthians, Galatians, Ephesians, Philippians, 2 Thessalonians, 1-2 Timothy, 1 Peter, and 1 John as well as the Apocryphal book of Tobit and I Clement.

Polycarp as martyr

As we have already noted in chapter 3, just as Ignatius was eventually martyred in Rome, so also Polycarp was eventually martyred in Smyrna in his extreme old age, According to the eyewitness account of his death distributed by the church in Smyrna, he accepted his death willingly. seeing it as the culmination of his service of God. The account tells us that his final prayer was as follows:

O Lord God Almighty, Father of your beloved and blessed Son Jesus Christ, through whom we have received knowledge of you, the God of angels and powers and of all creation, and of the whole race of the righteous who live in your presence, I bless you because you have considered me worthy of this day and hour, that I might receive a place among the number of martyrs in the cup of your Christ, to the

---

[508] Polycarp, *To the Philippians* 5:1 in in Lightfoot, Harmer and Holmes, p.125.

resurrection to eternal life, both of soul and of body, in the incorruptibility of the Holy Spirit. May I be received among them in your presence today, as a rich an acceptable sacrifice, as you have prepared and revealed beforehand, and have now accomplished, you who are the undeceiving and true God. For this reason, indeed for all things, I praise you, I bless you, I glorify you, through the eternal and heavenly High Priest, Jesus Christ, your beloved Son, through whom to you with him and the Holy Spirit be glory both now and for the ages to come. Amen.[509]

Irenaeus of Lyons

As we saw in chapter 3, Irenaeus of Lyons was a pupil of Polycarp and was Bishop of Lyons in the second half of the second century. His understanding of what a bishop should be like is set out in chapter 26 of Book 4 of his work *Against Heresies*:

In this chapter Irenaeus refers to bishops using the term 'presbyter.' In section 3 of the chapter, he describes those who are considered to be presbyters, but who are shown not to be so by the way they behave:

Those, however, who are believed to be presbyters by many, but serve their own lusts, and, do not place the fear of God supreme in their hearts, but conduct themselves with contempt towards others, and are puffed up with the pride of holding the chief seat, and work evil deeds in secret, saying, 'No man sees us,' shall be convicted by the Word, who does not judge after outward appearance (secundum gloriam), nor looks upon the countenance, but the heart; and they shall hear those words, to be found in Daniel the prophet: 'O you seed of Canaan, and not of Judah, beauty has deceived you, and lust perverted your heart.[Susanna 56] You that are waxen old in wicked days, now your sins which you have committed aforetime have come to light; for you have pronounced false judgments, and have been accustomed to condemn the innocent, and to let the guilty go free, albeit the Lord says, The innocent and the righteous shall you not slay.' [Susanna 52-53] Of whom also did the Lord say: 'But if the evil servant shall say in

---

[509] *The Martyrdom of Polycarp*, 14 in Lightfoot, Harmer and Holmes, pp.140-141.

his heart, My lord delays his coming, and shall begin to smite the man-servants and maidens, and to eat and drink and be drunken; the lord of that servant shall come in a day that he looks not for him, and in an hour that he is not aware of, and shall cut him asunder, and appoint him his portion with the unbelievers.' [Matthew 24:48-51]. [510]

In section 4 he then goes on to describe what true bishops are like. Christians, he writes, should 'keep aloof' from the false bishops he has just described. Instead, they should adhere to presbyters:

...who, as I have already observed, do hold the doctrine of the apostles, and who, together with the order of priesthood (presbyterii ordine), display sound speech and blameless conduct for the confirmation and correction of others. In this way, Moses, to whom such a leadership was entrusted, relying on a good conscience, cleared himself before God, saying, 'I have not in covetousness taken anything belonging to one of these men, nor have I done evil to one of them.' [Numbers 16:15] In this way, too, Samuel, who judged the people so many years, and bore rule over Israel without any pride, in the end cleared himself, saying, 'I have walked before you from my childhood even unto this day: answer me in the sight of God, and before His anointed (Christi eius); whose ox or whose ass of yours have I taken, or over whom have I tyrannized, or whom have I oppressed? Or if I have received from the hand of any a bribe or [so much as] a shoe, speak out against me, and I will restore it to you.' [1 Samuel 12:3] And when the people had said to him, 'You have not tyrannized, neither have you oppressed us, neither have you taken ought of any man's hand,' he called the Lord to witness, saying, 'The Lord is witness, and His Anointed is witness this day, that you have not found ought in my hand. And they said to him, He is witness.' In this strain also the Apostle Paul, inasmuch as he had a good conscience, said to the Corinthians: 'For we are not as many, who corrupt the Word of God: but as of sincerity, but as of God, in the sight of God speak we in Christ;' [2 Corinthians 2:17] 'We have

---

[510] Irenaeus of Lyons, *Against Heresies,* Bk IV.26.3, p. 497

injured no man, corrupted no man, circumvented no man.' [2 Corinthians 7:2] [511]

For Irenaeus, then, a true bishop is someone who is not swollen with pride and who does not rule over the church for his own benefit, and in a way that exploits and oppresses those for whom he is responsible. Instead, he teaches the doctrine of the apostles, and his speech and conduct are such that he is able to strengthen and correct the members of his flock.

What Irenaeus understood teaching the doctrine of the apostles to involve is demonstrated in the two major works of his which have survived, *Against Heresies* and *Demonstration of the Apostolic Preaching*. The first is a systematic refutation of the Gnostic heresies which were threatening the Church of his day and the second is brief introduction to the orthodox Christian faith, what Irenaeus describes as 'a manual of essentials' intended to set out 'in short space all the members of the body of truth.'[512]

At the heart of both these works is a clear understanding of what the apostolic faith involves. Irenaeus sets this out in summary form in chapter 10 of Book 1 of *Against Heresies*. In this chapter he declares:

The Church, though dispersed throughout the whole world, even to the ends of the earth, has received from the apostles and their disciples this faith: [She believes] in one God, the Father Almighty, Maker of heaven, and earth, and the sea, and all things that are in them; and in one Christ Jesus, the Son of God, who became incarnate for our salvation; and in the Holy Spirit, who proclaimed through the prophets the dispensations of God, and the advents, and the birth from a virgin, and the passion, and the resurrection from the dead, and the ascension into heaven in the flesh of the beloved Christ Jesus, our Lord, and His [future] manifestation from heaven in the glory of the

[511] Irenaeus of Lyons, *Against Heresies,* Bk IV.26.4, pp. 497-498.
[512] Irenaeus of Lynons, *Demonstration of the Apostolic Preaching* 1, in Iain MacKenzie, *Irenaeus' Demonstration of the Apostolic Preaching* (Aldershot: Ashgate, 2002), p. 1.

Father 'to gather all things in one,' Ephesians 1:10 and to raise up anew all flesh of the whole human race, in order that to Christ Jesus, our Lord, and God, and Saviour, and King, according to the will of the invisible Father, 'every knee should bow, of things in heaven, and things in earth, and things under the earth, and that every tongue should confess' Philippians 2:10-11 to Him, and that He should execute just judgment towards all; that He may send 'spiritual wickednesses,' Ephesians 6:12 and the angels who transgressed and became apostates, together with the ungodly, and unrighteous, and wicked, and profane among men, into everlasting fire; but may, in the exercise of His grace, confer immortality on the righteous, and holy, and those who have kept His commandments, and have persevered in His love, some from the beginning [of their Christian course], and others from [the date of] their repentance, and may surround them with everlasting glory.[513]

As can be seen from this quotation, for Irenaeus the 'faith received from the apostles and their disciples' is identical with the teaching of Scripture. What the apostles taught, and what the orthodox succession of bishops taught after them, is contained in written form in the writings of the New Testament[514] and the content of their teaching, the creation of the world by God the Father and the incarnation, death, resurrection, ascension and coming in glory of Jesus Christ was also testified to by the writers of the Old Testament, inspired by the Holy Spirit.

In line with this conviction, Irenaeus' exposition of the apostolic faith in both *Against Heresies* and in *Demonstration of the Apostolic Faith*

[513] Irenaeus of Lyons, *Against Heresies*, Bk I.10.1, p. 330.
[514] As Michael Kruger notes: Irenaeus quotes New Testament books extensively, even more than the Old Testament and clearly regards then as Scripture. These include the four Gospels, Acts, the entire Pauline corpus (minus Philemon), Hebrews, James, 1 Peter, 1 and 2 John, and Revelation – over one thousand New Testament passages in total. There is no indication that he rejects the unmentioned New Testament books (2 Peter, 3 John and Jude); the extant writings of Irenaeus simply do not refer to them (Michael Kruger, *Canon Revisited*, Wheaton: Crossway, 2012, Kindle edition, Loc.6260).

consists in the quotation and exposition of relevant biblical texts. For him, as for Ignatius and Polycarp before him, being, as a bishop, a teacher of the apostolic faith, and being what we would now call a biblical theologian is one and the same thing. As a teacher of the apostolic faith a bishop is necessarily a teacher of Scripture.

The Apostolic Tradition of Hippolytus

In chapter 4 we saw that the *Apostolic Tradition* attributed to Hippolytus bears witness to the existence of a threefold ministry of bishops, presbyters and deacons in the church in Rome at the beginning of the third century. What this work also tells us is the view taken at that time about the role of the bishop in the life of the church and the sort of person a bishop ought to be.

As we saw in chapter 4, the account in the *Apostolic Tradition* of the ordination of a bishop runs as follows:

He who is ordained as a bishop, being chosen by all the people, must be irreproachable. When his name is announced and approved, the people will gather on the Lord's from day with the council of elders and the bishops who are present. With the assent of all, the bishops will place their hands upon him, with the council of elders standing by, quietly. Everyone will keep silent, praying in their hearts for the descent of the Spirit. After this, one of the bishops present, at the request of all, shall lay his hand upon him who is being ordained bishop, and pray, saying

God and Father of our Lord Jesus Christ, Father of mercies and God of all consolation, you who live in the highest, but regard the lowest, you who know all things before they are, you who gave the rules of the Church through the word of your grace, who predestined from the beginning the race of the righteous through Abraham, who instituted princes and priests, and did not leave your sanctuary without a minister; who from the beginning of the world has been pleased to be glorified by those whom you have chosen, pour out upon him the power which is from you, the princely Spirit, which you gave to your beloved Son Jesus Christ, which he gave to your holy apostles, who founded the Church in every place as your sanctuary, for the glory and endless praise of your name. Grant, Father who knows the heart, to your servant whom you chose for the episcopate, that he will feed your holy flock, that he will wear your high priesthood without reproach, serving night and day, incessantly making your face favourable, and offering the gifts of your holy church; in the spirit of high priesthood having the power to forgive sins according to your command; to assign lots according to your command; to loose any bond according to the authority which you gave to the apostles; to please you in mildness and a pure heart, offering to you a sweet scent, through your son Jesus Christ, through whom to you be glory, power, and honour, Father and Son, with the Holy Spirit, in the Holy Church, now and throughout the ages of the ages. Amen.[515]

What we see in this account is that a bishop is someone chosen by the local church and whose ordination has the assent of the laity, the presbyters and the bishops of other churches. The bishop is to be 'irreproachable' (i.e. someone with whom there are no problems with regard to either their faith or their morals) and it is prayed that he will be someone who possesses 'mildness' and a 'pure heart.'

As the 'high priest' (i.e. chief presbyter) the bishop is to ensure that the church is spiritually fed, preside over its worship, declare the forgiveness of sins, ordain ('assign lots') and exorcise and heal ('loose any bond').

In addition, what we also saw in chapter 4 is that in the *Apostolic Tradition* the bishop has a specific role to play in the process of Christian initiation. After someone has been baptised, it says, they are to be an anointed by a presbyter with the 'Oil of Thanksgiving' and after that:

The bishop will then lay his hand upon them, invoking, saying, 'Lord God, you who have made these worthy of the removal of sins through the bath of regeneration, make them worthy to be filled with your

---

[515] *The Apostolic Tradition of Hippolytus of Rome*, 2-3 at
www.bombaxo.com/hippolytus.html

Holy Spirit, grant to them your grace, that they might serve you according to your will, for to you is the glory, Father and Son with the Holy Spirit in the Holy Church, now and throughout the ages of the ages. Amen. After this he pours the oil into his hand, and laying his hand on each of their heads, says, 'I anoint you with holy oil in God the Father Almighty, and Christ Jesus, and the Holy Spirit.'[516]

What is said here does not mean that the Holy Spirit is received by the new Christian for the first time through the laying on of hands by the bishop. Rather, following the biblical pattern of initiation found in Acts 8:14-17, 19:1-7, 2 Timothy 1:6 and Hebrews 6:2, what is envisaged here is that those who have been regenerated by the Spirit in their baptism have hands laid on them in order that they will receive power through the Spirit to serve God in the new life which he has given them.

This section of the *Apostolic Tradition* is the first explicit mention of the bishop's role in what later came to be known as confirmation, although Tertullian describes a similar pattern of Christian initiation in his work *On Baptism* written in about 193 without ascribing the laying on of hands to the bishop. It has been suggested that the laying on of hands after baptism only became part of Christian initiation during the second half of the second century, but a better reading of the evidence suggests that it was already in existence in the first half of the century at a time when there were still people around who remembered the practice of the Church in the apostolic period and that it was a conscious continuation of the biblical pattern of initiation referred to above.

---

[516] *The Apostolic Tradition of Hippolytus of Rome*, 21.

From the *Apostolic Tradition* onwards the role of the bishop in confirming those who have been baptised is an accepted part of Christian teaching and practice.[517]

The Didascalia Apostolorum

The *Didascalia Apostolorum* ('The teaching of the Apostles') is a compendium of instructions for the life of the Church that was written in Northern Syria sometime around 230. Chapters 4-8 of the *Didascalia* are concerned with who should be chosen as bishops and how bishops should behave.

Concerning who should be appointed to be a bishop, the *Didascalia* declares that a bishop should be someone of good character, preferably a teacher, and advanced in years:

...it is required that he be without reproof, irreprehensible, that he be far from all evil things, a man who is not less than fifty years (of age) and therefore far from the vehement manners of youth, from the desires of the Enemy, and from calumny, and from the blasphemy of false brethren which they bring against many, because they do not understand the word which is spoken in the Gospel, that 'everyone who speaks an idle word shall give account of ' it to the Lord in the day of judgment, for by thy words thou shalt be justified, and by thy words thou shalt be condemned.' [Matthew 12:36-37] If it be possible let him be a teacher, and if he be illiterate, let him be persuasive and wise of speech: let him be advanced in years.[518]

The requirement that a bishop should be advanced in years is not, however, absolute. Provision is made that:

...If the assembly be small and there be not found a man advanced in years, [one] about whom there be witnesses that he is wise and

[517] For confirmation in the New Testament and Patristic periods see Theodore Wirgman, *The Doctrine of Confirmation* (London: Longmans, Green and Co, 1902).
[518] Margaret Gibson, *The Didascalia Apostolorum in English* (London: C J Clay, 1903), p. 23.

suitable to be appointed Bishop; one being found who is a youth, whose companions testify about him, and those who are with him, that he is worthy to be appointed to the Bishopric; he though yet a youth shewing the works of age in humility and meekness, if all men testify about him, being proved by all the people; thus let him sit in peace. [519]

The *Didascalia* goes on to say that a bishop should be morally upright, humble, upstanding in his family life, loving, and generous to those in need:

Let him be watchful, and chaste, and stable, and well-regulated, and let him not be turbulent, nor trespass in wine, nor be a calumniator, nor let him be contentious, nor a lover of money, nor have a childish mind, nor let him exalt himself and fall into the condemnation of Satan; for it is said that 'everyone that exalteth himself shall be abased.' [Luke 14:11]

Thus the Bishop is required to be; a man who has taken one wife, who ruleth his house well; and thus let him be proved when he receives the laying on of hands, that he may sit in the place of the Bishops, if he be chaste, and if also his wife be believing and chaste, and if he have brought up his children in the fear of God, and if he have admonished and taught them, and if they reverence and respect him at home, and if all of them be obedient to him; for if his household according to the flesh oppose him and do not obey him, how shall those who are without belong to him and submit to him ?

Let it also be proved that he is blameless in the affairs of the world, and in his body, for it is written; 'See that there be no blemish in him who is appointed priest.' [Leviticus 21:17] Let him be also without anger, for the Lord hath said that anger destroyeth even the wise. Let him be merciful and gracious and full of love, for the Lord hath said that love shall cover a multitude of sins. Let his hand be stretched out to give; let him love both orphans and widows. Let him love the poor,

[519] *The Didascalia Apostolorum*, p.23.

and also strangers. Let him be apt in his service, and let him be constant in service. [520]

Concerning the bishop's teaching responsibilities the *Didascalia* declares:

Let him be very diligent in his instruction; let him be constant in the reading of the divine books assiduously, that he may interpret and explain the Scriptures accurately. Let him compare the Law and the Prophets with the Gospel, how that the commandments of the Law and the Prophets agree with the Gospel. Before all things then let him be a good discriminator of the Law, and of Deuteronomy, so that he may distinguish and shew what is the law of believers, and what are the chains of the unbelievers; lest any man of those who are under thy hand should take the chains to be the Law, and should put heavy burdens upon his soul, and should become a son of perdition. Be therefore diligent and careful about the Word, O Bishop, if thou canst, explain every commandment as it is in the doctrine. [521]

The point of the sentence starting 'Before all things' is that in his teaching the bishop needs to make clear which bits of the Old Testament law (such as the Ten Commandments) are still binding on Christians and which parts are not.

The *Didascalia* emphasises the necessity for the bishop to teach clearly about the judgement of God against sin.

It is required of thee, therefore, O Bishop, that when thou preachest thou shouldst testify and affirm about judgment, as in the Gospel, because the Lord hath said also to thee, 'Also thou, O son of man, I have set thee for a watchman unto the house of Israel, that thou mayest hear the word at My mouth and take heed, and preach it as from Me. When I say unto the wicked, That the wicked shall surely die, and thou dost not preach and say, so that the wicked may turn from his iniquity, the wicked man shall die in his iniquity, but his blood will

[520] *The Didascalia Apostolorum*, pp.23-24.
[521] *The Didascalia Apostolorum*, pp.24-25.

I require at thy hands. But thou, if thou warn the people from its way and it be not warned, the wicked shall die in his iniquity, but thou shalt deliver thy soul.' [Ezekiel 33:7-9] Therefore ye also, because upon you will fall the accusation of those who have sinned without knowing, preach and testify, and those who walk without discipline, admonish and reprove them publicly. [522]

However, it also stresses that the bishop need to show mercy on those who have sinned, excluding them from the life of the Church because of their sins, but then also instructing them about the way back:

It is required of you, O Bishops, according to the Scriptures, that ye judge those who sin with pity and mercy. For him that walketh on the brink of a river and falleth, if thou leave him in the river, thou pushest and throwest him down and committest murder; or when a man has fallen by a the side of a river's brink, and nearly perishes, stretch out thy hand to him quickly and draw him up that he perish not: thus therefore do, that thy people may learn and be wise, and also that he that sinneth, may not perish utterly, but that thou mayest look to him that hath sinned, be angry with him, and command them to put him out. And when he is put out, be ye not angry with him, and contend with him, but let them keep him outside of the Church, and then let them go in and make supplication for him, for even our Saviour made supplication to His Father for those that had sinned, as it is written in the Gospel, 'My Father, they know not what they do, nor what they speak, yet, if it be possible, forgive them.' [Luke 23:34] Then thou, O Bishop, command him to come in, and thyself ask him if he repents. If he be worthy to be received into the Church, appoint him days of fasting according to his fault, two, or three, or five, or seven weeks, and thus allow him to go, saying to him all that is proper for admonition and doctrine. Reprove him, and tell him to be humble-minded, and to pray and make supplication in the days of fasting, that he be found worthy of the forgiveness of sins, as it is written in Genesis, 'Thou hast sinned, cease. Let thy repentance be with thee, and

---

[522] *The Didascalia Apostolorum*, p.26.

thou shalt have power over it.' [Genesis 4:7] Look also at Miriam the sister of Moses, when she had spoken against Moses, and afterwards she repented, and was thought worthy of forgiveness, it was said by the Lord, 'If her father had but spit in her face, would she not have been ashamed and separated for seven days without the camp, and then she would have come in?' [Numbers 12:14] Thus also it is required of you to act towards those who promise to repent of their sins. Put them out of the Church as it is proper for their faults, and afterwards receive them as a merciful Father. [523]

The *Didascalia* underlines the point in the last sentence of this quotation by declaring that the calling of the bishop is to be a physician who gives the appropriate medicine to those who are spiritually sick because of their sins and that the bishop will be responsible before God for their ruin should he fail to do this:

Thou also, O Bishop, art made the physician of His Church, therefore do not restrain the medicine that thou mayest heal those that are sick in their sins, but cure them by every means and make them whole and establish them safe in the Church; that thou be not taken by this word which the Lord spake, 'Ye have ruled them with violence and levity.' [Ezekiel 34:4] Lead not therefore with violence; be not vehement, nor judge sharply, nor be merciless, nor deride the people who are under thy hand, nor hide from them the word of repentance, for that would be to have ruled them with violence and levity. But if ye oversee my people harshly and punish them with violence, and drive them and expel them, and do not receive them that have sinned, but harshly and mercilessly hide repentance from them, thou wilt even be a helper in their conversion to evil, and in scattering the flocks to be food for the beasts of the field, that is to say, to the wicked men of this world, but not to men in truth, but to the beasts, to the heathen, to the heretics; for him who goes out of the Church they follow immediately, like evil beasts, to swallow him for food; because of thine own harshness, he then that goeth out of the Church, either goeth and entereth in unto

---

[523] *The Didascalia Apostolorum*, pp.32-33.

the heathen, or plunges into heresies; he will be entirely a stranger, and be removed from the Church, and from the hope of God, and thou wilt be guilty of his ruin, because thou wert ready to put out and to cast away those who sin; and when they repented and returned, thou didst not wish to receive them.[524]

Cyprian of Carthage

Cyprian was a convert to Christianity from paganism who was bishop of Carthage in North Africa from 248 until his martyrdom a decade later.

For Cyprian, like Ignatius of Antioch before him, the Church consists of those who are in unity with their bishop. As he puts it in Epistle LXVIII, using the words 'priest,' 'pastor' and 'bishop' to describe the same office:

...they are the Church who are a people united to the priest, and the flock which adheres to its pastor. Whence you ought to know that the bishop is in the Church, and the Church in the bishop; and if anyone be not with the bishop, that he is not in the Church.[525]

Cyprian bases his understanding of the importance of the bishops in Jesus words to Peter as recorded in Matthew 16:18-19. We can see this in Epistle XXVI and in his treatise *On the Unity of the Church*.

In Epistle XXVI Cyprian writes:

Our Lord, whose precepts and admonitions we ought to observe, describing the honour of a bishop and the order of His Church, speaks in the Gospel, and says to Peter: I say unto you, That you are Peter, and upon this rock will I build my Church; and the gates of hell shall not prevail against it. And I will give unto you the keys of the kingdom of heaven: and whatsoever you shall bind on earth shall be bound in heaven: and whatsoever you shall loose on earth shall be loosed in heaven. Thence, through the changes of times and successions, the

---

[524] *The Didascalia Apostolorum*, pp.35-36.
[525] Cyprian *Epistle LXVIII*.8, in *The Ante-Nicene Fathers*, vol.V (Edinburgh and Grand Rapids, T&T Clark/Eerdmans, 1995), pp.374-375

ordering of bishops and the plan of the Church flow onwards; so that the Church is founded upon the bishops, and every act of the Church is controlled by these same rulers. Since this, then, is founded on the divine law, I marvel that some, with daring temerity, have chosen to write to me as if they wrote in the name of the Church; when the Church is established in the bishop and the clergy, and all who stand fast in the faith. [526]

In *On the Unity of the Church* he writes:

If anyone consider and examine these things, there is no need for lengthened discussion and arguments. There is easy proof for faith in a short summary of the truth. The Lord speaks to Peter, saying, I say unto you, that you are Peter; and upon this rock I will build my Church, and the gates of hell shall not prevail against it. And I will give unto you the keys of the kingdom of heaven; and whatsoever you shall bind on earth shall be bound also in heaven, and whatsoever you shall loose on earth shall be loosed in heaven. [Matthew 16:18-19] And again to the same He says, after His resurrection, Feed my sheep. And although to all the apostles, after His resurrection, He gives an equal power, and says, As the Father has sent me, even so send I you: Receive the Holy Ghost: Whose soever sins you remit, they shall be remitted unto him; and whose soever sins you retain, they shall be retained; [John 20:21] yet, that He might set forth unity, He arranged by His authority the origin of that unity, as beginning from one. Assuredly the rest of the apostles were also the same as was Peter, endowed with a like partnership both of honour and power; but the beginning proceeds from unity. Which one Church, also, the Holy Spirit in the Song of Songs designated in the person of our Lord, and says, my dove, my spotless one, is but one. She is the only one of her mother, elect of her that bare her. [Song of Songs 6:9] Does he who does not hold this unity of the Church think that he holds the faith? Does he who strives against and resists the Church trust that he is in the Church, when moreover the blessed Apostle Paul teaches the same thing, and sets forth the sacrament of unity, saying, There is one body

[526] Cyprian *Epistle XXVI*:1, p. 305.

and one spirit, one hope of your calling, one Lord, one faith, one baptism, one God?' [Ephesians 4:4].

And this unity we ought firmly to hold and assert, especially those of us that are bishops who preside in the Church, that we may also prove the episcopate itself to be one and undivided. Let no one deceive the brotherhood by a falsehood: let no one corrupt the truth of the faith by perfidious prevarication. The episcopate is one, each part of which is held by each one for the whole. [527]

From these two quotations we learn that Cyprian held that the foundational role of leadership and oversight first given by Jesus to Peter has passed down to the bishops and that it is for this reason that the Church consists of the bishops and the clergy and faithful laity who are united with them. Furthermore, just as there was one apostolic commission first given to Peter and then given to the other apostles, so also there is one episcopate equally shared by all bishops. In this way the unity of the Church is maintained.

It is important to note, however, that the bishops with whom the clergy and laity have to maintain unity are exclusively godly bishops. When bishops become ungodly the faithful are to separate themselves from them and appoint godly bishops in their place.

We can see this in Epistle LXVII in which Cyprian writes to the Christians in Spain congratulating them on appointing Sabinus and Felix as their bishops in the place of their previous bishops Basilides and Martial who had given way in the face of persecution by obtaining certificates saying that they had offered sacrifices to the gods.

In this letter Cyprian declares:

Nor let the people flatter themselves that they can be free from the contagion of sin, while communicating with a priest who is a sinner, and yielding their consent to the unjust and unlawful episcopacy of

---

[527] Cyprian, *On the Unity of the Church*, 4-5, in in *The Ante-Nicene Fathers*, vol.V (Edinburgh and Grand Rapids, T&T Clark/ Eerdmans, 1995), pp.422-423.

their overseer, when the divine reproof by Hosea the prophet threatens, and says, 'Their sacrifices shall be as the bread of mourning; all that eat thereof shall be polluted' [Hosea 9:4]; teaching manifestly and showing that all are absolutely bound to the sin who have been contaminated by the sacrifice of a profane and unrighteous priest. Which, moreover, we find to be manifested also in Numbers, when Korah, and Dathan, and Abiram Claimed for themselves the power of sacrificing in opposition to Aaron the priest. There also the Lord commanded by Moses that the people should be separated from them, lest, being associated with the wicked, themselves also should be bound closely in the same wickedness. Separate yourselves, said He, from the tents of these wicked and hardened men, and touch not those things which belong to them, lest you perish together in their sins [Numbers 16:26]. On which account a people obedient to the Lord's precepts, and fearing God, ought to separate themselves from a sinful prelate, and not to associate themselves with the sacrifices of a sacrilegious priest, especially since they themselves have the power either of choosing worthy priests, or of rejecting unworthy ones.[528]

He then goes on to explain that the Bible (Numbers 20:25-26, Acts 1:15, 6:2) makes clear that the appointment of a new bishop:

...ought not to be solemnized except with the knowledge of the people standing near, that in the presence of the people either the crimes of the wicked may be disclosed, or the merits of the good may be declared, and the ordination, which shall have been examined by the suffrage and judgment of all, may be just and legitimate.[529]

For this reason, he says:

...you must diligently observe and keep the practice delivered from divine tradition and apostolic observance, which is also maintained among us, and almost throughout all the provinces; that for the proper

---

[528] Cyprian *Epistle LXVII*.3 p.370.
[529] Cyprian *Epistle LXVII*, 4, p.370.

celebration of ordinations all the neighbouring bishops of the same province should assemble with that people for which a prelate is ordained. And the bishop should be chosen in the presence of the people, who have most fully known the life of each one, and have looked into the doings of each one as respects his habitual conduct. And this also, we see, was done by you in the ordination of our colleague Sabinus; so that, by the suffrage of the whole brotherhood, and by the sentence of the bishops who had assembled in their presence, and who had written letters to you concerning him, the episcopate was conferred upon him, and hands were imposed on him in the place of Basilides. [530]

For Cyprian a bishop has not only to be a godly individual, but he also needs to be someone who is known to be a godly individual.

Gregory Nazianzen
Gregory Nazianzen was ordained to the presbyterate by his father, the Bishop of Nazianazus on what is now Eastern Turkey, in 361, but afterwards he fled the diocese and went to the neighbouring district of Pontus for several months. Following his eventual return, he faced criticism for having rejected ordination within a week of receiving it and in order to explain his conduct he composed a defence of his actions. In this defence, known as *Oration II*, he explains that a key reason for his flight was a feeling that he was inadequate to perform the presbyteral role. To explain this point Gregory sets out what he thinks the presbyteral role involves and the characteristics someone has to have if they are to perform this role properly.

Although Gregory is writing specifically about the presbyterate, what he says is also applicable to the episcopate and it was drawn on by later writers such as Gregory the Great when they wrote about episcopal ministry in line with the principle that a bishop is a senior presbyter.

[530] Cyprian *Epistle LXVII*, 45, p.371,

Gregory's understanding of the role of the presbyter is that he is someone who is called to be a 'physician of souls.'[531] As such the role of the presbyter is to:

...provide the soul with wings, to rescue it from the world and give it to God, and to watch over that which is in His image, [Genesis 1:26] if it abides, to take it by the hand, if it is in danger, or restore it, if ruined, to make Christ to dwell in the heart [Ephesians 3:17] by the Spirit: and, in short, to deify, and bestow heavenly bliss upon, one who belongs to the heavenly host.[532]

This is a complex task, because just as physicians of the body have to give different treatments to different people so also do the physicians of the soul:

As then the same medicine and the same food are not in every case administered to men's bodies, but a difference is made according to their degree of health or infirmity; so also are souls treated with varying instruction and guidance. To this treatment witness is borne by those who have had experience of it. Some are led by doctrine, others trained by example; some need the spur, others the curb; some are sluggish and hard to rouse to the good, and must be stirred up by being smitten with the word; others are immoderately fervent in spirit, with impulses difficult to restrain, like thoroughbred colts, who run wide of the turning post, and to improve them the word must have a restraining and checking influence.

Some are benefited by praise, others by blame, both being applied in season; while if out of season, or unreasonable, they are injurious; some are set right by encouragement, others by rebuke; some, when taken to task in public, others, when privately corrected. For some are wont to despise private admonitions, but are recalled to their senses by the condemnation of a number of people, while others, who would

[531] Gregory Nazianzen *Oration II*,16 in *The Nicene and Post Nicene Fathers*, series 2, vol. VII. (Edinburgh and Grand Rapids: T&T Clark/Eerdmans, 1996), p. *208*.
[532] Gregory Nazianzen *Oration II,* 22, p.209.

grow reckless under reproof openly given, accept rebuke because it is in secret, and yield obedience in return for sympathy.[533]

In order to undertake this task properly, those called to be presbyters have first of got to be able to expound Scripture and to explain correctly the theology which Scripture contains. In Gregory's words:

In regard to the distribution of the word, to mention last the first of our duties, of that divine and exalted word, which everyone now is ready to discourse upon; if anyone else boldly undertakes it and supposes it within the power of every man's intellect, I am amazed at his intelligence, not to say his folly. To me indeed it seems no slight task, and one requiring no little spiritual power, to give in due season [Luke 12:42] to each his portion of the word, and to regulate with judgment the truth of our opinions, which are concerned with such subjects as the world or worlds, matter, soul, mind, intelligent natures, better or worse, providence which holds together and guides the universe, and seems in our experience of it to be governed according to some principle, but one which is at variance with those of earth and of men.

Again, they are concerned with our original constitution, and final restoration, the types of the truth, the covenants, the first and second coming of Christ, His incarnation, sufferings and dissolution, with the resurrection, the last day, the judgment and recompense, whether sad or glorious; to crown all, with what we are to think of the original and blessed Trinity.[534]

In addition, a presbyter must be someone who himself possesses what he then passes on to others:

A man must himself be cleansed, before cleansing others: himself become wise, that he may make others wise; become light, and then give light: draw near to God, and so bring others near; be hallowed,

---

[533] Gregory Nazianzen, *Oration II*, 30-31, p.211.
[534] Gregory Nazianzen, *Oration II*, 35-36, p.212.

then hallow them; be possessed of hands to lead others by the hand, of wisdom to give advice.[535]

This means he needs to be someone who is not only free from vice, but also pre-eminent in goodness. As Gregory puts it:

In the second place, although a man has kept himself pure from sin, even in a very high degree; I do not know that even this is sufficient for one who is to instruct others in virtue. For he who has received this charge, not only needs to be free from evil, for evil is, in the eyes of most of those under his care, most disgraceful, but also to be eminent in good, according to the command, 'Depart from evil and do good.[Psalm 37:27] And he must not only wipe out the traces of vice from his soul, but also inscribe better ones, so as to outstrip men further in virtue than he is superior to them in dignity. He should know no limits in goodness or spiritual progress, and should dwell upon the loss of what is still beyond him, rather than the gain of what he has attained, and consider that which is beneath his feet a step to that which comes next: and not think it a great gain to excel ordinary people, but a loss to fall short of what we ought to be: and to measure his success by the commandment and not by his neighbours, whether they be evil, or to some extent proficient in virtue: and to weigh virtue in no small scales, inasmuch as it is due to the Most High, 'from Whom are all things, and to Whom are all things.' [Romans 11:35][536]

In addition to what he writes in Oration II, Gregory also makes clear what he thinks a bishop should be like in *Orations XVIII* and *XLIII* in which he gives funeral orations for his father, the Bishop of Nazianus, and his friend Basil, the Bishop of Caesarea.

In the former he explains how his father was generous to the poor, rebuked pride and fostered lowliness, was free from guile and resentment, was prepared to stand up against the Imperial government, was concerned with the Church's unity and well-being and who eventually passed from the world 'with the words and forms

[535] Gregory Nazianzen, *Oration II*, 71, p.219.
[536] Gregory Nazianzen, *Oration II*, 14, pp.207-208.

of prayer, leaving behind no trace of vice, and many recollections of virtue.'[537]

In the latter he records Basil's ascetic lifestyle, his celibacy, his care for the poor and the sick, his honouring of virtue and castigation of vice, his deep knowledge of the things of God and his ability to instruct others in them, his overthrowing of heretics and his pastoral care, which made him fruitful in spiritual children and established many in the faith. [538]

It is also important to note that in his oration on Athanasius of Alexandria (*Oration XXI*) Gregory sets out what exactly he understands by the idea of episcopal succession. In chapter 8 he describes Athanasius appointment as Bishop of Alexandria ('the throne of Saint Mark') in the following terms:

Thus, and for these reasons, by the vote of the whole people, not in the evil fashion which has since prevailed, nor by means of bloodshed and oppression, but in an apostolic and spiritual manner, he is led up to the throne of Saint Mark, to succeed him in piety, no less than in office; in the latter indeed at a great distance from him, in the former, which is the genuine right of succession, following him closely. For unity in doctrine deserves unity in office; and a rival teacher sets up a rival throne; the one is a successor in reality, the other but in name. For it is not the intruder, but he whose rights are intruded upon, who is the successor, not the lawbreaker, but the lawfully appointed, not the man of contrary opinions, but the man of the same faith; if this is not what we mean by successor, he succeeds in the same sense as disease to health, darkness to light, storm to calm, and frenzy to sound sense.[539]

[537] Gregory Nazianzen, Oration XVIII, 20-38 in *The Nicene and Post Nicene Fathers*, series 2, vol. VII. (Edinburgh and Grand Rapids: T&T Clark/Eerdmans, 1996), pp. 20-38.

[538] Gregory Nazianzen, Oration XLIII, 63-71 in *The Nicene and Post Nicene Fathers*, series 2, vol. VII. (Edinburgh and Grand Rapids: T&T Clark/Eerdmans, 1996), pp. 416-419.

[539] Gregory Nazianzen, *Oration XXI*, 8 in *The Nicene and Post Nicene Fathers*, series 2, vol. VII. (Edinburgh and Grand Rapids: T&T Clark/Eerdmans, 1996), p.271

Like Irenaeus before him, Gregory sees genuine episcopal succession as dependent on continuity in the apostolic faith. In the words of Christopher Beeley in his book *Leading God's People*, for Gregory:

...what makes one a bishop with 'the true right of succession' is not merely rightful ordination or the external credentials of office, but the truth of one's faith and doctrine – that one believes and teaches in 'an apostolic and spiritual manner.' [540]

John Chrysostom

John Chrysostom's treatise *On the Priesthood* was written in about 381. It takes the form of a dialogue between John and his friend Basil in which John explains why the nature of the priestly office made him initially unwilling to be ordained, since he was conscious both of the greatness of the priestly calling and his own unworthiness to undertake it.

As John makes clear in Book 1 of the treatise, the office which he sought to evade was that of bishop [541] and the fact that he writes about the priesthood to justify his action underlines the point which noted in chapter 4, namely that for John, as for other Patristic writers, the episcopate formed part of a larger category of priestly ministry to which the ministry of presbyters ('priests') also belonged.

In Book 3 of the treatise Chrysostom argues that the role of the priest is more exalted than that of any human monarch because of the supernatural authority given to those who hold the priestly office to celebrate Holy Communion, to exercise the power of binding and losing sin, and to oversee the grant of eternal life at baptism. He also declares that the priest needs to be 'skilful in the management of property' and that he will need to oversee widows and consecrated

---

[540] Christopher Beeley, *Leading God's People* (Grand Rapids: Eerdmans, 2012), p.101.
[541] Philip Schaff and William Stephens, John Chrysostom, *On the Christian Priesthood Bk 1.6.* (New York: Christian Literature Company, 1889), Kindle Edition, p.12.

virgins, give judgement in temporal affairs, and be assiduous in pastoral visiting. [542]

In Book 4, like Gregory Nazianzen, John describes the priest as the physician of the soul and in an extended metaphor declares that the means given for this purpose is the application of the Word of God in Scripture:

...There is but one method and one way of healing appointed, after we have gone wrong, and that is, the powerful application of the Word. This is the one instrument, the only diet, the finest atmosphere. This takes the place of physic, cautery and cutting, and it be needful to sear and amputate, this is the means which we must use, and if this be of no avail, all else is wasted; with these we both rouse the soul when it sleeps, and reduce it when it is inflamed; with this we cut off excesses, and fill up defects, and perform all manner of other operations which are requisite for the soul's health.[543]

In Book 5 he goes on to say that in order to be able to apply the Word effectively, priests not only have to be willing to expend 'great labour upon the preparation of discourses to be delivered in public,' but also need to be indifferent to the praise of their hearers and have the power to preach well. If a priest becomes 'despised by the multitude' because of his inability to speak well 'he gains nothing from his nobleness of mind' and if he is 'overcome by the thought of applause' then 'harm is equally done in turn, both to himself and the multitude, because in his desire for praise he is careful to speak rather with a view to please than to profit.' [544]

In Book 6 he tells Basil that what really concerned him about the prospect of becoming a bishop was the eternal penalty for failing as a priest:

[542] John Chrysostom, *On the Christian priesthood,* Bk 3.16-17, pp.95-103.
[543] John Chrysostom, *On the Christian priesthood,* Bk 4.3, p.122.
[544] John Chrysostom, *On the Christian priesthood,* Bk 5.1-2, pp.142-144.

For if for him who causes one only, and that the least, to stumble, it is profitable at a great millstone should be hanging around his neck, and that he should be sunk in the depth of the sea [Matthew 18:6]; and if they who wound the consciences of the brethren, sin against Christ himself [1 Corinthians 8:12], what then will they one day suffer, what kind of penalty will they pay, who destroy not one only, or two, or three, but so many multitudes? [545]

To avoid this dreadful fate the priest needs even greater purity of soul than the hermit living in the desert. If those dwelling in the desert have to study: 'to speak and act with great circumspection, so that to the utmost extent they may draw near to God with assurance, and with unstained purity,' then:

...what power and strength, thinkest thou, does the ordained priest need so as to be able to turn his soul away from every defilement, and to keep its spiritual beauty unsullied? For he has need of a far greater purity than they; and whoever has need of greater purity, he too is subject to more pressing temptations than they, which are able to defile him, unless by using constant self-denial and much labour he renders his soul inaccessible to them. [546]

For Chrysostom, then, being a bishop is spiritually dangerous occupation and only by constant spiritual diligence can a bishop avoid incurring the judgement of God. Therefore, if someone desires to be a bishop he has not really understood what the role involves.

He then further adds that the priest also needs not only 'to be thus pure as one who has been dignified with so high a ministry,' but also 'well versed in the affairs of this life' so that he can understand the varying circumstances and needs of the different people for whom he is responsible: 'since neither is it well for physicians to apply one

[545] John Chrysostom, *On the Christian priesthood,* Bk 6.1, p.157.
[546] John Chrysostom, *On the Christian priesthood,* Bk 6.2, p.159

course of treatment for all their sick, nor for a pilot to know one of contending with the winds.'[547]

Ambrose of Milan

Ambrose of Milan seems to have written his work *On the Duties of the Clergy* in about 391. It presents a Christian alternative to the work *On the Duties* by the Roman philosopher and statesman Cicero. Ambrose takes Cicero's study of what is right, honourable, and expedient, as his model, but reworks it in a distinctively Christian direction in order to provide instruction for those whom he has ordained in his role as Bishop of Milan. In Ambrose's words:

I am speaking of the duties which I wish to impress upon and impart to you, whom I have chosen for the service of the Lord; so that those things which have been already implanted and fixed in your minds and characters by habit and training may now be further unfolded to you by explanation and instruction.[548]

Although Ambrose's work is thus primarily written for presbyters, as we shall see below what he writes shows that his work is intended to cover the duties of both bishops and presbyters together.

Ambrose begins his work by declaring that his calling as a bishop is to be a student of Christ and a teacher of the Bible. He writes:

I do not therefore claim for myself the glory of the apostles (for who can do this save those whom the Son of God Himself has chosen?); nor the grace of the prophets, nor the virtue of the evangelists, nor the cautious care of the pastors. I only desire to attain to that care and diligence in the sacred writings, which the Apostle has placed last among the duties of the saints [1 Corinthians 12:10]; and this very thing I desire, so that, in the endeavour to teach, I may be able to learn. For one is the true Master, who alone has not learned, what He taught

---

[547] John Chrysostom, *On the Christian priesthood*, Bk 6.4, p.165.
[548] Ambrose, *On the Duties of the Clergy* Bk 6:1:25, in *The Nicene and Post Nicene Fathers*, series 2, vol. X *(Edinburgh and Grand Rapids: T&T Clark/Eerdmans, 1997), p.47.*

all; but men learn before they teach, and receive from Him what they may hand on to others.[549]

Later on, Ambrose lays down that the language of the clergy should be marked by 'discussion without wrath, urbanity without bitterness, warning without sharpness, advice without giving offence'[550] and goes on to say that when teaching Scripture clergy need to observe this rule and also not speak at undue length:

Let our language be of this sort, more especially when we are speaking of the holy Scriptures. For of what ought we to speak more often than of the best subject of conversation, of its exhortation to watchfulness, its care for good instruction? Let us have a reason for beginning, and let our end be within due limits. For a speech that is wearisome only stirs up anger. But surely it is most unseemly that when every kind of conversation generally gives additional pleasure, this should give cause of offense![551]

He then adds that in terms of their teaching in general, clergy must pay attention both to the length of what they say, and the manner in which they say it:

The treatment also of such subjects as the teaching of faith, instruction on self-restraint, discussion on justice, exhortation to activity, must not be taken up by us and fully gone into all at one time, but must be carried on in course, so far as we can do it, and as the subject-matter of the passage allows. Our discourse must not be too lengthy, nor too soon cut short, for fear the former should leave behind it a feeling of aversion, and the latter produce carelessness and neglect. The address should be plain and simple, clear and evident, full of dignity and

---

[549] Ambrose, *On the Duties of the Clergy* Bk 1:1:3, in The *Nicene and Post Nicene Fathers*, series 2, vol. X (Edinburgh and Grand Rapids: T&T Clark/Eerdmans, 1997), p. 1.
[550] Ambrose, *On the Duties of the Clergy*, Bk 1:22:99, p.18.
[551] Ambrose, *On the Duties of the Clergy*, Bk 1:22:100, p.18.

weight; it should not be studied or too refined, nor yet, on the other hand, be unpleasing and rough in style.[552]

For Ambrose the essential virtues that bishops and other clergy must possess are wisdom, justice, fortitude and temperance:

First, you shall see the deep things of God, which needs wisdom. Next, you must keep watch for the people; this requires justice. You must defend the camp and guard the tabernacle, which needs fortitude. You must show yourself continent and sober, and this needs temperance.[553]

The 'deep things of God' are the truths of the Christian faith and the 'camp' and the 'tabernacle' are the Church. As part of his responsibility to defend and guard the Church the bishop must be prepared to exercise ecclesiastical discipline even though it causes him pain to do so. In Ambrose's words:

Not without pain is a limb of the body cut off which has become corrupt. It is treated for a long time, to see if it can be cured with various remedies. If it cannot be cured, then it is cut off by a good physician. Thus it is a good bishop's desire to wish to heal the weak, to remove the spreading ulcers, to burn some parts and not to cut them off; and lastly, when they cannot be healed, to cut them off with pain to himself.[554]

According to Ambrose, the clergy, while being 'hospitable to travellers' should 'avoid the banquets of strangers' since these lead to a love for feasting, and involve listening to tales 'about the world and its pleasures' and the consumption of excessive amounts of alcohol. [555] In order to avoid temptation, or even the appearance of impropriety the clergy should only 'go to the houses of widows or virgins' for the sake

---

[552] Ambrose, *On the Duties of the Clergy*, Bk 1:22:101, p.18.
[553] Ambrose, *On the Duties of the Clergy*, Bk 1:50: p.42.
[554] Ambrose, *On the Duties of the Clergy*, Bk 2:27:135, p.64.
[555] Ambrose On the Duties of the Clergy, Bk 1:20:86, p. 13.

of pastoral visitation and when this happens younger members of the clergy should normally be accompanied by the bishop.[556]

As he sees it, the clergy should spend the time they have free from liturgical responsibilities in prayer and the study of the Bible rather than in socialising:

Why do you not spend the time which you have free from your duties in the church in reading? Why do you not go back again to see Christ? Why do you not address Him, and hear His voice? We address Him when we pray, we hear Him when we read the sacred oracles of God. What have we to do with strange houses? There is one house which holds all. They who need us can come to us. What have we to do with tales and fables? An office to minister at the altar of Christ is what we have received; no duty to make ourselves agreeable to men has been laid upon us.[557]

Ambrose writes that in their day to day conduct the clergy must be '... be humble, gentle, mild, serious, patient. We must keep the mean in all things, so that a calm countenance and quiet speech may show that there is no vice in our lives.' [558] He further adds:

If we would please God, we must have love, we must be of one mind, we must follow humility, each one thinking the other higher than himself. This is true humility, when one never claims anything proudly for oneself, but thinks oneself to be the inferior. The bishop should treat the clerics and attendants, who are indeed his sons, as members of himself, and give to each one that duty for which he sees him to be fit.[559]

For Ambrose, an important part of the duties of the clergy is giving money to those in need, but he argues that they need to do this in a

---

[556] Ambrose On the Duties of the Clergy, Bk1:20:87, p. 13.
[557] Ambrose On the Duties of the Clergy, Bk1:20:88, p. 16.
[558] Ambrose, *On the Duties of the Clergy,* Bk1:20:89, p. 16.
[559] Ambrose, *On the Duties of the Clergy,* Bk2:27:134, p. 64.

methodical fashion that avoids giving away either too much or too little:

For they who see a good dispenser give him something to distribute in his round of duty, sure that the act of mercy will reach the poor. If they see him giving away either in excess or too sparingly, they contemn either of these; in the one case because he wastes the fruits of another's labours by unnecessary payments, on the other hand because he hoards them in his money bags. As, then, method must be observed in liberality, so also at times it seems as though the spur must be applied. Method, then, so that the kindness one shows may be able to be shown day by day, and that we may not have to withdraw from a needful case what we have freely spent on waste. A spur, because money is better laid out in food for the poor than on a purse for the rich. We must take care lest in our money chests we shut up the welfare of the needy, and bury the life of the poor as it were in a sepulchre. [560]

Finally, on the issue of clerical marriage, Ambrose interprets the New Testament injunction that 'the bishop must be the husband of one wife' (1 Timothy 3:2) to mean that the clergy may not re-marry if they have been widowed: 'As regards marriage, the law is, not to marry again, nor to seek union with another wife.'[561] He further argues that even those clergy who are married must be celibate because 'the ministerial office must be kept pure and unspotted, and must not be defiled by conjugal intercourse.'[562]This is because the Old Testament laws which demanded that those who offered sacrifice in Old Testament times needed to be ritually pure indicates that the clergy:

...must have a pure body wherewith to offer up the sacraments. If the people were forbidden to approach their victim unless they washed

[560] Ambrose, *On the Duties of the Clergy,* Bk 2: 16:78, p. 55.
[561] Ambrose, *On the Duties of the Clergy,* Bk 1: 50:257 p. 41.
[562] Ambrose, *On the Duties of the Clergy,* Bk 1: 50:258 p. 41.

their clothes, do you, while foul in heart and body, dare to make supplication for others? Do you dare to make an offering for them?[563]

Augustine of Hippo

Augustine reflects on the nature of the bishop's role and the qualities required of a bishop in three sermons which he preached at the beginning of the fifth century.

In Sermon 339, which was preached in about 425 on the anniversary on Augustine's ordination as a bishop. Augustine stresses that being a bishop is a serious burden because it involves being accountable to God for the people for whom he is the bishop. He writes:

This, you see, is the difference between each one of you and me, that you, practically speaking, are only going to render an account for yourselves alone, while I shall be giving one both for myself and for you. That's why the burden is so much greater; but carried well it wins greater glory, while if it is handled unfaithfully, it hurls one down into the most appalling punishment. [564]

Referring to Jesus' parable of the pounds in Luke 19:11-27, Augustine goes on to say that it terrifies him because it tells him of his responsibility as a bishop to pay out what he has been given by God, or, in other words, to teach his people what he himself has been taught by God through the Bible whether they want to hear it or not:

I could easily say, you see, 'What business is it of mine to be wearisome to people; to say to the wicked, 'Don't act wickedly, act like this, stop acting like that'? What business is it of mine to be burdensome to people? I've received instructions how I should live; let me live as I've been told to, as I've been commanded. Let me sign for what I have received; why should I give an account for others?' The gospel terrifies me; because nobody could outdo me in enjoying such anxiety-free leisure. There's nothing better, nothing more pleasant

---

[563] Ambrose, *On the Duties of the Clergy,* Bk 1: 50:258 p. 41.
[564] Augustine, Sermon 339:1 in Edmund Hill, *Augustine Sermons III/9* (Hyde Park: New City Press, 1994.) p.279.

than to search through the divine treasure chest' with nobody making a commotion; it's pleasant, it's good. But to preach, to refute, to rebuke, to build up, to manage for everybody, that's a great burden, a great weight, a great labour. Who wouldn't run away from this labour? But the gospel terrifies me. [565]

In sermon 340, a sermon which he preached in about 415, again on the anniversary of his ordination as bishop, Augustine, declares that being a bishop involves following the example of Peter by showing love for God by herding God's sheep. However, showing love for God in this way is not something for which a bishop can claim a reward because it is only through the grace of God, and not through his own efforts, that he is able to respond to God's love in this way:

I am certainly obliged to love the redeemer, and I know what he said to Peter: Peter, do you love me? Feed my sheep (Jn 21:16). This was said once, said again, said a third time. Love was being questioned and toil commanded, because where the love is greater, the toil is less. What shall I pay back to the Lord for all that he has paid-back for me? (Ps 1 1 6: 12). If I say that what I am paying back is my herding his sheep, even here it is not I who am doing it, but the grace of God with me (1 Cor 15: 10). So when can I be found to be paying him back, since he gets in first every time? And yet, because we love freely, because we are herding his sheep, we look for a reward. How shall this be? How can 'I love freely and that's why I'm herding sheep' be consistent with 'I request a reward, because I'm herding sheep'? This couldn't possibly happen, in no way at all could a reward be sought from one who is loved freely, unless the reward were the very one who is being loved. I mean, if what we are paying back for his having redeemed us is our herding his sheep, what are we paying back for his having made us shepherds? Being bad shepherds, you see —which God preserve us from —is something we are by our own badness; whereas good shepherds—which God grant we may be —is something we can only be by his grace.[566]

565 Augustine, Sermon 339: 4, p. 282.
566 Augustine, Sermon 340: 2, p. 293.

Augustine then goes on to emphasise what he calls 'the vast and varied activity' involved in a bishop caring for the individual pastoral needs of each of the sheep:

The turbulent have to be corrected, the faint-hearted cheered up, the weak supported; the gospel's opponents need to be refuted, its insidious enemies guarded against; the unlearned need to be taught, the indolent stirred up, the argumentative checked; the proud must be put in their place, the desperate set on their feet, those engaged in quarrels reconciled; the needy have to be helped, the oppressed to be liberated, the good to be given your backing, the bad to be tolerated; all must be loved

In order that a bishop can sustain this ministry, the bishop and his people need to pray for one another, as Paul asked his churches to pray for him (Romans 15:30, Colossians 4:3, 1 Thessalonians 5:2, 2 Thessalonians 3:1), that he may instruct them appropriately and that they may be obedient to what he tells them:

Just as I, you see, have to give thought with great fear and anxiety to how I may blamelessly carry out my duties as bishop; so you for your part must make a point of showing a humble and eager obedience to everything that is commanded you. So let us pray together, dearly beloved, that my tenure as bishop may be of profit both to me and to you. It will profit me, if I tell you what has to be done; and you, if you do what you hear. You see, if we all pray tirelessly, I for you and you for me, with the perfect love of charity, we shall all happily attain, with the Lord's help, to eternal bliss.[567]

In Sermon 340 A, which was preached in 411 at the ordination of another bishop, Augustine declares that a bishop is called to be a servant of his fellow Christians who, like him, are also servants of the same Lord:

[567] Augustine Sermon 340: 4, p. 294.

So, to put it in a nutshell, we are your servants; your servants, but also your fellow servants. We are your servants, but all of us here have one Lord and master. We are your servants, but in Jesus, as the apostle says: *ourselves, though, your servants through Jesus* (2 Corinthians 4:5). Through him we are servants, slaves, and through him we are also free; he said himself, after all, to those who believed in him, *If the Son sets you free, you shall be free indeed* (John 8:36).So shall I hesitate to become a slave through him, seeing that unless I had become a freeman through him, I would have remained in a hopeless slavery? We have been put in charge, and we are slaves; we are in authority, but only if we are of use.[568]

This call to be a servant, involving a willingness to suffer for the Lord's sheep, and even lay down one's life for them, is the 'good work' referred to by Paul in 1 Timothy 3:1 and Augustine comments that anyone who wants to be bishop but does not want to undertake this 'good work' is not really a bishop at all, even if he has the title:

Desiring the office of bishop is not desiring the office of bishop; it is setting your heart on a good work.

But doesn't he want to be a bishop, the one who doesn't do a good work, but his own work?

This man doesn't desire the office of bishop. It's what I was saying a moment ago; he's seeking the name, not the real thing.'

I want to be a bishop; oh, if only I were a bishop!'

Would that you were! Are you seeking the name, or the real thing? If it's the real thing you're seeking, you are setting your heart on a good work. If it's the name you're seeking, you can have it even with a bad work, but with a worse punishment.

So what shall we say? Are there bad bishops? Perish the thought, there aren't any; yes, I have the nerve, the gall to say, there are no bad

---

[568] Augustine, Sermon 340 A: 3, p. 296.

bishops; because if they are bad, they aren't bishops. You are calling me back again to the name, and saying, 'He is a bishop, because he is seated on the bishop's throne.' And a straw scarecrow is guarding the vineyard.[569]

On the other hand, Augustine also insists, over against the arguments of the Donatists, that the moral failures of bishops present no barrier to the faithful being fed by God through their ministry. What matters, he declares, is whose pantry the food comes from, not the vessel in which it is contained:

...don't let your hopes rest on men. We are good, we are ministers; we are bad, we are ministers. But if we are good, we are faithful ministers, really and truly ministers.

Pay attention to what we administer; if you're really hungry, and don't wish to be ungrateful, notice from whose pantry you are provided for. If you are eagerly longing to eat it, don't let it bother you what sort of dish it is set before you in. In the great house of a gentleman, there are not only vessel of gold and silver, but also of earthenware (2 Timothy 2:20). It's a silver vessel, a golden vessel, an earthenware vessel; what you have to consider is whether it contains bread, and whose bread this is, by whose gift it is being served you. He's the one you must fix your attention on, the one I'm talking about, the one by whose gift this bread is being served to you. He himself is the bread; I am the living bread, who have come down from heaven (John 6:51).[570]

On the subject of whether bishops should be married, Augustine acknowledges that Paul laid down that a bishop should the husband of one wife (1 Timothy 3:2), but then says that 'it would be much better if he didn't even have one.' He then goes on to argue that a bishop who does not have a wife can still have submissive and obedient children (1 Timothy 3:4-5) if the faithful (his spiritual children) are obedient to him:

---

[569] Augustine, Sermon 340 A:6, p. 300.
[570] Augustine, Sermon 340 A:9, p. 302.

...your bishop in the name of Christ, assisted by the grace of Christ, has decided not to have children according to the flesh, in order to have children according to the spirit. So it is your business to comply properly with his wishes, properly to obey him, to serve him with appropriate service; and then he will have children who are compliant—so many for just a few, heavenly ones for earthly ones, and instead of heirs, fellow heirs with him.[571]

Gregory the Great

Gregory the Great's *The Book of Pastoral Rule* was written at the start of his ministry as Bishop of Rome in 590. It was written in response to a letter from John, Bishop of Ravenna, in which John reproved Gregory 'for having wished by hiding myself to fly from the burdens of pastoral care.'[572] Gregory's response to this reproof was to write to John explaining why he viewed the burdens of pastoral care as being so heavy that he had sought to avoid them:

...lest to some they should appear light, I express with my pen in the book before you all my own estimate of their heaviness, in order both that he who is free from them may not unwarily seek them, and that he who has so sought them may tremble for having got them.[573]

The book is divided in four parts. In Part I he sets out the qualifications needed for being a bishop.

He explains that no one should become a bishop simply out of a desire for personal distinction if they have not already learned how to be an effective physician of souls:

No one presumes to teach an art till he has first, with intent meditation, learned it. What rashness is it, then, for the unskilful to assume pastoral authority, since the government of souls is the art of

---

[571] Augustine, Sermon 340 A:7 p.300.
[572] Gregory the Great, *The Book of Pastoral Rule*, Part I: Prologue, in The *Nicene and Post Nicene Fathers*, series 2, vol. XII (Edinburgh and Grand Rapids: T&T Clark/Eerdmans, 1997), p. 1.
[573] Gregory the Great, *The Book of Pastoral Rule*, Part I: Prologue, p.1.

arts! For who can be ignorant that the sores of the thoughts of men are more occult than the sores of the bowels? And yet how often do men who have no knowledge whatever of spiritual precepts fearlessly profess themselves physicians of the heart, though those who are ignorant of the effect of drugs blush to appear as physicians of the flesh! But because, through the ordering of God, all the highest in rank of this present age are inclined to reverence religion, there are some who, through the outward show of rule within the holy Church, affect the glory of distinction. They desire to appear as teachers, they covet superiority to others, and, as the Truth attests, they seek the first salutations in the marketplace, the first rooms at feasts, the first seats in assemblies Matthew 23:6-7, being all the less able to administer worthily the office they have undertaken of pastoral care, as they have reached the magisterial position of humility out of elation only. [574]

By contrast, the person who ought to be a bishop is someone who has a strong spiritual life, is committed to biblical and theological study, and is experienced in prayer:

That man, therefore, ought by all means to be drawn with cords to be an example of good living who already lives spiritually, dying to all passions of the flesh; who disregards worldly prosperity; who is afraid of no adversity; who desires only inward wealth; whose intention the body, in good accord with it, thwarts not at all by its frailness, nor the spirit greatly by its disdain: one who is not led to covet the things of others, but gives freely of his own; who through the bowels of compassion is quickly moved to pardon, yet is never bent down from the fortress of rectitude by pardoning more than is meet; who perpetrates no unlawful deeds, yet deplores those perpetrated by others as though they were his own; who out of affection of heart sympathizes with another's infirmity, and so rejoices in the good of his neighbour as though it were his own advantage; who so insinuates himself as an example to others in all he does that among them he has nothing, at any rate of his own past deeds, to blush for; who studies so

---

[574] Gregory the Great, *The Book of Pastoral Rule*, Part I: I, p.1

to live that he may be able to water even dry hearts with the streams of doctrine; who has already learned by the use and trial of prayer that he can obtain what he has requested from the Lord, having had already said to him, as it were, through the voice of experience, While you are yet speaking, I will say, Here am I [Isaiah 58:9]. [575]

In Part II Gregory goes on to list nine characteristics that need to be possessed by a bishop ('ruler').

1. The bishop should always be 'pure in thought' since:

...no impurity ought to pollute him who has undertaken the office of wiping away the stains of pollution in the hearts of others also; for the hand that would cleanse from dirt must needs be clean, lest, being itself sordid with clinging mire, it soil whatever it touches all the more. [576]

2. The bishop should always be 'chief in action' (i.e provide the clearest example of what it means to live out the Christian faith) so that:

...by his living he may point out the way of life to those that are put under him, and that the flock, which follows the voice and manners of the shepherd, may learn how to walk better through example than through words. For he who is required by the necessity of his position to speak the highest things is compelled by the same necessity to exhibit the highest things. For that voice more readily penetrates the hearer's heart, which the speaker's life commends, since what he commands by speaking he helps the doing of by showing. [577]

3. The bishop should know when to be silent and when to speak:

...lest he either utter what ought to be suppressed or suppress what he ought to utter. For, as incautious speaking leads into error, so

---

[575] Gregory the Great, *The Book of Pastoral Rule*, Part I: X, p. 7.
[576] Gregory the Great, *The Book of Pastoral Rule*, Part II: II, p.9.
[577] Gregory the Great, *The Book of Pastoral Rule*, Part II: III, p.10.

indiscreet silence leaves in error those who might have been instructed. For often improvident rulers, fearing to lose human favour, shrink timidly from speaking freely the things that are right; and, according to the voice of the Truth (John 10:12), serve unto the custody of the flock by no means with the zeal of shepherds, but in the way of hirelings; since they fly when the wolf comes if they hide themselves under silence.[578]

4. The bishop should know how to balance care for their neighbour with a life of contemplative prayer:

...a near neighbour to everyone in sympathy, and exalted above all in contemplation, so that through the bowels of loving-kindness he may transfer the infirmities of others to himself, and by loftiness of speculation transcend even himself in his aspiration after the invisible; lest either in seeking high things he despise the weak things of his neighbours, or in suiting himself to the weak things of his neighbours he relinquish his aspiration after high things.[579]

5. The bishop should know how to be companionable to those who live well while also being willing to use the authority of his office to take action against all forms of wrongdoing:

...a companion of good livers, and, through the zeal of righteousness, rigid against the vices of evil-doers; so that in nothing he prefer himself to the good, and yet, when the fault of the bad requires it, he be at once conscious of the power of his priority; to the end that, while among his subordinates who live well he waives his rank and accounts them as his equals, he may not fear to execute the laws of rectitude towards the perverse.[580]

---

[578] Gregory the Great, *The Book of Pastoral Rule*, Part II: IV, p.11.
[579] Gregory the Great, *The Book of Pastoral Rule*, Part II: V, pp.12-13.
[580] Gregory the Great, *The Book of Pastoral Rule*, Part II: VI, p.14.

6. The bishop should care for both people's spiritual and physical well-being:

The ruler should not relax his care for the things that are within, in his occupation among the things that are without, nor neglect to provide for the things that are without in his solicitude for the things that are within.[581]

7. The bishop should seek to be loved, but only in order to draw people to God:

It is right for good rulers to desire to please men; but this in order to draw their neighbours by the sweetness of their own character to affection for the truth; not that they should long to be themselves loved, but should make affection for themselves as a sort of road by which to lead the hearts of their hearers to the love of the Creator.[582]

8. The bishop should 'understand how commonly vices pass themselves off as virtues.' For example, 'inordinate laxity is believed to be loving-kindness, and unbridled wrath is accounted the virtue of spiritual zeal.'[583]

9. The bishop should know how to deal with sin differently in different circumstances:

It should be known too that the vices of subjects ought sometimes to be prudently connived at, but indicated that they are connived at; that things, even though openly known, ought sometimes to be seasonably tolerated, but sometimes, though hidden, be closely investigated; that they ought sometimes to be gently reproved, but sometimes vehemently censured. [584]

---

[581] Gregory the Great, *The Book of Pastoral Rule*, Part II: VII, p.17.
[582] Gregory the Great, *The Book of Pastoral Rule*, Part II: VIII, p.19.
[583] Gregory the Great, *The Book of Pastoral Rule*, Part II: IX, p.20.
[584] Gregory the Great, *The Book of Pastoral Rule*, Part II: X, p.20.

In order to be a person who has these characteristics, Gregory adds, the bishop needs to be someone who spends time daily in the study of the Bible.

But all this is duly executed by a ruler, if, inspired by the spirit of heavenly fear and love, he meditate daily on the precepts of Sacred Writ, that the words of Divine admonition may restore in him the power of solicitude and of provident circumspection with regard to the celestial life, which familiar intercourse with men continually destroys; and that one who is drawn to oldness of life by secular society may by the aspiration of compunction be ever renewed to love of the spiritual country. For the heart runs greatly to waste in the midst of human talk; and, since it is undoubtedly evident that, when driven by the tumults of external occupations, it loses its balance and falls, one ought incessantly to take care that through keen pursuit of instruction it may rise again. For hence it is that Paul admonishes his disciple who had been put over the flock, saying, Till I come, give attendance to reading 1 Timothy 4:13. Hence David says, How have I loved Your Law, O Lord! It is my meditation all the day Psalm 109:97.[585]

In Part III Gregory draws on the work of Gregory Nazianzen and emphasises that in his teaching the bishop needs to address different kinds of people differently. As he puts in the prologue:

Therefore according to the quality of the hearers ought the discourse of teachers to be fashioned, so as to suit all and each for their several needs, and yet never deviate from the art of common edification. For what are the intent minds of hearers but, so to speak, a kind of tight tensions of strings in a harp, which the skilful player, that he may produce a tune not at variance with itself, strikes variously? And for this reason the strings render back a consonant modulation, that they are struck indeed with one quill, but not with one kind of stroke. Whence every teacher also, that he may edify all in the one virtue of

---

[585] Gregory the Great, *The Book of Pastoral Rule*, Part II: XI, p.23.

charity, ought to touch the hearts of his hearers out of one doctrine, but not with one and the same exhortation.[586]

Gregory then develops this point by listing seventy-two types of people (arranged in thirty six matching pairs) who require to be 'admonished' (taught the meaning of obedience to God's word) in a different fashion. Three of these matching pairs will illustrate Gregory's approach.

Servants and masters:

Differently to be admonished are servants and masters. Servants, to wit, that they ever keep in view the humility of their condition; but masters, that they lose not recollection of their nature, in which they are constituted on an equality with servants. Servants are to be admonished that they despise not their masters, lest they offend God, if by behaving themselves proudly they gainsay His ordinance: masters, too, are to be admonished, that they are proud against God with respect to His gift, if they acknowledge not those whom they hold in subjection by reason of their condition to be their equals by reason of their community of nature. The former are to be admonished to know themselves to be servants of masters; the latter are to be admonished to acknowledge themselves to be fellow-servants of servants. For to those it is said, 'Servants, obey your masters according to the flesh' (Colossians 3:22); and again, 'Let as many servants as are under the yoke count their masters worthy of all honour' (1 Timothy 6:1); but to these it is said, 'And you, masters, do the same things unto them, forbearing threatening, knowing that both their and your

The whole and the sick:

Differently to be admonished are the whole and the sick. For the whole are to be admonished that they employ the health of the body to the health of the soul: lest, if they turn the grace of granted soundness to the use of iniquity, they be made worse by the gift, and afterwards

---

[586]Gregory the Great, *The Book of Pastoral Rule*, Part III, Prologue, p.24.

merit the severer punishments, in that they fear not now to use amiss the more bountiful gifts of God. The whole are to be admonished that they despise not the opportunity of winning health forever. For it is written, 'Behold now is the acceptable time, behold now is the day of salvation' (2 Corinthians 6:2) ...But, on the other hand, the sick are to be admonished that they feel themselves to be sons of God in that the scourge of discipline chastises them. For, unless He purposed to give them an inheritance after correction, He would not have a care to educate them by afflictions. For hence the Lord says to John by the angel, 'Whom I love I rebuke and chasten' (Revelation 3:19; Proverbs 3:11).[587]

Those at variance and those at peace

Differently to be admonished are those that are at variance and those that are at peace. For those that are at variance are to be admonished to know most certainly that, in whatever virtues they may abound, they can by no means become spiritual if they neglect becoming united to their neighbours by concord. For it is written, 'But the fruit of the Spirit is love, joy, peace' (Galatians 5:22) ...But, on the other hand, those that are at peace are to be admonished to take heed lest, while they love more than they need do the peace which they enjoy, they have no longing to reach that which is perpetual. For commonly tranquil circumstances more sorely try the bent of minds, so that, in proportion as the things which occupy them are not troublesome, the things which invite them come to appear less lovely, and the more present things delight, eternal things are the less sought after. Whence also the Truth speaking in person, when He would distinguish earthly from supernal peace, and provoke His disciples from that which now is to that which is to come, said, 'Peace I leave with you, My peace I give unto you' (John 14:27). That is, I leave a transitory, I give a lasting peace. If then the heart is fixed on that which is left, that which is to be given is never reached. Present peace, therefore, is to be held as

---

[587] Gregory the Great, *The Book of Pastoral Rule*, Part III, XII, pp.34-35.

something to be both loved and thought little of, lest, if it is loved immoderately, the mind of him that loves be taken in a fault.[588]

Having set out the admonition that needs to be given to these thirty-six pairs, Gregory then makes the further point that while it is difficult for the bishop to address the spiritual needs of individuals it is even more difficult, but nonetheless necessary, for the bishop to address the needs of several different types of people at once:

These are the things that a Bishop of souls should observe in the diversity of his preaching, that he may solicitously oppose suitable medicines to the diseases of his several hearers. But, whereas it is a matter of great anxiety, in exhorting individuals, to be of service to them according to their individual needs, since it is a very difficult thing to instruct each person in what concerns himself, dealing out due consideration to each case, it is yet far more difficult to admonish innumerable hearers labouring under various passions at one and the same time with one common exhortation. For in this case the speech is to be tempered with such art that, the vices of the hearers being diverse, it may be found suitable to them severally, and yet be not diverse from itself; that it pass indeed with one stroke through the midst of passions, but, after the manner of a two-edged sword, cut the swellings of carnal thoughts on either side; so that humility be so preached to the proud that yet fear be not increased in the timid; that confidence be so infused into the timid that yet the unbridled licence of the proud grow not; that solicitude in well doing be so preached to the listless and torpid that yet licence of immoderate action be not increased in the unquiet; that bounds be so set on the unquiet that yet careless torpor be not produced in the listless; that wrath be so extinguished in the impatient that yet negligence grow not in the easy and soft-hearted; that the soft-hearted be so inflamed to zeal that yet fire be not added to the wrathful; that liberality in giving be so infused into the niggardly that yet the reins of profusion be in no wise loosened to the prodigal; that frugality be so preached to the prodigal

---

[588] Gregory the Great, *The Book of Pastoral Rule*, Part III: XXII, pp. 48-49.

that yet care to keep perishable things be not increased in the niggardly; that marriage be so praised to the incontinent that yet those who are already continent be not called back to voluptuousness; that virginity of body be so praised to the continent that yet fecundity of the flesh come not to be despised by the married. Good things are so to be preached that ill things be not assisted sideways. The highest good is so to be praised that the lowest be not despaired of. The lowest is so to be cherished that there be no cessation of striving for the highest from the lowest being thought sufficient.[589]

In addition, Gregory also warns against the bishop giving people teaching that they are not yet ready to receive:

But the preacher should know how to avoid drawing the mind of his hearer beyond its strength, lest, so to speak, the string of the soul, when stretched more than it can bear, should be broken. For all deep things should be covered up before a multitude of hearers, and scarcely opened to a few. For hence the Truth in person says, 'Who, do you think, is the faithful and wise steward, whom his Lord has appointed over his household, to give them their measure of wheat in due season?' (Luke 12:42). Now by a measure of wheat is expressed a portion of the Word, lest, when anything is given to a narrow heart beyond its capacity, it be spilt. Hence Paul says 'I could not speak unto you as unto spiritual, but as unto carnal. As it were to babes in Christ, I have given you milk to drink, and not meat' (1 Corinthians 3:1-2). [590]

Finally in Part IV Gregory finishes the Pastoral Rule by warning against the danger of the bishop becoming proud and self-confident:

But since often, when preaching is abundantly poured forth in fitting ways, the mind of the speaker is elevated in itself by a hidden delight in self-display, great care is needed that he may gnaw himself with the laceration of fear, lest he who recalls the diseases of others to health by remedies should himself swell through neglect of his own health;

[589] Gregory the Great, *The Book of Pastoral Rule*, Part III, XXXVI, p.69.
[590] Gregory the Great, *The Book of Pastoral Rule*, Part III, XXXIX, pp.70-71.

lest in helping others he desert himself, lest in lifting up others he fall. For to some the greatness of their virtue has often been the occasion of their perdition; causing them, while inordinately secure in confidence of strength, to die unexpectedly through negligence. For virtue strives with vices; the mind flatters itself with a certain delight in it; and it comes to pass that the soul of a well-doer casts aside the fear of its circumspection, and rests secure in self-confidence; and to it, now torpid, the cunning seducer enumerates all things that it has done well, and exalts it in swelling thoughts as though super excellent beyond all beside. Whence it is brought about, that before the eyes of the just judge the memory of virtue is a pitfall of the soul; because, in calling to mind what it has done well, while it lifts itself up in its own eyes, it falls before the author of humility. For hence it is said to the soul that is proud, 'For that you are more beautiful, go down, and sleep with the uncircumcised' (Ezekiel 32:19): as if it were plainly said, Because you lift yourself up for the comeliness of your virtues, you are driven by your very beauty to fall.[591]

In order to combat this danger, writes Gregory:

...it is needful that, when abundance of virtues flatters us, the eye of the soul should return to its own weaknesses, and salubriously depress itself; that it should look, not at the right things that it has done, but those that it has left undone; so that, while the heart is bruised by recollection of infirmity, it may be the more strongly confirmed in virtue before the author of humility.[592]

How does the Patristic view of the role and necessary characteristics of bishops relate to the teaching of the New Testament?

The Patristic teaching about the role and necessary characteristics of bishops that we have looked at in this chapter is more developed than the teaching about these topics that is given in the New Testament.

---

[591] Gregory the Great, *The Book of Pastoral Rule*, Part IV, p.71
[592] Gregory the Great, *The Book of Pastoral Rule*, Part IV, p.72

Nonetheless, the essential content of this Patristic teaching is in line with what we find in the Bible.

In the Patristic writings, as in the New Testament, bishops are senior elders who are called by God to be the rulers and instructors of the churches, caring for the spiritual and physical needs of their flock, teaching those committed to their charge to believe in, and live according to, the gospel of the saving work of God in Jesus Christ, as taught in the Old and New Testaments. They are to guard the Church against those who would mislead and divide God's people, and they are to exercise pastoral discipline, to preside over the Church's worship, to ordain and to be involved in healing. In addition, though confirmation by bishops is first referred to in the *Apostolic Tradition* of Hippolytus, this too can be traced back to the practice of the Church in New Testament ties.

In the Patristic writings, as in the New Testament, bishops are to be Christians of good character who can provide models of godly living. They are to be people who are well versed in the teaching of Scripture, and who can effectively address the theological and pastoral issues that arise in the course of their ministry on the basis of this teaching. They are to be people who know themselves to be servants of God who are accountable to him for their service. They are to be people who are conscious of their own weakness and their need of God's help and the prayers of God's people. They are to be people who are willing to remain faithful to God even to the point of death, knowing that death is the gateway to life.

The idea of the bishop as the physician of souls, which recurs in the Patristic writings, is not directly taught in the New Testament, but it is a helpful metaphor which builds on the biblical idea that salvation is a form of healing (Malachi 4:2, Luke 4:18, 5:31-32) and emphasises the truth that we do find taught by the New Testament, that different people have different spiritual needs that need to be addressed differently.

For many Protestant theologians the insistence of Ignatius and Cyprian that the Church consists of the faithful united with their bishop is problematic because they do not see any such idea taught in the New Testament.

What this objection fails to note, however, is that the reason that Ignatius and Cyprian define the visible Church in the way that they do is because they believe, correctly, that the Church is meant to be a place in which God's people live in peace and unity with each other under the leaders that God has appointed, and in their context that meant living in peace and unity under the leadership of godly bishops. What they do not address, because this was not an issue for their time as it was at the Reformation, is what God's people should do if no godly bishops are available. However, it is not fair to criticise them for not tackling an issue which was not relevant for their time. In their own time what they said was perfectly reasonable.

Cyprian's idea that there is one episcopate in which all bishops share is not taught in the New Testament, but it makes perfectly good sense if we understand that he is thinking in terms of an office which all bishops equally exercise. It makes sense to say that the office of apostle was one office in which Peter, Paul and John equally shared. In a similar fashion it makes sense to say with Cyprian that there is one office of bishops in which Ignatius, Irenaeus and Cyprian equally shared. Another way of making the same point would be to say that just as there was a single apostolic college of which Peter, James and John were equally members, so also there is a single college of bishops of which Ignatius, Irenaeus and Cyprian were equally members.

Another aspect of Patristic teaching which is not taught in the New Testament, but which makes good sense in the light of what the New Testament does say is the idea that we find in Irenaeus, Cyprian and Augustine that a bishop who does not teach the apostolic faith, who is unwilling to embrace the responsibilities of the episcopal role, and who has departed from what the faith requires in a major way (such as not standing firm in the face of persecution) is not someone who can rightly be said to be a Catholic bishop (with the corollary that the faithful should seek another bishop instead)

This is because to be a bishop is not simply to hold the title, but to accept God's call be a certain kind of person, someone who holds the apostolic faith, who is willing to accept the responsibilities of being a bishop, and who faithfully exercises those responsibilities even when the going gets tough.

On the other hand, the teaching of the New Testament that the treasure of God's grace is contained in 'earthen vessels, to show that the transcendent power belongs to God and not to us' (2 Corinthians 4:7) means that Augustine was right to insist that the moral failures of bishops do not mean that we cannot received the grace of God through their ministry. To maintain this would be to wrongly limit the power of God.

Where Patristic teaching can legitimately be seen to depart from the teaching of the New Testament is in the insistence of Ambrose that widowed bishops should not re-marry and that married bishops must remain celibate and Augustine's declaration that although Scripture permits a bishop to have one wife it would be better for a bishop not to be married at all. There is nothing at all in the New Testament that suggests either that it would be better for bishops not to be married, or that they should be celibate if they are.

If Paul had held that elders, and hence bishops, should not be married he would have made this point in 1 Timothy 3:2 and Titus 1:6 rather than insisting that they should be faithful to their wives (which is what the phrase 'husband of one wife means[593]). Furthermore, Paul insists in 1 Corinthians 7:3-5 that Christian husbands and wives should have regular sex, an insistence which Ambrose's call for married bishops to be celibate contradicts.

---

[593] See Larry Hurtado, *Destroyer of the gods* (Waco: Baylor University Press, 2016), pp.166-167.

In this chapter we have looked at Patristic teaching about bishops in general. In the next chapter we shall go on to consider the teaching of the New Testament and the Patristic period about the role of the Bishop of Rome.

Chapter 9
The Biblical and Patristic Teaching about the role of the Bishop of Rome

1. The teaching of the Roman Catholic Church

At the end of chapter 4 it was noted that from the fifth century onwards a new group of churches emerged in Western Europe which acknowledged the overall authority of the Pope as not only the Patriarch of the Western Church, but the senior bishop of the Church as whole.

This is the position which continues to be upheld today by the churches belonging to the Roman Catholic Church. The teaching of the Roman Catholic Church is that as the successor of Peter the Bishop of Rome (the Pope) is the senior bishop of the Church throughout the world and has authority over all other bishops as well as the other clergy and the laity.

Pastor Aeternus
Thus, the *First Dogmatic Constitution on the Church of Christ* (*Pastor Aeternus*) agreed at the First Vatican Council in 1870 declares that the government of the Church was entrusted by Christ to Peter:

...the primacy of jurisdiction over the universal Church of God was immediately and directly promised and given to blessed Peter the Apostle by Christ the Lord. For it was to Simon alone, to whom he had already said: 'Thou shalt be called Cephas,' [John 1: 42] that the Lord after the confession made by him, saying: 'Thou art the Christ, the Son of the living God,' addressed these solemn words: 'Blessed art thou, Simon Bar-Jona, because flesh and blood have not revealed it to thee, but my Father who is in heaven. And I say to thee that thou art Peter; and upon this rock I will build my Church, and the gates of hell shall not prevail against it. And I will give to thee the keys of the kingdom of heaven. And whatsoever thou shalt bind on earth, it shall be bound also in heaven; and whatsoever thou shalt loose on earth, it shall be loosed also in heaven.' [Matthew 16:16-19] And it was upon Simon alone that Jesus after his resurrection bestowed the jurisdiction of chief pastor and ruler over all his fold in the words: 'Feed my lambs; feed my sheep.' [John 21:15-17] [594]

Peter, it says, continues to exercise the role given to him by Christ through his successors, the Popes:

That which the Prince of Shepherds and great Shepherd of the sheep, Jesus Christ our Lord, established in the person of the blessed Apostle Peter to secure the perpetual welfare and lasting good of the Church, must, by the same institution, necessarily remain unceasingly in the Church; which, being founded upon the Rock, will stand firm to the end of the world. For none can doubt, and it is known to all ages, that the holy and blessed Peter, the Prince and Chief of the Apostles, the pillar of the faith and foundation of the Catholic Church, received the keys of the kingdom from our Lord Jesus Christ, the Saviour and Redeemer of mankind, and lives, presides, and judges, to this day and always, in his successors the Bishops of the Holy See of Rome, which was founded by him, and consecrated by his blood. Whence, whosoever succeeds to Peter in this See, does by the institution of Christ himself obtain the Primacy of Peter over the whole Church.[595]

This being the case:

...resting on plain testimonies of the Sacred Writings, and adhering to the plain and express decrees both of our predecessors, the Roman Pontiffs, and of the General Councils, we renew the definition of the œcumenical Council of Florence, in virtue of which all the faithful of Christ must believe that the holy Apostolic See and the Roman Pontiff possesses the primacy over the whole world, and that the Roman Pontiff is the successor of blessed Peter, Prince of the Apostles, and is true vicar of Christ, and head of the whole Church, and father and

---

[594] *First Dogmatic Constitution on the Church*, Ch. I, in Philip Schaff, Creeds of *Christendom* at https://ccel.org/schaff/creeds2.v.ii.i.html,
[595] *First Dogmatic Constitution on the Church*, Ch. II.

teacher of all Christians; and that full power was given to him in blessed Peter to rule, feed, and govern the universal Church by Jesus Christ our Lord; as is also contained in the acts of the General Councils and in the sacred Canons.

Hence we teach and declare that by the appointment of our Lord the Roman Church possesses a superiority of ordinary power over all other churches, and that this power of jurisdiction of the Roman Pontiff, which is truly episcopal, is immediate; to which all, of whatever rite and dignity, both pastors and faithful, both individually and collectively, are bound, by their duty of hierarchical subordination and true obedience, to submit not only in matters which belong to faith and morals, but also in those that appertain to the discipline and government of the Church throughout the world, so that the Church of Christ may be one flock under one supreme pastor through the preservation of unity both of communion and of profession of the same faith with the Roman Pontiff.[596]

Lumen Gentium

In similar fashion, *The Dogmatic Constitution on the Church* (*Lumen Gentium*) agreed at the Second Vatican Council in 1964, while stressing the importance of episcopal collegiality, goes on to insist that:

...the college or body of bishops has no authority unless it is simultaneously conceived of in terms of its head, the Roman Pontiff, Peter's successor, and without any lessening of his power of primacy over all, pastors as well as the general faithful. For in virtue of his office, that is, as Vicar of Christ and pastor of the whole Church, the Roman Pontiff has full, supreme, and universal power over the Church. And he can always exercise this power freely.

The order of bishops is the successor to the college of the apostles in teaching authority and pastoral rule; or, rather, in the episcopal order the apostolic body continues without a break. Together with its head,

---

[596] *First Dogmatic Constitution on the Church,* Ch. III.

the Roman Pontiff, and never without this head, the episcopal order is the subject of supreme and full power over the universal Church. But this power can be exercised only with the consent of the Roman Pontiff. For our Lord made Simon Peter alone the rock and key-bearer of the Church (Cf. Matthew 16:18-19) and appointed him shepherd of the whole flock (c John 21:15ff). [597]

The theology of Papal authority found in *Pastor Aeternum* and *Lumen Gentium* can be also be found in the teaching of Pope Leo I in the fifth century and Pope Gregory the Great in the sixth century.

The teaching of Leo I

In a sermon delivered on the anniversary of his elevation to the Pontificate, Leo quotes the promise of Christ to Peter in Matthew 16:18-19 and declares that, in accordance with this promise, Peter remains present in the see of Rome and at the helm of the Church as a whole.

The dispensation of Truth therefore abides, and the blessed Peter persevering in the strength of the Rock, which he has received, has not abandoned the helm of the Church, which he undertook. For he was ordained before the rest in such a way that from his being called the Rock, from his being pronounced the Foundation, from his being constituted the Doorkeeper of the kingdom of heaven, from his being set as the umpire to bind and to loose, whose judgments shall retain their validity in heaven, from all these mystical titles we might know the nature of his association with Christ. And still today he more fully and effectually performs what is entrusted to him, and carries out every part of his duty and charge in Him and with Him, through Whom he has been glorified. And so if anything is rightly done and rightly decreed by us, if anything is won from the mercy of God by our daily supplications, it is of his work and merits whose power lives and whose authority prevails in his See. For this, dearly-beloved, was gained by that confession, which, inspired in the Apostle's heart by

---

[597] *Dogmatic Constitution on the Church*, Ch.III.22 in Walter Abbott (ed.), *The Documents of Vatican II* (London: Geoffrey Chapman, 1967), p.43.

God the Father, transcended all the uncertainty of human opinions, and was endued with the firmness of a rock, which no assaults could shake. For throughout the Church Peter daily says, 'You are the Christ, the Son of the living God,' and every tongue which confesses the Lord, accepts the instruction his voice conveys. This Faith conquers the devil, and breaks the bonds of his prisoners. It uproots us from this earth and plants us in heaven, and the gates of Hades cannot prevail against it. For with such solidity is it endued by God that the depravity of heretics cannot mar it nor the unbelief of the heathen overcome it.[598]

He then goes on to say that Peter continues to exercise the ministry given to him by Christ through his successors in the see of Rome, including even such a humble and unworthy successor as Leo himself:

And so, dearly beloved, with reasonable obedience we celebrate today's festival by such methods, that in my humble person he may be recognized and honoured, in whom abides the care of all the shepherds, together with the charge of the sheep commended to him, and whose dignity is not abated even in so unworthy an heir. And hence the presence of my venerable brothers and fellow priests, so much desired and valued by me, will be the more sacred and precious, if they will transfer the chief honour of this service in which they have deigned to take part to him whom they know to be not only the patron of this see, but also the primate of all bishops. When therefore we utter our exhortations in your ears, holy brethren, believe that he is speaking whose representative we are: because it is his warning that we give, nothing else but his teaching that we preach, beseeching you to 'gird up the loins of your mind' [1 Peter 1:13]. and lead a chaste and sober life in the fear of God, and not to let your mind forget his supremacy and consent to the lusts of the flesh. Short and fleeting are the joys of this world's pleasures which endeavour to turn aside from the path of life those who are called to eternity. The faithful and religious spirit, therefore, must desire the things which are heavenly,

[598] Leo I, *Sermon III.3* in *The Nicene and Post Nicene Fathers*, series 2, vol XII (Edinburgh and Grand Rapids: T&T Clark/Eerdmans, 1997), p.117.

and being eager for the Divine promises, lift itself to the love of the incorruptible Good and the hope of the true Light. But be sure, dearly-beloved, that your labour, whereby you resist vices and fight against carnal desires, is pleasing and precious in God's sight, and in God's mercy will profit not only yourselves but me also, because the zealous pastor makes his boast of the progress of the Lord's flock. 'For you are my crown and joy' [1 Thessalonians 2:20}, as the Apostle says; if your faith, which from the beginning of the Gospel has been preached in all the world has continued in love and holiness. For though the whole Church, which is in all the world, ought to abound in all virtues, yet you especially, above all people, it becomes to excel in deeds of piety, because founded as you are on the very citadel of the Apostolic Rock, not only has our Lord Jesus Christ redeemed you in common with all men, but the blessed Apostle Peter has instructed you far beyond all men.[599]

In a letter sent to Anastasius, Bishop of Thessalonica, in 446, Leo goes on to explain how there is a hierarchy in the episcopate which has at its centre the chair of Peter occupied by the Pope.

Bishops indeed, have a common dignity, but they have not uniform rank, much as even among the blessed apostles, notwithstanding the similarity of their honourable estate, there was a certain distinction of power. While the election of all of them was equal, yet it was given to one [i.e. St. Peter] to take the lead of the rest. From this model has arisen a distinction of bishops also, and by an important ordinance it has been provided that everyone should not arrogate everything to himself, but there should be in each province one whose opinion should have precedence among the brethren; and again certain whose appointment is in the greater cities should undertake a fuller responsibility, and that through them the care of the universal Church should converge towards Peter's one chair and nothing everywhere should be separate from its head.[600]

---

[599] Leo I, Sermon III.4, pp.117-118.
[600] Leo I. Epistle XIV.11, in John Kelly, *Early Christian Doctrines*, 4ed (London: A&C Black, 1980), p. 420.

The teaching which we find in such passages from Leo is helpfully summarised by John Kelly as follows:

First, the famous gospel texts referring to St. Peter should be taken to imply that supreme authority was confirmed by our Lord upon the apostle. Secondly, St. Peter was actually bishop of Rome, and his magisterium was perpetuated in his successes in that see. Thirdly, St. Peter being in this way, as it were, mystically present in the Roman see, the authority of other bishops throughout Christendom does not derive immediately from Christ, but (as in the case of the apostles) is mediated to them through St. Peter, i.e, through the Roman pontiff who in this way represents him, or, to be more precise, is a kind of *Petrus redivivus*. Fourthly, while their mandate is of course limited to their own dioceses, St. Peter's magisterium. and with it that of his successors, the popes of Rome, is a *plenitudo potestatis* extending over the entire church, so that its government rests ultimately with them, and they are its divinely appointed mouthpiece. [601]

The teaching of Gregory the Great.
Similar teaching about the role of the Pope can be found in the letters of Gregory the Great.

Thus, in a letter to the Emperor Maurice, Gregory writes:

For to all who know the Gospel it is apparent that by the Lord's voice the care of the whole Church was committed to the holy Apostle and Prince of all the Apostles, Peter. For to him it is said, Peter, do you love Me? Feed My sheep [John 21:17]. To him it is said, Behold Satan has desired to sift you as wheat; and I have prayed for you, Peter, that your faith fail not. And thou, when you are converted, strengthen your brethren [Luke 22:31-32]. To him it is said, You are Peter, and upon this rock I will build My Church, and the gates of hell shall not prevail against it. And I will give unto you the keys of the kingdom of heaven and whatsoever you shall bind an earth shall be bound also in heaven;

---

[601] Kelly, p.420.

and whatsoever you shall loose on earth shall be loosed also in heaven [Matthew 16:18].

Lo, he received the keys of the heavenly kingdom, and power to bind and loose is given him, the care and principality of the whole Church is committed to him, and yet he is not called the universal apostle; while the most holy man, my fellow priest John, attempts to be called universal bishop. I am compelled to cry out and say, *O tempora, O mores!*[602]

Gregory's rejection of the title 'universal bishop' and his objection to its use by the Patriarch of Constantinople has sometimes been interpreted as if Gregory rejected the whole idea that any one bishop had authority over Church as a whole. However, as the letter just quoted makes clear, this was not the case. As he goes on to say later on in the same letter:

...in honour of Peter, Prince of the apostles, it was offered by the venerable synod of Chalcedon to the Roman pontiff. But none of them has ever consented to use this name of singularity, lest, by something being given peculiarly to one, priests in general should be deprived of the honour due to them. How is it then that we do not seek the glory of this title even when offered, and another presumes to seize it for himself though not offered?

As this quotation shows Gregory's objection to the term 'universal bishops' was that it implied that there was only one bishop for the whole world, whereas his position was that there were numerous bishops, but that as the successor of Peter the Pope has authority over all of them.

A further example of Gregory's view of the authority of the Church of Rome can be found in letter written to a church official called John the Subdeacon about the election of a new Bishop of Milan [Medioloanum]. Gregory writes:

[602] Gregory the Great, *Letters Book 5:20* in *The Nicene and Post Nicene Fathers*, series 2, vol XII (Edinburgh and Grand Rapids: T&T Clark/Eerdmans, 1997*),* p.170.

Inasmuch as it is manifest that the Apostolic See is, by the ordering of God, set over all Churches, there is, among our manifold cares, special demand for our attention, when our decision is awaited with a view to the consecration of a bishop. Now on the death of Laurentius, bishop of the church of Mediolanum, the clergy reported to us that they had unanimously agreed in the election of our son Constantius, their deacon. But, their report not having been subscribed, it becomes necessary, that we may omit nothing in the way of caution, for you to proceed to Genua (Genoa), supported by the authority of this order. And, inasmuch as there are many Milanese at present there under stress of barbarian ferocity, you must call them together, and enquire into their wishes in common. And, if no diversity of opinion separates them from the unanimity of the election — that is to say, if you ascertain that the desire and consent of all continues in favour of our aforesaid son, Constantius — then you are to cause him to be consecrated by his own bishops, as ancient usage requires, with the assent of our authority, and the help of the Lord; to the end that through the observance of such custom both the Apostolic See may retain the power belonging to it, and at the same time may not diminish the rights which it has conceded to others.[603]

What we see in this letter is the belief that God has ordained that the Church of Rome, as the Church of the Apostle Peter, should have authority over all the other churches and that it is the role of the Pope exercise this authority, in this case by giving assent to the election of a new bishop.

What this evidence shows is that the view of the authority of the Popeas the successor of Peter that is found in subsequent Roman Catholic teaching can be found as far back as the fifth century. The question, however, is how far back this view goes. Can we trace this view of Papal authority back through the earlier Patristic period to the New Testament itself? As we shall see, the answer to this question is 'No.'

[603] Gregory the Great. *Letters Book 3:30* in *The Nicene and Post Nicene Fathers*, series 2, vol XII, p.128.

2. Peter in the New Testament.

In the Gospels we are told that Peter was one of the first disciples called to follow Jesus (Matthew 4:18-19, Mark 1:16-17, Luke 5:1-11, John 1:40-42), he always comes first when the twelve disciples are listed (Matthew 10:1-4, Mark 3:13-19, Luke 6:12-16) and along with James and John he formed an inner circle around Jesus (Mark 5:37, Matthew 17:1, Mark 14:33). Peter also acts as a spokesman for the twelve (Matthew 15:15, 18:21, Mark 1:36-38, 9:5, 10:28, 11:21, 14:29-32, Luke 5:5, 12:41). In particular he speaks for all the disciples when he confesses that Jesus is 'the Christ, the Son of the Living God' (Matthew 16:13-20, Mark 8:27-30, Luke 9:18-21).

After the resurrection Peter received an individual visitation and a personal recommissioning from the risen Jesus (Luke 24:34, 1 Corinthians 15:5, John 21:15-19) and in the early chapters of Acts it is Peter who is the leading figure in the life of the early church. Peter organises the appointment of a replacement for Judas Iscariot (Acts 1:15-26). Peter addresses the crowd on the day of Pentecost and after the healing of the lame man at the temple (Acts 2:14-41, 3:11-26). Peter enacts judgement on Ananias and Sapphira (Acts 5:1-11). Peter rebukes Simon Magus for seeking to purchase the power of the Spirit (Acts 8:17-24). It is Peter who raises Tabitha from the dead (Acts 9:46-53), and it is Peter who evangelises and baptises Cornelius and his household (Acts 10:1-18).

However, after his deliverance from prison in Acts 12:1-17 Peter largely drops out of view in the rest of Acts, only reappearing briefly at the Council of Jerusalem (Acts 15:7-11, 14) with the focus of the narrative switching to the missionary activity of Paul which is undertaken without any reference to Peter.

Furthermore, there is no evidence in the New Testament for the idea that Peter had authority separate from, and greater than, the authority given to the other apostles. This point is well made by Harold Browne who makes the following eight points in his commentary on the *Thirty Nine Articles*:

(1) If it had done so, we should have found some commission of this kind given to him in Scripture. There is plain enough commission to the Apostleship; but none to a hyper- apostleship, nor any mention of the existence of such an office in the history of the Gospels and Acts, or in the Epistles of the Apostles. (2) There is no title of pre-eminence given to St. Peter, such as Vicar of Christ, Sovereign Pontiff, or Arch-apostle. (3) There was no office known to the Apostles or the primitive Church higher than that of Apostleship. This, St. Chrysostom tells us, is 'the greatest authority, the very summit of authorities.' (4) Our Lord distinctly declared against any such superiority; and said that if any of the Apostles coveted it, he should be counted least of all (Matthew 20:27, 23:8, Mark 9:34-35, 10:44, Luke 9:46, 22:14, 24, 26). (5) St. Peter in his Epistles claims no peculiar authority (see 1 Peter 5:1, 2 Peter 3:2); and in the history there is no appearance of his taking it. The appeal in Acts 15 is not to St. Peter, but to the Apostles and elders: and the decree runs in their names, ver.22. If anyone presided there, it was not he, but St. James. Nay! The other Apostles took upon themselves to *send* Peter and John into Samaria (Acts 8:14); and 'he that is sent is not greater than he that sends him (John 13:16). (6) If St. Peter had been the visible head of the church, those who are of Paul or of Apollos might indeed been factious: but St. Paul as severely reproves for a schismatical spirit those who say, 'I am of Cephas' (1 Corinthians 1:12, 3:21). (7) The complete independence of the Apostles in all their proceedings, in their missionary journeys, their founding of Churches, etc. shews the same thing (see 1 Corinthians 4:14, 15, 9:2, Galatians 4:19 etc). (8) St. Paul's conduct especially proves, that he owned no dependence on St. Peter, nor subjection to him. He declares himself, 'in nothing behind the very chiefest Apostles' (2 Corinthians 12:11). On his conversion he took no counsel with men, not even with the Apostles (Galatians 1:16-17); but acted on his independent commission derive directly from Christ (Galatians 1:1). James, Cephas, and John gave him the right hand of fellowship, as their equal and co-Apostle (Galatians 2:9). He hesitated not to 'withstand St. Peter to the face, because he was to be blamed '(Galatians 2:11). And St. Chrysostom observes, that thus St. Paul shewed himself equal to St. Peter, St. John, and St. James, and that by comparing himself, not to the

others, but to their leader, he proved that each enjoyed equal dignity and importance. [604]

The three key New Testaments texts.

There are, however, three New Testament passages which are commonly appealed to as showing that Peter was given was given a special commission by Christ.

The first is Matthew 16:17-19, the text appealed to by Leo I and Gregory the Great, and then subsequently by *Pastor Aeturnus* and *Lumen Gentium*. In this passage we read that after Peter's confession of faith:

...Jesus answered him, 'Blessed are you, Simon Bar-Jona! For flesh and blood has not revealed this to you, but my Father who is in heaven. And I tell you, you are Peter, and on this rock I will build my church, and the powers of death shall not prevail against it. I will give you the keys of the kingdom of heaven, and whatever you bind on earth shall be bound in heaven, and whatever you loose on earth shall be loosed in heaven.'

As Leithart notes:

The text makes it clear that Jesus is speaking to Peter. Peter gives Jesus a title 'Christ;' Jesus in return gives Peter a title, *petros*, rock. Then He goes on to say that He will build His church on the *petra*. Jesus' pun identifies himself as foundational to the church (Matthew 16:18). Of course, it is the Peter-who-confesses-Jesus who is the rock. Of course, Jesus is *the* Rock, the chief cornerstone of the church. But there is no reason to deny that Jesus is calling Peter a foundation stone of the church. There is every reason to think this is exactly what he is saying.[605]

---

[604] E. Harold Browne, *An Exposition of the Thirty-Nine Articles*, 5ed (London: John W Parker and Son, 1840), p. 804.
[605] Peter Leithart, *The Gospel of Matthew Through New Eyes*, Vol 2 (West Monroe: Athanasius Press, 2018), Kindle edition, p.57.

However, what we find in Ephesians 2:20 and Revelation 21:14 is that it is not just Peter but all the apostles who are the foundation stones on which the Church is built. The Church is indeed built on Peter, but it is built on the other apostles as well. Similarly, the power of the keys given to Peter in Matthew 16:19, the power to admit and exclude people from the kingdom of God, is given to the apostles collectively in Matthew 18:18 and John 20:22-23. As before, what is true of Peter individually is true of the apostles collectively.

The second passage is Luke 22:31-32, referred to by Gregory the Great. Here we read:

Simon, Simon, behold, Satan demanded to have you, that he might sift you like wheat, but I have prayed for you that your faith may not fail; and when you have turned again, strengthen your brethren.

As William Kerr comments, these words 'lay the future duty on Peter as one who has fallen and been restored to be active in comforting and establishing others who might be wavering or who had gone astray like himself.'[606] What these words do not do, is give Peter any kind of unique authority among the apostles. In the words of Kerr:

The injunction to 'confirm' or 'strengthen' his brethren conferred no peculiar prerogative on Peter. The word is often used in the New Testament. St. Paul sent Timothy to the Thessalonians to 'strengthen' their faith. St. Paul himself longed to go to Rome for the 'strengthening' of the Christians there (Romans 1:11). [607]

The third passage is John 21:15-17, referred by Gregory the Great and then by *Pastor Aeternus* and *Lumen Gentium*. In this passage we are told that after the resurrected Jesus had breakfast with the disciples by the Sea of Galilee:

---

[606] William Kerr, *A Handbook on the Papacy* (London: Marshall, Morgan and Scott, 1950), p.51.
[607] Kerr, pp.50-51.

Jesus said to Simon Peter, 'Simon, son of John, do you love me more than these?' He said to him, 'Yes, Lord; you know that I love you.' He said to him, 'Feed my lambs.' A second time he said to him, 'Simon, son of John, do you love me?' He said to him, 'Yes, Lord; you know that I love you.' He said to him, 'Tend my sheep.' 17 He said to him the third time, 'Simon, son of John, do you love me?' Peter was grieved because he said to him the third time, 'Do you love me?' And he said to him, 'Lord, you know everything; you know that I love you.' Jesus said to him, 'Feed my sheep.'

To quote Kerr again:

The threefold query and the threefold charge 'Feed my lambs;' Tend my sheep;' 'Feed my sheep' correspond to Peter's threefold denial. It is the definite assurance that Peter had not finally forfeited his pastoral mission as one of the twelve by his apostasy.[608]

However:

To claim that it conferred on him special privileges of rulership or authority over the other disciples, or in any unique manner constituted him the supreme shepherd of the Church, is utterly unfounded. All the disciples had the duty of tending the Lord's sheep. The one who had terribly fallen away is now reinstated in his former place among the rest.

St. Peter himself has shown that the charge did not mean some special monopoly of authority but the general rule for all pastors or presbyters -a reminder of a duty already imposed: 'The elders there for among you I exhort who am a fellow elder…. tend the flock of God which is among you (1 Peter 5:1-2. St. Paul's words the presbyters of Ephesus are a parallel. Take heed unto yourselves, and to all the flock, in which the Holy Ghost hath made you bishops, to feed the Church of God, which he purchased with his own blood (Acts 20:28). The feeding and tending the sheep is the common duty of all pastors. The telling St.

---

[608] Kerr, p.52.

Peter then to fulfil it is accounted for by his lamentable personal history.[609]

None of these three passages therefore describe the giving of a special commission to Peter alone. No role is given to Peter that is not shared either with the other apostles, or with other leaders of the Church.

Furthermore, none of these passages suggests that any prerogative given to Peter will then be passed on to the Popes as his episcopal successors. This idea has to be read into these three passages. It cannot be found in them.

3. What do the Patristic writings say about the role of the Bishop of Rome?

What we have seen in the preceding section is that the sort of claims made for the Popes as the successors of Peter which can be found from the fifth century onwards cannot be found in the New Testament. The New Testament is silent about a special authority which is given to Peter, but not to the other apostles, and says nothing about the Popes being Peter's successors.

If we now turn to the writings of the Patristic period we find that the view of the authority of the Popes found in the sermons and letters of Leo I and Gregory the Great is not a view that can be found in the Patristic period as a whole.

The Second Century

Clement of Rome
If we begin by looking at the evidence of *First Clement* we find a letter written, as we saw in chapter 3, by one of the first Popes. However, this letter is completely silent about any authority possessed by the Pope over other churches. Clement nowhere tells the Corinthians that they should do what he is urging them to do because he is writing to them as the Bishop of Rome, or as the successor of Peter.

---

[609] Kerr, pp.52-53.

This fact is important, because Clement would have known what Peter himself had taught about the role of the Pope and if Peter had taught that the Pope possessed God given authority over all other churches one would expect Clement to have appealed to that fact when calling on the members of the Corinthian church to amend their ungodly behaviour. He would have said 'I urge by the authority given to Peter' or something to that effect. The fact that he makes no such appeal is best explained if Clement was unaware of any such teaching by Peter.

Ignatius of Antioch

Moving on to the letters of Ignatius of Antioch, here too we find no reference to authority possessed by the Pope over other bishops and churches. There are two phrases in the preface to his letter to the church in Rome which have been seen as giving a special authority to that church. The first is when he refers to the fact that the church 'presides in the place of the district of the Romans' and the second is when he refers to it 'presiding over love.' [610]

It has been argued by Roman Catholic apologists that the first phrase should be understood as referring to 'the church in the place of the district of the Romans which presides over the universal Church' and that in the second phrase 'love,' in the original literally 'the love,' means 'the Church' so that here also we have a reference to the universal authority of the church of Rome.[611]

The first point that needs to be made in response to this argument is that even if this interpretation of these two phrases is accepted, this would only show that Ignatius accepted the universal authority of the church of Rome. It would not show that he accepted the claims later made for the Pope as the successor of Peter.

Secondly, however, this interpretation of these two phrases should not be accepted. The idea that the Roman church presides over the Church

[610] Ignatius of Antioch, *To the Romans,* Preface, in Lightfoot, Harmer and Holmes, pp. 101-102.
[611] E Giles, *Documents Illustrating Papal Authority* (London: SPCK: 1952), p.5.

as whole has to be read into the first phrase. 'Presides' is most naturally understood in relation to the geographical qualifier that follows and the whole phrase then means that the church in the city of Rome presides (i.e has ecclesiastical jurisdiction) both in the city and the surrounding area. It is the same idea as is found in Tertullian's later statement that the churches founded by the apostles 'preside over their own places.'[612] This being, the case 'presiding over the love' cannot mean 'presiding over the universal Church.' 'Presiding' probably means 'preeminent,' and, in the words of Vall, what Ignatius is saying is that the Christians in Rome 'have a reputation among the churches for their practice of the corporal works of mercy.'[613] They are a church renowned for their loving actions.

The witness of Ignatius is important for the same reason as the witness of Clement. Ignatius too would have known the teaching and practice of the Church in the apostolic age and given his passionate interest in the role of the bishops in the life of the Church it is inconceivable that he would not have made mention of the universal Petrine authority of the Pope had this idea been known to him. His silence about the matter is a strong indication that no such idea had been taught by the Church in apostolic times.

Dionysius of Corinth

As mentioned in chapter 3, Bishop Dionysius of Corinth wrote to Soter, Pope in about 171 and in this letter he addresses the Christians in Rome as follows:

For this has been your practice from the beginning: to do good in various ways to all the brethren, and to send supplies to the many churches in every city, thus relieving the want of the needy, now making provision, by the supplies which you have sent from the beginning, for brethren in the mines; and thus as Romans you observed the hereditary custom of Romans, which your blessing bishop Soter has not only maintained, but even added to, by providing

---

[612] Tertullian, *On the Prescription of Heretics*, 36 in Giles, p. 22.
[613] Vall, p.151.

an abundance of supplies to the saints and by exhorting with blessed words, as a loving father his children, the brethren who come up. [614]

In this letter, 'the brethren who come up' are Christians who come to Rome from elsewhere and to whom Soter provides words of exhortation. What the letter shows us is that the Roman church, and Soter as their bishop, had continued to show the practical love mentioned by Ignatius and that is bishop was welcoming to visiting Christians. What it does not indicate is any idea of Soter, as Bishop of Rome, having any authority over the church in Corinth.

Irenaeus

As we saw in chapter 3, in his work *Against Heresies*, Irenaeus held that the true faith has been handed down through lines of episcopal succession which have their origin in the appointment of the first bishops by the apostles themselves, and to illustrate this point he referred to the apostolic succession in the churches of Rome, Smyrna and Ephesus.

In what he says about the church in Rome it is important to note that Irenaeus does not see the episcopal succession in Rome as going back solely to Peter. As we have seen, his view is that 'The blessed apostles, then, having founded and built up the Church, committed into the hands of Linus the office of the episcopate.'[615] The 'blessed apostles' are Peter and Paul and so what Irenaeus is saying is that Linus was jointly appointed as the first Bishop of Rome by both apostles together. What matters to him is not that Linus and the bishops that followed him were Peter's successors (and therefore the inheritors of unique episcopal privileges first given to him), but that they were the successors of the apostles, who in this case happened to be Peter and Paul. To put it another way, if the Roman episcopal succession went back to Paul alone (as in the case of the church in Ephesus), or had gone back to John, that would be equally significant as far as Irenaeus

---

[614] Dionysius of Corinth, letter to Soter, Eusebius, *Ecclesiastical History*, 4:23, text in Giles, pp.6-7.
[615] Irenaeus of Lyons, *Against Heresies*, Bk.III.3.3, p.416.

is concerned. His point about the apostolic basis of Catholic doctrine would still stand.

In the section of *Against Heresies* immediately preceding his account of the Roman episcopal succession Irenaeus writes concerning the Church in Rome:

Ad hanc enim ecclesiam propter potentiorem principalitatem necesse est omnem convenire ecclesiam, hoc est, eos qui sunt undique fideles, in qua semper ab his qui sunt undique conservata est ea quae est ab apostolis traditio.[616]

This is a very compressed statement and how to translate it is a matter of dispute. Roman Catholic writers have seen it is a statement that Christians everywhere need to be in communion with the See of Rome. For example, Charles Allnatt translates Irenaeus as follows:

For with this Church, on account of her more powerful headship (or supremacy), it is necessary that every Church, that is, the faithful everywhere dispersed, should agree (or be in communion); in which (in communion with which) Church has always been preserved by the faithful dispersed that tradition which is from the apostles.[617]

Even if this was a correct translation it would not establish that according to Irenaeus the reason for Rome's supremacy was the prerogatives given by Christ to Peter and then handed down to the successive Popes In any case, it can be seen to be an incorrect translation because it would make Irenaeus go against the basic argument he is putting forward in this section of *Against Heresies,* which is that in each orthodox church the Catholic faith has been separately preserved by being passed down a succession of orthodox bishops from the time of the apostles. The faith has not been preserved through communion with Rome, but through separate lines of faithful bishops.

---

[616] Irenaeus of Lyons, Against Heresies, BK III.3.2 in Giles, p. 10.
[617] Charles Allnatt, *Catheda Petri*, p.85 cited in Kerr p.90.

As George Salmon argues, what Irenaeus really seems to be saying is something along the following lines:

Rome is, on account of its civil greatness, a place to which every Church must resort: that is to say, every Church does not come thither officially, but Christians cannot help coming to the city from the Churches in every part of the world. We have no need, then, to examine the apostolic tradition of these churches in their respective lands. We can learn it from their members to be found in Rome, who, being in communion with the Roman Church, must agree with it in doctrine, and thus the Apostolic tradition preserved in the capital has been preserved not by native Romans only, but by the faithful collected in the city from every part of the world.[618]

To use an image later used to describe Constantinople, for Irenaeus Rome is like a reservoir into which Christians from all over the world flow, bringing the apostolic faith of their churches with them.

The controversy about the date of Easter

As we also saw in chapter 3, at the end of the second century Pope Victor tried to insist that Easter should always be celebrated on a Sunday. Synods across the Christian world agreed with this proposal, but the churches of Asia Minor, led by Polycrates Bishop of Ephesus, declared their intention of continuing to observe what they held to be the apostolic custom of celebrating Easter on the on the 14th day of Nisan (the day of the Jewish Passover) whatever day of the week that fell.

As Eusebius records, Victor's response was to excommunicate them:

Thereupon Victor, the president of the [church] of the Romans, endeavoured to cut off by a single stroke the communities of the whole of Asia, together with the neighbouring churches, from the common union, on the ground of unorthodoxy; and, indeed,

---

[618] George Salmon, *The Infallibility of the Church* (London: John Murray 1914), p.382.

371

denounced them in letters, proclaiming that the brethren in those parts were all wholly excommunicate.[619]

However, as Eusebius goes on to write:

This did not please all the bishops without exception. On the contrary they exhorted him in reply to have a mind for the things which make for peace and neighbourhood union and charity. And their words are extant also, in which they censure Victor somewhat sharply.

One of these was Irenaeus, who wrote in the name of the brethren in Gaul, whose leader he was; and while holding that the mystery of the Lord's resurrection should be celebrated on the Lords day and on that alone, he nevertheless suitably gives victor much counsel besides, not to cut off whole churches of God for observing an ancient custom handed down to them. And then he goes on to add in these very words:

'For not only is there a controversy about the day, but also about the very manner of the fast. For some think they ought to fast a single day, but others two, others again even more. and in the opinion of others, the 'day' amounts to forty continuous hours.

And this variety of observance did not originate in our time, but much further back, in the times of those before us, who, no doubt mistakenly, held closely, in their simplicity and ignorance, to this custom, and have transmitted it to posterity. Yet nonetheless they all lived in peace, and we live in peace, with one another; and the difference concerning the fast enhances the unanimity of our faith.' [620]

This is the first recorded occasion on which a Pope attempted to impose uniformity of practice and ecclesiastical discipline on the Church as whole. The fact that it failed, and that even those who agreed with Victor on the issue of when Easter should be celebrated were prepared to censure his action shows that they did not take the

---

[619] Eusebius, *Ecclesiastical History*, 4:23:9, text in Giles, p.16.
[620] Eusebius, *Ecclesiastical History*, 4:23, 10-13, text in Giles, pp. 16-17.

view that Victor as the Pope possessed unquestionable authority as the successor of Peter. They seem to have taken the view that even though Victor was the bishop of a very important church, he was still just another bishop and as such could and should be criticised by his fellow bishops when he got things wrong.

The Third Century

Tertullian

If we move on to the third century, we find that Tertullian refers to the position of the church in Rome in his work *The Prescription of Heretics* which was written at the turn of the second and third centuries. In chapter 22 of this work Tertullian responds to the claim made by the Gnostic heretics that there were matters of which the apostles were ignorant by declaring:

What man, then, of sound mind can possibly suppose that they were ignorant of anything, whom the Lord ordained to be masters (or teachers), keeping them, as He did, inseparable (from Himself) in their attendance, in their discipleship, in their society, to whom, 'when they were alone, He used to expound 'all things' [Mark 4:34] which were obscure, telling them that 'to them it was given to know those mysteries,' [Matthew 13:11] which it was not permitted the people to understand? Was anything withheld from the knowledge of Peter, who is called 'the rock on which the church should be built,' [Matthew 16:18] who also obtained 'the keys of the kingdom of heaven,' with the power of 'loosing and binding in heaven and on earth?' [Matthew 16:19] Was anything, again, concealed from John, the Lord's most beloved disciple, who used to lean on His breast [John 21:20] to whom alone the Lord pointed Judas out as the traitor, whom He commended to Mary as a son in His own stead? [John 19:26] Of what could He have meant those to be ignorant, to whom He even exhibited His own glory with Moses and Elias, and the Father's voice moreover, from heaven? [Matthew 17:1-8]. Not as if He thus disapproved of all the rest, but because 'by three witnesses must every word be established' [Deuteronomy 19:15, 2 Corinthians 13:1][621]

In this passage Tertullian refers to the Petrine texts in Matthew 16, but he does not view them as giving Peter greater status than the rest of the apostles. For him all the apostles equally were ordained by Christ to be the teachers of his Church and instructed by him accordingly.

In similar fashion, in chapter 36 all the churches founded by the apostles are seen as having equal importance as witnesses to the apostles' teaching. As he sees it, those who want to know the way of salvation can find it in the apostolic teaching preserved in any of these churches:

Come now, you who would indulge a better curiosity, if you would apply it to the business of your salvation, run over the apostolic churches, in which the very thrones of the apostles are still pre-eminent in their places, in which their own authentic writings are read, uttering the voice and representing the face of each of them severally. Achaia is very near you, (in which) you find Corinth. Since you are not far from Macedonia, you have Philippi; (and there too) you have the Thessalonians. Since you are able to cross to Asia, you get Ephesus. Since, moreover, you are close upon Italy, you have Rome, from which there comes even into our own hands the very authority (of apostles themselves). How happy is its church, on which apostles poured forth all their doctrine along with their blood! Where Peter endures a passion like his Lord's! Where Paul wins his crown in a death like John's where the Apostle John was first plunged, unhurt, into boiling oil, and thence remitted to his island-exile! See what she has learned, what taught, what fellowship has had with even (our) churches in Africa! One Lord God does she acknowledge, the Creator of the universe, and Christ Jesus (born) of the Virgin Mary, the Son of God the Creator; and the Resurrection of the flesh; the law and the prophets she unites in one volume with the writings of evangelists and apostles, from which she drinks in her faith. This she seals with the

[621] Tertullian, *On Prescription Against Heretics,* XXII, p.253.

374

water (of baptism), arrays with the Holy Ghost, feeds with the Eucharist, cheers with martyrdom, and against such a discipline thus (maintained) she admits no gainsayer.[622]

In this passage Tertullian attributes the status of the Church in Rome to its association with the apostles Peter, Paul and John, and to the orthodoxy of its faith and practice. There is no suggestion that it has special status because Peter continues to exercise a unique authority through its bishop.

In his later work *On Modesty,* Tertullian criticises a bishop for granting absolution to those guilty of adultery and fornication:

I hear that there has even been an edict set forth, and a peremptory one too. The Pontifex Maximus — that is, the bishop of bishops — issues an edict: 'I remit, to such as have discharged (the requirements of) repentance, the sins both of adultery and of fornication.' O edict, on which cannot be inscribed, 'Good deed!'[623]

He further writes that the bishop in question was wrong to appeal to the power of the keys granted to Peter as justification for his action because this power was granted to Peter personally:

If, because the Lord has said to Peter, 'Upon this rock will I build My Church,' 'to you have I given the keys of the heavenly kingdom;' or, 'Whatsoever you shall have bound or loosed in earth, shall be bound or loosed in the heavens,' you therefore presume that the power of binding and loosing has derived to you, that is, to every Church akin to Peter, what sort of man are you, subverting and wholly changing the manifest intention of the Lord, conferring (as that intention did) this (gift) personally upon Peter? 'On you,' He says, 'will I build My Church;' and, 'I will give to you the keys,' not to the Church; and,

---

[622] Tertullian, *On Prescription Against Heretics,* XXXVI, p.p.260-261.
[623] Tertullian, *On Modesty*, I, in *The Ante-Nicene Fathers* vol. IV. (Edinburgh and Grand Rapids: T&T Clark/Eerdmans, 1994), p.74.

'Whatsoever you shall have loosed or bound,' not what they shall have loosed or bound. [624]

Although Tertullian never names the bishop he is criticising, most scholars think that the bishop in question is one of two Popes, either Pope Zephyrinus (198-217) or Pope Callistus (217-222). If this is correct it is clear that Tertullian does not accept that the authority given by Christ to Peter was passed on to the Pope as his successor. In addition, if Tertullian is using the terms 'Pontifex Maximus' and 'bishop of bishops' to refer to the Pope he is using these terms in an ironic fashion to suggest that the bishop in question has an exaggerated view of his own importance. It does not mean that these were titles that were actually used by the Pope at the time when he was writing.

Cyprian of Carthage

Moving on to Cyprian, as we saw in chapter 8, his teaching was that the role of leadership and oversight of the Church first given by Jesus to Peter has passed on to all subsequent bishops. In the words of B J Kidd, Cyprian 'takes the *Tu es Petrus* as the charter not of the Papacy but of the Episcopate.' [625]

We can see this in Epistle XXVI where Cyprian declares that Christ's words to Peter describe 'the honour of a bishop and the order of His Church.' For him what these words show is 'that the Church is founded upon the bishops, and every act of the Church is controlled by these same rulers.' [626]

In his treatise on the *On Unity of the Church*, Cyprian again quotes Matthew 16:18-19 but this time he uses it to stress the oneness of the Church. In the words of Michael Fahey, Matthew 16:18-19 is not cited

...to argue a form of jurisdictional primacy for the Roman bishop; rather it is cited to emphasize the oneness of the Church founded by

---

[624] Tertullian, *On Modesty*, XXI, p.98.
[625] B J Kidd, *The Roman Primacy to 461*, (London: SPCK, 1936), p.24.
[626] Cyprian, *Epistle XXVI*, p.305.

Christ first upon the person of Peter in order to provide an effective symbol of its oneness.[627]

We can see this point if we look again at the words of Cyprian himself:

...that He might set forth unity, [Christ] arranged by His authority the origin of that unity, as beginning from one. Assuredly the rest of the apostles were also the same as was Peter, endowed with a like partnership both of honour and power; but the beginning proceeds from unity. Which one Church, also, the Holy Spirit in the Song of Songs designated in the person of our Lord, and says, my dove, my spotless one, is but one. She is the only one of her mother, elect of her that bare her. [Song of Songs 6:9]. [628]

In this quotation Cyprian makes two points.

First, all the apostles share the same 'honour and power' that was given to Peter.

Secondly, this honour and power was given first to one individual as a symbol of the oneness of the Church, a oneness which is also testified to by the Holy Spirit in the words of the Song of Songs.

To suggest that Cyprian is pointing to the institutional authority of the Pope is thus to miss the point that he is making.

Further evidence of Cyprian's view that Christ's words to Peter do not mean that the Pope has greater authority than other bishops can be found in Epistle LIV. In this letter he writes to Bishop Cornelius of Rome concerning disaffected members of the church in Carthage who had taken their case to Rome and he declares:

For it has been decreed by our whole body, and is equally equitable and just, that every cause should be heard where the offence has been committed. A portion of the flock has been assigned to the several

---

[627] Michael Fahey, *Cyprian and the Bible: a Study in Third- Century Exegesis* (Tübingen: J. C.B. Mohr, 1971), p. 309.
[628] Cyprian, *On the Unity of the Church*, p.422.

shepherds which each is to rule and govern, having here after to give account of his administration to the Lord; it therefore behoves those over whom we are set not to run about from place to place, nor, by their crafty and deceitful boldness, break the harmonious concord of the bishops, but there to plead their cause where they will have both accusers and witnesses of their crime; unless perhaps some few desperate and abandoned men count inferior the authority of the bishops established in Africa who have already given judgement concerning them…. Already has their cause being heard; already has sentence been given concerning them.[629]

For Cyprian each local bishop is a shepherd who is given authority to 'rule and govern' their own flock and Rome does not have a superior jurisdiction which can overrule what other bishops have decided.

Cyprian further underlined his view of the authority of each local bishop in his opening speech at a council of eighty-seven African bishops held in Carthage in 256. The African church held that heretics needed to re-baptised, whereas Pope Stephen held that they should be re-admitted to the communion of the Church through the laying on of hands. Stephen insisted that all the churches should take his view and threatened to excommunicate those churches that would not come into line. In response Cyprian declared:

It remains that we severally declare our opinion only same subject, judging no one, nor depriving anyone of the right of communion if he differs from us. For no one of us setteth himself up as a Bishop of bishops, or by tyrannical terror forces his colleagues to a necessity of obeying; in as much as every Bishop, in the free use of his liberty and power, has the right of forming his own judgement, and can no more be judged by another then he can himself a judge another. But we must all await the judgement of our Lord Jesus Christ, who alone has

---

[629] Cyprian, *Epistle LIV:14*, text in Kerr p.104.

the power both of setting us in the Government of His Church and of judging of our acts therein.[630]

The view taken by the later Church, following the teaching of Augustine, was that Stephen was right on the theological issue in question, but for our purposes the point to realise is that Cyprian and the African church he represented rejected the idea that the Pope possessed the authority to lay down what the position of other bishops and churches should be. The letter sent by Bishop Firmilian of Caesarea to Cyprian (Epistle LXXIV) indicates that this was also the view taken by the Eastern Christian churches. In this letter Firmilian denounces Stephen for his 'open and manifest folly' and for the 'strifes and dissensions' he has 'stirred up throughout the churches of the whole world.' [631]

The Fourth Century

The Council of Arles

In 313 a council of bishops summoned by the new Christian Emperor Constantine was held in Rome. The council, which was chaired by the Pope, met to decide the claim by a group in the Church of Africa (later known as the Donatists) that the consecration of Caecilian as Bishop of Carthage had been invalid. The council decided that that the claim was unjustified, but the group who had made the claim appealed against the decision.

In response Constantine summoned another council to meet in Arles in 314 to reconsider the matter. This council had representatives from across the Western Church, including Roman Britain, and was chaired by the Bishop of Arles, Marinus. Like the previous council, this council upheld the position of Caecilian and it also issued a number of canons on various points of Church discipline.

---

[630] Kerr, p.107.
[631] Cyprian, Epistle LVII, 17 & 24 in *The Ante-Nicene Fathers*, vol.5 (Edinburgh and Grand Rapids, T&T Clark/ Eerdmans, 1995), pp.394 & 396.

The Pope, Sylvester, did not attend the Council of Arles. He was informed of what it had decided by a number of letters which tell him 'what we have decreed in common council' so that 'all may know what in future they ought to observe' and ask him to make the decisions of the council known.[632]

A Kidd notes, these letters show the Pope as the acknowledged leader of the Western Church and 'the centre of communications.'[633] However, the letters do not ask Sylvester to ratify the council's decision. He is expected to accept the decision which the council has made. The idea that the Pope, as the successor of Peter, has the decisive voice in the affairs of the Church is completely missing.

The Council of Nicaea

The same is true with regard to the Council of Nicaea in 325, which was summoned by Constantine to consider the dispute between Arius and Bishop Alexander of Alexandria over the relationship between the Father and the Son in the Godhead. Pope Sylvester did not attend (he was represented by two presbyters) and the council was chaired by Bishop Hosius of Cordoba. There is no suggestion in the accounts of the council in the church histories of Eusebius, Socrates or Sozomen that what the Pope thought about the matter was considered by the council, and, as before, he was informed of the decisions made by the council and not asked to ratify them.

In addition, as we noted in chapter 4, while the Canons issued by the council acknowledge the metropolitical authority of the Pope in southern Italy, they also acknowledge that the Bishop of Alexandria has similar metropolitical authority in Egypt and Libya and the Bishop of Antioch has similar metropolitical authority in the area stretching from the Mediterranean to Mesopotamia. There is no suggestion that the Pope has jurisdiction over the Church as a whole.

---

[632] Kerr, p.117.
[633] Kidd, p.90.

The fourth century disputes about the Trinity

The history of the disputes about the doctrine of the Trinity between the Council of Nicaea in 325 and the Council Constantinople in 381 also shows that the voice of the Pope was not seen as decisive. The various councils that took place in the course of this dispute were not chaired by the Pope and what the Pope thought was not the decisive factor in their deliberations.

Furthermore, if we look at the writings of the champions of Nicene orthodoxy such as Athanasius of Alexandria, Hilary of Poitiers and Basil of Caesarea we find that they do not take into account the teachings of the Pope on the subject. These are simply not important to them. For them the matter has to be decided on the basis of Scripture and the orthodox Christian tradition, not on the basis of what the Pope thinks.

In addition, Liberius, Pope from 352-366, abandoned Nicene orthodoxy under pressure from the Emperor Constantius, and declared himself out of communion with Athanasius and in communion with the Arians. Athanasius laments his fall and Hilary anathematises him ('anathema, I say to thee, Liberius and thy associates'), but neither of them thinks that his apostasy should shape what the Church as whole should think. Ultimately, what he thinks does not matter. Orthodoxy is orthodoxy whether the Pope adheres to it or not [634]

The Council of Constantinople

The final and decisive decision in favour of Nicene orthodoxy was made at the First Council of Constantinople in 381. Pope Damasus was not invited to attend the council, which was a council of the Eastern church, and he was not even represented at it.

Until his death the president of the council was Bishop Meletius of Antioch, a bishop who was not even acknowledged as a bishop by

---

[634] For the fall of Liberius see Salmon, pp.425-429 and Kerr, pp. 126-128.

Rome, which viewed his rival Paulinus as the Bishop of Antioch. As Kerr comments:

This is one of the most convincing fact that history affords, that the modern claims of the Pope were unknown to the early church. A council universally acknowledged as Oecumenical meets without any recognition of the Bishop of Rome, and without his being in anyway concerned in it. Its president is a prelate, who was outside the communion of Rome. Not only so, but when Meletius died during the Council the assembled bishops agreed to the appointment of a successor at Antioch in opposition to Paulinus, who was obstinately maintained by Rome to be the lawful bishop. [635]

The second Canon issued by the council laid down the principle that 'The bishops are not go beyond their dioceses to churches lying outside of their bounds' and specified the areas to be administered by the metropolitan bishops of Alexandria, Antioch, Ephesus, Pontus and Thrace. However, 'No mention is made of the supreme 'immediate' authority of the Bishop of Rome.' [636] As we saw in chapter 4, in the third Canon the Pope has the 'prerogative of honour' in the Church as whole, but it is implied that this is because of the civic status of Rome as the old Imperial capital. Nothing is said about the Pope being the successor of Peter who exercises the authority given to Peter by Christ.

The Council of Serdica

It is important to note, however, that there is one fourth century council, the Council of Serdica in 344, that does give an authority to the Pope that goes beyond that given to other bishops.

Canons 3 and 4 of this council lays down that a bishop who has been condemned for some offence may appeal to the Pope for the case against him to be reconsidered. While his appeal is being heard by the

[635] Kerr, p.137.
[636] Kerr, p.137.

judges appointed by the Pope for this purpose his see is not to be filled by anyone else. The texts of the Canons run as follows:

Canon 3

Bishop Hosius said: This also it is necessary to add — that bishops shall not pass from their own province to another province in which there are bishops, unless perchance upon invitation from their brethren, that we seem not to close the door of charity.

But if in any province a bishop have a matter in dispute against his brother bishop, one of the two shall not call in as judge a bishop from another province.

But if judgment have gone against a bishop in any cause, and he think that he has a good case, in order that the question may be reopened, let us, if it be your pleasure, honour the memory of St. Peter the Apostle, and let those who tried the case write to Julius, the bishop of Rome, and if he shall judge that the case should be retried, let that be done, and let him appoint judges; but if he shall find that the case is of such a sort that the former decision need not be disturbed, what he has decreed shall be confirmed. Is this the pleasure of all? The synod answered, It is our pleasure.

Canon 4

Bishop Gaudentius said: It ought to be added, if it be your pleasure, to this sentence full of sanctity which you have pronounced, that — when any bishop has been deposed by the judgment of those bishops who have sees in neighbouring places, and he [the bishop deposed] shall announce that his case is to be examined in the city of Rome— that no other bishop shall in any wise be ordained to his see, after the appeal of him who is apparently deposed, unless the case shall have been determined in the judgment of the Roman bishop.[637]

[637] The Council of Serdica, Canons 3 and 4, in *Council of Serdica (344)* at https://newadvent.org/fathers/3815.htm

The role granted to the Pope in these Canons has to be acknowledged. However, it also needs to be noted that

(a) This is decision by a council to grant a new role to the Pope and it is a decision that the bishops are under no obligation to make ('if it be your pleasure'). This is not a role that the Pope possesses by right.

(b) The Bishop of Rome's authority in the matter is strictly limited. The right of appeal belongs only to bishops, the Pope cannot order a case to be re-tried unless a bishop appeals to him first, he cannot summon parties to Rome, and he cannot decide the matter himself (his role is limited to deciding if the case should be re-heard and, if so, appointing judges).

As Gore notes, the later Church was clear that these Canons did not give the Pope unlimited authority:

When in the case of the African presbyter Apiarius, the Roman bishops quoted these canons of Sardica, as canons of Nicaea, and used them to justify interference with the ordinary jurisdiction of an African bishop over his presbyter, the Church of Africa first ascertained by consulting the oriental authorities that these canons were not Nicene, and proceeded in council to guard jealously the rights of their own Church and to repudiate the papal interference: 'We find it enacted in no council of the fathers that any persons may be sent as legates of your holiness. Do not therefore, at the request of any, send your clergy as agents for you, lest we seem to introduce into the Church of Christ the ambitious pride of the world.'[638]

The Council of Rome and the Letter of Siricius

At the end of the fourth century we also find two examples in which a council of the Western Church and a Pope make claims for the See of Rome which point towards the claims subsequently made by Leo I and by the Roman Catholic tradition thereafter.

[638] Charles Gore, *Roman Catholic Claims*, 3ed (London: Rivingtons, 1890), pp.114-115.

384

In 382 Bishop Damasus convened a council in Rome which was attended by the major metropolitan bishops of the Western Church, including Bishop Ambrose of Milan. In response to the third Canon of the Council of Constantinople the previous year, this council declared that:

...though all the catholic churches diffused throughout the world are but one bridal chamber of Christ, yet the holy Roman church has been set before the rest by no conciliar decrees, but has obtained the primacy by the voice of our Lord and Saviour in the gospel: 'Thou art Peter and upon this rock ...shall be loosed in heaven.' There is added also the society of the most blessed Paul, 'a chosen vessel,' who was crowned on one and the same day, suffering a glorious death, with Peter in the city of Rome, under Caesar Nero; and they alike consecrated the above-named Roman church to Christ the Lord, and set it above all others in the world by their presence and venerable triumph. [639]

This is a clear claim by a Western council that the primacy of the Roman Church rests on Christ's words to Peter in Matthew 16. However, three things need to be noted.

First, this is a new claim. It does not reflect a pre-existing tradition but is a response to what had been decreed at Constantinople the previous year.

Secondly, no explanation is offered as to why Christ's words to Peter support the primacy of the Roman church. In addition, there is a confusion within the statement as to whether it is the words of Christ to Peter, or the presence and martyrdom of both Peter and Paul, that give the primacy to Rome.

Thirdly, the statement itself says nothing about what the primacy of the Roman Church means in relation to the Popes themselves. It leaves

[639] Council of Rome, A.D. 382 in Giles p.131.

unanswered the question of what precisely the primacy of the Roman church means in terms of the ministry exercised by its bishops.

In 384 Siricius became Pope in succession to Damasus and in the following year he wrote a letter to the Spanish bishop Himerius of Tarragona in which he makes three significant statements.

First, he writes:

We [Siricius as Bishop of Rome] bear the burdens of all who are heavy laden, or rather the blessed apostle Peter bears them in us, who in all things, as we trust, protects and defends those who are heirs of his government.

Secondly, he refers to the matters which Himerius has referred to 'the Roman Church, as to the head of your body.'

Thirdly, he declares that 'no priest of the Lord is free to be ignorant of the statutes of the apostolic see.'[640]

In these statements Siricius increases the claims made for the bishop and church of Rome. He claims that Peter is present and active in some unique way in the ministry of the Popes. He claims that the Roman Church is not just the most important church, but the head, that is the directing element, of the Church as a whole. Finally, he claims that clergy have a duty to be aware of (and presumably to obey) what is laid down by Church of Rome, a claim that necessarily implies that what is decided by Rome has the status of law for the Church a whole.

As with what was said about the primacy of the Church of Rome in the Council of Rome in 382, these claims made by Siricius are novel and are devoid of theological justification. We are not told why, and how, Peter is present and active in the ministry of the Popes, why the Roman church is the head of the church as a whole, and why decisions by Rome are binding on the Church as whole.

[640] Siricus, Epistle 1 in Giles pp.142-143.

The Fifth Century

The Letters of Innocent I

In 417 Pope Innocent I wrote to the Council of Carthage in relation to the Pelagian controversy. In this letter he congratulates those involved in the Council because:

...You have truly strengthened the vigour of our religion, no less now in consulting than before in passing sentence. For you decided that it was proper to refer to our judgement, knowing what is due to the apostolic see, since all we who are set in this place desire to follow the very apostle from whom the very episcopate and the whole authority of this name has emerged; following whom, we know how to condemn the evil and to approve the good. So also, you have by your priestly office preserve the institutions of the fathers, and have not spurned that which they decreed by a sentence not human but divine, that whatever is done, even though it be in distant provinces, should not be ended until it comes to the knowledge of this see, that by its authority the whole just pronouncement should be strengthened, and that from there the other churches (like waters proceeding from their natal sources and flowing through the different regions of the world, the pure strains of a uncorrupt head) should take out what they ought to enjoin, whom they ought to wash, and whom that water, worthy of pure bodies, should avoid as defiled with uncleansable filth.[641]

In the same year Innocent also wrote to Bishop Silvanus of Numidia and the members of the Council of Mileve on the same issue and in similar terms:

It is therefore with due care and fitness that you consult the secrets of the Apostolic office (that office, I mean, to which belongs, besides those things that are outside, the care of all the churches) as to what opinion should be held on doubtful matters, following the form of the ancient rule which, you and I know, has ever been kept in the whole world. But this I pass by, because I am sure your prudence is aware of

---

[641] Innocent, Epistle 29 to the Council of Carthage, in Giles, p.201.

it: for how could you by your actions have confirmed it, unless you knew that answers to questions always flow through all provinces from the apostolic spring? Especially as often as questions of faith are to be ventilated, I think all our brothers and fellow bishops ought to refer to none but Peter, that is to the author of their name and office, even as your affection has now referred [to us] a matter which may benefit all churches in common throughout the whole world. For they must needs be more cautious when they see the inventor of these evils, on the reports of two synods, cut off by the decree of our sentence from ecclesiastical communion. [642]

In this letter we see the claim later reiterated by Leo I and subsequent Roman Catholic tradition that, in accordance with the ancient tradition of the Church going back to apostolic times ('the institution of the fathers'), the Pope, as the occupant of the See of Peter, has the authority to make decisions and exercise discipline in a way that is binding for the Church as a whole.

As Kelly argues, when Leo I put forward his claims for the authority of the Pope in the middle of the fifth century he was 'gathering together and giving final shape to' the claims for Roman primacy that had already been put forward by the Council of Rome and then by Popes Siricius and Innocent I.[643]

However, in the fifth century these claims were definitely not accepted by the Church as a whole.

Augustine
Augustine was the major theologian of the first half of the fifth century. In his writings he never explicitly addresses the issue of the authority of the Popes and of the Church of Rome. However, the teaching we do find in his writings is incompatible with the view of Papal authority put forward by the Popes and the Roman Catholic Church in the fifth century and then subsequently.

[642] Innocent, Epistle 30 to the Council of Mileve, in Giles, p.202.
[643] Kelly, pp. 419-420.

First, Augustine teaches that the only head of the universal Church is the glorified Christ:

And since the whole Christ is head and body, which truth I do not doubt that you know well, the head is our Saviour himself, who suffered under Pontius Pilate, who now, after he is risen from the dead, sits the right hand of the Father; but his body is the Church: not this church or that, but diffused over all the world, nor that only which exists among men living, for those also belong to it who were before us and are to be after us to the end of the world. For the whole church made up of all the faithful, because all the faithful are members of Christ, has its head, which governs the body, situate in the heavens; although it is separated from sight, yet it is bound by love.[644]

Secondly, justifying his disagreement with the writings of Cyprian on re-baptism, Augustine teaches that authority in the Church lies not in the letters of individual bishops but primarily in the teaching of Scripture, and secondarily in the developing mind of the Church as whole, which finds expression in a variety of different ways:

But who cannot know that the sacred Canon of Scripture, of both of the Old and New Testament, is confined within its own limits, and that it stands above all later letters of the bishops, so that about it we can hold no matter of doubt or dispute as to whether what is written in it is true or right; but the letters of bishops which have been or shall be written since the closing of the canon are liable to be refuted, either by discourse of someone wiser, or by the weightier authority and more learned prudence of other bishops, or by councils; and these councils which are held in the several districts or provinces must yield without doubt to the authority of plenary councils which are formed for the whole Christian world; and that even of the plenary councils the earlier are often corrected by the later, when by some experiment

[644] Augustine, *Enarratio in Psalmum* LVI, in Giles, p.183.

things are brought to light which were concealed, and that becomes known which lay hid.[645]

Thirdly, in line with the teaching of Cyprian, Augustine views the commission given to Peter by Christ as being given not to him alone, or to him and to his successors in the See of Rome, but to all the apostles and to the whole Church, both of whom Peter represents. Thus, he writes:

For Peter in many places in the Scriptures appears to represent the Church; especially in that place where it was said 'I give to thee the keys...shall be loosed in heaven.' What! Did Peter receive these keys, and Paul not receive? Did Peter receive and John and James not receive, and the rest of the apostles? Or are not the keys in the Church where sins are daily remitted? But since in a figure Peter represented the church, what was given to him singly was given to the Church. [646]

Thus also, he writes:

For these keys not one man but the unity of the Church received. Here therefore the excellence of Peter is set forth, because he represented that universality and unity of the Church, when it's was said to him 'I give to thee' what was given to all. For that you may know that the Church did receive the keys of the kingdom of heaven, hear elsewhere what the Lord said to all the apostles, 'Receive the Holy Ghost' and forthwith 'Whose so ever sins you retain they are retained.' This pertains to the keys, of which it was said 'Whatsoever you shall lose on earth shall be loosed in heaven, and whatsoever ye shall bind on earth shall also be bound in heaven.' But this he said to Peter, that you may know that Peter then represented the person of the whole Church. Hear what is said to him, what to all the faithful Saints.

Deservedly also, after his resurrection, the Lord commended his sheep to Peter himself to feed; he was not the only one among the disciples who was thought worthy to feed the Lord's sheep, but when Christ

[645] Augustine, *De Baptismo contra Donatistas*, Book 2:3, in Giles, p. 191.
[646] Augustine, *Sermo 149*, in Giles, p.175.

speaks to one, unity is commended and to Peter for the first time, because Peter is first among the apostles. [647]

It is true that in a letter to the Donatist bishops Augustine declares with reference to Rome that 'the principality of the Apostolic chair has always been in vigour there.' However, as the Orthodox theologian Vladimir Guettee points out:

Augustine did not...recognize the superior jurisdiction of the Roman Church. What, then, does he mean by 'principality of the Apostleship'? He leaves no doubt upon the subject. After having ascribed this 'principality of the Apostleship' to St. Paul as well as to St. Peter, he observes that it is something 'higher' than the episcopate. "Who does not know," says he, "that the principality of the Apostleship is to be preferred to every episcopate?" (10th Sermon on Peter and Paul) The Bishops were considered, indeed, as successors of the Apostles; but while they inherited from them the apostolic ministry, they had no share in certain superior prerogatives, which only belonged to the first Apostles of Christ. These prerogatives constitutes the 'principality of the Apostleship', which thus belongs equally to all the first Apostles. And, in fact, the title of "Apostle-prince' is given to them all indifferently by the Fathers of the Church. Every Apostolic Church, therefore–that is, every Church that has preserved the legitimate Apostolic Succession–has preserved this principality of the see, that is, of Apostolic teaching. St. Augustine merely says that, in his time, the Church of Rome had preserved this succession of Apostolic teaching. [648]

It is also true that Roman Catholic apologists have appealed to the supposed epigram of Augustine '*Roma locuta est: causa finita est*' (Roman has spoken: the matter is finished) to support the idea that the Pope has the authority to make binding decisions on matters under dispute from which there can be no further appeal.

[647] Augustine, *Sermo 295*, in Giles, p.176.
[648] 'Fr. Vladimir (Guettee) on St. Augustine and the Papacy.' NFTU, 28 July 2017 at https://nftu.net/fr-vladimir-guettee-on-st-augustine-and-the-papacy/

However, as Kerr points out:

The phrase is not Augustine's. It misrepresents the passage from which it is supposed to be taken. His argument is that since two African Councils have decided against the Pelagians and have sent to the apostolic seat about the matter and 'from thence rescripts have come: the cause is finished.' [*Sermo 131*:10] His contention is that both the African Church and the Roman have condemned Pelagianism, so there is no more to be said.[649]

Augustine clarifies his meaning in a later work when he declares to the Pelagian leader Julian of Enclanum: 'In truth, your cause is anyhow finished by a competent decision of bishops in common.'[650] For Augustine what was decisive was a common decision of bishops in line with the teaching of Scripture, not simply a decision by the Pope.

Kerr helpfully sums up Augustine's attitude to the Papacy as follows:

Augustine's attitude to the Papacy was naturally one of deference to the holder of the Apostolic and Metropolitan See. He recognised no jurisdiction or superiority of teaching in him. He withstood him when he considered his theology was erroneous or his interference unwarranted. His position was well expressed in his own words to Pope Boniface. 'The pastoral watchtower is common to all of us who have the office of the episcopate although that on which you stand is a loftier height.' [651]

The Council of Carthage

That the attitude of respect to, but independence of, the Papacy found in Augustine represents the mind of the African Church as a whole is shown by a letter sent to Pope Celestine by a council held at Carthage in 424 (which Augustine attended). The Papal Legate, Bishop Faustinus, had argued that the African presbyter Apiarius should be

[649] Kerr, p.144.
[650] Augustine, *Contra Julianum Pelagianum*, Book 3 in Giles, p.222.
[651] Kerr, p. 143 citing Augustine *Ad Bonifacium Contra duas Epistolas Pelagianorum*, Book1:2.

restored to office because he had appealed to Rome and this was what Pope Celestine had decided.

On further examination of the case the council discovered 'such enormous crimes of his [Apiarius] that they were too much even for the patronage and pleading which Faustinus substituted for judgement and justice.' [652] As a result the council declined to reinstate Apiarius and wrote to the Pope asking him not to repeat such interference in their affairs in future because this was contrary to what had been decided at the Council of Nicaea:

Let your holiness reject, as is worthy of you, that impudent sheltering with you of presbyters and lower clergy, because by no definition of the fathers has the Church of Africa been deprived of this, and the Nicene decrees have plainly committed not only the clergy of inferior grade but the bishops themselves to their own metropolitans. For they prudently and justly perceive that all business should be concluded in the place where it arose; and they do not did not think that the grace of the Holy Ghost would be lacking in any province for the priests of Christ to discern wisely the right, and hold it firmly, especially since whoever thinks he is wronged by any judgement my appeal to the council of his province, or even to a general council; unless by chance there is anyone who believes that God can inspire a single individual with justice, and refuse it to numberless priests assembled in council. And how will the oversea judgement itself be valid, since it will be impossible to send thither the necessary witnesses, either on account of sex, or old age, or many other impediments? [653]

In the words of Kidd, in this letter:

Africa vindicated its right, in matters of ecclesiastical order, to remain *sui juris*, while continuing in the unity of the Faith and without breach

---

[652] Council of Carthage, *To Celestine*, in Giles p.234.
[653] To Celestine, in Giles pp.235-236.

of communion. She recognised the primacy of the Roman See, so long as Rome made no claim to primacy of jurisdiction.[654]

Furthermore, as the letter makes clear, underlying the African approach to the matter was the theological conviction that the Pope did not possess a special grace of the Holy Spirit that would be lacking in the priests [i.e. bishops] of the various provinces of the Church meeting together in council. The Africans thus took a conciliar rather than a Papal approach to the issue of where authority in the Church lay. That was why for them the decision made at Nicaea could simply be overruled by the Pope. The Pope was subject to a conciliar decision and not the other way around.

The Councils of Ephesus and Chalcedon

A similar conciliar approach was also taken by the Eastern Church at the third and fourth 'ecumenical councils,' the Council of Ephesus in 431 and the Council of Chalcedon in 451.

In 430, Pope Celestine had condemned the Christology of Nestorius, the Bishop of Constantinople, and had threatened to excommunicate him unless he recanted his errors and came into line with the theology of Rome and Alexandria.

The following year the Emperor Theodosius II summoned a council of bishops to meet a Ephesus to consider the matter. The council was presided over by Bishop Cyril of Alexandria and the Pope and the Western Church as whole was represented by a number of legates sent by Rome.

Two things are significant about this council in relation to the issue of Papal authority.

First, the Roman legates took the opportunity of the council to reiterate the claims now being made for the Pope by Rome. Thus, at the third session of the Council, the presbyter Philip, representing the Pope, declared:

654 Kidd, p.105.

There is no doubt, and in fact it has been known in all ages, that the holy and most blessed Peter, Prince and head of the apostles, pillar of the faith, and foundation of the Catholic Church, received the keys of the Kingdom from our Lord Jesus Christ, the Saviour and Redeemer of the human race and that to him was given the power of loosing and binding sins: who, even to this time and always, lives and judges in his successes. Or holy and most blessed Pope Celestine the Bishop is in according to due order his successor and holds his place, and he sent us to supply his presence in this holy Synod which the most humane and Christian emperors have convened, bearing in mind and continually guarding the Catholic faith. [655]

Secondly, however, the council itself did not show any sign of accepting the idea that the judgement of the Pope was in and of itself decisive. Rather than the council agreeing to a decision made by Pope Celestine, the Roman delegates were asked to, and did, sign up to a a sentence of excommunication of Nestorius previously drawn up by the council itself. As far as the council was concerned, the presence and signatures of the Roman delegates signified that the Western Church was 'likeminded with us in faith and religion' and therefore the judgement of the council represented 'the one common sentence of the whole world.'[656] It was the sentence of the Christian Church as whole, and not just what the Pope decided that mattered.

Writing to Pope Celestine the council also declared that having heard about the actions that the Pope has taken 'against the Pelagians and those inclined to like errors, we also considered it right that the decisions of your reverence concerning them should stand strong and firm.' [657] Here again, we do not see the Eastern Church simply signing up to what the Pope had decided. The Eastern bishops looked at what the Pope had done and then made their own independent decision that what he had done had been correct.

[655] Council of Ephesus, Third Session, July 431 in Giles p.252.
[656] Council of Ephesus, Letter to the Emperors Theodosius and Valentinian, in Giles, p. 255.
[657] Council of Ephesus, Letter to Pope Celestine, in Giles p. 256.

If we move on twenty years to the Council of Chalcedon we find the Eastern Church continuing to make its own independent assessment of whether the Pope was right. Leo I had written a letter to Bishop Flavian of Constantinople ('The Tome of Leo') setting out the position of the Papacy with regard to the issues concerning Christology that were then under dispute. At the fourth session of the Council of Chalcedon, rather than Leo's letter simply being accepted as authoritative, the Eastern bishops present were asked to declare whether it should be regarded as orthodox when viewed in the light of the teaching of the Councils of Nicaea and Constantinople:

...let each one of the bishops here assembled declare whether the epistle of archbishop Leo is in accordance with the exposition of the 318 fathers of Nicaea, and with the decrees of the 150 fathers afterwards assembled in the royal city. [658]

The bishops unanimously voted to approve what Leo had written, but the key point is that, as Giles puts it: 'before accepting the Pope's exposition of the faith, the bishops assured themselves that it agreed with the creeds and other statements of doctrine which they regarded as authentic.' [659]

In addition, when the Council came to set out what it believed it did not simply reproduce the teaching of Leo but issued its own authoritative statement of Christological orthodoxy, the Chalcedonian Confession. Here again we see that the Eastern bishops did not regard themselves as simply bound by what the Pope had written, but able independently to decide and declare the orthodox faith of the Church.

Furthermore, in the sixteenth session of the council voted for a Canon which re-affirmed the teaching of the Council of Constantinople that the See of Constantinople should have second place after the See of Rome:

[658] Council of Chalcedon, Fourth Session, in Giles, p. 310.
[659] Giles, p. 312.

Rightly have the fathers conceded to the see of Old Rome its privileges on account of its character as the Imperial City; and, moved by the same considerations, the hundred and fifty bishops have awarded the like privilege to the most holy see of New Rome, judging with good reason that the City which is honoured by the Imperial Power and the Senate, and enjoys the same privilege as the Imperial City, should also in ecclesiastical relations be exalted and hold the second place after that. [660]

This Canon was strongly resisted by the Papal legates who said that could not sit by and see 'The Apostolic see humiliated in our presence' but the council voted for it anyway. Implicit in this vote was a rejection of the claim that Rome's status was based on the continuing ministry exercised there by Peter in and through the Pope. The bishops at Chalcedon agreed with their predecessors at Constantinople that Rome's ecclesiastical status was based solely on its civic prestige as the old Imperial capital.

In their letter to Leo the bishops at Chalcedon wrote to Leo:

You are set as an interpreter to all of the voice of blessed Peter, and to all you impart the blessings of that faith. And so we too, wisely taking you as our guide in all that is good, have shown to the sons of the Church their inheritance of the truth. [661]

However, in view of their actions at Chalcedon these words by the bishops were really just flattery. They agreed with Leo's Christological teaching, but they did not accept his view of the Papal office as the direct continuation of the rule over the Church given to Peter by Christ. For them the leadership of the Church belonged to the bishops collectively and not in any exclusive way to the Bishop of Rome.

In Conclusion
If we review the evidence we have looked at in this chapter, what we discover is that although it is possible to draw a straight line from the

---

[660] Council of Chalcedon, Canon 28, in Kidd, p.145.
[661] Council of Chalcedon, To Leo, In Giles, p.322.

teaching about the role of the Pope found in the writings of Pope Leo I to contemporary Roman Catholic teaching on this subject, it is not possible to draw a straight line back from the teaching of Leo through the writings of the Fathers of the first five centuries to the ministry given to Peter by Christ.

What the biblical and Patristic material tells us is that although from New Testament times the Church of Rome was regarded as a very important church, because of its orthodoxy, because of its acts of love towards Christians in other churches, because Rome was the site of the ministry and martyrdom of Peter and Paul and because Rome was the capital city of the Roman Empire, the bishops of Rome were not regarded as having an unquestionable authority over the Church as a whole. This idea only really starts to develop at the end of the fourth century. Although prior to that Pope Victor and Pope Stephen claimed that all churches needed to accept their view of the date of Easter and the re-admission of heretics there is no evidence that this claim was rooted in any developed theology of the Petrine nature of the Papal office.

As Salmon notes, the fact that the later Roman theology of the Papacy seems to have only emerged in Rome at the end of the fourth century in the context of the claims then being made for the status of Constantinople as the 'New Rome,' tells us that unlike episcopacy it cannot be regarded as authentic part of apostolic tradition.

Salmon writes:

Whatever doctrines were delivered to the church by our Lord and His apostles must have been held by the Church at all times and in all places. Now it is owned the doctrine of Roman supremacy was not held by the church in all times; for it has to be confessed, as Newman dozen passages which I have quoted, that such a form of Church government was altogether unsuited to the condition of the Church in the first ages. But we argue further that if our Lord had put His disciples under the government of a single head, Christian missionaries, wherever they went, would have carried with them the knowledge of who their appointed ruler was, and would have taught the Churches which they founded to obey him. There would have been no difference between East and West as to the meaning of the texts which settled the constitution of the universal church. The teaching of the Church on this point would have been *in all places* the same; for this is not a subordinate doctrine, a true tradition concerning which might conceivably have been lost. The doctrine is a fundamental one; and those who had ever known it and received it must have kept up the memory of it by the perpetual practical application of it. [662]

Salmon's argument here is simply irrefutable.

It makes no sense to think that Christ gave universal and perpetual rule over the Church to Peter and the Bishops of Rome following him and yet this fact was either unknown to, or ignored, or suppressed by, the writers of the New Testament and almost all the bishops, theologians, and councils of the Church during the first five centuries of the Church's existence.

[662] Salmon, pp.402-403, italics his.

Chapter 10
The teaching of the Church of England about the role and character of bishops during the sixteenth and seventeenth centuries

In the last chapter we saw that the idea that the Pope has universal authority in the Church as a continuation of the ministry given by Christ to Peter is not taught in the New Testament and was not generally accepted by the Fathers of the first five centuries.

After the fifth century this idea continued to be rejected by the Orthodox churches of the East and by the Coptic churches in Egypt and Ethiopia and, as we saw in chapter 5, it was also rejected by the Church of England at the Reformation.

1. John Jewel's rejection of Papal authority

As we also saw in chapter 5, John Jewel's explanation of why the Church of England rejected the Papal claim to universal authority in his *Apology for the Church of England* runs as follows:

Yet notwithstanding we say that there neither is, nor can be any one man, which may have the whole superiority in this universal state: for that Christ is ever present to assist his church, and needeth not any man to supply his room, as his only heir to all his substance; and that there can be no one mortal creature, which is able to comprehend or conceive in his mind the universal church, that is to wit, all the parts of the world, much less able to put them in order and to govern them rightly and duly. For all the apostles, as Cyprian saith, were of like power among themselves, and the rest were the same that Peter was and that it was said indifferently to them all, 'Feed ye;' indifferently to them all, 'Go into the whole world;' indifferently to them all, 'Teach ye the gospel.' And, as Hierome saith, 'all bishops wheresoever they be, be they at Rome, be they at Eugubium, be they at Constantinople, be they at Rhegium, be all of like pre-eminence and of like priesthood.' And, as Cyprian saith, 'there is but one bishoprick, and that a piece thereof is perfitly and wholly holden of every particular bishop,' And, according to the judgment of the Nicene council, we say that the bishop of Rome hath no more jurisdiction over the church of God, than the rest of the patriarchs, either of Alexandria or Antiochia, have. And as for the bishop of Rome, who now calleth all matters before himself alone, except he do his duty as he ought to do, except he administer the sacraments, except he instruct the people, except he warn them and teach, we say that he ought not of right once to be called a bishop, or so much as an elder. For a bishop, as saith Augustine, 'is a name of labour, and not of honour;' because he would have that man understand himself to be no bishop, which will seek to have pre-eminence, and not to profit others. And that neither the pope, nor any other worldly creature, can no more be head of the whole church, or a bishop over all, than he can be the bridegroom, the light, the salvation, and life of the church: for these privileges and names belong only to Christ, and be properly and only fit for him alone. [663]

In this quotation Jewel gives three reasons for rejecting the authority of the Pope over the Church as whole, reasons which build on the Patristic teaching that we looked at in the last chapter.

First, it is Christ who assists and governs the universal Church, and no 'one mortal creature' either needs to, or has the ability to, undertake this role.

Secondly, just as there was an equality among the apostles, so there is equality among the bishops.

Thirdly, the Council of Nicaea did not give the Bishop of Rome any greater degree of jurisdiction than was enjoyed by the Patriarchs of Alexandria or Antioch.

Jewel also argues that the Pope should not even be regarded as a bishop 'except he do his duty as he ought to do, except he administer the sacraments, except he instruct the people, except he warn them

---

[663] Jewel, pp.59-60.

and teach.' This last point is important because it highlights the fact that for Church of England writers in the sixteenth and seventeenth centuries, as for their Patristic predecessors such as Augustine, to be a bishop involved more than having an ecclesiastical title. It meant exercising a particular role in the life of the Church.

In the rest of this chapter, we shall look in detail at what we learn from Church of England writings from the sixteenth and seventeenth centuries about the nature of this role and what sort of person someone needs to be in order rightly exercise it.

2. Individual Church of England writers on the role and character of a bishop

We shall start our exploration by looking at what eight individual Church of England writers from the sixteenth and seventeenth centuries, Hugh Latimer, John Hooper, Thomas Becon, James Pilkington, Thomas Bilson, Richard Hooker, Joseph Hall, and Jeremy Taylor have to say about the role and character of a bishop.

Hugh Latimer

Hugh Latimer was Bishop of Worcester between 1535 and 1539 and was eventually martyred for his Protestant beliefs in 1555 during the reign of Queen Mary.

In a sermon preached at St Paul's Cross in London in 1548 during the reign of Edward VI Latimer compares the work of a bishop (a 'prelate') in bringing people to faith and then confirming them in it to the work of a ploughman in ploughing a field. He declares:

A prelate is that man, whatsoever he be, that hath a flock to be taught of him; whosoever hath any spiritual charge in the faithful congregation, and whosoever he be that hath cure of souls. And well may the preacher and the ploughman be likened together: first, for their labour of all seasons of the year; for there is no time of the year in which the ploughman hath not some special work to do: as in my country in Leicestershire, the ploughman hath a time to set forth, and to assay his plough, and other times for other necessary works to be done. And then they also may be likened together for the diversity of works and variety of offices that they have to do. For as the plough man first setteth forth his plough, and then tilleth his land, and breaketh it in furrows, and sometime ridgeth it up again; and at another time harroweth it and clotteth it, and some- time diggeth it and hedgeth it, diggeth it and weedeth it, purgeth and maketh it clean: so the prelate, the preacher, hath many diverse offices to do. He hath first a busy work to bring his parishioners to a right faith, as Paul calleth it, and not a swerving faith; but to a faith that embraceth Christ, and trusteth to his merits; a lively faith, a justifying faith; a faith that maketh a man righteous, without respect of works: as ye have it very well declared and set forth in the Homily.[664] He hath then a busy work, I say, to bring his flock to a right faith, and then to confirm them in the same faith: now casting them down with the law, and with threatenings of God for sin; now ridging them up again with the gospel, and with the promises of God's favour: now weeding them, by telling them their faults, and making them forsake sin; now clotting them, by breaking their stony hearts, and by making them supplehearted, and making them to have hearts of flesh; that is, soft hearts, and apt for doctrine to enter in: now teaching to know God rightly, and to know their duty to God and their neighhours: now exhorting them, when they know their duty, that they do it, and be diligent in it; so that they have a continual work to do. [665]

Latimer then goes on to say that, because this is the case, bishops are called to work diligently at the tasks God has called them to do, just as a ploughman is called to work diligently at his ploughing, and that those who fail to do so are subject to God's judgement:

...it appeareth that a prelate, or any that hath cure of soul, must diligently and substantially work and labour. Therefore, saith Paul to Timothy, *Qui episcopatum desiderat, hie bonum opus desiderat*: 'He that desireth to have the office of a bishop, or a prelate, that man desireth a

---

[664] The homily 'Of the true, lively and Christian faith' in the *First Book of Homilies*.
[665] George Corrie (ed.), *Sermons of Hugh Latimer,* (Cambridge: CUP, 1844). pp.61-62.

good work.' [1 Timothy 3:1] Then if it be a good work, it is work; ye can make but a work of it. It is God's work, God's plough, and that plough God would have still going. Such then as loiter and live idly, are not good prelates, or ministers. And of such as do not preach and teach, nor do their duties, God saith by his prophet Jeremy, *Maledictus qui facit opus Dei fradulenter*; 'Cursed be the man that doth the work of God fraudulently, guilefully or deceitfully:' [Jeremiah 48:10] some books have it *negligenter,* 'negligently or slackly.' How many such prelates, how many such bishops, Lord, for thy mercy, are there now in England! And what shall we in this case do? shall we company with them? O Lord, for thy mercy! shall we not company with them? O Lord, whither shall we flee from them? But 'cursed be he that doth the work of God negligently or guilefully.' A sore word for them that are negligent in discharging their office, or have done it fraudulently; for that is the thing that maketh the people ill. [666]

In a sermon on Luke 2:18-22 preached in 1552 Latimer offers a different image for the calling of bishops and other ministers. In this sermon he compares unfavourably the care for their sheep shown by the shepherds mentioned in the nativity story with those clerks (those in holy orders) who have no care for their sheep, but only seek to feed off them:

Now these shepherds, I say, they watch the whole night, they attend upon their vocation; they do according to their calling; they keep their sheep: they run not hither and thither, spending the time in vain, and neglecting their office and calling. No, they did not so. Here, by these shepherds, all men may learn to attend upon their offices and callings. I would wish that clergymen, the curates, par sons, and vicars, the bishops, and all other spiritual persons, would learn this lesson by these poor shepherds; which is this, to abide by their flocks and by their sheep, to tarry amongst them, to be careful over them; not to run hither and thither after their own pleasure, but to tarry by their benefices and feed their sheep with the food of God's word; and to keep hospitality, and so to feed them both soul and body. For I tell you

[666] Corrie, pp.62-63.

these poor unlearned shepherds shall condemn many a stout and great learned clerk: for these shepherds had but the care and charge over brute beasts, and yet were diligent to keep them, and to feed them; and the other have the cure over God s lambs, which he bought with the death of his Son, and yet they are so careless, so negligent, so slothful over them: yea, and the most part intendeth not to feed the sheep, but they long to be fed of the sheep. They seek only their own pleasures, their own pastimes, they care for no more. But what said Christ to Peter? What said he? Peter, *amas me*? 'Peter, lovest thou me?'; Peter made answer, 'Yes:' 'Then feed my sheep' And so the third time he commanded Peter to feed his sheep. But our clergymen do declare plainly that they love not Christ, because they feed not his flock.[667]

Latimer's point is made clear in the middle section of this quotation. Bishops and other clergy are called to feed their flocks in soul and body. In soul by feeding the sheep with 'the food of God's word' and in body through the practice of hospitality.

John Hooper

John Hooper was Bishop of Gloucester and then Worcester from 1551-1554. Like Latimer, he was martyred for his Protestant views during the reign of Queen Mary in 1555.

In his *Answer to the Bishop of Winchester's Book* published in 1546 Hooper contends that the role of bishops is to govern the people in their care by faithfully proclaiming God's law to them, but that the bishops are negligent in doing this:

...every commonwealth ought to have but two governors, God and the prince, the one to make a law for the soul, the other for the body: all the king's officers to be ministers of the law made to the conservation of the commonwealth, and the bishops to be ministers in the church, of the law that is prescribed by God: as all justices, mayors, sheriffs, constables, and bailiffs, be ministers of the law made unto them, to

---

[667] George Corrie (ed.). *Hugh Latimer, Sermons and Remains* (Cambridge: CUP, 1844), pp.119-120.

govern the commonwealth; so must the bishops, priests, and all other preachers, be ministers of Christ, and govern the people in their vocation according unto the law prescribed by God. As Paul willed the 1 Cor. iv. people to judge of him and of his companions: *Sic nos aestimet homo ut ministros Christi., et dispensatores mysteriorum Dei; quod superest autem, illud reqiiiritur in dispensatoribus, ut fidus aliquis reperiatur.* ['This is how one should regard us, as servants of Christ and stewards of the mysteries of God. Moreover it is required of stewards that they be found trustworthy' - 1 Corinthians 4:1-2] There is no more required of the bishop, but that he be diligent and faithful in the execution of God's word. It is not required that he should make any law for the people, but to preach God's law with all diligence and study, as they do most negligently.[668]

As an example of the sort of episcopal negligence he has in mind Hooper goes on to explain that the previous year:

...at my being in England, for lack of expedition of mine affairs, I was compelled to remain in a town longer than I would, having communication with certain of the citizens of many matters, sought of my part only to have occasion to help their poor conscience from the snare of ignorancy. When I perceived I had obtained their willing audience, I demanded of them when their bishop (for of the town the bishop hath his name) preached among them, and the contents of his sermons. They told me that he never preached sermon in the town. I asked, what deputies he had in the town, appointed to preach. They said, none; and I believe it the better, for as long as I was in that town there was never sermon. I lamented the people; for I found a great many apt and ready, by inspiration of God's Spirit, to hear the truth, if they had a preacher; for, at one talk and communication, as much as they could comprehend they believed; the rest they stood in doubt of. Then I willed them diligently to learn the gospel, to avance[669] it in word, and to set it forth with the example of all honest life; and told

---

[668] Samuel Carr (ed.). *The Early Writings of John Hooper* (Cambridge: CUP, 1843) p. 142
[669] 'Avance' means 'advance.'

them that there were two general rules to learn and know God by: the first, by his Word, whereby our fathers before thousands of years knew him; the second was, to know God by his dear Son, opened and declared in Hierusalem unto the world, and that God can nor will be known none other ways than by his Word, and by his Son Christ Jesus. [670]

In this town, writes Hooper:

...the bishop of the diocese, from the time that he was appointed by the king's majesty unto that most painful office, he preached neither God, neither the devil, but let his flock wander as sheep without a shepherd. [671]

Hooper then goes on to say that despite such evident negligence the bishops nevertheless all say 'that their dioceses be well instructed and governed, and they do according unto their offices.'[672] His scathing response is:

Forsooth, as much their diligence is correspondent, and their facts agreeing with their name, (for they are called *dioecesani*, of *dioeceo*, that signifieth to govern and to defend,) as Absalom's facts agreed with his name. His name signifieth the peace and tranquillity of his father; but his facts was the affliction of his father, and banished him out of his realm [2 Samuel 17]. So doth the bishops govern the churches committed unto their charges, and defend them from false doctrine. [673]

In response to the claim that the bishops are doing their job properly because the people 'be instructed in the Paternoster, the creed, and the commandments, and hath the sacraments ministered unto them,'[674]

[670] Carr, pp.142-143.
[671] Carr, p.143.
[672] Carr, p.143.
[673] Carr, p.143.
[674] Carr, p.143.

Hooper argues that this is insufficient because unless the bishops regularly preach themselves, or make provision for others to do so, the people will remain ignorant concerning how to pray, and what it means to have faith, live rightly before God, and receive the sacraments beneficially. [675]

Hooper reiterates the importance of the bishop's preaching ministry in his sermons on Jonah published in 1550. Commenting on Jonah 4:4 'When Jonas had entered the city one day's journey, he cried and said, Within this forty days Ninive shall be destroyed,' he declares:

Of this text we learn, that Jonas lived not idle after he came to the place whether he was sent by God, but he walked abroad and cried. So should every man that is called to the office of a bishop or pastor. It is not enough he go to his diocese or parsonage, but he must walk abroad there, and cry out the commandment of the Lord; or else they be, with all their title, glory, pump, and name, dumb dogs, subject unto the vengeance and plague of God. And this is the mark thou shouldest know a bishop and priest by: by his tongue, that soundeth the word of the Lord, and not by his cap or outward vesture.[676]

Thomas Becon

Thomas Becon was a chaplain to Thomas Cranmer. In his work on the nature of the Christian life, *A Pleasant New Nosegay*, published in 1542, Becon gives a comprehensive summary of what he thinks the ministry of bishops and other Christian ministers involves. As he sees it, Bishops should live among the people for whom they are responsible, and must be diligent in ministering the sacraments, providing hospitality, and, above all, instructing their flock through both their words and their example about what it means to live a godly Christian life:

Art thou a bishop, priest, or spiritual minister of God's word? Look then well to thy office. Remember that it is thy duty reverently to

[675] Carr, pp.144-147.
[676] Carr, pP512.

minister the most blessed sacraments of Christ's church, and to preach the word of God to 'the flock upon whom 'the Holy Ghost hath made thee overseer, to govern the congregation of God, whom he purchased with his blood.' [Acts 20] Remember that it is said unto thee *Pasce, Pasce, Pasce*: 'feed,' 'feed,' 'feed.' [John 21] Feed therefore thy parish with good example of virtuous living. Feed them with the pure evangelium and true gospel of Christ. Feed them also with corporal food through the maintenance of hospitality. Teach them to forsake all idolatry and superstition, and only to cleave to the true and living God, the alone and omni-sufficient saviour. Teach them to honour and call on the name of their Lord God in all their adversities and troubles. Teach them faithful obedience toward their superiors. Teach them to love their wives as their own flesh, and to bring up their children and family in the fear and nurture of the Lord. Teach them to labour for their living, and not to take away any man's goods unjustly. Teach them to testify the truth, and to bear no false witness. Teach them to be no manslayers, but to love all men with a pure heart. Teach them to live of their own, and not to covet that which pertain to other men. Teach then to walk straight in the pathways of the Lord all the days of their life, lest the fierce plagues and cruel vengeance of God fall both upon thee and them. 'Cry, cease not: shew to the people their sins, offences, and wickednesses.' [Isaiah 58] Command the wicked to forsake his iniquity. Exhort the rich man unto the glad and ready distribution of his goods to the poor people.' [1 Timothy 6] 'Feed the flock of Christ,' so much as lieth in thy power.' [1Peter 5]. 'Be an example to the faithful in word, in conversation, in love, in spirit, in faith, in purity and cleanness of life.' [1 Timothy 4] 'Give attendance to thyself. and to doctrine: continue in these.' 'Reprove them that sin openly before all men, that the other may be afeard.' [1 Timothy 5] 'Keep thyself pure, clean, and honest.' 'Suffer affliction and trouble, as a good soldier of Jesus Christ.' 'Study to shew thyself acceptable to God, a workman that needeth not to be ashamed, dividing justly the word of truth.' [2 Timothy 2]. 'Fly the lusts of youth: follow righteousness, faith, charity, peace with them that call on the Lord with a pure heart.' 'Reprove the enemies of truth fiercely, that they mav be whole in faith.' 'Speak thou those things that become wholesome doctrine;' but 'above all things be an example to other of good works.' [1 Timothy 6] Be not absent from thy benefice. Live not dissolutely at the university or elsewhere. Be not that 'shepherd. and idol that forsaketh his flock,' [Zechariah 11] but give them meat in due time. Suffer not the wolf to devour Christ's sheep, whom he bought with no less price than with his own most precious blood. [John 10] Defend the glory of God, and not thine own dignity. Strive for the health of thy flock, and not for thy riches and possessions. The sinful of thy flock exhort unto faithful repentance. The desperate provoke thou unto the trust of God's mercy. The weak make thou strong. The diseased look thou heal. The bloody wounded look thou cure. The broken look thou make whole. The imperfect look thou make perfect. The strong in Christ look thou make ancient. To conclude, if thou be a true bishop, a faithful overseer, a diligent curate, a trusty shepherd, rather give thy life, and spend all the blood in thy body, than that one of the least of Christ's. flock should perish through thy fault. So makest thou be sure, 'when that prince of shepherds shall appear, to receive the incorruptible crown of glory.' [1 Peter 5] If thou dost not these things, which hitherto I have rehearsed, then look thou for none other, but with that unprofitable servant to be cast into utter darkness, where weeping and gnashing of teeth shall be. {Matthew 25] [677]

In his *Catechism*, published around 1552, Becon declares:

The bishops, pastors, and curates ought diligently to feed the flock of Christ with the true and pure word of God, to maintain hospitality for the relief of the poor and miserably afflicted Christians, and to be an example to the flock in all godliness and honesty.[678]

Here Becon is making the same basic point about the role of the bishop as in the *Nosegay*, although for some reason he omits here the call to minister the sacraments.

---

[677] John Ayre (ed.). *The Early Works of Thomas Becon* (Cambridge: CUP, 1843), pp. 224-225
[678] John Ayre (ed.). *The Catechism of Thomas Becon* (Cambridge: CUP, 1844). p. 114

James Pilkington

James Pilkington was Bishop of Durham from 1561-1576. In his 1563 work *The Burning of St Paul's Church: The Addition and Confutation of the Addition*, Pilkington argues that bishops are called to watch over the sheep of God's flock and protect them from the activity of the Devil, and that if they fail to do this they will have to answer to God for their negligence:

A bishop is a name of office, labour, and pains, rather than of dignity, ease, wealth, or idleness. The word *episcopus* is Greek, and signifies a scout watch, an overlooker, or spy; because he should ever be watching and warning, that the devil our enemy do not enter to spoil or destroy. And as in war the watchmen, scouts, or spies, if they fall on sleep or be negligent, they betray their fellows, and deserve death; so in God's church, if the bishops watch not diligently, and save their sheep, God has pronounced sentence of death against them by his prophet. 'I made thee a watchman to the house of Israel, says the Lord: thou shall hear the word of my mouth, and declare it them from me. If I say to the wicked. Thou wicked, thou shalt die, and thou wilt not warn him to take heed to his way, he shall die in his wickedness, but his blood I will require of thee.' [Ezekiel 33][679]

In the same work he further argues against his Roman Catholic opponent that the calling of a bishop is to rule, guide and teach God's flock, and that if someone fails to do this then he is not truly a bishop, even though he stands in the line of historic episcopal succession:

Does the see make the bishop and his doctrine good or bad? Does the place make him good or bad? If his saying be true, that they have such a succession, the man must needs be good because he is bishop of such a place or such, (for he means to have a continual succession of good bishops everywhere without interruption:) but whether they succeed in agreement of one true doctrine, as they do of one see or place, he cares not. If succeeding in place be sufficient to prove them good work

---

[679]James Scholefield (ed.). *The Works of James Pilkington* (Cambridge: CUP, 1842), p.494

bishops, then the Jews and Turks have their good bishops and religion still at Jerusalem, Constantinople, and elsewhere; for there they dwell where the apostles did, and have their synagogues, Levites, priests and bishops after their sort...

In temporal inheritance an evil man may succeed as right heir to a good; but in matters of pure religion a heretic, or he that differs from the truth, cannot be a lawful follower in God's church, and defender of the same religion and truth from which he is fallen, and become an enemy. Therefore, as the succession of good kings stands not only in enjoying the lands, goods, possessions and pleasures of the realm, but in the painful ministering of justice, defending his subjects from strangers, maintaining the good, and punishing the evil, by wholesome and Godly laws: so stands the succession of the church not in mitres, palaces, lands, or lordships, but in teaching true doctrine, and rooting out the contrary; by sharp discipline to correct the offenders, and godly exhortation to stir up the slothful, and encourage the good, to raise them that be fallen In comfortable promises, to strengthen them that stand, and bring home them that run astray. He that does these is the true successor of the prophets and apostles, though he live in wilderness, as Elias did, or be tied in chains, as Peter and Paul: he that does not, is not their successor indeed, but in name only, though he have the pope's blessing, cruche and mitre, lands and palaces, hallowings and blessings, or all that the pope has devised for his prelates.

To be a bishop is to be an officer, a ruler, a guide, a teacher of God's flock in God's church; and to be a true successor in a bishoprick, is to succeed in like pains, care, and diligent regard of God's people. Is he an officer that does not his office? Nay, surely, but only in name; for he is a thief in his office, and an usurer, that takes the profit and not the pain. An office stands properly in doing the duty of it, and not in talking of it, setting in deputies, bearing a shew, brag and face of a bishop. When they can bring the apostles' doctrine or life for example to be like their life and teaching, they may say they follow the apostles: but because they seek to be lords overt the flock, contrary to Peter's doctrine [1 Peter 5], and be enemies to the gospel, and murderers of the professors of it, they be traitors to their Lord God. [680]

Thomas Bilson

In his book *The Perpetual Government of Christ's Church*, which we have referred to before in the course of this study, Thomas Bilson declares:

The bishop then, or president of the presbyters (for I stand not on names while I discussed their powers,) is by Christ's own mouth pronounced to be the angel of the church; that is, the chief steward over God's household and overseer of his flock; and the authority he hath in the church is pastoral and paternal, even the same that hath continued in the church since the beginning of the world. this family kind of regiment began in the patriarchs, dured[681] in the priests and prophets of Moses' law, was derived to the apostles, and so descended to the chief priests of Christs' church to this day: who are to be honoured and obeyed in the word and the sacrament as fathers, of all their children.[682]

In Bilson's view there has been one church, or people of God, since the time of Adam and throughout this time there has been an unbroken succession of people called by God to exercise pastoral and paternal authority in the church. The first to exercise this role was Adam, and following him the other Patriarchs, they were followed by the chief priests and the prophets of the Mosaic dispensation, and they were in turn followed by the apostles, by the bishops appointed by the apostles, and by the bishops who have succeeded them as the chief steward of God's household and the overseers of his flock.

Bilson then goes on to argue that the witness of the New Testaments tells us that the bishop's role as steward and overseer involves the exclusive power to ordain and to exercise ecclesiastical discipline, a

---

[680] Scholefield, pp.598, 603-604.
[681] Endured.
[682] Bilson, p,379

power which is not shared by other presbyters. Thus he argues that it was Paul and not the presbyters who excommunicated the wrongdoer mentioned in 1 Corinthians 5 and who ordained Timothy ('you cannot convince that the presbytery did either excommunicate the malefactor of Corinth, or lay hands on Timothy'[683]) and this authority exercised by Paul is the same possessed by the bishops appointed to succeed him as the governors of the Church, first Timothy and Titus and then others in their stead. [684]

Richard Hooker

As we saw at the beginning of chapter 2, in Book VII of *The Laws of Ecclesiastical Polity*, written at the end of the sixteenth century, Hooker explains how a bishop is a presbyter who has the same basic ministry as all other presbyters, but who also has additional powers which set him apart from those presbyters who are not bishops:

A Bishop is a minister of God, unto whom with permanent continuance there is given not only power of administering the Word and the Sacraments, which power other Presbyters have; but also a further power to ordain ecclesiastical persons, and a power of chiefty in government over Presbyters as well as Laymen, a power to be by way of jurisdiction a Pastor even to Pastors themselves. So that this office, as he is a Presbyter or Pastor, consisteth in those things which are common unto him with other pastors, as in ministering the Word and Sacraments: but those things incident unto his office, which do properly make him a Bishop, cannot be common unto him with other Pastors.[685]

Joseph Hall

In his book *Episcopacy by Divine right asserted*, which we have also

referred to previously, Joseph Hall contends that bishops exercise the perpetual commission first given to the apostles. He writes:

---

[683] Bilson, p. 383.
[684] Bilson, pp.380-392.
[685] Hooker Bk. VII.ii.3, p. 334.

...we may not think, as one said well, that the Apostles carried their Commission with them up to heaven. They knew it was given them for a perpetuity of succession. He that said 'Go teach all Nations, and baptize,' added 'Behold I am with you to the end of the world.' He could not mean it of their persons which stayed not long upon earth after him; he meant it of their Evangelical successors.[686]

These successors are the bishops and, according to his promise, Christ is with them as he was with the apostles:

...in the effectual execution of those offices, which should be perpetuated to his Church, for the salvation of Mankind. Such were the preaching of the Gospel, and the administration of the Sacraments, the ordaining Church officers, the ordering of Church affairs, the infliction of censures, and, in short, the power of keys, which we justly say, were not tied to St. Peter's girdle, but were communicated to all his fellows, and to all his and their successors for ever.[687]

For Hall, the role of bishops is to execute these offices.

Jeremy Taylor

Jeremy Taylor was chaplain to Charles I and later Bishop of Down, Connor and Dromore from 1660-1673. In his 1647 work *Of the sacred order and offices of episcopacy by divine institution*, sometimes referred to as 'Episcopacy asserted,' he takes a similar approach to Hall in arguing that the 'superiority of jurisdiction' which was first delegated by Christ to the apostles was then also delegated to the bishops who came after them.

According to Taylor, when Christ promised the apostles keys of the kingdom of heaven:

...he promised them power to bind and loose, when he breathed on them the Holy Ghost, he gave them that actually, to which by the former promise they were intitled; and in the octaves of the Passion,

[686] Hall, p.200.
[687] Hall, p.201.

415

he gave them the same authority, which he had received from his Father, and they were the faithful and wise stewards whom the Lord made rulers over his household. [688]

This delegated power, writes Taylor, was not designed to pass away with the apostles themselves:

For when the Great Shepherd had reduced his wandering sheep into a fold, he would not leave them without guides to govern them, so long as the wolf might possibly prey upon them, and that is, till the last separation of the Sheep from the Goats. And this Christ intimates in that promise, *Ero vobiscum (Apostolis) usque ad consummationem saeculi.* Vobiscum; not with your persons, for they dyed long ago, but & *vostri similibus*, with Apostles to the end of the world. And therefore that the Apostolate might *vobiscum* be successive and perpetual, Christ gave them a power of ordination, that by imposing hands on others they might impart that power which they received from Christ.[689]

Taylor goes on to distinguish between the 'extraordinary' and ordinary' powers given to the apostles. The former were given for a limited period of time, whereas the latter were given to the Church as a gift of perpetual assistance, from which it follows there must be a succession of people able to exercise them:

...in the Apostles there was something extraordinary; something ordinary. Whatsoever was extraordinary, as immediate mission, unlimited jurisdiction, and miraculous operations, that was not necessary to the perpetual regiment of the Church, for then the Church should fail when these privileges extraordinary did cease. It was not therefore in extraordinary powers and privileges that Christ promised his perpetual assistance; not in speaking of tongues, not in doing miracles, whether in *materiâ censurae*, as delivering to Satan; or, in *materiâ misericordiae*, as healing sick people; or in *re naturali*, as in

---

[688] Jeremy Taylor, *Of the sacred order and offices of episcopacy* (London: Richard Royston, 1647), p.12, text at https://quod.lib.umich.edu/e/eebo/A64057.0001.001/1:1?rgn=div1;view=fulltext.
[689] Taylor, p.13.

resisting the venom of vipers, and quenching the violence of flames; in these Christ did not promise perpetual assistance, for then it had been done, and still these signs should have followed them that believe. But we see they do not. It follows, then, that in all the ordinary parts of power and office Christ did promise to be with them to the end of the world, and therefore there must remain a power of giving faculty, and capacity to persons successively for the execution of that, in which Christ promised perpetual assistance. For since this perpetual assistance could not be meant of abiding with their persons, who in few years were to forsake the world, it must needs be understood of their function, which either it must be succeeded to, or else it was as temporary as their persons. But in the extraordinary privileges of the Apostles they had no successors, therefore of necessity a succession must be constituted in the ordinary office of Apostolate.[690]

The 'ordinary office' of the apostles, argues Taylor, lay in performing those functions necessary to perpetuate the Church and it is this same office that has been passed on to the episcopate:

Now what is this ordinary office? Most certainly since the extraordinary (as is evident) was only a help for the founding and beginning, the other are such as are necessary for the perpetuating of a Church. Now in clear evidence of sense, these offices and powers are Preaching, Baptizing, Consecrating, Ordaining, and Governing. For these were necessary for the perpetuating of a Church, unless men could be Christians that were never Christened, nourished up to life without the Eucharist, become Priests without calling of God and Ordination, have their sins pardoned without absolution, be members and parts and sons of a Church whereof there is no coadunation[691], no authority, no Governor. These the Apostles had without all Question, and whatsoever they had, they had from Christ, and these were eternally necessary, these then were the offices of the Apostolate,

---

[690] Taylor, p.13-14.
[691] Membership in one body.

which Christ promised to assist for ever, and this is that which we now call the Order and Office of Episcopacy.[692]

For Taylor, then, the role of bishop is to preach, minister the sacraments, ordain and govern, with the power to govern including the ability to pardon sin.

What we learn from these eight writers

The eight writers we have just looked at have different emphases. The first four writers are reacting against the neglect of pastoral duties which, as we saw in chapter 5, was a feature of the Medieval episcopate. The last four, by contrast, are reacting to the argument of the radical Puritans that the roles of bishop and presbyter should be seen as identical. That is why the first four highlight the importance of the bishops' pastoral responsibilities, while the last four highlight what makes bishops different from presbyters.

However, if we put the writings of these eight writers together, we find a coherent overall picture of the bishop's role which is in line with the biblical and patristic teaching that we have looked at in chapters 7 and 8. According to this picture, bishops are primarily called to preach the Word and provide pastoral care, bringing people to faith in Christ, building them up in their faith, and protecting them from the attacks of the Devil. In addition, they are also called to minister the sacraments, provide for those in need, govern the clergy and laity in their dioceses, and ordain presbyters and deacons.

In terms of the character of bishops, we learn from Latimer that bishops need to be people who work diligently at the tasks God has given them to do, in the same way that ploughmen work diligently at their ploughing, or that the shepherds in the nativity story were diligent in caring for their flocks, and from Becon that bishops are to' Be an example to the faithful in word, in conversation, in love, in spirit, in faith, in purity and cleanness of life'

---

[692] Taylor, pp.14-15.

3. The Reformatio Legum Ecclesiasticarum

This picture of the bishop's role is filled out in more detail in the *Refomatio Legum Ecclesiasticarum.* ('The Reform of the Ecclesiastical Laws') the code of Canon Law for the Church of England put together by Archbishop Thomas Cranmer and others during the reign of Edward VI. [693]

The death of Edward VI in 1553 meant that work on the *Reformatio* stopped before it attained legal authority. However, it is nonetheless a very important document because it sets out what the first generation of English Reformers thought a reformed Church of England should be like and, as part of this, what a reformed episcopate should be like.

The part of the *Reformatio* concerned with bishops begins with a section which is said to describe 'the rank and dignity of bishops in the church,' but which in fact sets out the basic responsibilities of the bishops, which it sees as being to so govern and pastor the whole people of God, both clergy and laity, that people may be joined to Christ, grow in him and be led back to him if they should fall away.

The section runs as follows:

Bishops, because they hold the chief place among the other ministers of the church, must therefore govern and pastor the lower orders of the clergy, as well as the whole people of God, with sound doctrine, sober authority and wise counsel, not indeed in order to lord it over their faith but that they might prove themselves to be true servants of the servants of God. And they shall know that authority and ecclesiastical jurisdiction has been specially entrusted to them for no other reason than that by their ministry and dedication as many people as possible may be joined to Christ, and that those were already Christ's may grow in him and be built up, and that if some fail

---

[693] For details see Gerald Bray (ed), *Tudor Church Reform* (Woodbridge: Boydell Press/Church of England Record Society, 2005), pp.xll – liv.

in this, they shall be led back to their pastor who is Christ the Lord, and restored by salutary penance.[694]

The *Reformatio* then explains that it is the bishop's responsibility to promote harmony in the Church and that the clergy and laity have a corresponding responsibility to be obedient to their bishops, not only when they teach things that are laid down in Scripture, but also when they prescribe a course of action for the sake of good order, or obedience to ecclesiastical law:

Since everyone in the church must dwell in peace, and be concerned as much as they can with unity, therefore the bishop's primary responsibility shall be to foster harmony, and not only the dean, archdeacon arch presbyter and other ministers shall heed him, but also all other members of Christ committed to his care shall so conform themselves to his will, that they shall most readily obey, both in those matters which they teach according to the Word of God, and also in those which they shall ordain for the sake of Christian discipline and those which pertain to our ecclesiastical laws.[695].

The next section of the *Reformatio* explains in more detail the tasks a bishop needs to perform, namely, teaching the Word in person, or ensuring that others do so, ordaining, instituting and, when necessary, removing ministers, settling disputes between clergy and their churches, promoting virtuous behaviour and acting to curb vice and corruption, excommunicating persistent sinners and receiving penitents back into the Church, holding a visitation in their diocese at least once every three years, performing confirmations, certifying the validity of people's wills ('testaments') and in general terms to do everything commanded to bishops in Scripture and to uphold and enact ecclesiastical law:

---

[694] *Reformatio Legum Ecclesiasticarum,* 20:10 in Bray, p.357.
[695] *Reformatio Legum Ecclesiasticarum,* 20:11 in Bray, p.357. The reference to 'our ecclesiastical laws' is because after the breach with Rome the law of the Church was ultimately determined by the monarch and it is to the monarch that 'our' refers.

A bishop shall pass on the sound doctrine of the Word of God, first of all in person, and also through others, in his church, with as much diligence and dedication as he can; he shall confer holy orders at an appropriate time, but he shall not lay hands on anyone suddenly or because he has been bribed. He shall institute suitable ministers to ecclesiastical benefices, and he shall remove the unworthy wherever serious causes and bad behaviour require it, and put them out of the administration of the church; he shall listen to the testimonies of the church and complaints concerning his pastors; he shall settle quarrels which have arisen between ministers and their churches; he shall correct vices and corrupt behaviour by ecclesiastical censures; he shall prescribe edicts for the improvement of morals; he shall excommunicate persistent and deliberate gainsayers; he shall also receive penitents back into grace; he should also visit his entire diocese in places both exempt and not exempt every three years to deal with cases which have arisen and shall receive the usual procurations[696]; and he shall also be free to visit at other times, as often as seems right to him on account of new cases which might occur, but he should do so at his own expense and shall not demand fresh levies of stipends or procurations from the churches; he shall hold synods at stated times every year; it shall also be his responsibility to confirm those who have been instructed in the catechism at a particular time of the year; he shall also prove testaments. And lastly, everything which concerns bishops by the commandment of God shall be their responsibility, and our ecclesiastical laws have been committed to their hearing and judgements.[697]

After that, the *Reformatio* explains that it is necessary not only for the bishop to be a godly person, but for the members of the bishop's household and family to also be godly people who act in a godly manner. It further explains that bishops need to have chaplains who

---

[696] Procurations were sums of money to cover the expenses incurred by a bishop in undertaking a visitation.
[697] *Reformatio Legum Ecclesiasticarum,* 20:12 in Bray, p.359.

can make up for the deficiencies of the parochial clergy both by teaching the Scriptures themselves and by training others to do so:

As It is necessary for a Bishop to be adorned with sober and holy morals, so also it is essential for his household to be sober, modest and holy, and studious of the word of God to the extent that domestic duties allow, in order to be as useful to the church of God as possible in different ways, for men who can take charge of ecclesiastical posts can be obtained from his house, as from some treasure store. For surely they will be able to learn the doctrines of the faith soundly and solidly in the bishop's company (if he is the man he ought to be) and by his example in governing the church, acquire great knowledge. However, the Bishop must be careful not to sponsor the lazy, the useless, the unchaste or gamblers. For if he cannot control his own house, how shall he care for the church of God? And he shall have preaching chaplains around him who shall not only spread Holy Scripture by making up for the negligence and laziness of country parsons, but who will also prepare others in the household to undertake the same task, insofar as each one is able to do so. Indeed, this is one way among others of supplying the great lack of good and faithful ministers of the church. This was the way in which Augustine's house was set up, and that of other fathers who presided over the people of God in a holy manner. in addition, the wives of bishops must not be frivolous, lazy, caught up in desires or too richly clothed. For godly people are deeply offended by these things, and the ungodly insolently insult evangelical doctrine as a result. And what is laid down for wives, applies also to sons and daughters. [698]

The *Reformatio* next addresses the responsibility of bishops for the colleges at Oxford and Cambridge universities, which it sees as a 'seedbed' for future ministers of the Church. It lays down that when bishops have a responsibility for a college they must ensure that the head of the college is theologically orthodox and fosters orthodox theology among the college fellows. In addition, they must ensure that

---

[698] *Reformatio Legum Ecclesiasticarum,* 20:13 in Bray, p.359-361.

theology continues to be taught, and that there is a sufficient supply of orthodox theological teachers who will be able to serve as ministers of the Church in future:

In addition, some bishops have certain colleges of scholars committed to their defence and care. Therefore, they must look after them as diligently as possible, for there also the church has another seedbed for its ministers. Therefore, they shall diligently see to it that heads of houses are strong in Holy Scripture and retentive of sincere doctrine, and they shall spread it among the fellows of their college, reprimanding and compelling those who are its most persistent enemies. For if they do this, and if on the other hand they look after, advance and assist those who are devoted to evangelical godliness, they shall completely reform their colleges in a short space of time. The bishop shall not allow the reading of theology in these colleges (where it exists) to be suspended. Nor shall he allow a lecturer to be admitted to teach theology who either professes some strange doctrine or is over an empty and uncertain mind. He shall find out whether the full number of theologians is maintained in the college. Moreover, he shall also investigate to see which of them is doing well, and which are ignorant, so that he may know which and how many ministers he will have ready, when the need of the church shall require. [699]

As we saw in chapter 5, Medieval bishops were very often absent from their dioceses, and to counter this the the *Reformatio* insists that: '... bishops should in no circumstances ever be absent from their diocese or churches, unless some ecclesiastical cause or very great public need take them away.'[700]

It further adds that when they are resident at home bishops should participate in public worship in their cathedrals:

[699] *Reformatio Legum Ecclesiasticarum,* 20:14 in Bray, p.361.
[700] *Reformatio Legum Ecclesiasticarum,* 20:15 in Bray, p.361.

...it is hardly right for them to conduct the sacred offices on Sundays in their chapels, or to worship there. Instead, they should go to the cathedral church where they either preach themselves, or hear a preacher, and either administer the sacraments in communion themselves, auto part along with others. For services will be conducted more seriously when they attend, and their presence will grace the sacred assembly. [701]

Building on established Medieval practice, the *Reformatio* further lays down that each bishop must have a synod in their diocese:

...in which he, along with his presbyters, parish priests, vicars and clergy shall deal with those matters which need to be established or altered at the time. For a synod is the most perfect medicine for castigating negligence and removing errors, which are regularly sown in the churches by the devil and by evil people, and it may be by such synods that the links and the love between the bishop and his clergy may be increased and preserve. For the bishop will then know and address his clergy in a more familiar way, and they in turn will hear him directly and be able to question him when the nature of the matter demands it. [702]

The synod, it says:

...shall be convened by the bishop every year, and he shall ensure that the appointed day is made known to all the pastors who are scattered in rural deaneries in the countryside. Moreover, in his own city he shall order the said day to be announced by the preacher of the cathedral church and by notices posted on the doors, one full month before he opens the synod. But he should be free to choose whatever day he wishes for it after the second Sunday in Lent. Nevertheless, he shall see to it that parish priests and vicars will be able to return home in good time to be with their people on Palm Sunday. Moreover, the bishop shall designate a meeting place in the diocese which he judges

---

[701] *Reformatio Legum Ecclesiasticarum,* 20:15 in Bray, p.363.
[702] *Reformatio Legum Ecclesiasticarum,* 20:19 in Bray, p.365.

is most convenient for all those who will attend. Moreover, it shall not be lawful for any of the clergy to be absent from the Senate unless the bishop has approved his excuse. And above all, the bishop shall he present himself and (as is fitting) shall preside over the synod.[703]

Concerning what should be discussed at a synod, the *Reformatio* declares:

If some corruption of true doctrine has crept in, it must be condemned. Things in the Scriptures which are being expounded wrongly, to the offence of souls, shall be explained according to the pattern of orthodox faith, and things which perhaps have not been understood which disturb consciences shall be faithfully interpreted and clarified. If any ungodly and superstitious ceremonies have slipped in, they shall be removed. Ecclesiastical quarrels and controversies shall be heard and settled as far as time allows. And it shall be most diligently inquired as to whether the rites of all the sacred offices are conducted according to the form prescribed by our laws. And in sum, whatever seems to relate to the benefit of the people of God shall be discussed with complete confidence and singular diligence. There individual presbyters should be asked about questions pertaining to controversial matters. Moreover, the bishop shall listen patiently to the opinions of the more learned, and shall not allow any of the speakers to be rudely interrupted by any of those present until they have finished, for (as the apostle says), God is not a God of confusion, but of peace. [704]

The part of the *Reformatio* relating to bishops also has a section on archbishops which explains the specific responsibilities of the archepiscopal office. In this section 'us' and 'our' refer to the king:

Archbishops shall also recognize that everything ordained concerning bishops applies to them too, and in addition to those things it shall also be their responsibility to install bishops in their province, after

---

[703] *Reformatio Legum Ecclesiasticarum,* 20:20 in Bray, p.365-367.
[704] *Reformatio Legum Ecclesiasticarum,* 20:22 in Bray, p.367.

they have been chosen by us. And if possible, the archbishop should at some point travel across and visit his whole province in order to have a better understanding of the state of his entire province. And whenever it happens that some episcopal season are vacant, he will take the places of the bishops, not only in visitations but also in appointing to benefices and in all other ecclesiastical functions. But where there are bishops, if he notices that they are too slow in fulfilling their duties and especially in correcting vices and more negligent than can be tolerated in heads of the Lords flock, he shall first warn them in a fatherly way, and if that warning does not work it shall be lawful for him to appoint others in their stead. He shall also hear and judge the quarrels and causes of those who appeal to him. If bishops of his province dispute with or sue each other about something, the archbishop shall be the judge and final arbiter between them. In addition, he shall hear and judge accusations made against bishops of his province. And finally, if any disputes or lawsuits arise between the archbishops they shall be heard and decided by our judgement. In shall also be the archbishop's responsibility to convene provincial synods at our command.[705]

In summary, according to the *Reformatio Legum Ecclesiasticarum* the reformed bishops of the Church of England:

- Should be the governors and pastors of those in their dioceses.

- They are to be godly people with godly households and families.

- They are to reside in their dioceses and worship irregularly in their cathedral,

- They are to preach the Word, celebrate Holy Communion and, confirm,

- They are to foster harmony in the Church.

---

[705] *Reformatio Legum Ecclesiasticarum,* 20:17 in Bray, p.367.

- They are to combat vice and promote virtue, excommunicating persistent sinners, but also restoring the penitent.

- They are to ordain and institute new ministers, remove unworthy ministers, and take steps to ensure a supply of ministers for the future.

- They are to hold a visitation in their diocese at least once every three years and they are also to hold annual synods to act as an antidote to error and negligence and to be the means by which they can develop and sustain a loving relationship with their clergy.

The additional role of the archbishops is to install bishops after they have been appointed by the monarch, exercise episcopal functions in dioceses that are without a bishop, exercise pastoral discipline over the other bishops in their provinces, and act as judges, particularly when there is a dispute between bishops.

All this can be seen as an expansion of the basic vision for a reformed episcopacy found in the writings that we looked at in the first part of this chapter. It is also in line with the New Testament and Patristic teaching about the role and character of bishops which we looked at in chapters 7 and 8.

4. Bishops in the 1662 Ordinal

'The Form of Ordaining or Consecrating of an Archbishop or Bishop' contained in the 1662 Ordinal is a revision of the rite for the 'Consecrating of an Archbishop or Bishop' in the 1552 Ordinal which was in turn a revision of the rite of the same name in Cranmer's original Ordinal of 1550.[706] As we shall see below, the Ordinal contains a clear vision of what a bishop is called to do and what sort of character a bishop needs to have.

---

[706] For the history of the Ordinal see Paul Bradshaw, *The Anglican Ordinal: its history and development from the Reformation to the Present Day* (London: SPCK 1971).

The 1662 rite begins with a Collect that runs as follows:

Almighty God, who by thy Son Jesus Christ didst give to thy holy Apostles many excellent gifts, and didst charge them to feed thy flock: Give grace, we beseech thee, to all Bishops, the Pastors of thy Church, that they may diligently preach thy Word, and duly administer the godly discipline thereof; and grant to the people, that they may obediently follow the same; that all may receive the crown of everlasting glory; through Jesus Christ our Lord. Amen.

This Collect links the role of the bishop to that of the apostles in that it implicitly suggests that as the apostles were called to feed the sheep of Christ's flock, so also the bishops as called to do the same today, which is why the bishops are described as 'the Pastors of thy Church' (Pastor = shepherd). As shepherds, the Collect declares, bishops are called to preach God's Word and administer the sort of pastoral discipline laid down in Scripture.

The Collect is followed by the reading of the Epistle and the Gospel.

Two alternatives are offered for the Epistle.

The first is 1 Timothy 3:1-7:

This is a true saying, if a man desire the office of a bishop, he desireth a good work. A bishop then must be blameless, the husband of one wife, vigilant, sober, of good behaviour, given to hospitality, apt to teach; not given to wine, no striker, not greedy of filthy lucre; but patient, not a brawler, not covetous; one that ruleth well his own house, having his children in subjection with all gravity; (for if a man know not how to rule his own house, how shall he take care of the Church of God?) Not a novice, lest being lifted up with pride he fall into the condemnation of the devil. Moreover, he must have a good report of them which are without; lest he fall into reproach and the snare of the devil.

The second is Acts 20.17-35:

From Miletus Paul sent to Ephesus, and called the elders of the Church. And when they were come to him, he said unto them, Ye know, from the first day that I came into Asia, after what manner I have been with you at all seasons, serving the Lord with all humility of mind, and with many tears, and temptations, which befel me by the lying in wait of the Jews: and how I kept back nothing that was profitable unto you, but have shewed you, and have taught you publickly, and from house to house, testifying both to the Jews, and also to the Greeks, repentance toward God, and faith toward our Lord Jesus Christ. And now behold, I go bound in the spirit unto Jerusalem, not knowing the things that shall befal me there; save that the Holy Ghost witnesseth in every city, saying that bonds and afflictions abide me. But none of these things move me, neither count I my life dear unto myself, so that I might finish my course with joy, and the ministry which I have received of the Lord Jesus, to testify the Gospel of the grace of God. And now behold, I know that ye all, among whom I have gone preaching the kingdom of God, shall see my face no more. Wherefore I take you to record this day, that I am pure from the blood of all men. For I have not shunned to declare unto you all the counsel of God. Take heed therefore unto yourselves, and to all the flock over the which the Holy Ghost hath made you overseers, to feed the Church of God, which he hath purchased with his own blood. For I know this, that after my departing shall grievous wolves enter in among you, not sparing the flock. Also of your own selves shall men arise speaking perverse things, to draw away disciples after them. Therefore watch, and remember that by the space of three years I ceased not to warn every one night and day with tears. And now, brethren, I commend you to God, and to the word of his grace, which is able to build you up, and to give you an inheritance among all them which are sanctified. I have coveted no man's silver, or gold, or apparel: yea, ye yourselves know, that these hands have ministered unto my necessities, and to them that were with me. I have shewed you all things, how that so labouring ye ought to support the weak; and to remember the words of the Lord Jesus, how he said, It is more blessed to give than to receive.

The first reading indicates that that the bishop must be a mature Christian who lives in a godly manner and who shows his ability to exercise over the Church by the way he manages the life of his own family and household. The second indicates that, like the Ephesian elders, bishops are called to continue the ministry first exercised by Paul by acting as good shepherds who feed Christ's flock and guard it from those who seek to lead people away into heresy and schism.

Three possible readings are then offered for the Gospel.

The first is John 21:15-17:

Jesus saith to Simon Peter, Simon, son of Jonas, lovest thou me more than these? He saith unto him, Yea, Lord, thou knowest that I love thee. He saith unto him, Feed my lambs. He saith to him again the second time, Simon, son of Jonas, lovest thou me? He saith unto him, Yea, Lord, thou knowest that I love thee. He saith unto him, Feed my sheep. He saith unto him the third time, Simon, son of Jonas, lovest thou me? Peter was grieved because he said unto him the third time, Lovest thou me? And he said unto him, Lord, thou knowest all things; thou knowest that I love thee. Jesus saith unto him, Feed my sheep.

The second is John 20:19-23:

The same day at evening, being the first day of the week, when the doors were shut where the disciples were assembled for fear of the Jews, came Jesus and stood in the midst, and saith unto them, Peace be unto you. And when he had so said, he shewed unto them his hands and his side. Then were the disciples glad, when they saw the Lord. Then said Jesus to them again, Peace be unto you: As my Father hath sent me, even so send I you. And when he had said this, he breathed on them, and saith unto them, Receive ye the Holy Ghost. Whose soever sins ye remit, they are remitted unto them; and whose soever sins ye retain, they are retained.

The third is Matthew 28:18-20:

Jesus came and spake unto them, saying, All power is given unto me in heaven and in earth. Go ye therefore and teach all nations, baptizing them in the Name of the Father, and of the Son, and of the Holy Ghost;

teaching them to observe all things whatsoever I have commanded you: and lo, I am with you alway, even unto the end of the world.

These three readings indicate that bishops are called to follow in the footsteps of apostles by feeding Christ's flock, administering spiritual discipline, and fulfilling the Great Commission. The apostles did these things and bishops are called to do them too.

After the reading of the Gospel there is a sermon and the recitation of the Nicene Creed. After that follows the presentation of the bishop elect to the archbishop of the province (or the bishop appointed to represent him), the reading of the royal mandate for the consecration (which makes it lawful under the law of the state) and the making of an oath of canonical obedience to the archbishop by the bishop electing (indicating that he will exercise his episcopal ministry within the structure of provincial authority existing in the Church of England).

The archbishop then invites the congregation to pray for the bishop elect with the following words:

Brethren, it is written in the Gospel of Saint Luke, that our Saviour Christ continued the whole night in prayer, before he did choose and send forth his twelve Apostles. It is written also in the Acts of the Apostles, that the disciples who were at Antioch did fast and pray, before they laid hands on Paul and Barnabas, and sent them forth. Let us therefore, following the example of our Saviour Christ and his Apostles, first fall to prayer, before we admit and send forth this person presented unto us, to the work whereunto we trust the Holy Ghost hath called him.

The significance of these words is that they indicate that just as the original twelve apostles and then Paul and Barnabas were appointed to exercise apostolic ministry following a time of prayer so the same needs to be true with regard to bishops who are called to follow in their footsteps.

This summon s to prayer is followed by the Litany and by a further prayer which runs:

Almighty God, giver of all good things, who by thy Holy Spirit hast appointed divers Orders of Ministers in thy Church: Mercifully behold this thy servant now called to the work and ministry of a Bishop; and replenish him so with the truth of thy doctrine, and adorn him with innocency of life, that both by word and deed he may faithfully serve thee in this office, to the glory of thy Name, and the edifying and well-governing of thy Church; through the merits of our Saviour Jesus Christ, who liveth and reigneth with thee and the Holy Ghost, world without end. Amen.

In this prayer the role of the bishop is viewed as being to faithfully serve God in both word and deed, so that God may be glorified, and the Church may edified (i.e. helped to grow in its knowledge of the truth about God and what it means to live rightly before God) and well governed (i.e. governed in a way that is in line with God's desire for the welfare of his people).

The prayers are then followed by eight questions and answers that are asked by the archbishop and answered by the bishop elect in order that that the congregation may know how the candidate intends to act as a bishop (and so can be sure he is a fit person to be admitted 'to government in the Church of Christ'). These question and answers run as follows:

The Archbishop.

Are you persuaded that you be truly called to this ministration, according to the will of our Lord Jesus Christ, and the order of this Realm?

Answer. I am so persuaded.

The Archbishop.

Are you persuaded that the holy Scriptures contain sufficiently all doctrine required of necessity for eternal salvation through faith in

Jesus Christ? And are you determined out of the same holy Scriptures to instruct the people committed to your charge, and to teach or maintain nothing as required of necessity to eternal salvation, but that which you shall be persuaded may be concluded and proved by the same?

Answer. I am so persuaded and determined, by God's grace.

The Archbishop.

Will you then faithfully exercise yourself in the same holy Scriptures, and call upon God by prayer, for the true understanding of the same; so as ye may be able by them to teach and exhort with wholesome doctrine, and to withstand and convince the gainsayers?

Answer. I will so do, by the help of God.

The Archbishop.

Are you ready, with all faithful diligence, to banish and drive away all erroneous and strange doctrine contrary to God's Word; and both privately and openly to call upon and encourage others to the same?

Answer. I am ready, the Lord being my helper.

The Archbishop.

Will you deny all ungodliness and worldly lusts, and live soberly, righteously and godly in this present world; that you may shew yourself in all things an example of good works unto others, that the adversary may be ashamed, having nothing to say against you?

Answer. I will so do, the Lord being my helper.

The Archbishop.

Will you maintain and set forward (as much as shall lie in you) quietness, peace, and love among all men; and such as be unquiet, disobedient and criminous within your Diocese, correct and punish, according to such authority as ye have by God's Word, and as to you shall be committed by the Ordinance of this Realm?

Answer. I will so do, by the help of God.

The Archbishop.

Will you be faithful in ordaining, sending, or laying hands upon others?

Answer. I will so be, by the help of God.

The Archbishop.

Will you shew yourself gentle, and be merciful for Christ's sake to poor and needy people, and to all strangers destitute of help?

Answer. I will so shew myself, by God's help.

In these questions and answers we see that the bishop's role is to instruct people in the teaching of Scripture, to combat false teaching (i.e. teaching that is contrary to Scripture), to live in such a way as to provide an example of godly living, to encourage people to live lives of quietness, peace and love, and correct and punish those who do the opposite, to ordain and appoint other clergy, and to care for the poor and needy.

After these questions and answers the archbishop prays that God will give the new bishop the ability to perform what he has just declared he will do:

Almighty God, our heavenly Father, who hath given you a good will to do all these things; Grant also unto you strength and power to perform the same; that he accomplishing in you the good work which he hath begun, ye may be found perfect and irreprehensible at the latter day; through Jesus Christ our Lord. Amen.

The archbishop and all other present then say or sing the *Veni, Creator Spiritus* ('Come, Holy Spirit'), a prayer for the gift of the Holy Spirit, the liturgical logic being that it is through the work of the Spirit that God will fulfil the prayer that the archbishop has just offered.

The *Veni Creator Spiritus* is then followed by a further prayer by the archbishop:

434

Almighty God and most merciful Father, who of thine infinite goodness hast given thine only and dearly beloved Son Jesus Christ, to be our Redeemer and the Author of everlasting life; who, after that he had made perfect our redemption by his death, and was ascended into heaven, poured down his gifts abundantly upon men, making some Apostles, some Prophets, some Evangelists, some Pastors and Doctors, to the edifying and making perfect his Church: Grant, we beseech thee, to this thy servant such grace, that he may evermore be ready to spread abroad thy Gospel, the glad tidings of reconciliation with thee; and use the authority given him, not to destruction, but to salvation; not to hurt, but to help: so that as a wise and faithful servant, giving to thy family their portion in due season, he may at last be received into everlasting joy; through Jesus Christ our Lord, who with thee and the Holy Ghost liveth and reigneth, one God, world without end. Amen.

In this prayer the role of a bishop is to proclaim the Gospel, and to act as the 'wise and faithful steward' referred to by Jesus in Luke 12:42 by giving God's people 'their portion in due season,' this 'portion' being the spiritual food that they require so that they may attain eternal life.

After these prayers the archbishop and the other bishops present perform the actual act of ordination/consecration by laying their hands of on the head of the bishop elect, with the archbishop saying:

Receive the Holy Ghost for the office and work of a Bishop in the Church of God, now committed unto thee by the imposition of our hands; In the Name of the Father, and of the Son, and of the Holy Ghost. Amen. And remember that thou stir up the grace of God which is given thee by this imposition of our hands: for God hath not given us the spirit of fear, but of power, and love, and soberness.

The final sentence is a direct quotation of Paul's words to Timothy in 2 Timothy 1:6-7. It has the double purpose of emphasising that the ministry of a contemporary bishop is the same ministry to which Timothy was called and that this ministry is to be characterised by spiritual power, love and self-control ('soberness').

Following the act of ordination/consecration the archbishop gives the new bishop a Bible with a set of words that underline that the bishop must read, study and apply the teaching of Scripture in order to save both himself and those who hear his teaching:

Give heed unto reading, exhortation, and doctrine. Think upon the things contained in this Book. Be diligent in them, that the increase coming thereby may be manifest unto all men. Take heed unto thyself, and to doctrine, and be diligent in doing them: for by so doing thou shalt both save thyself and them that hear thee.

The archbishop also reiterates that a bishop is to be a shepherd feeding the flock of Christ rather than a wolf devouring it, and goes on to describes what acting as a shepherd needs to mean in practice:

Be to the flock of Christ a shepherd, not a wolf; feed them, devour them not. Hold up the weak, heal the sick, bind up the broken, bring again the outcasts, seek the lost. Be so merciful, that ye be not too remiss; so minister discipline, that you forget not mercy: that when the chief Shepherd shall appear ye may receive the never-fading crown of glory; through Jesus Christ our Lord.

The service them moves into the liturgy of Holy Communion with the final prayer by the archbishop before the benediction at the end of the service running as follows:

Most merciful Father, we beseech thee to send down upon this thy servant thy heavenly blessing; and so endue him with thy Holy Spirit, that he, preaching thy Word, may not only be earnest to reprove, beseech, and rebuke with all patience and doctrine; but also may be to such as believe a wholesome example, in word, in conversation, in love, in faith, in chastity, and in purity; that, faithfully fulfilling his course, at the latter day he may receive the crown of righteousness laid up by the Lord the righteous Judge, who liveth and reigneth one God with the Father and the Holy Ghost, world without end. Amen.

The 'servant' here is the new bishop, and what these words, partly based on 2 Timothy 4:2, again emphasise is that with God's blessing and empowered by God's Spirit, a bishop is to be an earnest preacher of the Word and to that he is to back up his preaching by providing a wholesome personal example of Christian living to his fellow believers.

Overall, what we learn from the Ordinal is that bishops are to be shepherds and stewards who:

- Preach and teach the Word of God and are diligent in challenging teaching that is opposed to it.

- Provide examples of godly living both in terms of their own conduct and in terms of how they manage their families and households.

- Encourage people to live godly lives marked by quietness, love and peace.

- Exercise spiritual discipline in a way that is neither too lenient, nor too severe.

- Ordain and appoint clergy.

- Care for the poor and needy.

5. The abolition of episcopal celibacy

In chapter 8 we saw that both Ambrose and Augustine argued in favour of bishops being celibate.

Their view gradually became the accepted view in the Western Church as part of a wider belief that the clergy as a whole ought to be celibate. This move towards an entirely celibate clergy received the support of the Popes. Nevertheless, as late as the eleventh century married clergy were still common in the Western Church. In 1074, however, Pope Gregory VII issues a decree forbidding the laity to receive ministry from married priests and in the English church, under the influence of Anselm, an absolute rule of clerical celibacy was imposed from 1102 onwards.

In the Eastern Church, by contrast, it remained normal for priests and deacons to be married and this position was formally endorsed by the Council of Trullo in 692. From the sixth century onwards, however, bishops came to be chosen from the ranks of the monks or from those parochial clergy who were unmarried.

At the time of the Reformation the Protestant side rejected compulsory clerical celibacy on the grounds that this practice lacked support from the Bible or the Early Church and had led to a situation in which it had been common for the clergy to have concubines and to engage in other forms of sexual immorality. Rome, on the other hand resisted calls to resist the abandonment of clerical celibacy and this position was maintained by the twenty fourth session of the Council of Trent in November 1563.

In the Church of England, clerical celibacy remained the law even after the breach with Rome, but in 1547 a large majority in Convocation agreed:

That all such canons, laws, statutes, decrees, usages and customs, heretofore made, had, or used that forbid any person to contract matrimony, or condemn matrimony already contracted by any person, for any vow or promise of priesthood, chastity or widowhood, shall henceforth cease, be utterly void, and of none effect. [707]

Then in 1549 the *Clergy Marriage Act* repealed all the laws and canons forbidding clerical marriage and declared that all were free to marry provided that they did so according to the rite in the new Prayer Book.

As Gilbert Burnet explains, the issue of whether clerical celibacy should be retained or abandoned was a matter of great controversy:

There was not any one point that was more severely examined at the time of the Reformation than this: for, as the irregular practices and

---

[707] John Strype, *Memorials of Archbishop Cranmer*, Bk II, Ch.4 cited in Edgar Gibson, *The Thirty Nine Articles of the Church of England* (London: Methuen, 1902), p.703.

dissolute lives of both seculars and regulars[708] had very much prejudiced the world against the celibate of the Roman Clergy, which was considered as the occasion of all these disorders; so, on the other hand, the marriage of the Clergy, and also of those of both sexes who had taken vows, gave great offence. They were represented as persons that could not master their appetites, but that indulged themselves in carnal pleasures and interests. Thus, as the scandals of the unmarried Clergy had alienated the world much from them; so the marriage of most of the Reformers was urged as an ill character both of them and of the Reformation; as a doctrine of libertinism, that made the Clergy look to like the rest of the world, and involved by them in the common pleasures, concerns and passions of human life. [709]

The issue was also a very personal one for Thomas Cranmer and Matthew Parker, both of whom had married.

In the face of the criticism of clerical marriage noted by Burnet, the legal right of the clergy (including bishops) to marry was defended theologically in Article XXXII of the *Thirty- Nine Articles* in 1563. The Article declares:

Bishops, Priests, and Deacons are not commanded by God's laws either to vow the estate of single life or to abstain from marriage. Therefore it is lawful also for them, as for all other Christian men, to marry at their own discretion, as they shall judge the same to serve better to godliness.

According to the Article, because there is nothing in the Bible to forbid clerical marriage it follows that it is as lawful according to the law of God for a member of the clergy to marry as for anyone else to do so. However, although the English Reformers therefore held that compulsory clerical celibacy should not be imposed upon the clergy this did not mean that they therefore felt that the clergy had to be married.

---

[708] That is, both ordinary parochial clergy and those in monastic orders.
[709] Gilbert Burnet, *An Exposition of the XXXIX Articles of the Church of England* (Oxford: Clarendon Press, 1819), p.485.

They were well aware that both Christ and St. Paul had affirmed the rightness of celibacy as a vocation to which some people may be called by God (Matthew 19:1-12, 1 Corinthians 7:1-9) and that, even for those without a specific celibate vocation, personal circumstances or the inability to find the right person to marry might rule out the possibility of marriage at any particular time. That is why the Article says that the decision about whether or not to marry is one that could only be made by each individual member of the clergy 'at their own discretion'

However, the Article also adds an important qualification to its declaration that it is lawful for the clergy to marry, namely that each individual needs to judge what will 'serve better to godliness.' That is to say, the decision whether or not to marry must not be simply made on the grounds of personal needs or desires, but on a judgement by an individual about what will help them to live a more godly life in the specific circumstances in which God has called them to serve him.

As Griffith Thomas suggests, this qualification may be a response to the *Injunctions* issued by Queen Elizabeth I in 1559 which note:

...there hath grown offence and some slander to the Church by a lack of discreet and sober behaviour in many ministers of the Church, both in choosing of their wives and in indiscreet living with them. [710]

In the face of what was said in the *Injunctions,* and the particular examples of clerical behaviour that lay behind it, Parker (who composed the Article in its final form) may have it felt necessary to emphasise that clerical marriage should be an aid to godliness and that both the choice of clergy wives and the behaviour of married clergy needed to reflect this fact. In other words, he is issuing a warning not to enter too lightly into marriage or to undertake marriage in a manner unbefitting the clerical calling.

[710] W H Griffith Thomas, The Principles of Theology, 4ed (London: Church Book Room Press, 1951), p. 548.

6. What we have learned in this chapter?

Putting together what we have seen in this chapter, we can say that the view of the role and character of bishops held in the Church of England in the sixteenth and seventeenth centuries was that bishops:

- Are to be godly people with godly households and families who labour diligently at the tasks God has called them to undertake.

- They, like other members of the clergy, are free to marry at their own discretion, but only

If they believe that this would be a aid to godly living.

- They are to be the governors and pastors of those in their dioceses, preaching the word, combatting error, providing pastoral care, bringing people to faith in Christ, building them up in their faith, and protecting them from the attacks of the Devil.

- They are baptize, celebrate Holy Communion, and confirm.

- They are to foster harmony in the Church and encourage people to live godly lives marked by quietness, love and peace.

- They are to exercise spiritual discipline, excommunicating persistent sinners, but also restoring those who are penitent.

- They are to care for the poor and needy.

- They are to ordain and institute new ministers, remove unworthy ministers, and take steps to ensure a supply of ministers for the future.

- They are to hold a visitation in their diocese at least once every three years and they are also to hold annual synods to act as an antidote to error and negligence, and as a means by which they can develop and sustain a loving relationship with their clergy.

As we have noted before in this chapter, this list of the role and characteristics of bishops is in line with the New Testament and Patristic teaching about the role and character of bishops which we looked at in chapters 7 and 8. In the sixteenth and seventeenth century the Church of England was not innovating, but rather remaining faithful to the existing biblical and Patristic pattern for episcopacy.

Even in its rejection of episcopal celibacy the Church of England followed the same approach, in that the argument of the English Reformers that bishops and other clergy should be allowed to marry was based on the fact that there is no prohibition of married clergy in the Bible, but that on the contrary the marriage of clergy was known and accepted in the New Testament, and was also something that was widely known and accepted in the Patristic period, the arguments of Fathers such as Ambrose and Augustine notwithstanding.

James Ussher and the *Reduction of Episcopacy*.
As noted in chapter 5, in 1641 the Archbishop of Armagh, James Ussher put forward an alternative approach to the Puritan criticism of the Anglican episcopate than that taken by writers such as Bilson, Hooker, Hall and Taylor. Rather than arguing that the Puritan critics of episcopacy are simply wrong in what they are saying, both historically and theologically, Ussher seeks to meet their concerns by proposing a form of church government in which episcopal and presbyterian forms of government are 'conjoined.'

Referring to the writings of Ignatius of Antioch, Justin Martyr, Tertullian and Cyprian, and Saxon and Medieval Canon Law, Ussher argues that there is precedent in the history of the Church for bishops and presbyters together ruling the Church and exercising ecclesiastical discipline.

He then declares:

True it is, but in our church this kind of presbyterian government has been long disused, yet seeing it still professeth that every pastor hath a right to rule the church (from whence the name rector also was given first unto him) and to administer the discipline of Christ, as well as to dispense the doctrine and sacraments, and the restraint of the exercise of that right proceeds only from the custom now received in this realm, no man can doubt come, but by another law of the land, this hindrance may well be removed.[711]

As Snoddy notes in his introduction to his collection of Ussher's writings on ecclesiology, Ussher's proposal was that a four-tier scheme of church government should be introduced into the Church of England;

...rising from the pastor administering discipline at the parish level, up through deanery, diocesan and national synods. The pastor or rector exercises a ministry of word, sacrament, and discipline in the parish. The right to administer discipline should be restored to the pastor who, with church wardens and sidesmen, will meet weekly to admonish those who 'live scandalously.' If they do not repent and mend their ways they can be barred from the Lord's Supper and presented at the next monthly synod. Suffragan bishops preside over these monthly synods which bring together all the pastors from an area equivalent to a rural deanery. The synod can pronounce the sentence of excommunication on unrepentant offenders and hold the parish ministers to account for their doctrine and conduct. Appeal may be made from this synod to a diocesan synod, meeting once or twice a year and chaired by 'the bishop, or superintendent (call him whether you will)' or a deputed suffragan serving as 'moderator.' More difficult matters could be referred to two provincial synods, Canterbury in the south and York in the north, which would comprise the bishops, suffragans, and elected clergy from every diocese, with an archbishop presiding. These should meet every third year, and if parliament is sitting they could join as one national synod.[712]

---

[711] Snoddy, p. 151.
[712] Snoddy, p.XXXIV.

As Snoddy goes on to say, Ussher's proposal failed to achieve its aim of bridging the gap between those who supported Presbyterianism and those who supported episcopacy:

The *Reduction* did not fare well as the parties polarized on this issue. The Scots were firmly opposed to any form of episcopacy and Parliament would become increasingly reliant on their support and unable to pursue such a compromise settlement. The King also signalled that a scheme such as Ussher's would not be acceptable. Speaking at Whitehall on 25 January 1641, Charles stated his intention to reduce 'all Matters of Religion and Government to what they were in the purest Times of Queen Elizabeth's Days.' He warned against petitions that would pull down episcopacy and proposals that would have bishops 'no better than Cyphers.' In October he would again affirm that 'I am constant for the doctrine and discipline of the Church of England as it was established by Queene Elis. and my father.' In all likelihood it was the King's disapproval of such reforms that prevented Ussher from distributing the manuscript of the *Reduction* more widely. For example, from March 1641 Ussher was called to consult a House of Lords committee on religion and there is no evidence that he submitted his scheme to the committee, whilst reform proposals from Sir Edward Dering, MP for Kent, and John Williams, Bishop of Lincoln, were debated in Parliament and the focus of much interest.

It seems that Ussher continued to harbour hopes that the *Reduction* would provide a way forward through the debates over polity. As late as May 1641 he was discussing the details of his plan with the Dutch ambassador. It seems that the King did give further consideration to Ussher's ideas and reduced episcopacy is reflected in the royal response to parliamentarian clergy during the negotiations at Newport on the Isle of Wight in September to November 1648, a response that was drafted before Ussher's arrival at Newport. Alan Ford notes the irony: 'royal stubbornness and political ineptitude meant that, when Ussher's proposal had the best opportunity for widespread acceptance, in 1641, Charles rejected it, and when it had little hope of success, in 1648, he endorsed it.' In 1641 the King had missed the opportunity to occupy the middle ground so carefully prepared by Ussher.[713]

Furthermore, as well as failing to achieve its purpose, it can also be argued that Ussher's proposal is theologically problematic. This is because it transfers the power to make decisions from the bishops to the various synods which he proposes should be created. As King Charles noted, this does seem to make bishops 'no better than Cyphers' They still have the title of bishops, but they cannot exercise effective power of government in the Church. It is the synods that decide things by what Ussher calls 'common consent,'[714] with the bishops' role in the Church's government being reduced to that of synodical moderators. This is essentially a presbyterian rather than an episcopal form of church government.

We can contrast this approach with that of the *Reformatio Legum Ecclesiasticarum*. As we have seen, the *Reformatio* lays down that bishops are to hold hold Synods. However, these synods are purely consultative bodies, with decisions being made by the bishops, either at the time or subsequently, in the light of their reflection on the advice they have received. The 'lower ministers' are to accept their bishop's 'decrees and sentences' as 'valid and firm,' but with a right of appeal to the archbishop or possibly the king in the event that the bishop's decisions are viewed as 'either unjust or absurd.' [715]

It can certainly be argued that the *Reformatio* gives insufficient weight to the need for the bishop to receive the consent as well as the advice of his fellow presbyters, but at least it recognises the distinctive role of the bishop in the government of the Church in a way that Ussher's proposal does not.

---

[713] Snoddy, p. XXXVI
[714] Snoddy, p. 153.
[715] *Reformatio Legum Ecclesiasticarum*, 20:23 in Bray p.269.

Chapter 11
The role and character of bishops in Church of England documents from the twentieth and twenty first centuries

The reformed Anglican vision of the role and character of bishops contained in the 1662 *Ordinal* still remains normative for those who belong to the Church of England today. This is because the *Ordinal*, alongside the *Thirty Nine Articles* and the *Book of Common Prayer*, is one of the 'historic formularies' in which, according to Canon A5, the Church of England's doctrine is to be found and to which Church of England ministers and lay workers must declare their assent, as specified in Canons C15, E5 and E8.

However, it is not sufficient simply to turn to the 1662 *Ordinal* and say, 'that is what the Church of England think about bishops.' That is because there are a range of other Church of England documents from the twentieth and twenty first centuries that need to be considered as well because they both reflect, and have helped to shape, contemporary Church of England thinking about the episcopate.

In this chapter we shall look at what is said in these documents and consider the strengths and weaknesses of the view of bishops that they put forward.

1. The Canons

The first document that needs to be taken into account is the *Canons of the Church of England*, first issued in 1969, but amended since.

In relation to bishops the key Canon is Canon C18, 'Of diocesan bishops, 'which runs as follows:

1. Every bishop is the chief pastor of all that are within his diocese, as well laity as clergy, and their father in God; it appertains to his office to teach and to uphold sound and wholesome doctrine, and to banish and drive away all

erroneous and strange opinions; and, himself an example of righteous and godly living, it is his duty to set forward and maintain quietness, love, and peace among all men.

2. Every bishop has within his diocese jurisdiction as Ordinary except in places and over persons exempt by law or custom.

3. Such jurisdiction is exercised by the bishop himself, or by a Vicar-General, official, or other commissary, to whom authority in that behalf shall have been formally committed by the bishop concerned.

4. Every bishop is, within his diocese, the principal minister, and to him belongs the right, save in places and over persons exempt by law or custom, of celebrating the rites of ordination and confirmation; of conducting, ordering, controlling, and authorizing all services in churches, chapels, churchyards and consecrated burial grounds; of granting a faculty or licence for all alterations, additions, removals, or repairs to the walls, fabric, ornaments, or furniture of the same; of consecrating new churches, churchyards, and burial grounds; of instituting to all vacant benefices, whether of his own collation or of the presentation of others; of admitting by licence to all other vacant ecclesiastical offices; of holding visitations at times limited by law or custom to the end that he may get some good knowledge of the state, sufficiency, and ability of the clergy and other persons whom he is to visit; of being president of the diocesan synod.

5. Where the assent of the bishop is required to a resolution of the diocesan synod it shall not lightly nor without grave cause be withheld.

6. Every bishop shall be faithful in admitting persons into holy orders and in celebrating the rite of confirmation as often and in as many places as shall be convenient, and shall provide, as much as in him lies, that in every place within his diocese there

shall be sufficient priests to minister the word and sacraments to the people that are therein.

7. Every bishop shall correct and punish all such as be unquiet, disobedient, or criminous, within his diocese, according to such authority as he has by God's Word and is committed to him by the laws and ordinances of this realm.

8. Every bishop shall reside within his diocese, saving the ancient right of any bishop, when resident in any house in London during his attendance on the Parliament, or on the Court, or for the purpose of performing any other duties of his office, to be taken and accounted as resident within his own diocese.[716]

This Canon deliberately draws on the language of the 1662 *Ordinal*. In line with the Ordinal and with the other writings from the sixteenth and seventeenth centuries that we looked at in the last chapter, paragraph 1 declares that a diocesan bishop is the pastor and father in God to all in the diocese, both clergy and laity alike, and that he or she[717] must be someone who can provide an example of godly living.

Paragraph 1 also says that in exercising this role it is the duty of the diocesan bishop to 'teach and to uphold sound and wholesome doctrine, and to banish and drive away all erroneous and strange opinion.' In the light of Canon A5 'sound and wholesome doctrine' means the doctrine that is found in the Holy Scriptures, in the writings of 'the Ancient Fathers and Councils of the Church' that are 'agreeable to the said Scriptures' and in the *Thirty Nine Articles*, the *Book of Common Prayer* and the *Ordinal*. 'Erroneous and strange option,' by contrast, means teaching that is contrary to this doctrine.

---

[716] Canon C.18 'Of diocesan bishops' at https://www.churchofengland.org/about/leadership-and-governance/legal-services/canons-church-england/section-c#b78
[717] The language of the Canon has not been updated to reflect the fact that the Church of England has had women bishops since 2014, but in the light of this fact the male pronoun has to be seen to refer to both men and women.

The paragraph also says that the diocesan bishop is to 'set forward and maintain,' that is to say teach and uphold, 'quietness love and peace' among all who are in the diocese.

Paragraphs 2-4 lay down the principle that the diocesan bishop has 'jurisdiction as Ordinary' in the diocese as a whole. What this means is that he or she has the permanent legal authority to act as pastor and father in God to all in the diocese. This jurisdiction may be exercised by the diocesan bishop directly or by someone authorised to act on his or her behalf.

The reference to 'places or persons exempt by law or custom' reflects the fact that there are what are known as 'peculiar jurisdictions' that are in a diocese but that do not come under the jurisdiction of the diocesan bishop. Examples include Westminster Abbey and other 'royal peculiars' that come under the jurisdiction of the monarch, certain college chapels at Oxford and Cambridge such as the chapels of King's College Cambridge and New College Oxford, and the Temple Church in London. In addition, in the case of cathedrals ordinary jurisdiction lies with the dean and chapter, although the diocesan bishop has rights of 'visiatorial jurisdiction' that enable him or her to supervise the life of the cathedral and take disciplinary action when necessary.

Paragraph 4 says that the exercise of such jurisdiction involves the right to ordain and confirm, to conduct or authorise services, to grant authority for repairs and alterations to churches and churchyards, to consecrate new churches, to install ministers into livings, to licence people to exercise other church offices, to hold visitations to gain a greater knowledge of the diocese and to preside over meetings of the diocesan synod.

The right to act as president of the diocesan Synod is laid down in Schedule 3 of the *Synodical Government Measure 1969* and is a reflection of the diocesan bishop's role as the minister who presides over the diocese as a whole. The diocesan synod is a meeting of the representative clergy and laity of the diocese to discuss matters relating to its life and mission and it is therefore right that the diocesan bishop should preside.

Paragraph 5 reflects the fact that under the *Synodical Government Measure* the diocesan bishop can block a resolution agreed by the clergy and laity in a diocesan synod. Because bishops are meant to act with the consent of the clergy and laity of the diocese, this veto is to not to be used 'without grave cause,' but the existence of this veto means that the diocesan bishop retains an authority independent of the rest of the Synod and can prevent the diocese adopting a course of action which is ungodly or otherwise ill advised.

Paragraph 6 sets out the duty of the diocesan bishop to ordain, confirm and ensure that there sufficient priests across the diocese.

Paragraph 7 sets out the duty of the bishop to 'correct and punish' ungodly behaviour and illegal behaviour by those in the diocese. This would include taking action under the *Ecclesiastical Jurisdiction Measure*, the *Clergy Discipline Measure* and the Church of England's Safeguarding Regulations and also includes the power of excommunication which according to Canon B16 can only take place in accordance with the 'order and direction' of the diocesan bishop. [718]

Finally, paragraph 8, like the *Reformatio Legum Ecclesiasticarum*, lays down that the diocesan bishop will normally reside in his or her own diocese.

It is important to note that Canon C18 is not an exhaustive account of a diocesan bishop's role. As Peter Beesley writes:

[718] Canon B.16, 'Of notorious offenders not to be admitted to Holy Communion' at
https://www.churchofengland.org/about/leadership-and-governance/legal-services/canons-church-england/section-b#b29.

...there is a vast web of primary legislation, both Acts of Parliament and Measures of the General Synod, that impose responsibilities and obligations on bishops or permit certain actions and prohibit others. [719]

No Canon could possibly outline everything that a diocesan bishop is called to do in relation to this legislation, and so Canon C18 does not attempt to do so. What it does instead is paint a broad-brush picture of what sort of person a diocesan bishop is to be and what the main parts of their role involve.

In addition to Canon C18 there are two other Canons which are directly concerned with bishops Canon C17 which is concerned with archbishops and Canon C20 which is concerned with suffragan bishops.

Canon C17, 'Of archbishops,' runs as follows:

1. By virtue of their respective offices, the Archbishop of Canterbury is styled Primate of All England and Metropolitan, and the Archbishop of York Primate of England and Metropolitan.

2. The archbishop has throughout his province at all times metropolitical jurisdiction, as superintendent of all ecclesiastical matters therein, to correct and supply the defects of other bishops, and, during the time of his metropolitical visitation, jurisdiction as Ordinary, except in places and over persons exempt by law or custom.

3. Such jurisdiction is exercised by the archbishop himself, or by a Vicar-General, official, or other commissary to whom authority in that behalf shall have been formally committed by the archbishop concerned.

---

[719] Peter Beesley, 'The legal role of bishops' in *Resourcing Bishops* (London: CHP, 2001), p. 248.

4. The archbishop is, within his province, the principal minister, and to him belongs the right of confirming the election of every person to a bishopric, of being the chief consecrator at the consecration of every bishop, of receiving such appeals in his provincial court as may be provided by law, of holding metropolitical visitations at times or places limited by law or custom, and of presiding in the Convocation of the province either in person or by such deputy as he may lawfully appoint. In the province of Canterbury, the Bishop of London or, in his absence, the Bishop of Winchester, has the right to be so appointed; and in their absence the archbishop shall appoint some other diocesan bishop of the province. The two archbishops are joint presidents of the General Synod.

5. By ancient custom, no Act is held to be an Act of the Convocation of the province unless it shall have received the assent of the archbishop.

6. By statute law it belongs to the archbishop to give permission to officiate within his province to any minister who has been ordained priest or deacon by an overseas bishop within the meaning of the Overseas and Other Clergy (Ministry and Ordination) Measure 1967, or a bishop in a Church not in communion with the Church of England whose orders are recognized or accepted by the Church of England, and thereupon such minister shall possess all such rights and advantages and be subject to all such duties and liabilities as he would have possessed and been subject to if he had been ordained by the bishop of a diocese in the province of Canterbury or York.

7. By the laws of this realm the Archbishop of Canterbury is empowered to grant such licences or dispensations as are therein set forth and provided, and such licences or dispensations, being confirmed by the authority of the Queen's

Majesty, have force and authority not only within the province of Canterbury but throughout all England. [720]

In the present set of Canons, unlike in the *Reformatio*, this Canon on archbishops precedes the Canon on diocesan bishops. The logic would seem to be to look at bishops in terms of descending scale of authority with the archbishops being considered first in Canon C17 because they have the most authority, diocesan bishops coming next in Canon C18 because they have lesser authority and suffragan bishops coming last in Canon C20 because they have least authority.

In terms of Canon C17 this order of Canons creates a problem because it leads to a failure to recognise that most of what archbishops are called to do is in fact covered not in Canon C17 but in Canon C18. The Archbishops of Canterbury and York are first and foremost the diocesan bishops of the dioceses of Canterbury and York. It is only because they are the bishops of these dioceses that they are also the Archbishops of Canterbury and York, the Metropolitan bishops of the Church of England's southern and northern provinces.

This means that to understand the responsibilities of the archbishops properly you have to do what we have done in this chapter and begin with Canon C17 and only then move on to Canon C18. The bulk of what the archbishops are called to do in so far as they are diocesan bishops is set out in Canon C17 and what you then get in Canon C18 is their additional responsibilities as archbishops.

These additional responsibilities are:

First, to exercise general oversight over the dioceses and bishops in their province and to exercise jurisdiction in diocese when they undertake a visitation within it (paragraphs 2-3).

Secondly, to confirm the election of bishops, act as the chief consecrator of other bishops, and receive such legal appeals as are

[720] Canon C17, 'Of archbishops' at https://www.churchofengland.org/about/leadership-and-governance/legal-services/canons-church-england/section-c#b77

specified by law (paragraph 4). The point of the reference to the election of bishops is that when a new diocesan bishop has been chosen by the monarch the person concerned is then formally elected to the post by the Dean and Chapter of the diocesan cathedral. The responsibility of the archbishop is to confirm that this election has taken place.[721]

Thirdly, to act as the presidents of the General Synod and to give or refuse assent to Acts of the Convocations of the Provinces of Canterbury and York (paragraphs 4 and 5). As was noted in chapter 5, the Convocations are the ancient provincial synods of the provinces of Canterbury and York. They consist of two Houses, the Upper House consisting of the diocesan bishops of the province plus ex officio (in the case of Canterbury) and elected suffragan bishops and the Lower House consisting of the elected representatives of the other clergy.[722] The Convocations have the right to pass Acts of Convocation which have moral but not legal force and these Acts only have validity if the archbishop of the province gives assent to them. Since 1970 the two Convocations, plus the Houses of Laity of the two provinces. have met together as the Church of England's General Synod and just as the archbishops have traditionally presided over the meetings of their Convocations, so also they act as the presidents of the joint General Synod.[723]

Fourthly, to give permission to clergy ordained by bishops outside the Church of England to serve as clergy in their province (paragraph 6).

---

[721] For the history behind the practice of election see Colin Podmore, 'The Choosing of Bishops in the Early Church and the Church of England: an historical survey' in *Working with the Spirit: choosing diocesan bishops* (London: CHP, 2001), pp.113-138.

[722] The constitution of the Convocations is specified in Canons H2 and H3.

[723] For the history of these arrangements see Colin Podmore, 'Synodical Government in the Church of England, History and Principles' in Colin Podmore, *Aspects of Anglican Identity* (London: CHP, 2005), pp. 103-123.

Fifthly, to grant certain licenses and dispensations (such as an archbishop's licence allowing a couple to marry in church) (paragraph 7).

Canon C20, 'Of bishops suffragan' runs as follows:

1. Every bishop suffragan shall endeavour himself faithfully to execute such things pertaining to the episcopal office as shall be delegated to him by the bishop of the diocese to whom he shall be suffragan.

2. Every bishop suffragan shall use, have, or execute only such jurisdiction or episcopal power or authority in any diocese as shall be licensed or limited to him to use, have, or execute by the bishop of the same.

3. Every bishop suffragan shall reside within the diocese of the bishop to whom he shall be suffragan, except he have a licence from that bishop to reside elsewhere.[724]

Just as Canon C18 needs to be read in conjunction with Canon C17, so this Canon also needs to be read in conjunction with Canon C17. What this Canon basically says is that a suffragan bishop can do those things that a diocesan bishop can do (as specified in Canon C17) but only to the extent that the power to do them is delegated to them by their diocesan. In addition, a suffragan bishop must reside in his or her diocese unless given permission by the diocesan to live elsewhere.

In summary, what we learn from Canons C17, 18 and 20 is that bishops are to be people who can provide examples of godly living, and that their basic responsibilities are to:

- Reside in their dioceses;

---

[724] Canon C20, 'Of bishops suffragan' at
https://www.churchofengland.org/about/
leadership-and- governance/legal-services/canons-church-england/section-c#b80.

- Be pastors and fathers in God to those in their dioceses;

- Teach and uphold 'wholesome and sound doctrine' and banish error;

- Undertake confirmations;

- Ensure that there are sufficient priests to minister the Word and the sacraments in their dioceses;

- Ordain clergy, institute clergy to benefices, and licence clergy and laity to exercise 'ecclesiastical offices;'

- Consecrate churches and church yards and grant faculties for the repair and alteration of churches and churchyards;

- Exercise ecclesiastical discipline;

- Exercise a veto over decisions by the clergy and laity in diocesan Synod when this is necessary.

Suffragan bishops exercise these responsibilities with the permission of their diocesan bishop and archbishops exercise a number of additional responsibilities.

2. Documents concerning the House of Bishops

In addition to what is said about bishops in the Canons, note also needs to be taken of what is said in various documents about the nature and responsibilities of the House of Bishops of the Church of England's General Synod.

According to the Standing orders of the General Synod, the House of Bishops is made up of the two archbishops, the other diocesan bishops, the Bishop of Dover, the Bishop of the Armed Forces and nine elected suffragan bishops. In addition, six female suffragan bishops and the Provincial Episcopal Visitors have the right to attend its meetings, but not to vote. [725]

The House of Bishops has two particular areas of responsibility.

The first of these areas is doctrine, liturgy and the administration of the sacraments. Under Article 7(1) of the constitution of the General Synod, matters to do with the doctrine and liturgy of the Church of England or the administration of the sacraments have to be referred to the House of Bishops and can only be given final approval in a form proposed by the House of Bishops.[726]

The second area is that of ministry. The House of Bishops has a particular responsibility for the selection and training of the clergy and nationally authorised lay ministers. This responsibility is exercised through the work of the Bishops Committee for Ministry, which oversees the work of the Church of England's Ministry Division.

In addition, under section 5 (i) of the constitution of the General Synod a Measure or Canon an only receive final approval if a majority of all three Houses of Synod vote in favour. This means that the House of Bishops has the same kind of veto in the General Synod as diocesan bishops have in their diocesan synods.[727]

---

[725] See Appendix A of the Standing Orders of General Synod at https://www.churchofengland.org/sites/default/files/2020-09/Standing%20order-%20updated%20Sept%202020.pdf
[726] 'A provision touching doctrinal formulae or the services or ceremonies of the Church of England or the administration of the Sacraments or sacred rites thereof shall, before it is finally approved by General Synod, be referred to the House of Bishops, and shall be submitted for such final approval in terms proposed by the House of Bishops and not otherwise.' *Constitution of the General Synod* 7(1) at http://peterowen.org.uk/articles/gs-constitution.html.
[727] 'A motion for the final approval of any Measure or Canon shall not be deemed to be carried unless, on a division by Houses, it receives the assent of the majority of the members of each House present.'. Constitution of General Synod 5(1) at http://peterowen.org.uk/articles/gs-constitution.html.

As well as meeting as part of the General Synod, the House of Bishops also meets separately in May and December each year to consider issues relating to these two areas of responsibility and any other issues relevant to the role of the bishops in providing oversight and leadership to the Church of England. There are also joint meetings for a similar purpose between the House of Bishops and the other bishops of the Church of England in what is known as the College of Bishops. [728]

The powers and responsibilities of the House of Bishops are a collective exercise at the national level of the ministry of oversight which bishops possess individually and which they exercise within their dioceses in the ways summarised in Canon C18. For example, the responsibility of the House of Bishops for the selection and training of the clergy and national authorised lay ministers is a national exercise of the responsibility of bishops to ensure that there are now, and will be in the future, sufficient ministers of word and sacrament in their dioceses.

3. The Ordinals in the Alternative Service Book and Common Worship

Although, as explained at the beginning of this chapter, the 1662 Ordinal remains doctrinally normative for the Church of England, since 1980 it has been supplemented by two other modern language ordinals. The first of these was the Ordinal contained in the *Alternative Service Book,* which was authorised for used from 1980 to 2007, and the second is the set of Ordination Services which form part of the Church of England's *Common Worship* resources and which have been authorised for used since 2007.

The Alternative Service Book

The service for 'The Ordination or Consecration of a Bishop' in the *Alternative Service Book* Ordinal contains three readings from the Old

---

[728] Bishops' information: House and College of Bishops' at
https://www.churchofengland.org/about/leadership-and-governance/general-synod/bishops-information-house-and-college-bishops.

and New Testaments. The Old Testament reading is Numbers 27:15-20 and 22-23, and the two New Testament readings are 2 Corinthians 4:1-10 and John 21:15-17.[729] The point of the Old Testament reading is to indicate that the ordination of a bishop involves commissioning someone to provide leadership for the people of God, just as Joshua was commissioned to provide leadership for the people of Israel, and the point of the New Testament readings is to indicate that bishops today are called to continue the apostolic role of making the gospel known and feeding the sheep of Christ's flock.

In this service the questions asked of the bishop elect by the archbishop are preceded by a 'declaration' in which the archbishop summarises the calling of a bishop. In this declaration the archbishop states:

A bishop is called to lead in serving and caring for the people of God and to work with them in the oversight of the Church. As a chief pastor he shares with his fellow bishops a special responsibility to maintain and further the unity of the Church, to uphold its discipline, and to guard its faith. He is to promote its mission throughout the world. It is his duty to watch over and pray for all those committed to his charge, and to teach and govern them after the example of the Apostles, speaking in the name of God and interpreting the gospel of Christ. He is to know his people and be known by them. He is to ordain and to send new ministers, guiding those who serve with him and enabling them to fulfil their ministry.

He is to baptize and confirm, to preside at the Holy Communion, and to lead the offering of prayer and praise. He is to be merciful, but with firmness, and to minister discipline, but with mercy. He is to have a special care for the outcast and needy; and to those who turn to God he is to declare the forgiveness of sins.[730]

---

[729] *The Alternative Service Book,* (London: SPCK, 1980), pp.382-385.
[730] *The Alternative Service Book*, p. 388.

Eight questions and answers then follow this declaration. They are as follows:

[Archbishop] Do you believe, so far as you know your own heart, that God has called you to the office and work of a bishop in his Church?

I believe that God has called me.

Archbishop Do you accept the holy Scriptures as revealing all things necessary for eternal salvation through faith in Jesus Christ?

I do so accept them.

Archbishop Do you believe the doctrine of the Christian faith as the Church of England has received it, and in your ministry will you expound and teach it?

I believe it, and will so do.

Archbishop Will you accept the discipline of this Church, and faithfully exercise authority within it?

By the help of God, I will.

Archbishop Will you be diligent in prayer, in reading holy Scripture, and in all studies that will deepen your faith and fit you to uphold the truth of the Gospel against error?

By the help of God, I will.

Archbishop Will you strive to fashion your own life and that of your household according to the way of Christ?

By the help of God, I will.

Archbishop Will you promote unity, peace, and love among all Christian people, and especially among those whom you serve?

By the help of God, I will.

Archbishop Will you then be a faithful witness to Christ to those among whom you live, and lead your people to obey the Saviour's command to make disciples of all nations?[731]

The prayer that accompanies the laying on hands by the archbishop and the other bishops present runs:

Almighty Father, fill this your servant with the grace and power which you gave to your apostles, that he may lead those committed to his charge in proclaiming the gospel of salvation. Through him increase your Church, renew its ministry, and unite its members in a holy fellowship of truth and love. Enable him as a true shepherd to feed and govern your flock; make him wise as a teacher, and steadfast as a guardian of its faith and sacraments. Guide and direct him in presiding at the worship of your people. Give him humility, that he may use his authority to heal, not to hurt; to build up, not to destroy. Defend him from all evil, that as a ruler over your household and an ambassador for Christ he may stand before you blameless, and finally, with all your servants, enter your eternal joy.[732]

As in the 1662 Ordinal, the new bishop is given a Bible by the archbishop and the words after the giving of the Bible are:

Receive this Book; here are words of eternal life. Take them for your guide, and declare them to the world. Keep watch over the whole flock in which the Holy Spirit has appointed you shepherd. Encourage the faithful, restore the lost, build up the body of Christ; that when the Chief Shepherd shall appear, you may receive the unfading crown of glory.[733]

Common Worship

The *Common Worship* Ordination Services contain an 'Introduction by the House of Bishops' which sets out its understanding of the roles of deacons, priests and bishops. In this introduction bishops are seen as

---

[731] *The Alternative Service Book*, pp.389-390.
[732] *The Alternative Service Book*, p. 394.
[733] *The Alternative Service Book*, pp. 394-395.

having the same basic ministry as deacons and priests, but with a number of additional responsibilities. The relevant paragraph of the introduction states:

Holy Orders help shape the Church around Christ's incarnation and work of redemption, handed on in the apostolic charge. The ministry of deacons is focused in being heralds of the kingdom and in bringing before the servant Church the needs of the world. The ministry of priests (who continue to exercise diaconal ministry) is focused in calling the Church to enter into Christ's self-offering to the Father, drawing God's people into a life transformed and sanctified. The ministry of bishops (as they embody the ministry of both deacon and priest) is focused in the apostolic responsibility of proclaiming and guarding the faith, of presiding at the sacraments, of leading the Church's prayer and of handing on its ministry, as they share with their fellow bishops in their apostolic mission.[734]

The *Common Worship* service for the 'The Ordination and Consecration of a Bishop' has fourteen suggested readings from the Bible.[735]

The six suggested Old Testament readings are: Isaiah 42.1-9; Isaiah 61.1-3; Ezekiel 34. [1-10,] 11-16, 23 Psalm: 40.1-14; 99 and 100. These readings indicate that a bishop is to be a herald of the gospel, a shepherd of God's flock and someone who leads God's people in prayer and praise.

The four suggested New Testament readings are Acts 20.17-35; 1 Timothy 3.1-7; 2 Timothy 3.14–4.5 and 1 Peter 5.1-11. These readings

---

[734] *Common Worship Ordination Services*, 'introduction by the House of Bishops' at https://www.churchofengland.org/prayer-and-worship/worship-texts-and-resources/common-worship/ministry/common-worship-ordination.
[735] Common Worship Ordination Services, 'The Ordination and Consecration of a Bishop' – Readings' at https://www.churchofengland.org/prayer-and-worship/worship-texts-and-resources/common-worship/ministry/common-worship-ordination-0#mm015. All other quotes from 'The Ordination and Consecration of a Bishop' are from this source.

indicate that bishops are to be chief elders who have the personal qualities listed in 1 Timothy 3 and who care for Christ's flock, proclaim the gospel and defend the faith against error.

The four suggested Gospel readings are Matthew 18.1-6; Matthew 28.16-20; John 17.1-9,18-21 and John 21.15-1. These reading indicate that bishops are exercise the power of the keys, fulfil the Great Commission, lead the Church into a unity rooted in Christ's word, and to care for Christ's sheep.

As in the case of the *Alternative Service Book*, the *Common Worship* service has a declaration by the archbishop preceding the questions to the bishop elect. This declaration states:

Bishops are called to serve and care for the flock of Christ. Mindful of the Good Shepherd, who laid down his life for his sheep, they are to love and pray for those committed to their charge, knowing their people and being known by them. As principal ministers of word and sacrament, stewards of the mysteries of God, they are to preside at the Lord's table and to lead the offering of prayer and praise. They are to feed God's pilgrim people, and so build up the Body of Christ.

They are to baptize and confirm, nurturing God's people in the life of the Spirit and leading in the way of holiness. They are to discern and foster the gifts of the Spirit in all who follow Christ, commissioning them to minister in his name. They are to preside over the ordination of deacons and priests, and join together in the ordination of bishops.

As chief pastors, it is their duty to share with their fellow presbyters the oversight of the Church, speaking in the name of God and expounding the gospel of salvation. With the Shepherd's love, they are to be merciful, but with firmness; to minister discipline, but with compassion. They are to have a special care for the poor, the outcast and those who are in need. They are to seek out those who are lost and lead them home with rejoicing, declaring the absolution and forgiveness of sins to those who turn to Christ.

Eleven questions and answers then follow this declaration. They are as follows:

Do you accept the Holy Scriptures as revealing all things necessary for eternal salvation through faith in Jesus Christ?

Ordinand **I do so accept them.**

Will you be diligent in prayer, in reading Holy Scripture, and in all studies that will deepen your faith and fit you to bear witness to the truth of the gospel?

Ordinand **By the help of God, I will.**

Will you lead your people in proclaiming the glorious gospel of Christ, so that the good news of salvation may be heard in every place?

Ordinand **By the help of God, I will.**

Will you teach the doctrine of Christ as the Church of England has received it, will you refute error, and will you hand on entire the faith that is entrusted to you?

Ordinand **By the help of God, I will.**

Will you be faithful in ordaining and commissioning ministers of the gospel?

Ordinand **By the help of God, I will.**

Will you promote peace and reconciliation in the Church and in the world; and will you strive for the visible unity of Christ's Church?

Ordinand **By the help of God, I will.**

Will you be gentle and merciful for Christ's sake to those who are in need, and speak for those who have no other to speak for them?

Ordinand **By the help of God, I will.**

Will you endeavour to fashion your own life and that of your household according to the way of Christ and make your home a place of hospitality and welcome?

Ordinand **By the help of God, I will.**

Will you work with your fellow servants in the gospel for the sake of the kingdom of God?

Ordinand **By the help of God, I will.**

Will you accept the discipline of this Church, exercising authority with justice, courtesy and love, and always holding before you the example of Christ?

Ordinand **By the help of God, I will.**

Will you then, in the strength of the Holy Spirit, continually stir up the gift of God that is in you, that the good news of Christ may be proclaimed in all the world?

Ordinand **By the help of God, I will.**

The prayer accompanying the laying on hands by the archbishop and other bishops runs:

Through your Spirit, heavenly Father,

fill *this your servant* with the grace and power which you gave to your apostles,

that as *a true shepherd he* may feed and govern your flock,

and lead them in proclaiming the gospel of your salvation in the world.

Make *him* steadfast as *a guardian* of the faith and sacraments,

wise as *a teacher*

and faithful in presiding at the worship of your people.

Through *him*, with *his* fellow servants in Christ,

increase your Church and renew its ministry,

uniting its members in a holy fellowship of truth and love.

Give *him* humility,

that *he* may use *his* authority to heal, not to hurt;

to build up, not to destroy,

Defend *him* from all evil,

that *he* may, as *a faithful steward*,

be presented blameless with all your household

and, at the last, enter your eternal joy,

through your Son Jesus Christ our Lord,

to whom, with you and your Holy Spirit,

belong glory and honour, worship and praise, now and for ever.

The words after the giving of the Bible are:

Receive this book,

as a sign of the authority given you this day

to build up Christ's Church in truth.

Here are words of eternal life.

Take them for your guide

and declare them to the world.

The *Common Worship* service is a development of the *Alternative Service Book* service, which in turn drew on the 1662 Ordinal and Canon C18. Overall, what we learn from these two services is that bishops are to be shepherds and stewards of God's people who:

- Promote the mission of the Church, guard its faith, further its unity and uphold its discipline;

- Preach the gospel;

- Teach the Christian faith as the Church of England has received it and refute error;

- Lead the Church in prayer and praise;

- Preside over the administration of the sacraments and confirm;

- Absolve those who are penitent;

- Ordain and commission new minsters and share in the ordination of new bishops;

- Care for the poor, the outcast and the needy and speak for those who have no one else to speak for them;

- Promote peace and reconciliation in the world.

In terms of their personal qualities, bishops are to be people who:

- Pray, read the Bible, and are diligent in other forms of theological study;

- Are humble, and exercise their authority with justice, courtesy and love;

- Fashion their own lives and those of their household after the way of Christ

- Make their homes place of hospitality and welcome.

4. Ecumenical Statements

In the course of the twentieth and twenty first centuries the Church of England has been involved in a series of bilateral and multilateral discussions about matters of faith and order with other churches.

These discussions have resulted in a number of statements about episcopacy to which the Church of England has given its assent in various ways.

ARCIC I statement on Ministry and Ordination

The first Anglican-Roman Catholic International Commission (ARCIC I) was established by the Anglican Communion and the Roman Catholic Church in 1968 in order to discuss issues concerning the Eucharist, the Ministry, and Authority in the Church which it was recognised the two Communions needed to address if they were to move towards the goal of 'full organic unity' between them.[736]

The ARCIC I statement on Ministry and Ordination was published in 1973. Together with the ARCIC I statement on the Eucharist it was recognised by the Church of England, along with the other churches of the Anglican Communion, as being 'consonant in substance with the faith of Anglicans.'[737]

The statement first considers the ministry of bishops in terms of the purpose of the ordained ministry as a whole. On this topic the statement declares:

Like any human community the church requires a focus of leadership and unity, which the Holy Spirit provides in the ordained ministry. This ministry assumes various patterns to meet the varying needs of those whom the church is seeking to serve, and it is the role of the minister to co-ordinate the activities of the Church's fellowship and to promote what is necessary and useful for the Church's life and mission. He is to discern what is of the Spirit in the diversity of the church's life and promote its unity.

In the New Testament a variety of images is used to describe the functions of this minister. He is servant, both of Christ and of the

[736] See *The Malta Report*, 1968, paragraphs 17-20 at
https://www.anglicancommunion.org/media/105272/the_malta_report.pdf
[737] See Roger Coleman (ed) *Resolutions of the Lambeth Conferences 1867-1988* (Toronto: Anglican Book Centre, 1992), pp.202-204.

Church. As herald and ambassador he is an authoritative representative of Christ and proclaims his message of reconciliation. As teacher he explains and applies the word of God to the community. As shepherd he exercises pastoral care and guides the flock. He is a steward who may only provide for the household of God what belongs to Christ. He is to be an example both in holiness and in compassion. [738]

The statement then goes on to consider the distinctive role of the bishop in symbolising and maintaining the 'communion of the churches in mission, faith and holiness, through time and space' as this is signified by his ordination by other bishops:

In the ordination of a new bishop, other bishops lay hands on him, as they request the gift of the Spirit for his ministry and receive him into their ministerial fellowship.

Because they are entrusted with the oversight of other churches, this participation in his ordination signifies that this new bishop and his church are within the communion of churches. Moreover, because they are representative of their churches in fidelity to the teaching and mission of the apostles and are members of the episcopal college, their participation also ensures the historical continuity of this church with the apostolic church and of its bishop with the original apostolic ministry.

The communion of the churches in mission, faith and holiness, through time and space, is thus symbolised and maintained in the bishop. Here are comprised the essential features of what is meant in our two traditions, by ordination in the apostolic succession. [739]

Baptism, Eucharist and Ministry

As its name suggests, *Baptism, Eucharist and Ministry* is an ecumenical report concerned with these three topics. It was published by the

---

[738] Anglican-Roman Catholic International Commission, *The Final Report* (London: SPCK, 1982), pp.32-33.
[739] Anglican-Roman Catholic International Commission, pp.37-38.

World Council of Churches in 1982 after a long process of consultation in which the Church of England was involved. Following its publication, the Church of England, like the other churches of the Anglican Communion, declared that it could recognise in this report 'the faith of the Church through the ages.'[740]

In a paragraph in the section on Ministry which has become widely influential, the report declares that all ordained ministers (including bishops) should exercise ministry in a personal, collegial and communal way:

It should be *personal* because the presence of Christ among his people can most effectively be pointed to by the person ordained to proclaim the Gospel and the call the community to serve the Lord in unity of life and witness. it should also be *collegial*, for there is need for a college of ordained ministers sharing in the common task of representing the concerns of the community. finally, be an intimate relationship between the ordained ministry and the community should find expression in a *communal* dimension with the exercise of the ordained ministry is rooted in the life of the community and requires the community's effective participation in the discovery of God's will and the guidance of the Spirit.[741]

The consensus statement in *Baptism, Eucharist and Ministry* on the distinctive function of bishops then states that in episcopally ordered churches:

Bishops preach the Word, preside at the sacraments, and administer discipline in such a way as to be representative pastoral ministers of oversight, continuity and unity in the Church. They have pastoral oversight of the area to which they are called. They serve the apostolicity and unity of the Church's teaching, worship and sacramental life. They have responsibility for leadership in the

---

[740] Coleman, pp.194-196.
[741] World Council of Churches, *Baptism, Eucharist and Ministry* (Geneva: World Council of Churches, 1982), p.26

Church's mission. They relate the Christian community in their area to the wider Church, and the universal Church to their community. They, in communion with the presbyters and deacons and the whole community, are responsible for the orderly transfer of ministerial authority in the Church.[742]

The Porvoo Common Statement

The Porvoo Common Statement, published in 1993, is a theological agreement between the Church of England, the Anglican churches in Wales, Scotland and Ireland, and the Lutheran churches of Sweden, Finland, Norway, Iceland, Estonia, Latvia and Lithuania.[743]

Chapter IV of this statement looks at the topic of 'Episcopacy in the service of the apostolicity of the Church.'

The chapter notes that 'God the Holy Spirit pours out his gift upon the whole Church (Ephesians 4:11-13, 1 Corinthians 12:4-11).'[744] It then goes on to declare that the diversity of these gifts:

...requires their co-ordination so that they enrich the whole Church and its unity. This diversity and the multiplicity of tasks involved in serving it calls for a ministry of co-ordination. This is the ministry of oversight, episcope, a caring for the life of a whole community, a pastoring of the pastors and a true feeding of Christ's flock, in accordance with Christ's command across the ages and in unity with Christians in other places. Episcope (oversight) is a requirement of the whole Church and its faithful exercise in the light of the Gospel is of fundamental importance to its life. [745]

Echoing the language of *Baptism, Eucharist and Ministry*, it says that the exercise of this oversight:

---

[742] World Council of Churches, pp.26-27.
[743] It was also later agreed by the Lutheran Church in Denmark.
[744] *The Porvoo Common Statement* (London: Council for Christian Unity, 1993), p. 23.
[745] *The Porvoo Common Statement,* p.25.

...is the particular responsibility of the bishop. The bishop's office is one of service and communication within the community of believers and, together with the whole community, to the world. Bishops preach the word, preside at the sacraments, and administer discipline in such a way as to be representative pastoral ministers of oversight, continuity and unity in the Church. They have pastoral oversight of the area to which they are called. They serve the apostolicity, catholicity and unity of the Church's teaching, worship and sacramental life. They have responsibility for leadership in the Church's mission. None of these tasks should be carried out in isolation from the whole Church. [746]

Again echoing the *Baptism, Eucharist and Ministry* report, the chapter also says that the bishop's ministry of oversight:

...is exercised personally, collegially and communally. It is personal because the presence of Christ among his people can most effectively be pointed to by the person ordained to proclaim the gospel and call the community to serve the Lord in unity of life and witness. It is collegial, first because the bishop gathers together those who are ordained to share in the tasks of ministry and to represent the concerns of the community; secondly, because through the collegiality of bishops the Christian community in local areas is related to the wider Church, and the universal Church to that community. It is communal, because the exercise of ordained ministry is rooted in the life of the community and requires the community's effective participation in the discovery of God's will and the guidance of the Spirit. In most of our churches today this takes synodical form. Bishops, together with other ministers and the whole community, are responsible for the orderly transfer of ministerial authority in the Church.[747]

As well as declaring that bishops exercise a necessary ministry of oversight, the chapter also declares that they are sign of the

[746] *Porvoo Common Statement,* p.25.
[747] *Porvoo Common Statement,* p.25.

apostolicity of the Church as whole. 'Apostolic succession in the episcopal office,' it argues, 'is a visible and personal way of focusing the apostolicity of the whole Church.' [748]

When a bishop is ordained or consecrated, it says, the laying on of hands by 'the ordaining bishop and other representatives' is a sign which does four things:

...first it bears witness to the Church's trust in God's faithfulness to his people and in the promised presence of Christ with his Church, through the power of the Holy Spirit, to the end of time; secondly, it expresses the Church's intention to be faithful to God's initiative and gift, by living in the continuity of the apostolic faith and tradition; thirdly, the participation of a group of bishops in the laying on of hands signifies their and their churches' acceptance of the new bishop and so of the catholicity of the churches: fourthly, it transmits ministerial office and its authority in accordance with God's will and institution. Thus in the act of consecration a bishop receives the sign of divine approval and a permanent commission to lead his particular church in the common faith and apostolic life of all the churches.[749]

Commenting further on the significance of episcopal ordination, the chapter also states that:

...the act of ordination is a sign of God's faithfulness to his Church, especially in relation to the oversight of its mission. To ordain a bishop in historic succession (that is, in intended continuity from the apostles themselves) is also a sign. In so doing the Church communicates its care for continuity in the whole of its life and mission, and reinforces its determination to manifest the permanent characteristics of the Church of the apostles. To make the meaning of the sign fully intelligible it is necessary to include in the service of ordination a public declaration of the faith of the Church and an exposition of the ministry to which the new bishop is called. In this way the sign of

[748] *Porvoo Common Statement,* p.26.
[749] *Porvoo Common Statement,* p.26.

historic episcopal succession is placed clearly in its full context of the continuity of proclamation of the gospel of Christ and the mission of his Church.[750]

The chapter acknowledges that:

The use of the sign of the historic episcopal succession does not by itself guarantee the fidelity of a church to every aspect of the apostolic faith, life and mission. There have been schisms in the history of churches using the sign of historic succession. Nor does the sign guarantee the personal faithfulness of the bishop.[751]

However, the use of the sign is nonetheless important because:

...the retention of the sign remains a permanent challenge to fidelity and to unity, a summons to witness to, and a commission to realise more fully, the permanent characteristics of the Church of the apostles. [752]

The Fetter Lane Common Statement and the Reuilly Common Statement

The Fetter Lane Common Statement of 1996, and the *Reuilly Common Statement* of 1999, from which we have already quoted in chapter 6, draw on what is said about the role of bishops In *Baptism, Eucharist and Ministry* and in the *Porvoo Common Statement*:

Echoing the Language of *Baptism Eucharist and Ministry*, the *Fetter Lane Statement* states:

Bishops guard the faith, preach the word, preside at the sacraments and ordain. Bishops meet collegially and in synods with clergy and laity, and are representative ministers of continuity and unity in the church. Bishops have a pastoral role and are pastors of the pastors. Bishops have a special responsibility for mission. They have a role in

---

[750] *Porvoo Common Statement,* p.27.
[751] Porvoo Common Statement, p.27.
[752] *Porvoo Common Statement,* p.27.

relating the local Christian community to the wider Church and the universal Church to their community. They, in communion with the presbyters and deacons and the whole community, are responsible for the orderly continuation of ministerial authority in the Church. [753]

Drawing on the *Porvoo Common Statement*, it also explains the threefold significance of the consecration or ordination of a bishop as follows:

The continuity of the Church in apostolic succession is signified in the consecration of ordination of a Bishop. In episcopal consecration the laying on of hands with prayer by the ordaining bishops (themselves so consecrated) bears witness to God's faithfulness to his people and to the promised presence of Christ with his Church to the end of time; secondly, it expresses the Church's intention to be faithful to God's initiative and gift, by living in the continuity of the apostolic faith and tradition; thirdly, the participation of a group of bishops in the laying on of hands signifies their churches' acceptance of the new bishop. This expresses the catholicity of the Church. Thus, in the act of consecration a bishop receives in faith the sign of divine approval and the commission to lead his particular church in the common faith and apostolic life of all the churches.[754]

Once again drawing on the *Porvoo Common Statement*, the *Reuilly Common Statement* declares that:

Anglicans believe that the historic episcopate is a sign of apostolicity of the whole church. The ordination of a bishop in historic succession (that is, in intended continuity with the apostles themselves) is a sign of God's promise to be with the Church and also the way the Church communicates its care for continuity in the whole of its faith, life and mission, and renews its intention and determination to manifest the permanent characteristics of the Church of the apostles. [755]

---

[753] *Anglican-Moravian Conversations* p. 22.
[754] *Anglican-Moravian Conversations*, p.25.
[755] *Called to Witness and Service*, p. 31.

An Anglican-Methodist Covenant

In its section on 'Oversight in practice,' the *Anglican- Methodist Covenant* of 2001 explains that in the Church of England:

Bishops have special (but not exclusive) responsibility for doctrine, worship and ministry. Bishops are the chief pastors in their dioceses and are called to lead the church in mission. They are the principal ministers of word and sacrament in the communities that they care for. They provide for and oversee the ministry of word, sacrament and pastoral care in all the parishes of the diocese. They share this ministry with parish priests in a collegial manner. Bishops normally have oversight of sector ministries within the diocese. They are responsible for the selection, training and licensing of ordained and accredited ministers. They have the ultimate responsibility for churches and church yards. They administer the law of the church. The bishop presides in the diocesan Synod, chairs the Bishops Council and is *ex officio* chairman or member of all statutory diocesan boards and committees. Bishops are also called to serve the mission and unity of the church. [756]

Taken together, what these ecumenical statements tell us is that bishops are heralds of Christ and shepherds and stewards of his people. They are called to exercise a ministry of oversight in the Church and should so in ways that are personal, but also collegial (together with other bishops and other ordained ministers) and communal (together with the people of God as a whole).

The specific roles of the bishop are to:

- Be a pastor to the pastors and to the whole people of God in their area

- Preach, and preside at the sacraments;

- Uphold the apostolicity of the Church's faith and practice and administer Church discipline;

[756] *An Anglican-Methodist Covenant*, p. 57.

- Be leaders in mission and promote the Church's unity;

- Represent the universal Church to the local Church and the local Church to the universal Church;

- Ordain and provide for the selection, training and licensing of ordained and lay ministers;

- Have ultimate responsibility for churches and church yards;

- Preside over the diocesan synod, chair the Bishop's Council (the synod's standing committee) and participate in other diocesan boards and councils.

We also learn that the ordination or consecration of a bishop in historic succession from the apostles has important symbolic significance. It bears witness to God's faithfulness to his people and Christ's continuing presence with his Church, it declares the catholicity of the Church as a whole and its acceptance of the church which the bishop represents, and it expresses a commitment by that church to maintain continuity with the church of the apostles in its faith, its life and its mission.

Ordaining a bishop in this way does not guarantee that a church will remain faithful to apostolic teaching and practice, but it is a constant challenge for it to do so.

5. Church of England Reports

Doctrine in the Church of England
As we saw in chapter 6, the 1938 report of the Archbishops' Commission on Christian Doctrine, *Doctrine in the Church of England*, highlights five key roles played by bishops in the life of the Church:

- To symbolize and secure 'in an abiding form the apostolic mission and authority within the church.'

- To 'guard the Church against erroneous teaching.'

- To represent 'the whole Church in and to his diocese, and his diocese in and to the Councils of the Church' and thus represent 'the unity and universality of the Church.'

- To exercise pastoral care in his diocese and thus represent the pastoral care of 'the Good Shepherd.'

- To be the appropriate agent for 'carrying on through ordination the authority of the apostolic mission of the Church.' [757]

Episcopal Ministry

The *Episcopal Ministry* report, which we have already referred to in chapter 6, has helped to shape the thinking about bishops in the Church of England and the wider Anglican Communion over the past three decades, particularly through its use of the concept of the bishop as the 'focus of unity.'

As we saw in chapter 6, the report suggests that there are three 'planes' to the life of the Church, the life of the local church, the relation of the local church to other local churches and to the Church as whole, and the relation of the local church to the Church as whole as this has existed since the time of the apostles.

It further suggests that since New Testament times bishops have played a central role in relation to each of these three planes. *Episcopal Ministry* sets out this idea in three key paragraphs in its fourth chapter:

In and after New Testament times, then, the bishop came to exercise the ministry of unity in relation first of all to his local community. That community might, in time, come to consist of several worshipping congregations in a 'diocese.' But in the episcopal churches it has remained spiritually and structurally the 'local church;' there, in acting as a focus of the community's worship and life, and in protecting it as guardian of its faith and order, the bishop stands in a relationship to

[757] *Doctrine in the Church of England*, p.123.

the community which makes it possible for him to act on its behalf. That is his responsibility in **the first plane of the Church's life**.

In the second plane of the Church's life, in keeping contact and communication with the leaders of other worshipping communities on his people's behalf, the bishop has, in every age, been the person who has held the local community together with other Christian communities. Through the episcopal office, by meetings; exchanges of letter; taking counsel together; visitations and prayer for one another, whole communities might remain constantly in touch with one another throughout the Church. So the bishop held in unity the local and the wider Church.

The third plane of the Church's life, witnessed in the succession of bishops from generation to generation, signifies and sustains size the unity of the Church through the years, marking a continuity in time from the Apostles. For already in the New Testament period It seems likely that there was some way of ensuring the succession of leadership (although authority to certify ministers appears also sometimes to lie within the local congregations, exercised by a council of presbyters).[758] But Timothy has the 'gift of God through the laying on of my hands' (2 Timothy 1:6) says Paul (cf Acts 14:23). [759]

The report then develops the idea of the relation of bishops to the three planes of the Church's life in its subsequent account of what it calls the 'emerging theology' of episcopacy.

In relation to the first plane, the unity of the local church, the report declares that there is a reciprocal relationship between a bishop and the local Christian community:

Christ's ministry is entrusted the whole people of God, to all the baptised; the episcopal ministry is called by the Holy Spirit from within that community and with the consent of that community; it is a ministry exercised in relation to the community and with the support

[758] A footnote refers to the commissioning of Paul and Barnabas in Acts 13:3.
[759] *Episcopal Ministry* p.21, bold in the original.

of the community. there is a mutuality of relation between bishop and people; he gives to his people but also receives from them. In the same way the people receive from their bishop but also give to him. This fundamental relational character implies that the bishop must know and be known by the people in the midst of whom he administers the sacraments. And in guarding the faith the bishop has the task of listening to his people, receiving their insights and discerning the mind of the whole people committed to his charge. The bishop is to be with and among his people: they are to act and think together. [760]

The report further declares that the pastoral role of the bishop in relation to the local church 'Is most clearly seen as the bishop fulfils the Commission of the Good Shepherd; 'feed my sheep' (John 21:17)' [761] In specific terms, this means that:

...in the local church the bishop has the special responsibility of ensuring the continuing fidelity of the Church: to the message transmitted from the Apostles; to the right ordering of the Sacraments; to the maintaining of the due order of the Church; and of seeing that the Apostolic mission is continued. It is of the nature of the bishop's office that he leads a local church by his presiding over the sacramental eucharistic celebration of Crucifixion and Resurrection which makes the Church. His ministry is focused in the Eucharist where he presides in the midst of his people and ministers Word and Sacrament, and in a different way in the local Synod where the Bishop gathers with his priests and people. His authority in all this is in no sense a personal possession, nor is it to be exercised according to the world's ideas of power or status. He feeds his sheep as the servant of Christ and servant of the servants of God. [762]

The relational character of the bishop's ministry in the local church is also seen in: 'the delegation of certain Episcopal functions to presbyters, deacons and the non-ordained ministers whose ministry

[760] *Episcopal Ministry*, pp. 162-163.
[761] *Episcopal Ministry*, pp.163.
[762] *Episcopal Ministry*, p.163.

meets particular needs and changing circumstances.' The fact that these ministries are thus ordered in relation to the bishop 'gives stability and harmony to the community in a way reflecting what we glimpse of the order and harmony in the relationship of the persons of the Trinity.' [763]

According to the report, by acting in the ways just described:

...the bishop focuses the life of the diocesan community he serves. That is to say, he becomes the focus of the community's corporate action, helping the people to act as one body: both in their sacramental life, and in everything else they do.[764]

In relation to the second plane, unity between churches, the report states that:

The bishop in his official capacity represents the whole Church in and to his diocese, and his diocese in and to the councils of the Church. He is thus a living representative of the unity and universality of the Church. [765]

It is this 'wider corporate role,' the report says, that is 'symbolized when bishops come together.'[766] It was for that reason that it was felt at the 1988 Lambeth Conference that the meetings of the Anglican Consultative Council, made up of bishops, clergy and laity, could not replace 'either symbolically or functionally' either the Lambeth Conference itself, or the Anglican Primates;' Meeting, both of which are meetings of bishops.[767]

Although in theory the bishop is the link between their diocese and the whole of the rest of the Church, the divided state of the Christian Church means that:

---

[763] *Episcopal Ministry*, p. 163.
[764] *Episcopal Ministry,* p.163.
[765] *Episcopal Ministry*, p,165, quoting the words of the *Anglican-Methodist Conversations*, Interim Report, 1958.
[766] *Episcopal Ministry,* p.165.
[767] *Episcopal Ministry*, p.165.

...the bishop's linking role must often in practice at present be confined to the diocesan churches of his own Communion. But it is still true that the bishop takes his people with him in spirit when he goes as representative of his Church to meet the representatives of other Churches for brotherly counsel in synods or councils. He may take clergy and laity with him in person in modern synodical structures, but it is the meeting of those with a ministry of oversight which is central to conciliar government. At this level the personal pastorate becomes corporate. 'Acting as a body' becomes possible in a further way. [768]

In relation to the third plane, the unity of the Church over the centuries since the apostles, the report states that:

...the bishop has the special task off safeguarding the continuing fidelity of the church to the message received and transmitted by the Apostles, maintaining the right order of the church and the continuation all the Apostolic mission. The orderly succession of bishops within an episcopal Church is intended to be a sign to the community that that church is teaching and acting as it is always taught and acted. The episcopal ministry thus symbolises and helps to secure in an abiding form the apostolic character of the Church's teaching, it's sacramental life and mission. So succession, properly understood, is not so much a succession of individuals as an unbroken continuity of communities (which are themselves made up of persons in relation).[769]

The report goes on to say that as guardians of the Church's faith and order bishops have a particular role to play in the process of reception, the process by which the Church as a whole comes to a mind about particular issues. In this process, the report argues, the role of bishops is to be: '

---

[768] *Episcopal Ministry*, p.166.
[769] *Episcopal Ministry*, p.166.

...the 'form' or 'vessel' which ensures that the 'matter' or 'content' of the faith is held safe. It is their responsibility to listen to, discern and guide the forming of the mind of their people, the synodical process and the reception of the decisions of the Councils.[770]

As well as overseeing the process of reception, bishops also have responsibility for 'dealing with crises and taking emergency action when the fundamentals are in question'[771] As the report sees it:

...when fundamental matters of faith and perhaps also of order are in question, the Church can make judgements, consonant with Scripture, which are authoritative, and...in such conditions these will normally need to be made by those with a responsibility for oversight for practical reasons of urgency and rapid communicability, and also as carrying an immediate and binding though provisional authority. [772]

There are 'rigorous conditions' that such a judgement must satisfy:

It must be consonant with Scripture. It must share the characteristic of all right decisions in matters of faith, in clarifying the truth, not seeking to add to it. It must be made with the intention that it be a statement of the whole fellowship. That means that such a pronouncement is made focally and representatively for the whole community, and remains ultimately to be received by the whole community. It must be made without duress (for example, political pressure), with the intention of issuing a decision on faith or morals which the mind of the Church will be able to recognise.[773]

When bishops produce a judgement that meets these conditions then:

...the truth expressed in the definition or decision on a matter of faith or order may be taken to be authoritative for the Church and to have

---

[770] *Episcopal Ministry,* p.168.
[771] *Episcopal Ministry,* p.168.
[772] *Episcopal Ministry,* pp.168-169.
[773] *Episcopal Ministry,* p.169.

been arrived at under the guidance of the Holy Spirit. [774]

However, the Church should only commit itself to the truth expressed in the judgement: 'on the understanding that it may come to be more fully grasped and more exactly expressed, or modified, as a result of its receiving by the whole people of God.'[775]

The final responsibility of a bishop identified by the report relates to the declaration in Article 34 of the *Thirty Nine Articles* that 'traditions and ceremonies' of the Church 'may be changed according to the diversities of countries, times, and men's manners,' always providing that 'nothing be ordained against God's Word.' As the report sees it, bishops carry 'special responsibilities of guardianship' in relation to such change:

...both as forming the College of bishops in a province or nation and as regards their collegial fellowship with one another in the wider Church. It is important that these two collegial 'corporate identities' be kept in balance, so that proper local needs are met and at the same time provincial or national Churches do not become inward looking. [776]

To put it another way, the bishops need to ensure that changes are made where necessary to suit the local context while at the same time care is taken to ensure that this does not result in a local church becoming unnecessarily idiosyncratic or insular.

Apostolicity and Succession
Apostolicity and Succession is a paper which was written by the Church of England's Faith and Order Advisory and published by the House of Bishops as a House of Bishops Occasional Paper in 1994. It was written after the debate in the General Synod on the *Episcopal Ministry* report resulted in a request for more work to be done on the subject of apostolic succession.

---

[774] *Episcopal Ministry,* p.169.
[775] *Episcopal Ministry*, p.169.
[776] *Episcopal Ministry*, p.170.

The paper's introduction notes that a fresh approach to the question of what the term 'apostolic succession' means, and how apostolic succession is maintained in the Church, has emerged in the course of ecumenical discussion, and lies at the heart of the ecumenical dialogues between Anglicans and Lutherans and Anglicans and Roman Catholics. The introduction goes on to say that in the light of this fact the aim of the paper is to 'begin testing the mind of the Church of England' about whether this fresh approach 'is one in which it can recognize the faith of the Church and from which it may learn lessons for its own understanding and practice.' [777]

On the subject of episcopacy and succession, the paper follows *Baptism Eucharist and Ministry* and the *Porvoo Common Statement* in emphasising the theological significance of what happens when a bishop is ordained. It declares:

To ordain by prayer and the laying on of hands expresses the Church's trust in its Lord's promise to empower disciples and it expresses the Church's intention in response to be faithful in carrying out the apostolic ministry and mission. The participation of three bishops in the laying on of hands witnesses to the catholicity of the churches. The laying on of hands by bishops who have had hands laid on them in succession signifies continuity back to the Apostles. Both the act of consecration and the continuity of ministerial succession witness to the Church's fidelity to the teaching and mission of the Apostles. This continuity is integral to the continuity of the Church's life as a whole. [778]

The paper then goes on to clarify that the existence of bishops who have been ordained in historic succession cannot guarantee the fidelity of the Church to the apostolic teaching and mission. Nevertheless, it contends, this does negate the importance of having such bishops:

[777] *Apostolicity and Succession (*London: Church House Publishing, 1994), p.4.
[778] *Apostolicity and Succession,* p.22.

It is not said that bishops 'guarantee' the fidelity of the church to the apostolic teaching and mission but rather that they serve, symbolise and guard the continuity of the apostolic faith and the communion of the Church. The bishop is, moreover, a sign of assurance to the faithful that the church remains in continuity with the apostles' teaching mission.[779]

Summarising its argument, the paper states that:

The historic episcopal succession is an expression first of Christ's faithfulness to the Church, second of the Church's intention to remain faithful to the apostles' teaching and admission. It is a means both of upholding that intention and of giving the faithful the confident assurance that the Church lives in continuity with the Lord's apostles and in anticipation of a glory yet to be fully disclosed.[780]

Bishops In Communion

Like *Apostolicity and Succession, Bishops in Communion*, which was published in 1991, is a House of Bishops Occasional Paper written by the Faith and Order Advisory Group. The purpose of this paper is to explore that nature of episcopal collegiality and its relationship to the communion ('koinonia') of the Church as a whole.

The paper's conclusion is first of all that:

Episcopal collegiality exists to ensure the Church's fidelity to the apostolic teaching and mission and to maintain the local church/diocese in fellowship - in communion - with the church around the world today and the church throughout the ages. It is a ministry which seeks to hold God's gift of himself in the present in continuity with the memory of the past and the anticipation of the future. It is a ministry with particular care for continuity and unity. [781]

Secondly, the college of bishops has:

---

[779] *Apostolicity and Succession*, p. 23.
[780] *Apostolicity and Succession*, p.24.
[781] *Bishops in Communion* (London: Church House Publishing, 1991), p.38.

...A special responsibility for leading the church in response to the complex issues on the contemporary world. This entails attentive listening to the challenges which come from new scientific knowledge and new model dilemma's, as well as the questions posed to the Christian faith by other faith communities add new movements of spirituality. Collegiality entails listening to those on the margins of the church, the prophetic voices, as well as to those outside the church in order to discern what should be the authentic witness to the gospel in today's world.[782]

Thirdly, the college of bishops is also called to provide 'leadership in the discernment of truth.' This involves:

...bringing into focus matters of concern, and determining what level of the Church's life is the appropriate one for exploring them. It entails determining what needs to be said at any particular moment and after that continuing to show care for the response and reception in the ongoing life of the Church. [783]

Furthermore, the report maintains that in order for episcopal collegiality to be exercised effectively in these three ways, individual bishops need to possess a list of qualities. These are:

- faithful discipleship to Jesus Christ grounded in a life of prayer:

- a readiness to listen to the Church and the world:

- sound learning which springs from the study of Scripture, the tradition of the church and contemporary theological research:

- a willingness to engage with new knowledge in various fields:

- an ability to weigh matters with wisdom:

- a recognition that the mystery of God is always seen 'as in a glass darkly':

[782] *Bishops in Communion*, p.39.
[783] *Bishops in Communion,* p.39.

- a patience to continue with difficult and seemingly intractable questions:

- a creative imagination to discern the signs of God's Kingdom:

- a willingness to make room for different positions when matters are complex and answers as yet unclear:

- a humility to confess mistakes:

- the skills to communicate wisely:

- the courage to take the lead, even when it makes one unpopular:

- the readiness always to be attentive to the prompting of the guidance of the Holy Spirit:

- the willingness and ability to work in partnership with others.[784]

Women Bishops in the Church of England?

Women Bishops in the Church of England? published in 2004, is a report by working party of the House of Bishops. The purpose of this report is to survey the theological issues that the Church of England will need to consider prior to deciding whether or not to ordain women bishops.

Chapter 2 of the report is concerned with 'Episcopacy in the Church of England.' At the end of this chapter the report notes that according to the Church of England:

- The ministry of a bishop is a continuation of the pattern of ministry found in the New Testament.

- It is a sign and instrument of apostolicity and catholicity.

---

[784] *Bishops In Communion,* p.39.

- It involves the proclamation and defence of 'wholesome doctrine.'

- It involves the oversight of the celebration of the sacraments.

- It involves the exercise of pastoral oversight and the promotion of unity.

- It involves overall responsibility for the life of a diocese.

- It involves the exercise of judicial authority.

- It involves leadership in mission.

- It is exercised in personal, collegial and communal ways.

- It is a representative ministry.

- It involves living in a manner that bears witness to the gospel.[785]

It then goes on to note that:

One of the things that is striking about the ministry of a bishop in the Church of England is that in general terms it remains the same ministry as that exercised by bishops in the patristic era.

- Like a bishop in patristic times a Church of England bishop is the principal minister of word and sacrament of the local church and has overall pastoral responsibility for his clergy and laity and he exercises his ministry together with his priests and deacons and as part of the wider episcopal college.

- Like a bishop in patristic times the role of a Church of England bishop is an instrument of unity

- Like a bishop in patristic times the Church of England bishop is called to declare and uphold the apostolic faith which is revealed

[785] *Women Bishops in the Church of England?* (London: Church House Publishing, 2004), p.63.

in Scripture and to which the Tradition of the Church bears witness.

- Like a bishop in patristic times a Church of England bishop has the sole right to ordain priests and deacons.

- Like a bishop in patristic times a Church of England bishop is called to be a leader in mission.

As the report see it, this convergence is not an accident. Rather, it exists because:

The Church of England has retained a traditional understanding of what the bishop's office involves in the same way that it has retained the office of bishop itself. The reason it has done so is the same in both cases, which is that it has wanted to maintain historical continuity with the early Church both as a sign of its identity as part of the one holy catholic and apostolic Church and as a means of upholding that identity.[786]

However, the report says, there has been change as well as continuity:

As we have explained, the office of bishop adapted to meet changing circumstances during the patristic period and it has continued to adapt ever since. What this means is that while the basic features of episcopal ministry today are the same as they were in the patristic era the way that this ministry is exercised is different. A bishop today simply does not operate in the same way that a bishop operated in the second century or the sixth century. [787]

---

[786] *Women Bishops in the Church of England?* pp.63-64.
[787] *Women Bishops in the Church of England?* p.69.

Writings on episcopacy by individual theologians

In this section of the chapter we shall look at what eight representative Church of England theologians have written about the role and character of bishops since 1970.

Colin Buchanan, Eric Mascall, J I Packer, and Graham Leonard – *Growing into Union*

The book *Growing into Union*, which was published in 1970, was a book by two Evangelicals (Buchanan and Packer)[788] and two Anglo-Catholics (Mascall and Leonard). The purpose of the book was to set out an alternative plan for a united church in England in the wake of the failure of the Anglican-Methodist unity scheme in 1968.

In chapter 4, the writers set out what they see as the 'true functions of a bishop' as follows:

First, with regard to pastoral care, he is the guardian of the preaching of the Word; this he must fulfil by his own teaching and study, by taking counsel with his presbyters and by teaching them, by taking counsel with his fellow bishops. In his liturgical ministry he gives sacramental expression to the headship of Christ over his Church. He who has the oversight ordains those who are called, and whose call is recognised by the faithful, to the ministry of oversight whereby they are empowered by the Spirit for the work of building up the body of Christ. In his administrative and disciplinary care, he acts as a father seeking to bring the family of God into a unity of love and trust in which each bears the burdens of others.

As a bishop of the whole Church of God his office is the sacramental expression of the unity of Christians in time and in space. Above all, his is a ministry of personal responsibility. He has to rule but 'he is set to rule in the Church and with the Church rather than over the Church' (A G Hebert); he must not be an autocrat, but neither must he be a neutral chairman, washing only the opinion of the majority to which you subject. He fulfils his office as bishop by serving the Church, but it

---

[788] A third Evangelical, Michael Green, contributed to two appendices).

must be a service in which, obedient to the Word himself, he brings others to obedience, and not a service in which he is servile to those whom he seeks to serve.[789]

Michael Ramsey - The Christian Priest Today

Michael Ramsey was an Anglican theologian who was successively Bishop of Durham, Archbishop of York and Archbishop of Canterbury between 1952 and 1974. His book *The Christian Priest Today* was first written in 1972 and then re-published in a revised edition in 1985.

Chapter 14 of this book is about 'The Bishop.' Ramsey begins the chapter by noting that 'despite the great difference between his days and our own' the life of Pope Gregory the Great 'exemplifies still the range and role of the bishop's office.'[790] Gregory, he writes:

...cared intensely about the spiritual movements, monastic and other, within the Church of his day, and at the same time he had an eye upon the impact of the Church upon the whole community. He was the teacher of the clergy and the people; and at the same time he was a missionary leader, as Gaul and England will never forget. and while he did not shrink from the tasks have ministration, he never forgot the contemplative ideal which had been his in earlier days. [791]

Ramsey next goes on to emphasize the continuing priestly nature of the bishop's ministry:

The bishop is still a priest, and unless he retains the heart and mind of a priest he will be a bad bishop. As man of theology he will teach the clergy and help them in their perplexities. As man of prayer he will help clergy and people to see their vocation in prayer and to practise it. As reconciler he will be perhaps less the observer of individual penitents then the one who unites peoples and groups and conflicting

---

[789] Colin Buchanan, Eric Mascall, J I Packer, and Graham Leonard, *Growing into Union* (London: SPCK, 1970), p.79.

[790] Michael Ramsey, *The Christian Priest Today* (London: SPCK, 1985), Kindle edition, p.94.

[791] Ramsey, p.95.

tendencies in the common service of Christ. As man of liturgy he fulfils his role not only in the Eucharist but in his distinctive office of the laying on of hands both in ordination and in confirmation. in all these ways he will be the priest's priest and the people's priest.[792]

The bishop, writes Ramsey, will be someone who listens: 'not least to those who are younger than himself' and who watches 'the new and uprising movements of thought and action in his own Church, in other Churches and beyond.'[793] By so doing he will be equipped to be:

...a minister of unity, interpreting his own church to others and others to his own, and encouraging those who interpret Christian faith to secular minds and secular minds to Christian faith. he will be aware of the upheavals in contemporary society. But at the same time he will know enough history to avoid facile enthusiasm for novelties for their own sake, and enough of the deeper things of theology to distinguish what is shallow and superficial from what is likely to be lasting. As the keeper of the tradition of Christ he will know what are the things which are not shaken. [794]

Finally, he declares:

...the bishop will always be pastor, teacher, missionary, sacramental minister, the servant of catholicity and apostolicity among priests and people. He must keep fresh, think, read, study, pray. The wise bishop guards what is called 'the one in four rule': he has one Sunday in every four free from preaching other engagements and keeps today quietly at home.[795]

Stephen Sykes – 'A Theology of Episcopacy'

Stephen Sykes was a Church of England theologian who was Bishop of Ely 1990-1999. In his essay 'A Theology of Episcopacy' which is Appendix D in the 2001 Church of England report *Resourcing Bishops,*

[792] Ramsey, pp.95-96.
[793] Ramsey, p.97.
[794] Ramsey, p.97.
[795] Ramsey, p.98.

he suggests that the role of a bishop is best understood with reference to the 'marks of mission' endorsed by the Lambeth Conference in 1988 and by General Synod in 1996. The reason he puts 'or five' in brackets is that the original version of the marks had the four marks he lists, but a fifth mark, on care for creation, was then added in 1990.

In looking at how bishops need to engage with each of the marks, Sykes repeatedly emphasizes that a bishops concerns cannot be limited to concern for the Church, for the diocese, or for the nation. The bishop needs to lead mission to those outside the Church and to address issues which affect everyone, and not just church members.

Sykes writes as follows:

The work of the Bishop is best presented by reference to the four (or five) marks of mission identified at the Lambeth Conference of 1988. These are:

- Evangelism: 'to proclaim the good news of the Kingdom'

- Teaching: to teach, baptise and nurture new believers'

- Care for the needy: 'to respond to human need by loving service'

- Justice:' to seek to transform unjust structures and society'

A substantial portion of a modern bishop's life in the Church of England will be concerned with the appointment, support, encouragement and (very occasionally) the disciplining of the clergy of his diocese. All these activities may readily have the four marks of mission in view. It is vital, however, that these activities do not absorb the entire life of a bishop, who also has responsibilities towards those outside the Church. Many of the most formative liturgical and ecclesiological emphases of the Church of England have been in the past are directed towards the instruction and sanctification of a baptized population. The Decade of Evangelism was necessary in England precisely because a balance had to be redressed in the context of a culture increasingly distant from the traditional message of the gospel. In the context of the Church of England baptizing fewer than 25% of babies, it is evident to all that England has become a mission field. A Bishop is bound, therefore, to be a leader of that mission.

Nor should the bishop's *teaching* activity be directed solely towards existing members of the church. Or rather, there is no absolute distinction between matters of concern to the life of church members and those of the wider society- as the example of teaching concerning marriage and divorce demonstrates. A range of major issues, concerning life and death, science and technology, entertainment, wealth and power impinge equally on professed members and there is a indeterminate allegiance. One of the tasks of the bishop is to understand as best he may the complex and many-sided culture in which the gospel is currently taught to outsiders and insiders alike.

Care for the needy embraces both the nature and causes of world poverty and also the distress which is absolutely local within the bishop's diocese. Precisely as bishop in the Church of God, there is no national boundary beyond which interest or responsibility fades out. Indeed in the light of the strongly prevailing political doctrines of national self-interest, a bishop has a duty to stimulate the conscience of people in his diocese to the reality and scale of preventable suffering in an interdependent world.

The addition of a fifth mark of mission, namely care for the environment, is an example of the fact that the marks of mission are themselves historically based. Again the bishop has no permission to draw the boundary of concern tightly around his diocese. But to understand the interconnections of the global economy by which the environment is being devastated is no small task. Again, there is a clear task of encouraging both teaching and local action, to outsiders and insiders alike.[796]

[796] Stephen Sykes, 'A Theology of Episcopacy' in *Resourcing Bishops* (London: Church House Publishing, 2001), pp.223-225.

Michael Nazir-Ali - 'Towards a theology of choosing bishops'

Bishop Michael Nazir-Ali is a theologian and ethicist who was Bishop of Raiwand in the Anglican Church of Pakistan from 1984-1986 and Bishop of Rochester in the Church of England from 1994-2009. His essay 'Towards a theology of choosing bishops' was published in the 2001 Church of England report *Working with the Spirit: choosing diocesan bishops.*[797]

In his essay, Nazir-Ali declares that bishops have a three-fold representative function:

First, bishops represent the wider Church to the local church and vice versa:

...the bishop...is not only the one who presides in a local church but...someone who brings the gifts and concerns of the wider Church to the local situation. At the same time, the bishop also has a responsibility for bringing the insights and needs of the local church to the attention of the wider family. [798]

Secondly, bishops, like the apostles, represent Christ to the Church and to the world as a whole:

If the office is to be understood as truly apostolic, bishops (and ministers who derive their authority from them) will be seen as representing Christ himself, in a particular way, to the people of God as well as to the world at large. This is in no way a denial of the authentic representativeness or the whole people of God: The New Testament often speaks the whole people of God being priests of God and of Christ and of Christ's presence amongst them. This gives them a role in the Church's discipline and decision making (Matthew 18:18-20, 1 Peter 2:5, Revelation 1:6, 5:10, 20:6).

---

[797] Dr Nazir-Ali was received into the Roman Catholic Church in 2021, but he wrote the essay as an Anglican theologian.
[798] Michael-Nazir Ali, 'Towards a theology of choosing bishops' in *Working with the Spirit: choosing diocesan bishops* (London: Church House Publishing, 2001), p.105.

Apostolic office is to be seen, however, as representative in a specific way. Jesus sends out the Twelve for mission on his behalf and gives them the assurance, 'He who receives you receives me, and he who receives me receives him who sent me' (Matthew 10:40). In Luke, in a similar way, the wider group of the Seventy (or Seventy-Two) are told that those who hear them, hear Christ and those who reject them, reject Christ (Luke 10:16). In the post resurrection commissionings, it is more difficult to tell whether it is all the disciples gathered together or the 'Twelve' only who are commissioned. As far as St. John's account is concerned, it is prudent to accept the view of both Hort and Barrett that the 'Twelve' received this commissioning as representatives of the Church about to be born (John 20:19-30).

Even so, it places them in a position of especial responsibility. The Matthean and Lucan (especially in the Act of the Apostles) accounts are clear that the prime responsibility for the worldwide mission is given to the 'Twelve' who exercise it with the assistance of many others, including, of course Paul and Barnabas (Matthew 28:16-20, Acts 1:1-11, Galatians 2:9). St Paul himself came to see his apostolic ministry as representative in a particular way (1 Corinthians 4:1-15 and 2 Corinthians 4:1-6:1), As to the latter, F.F. Bruce remarks that the plural 'we' here refers to the apostolic band unlike the 'we all' of chapter 3 which refers to all Christians. We may say, then, that this specific ministry is a gift of Christ, the head of the church, for the building up of the body (Ephesians 4:11, 15-16).

In some respects, as eyewitnesses, for example, the role of the apostles was unique and could not be repeated in subsequent ages. In other respects however, as we have seen, the apostles themselves provided for the continuance of their ministry. By the end of the second century, it is commonplace that, in specific ways, the bishops continue the ministry of the apostles. Traditionally these have been seen as teaching, leading and sanctifying. [799]

[799] Nazir-Ali, p.106.

Thirdly, like Moses and Paul, bishops represent their people and their prayers before God:

Just as the Bishop, like other ministers, represents Christ to the people, so also they bring the people and their gathered-up prayers to God. Moses is perhaps the clearest example of the Hebrew Bible of such intercession on behalf of the people. In the New Testament, however, we also find such a ministry. St Paul, for instance, commends the Ephesian elders to God (Acts 20:32) and prays for the Colossians (Colossians 1:9-11) or for Timothy (2 Timothy 1:3). There are many other examples of this ministry in the New Testament.[800]

Nazir-Ali also adds that in order to perform their ministries effectively bishops will need to be people who possess both theological competence and the gift of discernment, who have pastoral gifts and skills, who can motivate people and who are willing and able to bear public witness to gospel values. In his words:

It will be important to ensure that the new Bishop is an able guardian of the faith, as well as one who can encourage theological interpretation and exploration. In order to do this, the person chosen will be someone with basic competence in this area but, more importantly, with the gift of discernment. A bishop is not only 'pastor of the pastors,' but pastor of all who live within the geographical boundaries of the diocese (Canon C 18). This means that pastoral gifts and skills are required in those who are being chosen. A bishop is a leader in mission and has regularly to address the wider world, whether within the diocese, nationally or internationally. Those chosen to be bishops must be able to motivate clergy and laity alike for mission and service. From time to time, a bishop will be called to exercise a prophetic, and perhaps uncomfortable ministry in relation to a local or national issue. This requires a flexibility of approach and a

---

[800] Nazir-Ali, pp.106-107.

willingness to listen but also certain toughness in bearing faithful witness to gospel values.[801]

Paul Avis - Becoming a Bishop

Paul Avis is an Anglican theologian and ecumenist. His 2015 book *Becoming a Bishop* aims to provide 'a theological handbook of episcopal ministry.' In chapter 2 of this book he considers 'the bishop's identity and tasks.'

As he sees it, 'at bottom a bishop is a baptized disciple of Christ.'[802] In addition, a bishop is also a deacon and a priest. As a deacon a bishop has received 'the fundamental commission, given by Christ to his Church, to make him known in word and deed through the gospel.' [803] As a priest he or she is 'concerned with the worship of God, the celebration of the sacraments and the reconciliation of God's people to God and one another.' [804]

Avis then goes on to say that a bishop is '...the senior pastor or shepherd of the portion of the people of God committed to his or her care: 'the chief pastor to all that are within his diocese, as well laity as clergy, and their father in God.''[805] In carrying out this role the bishop's primary task is: 'to proclaim the gospel and to celebrate the sacraments of the gospel.' [806]

Bishops, he writes, have 'the responsibility of oversight within their diocese and, collectively with other bishops throughout their church, including a special responsibility for its doctrine, worship and ministry'[807] and as 'the guardian of the apostolic faith a bishop carries out his responsibility by teaching, preaching and (on advice)

---

[801] Nazir-Ali, p.107.
[802] Paul Avis, *Becoming a Bishop* (London: Bloomsbury/T&T Clark, 2015), p.17.
[803] Avis, p.18.
[804] Avis, p.19.
[805] Avis, p.20.
[806] Avis, p.21.
[807] Avis, p.22.

administering discipline.' [808] In addition, a bishop needs to be 'a competent Christian apologist, able to offer in the public forum a convincing an attractive account of Christian belief, 'a defence... of the hope that is in [us] (1 Peter 3:15).'[809]

In Avis' view:

...bishops are most truly at the heart of the church when they are leading their people in mission - that is to say essentially, reaching out in intelligent, credible persuasive ways to those who are not yet within the fold. They do this in person primarily through proclaiming the gospel, showing the way to personal faith and promoting the sacramental path of Christian initiation.[810]

Avis acknowledges that 'bishops cannot be successors of the apostles in respect of the apostles' unique irreplaceable role as witnesses to Christ's resurrection (Luke 24:48, Acts 1:8).' [811] However, he suggests that:

...bishops continue the work of the apostles in three ways: (a) upholding, expounding and promoting the apostolic faith; (b) leading the faithful in the apostolic mission of the gospel in the midst of the world; and (c) being a visible link through history, by continuous succession, with the Church of the apostles. In these three ways the episcopate -the historic episcopate- forms one of the building blocks of the visible, faithful continuity of the church through history, that is to say, its apostolicity.[812]

In line with the *Episcopal Ministry* report he declares that bishops are a 'focus and sign' of the Church's unity:

---

[808] Avis, p.23.
[809] Avis, p.23.
[810] Avis, p.26.
[811] Avis, p.24.
[812] Avis, p.24.

First, the Bishop is a *focus* of unity, the central point at which issues of unity converge, the place of intensity with regard to unity matters in a diocese and, collectively, in a church. The bishop is also a *sign* of unity: Through his or her visible continuity with the Church of the Apostles in the apostolic succession the bishop represents and manifests the unity that is an indestructible facet of Christ's Church.[813]

Finally, bishops are ministers of ordination. According to Avis: 'A crucial aspect of episcopal ministry and mission is when the bishop presides liturgically at ordination.'[814] It is crucial because it is 'an expression of episcopal oversight – the oversight of mission and ministry that is entrusted to the bishop,' and also a way in which a bishop acts as 'an agent or instrument of the apostolicity of the Church' by incorporating new bishops, priest and deacons 'within the historic ministry of the Church in continuity with the mission of the apostles, as a tangible sign that it is the same Church.' [815]

Conclusion: What we learn about the role and character of bishops from the writings we have looked at in this chapter
In this chapter we have looked at a variety of different accounts of the role and character of bishops. These accounts frequently derive both the ideas and language they employ from each other, or from common sources, but the result is not monochrome. What we find instead is a diversity of perspectives on what bishops do (or should be doing), and what sort of people they should be.

However, in spite of this diversity, if we look at these accounts as a whole, we find that a coherent picture of the bishop's role and character emerges. This picture can be summarised as follows.

In terms of what bishops are called to do:

   a.   Bishops are called to be Pastors to all in their dioceses, whether clergy or lay, whether in the Church or outside it.

---

[813] Avis p. 27
[814] Avis p,28.
[815] Avis p.29.

b. They are to be guardians of the Christian faith as the Church of England has received it and to oppose error.

c. They are to be leaders of the Church's mission in the world.

d. They are to teach and preach.

e. They are to lead worship, preside at the celebration of the sacraments and confirm.

f. They are to promote unity in their dioceses and in the wider Church, and encourage peace and reconciliation in the Church and the world.

g. They are to care for the poor and needy.

h. They are to ensure that there are sufficient ordained and authorised lay ministers in their dioceses and ordain and licence them to undertake their ministries.

i. They are to take part in the ordination and consecration of other bishops

j. They are to exercise ecclesiastical discipline and absolve the penitent.

k. They are to ensure that church buildings and churchyards are properly maintained and renovated.

l. They are to take counsel together with other bishops and with clergy and lay people in the synods, boards, and councils of their diocese and of the national church, using their power of veto when necessary.

In terms of the kind of people bishops are to be:

a. Bishops are to be baptized disciples of Jesus Christ.

b. They are to be deacons and priests before they are bishops and to continue a diaconal and priestly ministry as bishops.

c. They are to be people who personally accept the Christian faith as the Church of England has received it and committed to upholding and proclaiming it.

d. They are to be people with the ability to preach, teach and lead worship.

e. They are to be people of prayer who spend time studying the Scriptures and other writings that will enable them to understand and proclaim the faith.

f. They are to be people who have the capacity to understand new developments in the Church and in the world and interpret them in the light of the Bible and the orthodox Christian tradition.

g. They are to be people who can work with others and who treat others with justice, courtesy and love.

h. They are to be people who can handle the administrative aspects of the bishop's role efficiently.

i. They are to be people who make themselves accessible to others and who practice hospitality.

j. They are to be people of integrity who model the Christian faith in their personal behaviour and family life.

If we compare this picture of the bishop's role and character with what we have looked at in the other chapters in the second part of this book what we also find that it is a picture which is in continuity with the teaching about the role and character of bishops which can be found in the New Testament, in the writings of the Patristic period and in Church of England writings from the sixteenth and seventeenth centuries, including the 1662 Ordinal.

To quote again the words of the *Women Bishops in the Church of England?* report, we can therefore say that: 'The Church of England has retained a traditional understanding of what the bishop's office involves in the same way that it has retained the office of bishop itself.'

It is true that the Church of England has deployed new language with regard to the role of bishops in recent years, using terms like 'sign and focus of unity', 'leader in mission' and 'theological explorer.' However, in fact such language simply employs new words to describe old ideas.

Thus, 'sign and focus of unity' means that bishops are to be at the centre of the life of their diocese and the existence of their office as bishop symbolises the unity of the Church of Christ across space and time.

Thus, 'leader in mission' mean that bishops are to lead the Church in preaching the gospel, making disciples, founding new churches, and showing by word and example what it means to live in obedience to God.

Thus 'theological explorer' means that bishops need to be people who think seriously about how the unchanging truths of the Christian faith can best be expressed in the particular historical and cultural setting of their day.

As I have said, these are not new ideas. They describe what bishops have been doing ever since there have been bishops.

In parts I and II of this study we have looked at why it is right for the Church of England to have bishops, at what bishops are called to do, and at what sort of people they are called to be. In part III we shall go on to look at the issue of jurisdiction, the legal right of a bishop to exercise his or her ministry in a particular place, at what it means to exercise this jurisdiction in a 'good-enough' manner (or to fail to do so), and at what Christians should do if bishops fail to exercise their jurisdiction in a 'good-enough' manner in a significant way and over an extended period of time.

In the final chapter in this part, we shall conclude this study by reviewing what we have learned in the course of it and by considering how what we have learned can be applied to the challenges that Church of England bishops face today.

Part III

The nature and exercise of episcopal jurisdiction

Chapter 12
The nature, development and purpose of episcopal jurisdiction

In the previous chapters of this book we have already touched on the concept of jurisdiction. We have seen that at the Reformation the Church of England rejected the universal jurisdiction claimed by the Bishops of Rome from the end of the fourth century. We have also seen that Canons C17 and 18 gives 'ordinary jurisdiction' to diocesan bishops and that the Archbishops of Canterbury and York have 'metropolitical jurisdiction' and from Canon C20 that suffragan bishops have the jurisdiction that is delegated to them by the diocesan bishop.

In this chapter we shall go on to consider the nature and purpose of jurisdiction. We shall look in turn at what is meant by jurisdiction, how episcopal jurisdiction has developed in the Church in general, and in the Church of England and the Anglican communion in particular, how episcopal jurisdiction involves various different kinds of law, and what we learn from Ephesians 4 about the overall purpose of the exercise of episcopal jurisdiction. Finally, we shall look briefly at the issue of parallel episcopal jurisdiction.

1. The nature of jurisdiction

What is jurisdiction?
The New Oxford Dictionary of English defines the basic meaning of jurisdiction as 'the official power to make legal decisions and judgements.' It adds that it can also mean 'the territory or sphere of activity over which the authority of a court or other institution extends.'[816]

---

[816] 'Jurisdiction' in *The New Oxford Dictionary of English* (Oxford: OUP, 1998), p.992.

To put it another way, jurisdiction means both the official legal authority a person, or group of persons, possesses either to do something themselves, or to command something to be done (or not done), and the area over which this authority extends.

We can see what this means in practice if we consider the regulations that the United Kingdom government has introduced over the past couple of years to try to combat the spread of the Covid-19 virus.

These regulations, which have had legal force, have given the government and other bodies the power to tell people to do things (such as wear face masks) and not do other things (such as leave their homes without good cause, or travel abroad). The Government of the United Kingdom has been able to make and enforce these regulations because it has had the necessary jurisdiction to do so.

However, it has only been able to make and enforce these regulations in relation to England. This is because the jurisdiction of the United Kingdom government in these matters only covers England, with the devolved administrations in Wales, Scotland and Northern Ireland having jurisdiction over such matters in their own countries.

In addition, members of the government are subject to legal jurisdiction in the same way as everyone else. That is why the courts can decide that an individual minister, or the government as a whole, has acted unlawfully. By virtue of the jurisdiction they possess, the courts have the authority to do this. However, here again the principle of a geographical limit on jurisdiction comes into play. For instance, British courts can rule on matters to do with Covid-19 in this country, but they lack the jurisdiction to rule on such matters in other countries, such as France or the United States.

In the case of the Church of England episcopal jurisdiction means the legal authority that bishops have to do things themselves and to permit or instruct others do some things and not to do others. For example, bishops have the authority to ordain clergy, and to licence clergy to serve as the incumbent in a benefice, and they also have the authority not to ordain someone, or to grant them a licence.

However, just like the government of the United Kingdom, bishops only have jurisdiction in specific geographical areas. Thus, the Bishop of Rochester has the right to ordain throughout the Diocese of Rochester. However, the Bishop of Rochester has no right to ordain in the Diocese of Chichester. He, or she, would need special permission from the Bishop of Chichester to do so.

In addition, bishops are subject to legal jurisdiction under ecclesiastical law.

For example, the safeguarding section of the Church of England website states:

...under section 5 of the Safeguarding and Clergy Discipline Measure 2016 all authorised clergy, bishops, archdeacons, licensed readers and lay workers, churchwardens and PCCs **must have** 'due regard' to safeguarding guidance issued by the House of Bishops (this will include both policy and practice guidance). A duty to have 'due regard' to guidance means that the person under the duty is not free to disregard it but is required to follow it unless there are cogent reasons for not doing so. ('Cogent' for this purpose means clear, logical and convincing.) Failure by clergy to comply with the duty imposed by the 2016 Measure may result in disciplinary action.[817]

'Clergy' in the last sentence refers to bishops along with all other members of the clergy. They are subject to the jurisdiction of the 2016 Measure just like everyone else and so can be subject to ecclesiastical discipline if they fail to comply with its requirements.

The distinction between orders and jurisdiction
In order to understand episcopal jurisdiction properly it is also important to understand the distinction between orders and jurisdiction. This distinction is highlighted for example by the seventeenth century Archbishop of Armagh, John Bramhall, who in his

---

[817] 'Policy and practice guidance' at:
https://www.churchofengland.org/safeguarding/policy-and- practice-guidance

Protestants' Ordination defended argues that Roman Catholics need to recall that:

There is a double power ecclesiastical, of order and of jurisdiction; which two are so different the one from the other, as themselves both teach and practise, that there may be true Orders without any ecclesiastical jurisdiction, and an actual jurisdiction without holy Orders.[818]

Orders, in ecclesiological terms, are the right to perform certain spiritual acts conferred by ordination. Thus, a bishop properly ordained by other bishops using the 1662 Ordinal thereby receives the spiritual authority to do those acts proper to the office of a bishop, such as, for example, teaching, ordaining, and confirming. However, that bishop does not thereby have jurisdiction enabling him or her to perform such acts in all circumstances and in whatever way he or she chooses.

For example, the Bishop of Rochester would not have the inherent right, by reason of ordination, to take a confirmation service in the Diocese of Chichester, neither would he or she have the right to confirm using a Latin service which they had devised for themselves (because this rite would not be legally authorised for use in the Church of England). They would lack the necessary jurisdiction to perform either action.

Furthermore, there can be people who have episcopal orders, but are without any episcopal jurisdiction at all. For instance, a retired bishop without permission to officiate would still have episcopal orders, but that bishop would not have any episcopal jurisdiction and would therefore have no right to act as a bishop.

As Bramhall further notes, there can also be ecclesiastical jurisdiction without orders. This point is made in Article XXXVII of the *Thirty Nine Articles*, which states:

[818] John Bramhall, *Protestants' Ordination defended*, in *John Bramhall, Works*, vol. V (Oxford John Parker, 1845), p.230.

The Queen's Majesty hath the chief power in this realm of England and other her dominions, unto whom the chief government of all estates of this realm, whether they be ecclesiastical or civil, in all causes doth appertain, and is not nor ought to be subject to any foreign jurisdiction.

Where we attribute to the Queen's Majesty the chief government, by which titles we understand the minds of some slanderous folks to be offended, we give not to our princes the ministering either of God's word or of sacraments, the which thing the Injunctions also lately set forth by Elizabeth our Queen doth most plainly testify: but that only prerogative which we see to have been given always to all godly princes in Holy Scriptures by God himself, that is, that they should rule all estates and degrees committed to their charge by God, whether they be ecclesiastical or temporal, and restrain with the civil sword the stubborn and evil-doers.[819]

This article is clear that because English monarchs are not ordained they do not have the spiritual authority to minister the word or celebrate the sacraments that results from ordination. However, they do have the necessary jurisdiction to govern the Church of England and to authorise its laws. That is why the Queen is the 'supreme governor' of the Church of England, why the Canons and Measures of the Church of England have to receive the royal assent before they have authority as church law and why the Convocations, and hence the General Synod when a writ for them to do so has been issued by the Queen.

It is also why no one can act as a bishop within the Church of England, even if they have been ordained, and the actions they wish to undertake are otherwise lawful under the law of the Church of England, unless they have been duly appointed to a particular

---

[819] Article XXXVII in The Book of Common Prayer (Cambridge: CUP), pp.627-628.

bishopric by the Queen. Without this royal appointment they have no jurisdiction and so have no legal right to act.[820]

The basis of ecclesiastical jurisdiction

The basis of ecclesiastical jurisdiction, including episcopal jurisdiction, is the God-given authority that the Christian Church has to make laws that govern its affairs, and to which those who belong to it are subject. As Paul Welsby puts it in his book *How the Church of England Works*:

From the earliest times it has been conceded that a Church has the right to make its own laws for its members. Every society has its rules for the management of its own affairs, and the members of a particular society agree to abide by the rules of that society. In the case of the Church, however, there is a higher sanction for the formulation and enforcement of rules and regulations for its members. That sanction rests upon the commission given by Jesus Christ to his apostles: 'What things soever ye shall bind upon earth shall be bound in heaven; and what things soever ye shall loose on earth shall be loosed in heaven' (Matt. 18.18). The commission to 'bind' and to 'loose' means to 'declare forbidden' and to 'declare allowed'. The first apostles regarded rules and regulations as of considerable importance, and one only has to refer to St Paul's detailed rules for divine worship in the Church at Corinth (1 Corinthians) or to the regulations made at the first council of Jerusalem (Acts 15) concerning the admission of Gentiles into the Christian Church to see how necessary it was at a very early stage that corporate legislation needed to be promulgated. And so in every generation the Church, by virtue of Christ's commission, has made whatever rules have been necessary for the ordering of its corporate life. Now the Church is not a body of perfected saints but is made up of ordinary frail human beings. It follows, therefore, that unless chaos is to prevail the rules and regulations which it makes must be more than exhortations which

---

[820] For details of the current appointment process for bishops see the 'Senior Appointments' section of the Church of England website at:
https://www.churchofengland.org/resources/diocesan-resources/archbishops-advisers-appointments-and-development/senior-appointments

anyone can set aside when he wishes. Instead, they must be laws that can be enforced and to which are attached penalties for their non-observance.[821]

The Canons issued by the Councils of the Patristic period are an example of the Church making laws for itself in the way that Welsby describes, and from very early on in its existence we find the Church of England similarly making laws to govern its affairs.

The earliest example we have of this is Bede's account of the Council of Hertford. This took place on 24 September 673 and what Bede describes is an English Church, led by its bishops, which has an established diocesan and monastic structure that the Canons agreed at the Council seek to strengthen and regulate in line with the traditions established by the earlier Church Fathers.

Bede's account runs as follows:

In the name of our Lord God and Saviour Jesus Christ, in the perpetual reign and government of our Lord Jesus Christ. It seemed good that we should come together according to the prescription of the venerable canons, to treat of the necessary affairs of the church. We are met together on this 24th day of September, the first indiction; in a place called Hertford, I, Theodore, bishop of the Church of Canterbury, appointed thereto, unworthy as I am, by the Apostolic See, and our most reverend brother Bisi, bishop of the East Angles, together with our brother and fellow-bishop Wilfrid, bishop of the nation of the Northumbrians, who was present by his proper legates, as also our brethren and fellow-bishops, Putta, bishop of the Castle of the Kentishmen, called Rochester, Leutherius, bishop of the West Saxons, and Winfrid, bishop of the province of the Mercians were present; and when we were assembled and had taken our proper place, I said: I beseech you, beloved brethren, for the fear and love of our Redeemer, that we may faithfully enter into a common treaty for the sincere

---

[821] Paul Welsby *How the Church of England Works* (London: CIO Publishing 1985). p.68.

observance of whatsoever has been decreed and determined by the Holy and approved fathers. I enlarged upon these and many other things tending unto charity, and the preservation of the unity of the Church. And when I had finished my speech I asked them singly and in order whether they consented to observe all things which had been of old canonically decreed by the fathers? To which all our fellow-priests answered: we are all well agreed readily and cheerfully to keep whatever the canons of the holy fathers have prescribed. Whereupon I presently produced the book of canons, and pointed out ten particulars, which I had marked as being in a more special manner known by me to be necessary for us, and proposed that all would undertake diligently to observe them, namely:

1. That we shall jointly keep Easter Day on the Lord's Day after the fourteenth day of the moon in the first month.

2. That no bishop invade the diocese [parochia] of another, but be content with the government of the people committed to him.

3. That no bishop be allowed to offer any molestation to monasteries consecrated to God, nor to take away by violence anything that belongs to them.

4. That the monks themselves go not from place to place, that is from one monastery to another, without the leave of their abbot, but continue in that obedience which they promised at the time of their conversation.

5. That no clerk, leaving his own bishop, go up and down at his own pleasure, not be received wherever he comes without the commendatory letters of his bishop; but if he be once received and refuse to return when he is desired so to do, both the receiver and the received shall be laid under an excommunication.

6. That strange bishops and clerks be content with the hospitality that is freely offered them, and let not any of them exercise any

priestly function without permission of the bishop in whose diocese he is known to be.

7. That a synod be assembled twice in the year. But because many occasions may hinder this, it was jointly agreed by all that once in the year it be assembled on the first of August at the place called Clovesho.

8. That no bishop put himself before another out of an affectation of precedence, but that every one observe the time and order of his consecration.

9. We had a conference together concerning increasing the number of bishops in proportion to the number of the faithful, but we determine nothing as to this point at present.

10. As to matrimony: that none be allowed to any but what is lawful. Let none commit incest. Let no one relinquish his own wife, but for fornication, as the Gospel teaches. But if any shall have dismissed a wife to whom he had been lawfully married, let him not be coupled to another if he wish to be really a Christian, but remain as he is or be reconciled to his wife.

After we had jointly treated upon and determined these points, to the intent that no scandalous contention should be raised henceforth by any of us, and that there should be no mistake in the publication of them, it seemed proper that every one of us should confirm them by the subscription of his own hand, according as they had been determined. I dictated this our definitive sentence to be written by Titillus the notary. Done in the month and indiction above written. Whosoever therefore shall attempt to oppose and infringe this sentence, confirmed by our consent and the subscription of our hands as agreeable to the decrees of the canons, let him know that he is forbidden every function of a priest and all society with us. May the

Divine grace preserve us safe in the unity of the Church so long as we live.[822]

Six of the ten Canons listed by Bede make specific reference to bishops. They show that the English Church accepted the principle that bishops are not above the law of the Church but are subject to its jurisdiction and Canon 2 reflects the idea that each bishop has his own diocese as his area of jurisdiction ('government') and should not invade the jurisdiction of another bishop.

This idea was not a new one. As we saw in chapter 2, what was at first a general episcopal ministry exercised by the apostles became over the course of time a specific episcopal ministry relating to particular people and particular places, and it was this specific form of episcopal ministry that was exercised by the first bishops and has been exercised by other bishops ever since.

The development of episcopal jurisdiction
A helpful overview of the historical process involved in the development of episcopal jurisdiction is provided by Puller in *Orders and Jurisdiction.*

Puller, like Hooker before him, notes first of all that the apostles received from Christ a jurisdiction that was unlimited in its scope:

The apostles received a commission to go into all the world, and to gather into the church those who should accept and believe their message and to govern and feed them when they should have been gathered in (see Matthew 28:18-20; Mark 16:15-16, John 21:15-17, Acts 1:8, Matthew 18:18; John 20:21-23). Thus, the apostles collectively and individually received a worldwide mission to preach to all nations; and they received also an ecumenical jurisdiction over the Church and its members. In the original commission there was no

---

[822] Bede, *A History of the English Church and People*, Bk 4. 5. Text from H. Gee and W. J. Hardy, *Documents Illustrative of English Church History*, (London, Macmillan and Co.1869) pp. 10-13.

assignment of separate spheres of jurisdiction to particular apostles. All and each received authority to rule the whole flock.[823]

However, he observes that in the course of time:

After the work of evangelization had begun, the apostles, acting undoubtedly under the guidance of the Holy Spirit, in order to avoid confusion, limited themselves. To St. James was assigned the Mother - Church of Jerusalem [Acts 12:17, 21:18]. Outside that church St. Paul and St. Barnabas were to 'go unto the gentiles' [; St. Peter and St. John 'unto the circumcision' [Galatians 2:9]. St. Paul laid down a further rule for himself: he made it his aim so to preach the gospel, not where Christ was already named, that he might not build upon another man's foundation' [Romans 15:20] Undoubtedly St. Paul possessed an ecumenical jurisdiction, but he normally restrained himself in his exercise of it to the churches which he had himself founded and to 'the province which God had apportioned to him' [2 Corinthians 10:13]. [824]

What happened after that was that:

The apostles before they died consecrated others to succeed them, who shared with them their ecumenical jurisdiction, but who were also normally limited in the exercise of that jurisdiction to some special region, so that they might not clash with others who had received the same commission as themselves. Thus Timothy had jurisdiction in Ephesus and Titus in Crete; and St. Peter and St. Paul 'committed the ministry of the episcopate [at Rome] to Linus;' and St. Polycarp 'was constituted by the apostles bishop in the church in Smyrna;' and the seven churches of Asia in St. John's time each had their own 'angel' recognised by our Lord as being responsible for the spiritual condition of the church over which he presided; and

---

[823] Puller, pp.143 -144.
[824] Puller, p.144.

St. Irenaeus speaking generally, says: 'we are in position to reckon up those who were by the apostles instituted bishops of the churches.'[825]

However, in spite of the fact that each bishop thus had his own specific jurisdiction, it was nonetheless the case, writes Puller, that:

...the jurisdiction possessed by each bishop, though it was normally exercised within the limits of his diocese, in itself transcended those limits. Any bishop might without let or hindrance send missions into the unevangelized regions of heathenism; and, even within the circuit of Christendom, when proper occasions arose, bishops might perform acts of jurisdiction in dioceses which were not their own. The Church has made many disciplinary laws regulating this right of extra-diocesan intervention, but the right itself remains and is one of the fundamental prerogatives of the apostolic episcopate. Thus, when a see becomes vacant, the neighbouring bishops have the right of consecrating a successor, or of sanctioning and effecting the translation of one who has been previously consecrated to another see. If a Bishop is convicted of heresy or crime, his brethren have the right and duty of deposing him. Bishops sitting in synod may legislate for the churches of the province or of the nation or of the patriarchate, or it may be for the whole Church. Moreover, cases of extreme necessity sometimes arise, when the Church's by-laws of order have to give way, and bishops have the right and duty of exercising their ecumenical jurisdiction in abnormal ways. The restraining laws of the Church are intended to ward off confusion, but it is presupposed that they will be interpreted and applied so as to make for edification and not for destruction. [826]

---

[825] Puller, p.145.
[826] Puller, p.146.

Puller's overall conclusion is that the evidence from the Early Church tells us that even though the apostles had prerogatives which were not shared by the bishops who followed on after them,[827] nevertheless:

....the jurisdiction possessed and exercised by the bishops .... is substantially the same jurisdiction as that which was possessed by the apostles themselves. In both cases it was and is an ecumenical jurisdiction normally restrained as to its exercise within a limited sphere; this restraint being brought about either by the will of the apostles themselves or by the disciplinary laws of the Church; and its object being to secure that authorities, which, so far as the divine law is concerned, are co-equal and co-ordinate, shall not interfere with each other. [828]

We can see the same point in terms of the distinction between orders and jurisdiction that we noted earlier in this chapter. In terms of their episcopal orders all bishops, whoever they are, are equal. A bishop is a bishop, is a bishop. Moreover, these same orders give a bishop a right to act throughout the world. Thus, a bishop ordained to serve in a diocese in the United Kingdom would possess the spiritual authority to preach, ordain and confirm in Hong Kong, as is shown by the fact that he or she. would not need to undergo re-ordination in order to do so. Nevertheless, for the sake of good order the Church has laid down that bishops should normally exercise the spiritual authority stemming from their orders within a specific diocesan jurisdiction. However, this restriction is not absolute. It is perfectly proper for bishops to act as bishops outside their dioceses when it would benefit the Church for them to do so.

Canon 15 of the Council of Nicaea
We can see this if we consider Canon 15 of the Council of Nicaea. As we saw in chapter 4, this Canon declares:

---

[827] Puller notes that the apostles (unlike bishops subsequently) 'were the founders and foundations of the Church, they were the inspired channels of revelation; they had heard and seen and handled the Incarnate Word' (p.146 fn.2).
[828] Puller, p.146.

On account of the great disturbance and discords that occur, it is decreed that the custom prevailing in certain places contrary to the Canon, must wholly be done away; so that neither bishop, presbyter, nor deacon shall pass from city to city. And if any one, after this decree of the holy and great Synod, shall attempt any such thing, or continue in any such course, his proceedings shall be utterly void, and he shall be restored to the Church for which he was ordained bishop or presbyter.[829]

At first sight the meaning of this Canon is clear and absolute. No bishop may move from one place to another, and if a bishop does this then his episcopal acts will be without force, and he needs to be sent home forthwith.

In the history of the Church there have been theologians and churches who have argued that the Canon should be taken at face value and that therefore no bishop should ever be translated from one diocese to another.

However, the consensus of the later Church has been that the Canon should not be taken at face value and that translations are permissible.

There are two reasons for thinking that this consensus is correct.

First, if taken literally, the Canon forbids any bishop from *ever* moving outside their diocese. This would mean that all the bishops attending the Council of Nicaea, except the Bishop of Nicaea, had thereby rendered their episcopal acts (including drawing up Canon 15) 'utterly void.' A literal reading of the Canon thus undermines the Canon itself. It would also undermine the requirement of Canon 4 of Nicaea that a bishop should be ordained by three other bishops from other churches.

---

[829] The Canons of the Council of Nicaea, p. 32.

Secondly, as Henry Percival points out in his excursus on this Canon, the Canon: 'does not forbid Provincial Councils to translate bishops but forbids bishops to translate themselves.'[830] As he goes on to say:

...the thing prohibited is 'transmigration' (which arises from the bishop himself, from selfish motives) not 'translation' (wherein the will of God and the good of the Church is the ruling cause); the 'going' not the 'being taken' to another see. [831]

What the Canon is actually addressing is the problem of bishops moving from place to place of their own volition and disrupting the lives of other churches by so doing ('on account of the great disturbances and discords that may occur'). It is not intended to forbid bishops being translated from see to see, nor to prevent bishops from acting as bishops outside the boundaries of their dioceses when the good of the Church demands that they should.

Canon 7 of the Council of Serdica
As good example of the sort of situation in which the good of the Church requires bishops to act outside their dioceses in described in Canon 6 of the Council of Serdica, which reads as follows:

If it shall have happened, that in a province in which there have been very many bishops, one [i.e., but one] bishop remains, but that he by negligence has not chosen [to ordain] a bishop, and the people have made application, the bishops of the neighbouring province ought first to address [by letter] the bishop who resides in that province, and show that the people seek a ruler [i.e., pastor] for themselves and that this is right, so that they also may come and with him ordain a bishop. But if he refuses to acknowledge their written communication, and leaves it unnoticed, and writes no reply, the people's request should

---

[830] The Canons of the Council of Nicaea, p.33.
[831] The Canons of the Council of Nicaea, pp.33-34.

be satisfied, so that bishops should come from the neighbouring province and ordain a bishop.[832]

As Puller explains, the situation envisaged in this Canon is that:

...At some particular time a province might be almost denuded of its bishops; and those who remained might through remissness be unwilling to fill up the vacant sees or through some others cause might be hindered therefrom. Under such circumstances it would be the duty of the clergy in charge of the vacant dioceses to implore the bishops outside the borders of the province to come to their aid and to provide them with bishops. Ordinarily, for the sake of good order, the provision of bishops for sees within the province is committed to the bishops of the province, but this rule is not intended to be kept rigidly, when necessity and the preservation of the churches of the province require that it should be infringed. The fact that a state of things has arisen, in which the intervention of bishops outside the province has become necessary, lets loose their ecumenical jurisdiction, which is ordinarily tide up by the Church's laws...in such a case bishops who do not belong to the province have full jurisdiction to act; or in other words, the restraining laws give way before the necessity, and the external bishops are free to exercise their ecumenical jurisdiction.[833]

As the Catholic scholar Zeger Van-Espen explains, the basic principle affirmed by the Councils of the Patristic period is clear:

The jurisdiction of the bishops is circumscribed within certain limits for the greater commodity of the Church: but when this end ceases, and it is rather for the advantage of the Church that a bishop should go beyond the boundaries of his jurisdiction, he can freely do so. [834]

---

[832] Council of Serdica, Canon 6, in *The Nicene and Post-Nicene Fathers*, 2nd series, vol. XIV, p. 420.
[833] Puller, p.154.
[834] Zeger Van-Espen, *Dissertatio de Misero Statu Ecclesiae Ultrajectinae*, quoted in Puller, p.154.

The position of the Church of England and the Anglican Communion

If we return to the Canons of the Council of Hertford, we find that, as in the case of the Canons of the Council of Nicaea, the principle that bishops may legitimately act outside the confines of their dioceses is implicitly affirmed.

First, six bishops are recorded as having attended the Council. Five of these were outside their dioceses, and yet this is not something that is seen as the least bit problematic. Indeed, in Canon 7 it is agreed that a similar synod, which would also involve extra diocesan episcopal activity, should be held twice a year.

Secondly, as we have seen, Canon 6 lays down:

That strange bishops and clerks be content with the hospitality that is freely offered them, and let not any of them exercise any priestly function without permission of the bishop in whose diocese he is known to be.

This implies that there is no problem with bishops being outside their dioceses providing that they accept the hospitality offered to them in other dioceses and do not perform any 'priestly' (i.e. episcopal) functions without the permission of the local bishop. The latter point also implies that they may perform such functions if the local bishop's permission is given.

The idea that bishops in the Church of England may be present and act outside their dioceses has been accepted throughout the history of the Church of England and it continues to be accepted today.

Thus, as we have noted, Canon C18.8 of the Church of England's present Canons states that 'Every bishop shall reside within his diocese' but this does not mean that he or she can never leave their diocese. Indeed, the Canon itself envisages that bishops will absent from their dioceses in London when performing Parliamentary or Court duties 'or performing any other duties of his office.'

A prime example of such extra-diocesan duties is the coronation of the monarch. Because Westminster Abbey, where the coronation of the British monarch takes place, is a royal peculiar, it is outside the diocese of every bishop of the Church of England and yet this is not, and never has been, regarded as an impediment preventing a bishop (normally the Archbishop of Canterbury) [835] from crowning the monarch, with other bishops also being present and taking part in the service.

A coronation is of course a rare event, but episcopal ministry across diocesan boundaries is also something that happens on a day-to-day basis. Bishops are always going outside their dioceses to perform their episcopal duties, and this is regarded as a perfectly normal and natural thing to do. For example, bishops regularly go outside their dioceses to take part in meetings of the House and College of Bishops, to ordain other bishops, to take services, to preach, to teach and to confirm and no one thinks anything of it, providing what they are doing is not a deliberate intrusion into the normal diocesan ministry of the bishops in which these activities take place.

The acceptance by the Church of England that bishops may be present, and may act as bishops, beyond the boundaries of their dioceses has led to this principle also being accepted by the churches of the Anglican Communion. We can see this, for example, in the decisions made by the Lambeth Conferences of 1878 and 1988.

Recommendation 1.2 of the Lambeth Conference of 1878 declares that:

...when a diocese, or territorial sphere of administration, has been

---

[835] Other bishops who have performed a coronation are the Archbishop of York, the Bishop of Winchester, the Bishop of London and the Bishop of Carlisle who crowned Elizabeth I on the grounds that more senior bishops were 'either dead, too old and infirm, unacceptable to the queen, or unwilling to serve' (Patrick Collinson, "Elizabeth I (1533–1603)", Oxford Dictionary of National Biography, Oxford University Press, 2004; online edn, January 2012, doi:10.1093/ref:odnb/8636

constituted by the authority of any Church or province of this Communion within its own limits, no bishop or other clergyman of any other Church should exercise his functions within that diocese without the consent of the bishop thereof.[836]

In similar fashion, Resolution 72.12-2 of the Lambeth Conference of 1988 states that the Conference:

1. reaffirms its unity in the historical position of respect for diocesan boundaries and the authority of bishops within these boundaries; and in light of the above

2. affirms that it is deemed inappropriate behaviour for any bishop or priest of this Communion to exercise episcopal or pastoral ministry within another diocese without first obtaining the permission and invitation of the ecclesial authority thereof.

These two decisions reaffirm the historic principle that the jurisdiction of diocesan bishops should be respected.

However, once again it needs to be noted that both these statements also imply it is fine for a bishop to exercise episcopal ministry in another diocese providing the consent of the diocesan bishop has previously been obtained. This understanding of the matter is shown by the fact that Anglican bishops have frequently acted as bishops outside their own dioceses with the consent of the local bishop and this remains what happens today. It is normal, for instance, for bishops from the Church of England to visit their link dioceses in other parts of the Anglican Communion and to perform episcopal duties while they are there.

Furthermore, neither these statements, nor any other official Anglican statement, says what should happen in the sort of emergency situation envisaged by the Council of Serdica. There is no guidance, for example, on what should happen if the bishops of an Anglican province were to

---

[836] Lambeth Conference, 1878, Recommendation 1.2, in Coleman, p.4.

be wiped out as a result of persecution or civil war. Would it then be permissible for bishops from outside the dioceses concerned to act to re-establish episcopal ministry in them by consecrating new bishops? In the absence of any specific rules on the matter, Van-Espen's principle that a bishop is free to act when it is 'for the advantage of the Church that a bishop should go beyond the boundaries of his jurisdiction' would surely come into play and it would be legitimate for bishops to take the necessary action in the dioceses concerned.

The issue of when it is legitimate for bishops to take the sort of emergency action just described has become a contentious one in the Anglican Communion in recent years and we will return to in chapter 15. What needs to be noted at the moment is that the Christian tradition supports the principle of bishops taking such emergency action.

The personal, collegial and communal nature of Anglican episcopal jurisdiction

In both the Church of England and the other provinces of the Anglican Communion bishops exercise their episcopal jurisdiction in the personal, collegial, and communal ways outlined in the previous chapter. As individuals they exercise a personal episcopal ministry, but they also work together with other bishops and with the other clergy and the laity.

In the Church of England, the House and College of Bishops, the diocesan synods, and the General Synod provide the basic framework for bishops within which bishops exercise their episcopal jurisdiction in collegial and communal ways. However, they also act collegially and communally in numerous ways outside of these contexts. For example, bishops work collegially and communally in exercising oversight over the Church of England's theological colleges and courses, those bishops who are members of the House of Lords work collegially and communally in the course of their parliamentary activities, and Evangelical bishops are involved communally in the work of the Church of England Evangelical Council. In addition, bishops participate collegially and communally in other activities such as evangelistic campaigns, campaigns to address poverty and homelessness and work to support refugees and prevent modern day slavery.

Metropolitan and Patriarchal jurisdictions

As we saw in chapter 4, from the third century onwards the custom developed of the bishop of the capital city of each province of the Roman Empire having the title of 'metropolitan' bishop and of that bishop exercising additional jurisdiction not only over his own diocese, but over all the other dioceses in the province. For example, it was the role of the Metropolitan bishop to ratify the election of new diocesan bishops and to preside over the meetings of the bishops of the province.

It is important to note however, that the additional jurisdiction possessed by the Metropolitan bishops was an 'extraordinary' jurisdiction covering only a range of specified matters. The diocesan bishops retained 'ordinary' day to day jurisdiction over their dioceses. Thus, as we noted in chapter 4, Canon 9 of the Council of Antioch laid down that:

...each bishop has authority over his own parish [diocese], both to manage it with the piety which is incumbent on everyone, and to make provision for the whole district which is dependent on his city; to ordain presbyters and deacons; and to settle everything with judgement. But let him undertake nothing further without the bishop of the metropolis; neither the latter without the consent of the others. [837]

This Canon sets out a delicate balance. In matters to do with their dioceses, jurisdiction belongs to the diocesan bishops, but in matters outside their dioceses they come under the jurisdiction of the metropolitan and are to act with his consent. However, the metropolitan bishop also has to act in collegial fashion, acting with the consent of the diocesans.

[837] Council of Antioch, Canon 9, in *Nicene and Post Nicene Fathers* 2nd series vol. XIV, p.112.

As we also saw in chapter 4, over the course of time the chief metropolitan sees were seen as having primacy over the other metropolitan bishops in their area and their bishops came to be referred to as Patriarchs. These Patriarchal sees were originally Rome, Antioch, Alexandria and Carthage, with Constantinople eventually being added because of its status as the 'New Rome.'

As in the case of metropolitan bishops, the jurisdiction of the Patriarchal bishops was seen as limited and action outside of their jurisdiction was viewed as unacceptable. Thus, Canon 8 of the Council of Ephesus runs as follows:

Our brother bishop Rheginus, the beloved of God, and his fellow beloved of God bishops, Zeno and Evagrius, of the Province of Cyprus, have reported to us an innovation which has been introduced contrary to the ecclesiastical constitutions and the Canons of the Holy Apostles, and which touches the liberties of all. Wherefore, since injuries affecting all require the more attention, as they cause the greater damage, and particularly when they are transgressions of an ancient custom; and since those excellent men, who have petitioned the Synod, have told us in writing and by word of mouth that the Bishop of Antioch has in this way held ordinations in Cyprus; therefore the Rulers of the holy churches in Cyprus shall enjoy, without dispute or injury, according to the Canons of the blessed Fathers and ancient custom, the right of performing for themselves the ordination of their excellent Bishops. The same rule shall be observed in the other dioceses and provinces everywhere, so that none of the God beloved Bishops shall assume control of any province which has not heretofore, from the very beginning, been under his own hand or that of his predecessors. But if anyone has violently taken and subjected [a Province], he shall give it up; lest the Canons of the Fathers be transgressed; or the vanities of worldly honour be brought in under pretext of sacred office; or we lose, without knowing it, little by little, the liberty which Our Lord Jesus Christ, the Deliverer of all men, has given us by his own Blood.

Wherefore, this holy and ecumenical Synod has decreed that in every province the rights which heretofore, from the beginning, have belonged to it, shall be preserved to it, according to the old prevailing custom, unchanged and uninjured: every Metropolitan having permission to take, for his own security, a copy of these acts. And if anyone shall bring forward a rule contrary to what is here determined, this holy and ecumenical Synod unanimously decrees that it shall be of no effect.[838]

The background to this Canon was the holding of episcopal ordinations in Cyprus by the Patriarch of Antioch, which was objected to by the bishops in Cyprus on the grounds that the right to ordain bishops belonged to the province of Cyprus and that his actions were therefore a usurpation of jurisdiction.

The Council of Ephesus agreed with them and laid down the principle that the traditional rights of provinces ought to be upheld and that therefore no one had the right to claim jurisdiction over a province that had not traditionally been under their jurisdiction or the jurisdiction of their predecessors.

In the words of William Palmer:

The decree, in fact, recognises and establishes a great point of Christian morality. It was directed against usurpation; that is, against the assumption of power and jurisdiction, which had not been conferred by those who had the right to do so. Where power is conferred by legitimate authority, for good reasons, and conceded freely by those over whom it is to be exercised, the case is altogether different: for example, the jurisdiction of metropolitans and patriarchs over their respective provinces, sanctioned by the canons, was not based on usurpation or encroachment; it arose simply from motives of expedience or conveniency, and from the free choice of churches. But the Catholic Church never authorized any usurpations of jurisdiction: she always invariably acted on the same sacred principles; and though she may have been occasionally obliged to tolerate some infractions of

---

[838] Council of Ephesus, Canon 8, in Council of Antioch, Canon 9, in *Nicene and Post Nicene Fathers* 2nd series vol XIV, pp.234-235.

them, she has never approved or sanctioned such deviations from the gospel of Christ. [839]

As we saw in chapter 9, it was the principle that the traditional rights of the provinces should be upheld and that bishops should not unilaterally claim new rights of power and jurisdiction that led churches in the Eastern Empire and in Africa to reject the claim to a universal Petrine jurisdiction made by the Popes from end of the fourth century onwards.

Thus, as we noted, the Council of Carthage in 424 rejected the decision by Pope Celestine that the African presbyter Apiarius should be restored to office on the grounds that the Pope had no jurisdiction in the matter since: 'by no definition of the fathers has the Church of Africa been deprived of this, and the Nicene decrees have plainly committed not only the clergy of inferior grade but the bishops themselves to their own metropolitans.' By tradition and conciliar decision jurisdiction over African clergy belonged to the Church of Africa and not to the Pope, and therefore the Pope had exceeded his rightful authority. He did not have jurisdiction in the matter.

Metropolitan jurisdiction in the Church of England

We do not know precisely how jurisdiction operated in the dioceses that existed in Roman Britain. However, as we saw in chapter 5, it seems probable that by the fourth century there were four metropolitan sees (London, York, Lincoln and Cirencester) based in the four Roman provincial capitals in Britain.

With the collapse of Roman Britain this system of ecclesiastical organisation ceased to operate and, as we also saw, it was replaced during the Saxon period by a system in which there were two metropolitan sees, Canterbury and York. With the exception of the sixteen-year period in which there was an Archdiocese of Lichfield, this system of two metropolitan sees has remained in place ever since.

[839] William Palmer, *The Apostolical Jurisdiction and Succession of Episcopacy in the British Churches vindicated* (London: J G F & J Rivington, 1840), pp. 48-49.

What is important to note is that, in line with Patristic tradition, the jurisdiction possessed by the Archbishops of Canterbury and York outside their own dioceses is strictly limited. As we saw in chapter 11, they have certain specific responsibilities such as confirming the election of new bishops, hearing appeals in their provincial courts, and presiding in the Convocations and in General Synod. However, the ordinary jurisdiction in the dioceses other than Canterbury and York belongs to the bishops of those dioceses (except when it is suspended in the context of a formal metropolitical visitation). This means that the archbishops can normally only act in those dioceses with the permission of the diocesan. The Archbishop of Canterbury, for instance, could not simply decide to confirm or ordain in the Diocese of Birmingham, he or she would need to seek and receive permission to do so.

Although the Archbishops are often seen as 'super bishops,' with a higher rank than the other bishops, this is not in fact the case. To use the Latin phrase, the archbishops are *primus inter pares*, 'first among equals.' As bishops they have no greater rank than any other bishop, but for the sake of the good order of the Church they have by tradition and Canon some specific forms of additional jurisdiction. This means that the Archbishop of Canterbury is not the 'boss' of the Bishop of Birmingham and the Archbishop of York is not the 'boss' of the Bishop of Liverpool.

Papal jurisdiction in the Church of England

We do not have any specific evidence of how the Church in Roman Britain related to the Church in Rome. If we accept the tradition about King Lucius that we looked at in chapter 5, it seems to have been the case that Pope Eleutherius sent missionary bishops to Britain at the end of the second century. However, this action almost certainly did not mean that the Pope than claimed jurisdiction over the British church. This is because, as we saw in chapter 9, at this stage the Popes were not claiming jurisdiction over other churches.

What does seem likely, on the basis of the evidence we have from other churches, is that the British church did regard Rome as the leading see in the Western Empire because it was located in the Imperial capital, had been the site of the ministry and martyrdom of Peter and Paul, and had a long tradition for orthodoxy and for generosity to other churches.

By the sixth century, as we have seen, the Popes were claiming jurisdiction over other churches and what is clear from the pages of Bede is that, from the time Gregory the Great sent Augustine to evangelise the pagan English, the Popes saw themselves as having jurisdiction over the English church and the English church accepted this jurisdiction.

For example, we have a report sent to Pope Hadrian by his two legates, George and Theophylact, giving a report on synods of English church held in Chelsea and Mercia in 787. They write that:

We have written a capitular[840] of all the particulars, and rehearsed them in order in their hearing, who, with all humble submission and evident willingness, embracing your admonition and our poor selves, promised in all particulars to obey. Then we delivered to them your letters to read, enjoining them that they would see that the holy decrees be observed both by themselves and their subjects. [841]

To put it more simply, the Papal legates put forward a nineteen-point programme setting out how the Pope thought the leaders of the English church and the English kings should behave and the latter then agreed to obey what the Pope had laid down. As the legates go on to write:

We proposed these decrees, most blessed Pope Hadrian, in a public Council before Alfwald the king, and Eanbald the archbishop, and all the bishops and abbots of the country, and the senators and chief men and people of the land. And they, as we before said, vowed with all

---

[840] Summary
[841] Gee and Hardy, pp.32-33.

devotion of mind that they would keep them to the utmost of their power by the help of the heavenly mercy.[842]

Although Papal jurisdiction was accepted in principle there were disputes throughout the Middle Ages about what this jurisdiction should mean in practice. These tensions focussed on issues such as who had the right to appoint bishops (a right claimed by the Pope from the twelfth century onwards) and the right of appeal to the Papal courts about legal issues relating to England. These disputes are reflected, for example in two pieces of legislation passed during the reign of Richard II, the *Second Statute of Provisors* of 1390 and the *Second Statute of Praemunire* of 1391.

The former was designed to prevent the practice known as 'provision' whereby the Pope nominated people to vacant offices in the English church (including bishoprics) over the heads of the English patrons who would normally have had the right of nomination. This practice was seen as contrary to the legal rights of the English patrons and as undermining the well-being of the country by causing church offices and property to pass into the hands of foreigners. The latter was designed to limit the practice of appealing to the Papal courts in a way that was seen as undermining the authority of the Royal courts in England. [843]

As we saw in chapter 5, these disputes were eventually brough to an end by a series of Acts pf Parliament that were passed between 1532 and 1534 which, from the point of view of the English crown and the Church of England, brought all Papal jurisdiction in England to an end.

As we also saw in chapter 5, the theological basis for these Acts of Parliament were (a) that the claim to exercise worldwide jurisdiction made by the Pope involved an encroachment on the authority given to monarchs by God and (b) that the claim made by the Pope to have

---

[842] Gee and Hardy, pp. 43.
[843] The text of the two statutes can be found in Gee and Hardy, pp. 112-125.

authority over all other bishops was contrary to the teaching of Scripture and the Early Church.

Using the tools of humanist scholarship English scholars had gone back to the Scriptures and to the Fathers and saw that neither the Scriptures nor the Fathers gave the Pope greater legal authority than the rulers appointed by God and that neither Scripture nor the Fathers gave the Pope jurisdiction over all other churches in Christendom. In terms of the Canon 8 of the Council of Ephesus the jurisdiction claimed and exercised by the Pope over the English church and nation was thus an act of usurpation. It was a claim to have jurisdiction that did properly exist.

The position thus established in the 1530s still officially remains the case today. It is expressed in Article XXXVII, which still remains part of the official teaching of the Church of England, and which declares unequivocally 'The Bishop of Rome hath no jurisdiction in this realm of England.'

This position means that there is no higher human legal jurisdiction recognised by the Church of England than the legal authority of the Crown (exercised with the consent of Parliament) and there is no higher episcopal jurisdiction exercised in the Church of England than the metropolitical jurisdiction exercised by the Archbishops of Canterbury and York.

Jurisdiction in the Anglican Communion
When the Church of England began to spread overseas from the end of the sixteenth century it naturally took the view of jurisdiction established at the English Reformation with it. As a result, when self-governing overseas Anglican churches were formed from the eighteenth century onwards they too recognised the supreme juridical authority of the civil power[844] and recognised no higher episcopal

---

[844] Article XXXVII of the American revision of the Thirty Nine Articles of 1801 declares, for example, 'The power of the civil magistrate extendeth to all men, as well Clergy as Laity, in all things temporal; but hath no authority in things purely

jurisdiction than that of Metropolitan bishops. In the words of *The Principles of Canon Law Common to the Churches of the Anglican Communion*: 'The principal episcopal office in a province is that of archbishop, presiding bishop, or moderator, an office to which metropolitical authority customarily attaches.' [845] A metropolitan bishop can also be referred to as a 'primate' if he or she is the senior bishop of an Anglican province. In the Anglican Church of Australia, for example, there are several metropolitan bishops, but only one primate (currently the Archbishop of Adelaide, Geoffrey Smith).

When the Anglican Communion began to be formed from 1867 consideration was given to what sort of authority should exist within it. Two basic principles emerged as a result. The first was that there should be no centralised jurisdiction such as existed in the Roman Catholic Church. Each Anglican Church was to be self-governing. The second was that what should hold Anglican churches in union with each other should be a common loyalty to the fellowship, a common faith, and the practice of bishops meeting to take counsel together. Both these principles were a deliberate return to the position that existed with regard to jurisdiction and unity during the Patristic period, and which was still upheld by the churches of the Orthodox tradition.

These two principles were set out by the Lambeth Conferences of 1920 and 1930.

The encyclical letter from the 1920 Conference explains that:

spiritual. And we hold it to be the duty of all men who are professors of the gospel, to pay respectful obedience to the civil authority, regularly and legitimately constituted.' (text in J H Leith, *Creeds of the Churches*, rev. ed (Oxford: Basil Blackwell, 1973), p.279). The references to the monarch and to the Pope in the original article have gone, but the same basic point about the authority of the civil power is being made.
[845] *The Principles of Canon Law Common to the Churches of the Anglican Communion* (London: The Anglican Communion office, 2008), p.48.

For half a century the Lambeth Conference has more and more served to focus the experience and counsels of our Communion. But it does not claim to exercise any powers of control or command. It stands for the far more spiritual and more Christian principle of loyalty to the fellowship. The Churches represented in it are indeed independent, but independent with the Christian freedom which recognizes the restraints of truth and of love. They are not free to deny the truth. They are not free to ignore the fellowship. And the objects of our Conferences are to attain an ever deeper apprehension of the truth, and to guard the fellowship with ever increasing appreciation of its value.[846]

In this quotation 'the truth' means the truth of the Christian faith as set forth in the Scriptures and as witnessed to by the Fathers and the writings of the English reformers.

In line with what is said in the encyclical about the nature of the authority of the Lambeth Conference, Resolution 44 of the 1920 Conference also emphasises the advisory nature of the Central Consultative Body of the Communion:

In order to prevent misapprehension, the Conference declares that the Consultative Body, created by the Lambeth Conference of 1897 and consolidated by the Conference of 1908, is a purely advisory body. It is of the nature of a continuation committee of the whole Conference and neither possesses nor claims any executive or administrative power. It is framed so as to represent all branches of the Anglican Communion and it offers advice only when advice is asked for.[847]

The Conference of 1930 also spent time considering the nature Anglican Communion. The report of the committee that looked at this issue argues that there are:

---

[846] *The Six Lambeth Conferences 1867-1920* (London: SPCK 1920), pp.13-14, of the section on the 1920 Conference.
[847] *The Six Lambeth Conferences 1867-1920*, p.38.

...two prevailing types of ecclesiastical organisation. In one type there is 'centralised government.' The Roman Catholic Church is the great example of this type. In the other type there is 'regional autonomy within one fellowship.' This was the type of organisation that existed in the Church of the first centuries and which is upheld today by the Orthodox churches and by the Anglican Communion.[848]

As an organisation of the latter type the Anglican Communion is a fellowship of self-governing local churches, historically linked to the British Isles, 'whose faith has been grounded in the doctrines and ideals for which the Church of England has always stood.'[849]

The report describes these doctrines and ideals as follows:

What are these doctrines? We hold the Catholic faith in its entirety: that is to say, the truth of Christ, contained in Holy Scripture; stated in the Apostles' and Nicene Creeds; expressed in the Sacraments of the Gospel and the rites of the Primitive Church as set forth in the Book of Common Prayer with its various local adaptations; and safeguarded by the historic threefold Order of the Ministry.

What are these ideals? They are the ideals of the Church of Christ. Prominent among them are an open Bible, a pastoral Priesthood, a common worship, a standard of conduct consistent with that worship, and a fearless love of truth. Without comparing ourselves with others, we acknowledge thankfully as the fruits of these ideals within our Communion, the sanctity of mystics, the learning of scholars, the courage of missionaries, the uprightness of civil administrators, and the devotion of many servants of God in Church and State.[850]

The report goes on to add that 'while, however, we hold the Catholic Faith, we hold it in freedom.' What this means is that:

---

[848] *Report of the Lambeth Conference of 1930* (London: SPCK, 1930), p.153.
[849] *Report of the Lambeth Conference of 1930*, p.154.
[850] *Report of the Lambeth Conference of 1930*, p.154.

Every church our Communion is free to build up its life and development upon the provisions of its own constitution. Local churches (that quote the words of Bishop Creighton) 'have no power to change the Creeds of the universal Church or its early organisation. But they have the right to determine the best methods of setting forth to their people the contents of the Christian faith. They may regulate rites, ceremonies, usages, observances and discipline for that purpose, according to their own wisdom and experience and the needs of the people.'[851]

The report acknowledges that such freedom carries with it:

...the risk of divergence to the point even of disruption. In case any such risk should actually arise it is clear that the Lambeth Conference as such could not take any disciplinary action. Formal action would belong to the several churches of the Communion individually; but the advice of the Lambeth Conference, sought before executive action is taken by the constituent churches, would carry very great moral weight. And we believe in the Holy Spirit. We trust in His power working in every part of His Church as the effective bond to hold us together.[852]

The role of the Archbishop of Canterbury
The nature of the Anglican Communion means that the Archbishop of Canterbury is not the Anglican equivalent of the Pope. The Archbishop of Canterbury plays as important role in the life of the Communion. He is the personal 'focus of unity' in the Communion. To be a part of the Anglican Communion means to be in communion with him. He convenes and chairs the Lambeth Conference and the meetings of the Anglican Primates and is the President of the Anglican Communion Council. However, he has no power to determine the teaching or practice of the Anglican Communion. These are determined on a

---

[851] *Report of the Lambeth Conference of 1930*, p.154, quoting Mandell Creighton, *Church and Nation* (London: Longman Green and co., 1902), p.212, and also referencing Article XXXIV.
[852] *Report of the Lambeth Conference of 1930*, pp.154-155.

collegial and communal basis, by the Lambeth Conference, the Primates Meeting and the Anglican Consultative Council.

The current Anglican view of Papal primacy and jurisdiction.

Contemporary Anglican ecumenical thinking has become open to the possibility of the Pope exercising some form of universal primatial role as a world-wide personal focus of unity in a re-united Church. However, Anglicans are still unhappy, or at best cautious, about the claim made by the Popes for a world - wide Petrine jurisdiction.

For example, the response of the Executive Committee of the Evangelical Fellowship of the Anglican Communion to ARCIC I in 1988 states:

Although we do not believe the New Testament envisages any visible, human authority figure as head of the church, what we would contemplate, as not incompatible with the New Testament, would be a leadership somewhat similar to the role exercised by the Archbishop of Canterbury in the worldwide Anglican Communion, expressing historical continuity, visible unity, personal affection and a ministry of brotherly support, but not infallibility or universal jurisdiction. Similarly, within the fellowship of autonomous Orthodox churches the Ecumenical Patriarch possesses neither infallibility, nor universal jurisdiction, nor even 'primacy,' but rather a certain 'seniority' which 'is to be understood in terms not of coercion but of pastoral service.'.... As the first step towards such a servant image, which is already expressed in the title 'servant of the servants of God,' we dare to hope that the Pope will renounce such other traditional titles as 'the Vicar of Jesus Christ, the successor of the Prince of the Apostles, the Supreme Pontiff of the universal church. We would welcome such a gesture; it would reassure us that a reformed and remodelled primacy might be possible and acceptable. [853]

---

[853] 'Executive Committee of the Evangelical Fellowship of the Anglican Communion – An extract from an Open Letter to the Anglican Communion' in

Similarly, the 2006 statement *Growing Together in Unity and Mission* produced by the Anglican-Roman Catholic Commission for Unity and Mission notes that:

While some Anglicans are coming to value the ministry of the Bishop of Rome as a sign and focus of unity, there continue to be questions about whether the Petrine ministry as exercised by the Bishop of Rome exists within the Church by divine right; about the nature of papal infallibility; and about the jurisdiction ascribed to the Bishop of Rome as universal primate. [854]

2. How jurisdiction involves a range of different types of law

We have seen in this chapter that episcopal jurisdiction involves the exercise of lawful authority. However, this begs the question of what constitutes lawful authority. By what law, or laws, does a bishop have the authority to do things or to permit or instruct other people to do things? We have already seen that episcopal jurisdiction involves both civil and ecclesiastical law, but what about other laws, such as the law of nature, or the laws given by God in the Bible? Don't they also have significance in determining what is lawful?

Hooker on the different types of law

A helpful way into answering such questions in provided by Hooker's discussion of the various types of law in his *Laws of Ecclesiastical Polity*.

In Book I Hooker summarises the 'several kinds' of law that exist as follows:

The law which God with himself hath eternally set down to follow in his own works; the law which he has made for his creatures to keep; the law of natural and necessary agents; the law which angels in heaven obey; the law whereunto by the light of reason men find

Christopher Hill and Edward Yarnold (eds) *Anglicans and Roman Catholics: The Search for Unity* (London: SPCK/CTS, 1994), pp.295-296.
[854] *Growing Together in Unity and Mission* (London: SPCK, 2006), p.38.

themselves bound in that they are men; the law which belongeth unto each nation; the law that concerns the fellowship of all; and lastly the law which God himself hath supernaturally revealed. [855]

The last category here, 'the laws which God himself hath supernaturally revealed' means the law of God given to us in the Bible.

Against his Puritan opponents, Hooker argues that it is a mistake to think that the only law that God has given to human beings to live their lives to his glory is the law given in the Bible. What we need to realise, he maintains, is that God has given us both 'sacred Scripture' *and* other laws to teach us how to glorify him.

Hooker explains that:

By that which we work naturally, as when we breathe, sleep, move, we set forth the glory of God as natural agents do [Psalm 148:7-9], albeit we have no express purpose to make that our end, nor any advised determination therein to follow a law, but do that we do (for the most part) not as much as thinking thereon. In reasonable and moral actions another law taketh its place; a law by the observation whereof [Romans 1:21] we glorify God in such sort, as no creature else under man is able to do; because other creatures have not judgement to examine the quality of that which is done by them, and therefore in that they do they never can accuse or prove themselves. Men do both, as the apostle teacheth; yea, those men which have no written law of God to show what is good or evil, carry written in their hearts the universal law of mankind, the Law of Reason, whereby they judge as by a rule which God hath given unto all men for that purpose [Romans 2:15]. The law of reason doth somewhat direct men how to honour God as their Creator; but how to glorify God in such sort as required, to the end he may be an everlasting Saviour, this we are taught by divine law, which law both ascertaineth the truth and supplieth unto us was the want of that other law. So that in moral actions, divine law

---

[855] Hooker Bk I. XVI.1 p. 221.

helpeth exceedingly the law of reason to guide man's life; but in supernatural it alone guideth.[856]

What Hooker is saying here is that when we act as purely physical beings subject to the law of nature then we glorify God, even if we do not consciously intend do. Likewise, we glorify God when through the use of our innate God given power of reason we discern that it is right to do some things and not others and act accordingly. Finally, we glorify God when, under the direction of the 'divine law' in the Bible we act in such a way as to receive from God the everlasting salvation that he has provided through Jesus Christ.

Hooker then goes on to consider the laws which apply to humans as social beings:

Proceed we further; let us place man in some public society with others, whether civil or spiritual and in this case there is no remedy but we must add yet a further law. For although even here likewise the laws of nature and reason be of necessary use, yet somewhat over and besides them is necessary, namely human and positive law, together with the law which is of commerce between grand societies, the law of nations, and of nations Christians. For which cause the law of God hath likewise said 'let every soul be subject to the higher powers' [Romans 13:1] The public power of all societies is above every soul contained in the same societies. And the principal use of that power is to give laws onto all that are under it; which laws in such cases we must abide by unless there be reason shewed which may necessarily enforce that the Law of Reason or of God doth enjoin the contrary. Because except our own private and but probable resolutions be by the law of public determinations overruled, we take away all possibility of sociable life in the world. [857]

What Hooker is saying here is that as social beings we are subject to the laws which exist to regulate our lives in both 'civil' societies (such

---

[856] Hooker Bk I. XVI.7 p.227.
[857] Hooker Bk I. XVI.7 pp.227

as nations) and 'spiritual' societies (such as churches), and also those laws which regulate the relations between such societies. These laws build on the laws of nature and reason, but they apply to people not as single individuals, but as members of groups of individuals.

Concerning the laws which have been developed by the Church as a spiritual society, Hooker comments that it would be 'absurd' to argue that the Church lacks the authority to develop such laws, or to change them once they had been developed.

In his words:

...as all multitudes, once grown to the form of societies, are even thereby naturally warranted to enforce upon their own subjects particularly those things which public wisdom shall judge expedient for the common good: so it were absurd to imagine the Church itself, the most glorious among them, abridged of this liberty; or to think that no law, constitution, or canon, can be further made either for limitation or amplification in the practise of our Saviour's ordinances, whatsoever occasion be offered through variety of times and things, during the state of his un-constant world, which bringing forth daily such new evils as much of necessity by new remedies be redrest, did both of old enforce our venerable predecessors, and will always constrain others, some time to make, sometime to abrogate, sometime to augment, and again to abridge sometime; in sum, often to vary, alter, and change customs incident in the manner of exercising that power which does itself continue always one and the same. [858]

Following Hooker, we can thus say that as human beings we are subject to a range of laws. There is the law of nature, the law of reason, the divine law given in Scripture, the law governing behaviour in a particular society (civil or spiritual) and the law governing relations between particular societies.

[858] Hooker, Bk VI, II. 2 p. 238.

Within this this range of laws Scripture has a double importance. First, it confirms to us the truth shown to us by reason that we should do some things and not others, a truth which on our fallen state we are liable to forget or ignore (Romans 1:18-24). Secondly, and most importantly, it shows us how we may attain eternal salvation.

Earlier in Book I, Hooker explains that if we consider our state as human beings purely in the light of natural reason there appears to be no way in which we can be saved:

Our natural means therefore unto blessedness are our works; nor is it possible that Nature should ever find any other way to salvation than only this. But examine the works which we do, and since the first foundation of the world what one can say, My ways are pure? Since then all flesh is guilty of that for which God hath threatened eternally to punish, what possibility is there this way to be saved? [859]

In consequence, he writes:

There resteth therefore either no way unto salvation, or if any, then surely a way that is supernatural, a way which could never have entered into the heart of man as much as once to conceive or imagine, if God himself hath not revealed it extraordinarily. [860]

In response to this need for a way of salvation which addresses our fallen condition, God has revealed in the Bible:

...a way mystical and supernatural, a way directing unto the same end of life by a course which groundeth itself upon the guiltiness of sin and through sin desert of condemnation and death. For in this way the first thing is the tender compassion of God respecting us drowned and swallowed up in misery; the next is redemption out of the same by the precious death and merit of mighty Saviour, which hath witnessed

[859] Hooker Bk I. XI.5 p.203.
[860] Hooker Bk I. XI.5 p.203.

himself saying, 'I am the way the way' [John 14:6], the way that leadeth us from misery into bliss.[861]

Hooker and the teaching of the Articles

It is important to note at this point that Hooker's view (a) that the key function of Scripture is to provide us with the way of achieving eternal salvation and (b) that there are laws other than Scripture to which we are subject, is not Hooker's view alone. It is also the teaching of the *Thirty Nine Articles*, and as such a normative part of Anglican theology.

Article VI concerns 'the sufficiency of the holy Scriptures for salvation' and what it says is that:

Holy Scripture containeth all things necessary to salvation: so that whatsoever is not read therein, nor may be proved thereby, is not to be required of any man, that it should be believed as an article of the faith, or be thought requisite or necessary to salvation

What this article teaches is, positively, that what Scripture says is to be believed as a necessary part of the Christian faith, and that what it teaches us is what we need to know in order to be saved, and, negatively, that in consequence we do not have to believe anything that is not in Scripture as an article of faith, or as necessary for salvation.

Article XXXIV, 'Of the Traditions of the Church' then adds:

It is not necessary that traditions and ceremonies be in all places one or utterly alike; for at all times they have been diverse, and may be changed according to the diversity of countries, times, and men's manners, so that nothing be ordained against God's word.

Whosoever through his private judgement willingly and purposely doth openly break the traditions and ceremonies of the Church which be not repugnant to the word of God, and be ordained and approved by common authority, ought to be rebuked openly that other may fear

---

[861] Hooker Bk I. XI.6 p.205.

to do the like, as he that offendeth against the common order of the Church, and hurteth the authority of the magistrate, and woundeth the conscience of the weak brethren.

This article adds another source of law for the Christians in addition to the law of salvation revealed in Scripture. Ecclesiastical law, the law drawn up by the Church for the regulation of its activities, does not tell you how to be saved, but it should be obeyed nonetheless unless it can be seen to go against the higher authority of Scripture (which is why the English Reformers felt justified in rejecting large parts of Medieval church order).

Another source of law is given in Article XXXVII which, as we have seen previously, holds that 'Princes' (i.e, civil rulers) are given authority by God: 'that they should rule all estates and degrees committed to their charge by God, whether they be ecclesiastical or temporal, and restrain with the civil sword the stubborn and evil-doers.' What this article tells us is that out of obedience to God Christians need to obey the laws given by civil rulers, for these rulers act with authority from God.

Unlike Article XXXIV, this article does not qualify the authority of rulers by saying that their laws only have authority if they 'be not repugnant to the word of God.' However, we know that this was the position of those who drew up the articles. For example, the Homily 'Concerning Good Order and Obedience to Rulers and Magistrates' in the First Book of Homilies, a homily which was intended to be read alongside the Articles, emphasises like Article XXXVII that Christians have a God given obligation to obey their rulers. However, it also declares:

Yet let us believe undoubtedly, good Christian people, that we may not obey, kings, magistrates, or any other, though they be our own fathers, if they would command us to do anything contrary to Gods commandments. In such a case we ought to say with the Apostles, *We must rather obey God, than man* [Acts 5:29}. [862]

Bishops and the different kinds of law

If we return to the subject of episcopal jurisdiction, what we have just looked at indicates that bishops are subject to a range of laws in terms of both their possession and their exercise of episcopal jurisdiction.

Firstly, and most importantly, they are subject to Scripture, which is God's word written, and which uniquely reveals the way of eternal salvation through Jesus Christ. However, they are also subject to the law of nature, the law of reason, the law of the Church and the law of the state.

To explore this point in more specific terms, let us first of all imagine the case of Bishop Brian. He has just been made a bishop and as such he possesses episcopal jurisdiction. If we ask why he possesses this jurisdiction, the answer is that, firstly, he has it because, as we saw in chapter 2, the law of God in Scripture establishes that the office of bishop was established by God through the action of the apostles. Secondly, he has it because the law of the Church of England has made provision for the office of bishop should continue and has also laid down how bishops should be appointed and the extent of each bishop's jurisdiction. Thirdly, he has it because according to the provisions of United Kingdom law he has been appointed as a bishop by the Queen.

Moving on from the possession of episcopal jurisdiction to its exercise, let us also imagine a bishop going to preach in a church in her diocese.

- Bishop Margaret is preaching in her own diocese and is subject to the law of the Church which says she may do so without special permission.

---

[862] Concerning Good Order and Obedience to Rulers and Magistrates' in Robinson (ed), p. 84.

- She is subject to the law of reason which says she has a duty to be on time for the service and that this means that she must leave in good time in order that this should be the case.

- She is driving to the service and therefore she needs to obey the laws of nature in relation to the physical process of driving her car.

- As she drives her car, she is subject to the law of the state in terms of the rules of the road which she has an obligation to observe.

- When she gets to the service and preaches, her obligation as a bishop to point people to salvation means that she needs to expound the law of God in Scripture in which the way of salvation is set forth.

What all this shows is that there are many different types of law involved in the exercise of episcopal jurisdiction and they all need to be taken into account. Thus, Bishop Margaret cannot rightly obey her obligation to expound the law of God at the service, but ignore the law of the state by breaking the speed limit on her way to the service, since the law of God itself imposes an obligation on her to observe the rules of the road.

Three further examples of the different types of law that bishops need to take into account when exercising their jurisdiction are provided by the issues of food, church buildings and race.

On the issue of food:

- The law of nature means that people need food in order to live;

- The law of God teaches that Christians may eat all kinds of food (1 Timothy 4:3-5) but that it is also appropriate to fast as a form of spiritual discipline (Matthew 6:16-18, Matthew 9:15, Acts 14:23);

- The law of the Church lays down that there are certain times when fasting is particularly appropriate such as the seasons of Lent and Advent and special days set aside for prayer and fasting in relation to particular situations (see the discussion in Hooker Bk V. LXXII).

This being the case, it is the responsibility of bishops in the exercise of their jurisdictions to have regard to these laws and therefore to encourage those in their dioceses to make sure that their neighbours (both their immediate neighbours and those in other parts of the world) have access to sufficient food and to fast on appropriate occasions.

On the issue of church buildings:

- The law of God in Scripture teaches us by both example and precept that Christians should meet together for worship (Acts 2:46-27, 1 Corinthians 11:2-34, Hebrews 10:25);

- The law of nature means that human beings need protection from the weather and the law of reason therefore suggests that it is good for Christians to meet in buildings;

- The law of the Church has therefore made laid down that Christians should both erect churches and keep them maintained so that they remain useable;

- State law also comes into play because it too has provisions concerning the erection of new buildings and the maintenance of existing ones.

Because this is the case, part of the exercise of episcopal jurisdiction involves overseeing the building and maintenance of church buildings (see Canon C18.4)

On the issue of race, it is possible to imagine a government with a racist ideology passing a law to prohibit people from different races meeting together for worship and to further imagine church authorities, fearful of the government and of public opinion, including this prohibition in church law.

However, such laws would be against God's law in Scripture which holds that baptised believers, regardless of their racial background, are 'fellow citizens with the saints and members of the household of God' (Ephesians 2:19) and therefore cannot be excluded from sharing in the worship of God's people. In consequence, it would be the duty of a bishop to challenge the laws enacted by the state and the Church and to tell his or her people not to obey them (as the Confessing Church in Germany told Christians to reject the exclusion of Jewish clergy from the German church in the 1930s).

This third example is important because it underlines the point we have already noted in relation to Articles XXXIV and XXXVII that although Christians, including bishops, have a general obligation to be law abiding, when a human law (whether ecclesiastical or civil) contravenes God's law in Scripture then that law should be challenged and disobeyed. As we have seen, episcopal jurisdiction has to be exercised in accordance with law, but on occasion obedience to God's law may involve law breaking with regard to other laws.

The mutability of laws
A final point that bishops need to bear in mind is the mutability of law in two regards.

First, human law, whether civil or ecclesiastical, can and must change when new circumstances arise which make existing laws outdated. It is for this reason that Article XXXIV holds, as we have seen, that:

It is not necessary that traditions and ceremonies be in all places one or utterly alike; for at all times they have been diverse, and may be changed according to the diversity of countries, times, and men's manners, so that nothing be ordained against God's word.

A good example of such amendment of law is the way in which the laws of overseas Anglican churches had to adapt when the countries in which they existed became self-governing. Laws which reflected the relationship between the Church of England and the British parliament could no longer apply and needed to be updated.

What the mutability of human law means for bishops is that as leaders of the Church they need to be aware when law needs to change, encourage such change to take place, but ensure that the change does not bring about conflict with God's law.

Secondly, the move from the old covenant to the new means that many of the laws in the Old Testament are no longer directly applicable to Christians today. On the other hand, many of them still do.

As Article VII of the *Thirty Nine Articles* puts it:

Although the law given from God by Moses, as touching ceremonies and rites, do not bind Christian men, nor the civil precepts thereof ought of necessity to be received in any commonwealth; yet, notwithstanding, no Christian man whatsoever is free from the obedience of the commandments which are called moral.

The question that Article VII raises is how it is possible to affirm the continuing authority of the Old Testament as a whole as the law of God, while saying that large parts of it are not still binding for Christians today.

A helpful approach to this issue is provided by Oliver O'Donovan in his commentary on the Articles. He notes that:

It had been said consistently since the early fathers of the Church that the religious law of ancient Israel was determined by its structure in salvation-history, as an order of sacraments which communicated the benefits of Christ yet to appear. In the Middle Ages an additional point was made: that the law of ancient Israel was determined by its contingent character as a society; by its social, educational, moral structure within history. These two elements of contingency in Old Testament law are recognised in the remark that 'the law as touching ceremonies and rites, do (sic) not bind Christian men, nor the civil precepts thereof ought of necessity to be received in any commonwealth.' Thus, a division is set between the Christian era and

551

the society to which the Old Testament (as law) bears witness. The dialectic of historical development is acknowledged. The order by which the social good was mediated in ancient Israel cannot claim us immediately, but is part of the historical dialectic through which the gospel of Christ was revealed.[863]

He also notes, however, that:

...this contingent social order was also a mediation of the universal good: to understand it is not enough to understand its contingency, but we must understand its relation to the universal good as well. Hence we detect also within this law a revelation of created order and the good to which all men are called, a 'moral law' by which every human being is claimed and which belongs fundamentally to men's welfare. The theologian's task in expounding the Old Testament is to allow the contingent and the universal to emerge distinctly. If the universal does not shine through the contingent, then what is done is not theology, but only history: if the universal does not shine through the contingent, then what is done is bad theology, not founded in the narration of God's might deeds in saving history, and so inadequately Christian.[864]

What this means is that, in exercising their episcopal jurisdiction as teachers of the Church and as those responsible for thinking about the law of the Church today, bishops have to have in mind both the contingency and the continuing universal relevance of Old Testament law. They cannot view the law of God in the Old Testament as if all of it can be directly applied to the Church and society at large today, but they cannot view this law as simply outdated either. As O'Donovan says, they have to discern, guided by the New Testament, how the universal shines through the contingent.

---

[863] O' Donovan, *On the Thirty Nine Articles* (Exeter: Paternoster Press, 1986) pp. 63-64.
[864] O'Donovan p.64.

3.   The overall purpose of episcopal jurisdiction

So far in this chapter we have looked at what is meant by episcopal jurisdiction and how the possession and exercise of episcopal jurisdiction relates to various different kinds of law. In the final section of this chapter we shall go on to look at the overall purpose of episcopal jurisdiction. As we have seen being a bishop and exercising episcopal jurisdiction involves doing a multitude of different things and this raises the question of what, if anything, gives coherence to all this activity. To put it in terms of classical philosophy, what is the telos, or goal, of episcopal ministry and hence of the exercise of episcopal jurisdiction?

A clear answer to this question is provided by Paul in his letter to the church in Ephesus.

In Ephesians 4:8 Paul quotes the words of Psalm 68:18 'When he ascended on high he led a host of captives and he gave gifts to men.' As Tom Wright explains whereas first century Jewish interpretation saw this verse as referring to Moses, Paul sees it as referring to Christ:

A first century Jew might have understood this verse from the Psalm to be speaking of Moses. After the Exodus, when the Egyptians were defeated and the Israelites rescued from slavery, Moses went up Mount Sinai and came down with the stone tablets of the law, the Torah. in line with several early Christian writings, Paul sees the ascension of Jesus as being in a sense like that of Moses. After the 'new Exodus' which had been achieved in his death and resurrection, setting the human race free from bondage to sin and death, Jesus went up into the heavenly realm where he now reigns as Lord. Instead of coming down again with the law, as Moses had done, Jesus returned in the person of the spirit, through whom different gifts are now showered on the church.[865]

---

[865] Tom Wright, *Paul for Everyone – The Prison Letters, Ephesians, Philippians, Colossians and Philemon* (London: SPCK, 2002), p. 45.

In verses 11-16 Paul then goes on to specify what the nature of the gifts given by the ascended Christ are. He writes:

And his gifts were that some should be apostles, some prophets, some evangelists, some pastors and teachers, to equip the saints for the work of ministry; so that we may no longer be children, tossed to and fro and carried about with every wind of doctrine, by the cunning of men, by their craftiness in deceitful wiles. Rather, speaking the truth in love, we are to grow up in every way into him who is the head, into Christ, from whom the whole body, joined and knit together by every joint with which it is supplied, when each part is working properly, makes bodily growth and upbuilds itself in love.

As we saw in chapter 1, the 'pastors and teachers' to whom Paul refers in verse 11 are the presbyter-bishops, the leaders of the local church operating under the authority and direction of the apostles. As we then saw in chapter 2, during the course of the first century individual presbyter-bishops were appointed by the apostles to exercise oversight over the others and in the second century the title 'bishop' became exclusively attached to those who exercised this role.

What this means is that bishops, along with other presbyters, are among the gifts given by the ascended Christ to his Church, and the reason why they have been given to the Church is set out by Paul in the rest of the quotation.

What Paul says is helpfully expounded by the Evangelical biblical commentator Thomas Scott.

Commenting on Paul's words in verse 12 'to equip the saints for the work of ministry' (in his version 'for the perfecting, of the saints for the work of ministry') Scott writes:

...the ascended saviour, by sending forth able and faithful ministers, gave gifts unto men, as through their labours he communicated all other spiritual blessings. This appointment was intended for the perfecting of the Saints, in knowledge and holiness, as well as completing of their numbers by their performance of the several parts of the ministerial work; or for the perfecting of other holy persons to perform in their turn the work of the ministry, for edifying or building up the spiritual temple: by bringing sinners, through faith, to be built on the true foundation; and by increasing the fitness of believers for their several stations in the church; in order to the beauty, harmony, and proportion of the whole.[866]

Commenting on Paul's words 'for building up the body of Christ, until we all attain to the unity of the faith and of the knowledge of the Son of God, to mature manhood, to the measure of the stature of the fulness of Christ' he goes on to write:

...considering the church as the body of Christ, it was intended to nourish and mature that body till all believers were bought to that unity of faith and agreement in doctrine; and that spiritual and experimental knowledge of the Son of God, in his person, glory and salvation, as issuing in love, confidence, obedience and conformity; which would render the whole 'a perfect man' complete in every member, sense, and organ, and all grown up to maturity according to that measure of capacity, gifts, and grace, which Christ allotted to every individual, in order to the proportion of the stature of his mystical body, 'the fullness of him who filleth all in all!' That so the Church on earth might in each successive generation bear some proportion to the whole assembled company when perfected in number, in knowledge, holiness, union and felicity, in heaven. [867]

Finally, commenting on Paul's words in the remained of the quotation ('so that we may no longer be children' etc.) Scott comments that Christ's gifts are given:

That henceforth believers, should not be, as many had been, like children in knowledge and experience; and so through instability, want of judgement, and weakness of faith liable to be tossed to and fro, as ships without ballast, by the waves of the sea, or carried about

---

[866] Scott, vol III, on Ephesians 4:7-16.
[867] Scott, vol III, on Ephesians 4:7-16.

like clouds with the wind, by the false and pernicious doctrines, which subtle and ingenious men devised; and by the plausible reasonings and pretences with which they propagated them; and thus, as Satan's ministers, waylaid professors of the gospel, to deceive and pervert them for their own ambitious and selfish purposes. To prevent the division, scandals and delusions arising from the cunning craftiness of such deceivers, and the unsuspecting credulity of weak Christians, apostles, prophets, evangelists etc. had been appointed; and every believer had his measure of spiritual gifts bestowed on him; that he might improve it to promote the purity, peace and edification of the church. Thus all Christians as well as ministers, being taught to hold or maintain the truth in love; uprightly professing living upon, and defending the great truths of the gospel in meekness towards all men, and love of one another, might grow up in all things to an nearer communion with, and conformity to Christ, by influence derived from him and by observing his directions; as members in that body of which he is the Head from whom the whole receives all its life vigour and spiritual health; and being fitly proportioned and closely united through the gifts, grace and services of each individual and with the effectual operation of Christ by his Spirit according to his appointed measure in every part, continual increase is made to it both by the conversion of sinners and the sanctification of believers; and the whole is edified, united adorned and advanced in love of Christ and of everyone to the other with all the happy effects and fruits of love. [868]

What we learn from Paul's words in Ephesians 4, and from Scott's exposition of them, is that episcopal jurisdiction has to be understood in the light of the overall activity of the ascended Christ, in his Church, through his Spirit.

The ascended Christ has poured out spiritual gifts on all the individual members of his Church (1 Corinthians 12:1-13) that they may play their part of the building up on the body of Christ in unity, knowledge, holiness and love. The reason he has also given various types of

---

[868] Scott, vol III, on Ephesians 4:7-16.

leaders to the Church, bishops among them, is to bring people into the Church through the conversion of sinners, to help those in the Church to reach spiritual maturity though ever increasing knowledge of Christian truth, and to protect those in the Church from those who would lead them astray, the ' fierce wolves' and 'men speaking perverse things' referred to by Paul in Acts 20:29-30.

To put it another way, in the light of Ephesians 4:11-16 we can say that episcopal jurisdiction has a threefold purpose. It exists for the conversion of sinners, the sanctification of the saints, and the defeat of those who would lead the Church astray. As we have looked at what is said about the role of bishops in the New Testament and in the subsequent Christian tradition what we have found is that everything that bishops are called to do centres on these three tasks.

The purpose of granting episcopal jurisdiction is to prevent confusion by authorising particular individuals to perform these three tasks, and other tasks relating them, at a particular time, and in a particular place.

When we consider the granting of episcopal jurisdiction the natural tendency is to think in terms of the bishop of a diocese. However, as we have noted in the course of this study, matters are not as simple as that. In many dioceses around the world, and in the majority of the dioceses of the Church of England there are one or suffragan bishops alongside the diocesan bishop.

The existence of such suffragan bishops raises the question of how their role as bishops relates to the role of the diocesan bishop and the jurisdiction he or she possesses. It is to this issue that we shall turn in the next chapter. Before we do this, however, we shall finish this chapter by looking at the issue of parallel episcopal jurisdiction.

4. Parallel episcopal jurisdiction

Parallel jurisdiction exists when a particular group of people are subject to two or more jurisdictions. For example, in the United States there are both federal courts and a system of courts in the individual states, and those who live in the United States come under the jurisdiction of both these sets of courts.

Parallel episcopal jurisdiction, as a particular kind of parallel jurisdiction, exists when two or more bishops have a jurisdiction which covers people living in the same geographical area. For example, there is parallel episcopal jurisdiction in England because those living in England come under the episcopal jurisdiction not only of the bishops of the Church of England, but also of Roman Catholic bishops, bishops of various different Orthodox churches, bishops of various different Lutheran churches, and the bishops of the Moravian Church in Great Britain and Ireland.

In terms of purely Anglican episcopal jurisdiction in England there is parallel jurisdiction involving not only Church of England bishops, but also the bishops of the Free Church of England, and the bishop of the Anglican Mission in England.

Moving over to continental Europe, there is parallel Anglican episcopal jurisdiction between the bishops of the Church of England's Diocese in Europe, the Convocation of Episcopal churches in Europe, the Spanish Reformed Episcopal Church, and the Lusitanian Church.

Similar forms of parallel episcopal jurisdiction can be found right around the globe.

When thinking about parallel episcopal jurisdiction there are three key points that need to be understood.

First, parallel episcopal jurisdiction should not exist. As we saw in chapters 3 and 4 of this study, the principle which was established by the apostles and upheld by the Early Church was that there should be one bishop and one church in each geographical area. Thus, James was bishop of the church in Jerusalem, Timothy was the bishop of the church in Ephesus, Titus was the bishop of the church in Crete, the angels in Revelation 2 and 3 were the bishops of the seven churches of Asia and Ignatius was the bishop of the church in Antioch. Parallel jurisdiction goes against this principle because it involves different bishops exercising jurisdiction over different churches in the same geographical area. In terms of Canon 8 of the Council of Nicaea it involves the existence of 'two bishops in one city.'

Secondly, however, parallel episcopal jurisdictions do exist. It might be possible to evade the evidence for parallel episcopal jurisdictions previously noted by arguing that in each case only one bishop in each place genuinely possesses jurisdiction. The problem with this argument is that in the case of the parallel jurisdictions we have mentioned, and others around the globe, what we are dealing with is bishops of churches belonging to the one holy, Catholic and apostolic Church, who have been duly ordained in historic episcopal succession, and who have received authority, according to the laws of their various churches, to exercise jurisdiction in particular places. They are thus genuine bishops with genuine, but parallel, episcopal jurisdictions.

It is also not possible to argue that these jurisdictions are not genuinely parallel because each bishop only ministers to the members of his or her own church. The problem with this argument is that it ignores the fact that a bishop's ministry involves caring for everyone in their area of responsibility and not just for the people who belong to their particular church. A bishop's jurisdiction thus potentially extends to everyone living in the area their jurisdiction covers, and therefore necessarily parallels the jurisdiction of other bishops with responsibility for the same area.

Thirdly, as part of striving to make the Church's God given unity ever more visible Christians must seek to bring parallel episcopal jurisdictions to an end by moving towards a situation where there is only one church and therefore one episcopal jurisdiction in each place.[869] However, the fact that we live in a fallen world, and that this

---

[869] As the World Council of Church's *New Delhi Statement* put it in 1961: the unity which is both God's will and his gift to his Church is being made visible as all in each place who are baptized into Jesus Christ and confess him as Lord and Saviour are brought by the Holy Spirit into one fully committed fellowship,

fallenness continues to affect the Church, means that that it may sometimes also be necessary to create new parallel episcopal jurisdictions. There are two situations where this may be necessary.

The first is when an episcopally led church in a particular area is either unable, or unwilling, to proclaim the gospel to those outside the Church, or to provide appropriate pastoral care to existing Christian believers. In this situation it will be necessary to create a new church to undertake these tasks. This new church will need to come under the jurisdiction of a bishop and hence a parallel episcopal jurisdiction will come into being.

The second is when a church and/or bishop in a particular place departs from Christian orthodoxy in matters of belief or conduct to such a serious extent that faithful Christians have no alternative but to separate themselves from that church or that bishop. In this situation also it will be necessary to create a new church with its own bishop and hence to create a new parallel episcopal jurisdiction.

The principle at work in both these situations is that episcopal jurisdiction exists to serve the Church and its God given mission to the world, and if there is an emergency situation where the well-being of the Church and the effectiveness of its mission requires breaking the rules that normally limit the exercise of episcopal jurisdiction then breaking them may well be the right thing to do.

As previously indicated, we will look further at the question of what should happen in emergency situations in chapter 15.

holding the one apostolic faith preaching the one Gospel, breaking the one bread, joining in common prayer, and having a corporate life reaching out in witness and service to all and who at the same time are united with the whole Christian fellowship in all places and all ages in such wise that ministry and members are accepted by all, and that all can act and speak together as occasion requires for the tasks to which God calls his people. (https://www.oikoumene.org/resources/documents/new-delhi-statement-on-unity).

Chapter 13
Making sense of Suffragan Bishops

In the previous chapter we noted the important distinction between bishops' orders and episcopal jurisdiction. We saw that by virtue of their orders all bishops have a potentially universal episcopal jurisdiction based on the universal commission given by Christ to the apostles. However, we also saw that in order to prevent confusion and disorder the Church has limited the normal exercise of this universal jurisdiction to particular places. Thus, in the first century James had jurisdiction over the church in Jerusalem, in the third century Cyprian had jurisdiction over the church in Carthage, and today Dame Sarah Mulllally has jurisdiction over the Diocese of London.

In this chapter we shall go on to look at how the distinction between orders and jurisdiction enables us to make sense of the role of those whom the Church of England calls suffragan bishops. What we shall see is that there is no distinction between suffragan bishops and other bishops in terms of their orders, but only in terms of the particular forms of jurisdiction which they are called to exercise, forms of jurisdiction which involve providing assistance to diocesan bishops. To put it simply, we shall see that suffragan bishops are bishops who are given jurisdiction to exercise a ministry of assistance to other bishops.

We shall begin this chapter by defining the meaning of the term 'suffragan bishop.' We shall then look at the first emergence of suffragan bishops during the Patristic period. After that we shall look in more detail than we did in chapter 5 at the development of the role of suffragan bishop in the Church of England since the Middle Ages. Finally, we shall consider the role(s) of suffragan bishops in the Church of England today in the light of recent Church of England discussion of this issue.

1. The meaning of the term suffragan bishop

As noted above, in modern usage a suffragan bishop is a bishop who has been given jurisdiction to act as an assistant bishop to the bishop of a diocese. However, this use of the term is relatively modern. As the eighteenth century church historian Joseph Bingham writes:

...anciently suffragan bishops were all the city bishops of any province under a metropolitan, who were called his suffragans, because they met at his command to give their suffrage, counsel, or advice, in a provincial synod. And in this sense, the word was used in England, at the time when Linwood wrote his *Provinciale*, 'which was not above a hundred years before the Reformation, anno 1430. In his comment upon one of the constitutions of John Peckham, archbishop of Canterbury, which begins with these words, '*Omnibus et singulis coëpiscopis suffraganeis nostris:*' 'To all and singular our fellow bishops and suffragans:' upon the word Suffragans he has this note: 'They were called suffragans, because they were bound to give their suffrage and assistance to the archbishop, being summoned to take part in his care, though not in the plenitude of his power.'[870]

Bingham observes that the words of Linwood (the reference is to the English scholar and bishop Willlian Lyndwood, c.1375-1446) indicate that in the late Middle Ages the term 'suffragan' was used to refer to 'all the bishops of England under their archbishops or metropolitans'[871] He further adds 'Thus it was also in other Churches: the seventy bishops who were immediately subject to the bishop of Rome, as their primate or metropolitan, were called his suffragans.' [872]

However, it is clear from the words of Tyndale, Latimer, Bullinger and Ridley, which we shall look at below, that by the early sixteenth century the term suffragan had also come to be used in English in the specific modern sense of a non-metropolitan bishop whose role it is to

[870] Joseph Bingham, *Origines Ecclesiasticae*, (London: William Straker, 1843) p.190.
[871] Bingham, p.190.
[872] Bingham, pp.190-191.

act as an assistant to a diocesan bishop. This is also the meaning of the term in Henry VIII's *Suffragan Bishops Act* of 1534 after which the word comes to be generally used in the Church of England in its modern sense. [873]

We can thus say that the term suffragan has always been used to refer to a bishop who gives assistance to another bishop. However, whereas the term was originally used to refer to diocesan bishops who gave assistance to their metropolitan, by the sixteenth century it had come to be used to refer to bishops who gave assistance to their diocesan bishop, and this is the meaning it still has today.

2.   The emergence of assistant bishops in the Patristic period

Although the use of the term suffragan to describe bishops who assist diocesan bishops is thus relatively new, the existence of such assistant bishops goes all the way back to the early Patristic period.

Coadjutor bishops

In the Patristic period there were two types of bishops who assisted diocesan bishops. The first type were what is known as a 'coadjutor bishops,' that is to say, bishops who acted as assistant bishops to aged or infirm diocesan bishops with the normal understanding that they would eventually succeed them.

The first example we have of such a bishop is Alexander, who became co-adjutor bishop to bishop Narcissus of Jerusalem towards the end of the second century. According to the account given us by Eusebius:

And when he {Narcissus} was no longer able to perform the ministry on account of ripe old age, the aforementioned Alexander, being bishop of another community, was called by dispensation of God to a joint ministry with Narcissus, by revelation which appeared to him in a vision at night. Whereupon, as if in obedience to some oracle, he

---

[873] The Roman Catholic Church continues to use the term suffragan in the traditional sense of a non-metropolitan diocesan bishops. It uses the term 'auxiliary bishop' to refer what the Church of England calls suffragan bishops.

made the journey from the land of the Cappadocians, where he was first deemed worthy of the episcopate, to Jerusalem, for the purpose of prayer and investigation of the sacred places. The people there gave him the most cordial welcome and suffered him not to return home again, in accordance with another revelation which was seen by them also at night, and which vouchsafed an identical utterance of the clearest kind to those of them who were particularly zealous. For it indicated to them to go forth outside the gates and welcome as their bishop him who was fore-ordained of God. And doing this, with the common consent of the bishops who were administering the churches round about, they compelled him of necessity to remain. And in fact Alexander himself in a personal letter to the Antinoites which is still to this day preserved with us, mentions Narcissus as holding the chief place along with him, writing as follows, in these very words, at the close of the letter: 'Narcissus greets you, who before me was holding the position of bishop here, and is now associated with me in the prayers, having completed 116 years; and exhorts you, as I do likewise, to be of one mind.[874]

Commenting on this account from Eusebius, Bingham notes that while this reckoned to be 'the first instance of any coadjutor to be met with in ancient history' there are:

...several examples in the following ages. Theotecnus, bishop of Cæsarea, made Anatolius his coadjutor, designing him to be his successor: so that for some time they both governed the same church together. Maximus is said by Sozomen to be bishop of Jerusalem, together with Macarius. Orion, bishop of Palabisca, being grown old, ordained Siderius his coadjutor and successor, as Synesius informs us. So Theodoret takes notice that John, bishop of Apamea, had one Stephen for his colleague. And St. Ambrose mentions one Senecio, who was coadjutor to Bassus. In the same manner, Gregory Nazianzen was bishop of Nazianzum together with his aged father. Baronius, indeed, denies that ever he expressly asserts it; though some of them mistake

---

[874] Eusebius, *Ecclesiastical History*, VI.xi, pp. 37-39.

in calling him his father's successor: for he was no otherwise bishop of Nazianzum, but only as his father's coadjutor. He entered upon the office with this protestation, that he would not be obliged to continue bishop there any longer than his father lived; as he himself acquaints us in his own life, and other places: so that after his father's death he actually resigned; and getting Eulalius to be ordained in his room, he betook himself to a private life. All which evidently proves that he was not his father's successor, but only his coadjutor.

I will but add one instance more of this nature, which is the known case of St. Austin [Augustine], who was ordained bishop of Hippo whilst Valerius was living, and sat with him for some time as his coadjutor; which he did by the consent of the primate of Carthage, and the primate of Numidia, who ordained him. Possidius says, he had some scruple upon him at first, because he looked upon it as contrary to the custom of the Church: but being told that it was a thing commonly practised both in the African and Transmarine Churches, he yielded with some reluctancy to be ordained.[875]

Chorepiscopi

The second type of bishops were what is known as *chorepiscopi* (in the singular *chorepiscopus*) a Greek term referring to bishops who ministered in the countryside (the *chora*) rather than in a large town or a city.

To quote Bingham again:

As the bishops, when they were disabled by old age or infirmity, ordained themselves coadjutors in the city; so when their dioceses were enlarged by the conversion of Pagans in the country and villages at a great distance from the city church, they created themselves another sort of assistants in the country, whom they called Chorepiscopi: who were so named...because they were country - bishops, as the word properly signifies.[876]

[875] Bingham, pp. 177-180.
[876] Bingham, p. 181

There has been a long- standing debate as to whether chorepiscopi were bishops, or presbyters with certain delegated powers. However, there are six pieces of evidence that indicate that they were indeed bishops.

1. The name by which these people were known, *chorepiscopi*, itself indicates their episcopal status since, as noted above, the term means country bishops.

2. The Council of Antioch specifically refers to chorepiscopi being ordained as bishops.

3. The roles which they performed were distinctively episcopal ones.

4. They took part alongside other bishops in a number of the fourth century Church councils.

5. In chapter 85 of his *Defence against the Arians* Athanasius writes about country district near Alexandria called Mareotis:

...in which there has never been either a Bishop or a Chorepiscopus; but the churches of the whole district are subject to the Bishop of Alexandria, and each Presbyter has under his charge one of the largest villages, which are about ten or more in number. [877]

In this quotation bishop means a diocesan bishop, but chorepiscopus clearly also means bishop since the presbyters who rule the largest villages are distinguished from the chorepiscopus. There is no chorepiscopus in this district, says Athanasius, but there are presbyters.

6. As late as 864, Pope Nicholas I insists in a letter to the Archbishop of Bourges that chorepiscopi really are bishops

[877] Athanasius, *Defence against the Arians* 85, in *The Nicene and Post-Nicene Fathers*, 2nd series Vol. IV (Edinburgh and Grands Rapids: T&T Clark/Eerdmans, 1998), p.144.

and therefore their ordinations of presbyters and deacons should be regarded as valid.

The first chorepiscopus of which we have record is a bishop called Zoticus. Eusebius tells us that he was bishop of the village of Cumana in Phrygia in the latter half of the second century and that he opposed the Montanist movement.[878] However, Eusebius does not tell us anything else about him and we lack evidence from Eusebius or any other source that tells us precisely what the ministry of Zoticus and other chorepiscopi in the second and third centuries involved. It has been suggested that they exercised the full range of episcopal functions, but the fact is that we simply do not know.

When we reach the fourth century however, we do have evidence that tells us what jurisdiction they had at that time.

First, chorepiscopi had responsibility for the general oversight of the Church in their area. As Canon 10 of the Council of Antioch puts it:

The Holy Synod decrees that persons in villages and districts, or those who are called chorepiscopi, even though they may have received ordination to the Episcopate, shall regard their own limits and manage the churches subject to them, and be content with the care and administration of these.[879]

Secondly, chorepiscopi had the absolute right to ordain people to minor orders, but could only ordain presbyters and deacons with the agreement of the diocesan bishop. To quote Canon 10 of the Council of Antioch again:

...they may ordain readers, sub-deacons and exorcists, and shall be content with promoting these, but shall not presume to ordain either a presbyter or a deacon, without the consent of the bishop of the city to

---

[878] Eusebius, Ecclesiastical History, V.xvi, p.481.
[879] Council of Antioch, Canon 10 in *The Nicene and Post Nicene Fathers*, 2nd Series, vol. XIV (Edinburgh and Grand Rapids: T&T Clark /Eerdmans, 1997) p.113.

which he and his district are subject.[880]

The existence of this right to ordain is further proved by a letter from Basil of Caesarea to his chorepiscopi in which he reminds them that they need to examine carefully those who they ordain as ministers in the church and that according to the 'canons of the Fathers' only those who are ordained with the agreement of the diocesan are validly ordained:

I am much distressed that the canons of the Fathers have fallen through, and that the exact discipline of the Church has been banished from among you. I am apprehensive lest, as this indifference grows, the affairs of the Church should, little by little, fall into confusion. According to the ancient custom observed in the Churches of God, ministers in the Church were received after careful examination; the whole of their life was investigated; an enquiry was made as to their being neither railers nor drunkards, not quick to quarrel, keeping their youth in subjection, so as to be able to maintain the holiness without which no man shall see the Lord (Hebrews 12:14). This examination was made by presbyters and deacons living with them. Then they brought them to the Chorepiscopi; and the Chorepiscopi, after receiving the suffrages of the witnesses as to the truth and giving information to the bishop, so admitted the minister to the sacerdotal order.

Now, however, you have quite passed me over; you have not even had the grace to refer to me, and have transferred the whole authority to yourselves. Furthermore, with complete indifference, you have allowed presbyters and deacons to introduce unworthy persons into the Church, just any one they choose, without any previous examination of life and character, by mere favouritism, on the score of relationship or some other tie. The consequence is, that in every village, there are reckoned many ministers, but not one single man worthy of the service of the altars. Of this you yourselves supply proof

[880] Council of Antioch Canon 10 in *The Nicene and Post Nicene Fathers*, 2nd Series, vol. XIV, p.113.

from your difficulty in finding suitable candidates for election. As, then, I perceive that the evil is gradually reaching a point at which it would be incurable, and especially at this moment when a large number of persons are presenting themselves for the ministry through fear of the conscription, I am constrained to have recourse to the restitution of the canons of the Fathers.

I thus order you in writing to send me the roll of the ministers in every village, stating by whom each has been introduced, and what is his mode of life. You have the roll in your own keeping, so that your version can be compared with the documents which are in mine, and no one can insert his own name when he likes. So, if any have been introduced by presbyters after the first appointment, let them be rejected, and take their place among the laity. Their examination must then be begun by you over again, and, if they prove worthy, let them be received by your decision. Drive out unworthy men from the Church, and so purge it. For the future, test by examination those who are worthy, and then receive them; but do not reckon them of the number before you have reported to me. Otherwise, distinctly understand that he who is admitted to the ministry without my authority will remain a layman.[881]

Thirdly, chorepiscopi had the right to confirm. This is shown by the decision of the Council of Riez in 349 in the case of a diocesan bishop called Armentarius. The Council decided that because Armentarius had been consecrated in an uncanonical fashion he should be reduced to the rank of chorepiscopus. However, it still allowed him the privilege of confirming the newly baptised, which indicates that this was something that chorepiscopi were permitted to do in country areas.[882]

Fourthly, unlike presbyters, chorepiscopi had an unrestricted right to issue 'canonical letters' on behalf of Christians moving to a new area. Thus, Canon 8 of the Council of Antioch declares:

---

[881] Basil of Caesarea, Letter LIV, in The Nicene and Post Nicene Fathers 2nd Series, vol. VII (Edinburgh and Grand Rapids, T&T Clark/Eerdmans, 1996), p.157.
[882] Bingham, p. 186.

Let not country presbyters give letters canonical, or let them send such letters only to the neighbouring bishops. But the chorepiscopi of good report may give letters pacifical.[883]

Canonical letters or 'letters pacifical' were documents, normally issued by bishops indicating that someone moving to a new area was a Christian in good standing who should be admitted to the Eucharist and should be given material support if required. The point of this Canon is that such letters should only be sent by presbyters to neighbouring bishops, who would be in a position to know, or to verify, the truth of what the letter said, whereas chorepiscopi as bishops had a general authority to issue such letters.

Fifthly, unlike presbyters, chorepiscopi had the right to celebrate the Eucharist in the city church (what we would call the Cathedral) in the presence of the bishops or the presbyters of that church. Thus, Canon 13 and 14 of the Council of Neo Caesarea declare:

Country presbyters may not make the oblation in the church of the city when the bishop or presbyters of the city are present; nor may they give the Bread or the Cup with prayer. If, however, they be absent, and he [i.e., a country presbyter] alone be called to prayer, he may give them.

However:

The chorepiscopi, however, are indeed after the pattern of the Seventy; and as fellow-servants, on account of their devotion to the poor, they have the honour of making the oblation.[884]

What precisely 'after the pattern of the seventy' means is not entirely clear.[885] Nor is it clear why they are regarded as having a particular

---

[883] Council of Antioch, Canon 8 in *The Nicene and Post Nicene Fathers*, 2nd Series, vol. XIV, p.112.
[884] Council of Neo Caesarea, Canons 13 and 14 in *The Nicene and Post Nicene Fathers*, 2nd Series, vol. XIV, p.1.

devotion to the poor. However, what is clear is that these two Canons rank the chorepiscopi above the presbyters.

Sixthly, chorepiscopi had the right to attend and vote at the Councils of the Church. As Bingham notes, there are several instances of this fact:

...still remaining in the acts of the ancient councils. In the first Nicene council, Palladius and Selucius subscribe themselves Chorepiscopi of the province of Caelosyria: Eudaemon, Chorepiscopus of the province of Cilicia: Gorgonius, Stephanus, Euphronius, Rhodon, Theophanes, Chorepiscopi of the province of Cappadocia: Hesychius, Theodore, Anatolius, Quintus, Aquila, Chorepiscopi of the province of Isauria: Theustinus and Eulalius, of the province of Bithynia: so again in the Council of Neocaesarea, Stephanus and Rudus or Rhodon, two of the same that were in the Council of Nicaea, subscribed themselves. Chorepiscopi of the province of Cappadocia. And in the Council of Ephesus, Cæsarius, Chorepiscopus of Alce.[886]

The decline of the chorepiscopi
From the middle of the fourth century, however, the office of chorepiscopus went into decline.

Canon 6 of the Council of Serdica in 344, to which we referred to in the last chapter, rejected the idea of appointing bishops in villages or small towns (which was where the chorepiscopi were based). The Canon declares:

It is positively not permitted to ordain a bishop in a village or petty town, for which even one single presbyter is sufficient (for there is no necessity to ordain a bishop there) lest the name and authority of bishop should be made of small account, but the bishops of the province ought, as before said, to ordain bishops in those cities in which there were bishops previously; and if a city should be found

---

[885] The most likely explanation is that their ministry supplemented that of the diocesan ministry in the same way that the mission of the seventy in Luke 10: 1-24 supplemented the mission of the apostles.
[886] Bingham, p.187.

with a population so large as to be thought worthy of an episcopal see, let it receive one.[887]

Canon 57 of the Council of Laodicea in 380 then went further and declared that the chorepiscopi should be phased out in favour of 'visitors' (*periodeutai*), supervisory agents acting on behalf of the diocesan bishop:

Bishops must not be appointed in villages or country districts, but visitors; and those who have been already appointed must do nothing without the consent of the bishop of the city. Presbyters, in like manner, must do nothing without the consent of the bishop.[888]

From this point onwards we find the office of chorepiscopus gradually disappears in the Eastern Church. Although several chorepiscopi signed on behalf of their diocesans at the Council of Chalcedon in 451, and although chorepiscopi are still mentioned in the Canons of the Second Council of Nicaea in 787, in the long term the chorepiscopi were replaced by a system in which the reach of the diocesan bishop was extended either through the appointment of visitors or through the work of co-adjutor bishops.

It should be noted however, that the office of chorepiscopus survives to this day in some of the churches of the Syrian Orthodox tradition, and also in the Maronite church (an Eastern Rite Catholic Church in full communion with Rome).

In the Western Church the first mentions of the office of chorepiscopus are found in the fifth or sixth centuries when the chorepiscopi seem to have existed mainly in what is now Germany (especially Bavaria) and in what is now France.[889] Concern about competition between their ever-increasing influence and the authority

[887] Council of Serdica, Canon 6 in *The Nicene and Post Nicene Fathers*, 2nd Series, vol. XIV, p.420.
[888] Council of Laodicea, Canon 57 in *The Nicene and Post Nicene Fathers*, 2nd Series, vol. XIV, p.158.
[889] Jean Gaudemet, 'Chorepiscopus' in Andre Vauchez (ed,) *Encyclopedia of the Middle Ages* (London: Routledge, 2000) p. 294.

of diocesan bishops during the Carolignian period led to synodical legislations against them at the Synods of Paris (829), Aachen (836) and Meaux (845) and although the office of chorepiscopus was defended by writers such as the Archbishop of Mainz, Rabanus Maurus, in his work *De Chorepiscopis,* it gradually died out in the Western Church during the tenth and eleventh centuries, with the chorepiscopi being replaced by archdeacons.

3. The re-emergence of suffragan bishops in the Western Church

However, the office of suffragan bishop then re-appeared in the Western Church following the Fourth Lateran Council in 1215 which decreed that there was a pastoral need for 'coadjutors and assistants' to help bishops exercise their ministries especially with regard to preaching.

Canon 10 of the Council laid down that:

Among other things that pertain to the salvation of the Christian people, the food of the word of God is above all necessary, because as the body is nourished by material food, so is the soul nourished by spiritual food, since 'not in bread alone doth man live but in every word that proceedeth from the mouth of God' (Matt. 4: 4). It often happens that bishops, on account of their manifold duties or bodily infirmities, or because of hostile invasions or other reasons, to say nothing of lack of learning, which must be absolutely condemned in them and is not to be tolerated in the future, are themselves unable to minister the word of God to the people, especially in large and widespread dioceses. Wherefore we decree that bishops provide suitable men, powerful in work and word, to exercise with fruitful result the office of preaching; who in place of the bishops, since these cannot do it, diligently visiting the people committed to them, may instruct them by word and example. And when they are in need, let them be supplied with the necessities, lest for want of these they may be compelled to abandon their work at the very beginning. Wherefore we command that in cathedral churches as well as in conventual churches suitable men be appointed whom the bishops may use as

573

coadjutors and assistants, not only in the office of preaching but also in hearing confessions, imposing penances, and in other matters that pertain to the salvation of souls. If anyone neglect to comply with this, he shall be subject to severe punishment.[890]

This Canon paved the way for the use of suffragan bishops in the Church of England in the later Middle Ages that we noted in chapter 5. As the *Episcopal Ministry* report explains, in the absence of bishops from their dioceses their spiritual responsibilities, especially ordaining and confirming, were undertaken by suffragan bishops, while their legal and administrative responsibilities (the 'temporalities') were undertaken by co-adjutors who, unlike in the Patristic period, were not themselves bishops:

This permission was exploited in England from the thirteenth century, where suffragan bishops were appointed to carry on the spiritual work in diocese in the absence of the diocesan. In the days when a bishop had no ready means of contact with his diocese whilst absent on weighty affairs of Church or Crown, it can be readily seen that expediency warranted an arrangement whereby the bishop had another bishop to deputize for him. That was the position in England, such assistant bishops having titular sees normally located in non-Christian places (*in partibus infidelium*[891]) or being 'absentee' bishops of Irish dioceses. The principal functions of suffragans were conferring of orders and confirming. Their status was that of subordinate bishops. They were consecrated for the purpose of assisting the diocesan bishops who exercised an inherent power in delegating to them some of their episcopal functions. Such a suffragan was an episcopal deputy in respect of those spiritual ministrations which are performed by a bishop in virtue of his orders. So far as the temporalities were concerned, they were put under the management

---

[890] Text from *Fordham University, Medieval Sourcebook*: Twelfth Ecumenical Council: Lateran IV 1215 at https://sourcebooks.fordham.edu/basis/lateran4.asp.
[891] The Islamic invasions from the seventh century onwards meant that there were sees in Asia Minor and North Africa that still technically existed, but were not actually functioning.

of a coadjutor whenever a Bishop was too infirm in body or mind to carry his episcopal duties. There remained a clear distinction between the episcopal functions which could only be performed by someone in episcopal orders and matters such as collating to benefices, granting institutions, dispensations and the like, for which it was not necessary that the coadjutor should be episcopally ordained.[892]

4. Suffragan Bishops at the Reformation

At the beginning of the English Reformation, the early English Reformers were critical of the ministry of the medieval Catholic suffragan bishops, as part of a wider critique of medieval Catholic episcopal practice in general.

Thus, in his work *The Obedience of a Christian Man* William Tyndale sees the existence of suffragan bishops as the result of a combination of the diocesan bishops' neglect of their proper calling to preach the word of God in favour of performing quasi magical ceremonies of blessing ('conjurations') and the fact that they are too busy with other matters to engage even in these activities:

After that the bishops had left preaching, then feigned they this dumb ceremony of confirmation, to have somewhat at the leastway, whereby they might reign over their dioceses. They reserved unto themselves also the christening of bells, and conjuring or hallowing of churches and church-yards, and of altars and super-altars, and hallowing of

---

[892] *Episcopal Ministry*, pp.182-183. For studies of Medieval suffragan bishops in England see L A S Butler 'Suffragan Bishops in the Medieval Diocese of York,' *Northern History*, Vol. LXVIII, December 2000, pp 49-60 and David M Smith, 'Suffragan Bishops in the Medieval Diocese of Lincoln,' *Lincolnshire History and Archaeology*, Vo.17, 1982.

chalices, and so forth; whatsoever is of honour or profit. Which confirmation, and the other conjurations also they have now committed to their suffragans; because they themselves have no leisure to minister such things, for their lusts and pleasures, and abundance of all things, and for the cumbrance that they have in the king's matters and business of the realm.[893]

In his *Pious Lamentation* Nicholas Ridley likewise laments the fact that both diocesan and suffragan bishops perform ceremonies unknown to the Apostles:

...at every poor bishop's hands and suffragan, ye shall have hallowing of churches, chapels, altars, superaltars, chalices, and of all the whole household stuff and adornment, which shall be used in the church after the Romish guise; for all these things must be esteemed of such high price, that they may not be done, but by a consecrate bishop only. O Lord, all these things are such as thy Apostles never knew.[894]

In a sermon preached before Edward VI, Hugh Latimer is also critical of the sort of 'popish suffraganship' criticised by Tyndale and Ridley, but he does see precedent for the proper exercise of suffragan ministry in the action taken by the prophet Samuel in to discharge his prophetic office in his old age:

To be short, he was now come to age, he was an old man, an impotent man, not able to go from place to place to minister justice; he elected and chose two suffragans, two coadjutors, two co-helpers. I mean not hallowers of bells, nor christeners of bells; that is a popish suffraganship. He made them to help him to discharge his office: he chose his two sons rather than other, because he knew them to be well brought up in virtue and learning. It was not for any carnal affection; he cared not for his renown or revenues, but he appointed them for

---

[893] Henry Walter (ed.). *Tyndale - Doctrinal Treatises* (Cambridge: Parker Society/CUP, 1848), p.274.
[894] Henry Christmas (ed.). *Nicholas Ridley - Works* (Cambridge Parker Society/CUP, 1843), p.55.

the ease of the people, the one for to supply his place in Bethsabe, and the other in Bethlem...For the sake of his people, good father Samuel, and to discharge his office in places where he could not come himself, he set his two sons in office with him as his suffragans and as his coadjutors. Here I might take occasion to treat, what old and impotent bishops should do, what old preachers should do, when they come to impotency, to join with them preachers, (preachers, not bell-hallowers,) and to depart part of their living with them.[895]

Despite the criticisms of the ministry of medieval suffragan bishops made by reformers like Tyndale, Ridley and Latimer, the practice of appointing suffragan bishops continued in the Church of England after the breach with Rome.

As we saw in chapter 5, the *Suffragan Bishops Act* of 1534 provided a legal basis for the continuation of the ministry of suffragan bishops by providing for the existence a number of English suffragan sees to which bishops could be appointed by the king.

The preamble to the Act is quite conservative, in that it states that the purpose of the Act is to continue the existing medieval practice of appointing suffragan bishops:

Albeit that since the beginning of this present Parliament good and honourable ordinances and statutes have been made and established for elections, presentations, election, consecrations, and investing of archbishops and bishops of this realm, and in all other the king's dominions, with all ceremonies appertaining unto the same, as by sundry Provision statutes thereof made more at large is specified; yet nevertheless no provision hitherto has been made for suffragans, which have been accustomed to be had within this realm for the more speedy administration of the sacraments, and other good, wholesome, and devout things and laudable ceremonies, to the increase of God's

---

[895] Hugh Corrie (ed.). *Sermons by Hugh Latimer* (Cambridge: Parker Society/CUP, 1844), p.175.

honour, and for the commodity of good and devout people.[896]

However, when looked at carefully the Act can also be seen as a reforming measure. This is because as well as abolishing any role for the Pope in the appointment of suffragan bishops it also replaced the *ad hoc* system for appointing suffragan bishops that existed in the Middle Ages with an organised system in which there are specified sees to which suffragan bishops may be appointed. Furthermore, the sees concerned are English sees, there are no more appointments to Irish sees or to sees *in partibus infidelium*.

In addition, the Act removed any ambiguity about the extent of the jurisdiction that would be exercised by suffragan bishops by laying down that the archbishops and bishops would give commissions to each suffragan bishop that would specify the extent of the episcopal authority they could exercise and by emphasising that no suffragan bishop was allowed to receive any payment or perform any episcopal act that that exceeded the terms of their commission. To quote the Act itself:

...no such suffragans, which shall be made and consecrated by virtue and authority of this Act, shall take or perceive any manner of profits of the places and sees whereof they shall be named; nor use, have, or execute any jurisdiction or episcopal power or authority episcopal within their said sees, nor within any diocese or place of this realm, or elsewhere within the king's dominions, but only such profits, jurisdiction, power, and authority as shall be licensed and limited to them to take, do, and execute by any archbishop or bishop of this realm, within their diocese to whom they shall be suffragans, by their commission under their seals

And that every archbishop and bishop of this realm, for their own peculiar diocese, may and shall give such commission or commissions to every such bishop suffragan as shall be consecrated by authority of this Act, as has been accustomed for suffragans heretofore to have, or

[896] 'Suffragan Bishops Act, AD 1534' in Gee and Hardy, p.253.

else such commission as by them shall be thought requisite, reasonable, and convenient; and that no such suffragan shall use any jurisdiction ordinary or episcopal power, otherwise, nor longer time, than shall be limited by such commission to him to be given as is aforesaid,[897]

One of the reasons why the ministry of chorepiscopi had died out in the Western Church in the early mediaeval period was the way in which chorepiscopi were seen to be exercising an autonomous ministry outside, and in competition with, the authority of the diocesan bishops. The section of the Act we have just looked at was designed to prevent such a problem recurring in the Church of England.

There are two further things worth noting about the ministry of the suffragan bishops created under the 1534 Act.

First, in Patristic terms these suffragan bishops are more like chorepiscopi than co-adjutor bishops. That is to say, their function is to extend the reach of episcopal ministry within a diocese 'for the commodity of good and devout people,' rather than to provide a helper and successor for the diocesan bishop when he becomes incapable of exercising ministry due to illness or old age (the scenario envisaged by Latimer). [898]

Secondly, after the reformed ordinals were instituted from 1550 onwards, suffragan bishops were ordained according to these ordinals, which meant (as we saw in chapter 10) that the ministry they were consecrated to exercise was a reformed episcopal ministry which gave priority to preaching, teaching and pastoral care rather than the sort of medieval episcopal ministry focused on the blessing of buildings and objects which was criticised by Tyndale, Ridley and Latimer.

---

[897] Gee and Hardy, pp.255-256.
[898] Section 20:16 of the *Reformatio Ecclesiasticarum* does make provision for the archbishops to appoint co-adjutors to assist diocesan bishops when they can no longer serve because of illness or old age, but this provision never became law.

Suffragan bishops continued to be appointed under the 1534 Act throughout the sixteenth century and suffragan bishops are mentioned three times in the Church of England's Canons of 1604.

Canon XXXV lays down the penalty for suffragans who ordain unqualified people:

...if any Bishop or Suffragan shall admit any to sacred Orders, who is not so qualified and examined as before we have ordained; the Archbishop of his Province having notice thereof, and being assisted therein by one Bishop, shall suspend the said Bishop or Suffragan so offending, from making either Deacons or Priests for the space of two Years.[899]

Canon LX states that suffragans must engage in confirmation:

Forasmuch as it hath been a solemn, ancient and laudable Custom in the Church of God, continued from the Apostles times, that all Bishops should lay their hands upon Children baptized and instructed in the Catechism of Christian Religion, praying over them, and blessing them, which we commonly call Confirmation, and that this holy Action hath been accustomed in the Church in former Ages, to be performed in the Bishops Visitation every third Year: We will and appoint, that every Bishop, or his Suffragan in his accustomed Visitation, do in his own Person carefully observe the said Custom.[900]

Canon CXXXV lays down that suffragan must not receive a fee for ordaining people:

That no Fee or Money shall be received either by the Archbishop, or any Bishop or Suffragan, either directly or indirectly, for admitting of any into Sacred Orders. [901]

---

[899] Canon XXXV, *Constitutions and Canons Ecclesiastical* at https://www.anglican.net/doctrines/1604-canon-law/
[900] Canon LX, *Constitutions and Canons Ecclesiastical*.
[901] Canon CXXXV, *Constitutions and Canons Ecclesiastical*.

The inclusion of references to suffragan bishops in these Canons indicates that suffragan bishops were expected to continue to exist in the Church of England. However, the last Tudor suffragan bishops, John Sterne, Bishop of Colchester, died in 1607 and after him no more suffragan bishops were appointed. As the 2001 Church of England report *Suffragan Bishops* suggests:

The reason for this was a lessening in the need for additional episcopal ministry. There were, for instance, fewer clergy and so fewer ordination services. Diocesan bishops were now expected to reside in their diocese and fully available to perform episcopal duties. [902]

Nevertheless, the 1534 Act remained on the statute book and the concept of having suffragan bishops continued to be supported during the course of the seventeenth century.

Thus, in his work *The Reduction of Episcopacy*, which we have already noted in chapters 5 and 10 James Ussher suggested that the number of suffragan bishops should be increased to one for every rural deanery:

Whereas by a statute in the six- and- twentieth year of King Henry the eighth revived in the first year of Queen Elizabeth, suffragans are appointed to be erected in 26 several places of this Kingdom, the number of them might very well be conformed on to the number of the several rural deaneries, into which every diocese is subdivided; which being done, the suffragan supplying the place of those, who in the ancient church were called chorepiscopi, might every month assemble a synod of all the rectors, or incumbent pastors within the precinct, and according to the major part of their voices, conclude all matters that should be brought into debate before them.[903]

Thus also, Jeremy Taylor in his *Episcopacy Asserted* argued that suffragans may be required because of the involvement of diocesan bishops in public affairs. As *Episcopal Ministry* notes, his argument was that 'Bishops should not seek to involve themselves in secular affairs,

[902] *Suffragan Bishops* (The Church of England: GS Misc. 733, 2001), p.5.
[903] Snoddy, p.152.

but they ought to do what they can for the good of the community.'[904] This may involve the need for diocesan bishops be absent from their dioceses and therefore the need to delegate their episcopal functions to others, and there are ample precedents for such delegation in the early Church. To quote *Episcopal Ministry* again, according to Taylor:

In the early Church bishops 'delegated to presbyters so many parts of the bishop's charge and there are parishes in his diocese,' at first as common assistants, and later with parish cures of their own. Those functions which only a bishop can perform were not so delegated. But it was possible for a bishop to make 'express delegation of the power of jurisdiction,' as Paul did to Tychicus. Epaphroditus 'although he was then Bishop of Philippi' spent time with Paul and was then ' certainly non resident,' so that 'one in substitution,' would have been needed. In the post-apostolic period Jeremy Taylor finds various examples. Cyprian, for instance, had at some time two suffragans and two priests. [905]

For a third example, as we saw in chapter 5, Charles II, in his declaration on ecclesiastical affairs issued immediately before the Restoration in 1660, promised that suffragan bishops would be appointed in every diocese:

Because the dioceses, especially some of them, are thought to be of too large extent, we shall appoint such number of suffragan bishops in every diocese as shall be sufficient for the performance of their work. [906]

5. The appointment of suffragan bishops in the nineteenth century

Charles II's promise to appoint suffragan bishops was never carried out and there were no suffragan bishops in the Church of England for the rest of the seventeenth century and for the whole of the eighteenth

---

[904] p. 185.
[905] *Episcopal Ministry*, p.185.
[906] *Episcopal Ministry*, p.186.

century. However, as we also saw in chapter 5, from 1870 onwards suffragan bishops were once again appointed. The reason for this was a growing feeling that suffragan bishops were a practical solution to the fact that the size of Church of England dioceses meant that the diocesan bishops alone could not exercise effective episcopal ministry within them.

This feeling is expressed, for example, by Thomas Lathbury, who argues in his book *A history of the convocation of the Church of England* that provision to appoint suffragan bishops already exists, that they would not impinge on the role of the diocesan bishop and that they could be appointed on an economical basis.

It is obvious that the order might be revived with great advantage to the Church; and it is clear from the act by which suffragans are authorised, that no possible inconvenience or discomfort could arise to the diocesan, seeing that all the authority is vested in himself. The subject, therefore, is one which might be submitted to convocation; for though the act of parliament authorises the appointment, yet as more than three centuries have elapsed since it was enacted, and more than two since any suffragan was appointed, there are necessarily many matters which it might be desirable to review. If only one were appointed in each diocese, what incalculable good might result to the Church! The suffragan might also perform those duties which are now discharged by the chancellor of the diocese. The office is fully recognised by the canons of 1604, for it is appointed by the 60th that 'every bishop or his suffragan do in his own person carefully perform the office of confirmation; 'and Charles II, in his declaration in 1660, says, 'because the dioceses be thought to be of too large extent, we will appoint such a number of suffragan bishops in every diocese as shall be sufficient for the due performance of their work. 'It would be easy to constitute suffragans wherever they might be required; and as the individuals selected for the office would not be expected to live in a style beyond that of ordinary clergymen, the additional expenses incurred by travelling would be comparatively small. At all events the suffragan might be permitted to hold a second living, with a view to the defraying of the necessary expense; or a stall, or some preferment in each cathedral might be devoted to that purpose. These and similar points might be considered in convocation, who would devote to them that attention which their importance and the circumstances of the Church require. Now suffragans would go a great way towards a redress of the grievance; each of the present bishops would then be a sort of archbishop; and our two archbishops would then be patriarchs. The large extent of our dioceses could no longer be then complained of; nor the incapacity, which the bishop thence lies under, of acquainting himself much either with his clergy or his people.[907]

Campaigning for the re-institution of suffragan bishops began in the 1830s. The fact that it took until 1870 for the first suffragan bishop to be appointed reflects the fact that there was strong opposition to their reinstitution. As Arthur Burns explains in his book *The Diocesan Revival in the Church of England*, there were several reasons for this opposition.

- There was fear that suffragans who were not members of the House of Lords would set a precedent for the exclusion of bishops from Parliament.

[907] Thomas Lathbury, *A history of the convocation of the Church of England: from the earliest period to the year 1742* (London: J. Leslie, 1853), pp.520-521. See also Thomas Lathbury, *A letter respectfully addressed to the Right Hon. Sir Robert Peel, Bart., First Lord of the Treasury, on the Restoration of Suffragan Bishops* (London: John W. Parker, 1844), John Newman, *The Restoration of Suffragan Bishops Recommended* (London: Rivington, 1835) and George D'Oyly, *A Letter to the Ecclesiastical Commissioners of England on the subject of reviving the institution of Suffragan Bishops* (London: Rivington, 1843).

- There was a concern that suffragan bishops would be appointed without a named see, contradicting the practice of the universal Church.

- There was a feeling that increasing the size of the episcopate would lead to its quality being diluted by the appointment of less talented bishops, who might eventually become diocesans.

- There was a concern that 'if the suffragans relieved bishops of the burdens of pastoral duties diocesans might become the mere creatures of bureaucracy, court and parliament.'

- There was a concern that the existence of suffragan bishops would undermine the cohesion of dioceses and obscure the symbolic unifying role of the diocesan bishop and that suffragan bishops would create a barrier between the diocesan bishops and the clergy.

- There was a concern that appointing suffragan bishops would get in the way of plans to create more dioceses. [908]

However, as Burns further explains, by the end of the 1860s the balance of opinion had swung in favour of appointing suffragans with an accommodation being reached between those who wanted suffragans and those who wanted new dioceses 'as those demanding suffragans increasingly portrayed them as an intermediary stage on the way to the creation of more dioceses, by both overcoming prejudice and generating diocesan feeling in the districts to which they were assigned.'[909]

6. Suffragan bishops in the Church of England today

Since 1870 the number of suffragan bishops has steadily increased with the result that the majority of bishops in the Church of England are now suffragan bishops. There are currently 73 suffragan sees in

[908] Burns, pp. 212-213.
[909] Burns, pp.213-214.

the Church of England as opposed to 42 diocesan sees, which makes the Church of England the only church in the Anglican Communion that has more suffragan that diocesan bishops.

Every diocese except Hereford, Portsmouth and Sodor and Man have at least one suffragan see, and some dioceses such as London and Oxford have several. Thus, Rochester has the suffragan see of Tonbridge and Oxford has the suffragan sees of Buckingham, Dorchester and Reading.

As the *Suffragan Bishops* report notes, the growth in the number of suffragan bishops was linked to a change that took place in the twentieth century in the way that suffragan bishops were financed, to greater expectations of the ministry of bishops, and to a decision after the Second World War that it was simply not feasible to go on creating new dioceses. In the words of the report:

A major factor was the way suffragan bishoprics were financed. In the late Nineteenth Century and well into the Twentieth Century, most suffragan bishoprics were tied to wealthy livings. The suffragan bishopric of Burnley is a good case in point. In 1890 the Burnley Rectory Act was passed, which allowed for some of the income from the benefice of Burnley to be used to constitute a suffragan bishopric and which necessitated the Bishop to be also Rector of Burnley. Bishops of Burnley remained Rectors of Burnley through until 1987. It was usual practise throughout the Church of England for suffragan bishops to hold another ecclesiastical office which provided sufficient income to underwrite the expenses associated with the bishopric. These suffragan bishops were essentially priests in episcopal orders, who helped out with confirmations and Episcopal duties as required.

This model gradually became less the norm within the Church of England during the 1950s and 1960s when a whole raft of new suffragan bishoprics were founded, which were free standing, financially independent, and not tied to any other form of ecclesiastical office. This change in strategy towards full time suffragans came about as a result of some major reflection within the Church as to what could reasonably be expected of a d diocesan. There was considerable debate about the nature of episcopacy and what should be the proper episcopal charge. There was concern about the size of diocese and the wide variations in population from diocese to diocese. It was clear that in a large urban diocese the diocesan bishop could not hope to get round sufficiently and that his engagement with his clergy and his outreach to the laity was likely to be fairly limited.

The enormity of the task was coupled with a greater expectation on what was required of a bishop the expectation was increasingly that the bishop should be available to his clergy and laity as a high profile leader and that pastoral oversight was his primary task. There was a desire for more bishoping within the church. As in earlier times, the only way of meeting the expectations was either to carve up the diocese into smaller units or to create more suffragan bishops who would provide greater episcopal pastoral oversight. The former solution of dividing dioceses, which happened in 1926-27 was thought impractical in the 1960s and 1970s because of the financial implications. It would also quite simply have exhausted the legislative energies of the Church for a decade and have embittered it with local battles over the reduction of the size of dioceses. Increasing the number of suffragans was considered the simplest and most effective solution, in some cases like London and Oxford, the choice was starkly between the breakup of the diocese or an increased number of suffragan bishops with considerable delegated authority organised in an area system. Both London and Oxford chose the latter option.[910]

Filling and creating suffragan sees
The current processes for filling existing suffragan sees and for creating new ones is laid out in sections 17 and 18 of the *Dioceses, Pastoral and Mission Measure 2007.*[911] Both processes involve consultation by the diocesan bishop with the diocesan synod (or if the

[910] *Suffragan Bishops*, pp.5-6.
[911] *The Dioceses, Pastoral and Mission Measure* 2007 at
https://www.legislation.gov.uk/ukcm/2007/1/contents

appointment is urgent, with the bishops' council and diocesan synod's standing committee) the archbishop of the province to which the diocese belongs (unless the diocesan bishop in question is an archbishop), and the Church of England's Dioceses Commission. The General Synod also needs to be consulted either in the case of the creation of a new suffragan see, or if the Dioceses Commission feels the proposal to fill an existing suffragan see 'needs further consideration.' If, after the process of consultation, the diocesan bishop's proposal has the approval of the diocesan synod and, when necessary, the General Synod, the bishop may then petition the Queen to fill or create the suffragan see under the provisions of the 1534 *Suffragan Bishops Act.*

The only exception to the necessity to go through the process of deciding whether a suffragan see should be filled is in the case of the See of Dover. Because the Bishop of Dover acts as the *de facto* diocesan bishop of the Diocese of Canterbury a new Bishop of Dover is automatically appointed.

Every suffragan bishop in the Church of England has the same episcopal orders conferred on them when they are ordained as a bishop, however, as we saw in chapter 11 the precise jurisdiction of each suffragan bishop is determined by their diocesan bishop. In the words of Canon C20.2: 'Every bishop suffragan shall use, have, or execute only such jurisdiction or episcopal power or authority in any diocese as shall be licensed or limited to him to use, have, or execute by the bishop of the same.'

The process by which the diocesan bishop lays down the specific jurisdiction of a particular suffragan bishop is once again set out in the 2007 *Diocesan, Pastoral and Mission Measure.* Section 13 of the Measure states that 'the bishop of a diocese may by an instrument under his hand delegate to a suffragan bishop of the diocese such of his functions as may be specified in the instrument.'

What this means is that as the person who possess 'jurisdiction as Ordinary' within the diocese the exercise of all episcopal functions within the diocese belongs by law to the diocesan bishop. However, under the terms of the 2007 Measure the diocesan bishop may delegate the exercise of some of these functions to a suffragan bishop by means of a written document ('an instrument').

Under the Measure such delegation may be either permanent or temporary, and it may apply only to the current occupant of the suffragan see, or to subsequent occupants of the suffragan see as well.

Section 13.3 further lays down that may provide that 'the functions thereby delegated may be discharged by the suffragan bishop throughout the diocese or only in a particular area thereof specified in the instrument.' This provision means that there can be two different ways in which episcopal functions can be divided up between the diocesan and suffragan bishops. In the majority of dioceses the diocesan bishops delegates certain functions which the suffragan bishop then has responsibility for exercising across the whole of the diocese. In a minority of dioceses there is a geographical division of the diocese into areas and suffragan bishops are given delegated authority to function as the 'area bishop' of a particular area.

At present there are five dioceses which have formal area schemes. These are Chelmsford, Lichfield, Leeds, London, Oxford and Southwark. There are also informal area schemes in the dioceses of Peterborough, Winchester and York.

In terms of the understanding of episcopal jurisdiction that we looked at in chapter 12, what is happening in ecclesiological terms when the diocesan bishop issues an instrument is that the Church as whole, acting through the bishop in question, limits the universal jurisdiction that a suffragan bishop possesses by virtue of his her episcopal orders to a particular form of jurisdiction within a particular diocese, a jurisdiction which has the purpose of assisting the diocesan bishop in providing episcopal ministry within that diocese.

The Provincial Episcopal Visitors
Four of the Church of England's suffragan bishops, the Bishops of Beverley, Ebbsfleet, Maidstone and Richborough are what are known as Provincial Episcopal Visitors (PEVs). Under the terms of the 2014

House of Bishops' Declaration on the Ministry of Bishops and Priests,[912] the PEVs have the role of providing episcopal ministry to parishes in which the PCC has passed a resolution indicating that it wishes to receive priestly or episcopal ministry from men rather than women. The PEVs are suffragan bishops of the dioceses of Canterbury (Ebbsfleet, Maidstone and Richborough) and York (Beverley) who have been given jurisdiction to exercise this role within the dioceses of Canterbury and York and within other dioceses with the agreement of the diocesan bishop.[913] The Bishops of Beverley, Ebbsfleet, and Richborough minister to traditional Catholic parishes while the Bishop of Maidstone ministers to Conservative Evangelical ones.

It is important to note that, because the PEVs are suffragan bishops, the parishes to which they minister remain under the episcopal jurisdiction of their diocesan bishop and that this applies even if the diocesan bishop is a woman. Thus, traditionalist Catholic and Conservative Evangelical parishes in the Diocese of Chelmsford remain under the jurisdiction of the Bishop of Chelmsford, Guli Francis-Dehqani, even though they may also receive the episcopal ministry of the Bishops of Richborough or Maidstone.

Ecclesiologically the PEVs have exactly the same function as other suffragan bishops in that the purpose of their ministry is to assist a diocesan bishop in providing episcopal ministry within a particular diocese.

---

[912] *House of Bishops' Declaration on the Ministry of Bishops and Priests* (GS Misc 1077) at https://www.churchofengland.org/sites/default/files/2017-11/GS%20 Misc%201077%20House%20of%20Bishops%20Declaration%20on%20the%20 Ministry%20of%20Bishops%20and%20Priests%20-%20Guidance%20note%20from %20the%20House.pdf

[913] Technically, the PEVs are suffragan bishops of the Dioceses of Canterbury and York and assistant bishops in the other dioceses in which they serve. This is because their respective sees are situated within the dioceses of Canterbury and York.

In addition to suffragan bishops there are also what are known as 'honorary assistant bishops.' These are people who have bishops' orders but who have retired or who are currently acting in roles other than as diocesan or suffragan bishops, but who are given permission to perform episcopal duties within a diocese on an occasional basis. The appointment of such honorary assistant bishops is at the discretion of the diocesan bishop and because it does not involve the creation or filling of a suffragan see it does not involve the process set out in the 2007 Measure. Where honorary assistant bishops are in the same position as suffragan bishops is in regard to jurisdiction. They too only have such jurisdiction within a diocese as is delegated to them by the diocesan. For example, as bishops they have the authority to confirm, but they can only perform confirmations with the agreement of the diocesan bishop.

In the Church of England today there is little controversy about the existence of suffragan bishops. They are a familiar part of the life of the Church of England and their ministry is generally much valued. There are those who would ideally like to see the creation of additional dioceses in order to remove the need to have suffragan bishops and return to the model of one bishop in each diocese, but this is an option which was rejected by the Church of England in the 1960s and '70s for the reasons previously noted and there seems almost no appetite in the Church of England as a whole for going down this route.

There are also those who suggest more radical solutions for reforming the exercise of episcopacy. David Holloway, for example, in his 1994 Latimer study *Episcopal Oversight – A Case for Reform* argues that the role of bishop and Dean/Provost of the Cathedral ought to merge, that some of the presbyters of larger churches in the diocese should be made bishops by being given the authority to ordain and that parochial clergy as a whole should be given the right to confirm. [914] As with the idea of creating additional dioceses, there seems very little

[914] David Holloway, *Episcopal Oversight – A Case for Reform* (Oxford: Latimer House, 1994), p.32.

appetite for this sort of radical overhaul of the episcopal system, both because there seems to be very little prospect of agreement as to what shape such an overhaul should take and because of the sheer complexity of dismantling the present system and creating a new one in its place.

The general consensus seems to be that we should stick with the present system. However, where there is a lack of consensus is how the present system should be understood theologically and it is to this issue we now turn.

7. Making theological sense of the relationship between diocesan and suffragan bishops

As *Episcopal Ministry* notes, the current system of episcopacy within the Church of England raises the 'theological question how the concept of a unitary episcopate can cohere with the exercise of directly episcopal ministry by other bishops in the diocese on virtually a permanent basis.' [915] To put it another way, how is it possible to hold together the principle of monepiscopacy (one bishop having the oversight of each local church/diocese) with the reality that there is more than one bishop in most of the dioceses of the Church of England?

These questions are addressed in both *Episcopal Ministry* and *Suffragan Bishops* with the lack of consensus within the Church of England about how best to understand the role of suffragan bishops being illustrated by the fact that the two reports reach different conclusions on the matter.

Episcopal Ministry

Episcopal Ministry considers three 'models' by means of which 'the ministry of the suffragan bishop can be envisaged in the Church of England today.'[916]

---

[915] *Episcopal Ministry*, p.193.
[916] *Episcopal Ministry*, p.194,

The first model is 'A theology of episcopal collegiality of the diocesan and suffragan bishops within the diocese.' In relation to this model the report notes that:

One approach which has gained a measure of support is to see the ministry of the diocesan bishop with his suffragan or suffragans in collegial terms. Historically, episcopal collegiality has been understood in terms of the collegiality of bishops within a province or provinces or of the total episcopate of the whole church. Suffragans might be said to share in any case in a collegiality of all bishops by virtue of their consecration; but the intention of this particular approach is to create a new category of episcopal collegiality: that of episcopal collegiality within a diocese.[917]

As the report sees it this is a novel view of episcopal collegiality and one that involves substantial risks:

It is important to be clear but this is a novel extension of the concept of collegiality. Collegiality is an expression of the universal aspects of the bishop's office. There is a risk that the appropriation of the word 'collegiality' to describe the shared leadership that a chapter of bishops offers in a diocese, might lead unwittingly to situations in which the primacy of the diocesan bishop is obscured. Collegiality of bishops in a diocese could at its worst be little more than committee episcopacy, with a diocesan bishop able to be outvoted. No less seriously, an uncritical use of the notion of collegiality may compromise the *episcope* that a bishop shares with his clergy.[918]

The report goes on to say that it does not want:

...to deny that there are collegial elements in the relationship between a diocesan bishop and his suffragans, related particularly to their common episcopal office within the diocese, nor to disparage the

[917] *Episcopal Ministry*, p.194.
[918] *Episcopal Ministry,* p.194.

importance of responsible and harmonious personal working relationships. [919]

However, in its view:

...to invoke collegiality in too precise a sense must mean a departure in principle from the norm of monepiscopacy and endanger the theology which sees the focusing of the three planes of the church is life in the person of the bishop; and there is little evidence that that is desired. [920]

The second model is what the report calls the 'pragmatic solution' of giving a suffragan bishop responsibility for a particular geographical area within a diocese while retaining the responsibility of the diocesan bishop for the dioceses as a whole. The report acknowledges the strengths of this approach:

Such a development recognises the impossibility of one bishop's providing adequate Episcopal oversight within a large diocese. It takes seriously the integrity of each bishop by virtue of his consecration, and the authority that belongs to his office. It provides a framework for mutual support at an episcopal level. We believe that in a number of dioceses this pattern is working well and we believe it to be welcomed by the people. [921]

In addition:

...Inherent in this model of shared episcopal ministry is the desire to give formal recognition to the status of the suffragan as a bishop whilst at the same time retaining the overall leadership of the diocesan in the mission of the Church within and beyond the diocese. [922]

---

[919] *Episcopal Ministry*, p.195.
[920] *Episcopal Ministry*, p.195.
[921] *Episcopal Ministry*, p.197.
[922] *Episcopal Ministry*, p.198.

However, the report also sees it as also having a number of weaknesses.

First, it says:

...If division into areas became a standard pattern, a new level would appear to be created in the Church of England's hierarchy in which the existing diocesan has something of the role of a 'metropolitan,' and it may not always be clear what constitutes the basic 'diocesan' unit of the 'local church.' [923]

Secondly:

Whilst area schemes have made a Bishop more readily available to his clergy and people, the corresponding need to maintain a loyalty to the diocese and to the bishop of the diocese may lead to confusion as the area seeks to establish an identity and to give to its area bishop the recognition and the network of support he may require. [924]

Thirdly, if under an area scheme a diocesan bishop was to be a given their own area 'that might seem to imply some diminution of his relationship with the rest of the diocese.' [925]

In the light of the weaknesses identified in the first two models, the report puts forward a third model which in the view of most members of the Group that produced the report provides 'a good theological basis, with sound historical precedent' for understanding the ministry of suffragan bishops. This model involves seeing the suffragan bishop:

...in his relation to his diocesan as his specifically episcopal representative or 'vicar.' We suggest that the suffragan's presence enriches the episcopal ministry of the diocese because of what he personally brings to it in his gifts. He can be in the fullest sense an episcopal and focal minister in the example of personal holiness he

[923] *Episcopal Ministry*, p.197.
[924] *Episcopal Ministry*, p.197.
[925] *Episcopal Ministry*, p.198.

sets, and in meeting the people's need for a special minister in whatever ways the Church locally requires of him. [926]

The report explains that:

The model of the 'episcopal assistant curate' is unacceptable and we are arguing for something rather differently conceived; 'the bishop who acts in the place of his diocesan when delegation or occasion requires' is a better way of describing a suffragan's ministry. there are other 'vicarial' ministries of course. The archdeacon is the legal 'eye 'of the bishop; generally speaking the senior staff of a diocese share in pastoral oversight. But representative ministry in specifically episcopal matters should be seen as the task of the suffragan. This is more than a sharing in ordination or confirmation or institution. It is a sharing of identity. It is in a sense the exercising of the *personal* ministry of his diocesan. It may be too much to say that the suffragan is his diocesan's *alter ego*; but he might be described as taking his diocesan's 'episcopal presence' with him as he exercises an episcopal ministry of oversight, of guarding the truth, of ministering the Word and presiding at the Eucharist, and of discipline. He and the diocesan may share ordinations or confirmations, or take them alternately; they may share out vacancy meetings, institutions, special festivals in parishes; the suffragan may have special responsibility for some aspect of diocesan work. In all this, and however he exercises his *episcope*, the suffragan is exercising the unitary oversight of his diocesan as his vicar.[927]

In the view of the report, this way of seeing the suffragan's ministry:

...argues no diminution of his own episcopate. He is not *merely* an episcopal curate or assistant. He is himself fully a bishop. He exercises an episcopal and personal *episcope*, not the general *episcope* which the diocesan bishop shares with all his presbyters. We take the view that if the diocesan has divided the episcopal tasks between himself and his

---

[926] *Episcopal Ministry*, p.198.
[927] *Episcopal Ministry*, p.198-199.

suffragans so that the episcope within the diocese is shared, it need not follow that the episcope of the diocesan is thereby impaired.

On this theological model the diocesan bishop remains the diocesan bishop and the suffragan has a full and authentic episcopal ministry as a bishop; but it is a ministry understood within a clear theological context.[928]

Suffragan Bishops

The *Suffragan Bishops* report uses the three models for the ministry of suffragan bishops set out in *Episcopal Ministry* (what it calls *The Cameron Report*[929]) as the framework for its own discussion of the topic, offering 'both developments and fresh evaluation for each model.'[930]

Suffragan Bishops notes what it calls the 'hesitancy' of Episcopal Ministry about the collegial model, but argues that this hesitancy was misplaced. It declares:

Given that the early development move episcopacy took the church in the direction of the diocese gathered around one bishop and that the polity of the Church of England has normally held to this, there are fundamental approaches to shared *episcope* which give strength to the concept and exercise of a collegial episcopacy within the diocese rather than treating our inherited patterns in the way that *The Cameron Report* feared. These fears often congregate around the perceived damage that it could do to the concept of the bishop as a focus of unity. The personal dimension of the diocesan bishop's ministry is clearly central in the exercise of his episcopate (as it is in different ways for the suffragan) and the diocesan bishop is the personal focus for unity. however, this need not be solely an individualist model. There is diversity within true unity. Collaborative approaches to episcopal ministry offer a fuller and less one

---

[928] *Episcopal Ministry,* p.199.
[929] *Episcopal Ministry* came to be referred to as *The Cameron Report* because the group that produced it was chaired by Sheila Cameron QC.
[930] *Suffragan Bishops*, p. 19.

dimensional view of unity. Such an understanding proclaims that there is unity at the centre of the diocesan family that joyfully encompasses divergence and difference. it provides a rich view of unity which hopefully reflects in some way the fullness of unity within the persons of the Trinity. In arguing for a more collegial model we are not seeking to downgrade the importance of the personal character of the diocesan bishops primacy within the diocese. Rather we are advocating a dynamic and creative relationship between these two aspects of episcopal ministry. [931]

Suffragan Bishops also argues that the words 'koinionia'[932] and 'collaborative' should be linked to the word 'collegial' in describing the relationships between diocesan and suffragan bishops:

Along with collegial we link the words *koinonia* or *collaborative* to express the joint ministry of decision and suffragan bishops within the diocese. In their difference and individuality they bring a *pleroma*[933] to the episcopal ministry which is not possible for any one individual. They exhibit a oneness which can encompass difference, even disagreement, and this is the kind of unity that must exist within the church as a whole. In this way there is a positive advantage in such plurality within the unity of episcopal ministry. It is having to model this kind of unity which the rest of the church is striving to live out. There is still *one* episcopal ministry within the diocese but it is not individualistically focused. [934]

As *Suffragan Bishops* sees it, this kind of collegial approach represents a better way forward for the Church of England than simply creating more dioceses.

---

[931] *Suffragan Bishops*, p. 20.
[932] The Greek word used to describe the communion which exists between Christians within the body of Christ.
[933] The Greek word for fullness.
[934] *Suffragan Bishops*, p. 23.

We affirm that, rather than being merely a development that has happened over the past century because of population growth and growing demands upon episcopal ministry, the increasing deployment of suffragan bishops offers possibilities for a richer theology and practise of episcopacy in which theory and practise of episcopacy are better integrated. This is consistent with the tradition, not a rejection of it. *The Cameron Report* thought that the ideal would be an increase in the number of dioceses as the way to preserve our traditional understanding off the bishop within the diocese. We uphold that the best way forward would rarely be to create more dioceses but to develop the understanding of sharing within the one episcopate within the diocese. This understanding was reflected in Dr Anthony Russell's sermon when he was enthroned as Bishop of Ely when speaking of the ministry he shares with the suffragan Bishop of Huntingdon: *'Episcopacy in this diocese is a single function performed by two people.'* Under such a collegial understanding, the ministry of the Bishop as focus of unity involves the diocesan bishop operating collegially with his suffragans in such a way that the quality of unity in plurality is demonstrated within the Episcopal ministry of the diocese as it acts as a sign of unity for the whole of the diocese.[935]

In relation to the area model Suffragan Bishops notes the concern of *Episcopal Ministry* 'that area systems could blur the focus upon the diocesan as the one who exercises primary *episcope* within the diocese.' [936] However, *Suffragan Bishops* takes a much more positive view of the area approach:

We would wish to emphasise more advantages of an area system as one way of developing a collegial and collaborative approach to episcopal ministry where there is more than one, and especially where there are three or more, suffragan bishops. [937]

---

[935] *Suffragan Bishops*, p. 20, italics in the original.
[936] *Suffragan Bishops*, p. 23.
[937] *Suffragan Bishops*, p. 23.

While acknowledging the problems that one diocese experienced with operating an area scheme, which if strictly adhered to would mean that the diocesan bishop 'would take no part in appointments and never ordain or confirm except at the invitation of his suffragan,'[938] *Suffragan Bishops* argues that this should not discredit the area concept as such:

Such an experience points to the dangers the lurk within this approach to collaborative episcopal ministry that are waiting to catch out the unwary. However, diversity within episcopal ministry need not lead to fragmentation. When carefully devised and reflectively employed, it can promote a fuller expression of unity in depth and diversity. The important factor is the way in which the scheme is arranged, affirmed and monitored within the diocese. In particular the ministry of the diocesan has to be considered afresh within the light of such an area system. His ministry can often be most fully developed if he does not have an area of his own as this can minimise his presence within the whole of the diocese. The diocesan bishop is likely to be more heavily involved in national affairs, both in Church and State, than his suffragan(s), which usually frees the latter to take a more hands on approach in relation to the pastoral care of the clergy and as leader in mission. The task of being a leader in mission can be particularly strengthened by the very natural partnership which can exist between an area Bishop and other leaders in the wider community within his area. [939]

In relation to the 'episcopal vicar' model favoured by *Episcopal Ministry*, *Suffragan Bishops* notes that 'The important truth enshrined in this model is that there is one episcopate in the diocese.'[940] However, it then goes on to say that:

It is our view that such a concept is fully preserved in models one and two, which have the distinct advantage over this one that they also

---

[938] *Suffragan Bishops*, p. 24.
[939] *Suffragan Bishops*, p. 24.
[940] *Suffragan Bishops*, p. 24.

reflect the values of collegiality and collaborative ministry. Consequently, we do not believe that the concept of episcopal vicar is theologically broad enough to be used as a model for the ministry of suffragan bishops. [941]

Assessing the approaches taken in *Episcopal Ministry* and *Suffragan Bishops*

The first point to note about the approaches to understanding the ministry of suffragan bishops put forward in Episcopal Ministry and Suffragan Bishops is that the 'area model' considered in both reports is not in fact a model for understanding the ministry of suffragan bishops at all. It is a model for how the ministry of suffragan bishops may be exercised, but in itself it does not tell you anything about how to understand theologically the ministry of suffragan bishops and how their ministry relates to that of diocesan bishops.

If we therefore set the area model aside, we are left with the episcopal vicar and collegial approaches.

If we look at the episcopal vicar approach first of all, we can see that its great strength is that it takes seriously the fact that suffragan bishops are called to minister on behalf of, and under the authority of their diocesan bishops. Their role is to assist the diocesan bishop in exercising his or her jurisdiction across the whole of the diocese. *Episcopal Ministry* is thus correct to say that that a suffragan bishop 'acts in the place of his diocesan when delegation or occasion requires.'

The problem with the model lies with the idea that the ministry of the suffragan bishop involves 'the exercising of the *personal* ministry of his diocesan' and he or she can be described as 'taking his diocesan's 'episcopal presence' with him as he exercises an episcopal ministry of oversight, of guarding the truth, of ministering the Word and presiding at the Eucharist, and of discipline.'

---

[941] *Suffragan Bishops*, pp.24-25.

What this seems to suggest is that, in spite of the fact that *Episcopal Ministry* insists that suffragan bishops exercise 'an episcopal and personal *episcope*,' in reality suffragan bishops have no ministry of their own. Their role is solely to exercise the personal episcopal ministry of their diocesans.

It is hard to see in what sense it can then be said that 'the suffragan has a full and authentic episcopal ministry as a bishop.' Looking at the same point in another way, it is difficult to see why on this model a suffragan bishop needs to be a bishop at all. If the ministry that is being exercised is actually the ministry of the diocesan bishop then why couldn't the relevant acts be performed by a priest, a deacon, or even a member of the laity?

If the response is that this is impossible because someone has to be called and ordained or consecrated as bishop to perform these acts, then this response only highlights the problem because it points us to the fact that suffragan bishops can rightly perform episcopal acts because they *are in their own right* bishops. That is to say, they are people who have been called by God to be bishops and in response to this call have been set aside by the Church through the laying on of hands and have received the necessary gifts of the Spirit to perform episcopal ministry.

This fact cannot be ignored. Suffragan bishops have a personal episcopal ministry of their own given to them by God through the Church and it is this ministry of their own when they act in the diocese under the jurisdiction of their diocesan bishop.

Moving on the collegial approach, we can see that its great strengths are (a) that, unlike the episcopal vicar approach, it takes seriously the personal episcopal ministry possessed individually by each suffragan bishops and (b) that it correctly sees that the bishops in a diocese need to work together in a collaborative fashion.

There are, however, three problems with the collegial approach. The first problem relates to the appeal which the *Suffragan Bishops* report makes to the doctrine of the Trinity in support of the collegial approach.

As *Suffragan Bishops* itself explains, the doctrine of the Trinity teaches us that:

There is both order within the Trinity which governs the mutuality of working of the three persons and a full sharing in the divine nature which speaks of sharing and mutuality. The former equates to the necessity of order within the Church's threefold order while the latter supports the mutuality and collegiality within the episcopate. [942]

The problem with the concept of episcopal collegiality is that it can lead to a stress on mutuality and collegiality at the expense of order. Certainly, this is what we find in *Suffragan Bishops*. The report seems to see episcopal collegiality in entirely flat terms with no one member of the episcopal college having any more authority than any other. The idea that there might be an order within the episcopal college is entirely absent.

However, in traditional Christian thinking about episcopal ministry the existence of an order within the episcopal college has been seen as very important. In the classical Christian understanding of the Trinity the three Persons of the Trinity are ontologically equal since they all equally God,[943] but there is also an order in their working in which the Son and the Spirit are functionally subordinate to the Father.[944] In an analogous fashion, in the traditional Christian understanding of episcopacy going right back to the Patristic period all bishops are ontologically equal in regard to their episcopal orders, as previously noted, a bishop is a bishop is a bishop. However, there is also an order within the episcopate in which metropolitan bishops have authority

---

[942] *Suffragan Bishops*, p.22.

[943] In the words of the *Athanasian Creed* 'And in this Trinity none is afore, or after other: none is greater, or less than another; But the whole three Persons are co-eternal together and co-equal.'

[944] See Michael Ovey, *Your will be done – Exploring eternal subordination, divine monarchy and divine humility* (London: Latimer House, 2016).

over diocesan bishops and diocesan bishops have authority over suffragan bishops. In terms of Church law, metropolitan bishops have jurisdiction over diocesan bishops and diocesan bishops have jurisdiction over suffragan bishops.

This brings us to the second problem with the collegial approach which is that, as *Episcopal Ministry* correctly notes, there is the risk:

...that the appropriation of the word 'collegiality' to describe the shared leadership that a chapter of bishops offers in a diocese, might lead unwittingly to situations in which the primacy of the diocesan bishop is obscured. Collegiality of bishops in a diocese could at its worst be little more than committee episcopacy, with a diocesan bishop able to be outvoted.

Nothing that is said in *Suffragan Bishops* removes this risk. There is no recognition that the order that exists within episcopal ministry means that the diocesan bishop has the overall responsibility for the life of the diocese and the exercise of episcopal ministry within it and that therefore he or she has to have the final say.

The third problem is that the collegial approach as set out in Suffragan Bishops really amounts to a rejection of monepiscopacy itself. As we have seen in the course of this study, from apostolic times onwards the principle has been accepted that there should be a single person, 'the bishop,' with an overall responsibility for the Church in a given area. A collegial view of episcopacy as set out in Suffragan Bishops involves a rejection of this principle. As noted above, what the collegial approach really amounts to is giving a committee rather than a person the responsibility of a single person for the Church in a given area. Instead of a single shepherd there are a group of shepherds with no clarity about who is ultimately in charge – the very situation which monepiscopacy was instituted to avoid.

A further issue with what is said in *Suffragan Bishops* lies in its suggestion that because the diocesan bishops will be involved in national business in Church and State it will be the suffragan bishops who take on a 'more hands on approach in relation to the pastoral care of the clergy and as leader in mission.'

This suggestion is problematic for a couple of reasons.

It is increasingly the case that suffragan bishops are also taking on national roles. Thus, for many years the suffragan Bishop of Tonbridge, Brian Castle, was the Chair of the Mission Theology Advisory Group of Churches Together in Britain and Ireland, and today the suffragan Bishop of Swindon, Lee Rayfield, is the national spokesman for the Church of England on medical ethics and science and religion and is a member of the United Kingdom's Human Fertilisation and Embryology Authority. A neat binary division between diocesan bishops with national roles and suffragan bishops who undertake local ministry is therefore unrealistic.

It is also wrong in principle to suggest the pastoral care of the clergy and leadership in mission should be delegated to suffragans. As we have seen, these are integral parts of the calling of all bishops, and diocesan bishops cannot decide not be involved in them because of their national commitments. When the Canon C18.6 insists that a bishop must be resident in his or her diocese the subtext is that they need to be present in the diocese so that they can exercise their ministry there.

As we saw in chapter 5, the Victorians worked hard to get away from the eighteenth century concept of bishops as essentially national political figures who were only occasionally active in their dioceses and we need to avoid this notion returning in a new guise. As we saw earlier in this chapter, this is what Victorian critics feared the reintroduction of suffragan bishops into the Church of England would lead to and we do not want to have them proved right.

A better way of understanding the relationship between diocesan and suffragan bishops

A better way of understanding the relationship between diocesan and suffragan bishops, and hopefully one that could form the basis of consensus about the matter, is to focus on the distinction between orders and jurisdiction already highlighted in this chapter.

In the Christian tradition, episcopal orders are bestowed on all bishops when they are made bishops through the laying on hands. This gives someone the necessary authority in terms of their orders to exercise the overall leadership of a diocese as its chief presbyter and to perform certain specific functions, some of which (such as preaching and presiding at Holy Communion) can also be undertaken by those in priests' orders and some of which (such as ordaining and confirming) can only be undertaken by bishops.

As we have seen in the course of this study, in the earliest days of the Church the exercise of the overall leadership of a local church/diocese and the performance of the other functions of a bishop were carried out by one and the same person. However, as we have also seen, from the second century onwards the practical demands resulting from the growth of the Church meant that this early pattern was developed in two ways.

First, there was the emergence of the metropolitan system in which one bishop in a province was given the responsibility of exercising oversight over the other diocesan bishops in that province. To put it simply, there emerged a bishop of the bishops. Secondly, there was the emergence of coadjutor bishops and the chorepiscopi, who were bishops with the role of giving assistance in different ways to the diocesan bishops. This pattern of metropolitan bishops, diocesan bishops, coadjutor bishops and chorepiscopi was a matter of jurisdiction in the sense discussed in chapter 12. It was a matter of the Church setting different limits to the scope of the ministry exercised by different sorts of bishops.

In Anglican terms this development was a legitimate one because it comes under the terms of the freedom possessed by the Church to vary 'traditions and ceremonies' (i.e. ways of operating) providing that 'nothing be ordained against God's Word' (Article XXXIV) and because it was of practical benefit to the Church.

What also needs to be noted is that in this developed pattern of episcopal ministry the basic principle of monepiscopacy handed down from the time of the apostles was still maintained. In the metropolitical system there was one metropolitan (one 'bishop of the bishops') in each province and there was still one diocesan bishop in each diocese. In the system of coadjutors there remained one diocesan bishop with overall responsibility for the diocese with the coadjutor assisting him and normally also succeeding him as the next diocesan. In the system of chorepiscopi there was also one diocesan bishop with overall responsibility for the diocese with the chorepiscopi acting under his authority to extend the provision of episcopal ministry to the rural areas of the diocese.

As we have noted in the previous chapter, and in this one, the pattern of episcopal ministry in the Church of England is a deliberate continuation of the patristic model just outlined. There are two metropolitan bishops (the Archbishops of Canterbury and York) and alongside them diocesan bishops and suffragan bishops as the equivalent of the chorepiscopi. The metropolitans, the diocesans and the suffragans are all equally bishops, but they have different jurisdictions given to them as specified in Canons C17,18 and 20.

As with the patristic pattern, this Church of England pattern maintains the principle of monepiscopacy in the ways described above while allowing for a differentiation in jurisdiction to meet the developing needs of the Church.

In terms of Trinitarian theology, we can say that just as in the Holy Trinity there is an ontological equality between the persons, but also a functional subordination of the Son and the Spirit to the Father, so also in the Church of England all bishops are equal as regards their orders and the basic pattern of ministry to which they are called (as set out in the Canons and the Ordinals), but the diocesan and suffragan bishops are functionally subordinate to the metropolitans, and the suffragan bishops are functionally subordinate to the diocesans.

The functional subordination of the suffragan to the diocesan is, as we saw in the last chapter, very clearly set out in Canon C20. It is the diocesan bishop who gives the suffragan bishop the right to exercise episcopal jurisdiction in his or her diocese and who decides what the limits of that jurisdiction will be. Essentially, the suffragan does the episcopal work that is assigned to him or her by the diocesan. It should be noted, however, that contrary to what is suggested in *Episcopal Ministry*, the episcopal work that a suffragan does is his or her *own* work for God. It is not the work of the diocesan bishop done through them.

The concept of episcopal collegiality is true in so far as diocesans and suffragans are both members of the college of bishops and the concept of collaborative ministry is helpful in so far as it reminds us that a healthy relationship between diocesan and suffragan is one in which they work together by agreement alongside the other members of the senior leadership team in the diocese. However, neither concept negates the functional subordination of the suffragan bishop to his or her diocesan.

As suffragans are bishops it is right that they should be members of the House of Bishops of their diocesan synod, but the primary authority of the diocesan bishops in the life of the diocese makes it is right that it is the diocesan is the president of the synod who has the right to exercise an episcopal veto by withholding assent to what the synod has decided.

In terms of the national councils of the Church, because the diocesan bishops are the people with overall responsibility under God for their dioceses that they should be the people who represent their dioceses *ex officio* in the Convocations of Canterbury and York and therefore in the House of Bishops of the General Synod. However, it is also important that suffragans bishops should also be represented in the House of Bishops both because they may have particular expertise to bring to the Church's counsels and in order to ensure that the suffragan bishops' perspective is not overlooked.

The sheer number of suffragans makes it unreasonable for them all to be members of the House of Bishops, and having a representative number elected onto the House of Bishops and the opportunity for all bishops to take counsel together in regular meetings of the College of Bishops seems a reasonable compromise.

Coadjutor bishops?

The ancient office of coadjutor bishop does not formally exist in the Church of England (although it does in some other parts of the Anglican Communion[945]). However, although suffragan bishops have no official expectation of succession to the role of diocesan, other aspects of the coadjutor role are filled by suffragans. Thus, suffragan bishops will exercise the role of the diocesan bishop by delegation if he or she is incapacitated for some reason and will fill in if the death or retirement of a diocesan bishop creates a temporary vacancy in their own diocese or a neighbouring one.

In chapter 12 we looked at what is meant by episcopal jurisdiction. In this chapter we have looked at how the concept of jurisdiction helps us to make sense of the role of the suffragan bishop. In the next chapter we shall consider what it means for someone to be a 'good enough bishop' by rightly exercising episcopal jurisdiction.

---

[945] For example, in The Episcopal Church in the United States, when a diocesan bishop announces their retirement, a special diocesan convention is held to elect a coadjutor. Usually, the coadjutor serves with the incumbent for a short time before the latter's retirement, when the coadjutor becomes the diocesan bishop.

Chapter 14
Being a 'good-enough bishop'

1. Why bishops are only ever 'good-enough'

The subject of this chapter is what makes someone a 'good-enough bishop.' I have taken the term 'good-enough bishop' from Avis's book *Becoming a Bishop* in which he writes of the importance of the 'good-enough' bishop in the life of the Church:

A good-enough bishop is a precious gift of God to God's Church. While it is true that some dioceses revive after the bishop has moved on - just as some parishes spring back to life after the departure of their priest, whose presence acted like a wet blanket on lay initiative - a good bishop is a source of strength, inspiration and wisdom to his or her people. Bishops can make a qualitative difference for good or ill, to how church people experience their faith, worship and witness from day to day.[946]

Describing a bishop as 'good-enough' may seem rather grudging. After all, when we describe someone as being 'good-enough' there is an implied limitation of how good they are. They are not brilliant, excellent, outstanding, perfect, or even good. They are simply 'good-enough.' However, I would argue that the best we can ever say about a bishop, as about any other Christian minister, is that what they have done is 'good-enough' in the sense that that in their ministry they have performed the role to which God has called them in a reasonably competent fashion.

To understand why bishops are only ever 'good-enough' we need to turn first of all to what is said about original sin in Article IX of the *Thirty-Nine Articles*. This article declares that original sin:

---

[946] Avis, *Becoming a Bishop*, p.13.

...is the fault and corruption of the nature of every man that naturally is engendered of the offspring of Adam, whereby man is very far gone from original righteousness, and is of his own nature inclined to evil, so that the flesh lusteth always contrary to the spirit; and therefore in every person born into this world, it deserveth God's wrath and damnation. And this infection of nature doth remain, yea, in them that are regenerated, whereby the lust of the flesh, called in Greek φρόνημα σαρκὸς (which some do expound the wisdom, some sensuality, some the affection, some the desire of the flesh), is not subject to the law of God. And although there is no condemnation for them that believe and are baptized, yet the Apostle doth confess that concupiscence and lust hath itself the nature of sin.

In this quotation 'flesh' means our fallen human nature and what the article is reminding us is that our fallen nature and the sin that flows from it remain a permanent part of who we are even if we are baptised Christian believers. If we go on to ask what the effects of having a fallen nature are, there is a helpful explanation in the homily 'Of the Misery of all Mankind' in the *First Book of Homilies*. This tells us that our continuing fallenness means:

...there be imperfections in our best works: we do not love God so much, as we ought to do, with all our heart, mind, and power; we do not fear God so much, as we ought to do; we do not pray to God, but with great and many imperfections; we give, forgive, believe, love, and hope unperfectly; we speak, think, and do unperfectly; we fight against the devil, the world, and the flesh unperfectly.[947]

This being the case, it follows that no form of episcopal ministry is ever going to be anything other than imperfect. The ministry of every bishop will necessarily be marked by 'great and many imperfections' and they will necessarily 'speak think and do unperfectly.' That is why bishops, just like everyone else, are called to use the words of the general confession in the *Book of Common Prayer*:

[947] Robinson (ed.), *The Homilies*, p.14.

We have erred from thy ways like lost sheep, We have followed too much the devices and desires of our own hearts, We have offended against thy holy laws, We have left undone those things we ought to have done, And we have done those things which we ought not to have done, And there is no health in us.[948]

The imperfection of their episcopal ministry is something that has been generally accepted by bishops since the earliest days of the Church. For example, it what underlies Augustine's famous comment in Sermon 340 'for you I am a bishop, with you, after all, I am a Christian' which we noted at the start of chapter 7. The full quotation, of which these words are part, runs as follow:

But you too must all support me, so that according to the apostle's instructions we may carry one another's burdens, and in this way fulfil the law of Christ (Galatians 6:2). If he doesn't carry it with us, we collapse; if he doesn't carry us, we keel over and die. Where I'm terrified by what I am for you, I am given comfort by what I am with you. For you I am a bishop, with you, after all, I am a Christian. The first is the name of an office undertaken, the second a name of grace; that one means danger, this one salvation. Finally, as if in the open sea, I am being tossed about by the stormy activity involved in that one; but as I recall by whose blood I have been redeemed, I enter a safe harbour in the tranquil recollection of this one; and thus while toiling away at my own proper office, I take my rest in the marvellous benefit conferred on all of us in common.[949]

As we saw in chapter 8, Augustine was terrified of the fact that God had called him to be a bishop both because he was aware of the enormous importance of the bishop's role and of his inability, as a sinner, to undertake it in anything except an imperfect manner, and because he was aware that he would have to give account to God for his stewardship at the last judgement. What comforts him in the midst of his terror, he says in sermon 340, is the recollection that, just like

---

[948] The order for Morning Prayer, *The Book of Common Prayer*.
[949] Augustine, Sermon 340: 1, p. 292.

the members of his flock, he is a Christian who has received the 'marvellous benefit' of the forgiveness of sins because of the saving work of Jesus Christ.

What all this means is that there is no such thing as a perfect bishop any more than there is such a thing as a perfect Christian. All bishops are imperfect sinners, and this fact will be manifested in their ministries, as a careful study of episcopal biographies makes abundantly clear.

However, this does not mean that 'all cats are grey.' All professing Christians are imperfect sinners; however, some Christians live out their Christian calling more adequately than others. Similarly, all bishops are, as we have just noted, imperfect sinners, but some bishops fulfilling their episcopal calling more adequately than others That is why some bishops have generally been viewed as saints and heroes, whereas other have been viewed as villains. Thus, Athanasius and Augustine, despite all their imperfections, have generally been regarded as saints and heroes, whereas three of the Popes at the end of the Middle Ages, Innocent VIII (1484-92), Alexander VI (1492-1503) and Julius II (1503-13) are generally regarded even by devout Catholics, as villains because of their corruption, greed, cruelty, and sexual license.[950]

Turning to the history of the Church of England, the activist bishops of the nineteenth century, such as Samuel Wilberforce, Charles Longley, or J C Ryle are generally regarded as having performed their episcopal duties much more adequately than the largely absentee bishops of the previous century.

Because it is possible to make these kinds of distinctions between the adequacy of bishops it makes sense to say that, despite all bishops being imperfect, there are some bishops who are 'good-enough bishops' (that is, bishops who exercise their episcopal jurisdictions in a generally adequate fashion) and some who are not.

[950] See, for instance, Kerr, pp.227-230.

In the remainder of this chapter, we shall consider what makes someone a 'good-enough bishop'. We shall base this consideration on the teaching of the Church of England which we looked at in chapters 11 and 12, teaching which is in continuity with the teaching about the role and character of bishops in the New Testament, in the writings of the Patristic period, and in Church of England writings from the sixteenth and seventeenth centuries including the 1662 *Ordinal*.

2. What do good-enough bishops need to do?

a. They need to be pastors

The primary and overarching task which the good-enough bishop is called to perform is to be a pastor. To quote Canon C.18.1 again 'Every bishop is the chief pastor to all that are within his diocese, as well laity as clergy, and their father in God.' As we shall see below, everything that a bishop is called to do relates to this one basic calling.

In the history of the Church a persistent temptation for bishops has been to see themselves as having the right to rule over the faithful in an authoritarian and domineering fashion and to exploit the opportunities this provides to acquire money and material possessions for themselves. In 1 Peter 5:2-4 Peter makes clear, however, that this is a temptation to which bishops must not succumb. They are not to domineer over their flocks for their own benefit, but to tend their flocks as pastors, fulfilling this role willing and eagerly and for their flocks' benefit. 'Tend the flock of God that is your charge, not by constraint but willingly, not for shameful gain but eagerly, not as domineering over those in your charge but being examples to the flock.'

In unpacking what it means for a bishop to act as a pastor tending his or her flock, the first thing we need to note is what Canon C.18 tells us about the extent of a bishop's jurisdiction. Although, as we have seen, bishops have, by virtue of their episcopal orders, a potentially universal jurisdiction, the exercise of that jurisdiction is normally limited to a particular place. In the case of diocesan bishops (as C.18 indicates) that place is a particular diocese. As Canon C.20 indicates that is also true of a suffragan bishop. Finally, as Canon C.17 indicates the primary jurisdiction of a metropolitan bishop is his or her diocese, but he or she also has an additional jurisdiction covering a particular province.

The jurisdiction that each bishop has lays down the geographical limits within which they are primarily called to acts as a pastor and, as Canon C18 goes on to say, their calling is to act as the 'chief pastor' to everyone ('all') who live within those geographical limits whether they are laity or clergy. Just as a parish priest has a pastoral responsibility for everyone in the parish, regardless of whether they are churchgoers or not, regardless of whether they are Christians or not, so a bishop has a pastoral responsibility for everyone in their diocese.

The second thing we need to understand is what it means to for a bishop to be a pastor. To understand this means we need to go back to the verses from John 21 that we noted in chapters 7 and 9 where the risen Christ gives a fresh commission to Peter after the resurrection:

This was now the third time that Jesus was revealed to the disciples after he was raised from the dead. When they had finished breakfast, Jesus said to Simon Peter, 'Simon, son of John, do you love me more than these?' He said to him, 'Yes, Lord; you know that I love you.' He said to him, 'Feed my lambs.' A second time he said to him, 'Simon, son of John, do you love me?' He said to him, 'Yes, Lord; you know that I love you.' He said to him, 'Tend my sheep.' He said to him the third time, 'Simon, son of John, do you love me?' Peter was grieved because he said to him the third time, 'Do you love me?' And he said to him, 'Lord, you know everything; you know that I love you.' Jesus said to him, 'Feed my sheep. (Jn 21:15-17)

As John Marsh writes, in these verses Jesus tells Peter: 'He must guide and feed the flock of Christ, and become an 'under-shepherd' to Christ the great Shepherd of the sheep.' [951]

---

[951] John Marsh, *Saint John* (Harmondsworth: Penguin, 1968), p.672.

As we saw in chapter 9, this mandate given by Jesus to Peter cannot rightly be seen as restricted to the ministry of the Pope. In John 21 this command is given by Jesus to Peter personally as part of his restoration following his betrayal of Jesus. However, it can also be taken as a mandate to the wider Church since the command to provide pastoral care to the disciples of Jesus is also repeated subsequently by Paul (Acts 20:28-31) and by Peter himself (1 Pet 5:2-4) as a command to the leaders of the Early Church in general.

The pastoral mandate given by Jesus to Peter and to the Church in general fulfils the prophecies in Isaiah 40:11, Ezekiel 34: 23, Micah 5:4, that God will care for his people like a shepherd and will do this through the ministry of a descendant of David. These prophecies are fulfilled in the first instance through the ministry of Jesus the good shepherd (John 10:1-18) and this ministry of Jesus then continues in the ministry of the Church, the ministry of bishops included.

As we saw in chapter 7, the biblical descriptions of the work of the shepherd in passages such as Ezekiel 34:1-16, Acts 20: 28-31, John 21:15-17 and Matthew 18:12-14 indicate that it has three elements. A good shepherd feeds the flock, making sure it has adequate food and water, the shepherd tends the flock, making sure it is protected from those who would do it harm, and the shepherd goes out and searches for those sheep who have gone astray. In terms of pastoral care, this means feeding the faithful through word and sacrament, protecting them as far as possible from enemies, human and demonic, and seeking to recover those who are lost either as a result of the Fall or because they have fallen away from the Christian faith in their belief, their behaviour, or both together.

To be a good enough bishop involves fulfilling this triple calling to feed, protect and recover.

The idea of the bishop as shepherd overlaps with the other major Patristic image of the bishop as a physician of souls, which we looked at in chapter 8, and which involves an analogous calling to give people the spiritual treatment that they need to ensure that they stay spiritually healthy, to cure them when they are spiritually sick, and to help them return to heath when they have relapsed.

b. They need to be guardians of the Christian faith

The calling of bishops to be guardians of the faith follows on from their calling to feed the faithful. Sheep need a supply of appropriate physical food otherwise they starve and ultimately die, and it is the shepherd's responsibility to see that they get this food. Similarly, human beings need a supply of appropriate spiritual food or else they will starve spiritually in this world and die eternally in the world to come. The food that they need is the Christian faith and the role of the bishops as a guardian of the faith is to ensure that this supply of spiritual food is protected against those who want to do away with it or contaminate it.

This, of course, raises the question of what is meant by 'the Christian faith.' As we have already seen during this study, what is meant is the message taught by Jesus to the apostles, and then by the apostles to the Church. [952]

'The faith' in the New Testament
A significant feature of the New Testament writings, which is often overlooked, is the way that they presuppose the existence of a corpus of authoritative teaching which has been handed down to the faithful and which they are expected to believe and uphold.

We can see this idea in the letters of Paul in a variety of places. For example, in Romans 6:17 he refers to 'the standard of teaching to which you were committed', in Colossians 2:7 he exhorts the Colossians to be 'established in the faith as you have been taught it', in 2 Thessalonians 2:15 he tells the Thessalonians to 'stand firm and hold to the traditions which you were taught by us, either by word of mouth or by letter' and in Titus 1:9 he lays down that a bishop 'must

---

[952] The paragraphs that follow are an adaptation of part of Martin Davie and Paul Fiddes, 'How do we know what the faith is?' in Paul Fiddes (ed), *Sharing the Faith at the Boundaries of Unity* (Oxford: Regents Park College:2015), pp. 8-14.

hold fast to the sure word as taught, so that he may be able to give instruction in sound doctrine and also confute those who contradict it.'

The same idea is also put forward by a range of other New Testament writers. Thus in Hebrews 10:23 the writer to the Hebrews refers to 'the confession of our faith' to which he wants his readers to hold fast without wavering, in 1 Peter 1:25 Peter talks about 'the good news which was preached to you,' in Jude 3 and 20 Jude refers to 'the faith once delivered to the saints' and 'your most holy faith' and in 1 John 2:24 John's readers are exhorted 'let what you have heard from the beginning abide in you.'

If we ask where this authoritative teaching came from, the answer that the New Testament gives us is that it was given to the Church by the Apostles and those associated with them such as the Lord's brothers James and Jude. This is made clear by Luke in his two part account of the origins of Christianity in Luke and Acts. In Luke's Gospel and at the start of the first chapter of Acts Jesus instructs the Apostles and from then onwards it is the Apostles and those associated with them who give instruction to those who subsequently become Christians. It is this 'teaching of the Apostles' (Acts 2:42) that is the standard of faith for the Church. Although Paul was not part of the original group of Apostles he is commissioned as an additional Apostle by the risen Christ himself (Acts 9:1-31) and his teaching is in line with the teaching of the other Apostles.

This last point is also made by Paul himself in the opening chapters of Galatians. He emphasises his own independent commissioning as an a Apostle ('Paul an apostle – not from men nor through man, but through Jesus Christ and God the Father, who raised him from the dead' Galatians (1:1), but he also notes that what he preached as an Apostle was 'the faith he once tried to destroy', the faith that was believed by the Church in its earliest days (Galatians 1:23) and that it was recognised by the leaders of the Church in Jerusalem that he had been appointed to preach to the Gentiles the same gospel that they had been appointed to preach to the Jews (Galatians 2:6-10). His subsequent argument with Peter was not because he and Peter had a different understanding of what the gospel was but because St Peter was unwilling to behave in a way that was consistent with the gospel (Galatians 2:11-21). There were not two different gospels, a Pauline gospel and a Petrine one, but a single agreed gospel, which St Peter had failed to live out adequately.

It is these sort of New Testament passages that are in mind when subsequent Christian theologians have referred to 'the faith.' This term has been used as a shorthand for 'the apostolic faith' or 'the faith of the Church,' the multifaceted gospel that we looked at in chapter 7, that was first handed down by the Apostles and that has been taught, believed and confessed by orthodox Christians ever since.

'The faith' in the Canons

When the question is asked 'how do we know what the faith is?', what is being asked is how we know the content of this body of agreed belief handed down in the Church from its earliest days. In the Church of England the answer to this question is given in Canons A5 and C15.

In order to understand the answers given in these Canons it is necessary first of all to discuss the relationship between 'the faith' and 'doctrine'. The Greek word *didache* (teaching) used by Paul in Romans 6:17 was translated in Latin as *doctrina* and from there into English as 'doctrine'. Thus the Authorised Version of Romans 6:17 talks about 'that form of doctrine' to which the Romans were committed. This linguistic development meant that the term doctrine came to be used in English to refer to the understanding of the Apostolic teaching held by the Christian Church as a whole or by particular churches.

It is this meaning of the term doctrine that underlies what is said in Canon A5 When it talks about 'doctrine' this is shorthand for the understanding apostolic faith held by the Church of England and means the same as 'the faith' in Canon C15.

Canon A5 declares:

The doctrine of the Church of England is grounded in the Holy Scriptures, and in such teaching of the Fathers and Councils of the Church as are agreeable to the said Scriptures.

In particular such doctrine is to be found in the Thirty-nine Articles of Religion, the Book of Common Prayer, and the Ordinal. [953]

Canon C 15 states that the Church of England:

...professes the faith uniquely revealed in the Holy Scriptures and set forth in the catholic creeds, which faith the church is called upon to proclaim afresh in each generation. Led by the Holy Spirit, it has born witness to Christian truth in its historic formularies, the Thirty-nine Articles of Religion, the Book of Common Prayer and the Ordering of Bishops, Priests and Deacons. [954]

What we find in these two Canons is a threefold answer to the question of we know what 'the faith' is. They tell us that we know what the faith is through the Scriptures, the teaching of the Patristic period and the witness of the Church of England's three historic formularies. However, these three sources of our knowledge of the faith do not possess the same authority. The primary authority is the Holy Scriptures, the secondary authority is the teaching of the patristic period and tertiary authority is the witness of the historic formularies.

The Scriptures
Both Canon A5 and Canon C15 see the Holy Scriptures as primary place in which we gain knowledge of the faith. Although these Canons themselves do not say so, when they are seen in the context of other Church of England statements such as Article VI of the *Thirty-Nine Articles* it is clear that what they are talking about is the Scriptures of the Old and New Testaments, the thirty-nine books of the Old Testament and the twenty-seven books of the New.

---

[953] *The Canons of the Church of England*, Canon A.5.
[954] *The Canons of the Church of England*, Canon C.15.

To understand why the Church of England sees these books as primary, the point we have to grasp is that although the Apostolic witness was originally give orally, as in Peter's sermon on the Day of Pentecost (Acts 2:14-36) or Paul's speech before the Areopagus in Athens (Acts 17:22-31), the teaching of the Apostles and those associated with also came to be set down in writings which were intended to convey through the written word the same faith that had originally been proclaimed through the spoken word. In Galatians, for example, the gospel that Paul is seeking to expound through his letter is exactly the same one which he has previously preached to the Galatians and which he fears they are deserting.

As N T Wright notes, 'those who read these writings discovered, from very early on, that the books themselves carried the same power, the same authority in action, that had characterized the initial preaching of the word.'[955] Because the authority that had characterized the initial preaching of the word was a result of the work of the Holy Spirit given to the Apostles in accordance with Jesus' promise (Acts 1:8) the Early Church drew the conclusion that the fact that these books possessed the same authority as that possessed by the Apostles themselves meant that these books were inspired by the same Holy Spirit in order to preserve the apostolic teaching in permanent form in the Church. The canonisation of the New Testament books that gradually took place over the first four centuries was thus an act of acknowledgement, an acknowledgement that in this particular set of books the apostolic preaching and therefore the apostolic faith was recorded for posterity in a form inspired by God himself. '[956]

In the face of the arguments of those such as Marcion who held that these books (or in his case some edited form of them) were sufficient on their own the Early Church also acknowledged that these books had to be read alongside the books of the Old Testament. This was because the Apostles and the New Testament writings consistently

---

[955] N T Wright, *Scripture and the Authority of God* (London: SPCK, 2006), p.38.
[956] For the idea of canonization as an act of acknowledgement, see John Webster, *Holy Scripture* (Cambridge: CUP, 2009), pp.52-67.

taught that the Christian faith had to be understood against the background of the New Testament, because the story of the life, death, resurrection and ascension of Jesus was the story of how the God of the Old Testament had fulfilled his promises by sending his Son to free the world from sin and death so that God's people might share life with him for ever (for this see, for instance, Luke 1:67-79, Acts 2:14-36, Romans 1-8) and because the basic moral law set out in the Old Testament was still binding on Christian believers (Matthew 5:17-20, Romans 3:31, 1 Corinthians 6:9-11).

The Early Church therefore maintained a dual canon consisting of the books of both the Old and New Testaments, understood according to a scheme of promise and fulfilment, as the basis for its understanding of the faith and the Church of England has continued to do the same, and for the same reasons, as we saw when we looked at the issue of the law binding on bishops in chapter 12.

The writings of the Patristic period
The reason that the Church of England has seen the writings of the Patristic period as being the secondary source of our knowledge of the faith is because it has believed that patristic theologians such Irenaeus, Athanasius and Augustine, the great orthodox councils of the Patristic period such as the Councils of Nicaea, Second Constantinople and Chalcedon, and the three Catholic creeds that emerged out of the Patristic period, the Apostles, Nicene and Athanasian Creeds, teach us how to understand properly the faith contained in the Scriptures. They teach us, for example, that in order to understand the faith correctly we have to understand that the God of the Old and the New Testament is one and the same, that God is Father, Son and Holy Spirit, that Jesus is both truly human and truly divine and that salvation is a result of divine grace and not human effort.

The reason that the authority of the Patristic writings is secondary is because whereas the Scriptures, being inspired by God, have intrinsic authority, the Patristic writings have derived authority in the sense that their authority is dependent on their bearing faithful witness to the Apostolic faith as this is taught in the Scriptures. They are authoritative precisely because they point us beyond themselves to the witness of Scripture. That is why it is specified in Canon A5 that it is only those Fathers and Councils that are 'agreeable to the said Scriptures' that are authoritative for the church of England's understanding of the faith.

The historic formularies

The three historic formularies of the Church of England, the *Thirty-Nine Articles* of *the Book of Common Prayer* and the 1662 Ordinal were produced during the sixteenth and seventeenth centuries in order to give theological and liturgical expression to the faith contained in the Scriptures, and witnessed to by the writings of the Patristic period. The reason the Church of England views them as having authority as source for its knowledge of the faith is that it judges that they fulfil this objective.

Thus, Articles I and II of the *Thirty-Nine Articles* witness to the Biblical and Patristic teaching concerning the Trinity and the Incarnation, the general confession at Morning and Evening Prayer in the *Book of Common Prayer* reflects the Biblical and Patristic testimony to universal human sinfulness, and the service for the Ordering of Priests in the *Ordinal* reflects what the Bible and the Patristic writings have to say about the nature of priestly ministry.

The historic formularies bear a tertiary witness to the Apostolic faith in the sense that they are dependent on the Scriptures as read in the light of the Patristic writings. Like the Patristic writings they have derivative rather than an intrinsic authority, but in their case it is a double derivation.

Building on these foundations

If these three sources are where the faith is to be found, what this means in terms of bishops being guardians of the faith is that bishops must do three main things. First, they must constantly remind those for whom they have pastoral responsibility, and the Church of England as a whole, that these are the three primary sources to which people should turn first of all if they want to find spiritual food themselves or provide spiritual food to others. Secondly, they must ensure that they use what is taught in these three sources as the primary basis for their own teaching and practice. Thirdly, they must do whatever they can to ensure that ministers over whom they have jurisdiction also use what is taught in these three sources as the primary basis for their own teaching and practice.

Theological explorers?

As we saw in chapter 12, in the twentieth and twenty-first centuries the Church of England has adopted the idea that bishops should be 'theological explorers.' In *Becoming a Bishop* Avis suggests that there is an 'ambiguity' about how it is possible for a bishop to be both a guardian of the faith and a theological explorer. This is because:

...a bishop is ordained to teach the faith in a relevant way, to make judgments on the application of Scripture and tradition to topical issues, and to enter into dialogue with those of different beliefs or none. The openness of the quest for truth and the negotiation that arise from dialogue are inevitably in tension with the bishop's office as the guardian of doctrine and teacher of the faith. [957]

The problem with this argument is that it fails to recognise the point stressed by Lesslie Newbigin that all thinking starts from somewhere:

No coherent thought is possible without taking some things as given. It is not difficult to show, in respect of every branch of knowledge as it is taught in schools and colleges, that there are things taken for granted and not questioned, things which could be questioned. No coherent thought is possible without presuppositions. What is required for honest thinking is that one should be as honest as possible about what these presuppositions are. The presupposition of all valid and coherent Christian thinking is that God has acted to reveal and effect his purpose for the world in a manner made known in the Bible.[958]

---

[957] Avis, *Becoming a Bishop*, p.130.
[958] Lesslie Newbigin, *The Gospel in a Pluralist Society* (London: SPCK, 1999), p.8.

If we accept Newbigin's argument, it follows that there is nothing at all difficult with the idea that a bishop will engage in a quest for further understanding, or engage in dialogue with those who are not Christians, with the faith revealed in Scripture, and witnessed to by the Patristic writings and the historic Anglican formularies, as their presupposition.

Everyone starts from somewhere in their quest for a deeper understanding of truth and it is right that bishops start from a position of upholding the truth of the faith of which they are the guardians. To use the famous words of Anselm in his work the *Proslogion* it makes perfect sense for a bishop to work on the basis of the axiom *Credo ut intelligam*, 'I believe so that I may understand.'[959]

As the House of Bishops' 1986 statement *The Nature of Christian Belief* rightly says:

A bishop may properly enter into questionings on matters of belief, both because as a man of integrity he will feel any force that is in such questionings, and also because as a leader part of his responsibility on behalf of the Church is to listen honestly to criticisms of its faith and life. but in all he says he must take care not to present variant beliefs as if they were the faith of the Church; and he must always make as sure as he can that his hearers understand what that faith is and the reasons for it.[960]

In other words, bishops should seek to understand contemporary criticisms of the faith and help others to understand them as well, as for instance Augustine did in the fifth century,[961] but this does not mean that in so doing they should suspend their commitment to the faith of which they are the guardians, or that they should cease to

---

[959] Anselm, *Proslogion*, 1, in *Anselm of Canterbury – The Major Works* (Oxford: OUP, 1998), p.87.

[960] The House of Bishops, *The Nature of Christian Belief* (London: Church House Publishing, 1986) p.36.

[961] See, for example, Augustine, *City of God* (Harmondsworth: Penguin, 1972).

make clear what elements of contemporary thought, both inside and outside the Church are to be rejected as contrary to that faith.

c. They need to teach and preach

To feed the sheep with wholesome food (or, to vary the metaphor, to give the medicine of the gospel to those who are sick) bishops need to teach and preach. In the words of Paul in 2 Timothy 4:2 they are to: 'preach the word, be urgent in season and out of season, convince, rebuke, and exhort, be unfailing in patience and in teaching.'

In the modern Church of England taking the importance of teaching and preaching seriously is often seen as the hallmark of the Evangelical wing of the Church, whereas as those in the Catholic Anglican tradition have a greater emphasis on worship on the sacraments. However, this idea that one can rightly be focussed on sacramental ministry at the expense of preaching and teaching is something that the bishops of the early Church would have found completely baffling.

In the words of Christopher Beeley:

It is extremely significant- for all the churches – that the major theologians of the early church devote their reflections on pastoral leadership almost entirely to the ministry of the word. On the one hand, Gregory Nazianzen, Ambrose, John Chrysostom and Gregory the Great each ministered in a full sacramental context. They stressed the importance of baptism as the beginning of the Christian life, and their worship each week centered on the Holy Eucharist and was supported by regular prayers of various sorts. Yet they all believed, without exception, that the main focus of pastoral work and the heart of church leadership was not 'ritual activity' *per se,* but the administration of God's word through preaching, teaching and pastoral counsel within the celebration of the mysteries of the Church. [962]

---

[962] Beeley, p. 106.

Following the example of these bishops of the early Church, bishops today need to see teaching and preaching, whether in person, in writing, or using electronic media, as being at the heart of what they are called to do. They cannot simply devolve the teaching task to the parochial clergy, or to a Canon theologian, or content themselves by drawing attention to other sources of teaching that are available. They are called to feed the sheep themselves.

Furthermore, episcopal teaching and preaching must have a definite content, and that content needs to be the faith of which the bishops are guardians. It is not sufficient for a bishop's teaching and preaching to be filled with the latest cultural, political, and social ideas, and to focus on vague moral exhortation. What it needs to be filled with instead is the proclamation of mighty acts of the Triune God in creation and redemption, and what God has revealed about how he wants his human creatures to live in response.

The necessity for teaching and preaching to have this sort of definite doctrinal and moral content is well set out by the first Anglican Bishop of Liverpool, J C Ryle. In an address given in Wigan in 1881, as part of his Primary Visitation of the Diocese, Ryle warns the clergy and lay-workers of his diocese that what he calls 'a dislike to distinct doctrine' is 'a widespread evil of our times'[963] and draws their attention to a class of Christian teachers who, he says, illustrate this evil:

Search their sermons and books, and you find plenty of excellent negatives, plenty of great swelling words about 'the fatherhood of God, and charity and light and courage and manliness and large-heartedness and wide views and free thought;' plenty of mere wind-bags, high- sounding abstract terms, such as, 'the true and the just and the beautiful and the high-souled and the genial and the liberal' and so forth. But alas, there is an utter absence of distinct, solid, positive doctrine. And if you look for a clear systematic account of the way of pardon and peace with God, of the right medicine for a burdened

---

[963] J. C Ryle, *Charges and Addresses* (Hope Mills: Heritage Bible Foundation, 2011), Kindle edition, loc.891.

conscience, and the true cure for a broken heart, of faith and assurance and justification and regeneration and sanctification, you look in vain. The words indeed you may sometimes find, but not the realities; the words in new and strange senses, fair and good looking outside, like rotten fruits; but like them, empty and worthless within. But one thing, I repeat, is abundantly clear: positive doctrinal statements are the abomination of a certain class of Christian teachers in this day.[964]

Ryle then goes on to explain to his audience the seriousness of this dislike of distinct doctrine:

Whether we like to allow it or not, it is an epidemic which is just now doing great harm, and specially among young people it creates, fosters and keeps up an immense amount of instability in religion. It produces what I must venture to call, if I may coin the phrase, a jelly-fish Christianity in the land: that is, a Christianity without bone, or muscle, or power. A jellyfish, as everyone knows who has been much by the seaside, is a pretty and graceful object when it floats in the sea, contracting and expanding like a little delicate transparent umbrella. Yet the same jelly-fish, when cast on the shore, is a mere helpless lump, without capacity for movement, self- defence, or self-preservation. Alas! it is a vivid type of much of the religion of this day, of which the leading principle is –'no dogma, no distinct tenets, no positive doctrine. 'We have hundreds of ministers, both inside and outside the Church of England, who seemed not to have a single bone in their body of divinity. They have no definite opinions; they belong to no school or party; they are so afraid of 'extreme views' that they have no views at all. We have thousands of sermons preached every year, which are without an edge, or a point, or a corner, smooth as ivory balls, awakening no sinner, and edifying no saint. We have legions of young men annually turned out from our universities, armed with a few scraps of second-hand philosophy, who think it is a mark of cleverness and intellect to have no decided opinions about

---

[964] Ryle, loc.891-900.

anything in religion coma and to be utterly unable to make up their minds as to what is Christian truth....They are sure and positive about nothing. [965]

The result of this kind of religion, he declares, is that:

...We have myriads of worshippers, respectable church-going people, who have no distinct and definite views about any point in theology. They cannot discern things that differ, any more than colour blind people can distinguish colours. They think everybody is right and nobody wrong, everything is true and nothing is false, all sermons are good and none are bad, every clergyman is sound and no clergyman unsound. They are 'tossed to and fro like children by every wind of doctrine;' [Ephesians 4:14] carried away by some new excitement and sensational movement; ever ready for new things, because they have no firm grasp on the old; and utterly unable to render a reason of the hope that is in them.' [1 Peter 3:15] All this, and much more of which I cannot now speak particularly, is the result of that unhappy *dread of distinct doctrine* which has been so strongly developed and has laid such hold on many churchmen in these latter days. [966]

The particular details of the kind of preaching which Ryle describes are characteristic of his day rather than ours, but the general warning he issues is as applicable today as it was in 1881. As anyone who knows the Church of England will be able to testify, there are still huge numbers of clergy, lay ministers, and ordinary lay members of the Church of England, who are without any decided doctrinal opinions and who are therefore easily taken in by any prevailing religious or cultural movement, even when the tenets of that movement are contrary to the tenets of the Christian faith as the Church of England has received it.

In order to address this problem, bishops have to do all they can to ensure that clergy and lay ministers are properly trained and that

---

[965] Ryle, loc.900-910.
[966] Ryle, loc. 919.

those appointed as ministers are willing and able to engage in teaching and preaching that has a clear doctrinal and moral content (a point to which we will return later in this chapter), but they also have to take every opportunity to model this kind of preaching and teaching themselves. People will only begin to really take it seriously if they see the bishops doing it first.

In order to model teaching and preaching that has a clear doctrinal and moral content in contrast to the 'jelly-fish' approach criticised by Ryle bishops arguably need to do four things.

They need draw people's attention to the fact that the Church of England has a clear doctrinal basis to which those licensed to minister in the Church of England must give their assent (see Canons A5, C 15 and E5).

They need to explain how the teaching of the Fathers, the Councils, the Creeds, and the Anglican formularies reflect the faith taught in the Bible, the 'gospel,' so that those who accept the Bible can and should accept the teaching given in these other sources of Anglican doctrine.

They need to explain (and model) how preaching on a particular passage of Scripture needs to involve not only drawing people's attention to the specific message the author of that passage was inspired by God to convey, but also showing how this message fits into the overall message about God and humanity's relation to God that is taught in the Bible and then reflected in the other sources of Anglican doctrine.

They need to explain (and model) how preaching needs to involve applying the teaching of a particular passage and the Christian faith in general to the issues facing a congregation at a particular time and place. To use Gregory the Great's physician analogy, the preacher is like a doctor who understands what ails his or her patients and prescribes the appropriate medicine.

This last point highlights why it is vital for the bishops to know their people, and their people's particular circumstances. Gregory the

Great's list of multiple spiritual conditions which require a different prescription may be seen as over precise, but it makes the point that the application of doctrine in preaching, teaching and pastoral care in general must be as specific as possible, and this involves the bishop as shepherd knowing his or her flock and their needs at any given time.

As we saw in chapter 7, feeding the flock means providing teaching that meets the specific spiritual needs of both young Christians, and also those who have been Christians for some time. Bishops as shepherds need to provide milk for those who are babes in Christ and solid food for those who are more mature and they can only do this effectively if they know those whom they are teaching.

Because we live in an age in which the Christian faith is now often challenged and doubted the call to feed the flock also means persuading the flock to accept the food that God offers. This means, as Avis writes, that a good-enough bishop will also need to be: '...a competent Christian apologist, able to offer in the public forum a convincing and attractive account of Christian belief, 'a defence...of the hope that is in [us] (1 Peter 3;15).' [967]

d.   They need to provide an example to the flock

As we saw in Chapter 7, in 1 Timothy 4:12 Paul tells Timothy as Bishop of Ephesus:

Let no one underrate you because you are young, but be an example to believers in speech, in behaviour, in love, in faith, purity.[968]

Kelly comments that this instruction to Timothy:

...is a truly Pauline touch; the Apostle expected the Christian leader to be a model to others (Philippians 3:7, 2 Thessalonians 3:9). Five spheres in which it is important that he should do this are mentioned. First **in speech** refers to his day-to-day conversation (his preaching

---

[967] Avis, *Becoming a Bishop*, p.23.
[968] Translation in Kelly, *The Pastoral Epistles*, p.97.

will be touched on later), and **in behaviour** to the general conduct of his life; both should presumably be marked by great propriety and Christian grace. The remaining three terms denote interior qualities which nevertheless colour a man's outward deportment - **love**, i.e. fraternal charity in the full sense; **faith,** by which is probably meant 'faithfulness' or 'fidelity' (cf. Romans 3:3; Galatians 5:22) and **purity** which covers not only chastity in matters of sex but also the innocence and integrity of heart which are donated by the related noun *hagnotes* in 2 Corinthians 6:6. [969]

There are two reasons why Timothy, and bishops today, need to provide this kind of example as pastors of their flocks.

First, their example provides a non-verbal form of teaching. By providing this kind of example bishops not only declare in their teaching, but also show in their lives, what it means to live rightly as a member of Christ's flock. In Pauls words in 2 Thessalonians 3:9, it provides 'an example to imitate.'

Secondly, to quote Matthew Henry's commentary, it is because 'Those who teach by their doctrine must teach by their life, else they pull down with one hand what they build up with the other.' [970] A bishop who does not provide a godly example will necessarily undermine the good that they do by their teaching and preaching.

As Beeley notes, in his work *On Christian Doctrine* Augustine provides a penetrating discussion of the importance of the Christian leader's manner of life which expands these two points. To quote Beeley:

He [Augustine] stresses that, beyond all skills, technique, and effort, what matters most is the pastor's manner of life, as Paul directs in 1 Timothy. Yet Augustine also knows that Paul rejoices in the proclamation of Christ even if it comes from selfish or ulterior motives (Philippians 1:18, 2:21) - that one can 'speak wisely and eloquently

[969] Kelly, p.104.
[970] David Winter (ed), *Matthew Henry's Commentary, Acts to Revelation* (London: Hodder and Stoughton, 1975), p.368.

while living a worthless kind of life,' and still provide some real instruction. After all, even Jesus tells his followers to do what the Pharisees say but not what they do (Matthew 23:3).

At the same time, Augustine is keen to note the consequences of unrighteous preaching. First of all, any work that is not based on the character of holiness is of no benefit to ministers themselves, so they are deluding themselves to think that they are gaining anything from it. Whatever true teaching may come from those who live falsely does not even belong to them, he says but is stolen from others who possess it truly. Secondly, Augustine reminds us that we can't fool all the people all the time. In the long run, 'people will not hear and obey someone who does not listen to himself.' Unrighteous ministers undermine the effectiveness of the word, cheapen the gospel, and eventually cause people to despise it. How many souls have been led away from the gospel, Augustine asks, by the destructive conduct of one of its ministers? Thirdly, character based leadership is more effective than empty words. For all these reasons we must, as Paul says, 'act well in the sight of God and other people' (2 Corinthians 8:21) because our manner of life is itself an eloquent sermon.[971]

The ancient requirement that the life of a bishop's household, or in modern terms a bishop's family life, should be exemplary is a particular form of the general requirement that a bishop's life should be capable of being an example to his or her flock.

As Thomas Oden comments on Paul's teaching on this topic in 1 Timothy 3:4-5:

To guide other souls on a hazardous journey, the leader [in this case the bishop] must guide his own family fairly and well (v.6) as a good parent and caring spouse. 'For the Church is, as it were, a small household' (Chrysostom...). The implication is that the role of parent will have been enacted sufficiently fairly to elicit the legitimate respect with the family and to have an intrinsic dignity recognised by his

---

[971] Beeley, pp.44-45 quoting Augustine, *On Christian Doctrine*, 4.27.29-28.61.

children (v.5). Suppose a potential leader had not yet learned how to care for spouse and children. Would that be reassuring evidence that such a person is ready to care ably for the family of God? guiding the community of faith is something like parenting an extended family. The church needs evidences of competency in primary human relationships among those to whom one is most constantly and fully accountable.[972]

e. They need to combat error and exercise discipline

Alongside positively teaching and preaching the truth by word and personal example in the way just described, it has also been accepted since the earliest days of the Church bishops need to combat error. In the words of the 1662 *Ordinal*, they are called to act with 'all faithful diligence' to 'banish and drive away all erroneous and strange doctrine contrary to God's word.' This is because if godly teaching and preaching is good food that keeps the sheep healthy, doctrinal error is food that makes the sheep spiritually sick by preventing them from knowing the truth about God and themselves and living in the light of it, and bishops as shepherds need to do all they can to get rid of it.

The Nature of Christian Belief suggests that bishops should discharge this responsibility in two ways.

First, it says: 'In general, and most significantly, by the teaching of the faith within worship, in the pastoral community, and in mission.' Secondly, 'What the bishop can and should do is to foster a continuing process of theological education for all ministers, clerical and lay, and to share and guide their reflection on these matters, including reflection on questionings and speculations.' [973]

More recently, in the book published in the *Living in Love and Faith* suite of resources the bishops explain the injunction of the Ordinal as meaning that:

---

[972] Thomas Oden, *First and Second Timothy and Titus* (Louisville: John Knox Press, 1989), p.142.
[973] *The Nature of Christian Belief,* p.37.

Bishops will, collectively, look at how deeply the pattern of teaching in the church as a whole is sending down roots into the Bible, how richly it is informed by the Christian tradition, how attentive it is to what we know of the natural world, and how seriously participants in it are engaging with their mission context and with one another's deep convictions. They will look at how well the church is encouraging, resourcing, and making use of those who do have formal and informal teaching roles. They will make judgements about how present teaching relates to the limits that earlier generations of the church have identified as necessary to protect the overall health of the Christian faith.[974]

Neither of these approaches do justice to what is called for in the *Ordinal*. The first confines combatting error with teaching and ministerial education, and the second simply involves the bishops looking at what is going on. Neither approach involves what the *Ordinal* calls for, which is bishops acting to as far as possible identify and remove doctrinal error from the life of the Church.

To act in the way called for by the *Ordinal* bishops need to do three things.

First, bishops need to keep themselves informed about the forms of doctrine that are currently prevalent, take time to understand them, and exercise discernment to determine which of them are erroneous.

Secondly, bishops need to explain why it is that certain forms of doctrine are erroneous. For example, in his *ad clerum* sent out as Bishop of Jerusalem which we looked at in chapter 7, James explains why it is a serious error to say that true faith can exist apart from the works that are its fruit:

What does it profit, my brethren, if a man says he has faith but has not works? Can his faith save him? If a brother or sister is ill-clad and in lack of daily food, and one of you says to them, 'Go in peace, be

---

[974] *Living in Love and Faith* (London: Church House Publishing), p.319.

warmed and filled,' without giving them the things needed for the body, what does it profit? So faith by itself, if it has no works, is dead.

But someone will say, 'You have faith and I have works.' Show me your faith apart from your works, and I by my works will show you my faith. You believe that God is one; you do well. Even the demons believe—and shudder. Do you want to be shown, you shallow man, that faith apart from works is barren? Was not Abraham our father justified by works, when he offered his son Isaac upon the altar? You see that faith was active along with his works, and faith was completed by works, 23 and the scripture was fulfilled which says, 'Abraham believed God, and it was reckoned to him as righteousness'; and he was called the friend of God. You see that a man is justified by works and not by faith alone. And in the same way was not also Rahab the harlot justified by works when she received the messengers and sent them out another way? For as the body apart from the spirit is dead, so faith apart from works is dead. (James 2:14-26)

For another example, in his homily 'A fruitful exhortation to the reading and knowledge of Holy Scripture' Thomas Cranmer explains why it is erroneous for people to say that 'they dare not read holy Scripture, lest through their ignorance, they should fall into any error.' Cranmer declares:

...ignorance of God's word is the cause of all error, as Christ himself affirmed to the Sadducees, saying, that *they erred, because they knew not the Scripture.* [Matthew 22:29] How should they then eschew error, that will still be ignorant? And how should they come out of ignorance, that will not read nor hear, that thing which should give them knowledge? He that now has the most knowledge, was at the first ignorant: yet he forbare not to read, for fear that he should fall into error; but he diligently read lest he should remain in ignorance, and through ignorance in error. And, if you will not know the truth of God (a thing most necessary for you), lest you fall into error, by the same reason that you may then lie still, and never go, lest if you go, you fall in the mire; nor eat any good meat, lest you take a surfeit, nor sow your corn, nor labour in your occupation, nor use your merchandise, for fear you lose your seed, your labour, your stock: and so, by that reason, it should be best for you to live idly, and never to take in hand, to do any manner of good thing, last peradventure some evil thing may chance thereof. [975]

Thirdly, bishops need to take whatever action they can to stop people spreading error, preferably by persuasion and leading them back to the truth, but if this does not work, through whatever kind of disciplinary action is available.

The need to take disciplinary action to combat erroneous ideas and teaching is only part of a bishop's wider responsibility to exercise ecclesiastical discipline which covers the actions of all who are 'unquiet, disobedient, criminous within his diocese.' [976] This responsibility has two aspects.

First, as part of his or her episcopal jurisdiction a bishop has the responsibility to discipline clergy and lay ministers who have erred in either faith or morals. This responsibility is laid down in Article XXVI of the *Thirty-Nine Articles* which declares:

...it appertaineth to the discipline of the Church, that inquiry be made of evil Ministers, and that they be accused by those who have knowledge of their offences; and finally being found guilty by just judgement be deposed.

In the words of Gerald Bray, the principle behind what is said here is that:

...there is no excuse for tolerating either moral laxity or doctrinal deviance in the Christian ministry. It may be true that God's grace is able to overcome the defects caused by such things, but we also have a responsibility to make sure that the preaching of the Gospel and its preachers are as pure as they can reasonably be expected to be.[977]

---

[975] *The Homilies*, p.8.
[976] *The Canons of the Church of England,* Canon C18.7.
[977] Gerald Bray, *The Faith We Confess* (London: Latimer Trust, 2009) p.248.

The legal tools bishops have to exercise clergy discipline are the *Clergy Discipline Measure*[978] and the *Ecclesiastical Jurisdiction Measure*[979] and bishops should be prepared to use them. It should be noted that the deposition from orders mentioned in Article XXVI is the highest penalty that can be inflicted not one that must be imposed for every category of offence. The judgement that has to be made is what penalty is appropriate for a particular offence.

Lay ministers are not covered by either the *Clergy Discipline Measure* or the *Ecclesiastical Jurisdiction Measure* but there is Canonical provision for a bishop to exercise discipline by revoking their license to minister.[980]

Secondly, in cases of extreme misconduct ('grave and open sin without repentance') the bishop has the responsibility to exercise the 'power of the keys' by excommunicating clergy or laity in sense of prohibiting them from receiving communion. This is laid down in Canon B.16 which provides for the bishop to have the final say on the matter after giving the alleged offender the opportunity for a personal interview. [981]

The power of excommunication granted by Canon B.16 is currently very rarely used, but that does not mean it should not be used.

As Stanley Hauerwas observes in his commentary on Matthew, paradoxical though it may seem at first sight:

...excommunication is a form of love. Excommunication is not to throw someone out of the church, but rather to help them to see that they have become stumbling block and are, therefore, already out of the

[978] *The Clergy Discipline Measure 2003* as amended at https://www.churchofengland.org/sites/default/files/2017-10/cdm-2003-as-amended-by-scdm-jan-2017-as-published_0.pdf
[979] *The Ecclesiastical Jurisdiction Measure 1963* at https://www.legislation.gov.uk/ukcm/1963/1/contents
[980] *The Canons of the Church of England*, Canon E.6.3, E8.5.
[981] *The Canons of the Church of England* Canon B.16:1-2.

church. Excommunication is a call to come home by undergoing the appropriate penance. [982]

However, because excommunication is a call to the sinner to come home the proper end of the process of excommunication is only achieved when the person who has undergone discipline is restored to full participation in the life of the Church. As P E Hughes comments on Paul's plea for the restoration of a penitent offender in 2 Corinthians 2:5-11, the primary end of all discipline within the Christian community is 'the reformation and therefore the restoration of the guilty person.' In consequence:

Discipline which is so inflexible as to leave no place for repentance and reconciliation has ceased to be truly Christian; for it is no less a scandal to cut off the penitent sinner from all hope of re-entry into the fellowship of the redeemed community than it is to permit flagrant wickedness to continue unpunished in the Body of Christ.[983]

In the words of Article XVI, we cannot 'deny the place of forgiveness to such as truly repent.' This means that there not only needs to be a process for excommunicating people, but also a process, known to the sinner, by which he or she may be restored.

As we have noted, it is the shepherd's job to recover the lost sheep and as we saw in chapter 8 this has traditionally been understood in terms of bishops having the responsibility of both binding and losing, of both excommunicating and restoring the penitent. Both are equally important and the good-enough bishop will do both.

f. They need to lead worship and preside over the celebration of the sacraments

As we have seen in this study, from the earliest times of which we have evidence bishops have led the worship of the Church and

---

[982] Stanley Hauerwas, *Matthew* (London: SCM,2006), p.165.
[983] P E Hughes, *The Second Epistle to the Corinthians* (Grand Rapids: Eerdmans, 1992), pp. 66-67.

presided at the celebration of the sacraments. As time went on, the growth of the Church led to the exercise of this responsibility being partially delegated to other members of the clergy in parish churches and elsewhere, but it is nonetheless a responsibility which bishops are still called to exercise.

In their exercise of this responsibility bishops, like all others leading worship in the Church of England, need to observe three key principles.

First, the form of worship needs to be in accord with what is legal in the Church of England, in line with the declaration made by all bishops at their consecration: 'I will use only the forms of service which are authorised or allowed by Canon.'[984] The form of worship should also respect local practice in so far as this would not conflict with that declaration.

Secondly, the language of worship needs to be accessible to those attending worship in line with the principle set out in Article XXIV:

It is a thing plainly repugnant to the word of God and the custom of the primitive Church, to have public prayer in the Church, or to minister the sacraments in a tongue not understanded of the people.

Thirdly, the content of worship needs to involve the reading and exposition of Scripture, a creedal affirmation of faith, the praise of God, the confession and absolution of sins, and intercessions.

If a service involves Baptism or Holy Communion these principles still apply. However, as part of their overall teaching responsibility bishops also have a responsibility to try to ensure that those in their diocese are properly instructed in the meaning and requirements of Baptism and Holy Communion as these are set out in normative fashion in the Catechism of the *Book of Common Prayer*.

---

[984] *The Canons of the Church of England,* Canon C.15, 1 & 3.

In the case of Baptism, the meaning and requirements are set out in question-and-answer form as follows:

Question. What is the outward visible sign or form in Baptism?

Answer. Water: wherein the person is baptized, In the Name of the Father, and of the Son, and of the Holy Ghost.

Question. What is the inward and spiritual grace?

Answer. A death unto sin, and a new birth unto righteousness: for being by nature born in sin, and the children of wrath, we are hereby made the children of grace.

Question. What is required of persons to be baptized?

Answer. Repentance, whereby they forsake sin: and faith, whereby they steadfastly believe the promises of God, made to them in that Sacrament.

Question. Why then are infants baptized, when by reason of their tender age they cannot perform them?

Answer. Because they promise them both by their sureties: which promise, when they come to age, themselves are bound to perform. [985]

In the case of Holy Communion, they are set out as follows:

Question. Why was the Sacrament of the Lord's Supper ordained?

Answer. For the continual remembrance of the sacrifice of the death of Christ, and of the benefits which we receive thereby.

Question. What is the outward part or sign of the Lord's Supper?

Answer. Bread and Wine, which the Lord hath commanded to be received.

Question. What is the inward part, or thing signified?

---

[985] A Catechism, *The Book of Common Prayer*

Answer. The Body and Blood of Christ, which are verily and indeed taken and received by the faithful in the Lord's Supper.

Question. What are the benefits whereof we are partakers thereby?

Answer. The strengthening and refreshing of our souls by the Body and Blood of Christ, as our bodies are by the Bread and Wine.

Question. What is required of them who come to the Lord's Supper?

Answer. To examine themselves, whether they repent them truly of their former sins, steadfastly purposing to lead a new life; have a lively faith in God's mercy through Christ, with a thankful remembrance of his death; and be in charity with all men. [986]

If people do not properly understand the meaning and requirements of the sacraments as set out in these questions-and-answers, not only will they not benefit from the sacraments in the way that God intends, but they will instead be the object of God's judgement as those who remain in a state of unbelief and consequent ungodliness (see 1 Corinthians 11:29-34). To avoid this pastoral disaster, bishops need to ensure that those called to do all that is humanly possible to ensure that such understanding exists.

In addition to their other responsibilities in relation to worship, bishops also have the unique responsibility of conducting services of confirmation. The principles for the form and content of confirmation services are the same as those for services of worship in general, but as with Baptism and Holy Communion the bishop needs to ensure that those being confirmed properly understand the purpose of the service.

In line with the teaching of New Testament passages such as Acts 8:14-17, 19:1-7, 2 Timothy 1:6-7 and Hebrews 6:2[987] and the historic teaching of the Christian Church as a whole, the Church of England

---

[986] A Catechism, *The Book of Common Prayer*
[987] For the interpretation of these passages see Theodore Wirgman. *The Doctrine of Confirmation* (London: Longman, Green and Co, 1902) and Frederick Chase, *Confirmation in the Apostolic Age* (London: Macmillan, 1909).

holds that confirmation is not simply, as is widely but mistakenly thought, an opportunity for those baptised as infants to 'ratify and confirm' for themselves the promises that were made on their behalf by their parents and godparents.

It is this, but it is also a rite additional to baptism in which by means of prayer and the laying on of hands by a bishop, those who have received new life in Christ through faith and baptism are given the gifts of the Spirit, and particularly the sevenfold gifts prophesied in Isaiah 11:2-3, to strengthen them as they live for God and engage in battle against the world, the flesh and the devil. This second understanding of the purpose of confirmation is made clear in the prayer said by the confirming bishop in the *Book of Common Prayer* confirmation service prior to the laying on of hands, which runs:

Almighty and ever living God, who hast vouchsafed to regenerate these thy servants by Water and the Holy Ghost, and hast given unto them forgiveness of all their sins: Strengthen them, we beseech thee, O Lord, with the Holy Ghost the Comforter, and daily increase in them thy manifold gifts of grace; the spirit of wisdom and understanding; the spirit of counsel and ghostly strength; the spirit of knowledge and true godliness; and fill them, O Lord, with the spirit of thy holy fear, now and for ever. Amen.[988]

Bishops need to ensure that those preparing candidates for confirmation make sure that the candidates understand the promises made by them, or on their behalf, at their baptism and are willing to personally ratify and confirm them, and that they understand and sincerely desire the strengthening gifts of the Spirit given at confirmation and purpose with God's assistance to live a godly life with the help of them. They also need to underline the importance of confirmation to the candidates and the wider congregation at the time of the service, challenging those who have not yet been confirmed to get confirmed, and those who have been confirmed to repent of their

---

[988] The Order of Confirmation, *The Book of Common Prayer*.

failures to live rightly in the light of that fact and to seek God's help to do better in future.

g.   They need to be leaders in mission

As we saw in chapter 11, in the twentieth and twenty-first centuries the Church of England has come to emphasise that bishops are to be leaders in mission. What is important to note is that this is not a separate category of activity from the other episcopal activities noted in this chapter. Being involved in mission means being involved in the activity of God in the world, what theologians have come to call the *missio dei*. Bishops do this as they act as pastors and physicians, guardians of the faith, teachers and preachers, provide examples of holy living, combat error, lead worship and preside over the celebration of the sacraments. In all these activities they take part in the work of God in the world.

As we noted in chapter 11, in the course of the twentieth century the Anglican Communion identified 'five marks of mission' which were then adopted by the Church of England. These marks of mission are what are seen as the five key aspects of Christian participation in the work of God in the world. They are:

1.   To proclaim the Good News of the Kingdom

2.   To teach, baptise and nurture new believers

3.   To respond to human need by loving service

4.   To transform unjust structures of society, to challenge violence of every kind and pursue peace and reconciliation

5.   To strive to safeguard the integrity of creation, and sustain and renew the life of the earth.[989]

---

[989] 'Marks of Mission' at https://www.anglicancommunion.org/mission/marks-of-mission.aspx For discussion of the Five Marks of Mission see Andrew Walls and

When bishops are said to be leaders of mission, what this means is that as part of their episcopal calling they are to engage in these activities themselves (thus leading by example) and to teach and support those in their flocks to do the same. Seen from this perspective, the question and answer in the 1662 *Ordinal*:

Will you shew yourself gentle, and be merciful for Christ's sake to poor and needy people, and to all strangers destitute of help? Answer. I will so shew myself by God's help

is a question and answer about whether a bishop is prepared to act as a leader in mission, taking part in this aspect of the work of God themselves and providing an example to others to do the same.

There are those who have difficulty with the five marks of mission because they can see how the first two are mandated by the great commission in Matthew 28:19-20 but are not sure what the biblical mandate is for the last three.

The answer to this difficulty is that marks 3-5 do have a biblical mandate. This is because the point of proclaiming the good news, and teaching, baptising and nurturing new believers, is not simply so that people have their sins forgiven, but so that they live in the way God created them to live, both in this world and in the world to come. And if we ask what it means to live in this way it involves showing love for God by showing love for our neighbours (hence marks 3 and 4) and for the rest of the created order (hence mark 5).

This point is well made in the 2010 House of Bishops report *Living thankfully before God: Living fairly before each other* from which the following paragraphs are taken in a slightly adapted form: [990]

Cathy Ross (eds), *Mission in the 21st Century: Exploring the Five Marks of Global Mission* (London: Darton, Longman and Todd, 2008).
[990] The House of Bishops, *Living thankfully before God: Living fairly before each other* (London: The Archbishops' Council, 2010), pp. 5-7.

The first two chapters of the book of Genesis set the stage for the rest of the biblical account of what it means to live rightly before God. They tell us that living out our vocation to show what God is like involves expressing our love for him by taking responsibility for the world that he has created. The created order as a whole, and not just the human part of it, has value in God's sight and human beings are called to share in God's care for it.

In Genesis 1:28 God tells the first human beings:

Be fruitful and multiply, and fill the earth and subdue; and have dominion over the fish of the sea and over the birds of the air and over every living thing that moves upon the earth.

This command gives human beings authority over rest of the created order and it also involves the right to use the resources provided by the natural world. As God goes on to say in the next verse 'I have given you every plant yielding seed that is upon the face of all the earth, and every tree with seed in its fruit; you shall have them for food.'

In our day many people have come to see this command in Genesis as lying at the root of the environmental problems that we face. This is because it can be (and has been) viewed as giving human beings the right to treat the rest of creation in any way they see fit. However, to view this God-given calling to exercise 'dominion' over creation as giving us a right to engage in unlimited exploitation of it for our own benefit is fundamentally to misrepresent what Genesis is saying. God's rule over creation is for the benefit of creation as a whole. 'The Lord is good to all and his compassion is over all that he has made' (Psalm 145:9). The same is meant to be true of the human vice-regency over creation exercised on his behalf.

As the second creation account in Genesis 2:15 tells us, human beings have the vocation to 'till and keep', that is to say to serve and preserve, the created order in the same way that someone might be given the task of taking care of a garden or a park and the animals living in it in order to enable them to flourish. This in turn means that while human beings have the right to make use of the rest of the created order in order to live, this should be done with appropriate restraint, in a way that recognises that the non-human creation has its own intrinsic value in the sight of God. That is why, for example, the Old Testament law sets limits to the way in which the people of Israel can use the natural order (see Exodus 20:10, Leviticus 25:7, Deuteronomy 25:4).

This is made clear by the way in which God creates human beings as male and female to be his image bearers (Genesis 1:27), by his command to them to be fruitful and multiply (Genesis 1:28) and by the story of the creation of Eve (Genesis 2:18-25). The human vocation to care for creation was not intended by God to be fulfilled by a single individual, but by a community of people. Just as God himself exists in an eternal communion of love as Father, Son and Holy Spirit, so also he has created his human image bearers to exist in relationships of mutual love for which the relationship between men and women is the basis and the paradigm. As a result we are called to express the reality of our love for God not simply by caring for the non-human creation but also by showing love to other people (see 1 John 4:20-21).

This is where the command to love our neighbour comes into the picture. God gives himself to be loved by us in the shape of other people and, as Jesus' story of the Good Samaritan (Luke 10:29-37) explains, our neighbour is that particular individual in whom God gives himself to be loved by us at any given moment. Furthermore, true love for our neighbour will be shaped by our awareness that our neighbour's highest good will be served by helping them to live in a way that is in accordance with God's will for them.

This means that there can be no conflict between the two commandments. We express love for God as we show love to our neighbour, and we show love for our neighbour as we act towards them in a way that enables them to fulfil God's good purposes for them. Loving someone means wanting what is best for them and what is best for all human beings is that they should flourish in the manner for which God created them.[991] This in turn means that just as love of God and love of neighbour necessarily belong together, so also do love of God, love of neighbour and care for the rest of creation. This is so for two reasons.

First, as we are coming increasingly to realise, human beings are dependent on the natural world for their existence and so when the creation is not cared for human beings are unable to flourish in the way that God intends.

Then, as has already been noted, love for neighbour means acting in a way that enables them to fulfil God's good purposes for them. Therefore, our dealings with them will need to reflect the fact that, like us, they too are people who are called by God to exercise responsible care for the whole of the world that God has created.

All this being the case, it is not only permissible but mandatory for the good-enough bishop to seek to fulfil the five marks of mission and to teach, exhort and support others to do the same.

h.   They need to promote unity in the Church

As we saw in chapter 11, in the twentieth and twenty first centuries the Church of England has emphasised the idea that the bishop is the 'focus of unity' in a diocese in the sense that as a bishop of the Catholic Church in historic succession he or she symbolises the unity of the local Church with the whole Church of Christ down the ages and across the world.

In addition, an unofficial understanding of the bishop as focus of unity has developed which stresses the role of the bishop as the person who is responsible for holding together the diversity of Anglican belief and

---

[991]'To respond to human need by loving service' and 'To transform unjust structures of society, to challenge violence of every kind and pursue peace and Reconciliation' are ways of helping human beings to flourish in the manner for which God created the. God did not create his human creatures to live in want, to suffer injustice and violence and to live unreconciled to each other. These are the results of the Fall.

practice within a diocese by being the focal figure to whom everyone looks regardless of their differences with each other.

The problem with the first of these approaches is that can reduce the bishop's role to a purely symbolic one. He or she is a focus of unity simply by reason of being a bishop regardless of what he or she does.

The problem with the second is that it can lead to a situation in which the bishop seeks to be all things to everyone, not expressing any specific opinions on divisive topics so that everyone will be willing to continue to be happy to accept their ministry.

Furthermore, neither of these approaches reflects the most important role of the bishop which is, as we saw in chapter 12 to exercise episcopal jurisdiction in such as way as to help God's people grow into the unity referred to by Paul in Ephesians 4:13, 'the unity of the faith and of the knowledge of the Son of God.'

To quote Thomas Scott again, the purpose of a bishop's ministry, like the purpose of other ministries given by God to the Church as the body of Christ, is:

...to nourish and mature that body till all believers were bought that unity of faith and agreement in doctrine; and that spiritual and experimental knowledge of the Son of God, in his person, glory and salvation, as issuing in love, confidence, obedience and conformity; which would render the whole 'a perfect man' complete in every member, sense and organ, and all grown up to maturity according to that measure of capacity, gifts, and grace, which Christ allotted to every individual, in order to the proportion of the stature of his mystical body, 'the fullness of him who filleth all in all.' That so the Church on earth might in each successive generation bear some proportion to the whole assembled company when perfected in number, in knowledge, holiness, union and felicity, in heaven. [992]

---

[992] Scott, vol III, on Ephesians 4:7-16.

It is this sort of unity that the bishop is called God to foster, and he or she cannot fulfil that calling simply by being a bishop in historic succession, or simply by being someone who people of all shades of opinion in a diocese are happy to relate to, but rather by engaging in the sort of active pastoral ministry described in this chapter, guarding the faith, teaching and preaching, setting an example of holy living, leading worship, presiding over the sacraments, confirming, combatting error, exercising discipline, and restoring the penitent.

The role of bishops within the Church of England, in the Anglican Communion, and in the ecumenical sphere must also be to foster the kind of unity described in Ephesians 4. What bishops must strive to achieve to the best of their ability is not simply a Church of England, or an Anglican Communion, or world-wide Church, that is structurally united and has bishops in historic succession, but one in which the kind of unity described by Paul becomes an ever-greater reality.

Only in this way will Christ's prayer in John 17:23 be fulfilled: 'that they may become perfectly one, so that the world may know that thou hast sent me and hast loved them even as thou hast loved me.'

i.   They need to ordain and appoint ministers

Bishops are the chief shepherds within their area of jurisdiction, but they are not the only shepherds. If the Church is to be the built up so it has the kind of unity described in Ephesians 4 the bishops will need the help of a whole range of assistant shepherds, suffragan bishops, priests, deacons, and lay ministers of various kinds.

It is the role of bishops, working with their fellow bishops and with others in the Church, to ensure that the right people are selected, trained, and appointed to fulfil these roles. In more specific terms, the 'right people' means those who understand and believe the Christian faith as the Church of England has received it, who have already shown themselves to be examples of godliness in their personal and family lives, and who indicate that they are willing and competent to teach and preach, to lead worship and preside at the sacraments, to correct error, to rebuke sin, and to restore the penitent.

There are two ways in which bishops can fail to fulfil this role properly.

One is when, for the sake of a quiet life, or simply to fill ministerial posts, bishops allow people who do not fulfil these criteria to be ordained, licensed and appointed to positions in the Church, or to continue in such positions. This matters because it means that portions of the flock will not be properly fed, or protected from harm, and those who have gone astray will not be reclaimed.

The other is when people who do fulfil these criteria, or who have the potential to do so with the right support, are turned down for selection, training, or appointment, because of their social or educational background, because they are disabled in some way, or because they come from a minority ethnic background. This matters because it involves bishops rejecting for no good reason those who have the potential to be good-enough shepherds and who may have a genuine call from God.

j.   They need to oversee the creation and maintenance of church buildings and churchyards

As we saw in chapter 12, the law of God, the law of nature and the law of the Church together make clear that Christians should both erect churches and keep them maintained so that they remain useable as place for worship and bases for mission.[993]

Furthermore, although there is no specific biblical command to do so, since at least the time of Abraham and Sarah (Genesis 25:9-10) God's people have reverently disposed of the dead in places set aside for that purpose. To do this shows due respect to the person whose mortal remains are disposed of in this way. Having churchyards and consecrated burial grounds[994] is a way of continuing this tradition and

---

[993] For the spiritual importance of maintaining church buildings see the homily 'For Repairing and Keeping Clean of Churches' in Robinson (ed.) *The Homilies*, pp.194-198

[994] A churchyard is around a church, whereas a burial ground is separate from it.

keeping them in good order is a sign of continuing respect to the dead buried in them and as such a witness to the watching world.

It has also been realised recently that churchyards can also provide a means for caring for God's world by providing a have for native flora and fauna.[995]

The Canonical role of the diocesan bishop relation to church buildings and churchyards involves 'granting a faculty or licence for all alterations, additions, removals, or repairs to the walls, fabric, ornaments, or furniture of the same' and 'consecrating new churches, churchyards, and burial grounds.'[996] The first is a way of ensuring that all repair and alterations are properly done in accordance with the laws of the Church and the state and the second is an appropriate symbolic way of dedicating new buildings and places of burial to the service of God.

It is important to note, however, that this should not be the limit of the bishop's role. He or she should be doing all that they can to encourage, support and helping facilitate the erection of new church buildings, the maintenance and development of existing ones and the maintenance and creation of church yards and burial grounds.

A good modern example of a bishop acting in this sort of way is the decision by the then Bishop of Rochester, Christopher Chavasse, to launch an appeal in the diocese in 1944 to raise £250,000 to rebuild bombed out churches and halls and build new churches in areas of new housing, and the way he subsequently worked hard to ensure that the money was raised, and that the rebuilding and building took place. Chavasse did not undertake the work of rebuilding and building himself, but his support and encouragement galvanised the diocese and made sure that it got done.

[995] For this last point see the website of Caring for God's Acre at
https://www.caringforgodsacre.org.uk/
[996] *The Canons of the Church of England,* Canon C.18:4.

k. They need to work with others, but also stand *contra mundum*

As we have seen during this study, a bishop is called to work in a collegial and communal manner. In other words, a bishop needs to work with other bishops and with other clergy and laity both through the formal structures of church government and in numerous more informal ways.

A good-enough bishop will welcome this calling, realising that he or she cannot do everything themselves and that they do not have a monopoly of knowledge, spiritual insight, or practical wisdom, and that they will therefore need the assistance and advice of others to fulfil the role to which God has called them.

On the other hand, a good-enough bishop will also understand two other things.

First, they cannot rightly devolve to others work that they should be doing themselves simply because they find it difficult or uninteresting. There must be a proper reason for devolving work to others.

Secondly, they cannot avoid their own individual responsibility before God. They cannot go along with decisions made by others, even if they have, for instance, majority support in the House of Bishops, the diocesan synod or the General Synod, if they have good reason to believe that they are unwise or contrary to the Christian faith. A good-enough bishop will not allow him or herself to simply become the puppet of others, but knowing their personal answerability to God, will do what is right even if this brings opposition and personal criticism from inside or outside the Church and will use their episcopal power of veto when this is necessary.

Like Athanasius in the fourth century, bishops should therefore work with others, but should also be prepared to stand *contra mundum*, against the world,[997] when occasion demands it. As Athanasius stood

---

[997] These were the words inscribed on Athanasius' tomb.

firm for Trinitarian truth in spite of being exiled five times and being the subject of numerous false allegations of personal misconduct, so a good-enough bishop must stand firm for truth today whatever the consequences.

1. They need to keep on top of administration

The bishop's role is not primarily that of administration. Nevertheless, there is inevitably a large amount of administration involved in being a bishop and a good-enough bishop will keep on top of it. This is because if he or she fails to do so, by, for instance, failing to read or answer correspondence, failing to make decisions within an appropriate time frame, failing to read or produce papers for meetings, or failing to delegate work efficiently, then things that need to happen will either not happen, or will happen more slowly than they should, and people will becoming will become increasingly frustrated (or even angry) with the bishop as a result.

If a bishop knows that he or she does not have a natural bent for administration, then they should be prepared to admit the fact and seek assistance from others to avoid or mitigate the problems this would otherwise cause. A bishop's staff will be able to help a bishop keep on top of administration, but he or she must be willing to let them do so.

3. What sort of people will make good-enough bishops?

Although it is impossible to say with absolute certainty whether someone will make a good-enough bishop, what it is possible to say is what sort of people are likely to make good-enough bishops based on the role description of a good-enough bishop given above.

- They will be committed followers of Jesus Christ.

- They will be baptised and confirmed.

- They will understand and whole-heartedly assent to the Christian faith as this is set out in the Scriptures and witnessed to by the Creeds and other Patristic writings and by the Church of England's historic formularies.

- They will be people whose personal and family lives model Christian holiness

- They will have shown their ability to undertake the various aspects of the bishop's role during an extensive period serving as deacons and priests. As stressed throughout this study, a bishop is a senior presbyter/priest with additional responsibilities and so the right test for how someone will be as a bishop is how they have been as a priest (the close overlap between the specifications for priests and those for bishops in the 1662 *Ordinal* underlines this point).

- They will have shown that they are prepared to work with others, but also prepared to stand firm against others for the sake of Christian truth when it Is necessary to do so.

- They will have shown that they can keep on top of administration.

The question is often raised as to whether a bishop needs to have a higher academic qualification in theology (M.Phil. or above). The answer to this question is 'no' because although a bishop needs to be intellectually qualified to teach and defend the faith in the Church and in the public square having a higher degree is not the only criteria for showing whether this is case. Furthermore, the specialist nature of higher degrees means that by themselves they do not show whether someone is a good overall teacher and advocate for the Christian faith. [998]

---

[998] It is perhaps worth noting that having a higher degrees as a mark of academic distinction is a very recent idea. C S Lewis, William Temple and Michael Ramsey were three of the great Anglican intellectuals of the twentieth century. None them studied for a higher degree. The same was also true of the great Swiss theologian Karl Barth.

The question is also raised as to whether bishops need management qualifications (such as MBAs). Again, the answer is 'no,' because it is perfectly possible for people to be capable of the bishop's role without having studied modern organisational theory and practice. The Church has its own criteria for successful leadership and it possible to know about these from a study of the Bible and the Christian tradition without having not rely on input from outside sources.

4. The Pastoral letter and directive from Bishop Love

The attached pastoral letter and directive from Bishop William Love, formerly a bishop in The Episcopal Church and now a bishop in ACNA, is included at the end of this chapter as a clear up-to-date example of what being a good-enough bishop means.

The occasion for the letter was the attempt by the authorities of The Episcopal Church to force Bishop Love to use General Convention resolution BO12 to force him to allow same-sex marriages to take place in the Diocese of Albany.

The letter shows what it means to be a good-enough bishop because in the letter Bishop Love shows that he understands what is involved in the office of bishop and carries out this office by teaching the truth about sex and marriage and countering the error of The Episcopal Church's demand on the basis of Scripture, the orthodox Christian tradition and the Anglican formularies. Like Athanasius, Bishop Love is also prepared to stand *contra mundum* himself and to call on others to the same.

Here is a good shepherd feeding his flock and protecting it against those who want to lead it astray.

A Pastoral Letter and Pastoral Directive
By the Rt. Rev. William H. Love
Bishop of Albany

November 10, 2018

To the People of God in the Diocese of Albany and throughout the World, I speak to you today both as your Brother in Christ, and as the Bishop, Chief Pastor and Ecclesiastical Authority of the Diocese of Albany. As Brothers and Sisters in Christ, Jesus commands us to love God first and foremost with all our heart, soul, mind and strength, and secondly, to love one another (Mark 12: 28-31), remembering as Paul points out in (I Corinthians 12:13), we are all part of the One Body of Christ. What impacts any one part or member of the Body, ultimately impacts the entire body, either directly or indirectly. That is true not only for individuals, but also for congregations, dioceses, provinces, the world wide Anglican Communion and the wider catholic or universal Church. Resolution B012 recently passed at the 79th General Convention of The Episcopal Church is one of those things that will impact all of us either directly or indirectly.

As members of the One Body, not only are we given different gifts, but we are entrusted with different ministries. In Paul's Letter to the Ephesians, he states that 'Christ Himself gave the apostles, the prophets, the evangelists, the pastors and teachers, to equip the people for works of service, so that the body of Christ may be built up until we all reach unity in the faith and in the knowledge of the Son of God.' (Ephesians 4:11-13 NIV). With every ministry comes certain responsibilities, all of which will ultimately be judged by Christ. As we prepare to talk about B012, I would like to focus for just a moment on the responsibilities the Lord has entrusted to me as a bishop in the Church.

As stated in the Examination of a Bishop in the Ordination Service in the Book of Common Prayer (BCP), I, as a bishop in God's holy Church, have been 'called to be one with the apostles in proclaiming Christ's resurrection and interpreting the Gospel, and to testify to Christ's sovereignty as Lord of lords and King of kings' (BCP 517). I have been 'called to guard the faith, unity, and discipline of the Church' (BCP 517). Along with my fellow bishops, I have been called to 'share in the leadership of the Church throughout the world, [whose] heritage is the faith of patriarchs, prophets, apostles, and martyrs, and those of every generation who have looked to God in hope' (BCP 517). I have been called to 'be faithful in prayer, and in the study of Holy Scripture, that [I] may have the mind of Christ...[to] boldly proclaim and interpret the Gospel of Christ, enlightening the minds and stirring up the conscience of [the] people [entrusted to my care]' (BCP 518). On three separate occasions (my ordinations as deacon, priest, and bishop) I have solemnly declared 'that I do believe the Holy Scriptures of the Old and New Testaments to be the Word of God, and to Contain all things necessary to salvation' (BCP 513). Upon my consecration as Bishop, I was given a Bible and was issued the following charge by the Presiding Bishop: 'Receive the Holy Scriptures. Feed the flock of Christ committed to your charge, guard and defend them in His truth, and be a faithful steward of his holy Word and Sacraments' (BCP 521). I take this charge very seriously. I share all of this with you in an effort to help you understand the charge and responsibilities that Christ has given to me as I attempt to carry out the ministry entrusted to me as the Bishop of Albany and deal with the various issues such as B012 confronting the Church, particularly as they pertain to this Diocese. By God's grace and the guidance and empowerment of the Holy Spirit, I have tried throughout my 12 years as Bishop of Albany, to be faithful and obedient to the Great Commandment, to God's Holy Word, and to my ordination vows and the responsibilities entrusted to me as outlined above.

With the passage of B012, the 79th General Convention of The Episcopal Church in effect is attempting to order me as a Bishop in God's holy Church, to compromise 'the faith that was once for all delivered to the saints' (Jude 3 ESV), and to turn my back on the vows I have made to God and His People, in order to accommodate The Episcopal Church's 'new' understanding of Christian marriage as no longer being 'a solemn and public covenant between a man and a woman in the presence of God' as proclaimed in the rubrics of the Book of Common Prayer (BCP 422), but now allowing for the marriage of same-sex couples. The 8th Resolve of B012 states: 'Resolved, That in dioceses where the bishop exercising ecclesiastical authority (or, where applicable, ecclesiastical supervision) holds a theological position that does not embrace marriage for same-sex couples, and there is a desire to use such rites by same-sex couples in a congregation or worshipping community, the bishop exercising ecclesiastical authority (or ecclesiastical supervision) SHALL invite, as necessary, another bishop of this Church to provide pastoral support to the couples, the Member of the Clergy involved and the congregation or worshipping community in order to fulfil the intention of this resolution that all couples have convenient and reasonable local congregational access to these rites;' (B012 Marriage Rites for the Whole Church).

When B012 was presented to the House of Bishops at the 79th General Convention, I both spoke and voted against it, sharing my concerns, all to no avail. A few weeks ago, I met with the Presiding Bishop, the Most Reverend Michael Curry, to once again share my concerns regarding B012 and the tremendous damage I believe it will cause not only in the Diocese of Albany, but throughout The Episcopal Church and wider Anglican Communion. I now share with each of you, those same concerns regarding B012, and why it is that I am issuing the Pastoral Directive which follows this Pastoral Letter.

First: B012's stated intent of making liturgies for same-sex marriages available for use in every Diocese and parish of the Episcopal Church (where civil law authorizes same-sex marriage) is in direct conflict and contradiction to God's intent for the sacrament of marriage as revealed through Holy Scripture. In so doing, B012 ignores God's Word regarding marriage and thus ignores the authority of Holy Scripture. When asked about marriage and divorce, Jesus stated, 'But from the beginning of creation, 'God made them male and female.' 'Therefore a man shall leave his father and mother and hold fast to his wife, and the two shall become one flesh.' What therefore God has joined together let not man separate' (Mark 10:6-9 ESV). As the 'Son of God,' God incarnate, God -- 'the Word became flesh' (John 1:14, NIV), it would stand to reason that Jesus would know God's purpose or intent

659

for marriage. Jesus could have allowed for, or made provision for, a wider interpretation of marriage (to include that between two men or two women), but He didn't. Despite what some would have you believe, homosexuality, or same-sex attractions (even that found in monogamous loving relationships) is not unique to our generation. It existed long before Jesus walked the face of the earth, as evidenced in a study of the Ancient Greco-Roman World. Yet from the very beginning of creation (as referenced above), marriage has been between a man and woman. The fact that some in today's sexually confused society (to include 5 of the 9 U.S. Supreme Court Justices in 2015) may have broadened their understanding of marriage to be more inclusive, allowing for same-sex marriages, doesn't mean that God, 'the Father Almighty, creator of heaven and earth' (BCP 96) has changed His mind or His purpose or intent for marriage as revealed in Holy Scripture which is the living Word of God.

Second: B012 turns upside down over 2000 years of Church teaching regarding the Sacrament of Holy Matrimony, and is in direct contradiction of The Episcopal Church's 'official teaching' on marriage as outlined in the rubrics and the opening preface of the marriage service in the Book of Common Prayer, as well as the Catechism (BCP 861). In the preface to the marriage service we read: 'Dearly beloved, we come together in the presence of God to witness and bless the joining together of this man and this woman in Holy Matrimony. The bond and covenant of marriage was established by God in creation.' (BCP 423). The rubric in the marriage service states: 'Christian marriage is a solemn and public covenant between a man and a woman in the presence of God.'(BCP 422). None of this was changed in the Book of Common Prayer at the 79th General Convention, therefore they remain in effect as the official teaching of the Church regarding marriage. The marriage canon of the Diocese of Albany, recognizes and upholds this traditional understanding of marriage, and as a result prohibits its clergy from officiating at or allowing any marriage to take place on any church property other than that between a man and woman. Thus, to carry out the dictates of B012 would be a direct violation of our own diocesan canons.

Third: B012 by its very intent of making liturgies available for same-sex marriages, (while perhaps well intended) is in fact doing a great disservice and injustice to our gay and lesbian Brothers and Sisters in Christ, by leading them to believe that God gives his blessing to the sharing of sexual intimacy within a same-sex relationship, when in fact He has reserved the gift of sexual intimacy for men and women within the confines of marriage between a man and woman as expressed in the above passage from Mark's Gospel.

Fourth: B012 through the actions mentioned above, encourages Brothers and Sisters in Christ who have same-sex attractions, to act on those attractions engaging in sexual behavior that God through Holy Scripture has not only NOT blessed, but has identified as sinful and forbidden. In Leviticus, in the midst of a long list of forbidden sexual acts, we read, 'The Lord said to Moses [and the Israelites]...Do not have sexual relations with a man as one does with a woman; that is detestable.' (Leviticus 18:1, 22). In Romans, Paul states, 'Therefore God gave them over in the sinful desires of their hearts to sexual impurity for the degrading of their bodies with one another. They exchanged the truth about God for a lie...Because of this God gave them over to shameful lusts. Even their women exchanged natural sexual relations for unnatural ones. In the same way the men also abandoned natural relations with women and were inflamed with lust for one another. Men committed shameful acts with other men, and received in themselves the due penalty for their error.' (Romans 1:24-25,26-27).

These are just two of numerous passages in both the Old and New Testament that speak to the issue of homosexual behavior as well as well as a variety of inappropriate or sinful heterosexual acts. For those who would argue that these passages don't apply to the 'loving, committed same-sex relationships' we are speaking of in today's modern Western Society, I would encourage you to read the excellent, well researched article written by the Rt. Rev. Grant LeMarquand (a Greek and New Testament scholar) entitled: 'Homosexuality: The Bible and the Anglican Crisis.' It is posted on the Diocese of Albany Website.

Fifth: B012 is contributing to false teaching in the Church regarding marriage and human sexuality, thus opening the door for people with same-sex attractions to fall into sin by disordering God's original design in creation, exchanging the complementary nature of the male and female body to 'become one in flesh,' with a distorted unnatural expression of sexual intimacy between people of the same sex. In so doing, not only does the same-sex couple come under God's judgement and condemnation, but it also brings God's judgement and condemnation against The Episcopal Church. Jesus said, Things that cause people to stumble are bound to come, but woe to anyone through whom they come. It would be better for them to be thrown into the sea with a millstone tied around their neck than to cause one of these little ones to stumble.' (Luke 17:1-2 NIV). Recent statistics show that The Episcopal Church is spiraling downward. I can't help but believe that God has removed His blessing from this Church. Unless something changes, The Episcopal Church is going to die.

Sixth: B012, as stated earlier, is attempting to force me and every other bishop in this Church to violate our ordination vows, particularly in regard to upholding the Holy Scriptures as the Word of God; interpreting the Gospel of Christ; being a faithful pastor to those entrusted to our care; and guarding the faith, unity and discipline of the Church. To follow the dictates of B012, would require that I ignore what God has revealed in Holy Scripture regarding His intent for marriage and to share a false teaching on marriage, thus preaching a false gospel which could lead the very people entrusted into my care to fall into sin – all of which will contribute to the destruction (rather than the guarding) of the faith, unity and discipline of the Church. There are many in the Diocese of Albany who have made it clear that they will not stand for such false teaching or actions and will leave – thus the blood bath and opening of the flood gates that have ravaged other dioceses will come to Albany if B012 is enacted in this Diocese.

Seventh: B012 places a major obstacle in my ability as Bishop, to 'share in the leadership of the Church throughout the world.' To date, the Diocese of Albany has upheld and honored everything asked of us by the wider Anglican Communion through the 1998 Lambeth Resolution 1.10, the Windsor Report of 2004, and the various requests of the Primates of the Anglican Communion shared through their numerous Communiques in recent years.

As a result of our faithfulness in upholding God's Word and honoring what has been asked of us, I am one of the very few Episcopal bishops and the Diocese of Albany is one of the very few dioceses of The Episcopal Church that are still welcome and in good relations with the other bishops and dioceses of the wider Anglican Communion, particularly in the Global South. The Diocese of Albany has a long standing history and has been richly blessed by our strong relationship with our fellow Brothers and Sisters in Christ throughout the Anglican Communion. B012, if implemented in this Diocese will destroy all of that. The open doors we currently enjoy throughout the Anglican Communion will be slammed shut.

There are some within the Church who believe that The Episcopal Church is being 'prophetic' in promoting same-sex marriage – that God is doing 'a new thing' in our generation, and that ultimately the rest of the Church will come to see that. In the mean time because this is seen as a justice issue for our Gay and Lesbian Brothers and Sisters in Christ, if necessary they are willing to walk away from others in the Communion who can't embrace this 'new thing' that they believe God is doing.

I would argue such beliefs are exactly what the Prophet Jeremiah was speaking of when he proclaimed: 'Thus says the Lord of hosts; Do not listen to the words of the prophets who prophesy to you filling you with vain hopes. They speak visions of their own minds, not from the mouth of the Lord. They say continually to those who despise the Word of the Lord, 'It shall be well with you'; and to everyone who stubbornly follows his own heart, they say, 'No disaster shall come upon you." (Jeremiah 23:16-17)

Or perhaps our generation is the one the Apostle Paul warned Timothy about when he stated: 'For the time is coming when people will not endure sound teaching, but having itching ears they will accumulate for themselves teachers to suit their own passions.' (II Timothy 4:3). B012 is a blatant attempt to silence theologically conservative and orthodox bishops in the Church. While I don't question the sincerity or the well intentions of many in the Episcopal Church who believe the best way to love and minister to our Gay and Lesbian Brothers and Sisters in Christ is to embrace them in their sexuality and make provisions for their same-sex attractions through same-sex marriage rites, I do believe they have been deceived into believing a lie that has been planted in the Church by the 'great deceiver' – Satan. In his letter to the Ephesians, Paul states: '...stand against the schemes of the devil. For we do not wrestle against flesh and blood, but against the rulers, against the authorities, against the cosmic powers over this present darkness, against the spiritual forces of evil in the heavenly places.' (Ephesians 6:11-13). The Episcopal Church and Western Society have been hijacked by the 'Gay Rights Agenda' which is very well organized, very strategic, very well financed, and very powerful. Satan is having a heyday bringing division into the Church over these issues and is trying to use the Church to hurt and destroy the very ones we love and care about by deceiving the leadership of the Church into creating ways for our gay and lesbian brothers and sister to embrace their sexual desires rather than to repent and seek God's love and healing grace. B012 plays right into this. As a lifelong Episcopalian and as a Bishop of this Church, I call upon my fellow bishops and the leadership of this Church to rethink the path we are currently on regarding same-sex marriages. It is not out of mean-spiritedness, hatred, bigotry, judgmentalism, or homophobia that I say this – but rather out of love – love for God and His Word; love for The Episcopal Church and wider Anglican Communion; love for each of you my Brothers and Sisters in Christ, especially love for those who are struggling with same-sex attractions.

In calling for The Episcopal Church to rethink and change its current teaching and practices regarding same-sex marriages, in NO way am I suggesting that we should return to the days of old where our gay and lesbian Brothers and Sisters in Christ were despised and treated shamefully; when they were branded as being worse sinners than everyone else; and when they were told or led to believe that God didn't love them and that they were not welcome in the Church. Such behavior is not of God and needs to be repented of.

While we need to resist the temptation to place ourselves in the judgement seat judging and condemning others, recognizing that we are all fallen sinners in need of God's love, and mercy and redeeming grace, we must also resist the temptation to bless and give permission to sexual behaviors that are in opposition to God's will and design as revealed through Holy Scripture as B012 would have us do. To do so, does an equal or greater injustice to our gay and lesbian Brothers and Sisters in Christ. When the woman caught in adultery was brought to Jesus, He didn't condemn her, as all those with stones in their hands had done, but neither did he bless her inappropriate sexual behavior. Jesus said, 'Woman...Neither do I condemn you; go, and from now on sin no more.' (John 8:11 ESV).

Jesus is calling the Church to follow His example. He is calling the Church to have the courage to speak His Truth in love about homosexual behavior – even though it isn't politically correct. Sexual relations between two men or two women was never part of God's plan and is a distortion of His design in creation and as such is to be avoided. To engage in sexual intimacy outside of marriage between a man and women, is against God's will and therefore sinful and needs to be repented of, NOT encouraged or told it is ok. The same is true for heterosexuals. To continue in such behavior, regardless of how much you may love the person is harmful to both your physical and spiritual health and wellbeing. Sometimes the greatest act of love we can share with a loved one is to say: 'NO! We love you, we are here for you and will help you in any way that we can, but we cannot give our blessing to a behavior that will ultimately hurt you.' The Lord is calling the Church to help our Brothers and Sisters in Christ who have same-sex attractions to come to understand that their 'identity' and value is not found in their sexual orientation, as they have been led to believe, but rather in their relationship with God, in and through Jesus Christ – the

One in whose 'image' they were created. (Genesis 1:27); the One who died for them, offering Himself as a sacrifice for their sins and the sins of the world. With that said, the Bible does not forbid two people of the same sex from loving one another in the sense of caring deeply or having a strong sense of affection for one another. Strong friendships are a blessing and gift. As already mentioned, God commands us to love one another both male and female. The Bible doesn't forbid two people of the same sex from sharing a home or life together. It doesn't forbid two people of the same sex from being legal guardians for one another or health care proxies for one another. All God has said through Holy Scripture regarding relations between two men or two women is that they should not enter into sexual relations with one another, and that marriage is reserved for the joining together of a man and woman.

While the state may have chosen to expand its definition of marriage to accommodate for some of the above legal benefits normally given to a husband and wife, it is not necessary for the Church to change its definition or understanding of the sacrament of Holy Matrimony to match the State's definition. It is time for the Church to stop functioning as an agent of the State in issuing marriage licenses.

I know I have said several things in this Pastoral Letter that some of the clergy and people of the Diocese of Albany and many in the wider Episcopal Church do not agree with. It has not been my intent to create conflict or divisions amongst us, but rather to share the message that I believe in all my heart God has given me share at this time in the life of the Church. Those of you, who know me, know that I have agonized over this letter and how best to address B012 in the Diocese of Albany and the wider Church. There has not been a single day since General Convention that I have not thought and prayed about B012. I give thanks to God for all of you here in the Diocese and throughout the world who have been holding me and the Diocese up in your prayers. It means more than I can ever express.

There is no doubt The Episcopal Church and now the Diocese of Albany are in the midst of a huge storm that can rip us apart if we are not careful. That is exactly what Satan wants. We don't have to play his game. If we focus on what divides us, we will be destroyed. If we focus on what unites us – our Lord Jesus Christ - He will get us through to the other side. I pray the Lord will help us to see one another as He sees us; to love one another as He loves us; to forgive one another as He forgives us.

I know there are people of good will on both sides of this issue, and that ultimately, we want the same thing – to know how best to show God's love, and minister to our Brothers and Sisters in Christ who have same-sex attractions. The problem is, we have a very different understanding of how to go about it. I know that for the majority at the 79th General Convention, B012 was seen as the way forward. However, as I have already alluded to, I believe B012 is misguided, heavily flawed and will ultimately do far more damage than good. As a result, I cannot in good conscience as a bishop in God's holy Church agree to what is being asked for in B012. While I respect the authority of General Convention as an institutional body, my ultimate loyalty as a bishop in God's holy Church is to God.

Therefore, for all the reasons mentioned in the above Pastoral Letter, in my capacity as Bishop Diocesan - pastor, teacher and overseer of the Clergy of the Diocese, and pursuant to Canons III.9.6 and IV.7 of the Constitution and Canons of The Episcopal Church, I hereby issue the following Pastoral Direction to all the clergy canonically resident, resident or licensed in the Episcopal Diocese of Albany:

Until further notice, the trial rites authorized by Resolution B012 of the 79th General Convention of the Episcopal Church shall not be used anywhere in the Diocese of Albany by diocesan clergy (canonically resident or licensed), and Diocesan Canon 16 shall be fully complied with by all diocesan clergy and parishes.

May God the Father, Son, and Holy Spirit guide and lead us as we go forth in His Name, attempting to discern and carry out His will. In all we say and do, may God be honored and glorified and His Church and people be blessed. Amen!

Faithfully Yours in Christ,
William Love
Bishop of Albany

Chapter 15
When someone is a not good-enough bishop

In the previous chapter we looked at why bishops will only ever be 'good-enough' and what it means for someone be a good-enough bishop. In this chapter we shall go on to look at what it means for someone to be a not good-enough bishop, or in other words someone who does not exercise their jurisdiction in a good-enough fashion.

We shall look in turn at three categories of bishop who are not good-enough:

- Those who sincerely desire to be a good-enough bishop but are simply not up to the job.

- Those who want to be a bishop because of the benefits it brings them, but who do not take seriously what being a bishop involves.

- Those who sincerely desire to be a good-enough bishop, but who use their role to propagate heretical beliefs and practices.

In this chapter we shall also consider what Christians should do when someone comes into one of these three categories.

1. Those who want to be good-enough bishops, but are not up to the job

It is possible to envisage someone who is a committed follower of Jesus Christ, who is baptised and confirmed, who has been consecrated as a bishop, who lives a holy life, who accepts orthodox Christian teaching, and who sincerely wishes to serve God and God's people as a bishop, and yet is not in fact a good-enough bishop. The reason for not being a good-enough bishop in this case would be some sort of incapacity that means that they are simply not up to the demands of the bishop's role in one or more respects.

This incapacity could take a variety of forms.

First, the bishop in question could sincerely accept orthodox Christian teaching in so far as they understand it, but that understanding could be relatively superficial, either because they lack the intellectual capacity for any deep understanding of the Christian faith, or because their theological education has been insufficient.

A bishop in this position could make the Declaration of Assent since it would be possible for them to believe 'in the faith which is revealed in the Holy Scriptures and set forth in the catholic creeds and to which the historic formularies of the Church of England bear witness' [999] even though their understanding of this belief was superficial.

However, the superficiality of their understanding would make it difficult, if not impossible, for them to act as an effective guardian of the faith, to teach or preach effectively, to combat error, or to be an effective apologist. This is because to do any of these things requires an understanding of the Christian faith that goes beyond the superficial. If someone is going to guard the faith, teach or preach it persuasively, or defend its truthfulness and relevance when these are called into question, then they need to have a deep rather than superficial understanding of what the Christian faith is, why it is truthful, and why it remains relevant today.

Secondly, they could have a deep understanding of the Christian faith, but a poor understanding of the contemporary world due to a lack of education or of interest.

This would create problems in terms of their capacity to teach and preach and to be a leader in mission. Effective teaching and preaching which will be of use to the flock of Christ today needs to not only expound the Christian faith, but also to show how it relates to the modern world. To use a traditional analogy, teaching and preaching needs to be like a sturdy bridge that is firmly grounded at both ends. It needs to be grounded at one end in the truths of the Christian faith and grounded at the other in the realities of the modern world. A

---

[999] *The Canons of the Church of England,* Canon C.15 1 (1).

bishop who does not understand the contemporary world will not be able to achieve this double grounding.

In addition, they will not be able to be an effective leader in mission because they will not understand what needs to be said or done to explain the Christian message to those outside the Church, and to show its relevance to the ethical, social, political, and environmental issues they are facing. Thus, they will not be able to commend the Christian message of salvation to people today in way that relates to their experiences, hopes, and fears unless they first understand them. Similarly, they will not be able to explain what the Christian faith has to say about the ethics of reproductive technology unless they understand reproductive technology, or to provide a Christian perspective on the political situation of the day unless they understand that situation.

Thirdly, they could have a lack of pastoral knowledge and experience that means they are unable to understand or empathise with the day-to-day problems and temptations facing the clergy and laity for whom they are responsible or know how the Christian message addresses these.

A bishop in this situation would be like a shepherd who was ignorant of how to tend sheep or a doctor who could not diagnose the ailments of their patients or know how these might be cured. A good-enough bishop needs to have not only theoretical theological knowledge but practical knowledge of the cure of souls, and if someone lacks this practical knowledge, they will be a not good-enough bishop.

Fourthly, they could have a deep understanding of both the Christian faith and the contemporary world and have practical knowledge of the cure of souls, but not be able to communicate effectively to either groups or individuals because of a lack of training or natural incapacity.

Without the ability of communicate effectively either orally or in writing a bishop will be unable to be effective as a teacher, a preacher, a leader in mission, or a physician of souls. To switch back to the image of a bishop as a shepherd, the shepherd will be unable to lead the sheep where they need to go if they cannot comprehend what the shepherd is saying.

Fifthly, they could be poor at leading worship.

Leading worship well is a skill which some people seem to possess naturally, and which others can learn, but it is also something that some people never seem to get the hang of. It is possible that a bishop could come into this latter category and if this was the case it would follow that they were not good-enough at what is a central part of a bishop's ministry.

Sixthly, they could be a poor judge of people.

One of the key aspects of the bishop's role, acknowledged from the Pastoral Epistles onwards, is ensuring that the right people are appointed to positions within the Church, or continue to hold such positions. The people involved will primarily be members of the clergy but will also include members of the laity. If a bishop is a poor judge of people, this can very well lead to unsuitable people being appointed to posts or remaining in post with the potential for lasting harm to the life and mission of the Church as a result. A bishop whose incapacity to make right judgements about people results in large amounts of such harm must therefore be regarded as a not good-enough bishop.

Seventhly, they could be bad at working with others.

Like communicating, or leading worship well, working well with others is a skill which some people seem to possess innately, and which others learn, but which some remain bad at. As we have seen in this study, bishops are called to work collegially with other bishops, and communally with other members of the clergy and with the laity. If they cannot do this well because they are bad at working with others, then this too can result in lasting harm to the life and mission of the Church since it can prevent the Church's processes for corporate decision-making and action operating effectively. For this reason, a bishop who is seriously bad at working with others must be viewed as a not good-enough bishop.

Eighthly, they could be bad at handling conflict.

There are two forms that this can take. On the one hand, a bishop can handle conflict in a way which causes serious and lasting damage to other people or to the bishop's pastoral relationship with them. On the other hand, a bishop can be so afraid of conflict that he or she is unwilling to act in a way which will lead to conflict, even when that action is necessary for Christian truth to be proclaimed or protected or for the work of the Church to go forward effectively. As the saying goes, they will do 'anything for a quiet life.' A bishop who habitually engages in either error can seriously harm the Church and the people within it and is thus a not good-enough bishop.

Ninthly, they could be unable to keep on top of administration.

As we saw in the previous chapter, although a bishop is not primarily an administrator, being a bishop does involve administration and if a bishop does not keep on top of it then there can be harmful consequences to the work and morale of the diocese. If a bishop simply cannot keep on top of the administration that needs to happen, even with the administrative assistance available to a bishop then in this regard he or she is a not good-enough bishop.

Tenthly, they could be incapable of getting the right balance between their primary diocesan commitment and work outside the diocese.

In addition to their diocesan responsibilities, bishops (both diocesan and suffragan) are expected to attend meetings (both national and international) outside their dioceses, to serve on committees and working parties, and to undertake specific areas of national episcopal responsibility, such as being the bishop for prisons or the bishop for healthcare. Those bishops who are in the House of Lords also have extra commitments related to this. All this extra-diocesan activity is a legitimate part of the bishop's role, but if a bishop gets the balance wrong it can leave them with insufficient time for their primary calling to act as shepherds within their primary area of jurisdiction. A bishop who is unable to get the balance right and ends up neglecting their diocesan work in consequence is a not good-enough bishop in this respect.

2. Those who want the benefits of being a bishop, but without the obligations

Because over the centuries the office of bishop has come to carry with it money, power and social prestige, there is a danger that it can be sought by those 'bad bishops' we saw referred to by Augustine in chapter 8. These bad bishops want the benefits of being a bishop, but who have no intention of fulfilling the obligation that the office brings with it to be a faithful shepherd to a part of God's flock and an example of holy living.

Scott highlights this danger in his commentary on the words of Jesus in John 10:1 about the thieves and robbers who enter into God's sheepfold but not through him. These words refer, he says, to those who:

...intrude into the pastoral office...abusing human appointments though good in themselves, and even divine institutions, to subserve their love of ease, wealth, authority, or reputation; and employing the influence of rich and powerful connexions, or that acquired by natural abilities and human learning, as a passport into stations in the church, for which they have not one correspondent disposition or qualification. Such men, like the thieves and robbers of our Lords time, are the thieves and robbers, who enter the fold in an unauthorised manner, to fleece or butcher, not to feed the flock; who rob Christ of his honour, and starve the souls of the people, in order to enrich themselves, and aggrandize their families.[1000]

Archbishop Lancelot Blackburne

The late medieval Popes mentioned at the beginning of the previous chapter are examples of the sort of people Scott has in mind, but the

---

[1000] Scott vol III, on John 10:1-5.

history of the Church of England also provides numerous examples of the same phenomenon. A particularly striking example is provided by the career of Lancelot Blackburne who was Bishop of Exeter from 1717-1724 and Archbishop of York from 1724-1743.

A good account of Blackburne is given by Fergus Butler-Gallie who writes as follows:

There are many leaders in history of the Church of England who were promoted due to their great holiness, the administrative skill or their inspirational leadership abilities. Lancelot Blackburne was not one of them. He is one of the most astonishing figures in the history of the church, beginning his career as a pirate in the Caribbean and ending it as the second most senior clergyman in the country. Blackburne went up to Christ Church in 1676 and five years later was made a Deacon by the Bishop of Oxford. It was at this point that he mysteriously decided to go to the West Indies, spending most of his time on Nevis, an island known to be the operating centre for piracy against Spanish and French galleons. Exactly what Blackburne did there is not known. However, by the end of 1681 he was being furnished with payments by the British crown for 'secret services' a poorly disguised seventeenth-century euphemism for privateering.

After three years in the Caribbean, clerical advancement beckoned. Blackburne returned to England, was ordained priest and took up a series of sinecures in the Diocese of Exeter, conveniently far from serious oversight in London. He rose quickly and, even though as a Canon at Exeter he was briefly suspended for employing builders to construct a tunnel in order to enjoy late night trysts with his neighbour's wife, eventually became Dean. There he might have remained were it not for the accession of George I. The womanising Hanoverian was on the lookout for a clergyman unscrupulous enough to marry him (bigamously) to his mistress. Blackburne was more than happy to do so, displaying remarkable pastoral flair when he counselled the incumbent queen: 'Madam I have been with your minister Walpole, and he tells me you are a wise woman, and do not mind your husband's having a mistress.'

Blackburne's reward was to be made Bishop of Exeter and then, in 1724, Archbishop of York, a job he miraculously managed to keep for the next nineteen years. He neglected his duties, stopping any ordinations after his first few years in the post and refusing to conduct confirmations after an incident in Nottingham parish church. (Blackburne began the service but, having swiftly become bored, sent his servant to fetch him his pipe, some tobacco and a pint of ale to help pass the time. Such was the Vicar's fury that he forced the Archbishop out of the church with the words, 'No Archbishop shall make a tippling houses of St Mary's so long as I am its Vicar.) He didn't set aside his interest in women after his archepiscopal appointment either. Horace Walpole recalled dining at Blackburne's London home in Downing St (the home of many a rogue since) with his wife, his mistress Mrs Conwys and Thomas, his illegitimate son by a third woman, whom, in a show of paternal affection, he had made his Chaplain.

His trips to York were rare, but not wasted; on one visit he employed Dick Turpin as his Butler and on another he was supposedly caught in what tabloid newspapers would now call 'a romp' involving among others a local milkmaid. It was said that, close to death, he mellowed somewhat, with the only remnant of his pirating past being his seraglio. Such were his carnal appetites that on his death a wit penned the lines, 'All the buxom damsels of the North,/Who knew his parts, lament their going forth.'

Other contemporaries were kinder, Walpole calling him 'a gentleman to the last...[although] a man of this world.' Perhaps the best summing up of his extraordinary figure was that of the satirist William Donaldson, who remarked that his behaviour was seldom of a standard to be expected of a cleric; and seldom of a standard to be expected of a pirate. [1001]

[1001] Fergus Butler-Gallie, *A Field Guide to the English Clergy* (London: Oneworld Publications, 2018), pp.41-43. The *Dictionary of National Biography* gives a more sanitised version of Blackburne's career, but Butler-Gallie's account is supported

What is clear from this account and the original sources on which it is based, is that Blackburne fits exactly Scott's description of those who wrongly intrude into the pastoral office, in this case the office of bishop. He was, in Augustine's terms a bad bishop, a man who does not seem to have had any sense of a genuine call to Christian ministry, regarding it simply as a way to provide himself with a comfortable living. He seems to have almost completely neglected his pastoral responsibilities and was unwilling to restrain his sexual activities so as to provide an example of holy living.

In biblical terms he was like the unfaithful steward described by Jesus in his parable recorded in Luke 12:21-48:

Peter said, 'Lord, are you telling this parable for us or for all?' And the Lord said, 'Who then is the faithful and wise steward, whom his master will set over his household, to give them their portion of food at the proper time? Blessed is that servant whom his master when he comes will find so doing. Truly, I say to you, he will set him over all his possessions. But if that servant says to himself, 'My master is delayed

by the eighteenth-century sources. In a letter written in 1780, for example, Horace Walpole writes as follows:
'I was much better acquainted with bishop Blackbourne. He lived within two doors of my father in Downing Street, and took much notice of me when I was near man. It is not to be ungrateful and asperse him, but to amuse you, if I give you some account of him from what I remember. He was perfectly a fine gentleman to the last, to eighty-four; his favourite author was Waller, whom he frequently quoted... I often dined with him, his mistress, Mrs. Conwys, sat at the head of the table, and Hayter, his natural son by another woman, and very like him, at the bottom, as chaplain: he was afterwards Bishop of London. I have heard, but do not affirm it, that Mrs. Blackbourne, before she died, complained of Mrs. Conwys being brought under the same roof. To his clergy he was, I have heard, very imperious. One story I recollect, which showed how much he was a man of this world: and which the Queen herself repeated to my father. On the King's last journey to Hanover, before Lady Yarmouth came over, the Archbishop being With her Majesty, said to her, "Madam, I have been with your minister Walpole, and he tells me that you are a wise woman, and do not mind your husband's having a mistress.' (Horace Walpole to David Dalrymple, December 11, 1780 in *The Letters of Horace Walpole*, vol.4, https://www.gutenberg.org/cache/epub/4919/pg4919.html

in coming,' and begins to beat the menservants and the maidservants, and to eat and drink and get drunk, the master of that servant will come on a day when he does not expect him and at an hour he does not know, and will punish[a] him, and put him with the unfaithful. And that servant who knew his master's will but did not make ready or act according to his will, shall receive a severe beating. But he who did not know, and did what deserved a beating, shall receive a light beating. Everyone to whom much is given, of him will much be required; and of him to whom men commit much they will demand the more.

As David Wenham notes in his commentary on the parables, this parable was addressed in the first instance to Peter and the other apostles, and it indicates what Jesus expects from the leaders of the Church (such as bishops). In Wenham's words, what the parable tells us is that:

...the faithful leader is one who (1) honours his master in his absence and is ready to give account to him at any time; (2) does so positively by feeding his fellow servants at the proper time - we are reminded of Paul's instructions on the pastors teaching responsibility to Timothy and Titus; (3) does so negatively by not exalting himself over his fellow servants or indulging himself. [1002]

Blackburne appears to have failed on all three counts and the same would be true of any other bishop who behaved in a similar fashion. They would simply not be a good-enough bishop.

The one redeeming feature of Blackburne is that he was at least what we might call an honest rogue. That is to say, he sees to have been quite open about his sexual misconduct and his use of the Church as means for his own personal benefit. He never appears to have claimed to be more pious and holy than he actually was.

[1002] David Wenham, *The Parables of Jesus* (London: Hodder and Stoughton, 1989), p.79.

Bishop Peter Ball

There is one thing worse than an honest rogue such as Blackburne and that that is a dishonest rogue. Bishops who come into this category are bad bishops who use the office of bishop for their own personal benefit and gratification, but who keep what they are doing concealed behind a veneer of dedication and holiness. Such bishops are the sort of wolves in sheep's clothing referred to by Christ in Matthew 7:15.

A recent and particularly shocking example of a Church of England bishop who falls into this category is the late Bishop Peter Ball, who was suffragan Bishop of Lewes from 1977-1992 and Bishop of Gloucester from 1992-1993. It was subsequently discovered that Ball had been sexually abusing young men during the whole of his time as a bishop and having received a Police caution for gross indecency in 1993 he was subsequently convicted in 2015 of two charges of indecent assault and an additional charge of misconduct in public office and sentenced to thirty-two months in prison.

What was particularly shocking about Ball's conduct is that he used a carefully cultivated reputation for personal holiness as the founder of the new monastic community of The Glorious Ascension, and the position he had as a bishop, to give him the opportunity to fulfil his desire to engage in sexual activity with young men.

As Bobbie Cheema QC, the prosecution counsel, said at Ball's trial:

[Ball] was highly regarded as a godly man who had a special affinity with young people. The truth was that he used those 15 years in the position of bishop to identify, groom and exploit sensitive and vulnerable young men who came within his orbit. For him, religion was a cloak behind which he hid in order to satisfy his sexual interest in those who trusted him.[1003]

Not only did Ball engage in sexual activity with the young men involved, but he explained what he was doing to them in terms of it

---

[1003] Sandra Laville, 'Former bishop admits sexually abusing young men,' *The Guardian,* 8 September 2015.

being a way in which they could draw nearer to God by becoming more like Jesus through the self-humiliation involved in activities such as becoming naked with Ball and submitting to flagellation. He thus not only misused his own position as a bishop by using it as an opportunity to engage in sexual abuse of young men, but what was worse, sought to convince them that this abusive activity was something willed by God, thus bearing false witness against God himself.

Ball's activities, were entirely contrary to the promises he made when was ordained, caused serious and lasting psychological damage to the young men involved (one of whom subsequently committed suicide), and did great damage to the reputation and hence the mission of the Church. On all these counts Ball is a prime example of a not good-enough bishop.[1004]

3. Those who desire to be good enough bishops but propagate heresy

As we have noted, the third category of not good-enough bishops consists of those bishops who, unlike those in the second category, sincerely desire to be good-enough bishops, but who propagate heresy in relation to Christian belief or Christian behaviour, heresy meaning teaching and practice which is contrary to the Christian faith as taught by the apostles and witnessed to by Scripture.

I have chosen five bishops to illustrate this category, two bishops from the Patristic period, two bishops from the Church of England in the twentieth century, and one bishop from the Anglican Church of Canada in the twenty-first century.

[1004] The independent report for the Church of England on the case of Bishop Peter Ball undertaken by Dame Moira Gibb, *An Abuse of Faith*, can be found at: https://gallery.mailchimp.com/50eac70851c7245ce1ce00c45/files/28fa6c7e-0bf4-476b-ba2d-81d2c85503c3/Report_of_the_Peter_Ball_Review_21.06.17.pdf The BBC documentary about Ball *'Exposed: The Church's Darkest Secret'* is available on You Tube.

Bishop Apollinarius of Laodicea

The first is Apollinarius, who was Bishop of Laodicea in the fourth century.

Prior to his lapse into heresy Apollinnarius was highly regarded as a scholar and a pillar of Nicene orthodoxy. During the reign of the pagan Emperor Julian (361-363) when Christians were forbidden to read or teach Greek or Latin classical texts, Apollinarius and his father, who was a schoolmaster, responded by paraphrasing the Old Testament in the form of the poetry of the classical poets Homer and Pindar and the New Testament in the fashion of the dialogues of Plato. Apollinarius also undertook a scholarly defence of Christianity again Julian and the Neo-Platonist philosopher Porphyry, wrote against the Arians and other heretics, and produced commentaries on many of the books of the Bible. He was a friend of both Athanasius and Basil of Caesarea the great champions of Nicene orthodoxy.

It therefore came as a great shock when it was realised from about 371 onwards that this venerable figure had fallen into heresy.

The issue which Apollinarius' heresy sought to address was how Christ could be both God and Man at the same time. In common with other pro-Nicene theologians, Apollinarius began with the presupposition that Christ was perfectly and completely divine. Like Athanasius, he held that only God could save the world, Christ was saviour, therefore Christ must be fully divine. The issue that followed from this affirmation was how to reconcile Christ's full divinity with his humanity. Where Apollinaris became heretical was in the way that he tried to achieve this reconciliation.

As Alan Richardson explains:

Apollinarius accepted St. Paul's familiar division of human personality into body, soul and spirit (1 Thessalonians 5:23]. Thus, for his psychology spirit is the rational, moral and spiritual faculty of man. his distinctively human element; soul is the physical life - the faculties which men and animals have in common. He then proceeded to say that in the personality of Christ there is no human spirit; for the place of spirit in Christ was taken by the Logos: Christ was thus Logos, soul and body. The Logos of God was, as it were, united to the body and soul of a man: the Scriptural text on which he chiefly relied was: 'The Word (Logos) was made flesh' (John 1:14). Thus, soul and body in Christ were governed by the divine Logos to which they were united: Christ had no human spirit, or mind, and was therefore completely sinless, sin has its seat in the higher human faculties. The Logos is, as it were, living a divine life in human flesh.[1005]

As Richardson goes on to explain, Apollinarius' Christology was 'not a satisfactory solution of the Christological problem.' This is because it did really hold:

...that the Logos became man. Spirit – the distinctively human part of man which is lacking in animals, our rational, moral and spiritual faculties – was not assumed by the Logos; and therefore Christ was not a man at all: the Logos has, as it were, assumed an animal soul and body; but it could not be said that in Christ Godhead and manhood were united, because that which distinguishes a man from the animals was not present in his personality at all. This theory, attractive at first sight involves the corollary that the historical Jesus was not human at all! The words of the Nicene Creed, 'and was made man,' become meaningless on the Apollinarian position. [1006]

Furthermore, just as much as Arianism, Apollinarius' theology undermined the gospel message of salvation. This is because a Jesus who was not truly human was a Jesus could not save. Salvation occurs because in Christ God took our humanity upon himself and fashioned it anew in an act of divine recreation. However, according to Apollinarius God in Christ did not take our whole humanity upon himself – the most important part was missing.

[1005] Alan Richardson, *Creeds in the Making* (London: SCM, 1982), p.72. For a more detailed account of Apollinarius' Christology see John Kelly, *Early Christian Doctrines*, pp. 290-295.
[1006] Richardson, pp.72-73.

Gregory Nazianzen makes this point in a famous passage from his letter to a priest called Cledonius:

If anyone has put his trust in Him [Christ] as a Man without a human mind, he is really bereft of mind, and quite unworthy of salvation. For that which He has not assumed He has not healed; but that which is united to His Godhead is also saved. If only half Adam fell, then that which Christ assumes and saves may be half also; but if the whole of his nature fell, it must be united to the whole nature of Him that was begotten, and so be saved as a whole. Let them not, then, begrudge us our complete salvation, or clothe the Saviour only with bones and nerves and the portraiture of humanity. For if His Manhood is without soul, even the Arians admit this, that they may attribute His Passion to the Godhead, as that which gives motion to the body is also that which suffers. But if He has a soul, and yet is without a mind, how is He man, for man is not a mindless animal? And this would necessarily involve that while His form and tabernacle was human, His soul should be that of a horse or an ox, or some other of the brute creation. This, then, would be what He saves; and I have been deceived by the Truth, and led to boast of an honour which had been bestowed upon another.[1007]

For these reasons Apollinarius was correctly judged to have fallen into heresy and he was condemned as a heretic at councils held in Rome in 377, in Alexandria in 378 and in Antioch in 379. Finally, and most decisively, his theology was anathematized alongside other heresies In Canon I of the Council of Constantinople, the second ecumenical council, in 381, and in 388 the followers of Apollinarius were forbidden to take part in the worship of the Church.

[1007] Gregory Nazianzen, 'To Cledonius the Priest against Apolinarius' (Ep.CI) in *The Nicene and Post Nicene Fathers*, 2nd series Vol, VII (Edinburgh and Grand Rapids: T&T Clark/Eerdmans, 1996), p. 440.

Patriarch Nestorius of Constantinople

Nestorius of Constantinople was a priest and a monk whose reputation as preacher led to his appointed as Patriarch of Constantinople in in 428.

In a sermon preached on Christmas morning 428, shortly after his arrival in Constantinople, Nestorius told the congregation, including many visiting clergy and members of the imperial court that it was wrong to use the traditional title *theotokos* ('God bearer' or 'Mother of God') to describe the Virgin Mary. This was because the divine nature cannot be born any more than it can die, and so while Mary could be the mother of Christ's human nature (and therefore be called *Christotokos*, 'Christ-bearer') she could not be the mother of his divine nature (and therefore *theotokos*).

This argument, which he reiterated in his circular letter at Easter in 429, was linked to Nestorius' wider understanding of the person of Christ, which he expressed in letters to his main theological opponent, Cyril, Patriarch of Alexandria. As Roger Olson explains:

Nestorius argued that the incarnation is a mutual indwelling of two persons- the eternal Son of God and the mortal human Jesus. To that union we assign the name Jesus Christ, or just Christ, and consider the union itself as a 'person' in the compound or corporate sense. Thus for Nestorius 'in Jesus Christ, God has united the divine *prosopon* [person} to a human nature – but this in no way destroys the two natural *prosopa* [persons], which correspond to each of the two 'complete natures' or *hypostases* which are united in Christ.' [1008]

For Nestorius, therefore, Jesus Christ was what he called a *synapheia* or conjunction between the divine Son of God with his divine nature, and the human person Jesus with his human nature. In this conjunction it was the Son of God who possessed divine power and

[1008] Roger Olson, *The Story of Christian Theology* (Leicester: Apollos, 1999), p.216. A summary of Nestorius' position in his own words can be found in in his letter to Pope Celestine in Edward Hardy (ed, *Christology of the Later Fathers* (Philadelphia: Westminster Press, 1954), pp. 346-348

therefore performed miracles, and the human Jesus who possessed human weakness and therefore suffered and died.

It appears from the witness of Cyril, that Nestorius used the analogy of a marriage to describe this conjunction. In Olson's words:

Nestorius apparently argued that just as two independent persons come together to form a union transcending their differences in marriage, so in the incarnation the Son of God and the Son of David formed a union (initiated by the son of God) that transcended their different natures. That union is a fellowship and cooperation of wills that is stronger than any human friendship or marriage. These can only provide a dim analogy for it.[1009]

Nestorius was eventually condemned as a heretic, deposed as a bishop, and excommunicated by the Council of Ephesus in 431, which declared:

We discovered that he had held and published impious doctrines in his letters and treatises, as well as in his discourses which he delivered in this city, and which have been testified to. Compelled thereto by the canons and by the letter of our most holy father and fellow-servant Celestine, the Roman bishop, we have come, with many tears, to this sorrowful sentence against him, namely, that our Lord Jesus Christ, whom he has blasphemed, decrees by the holy Synod that Nestorius be excluded from the episcopal dignity and from all priestly Communion. [1010]

This condemnation was a result of political manoeuvring by Cyril of Alexandria who made sure it was agreed before bishops supporting Nestorius arrived at the council. Nevertheless, the general judgement of the Church has been that the Council was right to reject Nestorius' Christology as heretical.

[1009] Olson, p.216.
[1010] Decree of the Council of Ephesus against Nestorius in *Nicene and Post Nicene Fathers*, vol. XIV, p.218.

To quote Olson again:

There is no doubt that Nestorius' intentions were sound. He wished to preserve the integrity of God's nature and human nature even in the incarnation by positing a 'union of natures.' He wanted also to do full justice to the humanity of Jesus Christ and not allow it to be swallowed up in the divinity or truncated or in any way made less than like ours. After all, Nestorius would argue, does not Scripture itself say that Jesus Christ 'increased in wisdom and in years, and in divine and human favour' (Luke 2:52 NRSV)? Yet it in spite of his laudable intentions - many of which were shared by more orthodox Christians- Nestorius could not account for the unity of Christ. In the end, in spite of his valiant attempt to explain how a conjunction of two persons could count as one person (*prosopon*), his Christ turns out to be two individuals and not one. The Son of God did not truly experience human existence 'in the flesh' but only 'through association with the man.' [1011]

The fundamental problem with Nestorius' two-person approach to Christology, and what made it heretical, was that it involved a rejection of the apostolic witness in the New Testament that it is the eternal Son of God who is the person who unites the two natures of Christ is made clear by the New Testament.

Throughout the New Testament there is one person described or referred to, never two, and if we ask who that person was, the answer is, as we have already indicated, that it was the eternal Word or Son of God who took human nature upon Himself at the incarnation (John 1:14). It was the one who was rich with the glory of heaven who became poor for our sake (2 Corinthians 8:9). It was the one who 'descended' from heaven to earth at the incarnation who ascended 'far above all the heavens' (Ephesians 4:9–10). It was the one who was eternally 'in the form of God' who 'emptied himself', took upon himself 'the form of a servant' and was 'born in the likeness of men' (Phil 2:7). It was the one who 'reflects the glory of God and bears the very stamp

[1011] Olson, pp.217-218.

of his nature, upholding the universe by his word of power' who partook of our nature for the sake of our salvation (Hebrews 1:3 and 2:14–18).

Furthermore, because it rejected this New Testament teaching, Nestorius' theology ultimately undermined the possibility of salvation just as much as Apollinarius' theology had done. Gregory of Nazianzen's axiom 'the unassumed is the unhealed' applies just as much to Nestorius' Christology as to that of Apollinarius. This is because for Nestorius the human nature of Christ was never assumed by the eternal Word but always remained separate from it, and so his humanity (and therefore ours) was never healed of sin and death.

Bishop Ernest Barnes

Moving on from the fourth to the twentieth century, Ernest Barnes was a mathematician, scientist and theologian who was Bishop of Birmingham from 1924 - 1952. During his period as a bishop, he attracted widespread controversy both because of his conflict with the Anglo-Catholics in his diocese (he attacked Anglo-Catholic ritual, and in 1929 he refused to install an Anglo-Catholic priest to a living in the diocese) and because of his uncompromisingly liberal approach to Christian theology. To use the terminology of the time, Barnes was a 'modernist,' someone who believed that traditional Christian thought need to be adapted in the light of scientific discovery and biblical criticism.

The book in which he gave clearest expression to his liberal views, and which provoked a great furore in consequence, was his book *The Rise of Christianity*, which was published in 1947.

As its title suggests, this book is concerned with the question of how Christianity came into being and developed thereafter.

The presupposition on which the book is based is that modern man now knows that miracles do not occur. In Barnes' words:

...modern man, with his thought shaped by scientific investigation, is certain that miracles, in the sense of finite-scale activities contrary to the normal ordering of nature, do not happen. Only figuratively can the blind receive their sight, or the lame be made to walk, or the lepers be cleansed, or the deaf be made to hear, or the dead be raised up.[1012]

In line with this presupposition Barnes contends that not only did Jesus himself not perform miracles, but that Jesus' virgin birth, resurrection, and ascension did not happen either.

With regard to the virgin birth, Barnes contends that the stories of the virgin birth in Matthew and Luke are simply one of five attempts to express the idea of Jesus as the Son of God, of which only the picture given in Mark is to be accepted:

We have now passed under rapid review five different attempts in the New Testament to present Jesus as son of God. That in the Apocalypse is fantastic; and the speculations of the writer of Hebrews are hardly less extravagant. The legend of the virgin birth proved widely popular: unfortunately, if analytical scholars are right, it depends upon dubious history. There remain the story preserved by Mark and the theory of the philosophical mystic who wrote the gospel according to John. In Mark we read of the Galilean peasant-craftsman who, by his quality of spirit, his rare perfection of character, his profound wisdom and brave loyalty to his Father in heaven, showed himself to be God's son. In John we meditate upon the man in whom the divine Logos came to dwell. The mysticism of John is sublime: but, when from its heights we come down to earth, we ask whether it is actually true of Jesus that all things were made by, or through, him. Had he the knowledge of One who from the beginning was with God? Was the future not hid from him as from us? John, if we apprehend him aright, claims too much. His

Christ has ceased to have the limitations of humanity.[1013]

With regard to the resurrection, Barnes holds that after the crucifixion Jesus' 'body: 'quite possibly had been flung ignominiously into a

---

[1012] Ernest Barnes, *The Rise of Christianity* (London: Longmans, Green and Co, 1947), p. 66.
[1013] Barnes, pp.96-97.

common malefactors' grave.'[1014] The stories of Jesus' burial in the tomb of Joseph of Arimathea and his subsequent bodily resurrection are not historical accounts, but mythological expressions of the conviction that in spite of his death Jesus was still present with his followers. To quote Barnes again:

...the resurrection stories which gradually arose express the conviction the absolute certainty of the earliest members of the community that Jesus was present with them. In the power given by his Spirit they became missionaries: they grew increasingly confident that they had a religious message of supreme importance. Probably almost from the beginning, before the stories of the empty tomb and of the post-resurrection appearances took shape as Christian beliefs, the earliest disciples of Jesus expressed their spiritual certainty by words such as 'Christ is risen.' Luke records (Acts 4:2) that Peter and his associates in their early preaching 'proclaimed in Jesus the resurrection from the dead.' The followers of the Saviour-Lord thought of themselves as sharing his resurrection: they 'were raised together with Christ' and therefore seeking 'the things that are above, where Christ is, seated on the right hand of God' (Colossians 3:1). Metaphor changes easily into myth, and myth into what is supposed to history.[1015]

The story of the ascension is a further mythological embellishment of the resurrection stories which emerged in the early second century, and in which: 'the appearance of the angels is itself a warning that we are in the domain of religious romance.'[1016]

If we ask who Jesus actually was, the answer which Barnes gives is

that Jesus was a Galilean peasant who: 'seems always to have felt God's presence: the unity was to him so natural and complete that he never suggested that it was something exceptional or abnormal.[1017]

[1014] Barnes, p.174,
[1015] Barnes, pp.174-175.
[1016] Barnes, p.177.
[1017] Barnes, p.143.

Jesus was not God incarnate, he was simply a human being. However: 'In things of the spirit, the words of Jesus show the wisdom of God. His life was that which God would have lived under human limitations.'[1018]

At the end of the book Barnes draws the threads of his argument together and presents the following overall account of how he thinks Christianity arose and developed:

In the preceding pages we have carried the story of Christianity from its obscure beginning to its worldly triumph. It is a most strange tale, which would be incredible were it not true. In the background of the story we have a succession of men, prophets who during several centuries arose within two obscure, and none too highly civilized, groups of Semitic tribes. These men fashioned ethical monotheism, the conviction that humanity is the creation of a God who is good and who demands the service of goodness.

Then there emerged in Galilee a peasant artisan, profoundly, convinced of the truth of the prophets message, who felt that he knew God and was called to serve Him. This man for a brief year or so taught in a remote district, speaking of God with an intimate and beautiful certainty. Finally, because of teaching which expressed his loyalty to God, he was executed as a common criminal.

All memory of him ought rapidly to have vanished. But it would seem that his personality was so strong, his religious sureness so great, his moral and spiritual influence so powerful that his followers could not forget him. As they repeated his teaching they gained an unshakable certainty of his continuing presence. So a new religion grew up, ethical monotheism centred on Jesus the Christ.

The new faith, like its founder, taught its adherents to lead clean,

honourable and kindly lives. It led them to ignore many of the motives of worldly prudence, by which men are normally guided. Christians believed that the Spirit of Christ bade them distrust the use of armed

---

[1018] Barnes, p.143.

force, renounce the power of wealth and even forgo the appeal to established law. They lived in 336 the conviction that, apart from such help, goodness and good-will shown in speech and deed would in the end prevail. After being persecuted for well-nigh three centuries by the authorities of an empire to whom its tenets were an affront, the Christian faith triumphed and forthwith its adherents began to forsake their distinctive outlook on life. The salt lost its savour. An opportunist monotheism, at its best stoic rather than Christian, remained. Expediency the higher expediency which God may be thought to approve became the all too common guide of the Christian in the perplexities and dangers of his earthly life.

Yet there remained and remains the memory of him whom men still call God's anointed, the Christ. The Spirit of Christ perturbs even the churches which have largely forsaken his teaching. Beyond the churches his influence persists. Amid unpromising surroundings it repeatedly emerges with renewed strength in a way that confounds critics and joyfully surprises anxious followers of Jesus. Men captured by the thought and personality of the Christ never apologize for their faith, though they may often be ashamed of the weakness of their loyalty. Some exalt the importance of religious forms and ceremonies and thus instinctively seek to excuse to themselves their failings. Uneasiness is seldom, if ever, thus overcome. But after failure the search for religious reality begins anew. Out of apparently dead formulae and empty ritual the Spirit of Christ emerges as bulbs in springtime appear on what seemed lifeless twigs. Intellectual groups, perplexed by a struggle to understand a Universe obviously too vast for man's apprehension, joining heart to mind, give homage to Christ. So his followers are led to claim for Jesus the Christ a supremacy that time cannot end. Because his Spirit does not die they worship him as Son of God.[1019]

Barnes' book was publicly repudiated by the Archbishops of Canterbury and York in speeches to their respective Convocations, but

[1019] Barnes, pp.335-336.

no formal ecclesiastical action was taken against Barnes. Unlike Apollinarius and Nestorius his teaching was never formally declared to be heretical and unlike them he remained a bishop until he resigned his see in 1952 on grounds of ill health. [1020]

However, there can be no doubt that his teaching was in fact heretical. Barnes' reading of the New Testament is unquestionably at odds with what the Bible teaches about the origins of Israelite monotheism and about Jesus' life and identity and is also unquestionably at odds with the teaching of the Fathers, the Creeds and the historic Anglican formularies. What Barnes presents us with is a unitarian rather than Trinitarian view of God, and a Jesus who was not God incarnate, did not work miracles, did not die and rise to save humankind from sin and death, did not ascend to the right hand of the Father and will not come again to judge the quick and the dead. Barnes' Jesus is a Jewish religious teacher and mystic who is dead and lives on only though the continuing influence of his memory upon on his followers.[1021]

As we have seen, Barnes' calling as a bishop was to be the guardian and teacher of the faith taught in the Bible, the Fathers, the Creeds and the Anglican formularies. That was the calling to which he pledged himself when he became a bishop. *The Rise of Christianity* shows that he was a not good-enough bishop because he failed radically to fulfil this calling.

Bishop John Robinson

Bishop John Robinson was a New Testament scholar and theologian who was suffragan bishop of Woolwich from 1959-1969. The book for which he is best known is *Honest to God*, which was published in 1963, and which has remained in print ever since.

In the Preface to this book, Robinson writes:

[1020] Charles Smyth, *Cyril Foster Garbett, Archbishop of York* (London: Hodder and Stoughton 1959), pp. 469-474.
[1021] Barnes' thought is less than clear, but when he talks about Jesus' continuing presence or the presence of the Spirit of Christ this seems to be what he means.

It belongs to the office of a Bishop in the Church to be a guardian and defender of its doctrine. I find myself a bishop at a moment when the discharge of this burden can seldom have demanded greater depth of divinity and quality of discernment.

For I suspect that we stand on the brink of a period in which it is going to become increasingly difficult to know what the true defence of Christian truth requires. There are always those (and doubtless rightly they will be in the majority) who see the best, and indeed the only, defence of doctrine to lie in the firm reiteration, in fresh and intelligent contemporary language, of 'the faith once delivered to the Saints.' And the Church has not lacked in recent years theologians and apologists who have given themselves to this task. Their work has been rewarded by a hungry following, and there will always be need of more of them. Nothing that I go on to say should be taken to deny their indispensable vocation.

At the same time, I believe we are being called, over the years ahead, to far more than a restating of traditional orthodoxy in modern terms. Indeed, if our defence of the Faith is limited to this we shall find in all likelihood that we have lost out to all but a tiny religious remnant. A much more radical recasting, I would judge, is demanded, in the process of which the most fundamental categories of our theology - of God, of the supernatural, and of religion itself - must go into the melting.[1022]

The reason this is the case, he declares, is because of the: 'growing-gulf between the traditional orthodox supernaturalism in which our Faith has been framed and the categories which the 'lay' world (for want of a better term) finds meaningful today.' [1023]

Robinson's purpose in writing *Honest to God* was to try to find a way of talking about the Faith that the 'lay' world be able to find meaningful.

[1022] John Robinson, *Honest to God* (London: SCM, 1963, p.7.)
[1023] Robinson, p.8.

The book covers the topics of God, Christology, worship and prayer, and ethics.

About God, Robinson contends that just as we have stopped thinking of a God who exists literally or physically beyond the sky, so we now have to stop thinking of a God who is metaphysically 'out there' in the sense of being a :

...supreme Person, a self-existent subject of infinite goodness and power, who enters into a relationship with us comparable with that of one human being with another. [1024]

What Robinson proposes instead is a new way of thinking in which:

To say that God is personal is to say that 'reality at its very deepest level is personal,' that personality is of *ultimate* significance in the constitution of the universe but in personal relationships we touched the final meaning of existence as nowhere else. 'To predicate personality of God' says Feuerbach, 'is nothing else than to declare personality as the absolute essence.' to believe in God as love means to believe that in pure personal relationship we encounter, not merely would ought to be, but what is, the deepest, veriest truth about the structure of reality. This, in face of all the evidence, is a tremendous act of faith. but it is not the feat of persuading oneself of the existence of a super being beyond this world endowed with personal qualities. Belief in God is the trust, the well-nigh incredible trust, that to give ourselves to the uttermost in love is not to be confounded but to be 'accepted,' that love is the ground of our being, to which ultimately we 'come home.'[1025]

In this way of thinking, declares Robinson:

A statement is 'theological' not because it relates to a particular Being called 'God,' but because it asks *ultimate* questions about the meaning

[1024] Robinson, p.48.
[1025] Robinson, pp.48-49 italics in the original quoting Ludwig Feuerbach in *The Essence of Christianity.*

of existence: it asks what, at the level of *theos*, at the level of its deepest mystery, is the reality and significance of our life.[1026]

In line with this understanding of how we should understand God, Robinson rejects as 'mythical' the traditional Christian belief in: "a God' who 'visits' the earth in the person of 'his Son'"[1027] Instead Robinson proposes an alternative Christology in which:

Jesus is 'the man for others,' the one in whom Love has completely taken over, the one who is utterly open to, and united with the Ground of his being. And this 'life for others, through participation in the Being of God,' is transcendence. For at this point of love 'to the uttermost,' we encounter *God*, the ultimate 'depth' of our being, the unconditional in the conditioned. This is what the New Testament means by saying that 'God was in Christ' and that 'what God was the Word was. Because Christ was utterly and completely 'the man for others,' because he *was* love, he was 'one with the Father' because 'God is love.' But for this very reason he was most entirely man, the Son of man, the servant of the Lord. [1028]

Robinson further suggests that we need to reject the traditional Christian belief in 'a supernatural Being coming down from heaven to 'save' mankind from sin' since such a belief 'is frankly incredible' to people today.[1029] Instead, he suggests that the grace of God given to us in Jesus Christ:

...is the life of 'the man for others,' the love whereby we are brought completely into one with the Ground of our being, manifesting itself in the unreconciled relationships of our existence. It was manifested supremely on the Cross, but it is met whenever the Christ is shown forth and recognized in 'an entirely different mode of living-in-

---

[1026] Robinson, p.49 italics in the original.
[1027] Robinson, p.67.
[1028] Robinson, pp.76-77 italics in the original.
[1029] Robinson, p.78.

relationship from anything known in the world.' For there. In however 'secular' a form, is the atonement and the resurrection.[1030]

On worship Robinson writes that its purpose is to foster a better engagement with the world and the people in it:

The purpose of worship is not to retire from the secular into the department of the religious, Let alone escape from 'this world' into the 'other world,' but open oneself to the meeting of the Christ in the common, to that which has the power to penetrate its superficiality and redeem it from its alienation. The function of worship is to make us more sensitive to these depths; to focus, sharpen and deepen our response to the world and to other people beyond the point of proximate concern (of liking, self -interest, limited commitment, etc,) to that of ultimate concern; to purify and correct our loves in the light of Christ's love; and in him to find the grace and power to be the reconciled an reconciling community.[1031]

On prayer, Robinson focusses on prayer as intercession and suggests that this means opening 'oneself to another unconditionally in love.' [1032] This, he says:

...may consist simply in listening, when we take the otherness of the other person most seriously. It may not be talking to God, as though to a third person, about him at all. The *Thou* addressed may be his own *Thou*, but it may be addressed and responded to at such a level that we can only speak of knowing him in God and God in him. [1033]

Finally, on ethics Robinson builds on the work of the American Anglican ethicist Joseph Fletcher and argues that for the Christian there are no moral 'absolutes,' but the sort of love shown by Christ. This means, he says, that:

[1030] Robinson, p.82 quoting John Wren-Lewis in *They became Anglicans*.
[1031] Robinson, p.87.
[1032] Robinson, p.99.
[1033] Robinson, p.100 italics in the original.

...nothing can of itself always be labelled as 'wrong.' One cannot, for instance, start from the position 'sex relations before marriage' or 'divorce' are wrong or sinful in themselves. They may be in 99 cases or even 100 cases out of 100, but they are not intrinsically so, for the only intrinsic evil is lack of love.[1034]

Honest to God was a very divisive book, being strongly welcomed by many and equally strongly opposed by others.[1035] In the Church of England the Archbishop of Canterbury, Michael Ramsey, criticised in the Canterbury Convocation the way Robinson had trailed his book in an article in the *Observer* entitled 'Our image of God must go,'[1036] and published a gently critical response to *Honest to God* in a pamphlet entitled *Images Old and New*.[1037] However, like Barnes before him, Robinson was never disciplined by the Church of England for his views, and he remained Bishop of Woolwich until he moved back to academia in 1969.

Nevertheless, as with the teaching of Barnes in *The Rise of Christianity*, there can be no doubt that the views expressed by Robinson in *Honest to God* were heretical.

First, Robinson completely removes the key biblical distinction between God and creation by subsuming God into the general category of 'reality' (i.e. everything that is). For him, as we have seen, belief in God does not mean belief in the transcendent, personal, self-existent, loving God of the Bible, but the belief that reality is personal, and that love is the deepest truth about reality. For him reality is God and love is what reality is like (what it means to say that everything that exists is 'personal' and 'love' is something which he never explains).

Secondly, for Robinson Jesus was in the last resort simply a supremely loving human being. He was not as the Bible, the Creeds, and the

---

[1034] Robinson, p.120.
[1035] For a good overview of reactions to *Honest to God* see John Robinson and David Edwards (eds) *The Honest to God Debate* (London: SCM 2012).
[1036] Owen Chadwick, *Michael Ramsey- A life* (London: SCM, 1998), p.371.
[1037] Michael Ramsey, *Images Old and New* (London: SPCK, 1963).

Anglican formularies declare the eternally existent second Person of the Trinity who assumed human nature at the incarnation, but a man who manifested love. In biblical terms Robinson once again blurs the creator-creature distinction. For a human being to be supremely loving does not make them God, they are still just a creature.

Thirdly, Robinson wrongly views the atonement and the resurrection as meaning a loving way of living and encountering the grace of God as encountering this. In the Bible, and the Christian tradition following the Bible, the terms 'atonement' and 'resurrection' refer to the historical and supernatural acts of God by which sin and death were overcome and the grace of God is God's gift of new life to all those who accept in faith that these acts have taken place.

Fourthly, Robinson wrongly restricts the purpose of worship to helping us to engage better with the world and the people we encounter in it. What he ignores in that the purpose of worship is also to acknowledge who God is, to hear what he has done for us and praise him for it, to confess our sins to God and receive absolution for them, to receive supernatural spiritual life from God through the sacraments, and to bring our needs and the needs of the world before God in intercessory prayer.

Fifthly, Robinson wrongly suggests that intercessory prayer means giving oneself unconditionally to another human being and may not involve talking to God at all. In the Bible and the Christian tradition, prayer in all its forms always means activity directed towards God, engaging with another human being is not the same thing.

Sixthly, Robinson wrongly sees love as the only moral absolute. What he fails to acknowledge is that what constitutes loving action is determined by the order put into creation by God, an order which is made known to us by creation itself and, most clearly by God's word in the Bible. In relation to this order one can say that certain things such as adultery, theft and murder are absolutely wrong and that loving God and neighbour means refraining from doing them.

One can sympathise with what Robinson was seeking to do in *Honest to God*. As we noted in the last chapter, it is an important part of a bishop's role to act as a Christian apologist by showing how the Christian faith continues to make sense in the contemporary world. Unfortunately, in seeking to undertake this apologetic task Robinson ended up by publicly misrepresenting in the ways outlined above the very faith which as a bishop he was called to guard and defend.

Bishop Michael Ingham

The four examples of bishops lapsing into heresy given above all relate to their teaching. It is what they taught that was heretical. However, a bishop can also act heretically when he or she performs heretical actions, or gives permission to others to do so.

This is illustrated by the case of Michael Ingham, who was Bishop of the Canadian diocese of New Westminster from 1994-2013. On 15 June 2002 he gave his consent as bishop of the diocese to a motion in the diocesan synod to allow the blessing of gay and lesbian unions in those churches in the diocese which wanted to offer them.

In a statement following the passing of the synod motion, Bishop Ingham declared that agreeing to offer such blessings was a legitimate thing to do:

We are not compromising the Christian faith nor relativising its moral teaching. We are extending to gay and lesbian Christians the same freedom that is enjoyed by others to commit their lives to Jesus Christ together, and the same obligation to grow in the costly demands of love. We are calling them to fidelity, permanence and stability in relationships. We are offering them the support of the Christian community as they grow into the fullness of the stature of Christ through the struggles and challenges of mutual commitment.[1038]

[1038] 'Statement by Bishop Michael Ingham following the vote on motion 7' at https://www.anglican.ca/news/statement-by-bishop-michael-ingham-following-the-vote-on-motion-7/3005742/

However, agreeing to the offering of such blessings was in fact a heretical move. Why this is so is helpfully explained by J I Packer in his article 'Why I walked' which explains why he was one of those Anglicans who left the diocese of New Westminster rather than accept what the synod and Bishop Ingham had decided. Packer explains:

To bless same-sex unions liturgically is to ask God to bless them and to enrich those who join in them, as is done in marriage ceremonies. This assumes that the relationship, of which the physical bond is an integral part, is intrinsically good and thus, if I may coin a word, blessable, as procreative sexual intercourse within heterosexual marriage is. About this assumption there are three things to say.

First, it entails deviation from the biblical gospel and the historic Christian creed. It distorts the doctrines of creation and sin, claiming that homosexual orientation is good since gay people are made that way, and rejecting the idea that homosexual inclinations are a spiritual disorder, one more sign and fruit of original sin in some people's moral system. It distorts the doctrines of regeneration and sanctification, calling same-sex union a Christian relationship and so affirming what the Bible would call salvation in sin rather than from it.

Second, it threatens destruction to my neighbor. The official proposal said that ministers who, like me, are unwilling to give this blessing should refer gay couples to a minister willing to give it. Would that be pastoral care? Should I not try to help gay people change their behavior, rather than to anchor them in it? Should I not try to help them to the practice of chastity, just as I try to help restless singles and divorcees to the practice of chastity? Do I not want to see them all in the kingdom of God?

Third, it involves the delusion of looking to God—actually asking him—to sanctify sin by blessing what he condemns. This is irresponsible, irreverent, indeed blasphemous, and utterly unacceptable as church policy. How could I do it?[1039]

Because, it involves deviation from the biblical gospel and the historic Christian creed, involves spiritual destruction rather than pastoral care, and blasphemously asks God to sanctify sin, blessing gay and lesbian relationships is a heretical thing to do and Bishop Ingham himself lapsed into heresy when he agreed to it.

As Thomas Aquinas once noted, approving of fornication is just as heretical as denying the Trinity: 'if a person were to maintain that God is triune and not one, or that fornication is not a sin, he would be a heretic.'[1040] Fornication means all sexual activity outside heterosexual marriage, including same-sex sexual relationships, and so in agreeing to the blessing of such relationships Bishop Ingham was acting in just as a heretical a fashion as if he had given his consent to churches in the diocese deciding to formally reject the Nicene Creed. By so doing he showed himself to be, to a very serious extent, a not good-enough bishop.

Why heresy by bishops matters

Many people today find it difficult to understand why bishops being heretical matters. They can understand why it is a bad thing if bishops are simply not up to the job, exploit the office of bishop for their own gain, or use it as a cover for abuse, but they cannot see why it is a matter for concern if a bishop is heretical.

As we noted in the last chapter, the fashion for doctrinal indefiniteness noted by Ryle back in the nineteenth century is still with us today, and it leads many people to think that providing a bishop is kindly and hard-working and holds the diocese together in a reasonable degree of

---

[1039] J I Packer, 'Why I Walked - Sometimes loving a denomination requires you to fight' at https://www.gafcon.org/sites/gafcon.org/files/resources/files/why_i_walked_by_ji_packer.pdf
[1040] Thomas Aquinas, *Commentary on the Letters of Saint Paul to the Philippians, Colossians, Timothy, Titus and Philemon* (Lander, Wyoming: The Aquinas Institute, 2012), p. 457.

unity, then the fact that he or she may have some rather untraditional ideas about theology or ethics is really not that important.

To understand why a bishop having or supporting heretical ideas does matter it is helpful to turn to the opening words of the *Athanasian Creed*, one of the three ancient Creeds authorised for use in Church of England services. [1041]

The *Athanasian Creed* begins with the uncompromising words: 'Whosoever will be saved: before all things it is necessary that he hold the Catholick Faith. Which Faith except every one do keep whole and undefiled: without doubt he shall perish everlastingly.'[1042]

Following a decision by the Upper and Lower Houses of the Canterbury Convocation in 1873 these words remain part of the accepted doctrinal teaching of the Church of England.[1043] What they

---

[1041] What follows is adapted from material in Martin Davie, *The Athanasian Creed* (London: Latimer Trust, 2019).

[1042] *The Athanasian Creed*, vv.1-2.

[1043] In May the following year the upper and lower houses of Convocation then produced a joint synodical declaration which ran as follows:
For the removal of doubts and to prevent disquietude in the use of the creed commonly called the Creed of St. Athanasius, this synod doth solemnly declare:
1. That the confession of our Christian faith, commonly called the Creed of St. Athanasius, doth not make any addition to the faith as contained in the Holy Scripture, but warneth against errors which from time to time have arisen in the Church of Christ.
2. That as Holy Scripture in divers places doth promise life to them that believe and declare the condemnation of them that believe not, so doth the Church in this confession declare the necessity for all who would be in a state of salvation of holding fast the Catholic faith, and the great peril of rejecting the same. Wherefore the warnings in this confession of faith are to be understood no otherwise than the like warnings in Holy Scripture, for we must receive God's threatenings even as His promises, in such wise as they are generally set forth in Holy Writ. Moreover, the Church doth not herein pronounce judgment on any particular person or persons, God alone being the judge of all. (*Chronicle of Convocation*, 9 May 1873, 405–406) The Church of England has never rescinded what is said in this declaration.

set out is the basic principle that holding fast to the orthodox Christian faith is necessary in order to avoid eternal damnation.

The theological basis for this principle is the New Testament teaching that belief brings salvation whereas failure to believe brings condemnation. Mark 16:16 states 'He who believes and is baptized will be saved; but he who does not believe will be condemned.' [1044] In similar fashion we are told in John 3:16-18 'For God so loved the world that he gave his only Son, that whoever believes in him should not perish but have eternal life. For God sent the Son into the world, not to condemn the world, but that the world might be saved through him. He who believes in him is not condemned; he who does not believe is condemned already, because he has not believed in the name of the only Son of God.' For these verses, and for the New Testament as a whole, belief is the thing that is of primary significance (necessary 'before all things' as the Creed puts it) because, although belief has to express itself in a changed pattern of behaviour, it is belief that places us in a state of salvation. As Romans 3:28 puts it, 'we are justified (i.e. have a right relationship with God) by faith.'

The link between what is said in these verses from the New Testament and what is taught in the opening verses of the Athanasian Creed lies in the fact that belief in Jesus leading to salvation means belief in the teaching of the apostles. Because Christ has ascended to the right hand of the Father he no longer presents himself directly to us as the object of our belief as was the case during the years of his earthly ministry. Instead, he is presented to us in the form of the teaching of the apostles. As Paul says, the apostles are the 'ambassadors' of Christ (2 Corinthians 5:20) appointed by him to speak and act on his behalf.

[1044] Mark 16:9-20 are generally regarded today as an addition to the original text of Mark and therefore as non-Canonical. However, in the history of the Church they have been regarded as the original ending of Mark and this historic position can still be defended. See for example J. W. Burgon *The Last Twelve Verses of the Gospel according to S. Mark* (Oxford: OUP, 1871) and W. R. Farmer, *The Last Twelve verses of Mark* (Cambridge: CUP, 1974).

This means that our belief or unbelief in the apostles' teaching is our belief or unbelief in Christ himself.

The 'Catholic faith' to which the Athanasian Creed refers is the teaching of the apostles as this is expounded in the New Testament and has been handed down in the Church (what we referred to as 'the faith' in the last chapter). It follows that belief or unbelief in the Catholic faith is also belief or unbelief in Christ and that if we wish to be saved rather than condemned we must believe what the Catholic faith teaches (which in Church of England terms means what is taught in the Bible, the Fathers, the Creeds and the Anglican formularies).

Furthermore, we have to go on believing it even when, like the Catholic Christians in Gaul and Spain in the fifth and sixth centuries for who the Athanasian Creed was first written, we face pressure to do otherwise. As the parable of the sower (Mark 4: 1-20) makes clear, it is persistence in the faith that brings salvation.

We must also go on believing the Catholic faith in its entirety, 'whole and undefiled' as the Athanasian Creed puts it. This is because we cannot legitimately choose to believe some bits of the faith and reject others. It is the Catholic faith as a whole that has been presented to us to be the object of our belief and if we decide not to believe parts of it then we enter into a state of unbelief and therefore become subject to condemnation.

When the Creed says that the person who fails to keep the faith will 'without doubt' perish everlastingly, what it has in view is someone who persists in a state of unbelief. It does not rule out extenuating circumstances [1045] or the possibility that someone who is currently in

---

[1045] As the eighteenth century commentator on the Creed, Daniel Waterland, notes, the verses are not intended '...to exclude any such merciful abatement, or allowances, as shall be made: for man's particular circumstances, weaknesses, frailties, ignorance, inability, or the like; or for their sincere intentions, and honest desires of knowing, and doing the whole will of God; accompanied with a general repentance of their sins, and a firm reliance on God's mercy, through the

a state of unbelief may repent and be forgiven and therefore be saved. What it does do is warn that deliberate departure from the Catholic faith is an ultimately serious matter because if we persist in it eternal loss will be the result.

The reason all this is relevant to the issue of heretical bishops is because a bishop who lapses into heresy is by definition someone who has departed from the Catholic faith and has thus placed themselves in real danger of eternal damnation. Furthermore, if that bishop than goes on to teach heresy, or to encourage or permit heretical forms of behaviour, then he or she is putting the souls of the faithful at real risk of the same fate.

We would rightly regard a bishop who put people in risk of very serious physical harm as a not good-enough bishop. In the same way we should regard a bishop who puts people in the risk of the ultimate spiritual harm of eternal damnation as being to a very serious extent a not good-enough bishop.

4. What Christians should do when faced with a not good-enough bishop

In think about what to do when faced with not good-enough bishops, it is important to make a clear distinction between the first category of such bishops and the second and third. This is because someone being a 'bad bishop' or a heretical bishop is a far more serious issue than someone who is simply not up to the job.

How to respond when a bishop is not up to the job

When a Christian suspects that a bishop is not up to the job, they should first give the bishop concerned the benefit of the doubt. This is because their experience of the bishop may well not be representative of how the bishop normally behaves. All Christian ministers, bishops included, have 'off days' and it is not just to judge a bishop's ministry on the basis of what happens on such a day.

sole merits of Christ Jesus.' (Daniel Waterland, *A Critical History of the Athanasian Creed* (London: Forgotten Books, 2015), p.150).

What this means is that a Christian should not start alleging that a bishop is not up to the job on the basis of limited evidence. It is only if there is a range of evidence, verified by a range of people who have no particular axe to grind against the bishop, that someone should start to suggest that this might be the case.

When it becomes clear that there is a real problem with the bishop's ministry, a Christian must pray for the bishop concerned. That bishop is a Christian brother or sister who wants to serve God but is having difficulty doing so. Christian charity requires that in this situation a Christian should pray that God will strengthen and help them in the face of this difficulty.

Having prayed for the bishop, a Christian should not grumble or gossip about the bishop's shortcomings, but should bring their concerns either directly to the bishop, or to those in the diocese who have particular responsibility to assist the bishop in his or her ministry such as the diocesan bishop, the suffragan bishop, the archdeacons, the diocesan secretary, the chairs of the Houses of Clergy and Laity in the diocesan synod, the bishop's chaplain, or the bishop's PA. Who should be approached will depend on the particular issue or issues that have arisen.

Those who receive such concerns about the bishop then need to decide whether they think these concerns are justified and, if they consider that they are, they too need to pray for the bishop and then approach the bishop to let them know about these concerns and to discuss how they should be addressed.

If the concerns are the result of misunderstanding, then the issue is how this misunderstanding can be rectified. If, however, they have real substance the issue then becomes how the bishop can be helped to address them. Thus, a bishop who lacked a sufficiently deep understanding of the Christian faith could be helped to deepen their understanding, a bishop who was bad at handling conflict could be helped to learn how to handle conflict better, and bishop who had difficulty keeping on top of administration could be helped with skills such as time management and learning how to prioritise pieces of work.

Another way forward would be for others in the diocese to take on matters that a bishop is not good at. For example, if a diocesan bishop is not very good as a teacher, but a suffragan bishop is talented in this area, then the best way forward would be for the episcopal workload in the diocese to be arranged so as to allow the suffragan the major responsibility for teaching. For another example, if a bishop struggles to lead worship well then then the best way forward would be to delegate the responsibility for leading worship as much as possible to those who can do it better.

It would only be if a bishop refused help, refused to delegate in the way just suggested, or showed no ability to improve in those areas of ministry where they fell short, and this had a serious impact on the life of the diocese, that the further step would need to be taken of suggesting to the bishop concerned that they should consider resignation or retirement. This would have to be a suggestion, because unless their failure had been so serious as to contravene church law it would be difficult, if not impossible, to force them to go.

Should the bishop concerned agree to resign or retire their departure should be accompanied by as much support and dignity as possible and where appropriate arrangements should be made for them to continue to serve God in some other form of ministry.

When the issue is a bishop who sincerely does their best to be a good-enough bishop, but nonetheless fell short it would not be appropriate for people to seek to disassociate themselves from the bishop's ministry by, for example, requesting ordination or licensing from some other bishop, or asking for another bishop to take confirmation. What would be appropriate would be to avoid creating circumstances in which their shortcomings were a problem. For instance, it would not be sensible to ask a bishop to preach if he or she was bad at preaching. Similarly, it would not be sensible to ask a bishop to lead an apologetics course if they had little knowledge or ability in this area.

How to respond when someone is a 'bad bishop'

When we come to the second category of not good-enough bishop, the 'bad bishop' identified by Augustine who desires the bishop's role but not the obligation of faithful service that goes with it then what is said in Article XXVI 'Of the Unworthiness of the Ministers which hinders not the effect of the Sacrament' comes into play. This Article runs as follows:

Although in the visible Church the evil be ever mingled with the good, and sometime the evil have chief authority in the ministration of the word and sacraments; yet forasmuch as they do not the same in their own name, but in Christ's, and do minister by His commission and authority, we may use their ministry both in hearing the word of God and in the receiving of the sacraments. Neither is the effect of Christ's ordinance taken away by their wickedness, nor the grace of God's gifts diminished from such as by faith and rightly do receive the sacraments ministered unto them, which be effectual because of Christ's institution and promise, although they be ministered by evil men.

Nevertheless it appertaineth to the discipline of the Church that inquiry be made of evil ministers, and that they be accused by those that have knowledge of their offences; and finally, being found guilty by just judgement, be deposed.

The first part of this article reflects the teaching of Augustine against the Donatists which we noted in chapter 8. The basic principle it sets out is that the wickedness of ministers (including bishops) is no barrier to people receiving Christ's grace through their ministry.

As William Beveridge puts it in his commentary on this article:

It is not their own word they preach, but Christ's; not their own sacraments they administer, but Christ's; and therefore, be their own sins what they will, the ordinance is still Christ's ordinance; the institution of it is from Christ; the promises annexed to it are made by Christ; and we cannot think that Christ's grace should be hindered by man's sin; or that because ministers are not faithful to Christ, Christ should not therefore be faithful to his people in performing the promises made to them; which promises were not made to the administration of the promises by faithful persons, but to the ordinances in general, as duly administered even by such as are truly and rightly called to it. So that the ordinance is never the better for being administered by worthy, nor is it the worse for being administered by unworthy persons. Whether the ministers be worthy or unworthy, it is still by the grace of Christ his ordinances are made effectual.[1046]

What Article XXVI principally has in mind is parish ministry and the preaching of the word and celebration of the sacraments by a parish priest. However, since the Patristic period it has been accepted that the basic principle involved 'it is still by the grace of Christ his ordinances are made effectual' also extends to the acts performed by bad bishops. Thus, not only may people receive grace through a bad bishop preaching the word and celebrating the sacraments, but people may receive the gifts of the Spirit when hands are laid on by a bad bishop at confirmation and be validly ordained or consecrated in services in which bad bishops take part. This means not only that those baptised, confirmed, ordained or consecrated in such circumstances do not need to have these ordinances repeated, but it would be positively wrong for this to happen since it would in effect be asking God to do again what he has already done.

However, as we saw in last chapter, the second half of the article has to be taken equally seriously and it too applies to bishops and not just to ordinary parish ministers. To reword the second part of Article XXVI slightly we can therefore say that it appertaineth to the discipline of the Church that inquiry be made of evil bishops, and that they be accused by those that have knowledge of their offences; and finally, being found guilty by just judgement, be deposed.

[1046] William Beveridge, *Ecclesia Anglicana, Ecclesia Catholica* (Oxford: OUP, 1846), p. 448.

What all this means in practical terms is that if someone suspects that someone is a 'bad bishop' their first move should be not be to spread rumours to this effect, but to ascertain whether there are good grounds for believing that the suspicion is true, and that the bishop concerned is seriously negligent in the performance of their duties, or seriously ungodly in their behaviour.

If upon further investigation it becomes apparent that this is true, then they should contact the bishop concerned and raise the issue (s) involved privately with them in line with Jesus' words in Matthew 18:15. If the bishop's response was unsatisfactory then the appropriate course of action would be to inform the relevant diocesan authorities and then make a formal allegation of misconduct against the bishop concerned in order to precipitate the disciplinary procedure set out in the *Clergy Discipline Rules 2005*.[1047] If the allegation involved criminal activity (as in the case of Bishop Ball) the police would also need to be informed so that there could be a separate criminal investigation.

The Church's disciplinary procedure may involve the suspension of the bishop concerned from office and the outcome of the procedure could, if the issue was serious enough, involve deposition from office and a permanent prohibition from exercising ministry in the Church of England (this would be in addition to any penalties imposed as a result of a criminal prosecution).

Given that this disciplinary procedure exists, the appropriate response if someone believes that there is good evidence that a bishop (or archbishop) is seriously negligent in the conduct of their ministry, or involved in seriously ungodly conduct, is to make use of it.

[1047] The *Clergy Discipline Rules 2005* can be found at https://www.churchofengland.org/sites/default/files/2021-07/C%20D%20Rules%20%282021%29.pdf

There are two further points that need to be noted. First, someone responding to a 'bad bishop' in the way outlined above should seek to avoid any sense of moral superiority to the bishop concerned but should instead constantly pray 'God be merciful to me a sinner!' (Luke 18:9-14). Secondly, someone responding in this way has an obligation to pray for the bishop concerned that they may repent and receive God's forgiveness for their wrongdoing.

How to respond when a bishop is heretical

When we come to the third category of not good-enough bishops, those who are heretical in their teaching or actions, what is said in the first half of Article XXVI still applies. This means, for instance. that if someone was baptised, confirmed, or ordained by Bishop John Robinson their baptism, confirmation or ordination would be valid and efficacious in spite of his lapse into heresy.

However, in spite of the fact that the episcopal acts performed by heretical bishops should be regarded as valid and efficacious, it is nevertheless the case that faithful Christians should seek to separate themselves from such bishops.

The New Testament is clear that those propagating heretical teaching should be avoided. This is mentioned at various points in the New Testament. Thus Titus 3: 10 speaks of avoiding foolish controversies and 'having nothing more to do' with a person who stirs up division and Romans 16:17 refers to 'watching out for those who cause divisions and create obstacles contrary to the doctrine that you have been taught; avoid them.' 1 Timothy 6: 11 uses the language of 'fleeing' from those who follow a 'different' doctrine (vv 3 and 11). Elsewhere the New Testament refers to not 'partnering' with those spreading dangerous teaching (Ephesians 5: 6-7 and 2 John 10-11) and not tolerating those who teach or practise sexual immorality (Revelation 2: 20).

The subsequent tradition of the Church has understood this to mean that Christians should separate themselves from the ministry of ungodly bishops, including those bishops who have fallen into heresy.

For example, referring to bishops as 'priests' Cyprian writes as follows to Christians in Spain:

Nor let the people flatter themselves that they can be free from the contagion of sin, while communicating with a priest who is a sinner, and yielding their consent to the unjust and unlawful episcopacy of their overseer, when the divine reproof by Hosea the prophet threatens, and says, 'Their sacrifices shall be as the bread of mourning; all that eat thereof shall be polluted; ' Hosea 9:4 teaching manifestly and showing that all are absolutely bound to the sin who have been contaminated by the sacrifice of a profane and unrighteous priest. Which, moreover, we find to be manifested also in Numbers, when Korah, and Dathan, and Abiram Claimed for themselves the power of sacrificing in opposition to Aaron the priest. There also the Lord commanded by Moses that the people should be separated from them, lest, being associated with the wicked, themselves also should be bound closely in the same wickedness. 'Separate yourselves,' said He, 'from the tents of these wicked and hardened men, and touch not those things which belong to them, lest you perish together in their sins.' Numbers 16:26 On which account a people obedient to the Lord's precepts, and fearing God, ought to separate themselves from a sinful prelate, and not to associate themselves with the sacrifices of a sacrilegious priest, especially since they themselves have the power either of choosing worthy priests, or of rejecting unworthy ones.[1048]

Similarly, Augustine writes 'We should not obey those bishops who have been duly elected, if they commit errors, or teach or ordain anything contrary to the divine Scripture.' [1049]

In the same vein Luther writes that:

[1048] Cyprian, Epistle 67:3, in *The Ante-Nicene Fathers*, Vol.5, p. 370. The specific reference is to bishops who have lapsed into idolatry in the face of persecution but from Cyprian's other letters it is clear that the principle extends to bishops who have fallen into heresy.
[1049] Augustine, *Ad Catholicos Fratres Liber Unos*, Chapter 28, cited in Lee Gatiss (ed) *Fight Valiantly!* (Watford: Church Society, 2019), p. 160.

...wherever there is a Christian congregation in possession of the gospel, it not only has the right and power but also the duty – on pain of losing the salvation of its souls and in accordance with the promise made to Christ in baptism – to avoid, to flee, to depose, and to withdraw from the authority that our bishops...and the like are now exercising. For it is clearly evident that they teach and rule contrary to God and his word... it is a divine right and a necessity for the salvation of souls to depose or avoid such bishops...and whatever is of their government. [1050]

If we ask how Christians in the Church of England today should act in the light of this teaching, the answer is that first of all, they should make as sure as possible that the bishop concerned really has become heretical (rather than simply being confused or expressing themselves badly). An accusation of heresy is extremely serious and it should never be made lightly or without proper evidence.

Secondly, if it becomes apparent that the heresy is real then they should warn others of its existence and call on (and pray for) the bishop concerned to repent of the heresy and return to orthodoxy.

If the bishop refuses to acknowledge the heresy and repent of it, the second half of Article XXVI suggests that they should then seek the deposition of the bishop concerned through due legal process, such deposition then allowing the appointment of an orthodox bishop in their place.

The way to do this would be to initiate proceedings against the bishop concerned under the terms of the *Ecclesiastical Jurisdiction Measure* on the basis that the bishop had committed 'an offence against the laws ecclesiastical involving matters of doctrine, ritual or ceremonial.' [1051] If proceedings were brought in this way, and if a bishop was found to

---

[1050] Martin Luther, 'That a Christian assembly or congregation has the right and power to judge all teaching and to call, appoint and dismiss teachers, established by Scripture' LW 39:308-309 cited in Gatiss p.160.
[1051] *Ecclesiastical Jurisdiction Measure*, 14.1(a).

have committed such an offence, then under the measure one of the possible penalties would be for such a bishop to be deposed.[1052]

Proceedings under the *Ecclesiastical Jurisdiction Measure* are the only way to legally remove a Church of England bishop for heresy and clear the way for a replacement to be appointed. However, it is important to be aware that the prevailing view in the Church of England is 'that such proceedings do more harm than good'[1053] and so great pressure would be brought to bear to prevent proceedings being initiated or to halt them once they had been initiated.

Furthermore, given the present culture of doctrinal confusion in the Church of England there is no guarantee that a heretical bishop would be found guilty of a doctrinal offence, and even if they were found guilty there is no guarantee that the penalty of deposition would be imposed as a result.

Given that this legal route might well not prove successful for the reasons just given, what other options do those in the Church of England have if a bishop is heretical?

The only other option within the Church of England's existing canonical framework would be for the Christians concerned to request that they should receive pastoral oversight from some other bishop. Under Canon C.18 this request would need to be agreed by the diocesan bishop, who would also need to agree who the substitute bishop would be. Furthermore, if the heretical bishop was a diocesan bishop those in their diocese would still come under his or her jurisdiction as the ordinary, even If pastoral care was exercised by some other bishop. Under Canon law there is simply no way for a diocesan bishop not to remain the bishop of all those in his or her diocese.

If a heretical bishop was not deposed as a result of proceedings under *the Ecclesiastical Jurisdiction Measure,* and if a request for alternative

---

[1052] *Ecclesiastical Jurisdiction Measure* 49:1 (a)
[1053] *The Nature of Christian Belief*, p. 38.

episcopal oversight was not granted, or if it was granted but the Christians concerned felt they could not rightly accept still having a heretical diocesan bishop as their ordinary, then there would only two other options.

The first option would be for the Christians concerned to break Canon law by remaining in the Church of England but placing themselves under what would be in Church of England terms the irregular jurisdiction of some bishop from the Church of England or elsewhere. Going down this route would lead to proceedings being brought against them (and against the bishop concerned if he or she was from the Church of England) and those concerned would need to be aware of this and willing to accept the consequences.

As we noted in chapter 12, the question of whether it would be right for a bishop to offer irregular jurisdiction in this way has been hotly debated in the Anglican Communion in recent years. The official line that has been taken by the Anglican Communion is that such action is always illegitimate. GAFCON, on the other hand has maintained that it can be legitimate.

The material we looked at in chapter 12 indicates that GAFCON has got the better case. What we saw in that chapter is that all bishops have a potentially universal jurisdiction by virtue of their episcopal orders. The exercise of this universal jurisdiction is normally limited to particular jurisdictions. However, such limitation exists to serve the Church and its God given mission to the world, and if there is an emergency situation where the well-being of the Church and the effectiveness of its mission requires breaking the rules that normally limit the exercise of episcopal jurisdiction then breaking them may well be the right thing to do.

One such situation is where a bishop has become heretical and the Christians in the diocese concerned need alternative episcopal oversight. As Cyprian explains in Epistle 66, in a situation like that in Arles where Bishop Marcian had succumbed to the Novationist heresy, other bishops have not only the right, but the obligation, to provide such oversight:

Let letters be directed by you into the province and to the people abiding at Arles, by which, Marcian being excommunicated, another may be substituted in his place, and Christ's flock, which even to this day is contemned as scattered and wounded by him, may be gathered together. Let it suffice that many of our brethren have departed in these late years in those parts without peace; and certainly let the rest who remain be helped, who groan both day and night, and beseeching the divine and fatherly mercy, entreat the comfort of our succour. For, for that reason, dearest brother, the body of priests is abundantly large, joined together by the bond of mutual concord, and the link of unity; so that if any one of our college should try to originate heresy, and to lacerate and lay waste Christ's flock, others may help, and as it were, as useful and merciful shepherds, gather together the Lord's sheep into the flock. For what if any harbour in the sea shall begin to be mischievous and dangerous to ships, by the breach of its defences; do not the navigators direct their ships to other neighbouring ports where there is a safe and practicable entrance, and a secure station? Or if, on the road, any inn should begin to be beset and occupied by robbers, so that whoever should enter would be caught by the attack of those who lie in wait there; do not the travellers, as soon as this its character is discovered, seek other houses of entertainment on the road, which shall be safer, where the lodging is trustworthy, and the inns safe for the travellers? And this ought now to be the case with us, dearest brother, that we should receive to us with ready and kindly humanity our brethren, who, tossed on the rocks of Marcian, are seeking the secure harbours of the Church; and that we afford such a place of entertainment for the travellers as is that in the Gospel, in which those who are wounded and maimed by robbers may be received and cherished, and protected by the host.[1054]

To put it simply, where part of the Lord's flock lacks a true shepherd then other shepherds have a responsibility to step in and remedy the situation even if they break the normal pattern of ecclesiastical jurisdiction in doing so. To quote Van-Espen again:

[1054] Cyprian, Epistle 66:3, in *The Ante-Nicene Fathers*, vol.5, p. 368.

The jurisdiction of the bishops is circumscribed within certain limits for the greater commodity of the Church: but when this end ceases, and it is rather for the advantage of the Church that a bishop should go beyond the boundaries of his jurisdiction, he can freely do so.

Note 1 below gives examples of how two orthodox bishops of the fourth century, Athanasius and Eusebius of Samosata were willing to act outside the normal bounds of their jurisdiction during the Arian controversy

The argument against allowing the possibility of such extraordinary exercise of episcopal jurisdiction that is often heard in the Church of England is that it would mean that people could 'pick and choose' their own bishop. This argument is unconvincing, because it fails to understand is that what is being proposed is not that Christians can reject one bishop and choose another one whenever they feel like it, but that in an emergency situation where a bishop has become heretical the faithful can and should respond by seeking the oversight of an orthodox bishop.

The second option would be for the Christians concerned to leave the Church of England and place themselves under the episcopal oversight of a bishop in another Anglican church such as, the Free Church of England or the Anglican Mission in England, or a church in a different tradition such the Roman Catholic Church or one of the Orthodox churches.

5. Responding well to not good-enough bishops

In this chapter we have looked at what makes someone a not good-enough bishop and suggested appropriate ways of responding when someone is a not good-enough bishop. We have seen that Christians should seek to help bishops who are not up to the job to do better, and we have also seen that it is necessary for faithful Christians to contend against the ungodliness of ungodly bishops and the heresy of heretical ones, using the *Clergy Discipline Measure* and the *Ecclesiastical Jurisdiction Measure* to try to depose bishops from office if they are not willing to repent and change their behaviour, their teaching, or their heretical practice.

We have also noted that as a last resort Christians may need to call upon the help of orthodox bishops in a way that goes against Canon law or may need to leave the Church of England entirely and place themselves under the oversight of a bishop from another church.

Two final points that need to be noted are, firstly, that when contending against the ungodliness of ungodly bishops Christians always need to remember that they do stand in a position of moral superiority. If the bishop is ungodly then so also are they and so they need to issue calls for repentance, and initiate disciplinary procedures in much fear and trembling over their own weaknesses.

Secondly, as Lee Gatiss notes, in contending against the heresy of heretical bishops Christians:

...need to remember to contend by spiritually applying the gospel and drawing the necessary lines, in *a way that pleases God*. There is a danger that if we don't stand firm and oppose heresy we end up sliding into compromise and heresy ourselves, since we are always inclined to corruption no matter how pure our church may be on paper. But it is equally dangerous to fight in a way that loses sight of our Lord Jesus. It is true that we may sometimes be tempted to act or not to act because of worldly considerations and calculations, being more concerned for what our friends may say about us, or how the diocese might take it, then we ought to be. That is human nature, sadly. On the other hand we should be more focused on people than on arguments: note how Jude and James say we contend by having mercy on those who doubt and by saving those who wander. If we are servants of the Lord and not just of some ecclesiastical faction, we will not be quarrelsome but kind to everyone, able to teach (2 Timothy 2:24). Our relationships to our human opponents must always be sufficiently respectful and dignified that we are able to speak in a way that they can hear and learn and by God's grace possibly repent. [1055]

Note 1: Athanasius and Eusebius of Samosata exercising extraordinary jurisdiction

Athanasius

Immediately on his arrival in Egypt, Athanasius displaced those whom he knew to be attached to Arianism, and placed the government of the Church and the confession of the Nicæan council in the hands of those whom he approved, and he exhorted them to hold to this with earnestness. It was said at that time, that, when he was traveling through other countries, he effected the same change, if he happened to visit churches which were under the Arians. He was certainly accused of having dared to perform the ceremony of ordination in cities where he had no right to do so.[1056]

Athanasius passed through Pelusium on his way to Alexandria, and admonished the inhabitants of every city to beware of the Arians, and to receive those only that professed the Homoousian faith. In some of the churches also he performed ordination; which afforded another ground of accusation against him, because of his undertaking to ordain in the dioceses of others.[1057]

Eusebius of Samosata

Him, too, Valens relegated to Arabia, the divine Meletius to Armenia, and Eusebius, that unflagging labourer in apostolic work to Thrace. Unflagging he was indeed, for when apprised that many churches were now deprived of their shepherds, he travelled about Syria, Phœnicia and Palestine, wearing the garb of war and covering his head with a tiara, ordaining presbyters and deacons and filling up the other

---

[1055] Gatiss, p.179. Italics in the original.

[1056] Sozomen, *Ecclesiastical History* 3:21, in *The Nicene and Post-Nicene Fathers* 2nd series, vol. II (Edinburgh and Grand Rapids, T&T Clark Eerdmans, 1997), p.299.

[1057] Socrates *Ecclesiastical History*, 2:24, in *The Nicene and Post-Nicene Fathers* 2nd series, vol. II, p.253.

ranks of the Church; and if haply he lighted on bishops with like sentiments with his own, he appointed them to empty churches.[1058]

Lastly the divine Eusebius ordained Maris, Bishop of Doliche, a little city at that time infected with the Arian plague. With the intention of enthroning this Maris, a right worthy man, illustrious for various virtues, in the episcopal chair, the great Eusebius came to Doliche. As he was entering into the town a woman thoroughly infected with the Arian plague let fall a tile from the roof, which crushed in his head and so wounded him that not long after he departed to the better life. As he lay a-dying he charged the bystanders not to exact the slightest penalty from the woman who had done the deed, and bound them under oaths to obey him. Thus he imitated his own Lord, who of them that crucified Him said 'Father forgive them for they know not what they do.'[1059]

[1058] Theodoret, *Ecclesiastical History*, 4:12, in *The Nicene and Post-Nicene Fathers* 2nd series, vol. III (Edinburgh and Grand Rapids, T&T Clark Eerdmans, 1996), p.116.
[1059] Theodoret, *Ecclesiastical History*, 5:4, in *The Nicene and Post-Nicene Fathers* 2nd series, vol. III (Edinburgh and Grand Rapids, T&T Clark Eerdmans, 1996), p.134.

Chapter 16
Bishops past, present and future

As we indicated at the end of chapter 11, we shall do two things in this final chapter. First, we shall review what we have learned in the course of this study about why the Church has had bishops in the past and should continue to have bishops today and about the nature of episcopal ministry, both in the Church in general and the Church of England in particular. Secondly, we shall apply what we have learned as we consider the challenges that Church of England bishops face today, and will face in the future, because of the way that a secular ideology now dominates Western society.

A. What we have learned in the course of this study

1. Why the Church has had bishops

We can summarise what we learned in Part I of this study about why the Church has had bishops by saying that the reason the Church has always had bishops is because the first bishops of the Church were the apostles themselves, and the apostles then appointed other bishops to succeed them in the role of exercising pastoral oversight over the clergy and laity of the churches they had founded.

This is the view that has traditionally been taken in the Church of England and that finds expression in the famous words of the preface to the 1662 *Ordinal*:

It is evident to all men diligently reading holy Scripture and ancient Authors, that from the Apostles' time there have been these Orders of ministers in Christ's Church; Bishops, Priests and Deacons.

Until the sixteenth century there does not seem to have been anybody who would have questioned the truth of this statement. People disagreed about the precise reasons why the apostles introduced bishops, and the precise nature of the distinction between priests/presbyters and bishops, but no one seems to have doubted that the practice of having bishops was of apostolic origin. However, from the sixteenth century onwards this traditional consensus has been completely reversed with the scholarly consensus today, including among Anglican scholars, being that the apostles did not institute episcopacy, but that bishops were first introduced into the Church in the second century in response to the challenges the Church was facing at that time. However, what we have seen in this study shows that the traditional consensus was correct, and the modern consensus is wrong.

In chapter 1 we saw that in the New Testament itself and in the two earliest post New Testament writings known as the *Didache* and *1 Clement* the two terms *presbuteros* (elder/presbyter) and *episkopos* (bishop) are used as synonyms. However, although the term *episkopos* is thus not used in the New Testament to refer to the distinctive form of ministry which would later be called episcopacy, the evidence we have indicates that such a ministry existed in New Testament times.

In chapters 2 and 3 we saw that episcopal oversight, in the sense of the overall oversight or 'government' of the churches, was first exercised by the apostles themselves:

They which were termed Apostles, as being sent of Christ to publish his gospel throughout the world, and were named likewise Bishops, in that the care of government was also committed unto them, did no less perform the offices of their episcopal authority by governing, than of their apostolical by teaching.[1060]

The apostles' episcopal oversight was originally universal in extent (see Matthew 28:18-20), but the geographical areas in which they exercised oversight gradually became divided up, and the combined evidence of the New Testament, the other sources which we have from the first and second centuries, and later writings such as Eusebius' *Ecclesiastical History*, tells us that the apostles gradually appointed others to exercise episcopal oversight over churches for which they had originally been personally responsible. In this way James was

[1060] Hooker, Bk. VII.iv.1. pp.336-337.

given episcopal oversight over the church in Jerusalem, Timothy was given episcopal oversight in Ephesus, Titus was given episcopal oversight in Crete, and the angels of the churches in Revelation 2 and 3 were given episcopal oversight over the seven churches of Asia. This means that although the term 'bishop' (*episkopos*) is first used as a specific title for those exercising this sort of episcopal oversight in the letters of Ignatius at the beginning of the second century, the office to which the title refers seems to have existed, at least as far as the church in Jerusalem is concerned, from very early on in the Church's history. Thus, James appears to have already been Bishop of Jerusalem by the time of peter's miraculous escape from prison recorded in Acts 12.

From the second century onwards, we find no evidence for the existence of any church that did not have an episcopal form of church government and the universal consensus, reflected by early writers such as Irenaeus, Hegesippus and Tertullian, was that later bishops were in a line of historical succession that could be traced back to the apostles themselves. For instance, Timothy was understood to have been appointed as the first bishop of Ephesus by Paul and all subsequent bishops of Ephesus traced their episcopal lineage back through to Timothy to Paul. The accuracy of these lines of historic episcopal succession has been questioned by church historians, but no good reason has been produced to show that they are incorrect and the evidence for them can be traced back to the testimony of people who were still alive in the time of the apostles.

In chapter 4 we saw that the evidence we have tells us that from the very first bishops had responsibility for more than one church, with James, Timothy, Titus, and the angels of the churches having responsibility for multiple churches in Jerusalem, Ephesus, Crete and the seven cities referred to in Revelation (such groups of churches constituting what later came to be called dioceses). During the second century ecclesiastical provinces made up of the dioceses overseen by a group of bishops were formed based on the civil provinces of the Roman Empire and during the third century the bishop of the metropolitan city of the province (the 'metropolitan' bishop) came to be viewed as having a position of superiority over the other bishops of the province and he was referred to as the 'arch' or chief bishop to mark his consequent superiority. Finally, a further distinction emerged between the metropolitans, with the bishops of the most important metropolitan cities being given the titles of primates and patriarchs. In the councils of the fourth century the bishops of Rome, Alexandria, Antioch and Constantinople were acknowledged as having this patriarchal position.

In chapter 5 we traced the history of episcopacy in the Church of England and what we saw was that such evidence as we have indicated that the Church in Roman Britain was episcopal from the outset and that by the fourth century it had its own system of provinces and metropolitan bishoprics. This provincial system collapsed following the Saxon conquest of most of England from the fifth century onwards However, following the emergence of a new English church (the 'Church of England') as a result of the evangelization of the Saxon kingdoms led by missionary bishops from Europe and from the Scottish Celtic tradition, a new diocesan and provincial system eventually emerged in the eighth century with two provinces, one southern and one northern, presided over by the two archbishops of Canterbury and York.

What we also saw in chapter 5 was that the episcopal and provincial system instituted during the early Saxon period was deliberately and carefully maintained in the centuries that followed, even in the face of the religious and political turmoil of the Reformation, the English Civil War and the Commonwealth. As a result, all the dioceses of the present-day Church of England (except for the diocese of Sodor and Man which originally formed part of a Norwegian diocese) can trace their origins back to the original dioceses of the Saxon Church of England and all the bishops of the Church of England can trace their episcopal lineage back to the first bishops of that church and through them to the first bishops appointed by the apostles themselves.

All this is relevant to the question of why the Church has bishops. As we saw in chapter 6 the tendency of the Church of England in recent times has been to argue that it is right to have bishops because episcopacy is the historic form of church government and bishops perform a variety of useful practical and symbolic functions in the life of the Church. However, we also saw that these are not the fundamental reason why it is right for the Church of England (and all other churches) to have bishops in historic succession.

As we also saw in chapter 6 the fundamental reason is that an episcopal system of church government was introduced by the apostles, who were acting with the authority of God. To quote once again the words of Hooker:

...whether the Apostles alone did conclude of such a regiment, or else they together with the whole Church judging it a fit and a needful policy did agree to receive it for a custom; no doubt but being established by them on whom the Holy Ghost was poured in so abundant measure for the ordering of Christ's Church, it had either divine appointment beforehand, or divine approbation afterwards, and is in that respect to be acknowledged the ordinance of God, no less than the ancient Jewish regiment, whereof though Jethro were the deviser (Exodus 18: 19), yet after that God had allowed it, all men were subject unto it, as to the polity of God, and not of Jethro.[1061]

A church which wants to be faithful to the pattern of church government ordained by God himself through the apostles should therefore have bishops, and it would make sense for these bishops to be consecrated in historic succession (as happened at the English Reformation) as a visible sign that these bishops are intended to be in continuity with the bishops who were first appointed by the apostles.

This does not mean, however, that having bishops is a benchmark by which it can be decided whether a particular group of people is a church at all. As Article XIX explains, there are two 'essential' notes of the church, the true preaching of the word and the right administration of the sacraments, and from this it follows that a

[1061] Hooker, Bk. VII.5.2. p. 341.

church that has these two notes is a church, regardless of the kind of government it has. It would be better if it had bishops, but it is nonetheless still a church, and the Church of England would be able to recognise it as such.

2. The role and character of bishops

In part II of this study, we considered the role and character of bishops, exploring what tasks bishops are called to perform and what sort of people they need to be. We looked in turn at what we learn about this subject from the New Testament, from the writers of the Patristic period, from Church of England writers in the sixteenth and seventeenth centuries, and from recent Church of England writings about the matter.

What we have seen is that Church of England writings contain a variety of different accounts of the role and character of bishops. However, despite this variety, if we consider these accounts as a whole, we find that a coherent picture of the bishop's role and character emerges from them. This picture can be summarised as follows.

As we saw at the end of chapter 11, in terms of what bishops are called to do:

a. Bishops are called to be Pastors to all in their dioceses, whether clergy or lay, whether in the Church or outside it.

b. They are to be guardians of the Christian faith as the Church of England has received it and to oppose error.

c. They are to be leaders of the Church's mission in the world.

d. They are to teach and preach.

e. They are to lead worship, preside at the celebration of the sacraments and confirm.

f. They are to promote unity in their dioceses and in the wider Church and encourage peace and reconciliation in the Church and the world.

g. They are to care for the poor and needy.

h. They are to ensure that there are sufficient ordained and authorised lay ministers in their dioceses and ordain and licence them to undertake their ministries.

i. They are to take part in the ordination and consecration of other bishops

j. They are to exercise ecclesiastical discipline and absolve the penitent.

k. They are to ensure that church buildings and churchyards are properly maintained and renovated.

l. They are to take counsel together with other bishops and with clergy and lay people in the synods, boards, and councils of their diocese and of the national church, using their power of veto when necessary.

In terms of the kind of people bishops are to be:

a. Bishops are to be baptized disciples of Jesus Christ.

b. They are to be deacons and priests before they are bishops and to continue a diaconal and priestly ministry as bishops.

c. They are to be people who personally accept the Christian faith as the Church of England has received it and committed to upholding and proclaiming it.

d. They are to be people with the ability to preach, teach and lead worship.

e. They are to be people of prayer who spend time studying the Scriptures and other writings that will enable them to understand and proclaim the faith.

f. They are to be people who have the capacity to understand new developments in the Church and in the world and interpret them in the light of the Bible and the orthodox Christian tradition.

What we also saw is that a comparison of this picture with the teaching about the role and character of bishops which can be found in the New Testament, in the writings of the Patristic period and in Church of England writings from the sixteenth and seventeenth centuries, including the 1662 *Ordinal,* shows that there is a continuity between this picture and this earlier teaching. The Church of England has remained a traditional church in its understanding of the role and character of bishops, just as much as it has remained a traditional church by continuing to have bishops in historic succession.

In chapter 9 of part II, we also considered what we learn from the New Testament and the Patristic tradition about the specific role of the Bishop of Rome. What we discovered is that there is a straight line of historical continuity between the claims for the universal Petrine authority of the Pope made by Pope Leo I in the mid fifth century and the claims for the authority of the Pope contained in the two key modern Roman Catholic documents on the topic, *Pastor Aeternus* in 1870 and *Lumen Gentium* in 1964. However, what we also discovered is that there is no direct line of historical continuity the extends back from the teaching of Pope Leo through the writings of the Fathers of the first five centuries to the ministry given to Peter by Christ. Although from New Testament times onwards the Church of Rome was regarded as very important church, it is only at the end of the fourth century that the idea came to be put forward by the Popes that the bishops of Rome had an unquestionable authority over the Church as a whole based on the commission given by Christ to Peter. This was a new idea, and it was not one that was ever accepted by the ecumenical councils, or by the Church as whole.

The claims for the Papacy made by the Roman Catholic Church thus fail the test of Catholicity in that they are not part of the apostolic witness contained in the New Testament, or the teaching of the Early Fathers, and they have never been accepted across the Church as whole. The Church of England was therefore right to reject these claims at the time of the Reformation.

3.   Episcopal Jurisdiction

In part III of this study, we have considered the nature and exercise of episcopal jurisdiction.

In chapter 12 we saw that the term 'jurisdiction' means both the official legal authority a person, or group of persons, possesses either to do something themselves, or to command something to be done (or not done) by others, and the area over which this authority extends.

We also saw that the purpose of episcopal jurisdiction is the building up of the Church as the body of Christ in the way described by Paul in Ephesians 4:11-16.

We noted that by virtue of their episcopal orders bishops have in principle the same kind of universal jurisdiction originally given to the apostles, but that the exercise of this universal jurisdiction is normally limited by the Church to specific places to avoid confusion and conflicting claims to authority. However, it has also been accepted both by the Church as a whole, and by the Church of England and the Anglican Communion, that bishops may act outside the normal limits of their jurisdiction if circumstances mean that it would be right for them to do so. In the words of Van-Espen:

The jurisdiction of the bishops is circumscribed within certain limits for the greater commodity of the Church: but when this end ceases, and it is rather for the advantage of the Church that a bishop should go beyond the boundaries of his jurisdiction, he can freely do so.[1062]

[1062] Zeger Van-Espen, *Dissertatio de Misero Statu Ecclesiae Ultrajectinae*, quoted in Puller, p.154.

In addition, parallel episcopal jurisdictions should not exist because they violate the principle established by the apostles and upheld by the Early Church that there should be one bishop and one church in each geographical area. In normal circumstances Christians should work to bring parallel episcopal jurisdictions to an end. However, it may also be necessary to establish new ones in emergency situations where a bishop is unable, or unwilling, to proclaim the gospel to those outside the Church, or to provide appropriate pastoral care for those inside it, or where a bishop or church has fallen into heresy and faithful Christians need to separate themselves from that bishop or that church as a result.

We further noted that in the Early Church metropolitan and patriarchal jurisdictions came into existence alongside diocesan jurisdictions. However, these jurisdictions were limited both in extent and the degree of authority involved, and action taken outside of these limits was viewed as unacceptable. It was for this reason that the claims for universal and unlimited jurisdiction made by the Popes from the end of the fourth century were regarded as illegitimate by the churches in the Eastern Empire and Africa.

In the Church of England bishops exercise their jurisdiction in personal, collegial and communal ways, acting as individuals, but also in collaboration with other bishops, other members of the clergy and with the laity. Following the rejection of Papal jurisdiction at the Reformation, there is no higher jurisdiction in the Church of England than the legal jurisdiction exercised by the Queen as the Church of England's supreme governor and the metropolitical jurisdictions exercised by the Archbishops of Canterbury and York.

In the Anglican Communion each province has its own diocesan and metropolitan bishops, but there is no bishop with jurisdiction over the Communion as whole. The Archbishop of Canterbury has certain specific roles within the Communion, but he is not the Anglican equivalent of the Pope and has no power to determine the teaching or practice of the Anglican Communion. These are determined on a collegial and communal basis, by the Lambeth Conference, the

Primates Meeting and the Anglican Consultative Council. Contemporary Anglican ecumenical thinking has become open to the possibility of the Pope acting as a world-wide personal focus of unity in a re-united Church. However, Anglicans are still unhappy, or at best cautious, about the claim made by the Popes for a world-wide Petrine jurisdiction.

Finally, we noted that in the exercise of their jurisdiction bishops are subject to a range of laws. They are subject to Scripture, which is God's word written, and which uniquely reveals the way of eternal salvation through Jesus Christ. However, they are also subject to the law of nature, the law of reason, the law of the Church and the law of the state. While bishops should normally obey the laws of the Church and the state, they should be prepared to disobey them if they go against the law of God as revealed in Scripture. Similarly, bishops should support appropriate changes in the laws of the Church and the state to meet new circumstances, but only if these changes do not contravene the law of God.

In chapter 13 we looked at how the distinction between episcopal orders and jurisdiction enables us to make sense of the distinction between diocesan bishops and suffragan bishops, that is bishops who give assistance to their diocesan bishop.

In this chapter we saw that there were suffragan bishops from the second century onwards and that there were two types of such bishops. There were coadjutor bishops who assisted aged or infirm diocesan bishops with the expectation that they would succeed them, and there were rural bishops (*chorepiscopi*) who served in the rural areas of dioceses under the jurisdiction of the diocesan.

In the Church of England there were suffragan bishops in the Middle Ages whose responsibility it was to undertake the spiritual responsibilities of diocesan bishops, especially ordaining and confirming, when the latter were absent from their dioceses. At the Reformation provision was made for the appointment of suffragan bishops by the *Suffragan Bishops Act* of 1534, and although the practice of appointing suffragan bishops lapsed at the beginning of the seventeenth century it was revived in 1870, and today there are more suffragan bishops in the Church of England than diocesan bishops.

We also saw that suffragan bishops are bishops who exercise particular roles within dioceses under the authority of the diocesan bishop. These roles may be exercised across a diocese, or mainly exercised in a particular area of a diocese in what are known as 'area schemes.' The five Provincial Episcopal Visitors are suffragan bishops whose role is to provide episcopal ministry to parishes that wish to receive priestly or episcopal ministry from men rather than women.

We further saw that there has been debate about the ministry of suffragan bishops and how it relates to that of diocesan bishops since Patristic times. This debate continues in the Church of England today and is reflected in the different models for the ministry of suffragan bishops put forward by the two Church of England reports *Episcopal Ministry* and *Suffragan Bishops*. The former sees a suffragan bishop as an 'episcopal vicar' exercising ministry on behalf of his or her diocesan. The latter sees a suffragan bishop as a member of a college of bishops, the members of which exercise episcopal ministry in a diocese on an equal basis. We noted that there are serious problems with both these models, and that a better approach is to see the distinction between diocesan and suffragan bishops in terms of jurisdiction.

A suffragan bishop is like all other bishops in virtue of his or her orders and hence is able to exercise the full range of episcopal ministry. However, a suffragan bishop is distinguished from a diocesan bishop in that he or she is given jurisdiction to exercise his or her ministry in a particular diocese, under the authority of its diocesan, and in a manner laid down by that diocesan.

This understanding of the suffragan bishop's role preserves the truth that a suffragan bishop exercises his or her own ministry, while at the same time preserving monepiscopacy, the principle that there is one bishop with overall responsibility for the oversight of each diocese.

In chapter 14 we considered what it means for a bishop to exercise their ministry in a 'good enough fashion.' We saw that the continuing presence of sin in the life of every Christian means that no bishop ever exercises their ministry in a perfect fashion. Every bishop always falls short. Nevertheless, there can be bishops who are 'good-enough' because, despite their imperfections, they exercise their episcopal jurisdiction in a generally adequate fashion.

We noted that such bishops need, first, to be pastors. This means that they need to feed the sheep of Christ's flock with the spiritual food of the Christian faith, protect them from those who would lead them astray in terms of belief or behaviour, and recover them when they have gone astray.

Secondly, they need to be guardians of the Christian faith as revealed in Holy Scripture and witnessed to by the writings of the Patristic period and the historic Anglican formularies. As guardians they need to point people to these sources of Christian truth, use them as the basis for their own teaching and practice, and do whatever then can to ensure that those ministers under their jurisdiction do the same.

Being a guardian of the faith in this way is not in tension with the idea that bishops are to be theological explorers. Everyone starts from somewhere in their quest for a deeper understanding of truth and the starting point for bishops is the faith of which they are the guardians.

Thirdly, they need to teach and preach. This is the heart of what bishops are called to do. They are called to feed the sheep themselves and cannot simply leave this role to others. Furthermore, their teaching and preaching needs to have a definite content and this content needs to be the faith of which they are the guardians. In addition, they need to know how to apply the truths of the Christian faith to the particular situations their flocks are facing, and they need to have the ability to act as apologists, able to commend and defend the faith to those outside the flock.

Fourthly, they need to be able to provide examples of holy living in their personal lives so that what they teach and preach is supported rather than undermined by how they behave.

Fifthly, in order to protect and recover the sheep, they need to combat error and exercise discipline. This means discerning and combatting doctrinal error and disciplining those ministers who teach it. It also means using the disciplinary tools available to them to exercise the power of the keys to both discipline and restore those members of the clergy who have erred in their behaviour.

Sixthly, they need to lead worship and preside over the celebration of the sacraments. When leading worship, they need to make sure that the form of worship conforms to church law, that the language of worship will be accessible to those who are present and that the content of worship will include the key elements of the reading and exposition of Scripture, a creedal affirmation of faith, the praise of God, the confession and absolution of sins, and intercessions. They will also need to be diligent in taking confirmation and in seeking to ensure that those in their dioceses understand the meaning of Baptism, Holy Communion and Confirmation and the responsibilities they involve as

Seventhly, they need to be leaders in mission. This means that they are to fulfil the five marks of mission themselves and to teach, exhort and support others to do the same.

Eighthly, they need to promote unity in the Church. They cannot do this simply by being bishops in historic succession, or by being bishops to people of all shades of opinion are happy to relate to, but by helping God's people grow into the unity referred to by Paul in Ephesians 4:13, 'the unity of the faith and of the knowledge of the Son of God,' by undertaking the activities previously listed.

Ninthly, they need to ordain and appoint ministers, other shepherds to help care for the sheep. In specific terms this means that working with their fellow bishops and with others in the Church they need ensure that there is a supply of ordained and lay ministers who understand and believe the Christian faith as the Church of England has received it, who are able to provide examples of godly living, and who have shown that they are willing and competent to teach and preach, to lead worship and preside at the sacraments, to correct error, to rebuke sin, and to restore the penitent.

Tenthly, they need to oversee the creation and maintenance of church buildings and churchyards in accordance with the laws of the Church and the state so that there are buildings in good order that can be used as places for worship and bases for mission and so that there are places where the bodies of the dead can be reverently laid to rest and where nature can be encouraged to flourish.

Eleventhly, they need to work with others in a collegial and communal fashion, but they cannot use this as an excuse to avoid their own personal responsibilities, and like Athanasius they need to be prepared to stand up against others for the sake of Christian truth and to use their powers of veto when it is necessary to do so.

Twelfthly, they need to keep on top of the administration which is an unavoidable part of being a bishop and when necessary, they need to be willing to accept help from others on their staff in order do to this.

We further noted that in the light of this role description for a good-enough bishop, those selected to be bishops should be:

- People who are committed followers of Jesus Christ.

- People who are baptised and confirmed.

- People who understand and whole-heartedly assent to the Christian faith as this is set out in the Scriptures and witnessed to by the Creeds and other Patristic writings and by the Church of England's historic formularies.

- People whose personal and family lives model Christian holiness.

- People who have shown their ability to undertake the various aspects of the bishop's role during an extensive period serving as deacons and priests.

- People who have shown that they are prepared to work with others, but also prepared to stand firm against others for the sake of Christian truth when it Is necessary to do so.

- People who have shown that they can keep on top of administration.

What is not necessary, however, is that they should have higher degrees in theology or qualifications in business administration.

Finally, the pastoral letter and directive from Bishop William Love on the issue of same-sex marriage. was included at the end of the chapter as a prime example of someone acting as a good-enough bishop by feeding his flock and protecting it from those who would lead it astray.

Having looked at what makes someone a good-enough bishop, we went on to look in chapter 15 at what makes someone a not good-enough bishop and what Christians should do when this is the case.

In this chapter we distinguished three categories of not good-enough bishops.

First, there are those who want to be good-enough bishops but are simply not up to the job. Ten reasons were identified as to why this might be the case:

1. They could have only a superficial understanding of the Christian faith.

2. They could have a deep understanding of the Christian faith, but a poor understanding of the contemporary world.

3. They could have a lack of pastoral knowledge and experience.

4. They could have a deep understanding of both the Christian faith and the contemporary world and have practical knowledge of the cure of souls, but not be able to communicate effectively to either groups or individuals because of a lack of training or natural incapacity.

5. They could be poor at leading worship.

6. They could be a poor judge of people and therefore make poor appointments or continue to hold positions for which they are unsuited.

7. They could be bad at working with others.

8. They could be bad at handling conflict, either because they handle it in a way which causes serious and lasting damage or because they seek to avoid at all costs it even when it is necessary.

9. They could be unable to keep on top of administration.

10. They could be incapable of getting the right balance between their primary diocesan commitment.

Secondly, there are what Augustine called 'bad bishops,' those who want the benefits of being a bishop, but who have no intention of fulfilling the obligation that the office brings with it to be a faithful shepherd to a part of God's flock and an example of holy living.

We saw that Archbishop Lancelot Blackburne and Bishop Peter Ball were examples of such 'bad bishops, with the case of Bishop Ball being the more heinous since while Blackburne did not pretend to be godly, Ball used a pretence of godliness as a means to facilitate sexual abuse.

Thirdly, there are those who propagate heresy in relation to Christian belief or behaviour. We saw that Bishop Apollinarius of Laodicea and Patriarch Nestorius of Constantinople were examples of heretical bishops from the Patristic period and Bishop Ernest Barnes, Bishop John Robinson and Bishop Michael Ingham were examples of heretical bishops from recent times.

We noted that the reason heresy has to be regarded as extremely serious is because of the truth highlighted by the Athanasian Creed that salvation involves holding fast to the Catholic (i.e. orthodox) faith in both belief and behaviour and heresy and that heresy therefore brings with it the risk of the ultimate spiritual harm of eternal damnation.

Having identified these three categories of not good-enough bishops we then considered how Christians should respond to each of them.

Regarding the first category, we saw that the correct approach is for people to pray for the bishop concerned and work with him or her to help them become good-enough. If in the long term it becomes apparent that this is not going to happen the bishop should be encouraged to resign or retire with as much dignity and support as possible so that a bishop who will be good-enough can then be appointed.

Regarding the second and third categories, we saw that the teaching of Article XXVI comes into play. This means that the episcopal acts or bad or heretical bishops (such as confirmation or ordination) should be regarded as valid, but that nevertheless that it is necessary for faithful Christians to contend against the ungodliness of ungodly bishops and the heresy of heretical ones, using the *Clergy Discipline Measure* and the *Ecclesiastical Jurisdiction Measure* to try to depose bishops from office if they are not willing to repent and change their behaviour, their teaching, or their heretical practice.

We further saw:

a.   That Christians should avoid any feeling of moral superiority over not good-enough bishops.

b.   That they should contend against heresy in a godly way, treating those involved in heresy with dignity and respect.

c.   That if heretical bishops remain in office faithful Christians need to seek some form of alternative episcopal oversight and that in this situation bishops should be prepared to follow Patristic precedent by offering such oversight outside the bounds of their normal jurisdiction.

B. Applying what we have learned to the challenges facing bishops today because of the secularisation of Western society

Church of England bishops today all face a range of specific local challenges that are much the same as the problems that other bishops have faced during the history of the Church. Such challenges are, for instance, the existence of difficult working relationships, clergy and laity going off the rails, a lack of resources and excessive demands on the bishop's time.

They also face the challenge of helping people both inside and outside the Church to deal with the multiple social problems facing Britain today including, for example, the continuing effects of Covid-19, the rising cost of living, lack of affordable housing, and the existence of modern forms of slavery.

However, in addition to these specific challenges, there is one overarching challenge which is new and which all bishops (and indeed all Christians) now face, which is how to respond to the dominance of a secular ideology in Western society and the potential effects of this ideology on the life of the Church both now and in the years to come.

How the dominant secular ideology has developed [1063]

Carl Trueman's important study *The Rise and Triumph of the Modern Self* addresses the question of why it is that in contemporary Western society it has come to be regarded as meaningful to say 'I am a woman trapped in a man's body' (and unacceptable to question this statement) when previous generations would have dismissed this statement as completely absurd.

Trueman's answer to this question is that the reason the statement is

now regarded as meaningful is because a number of interrelated developments that have taken place across the Western world since

---

[1063] The paragraphs that follow are adapted from Martin Davie, *Living in Love and Faith – A biblical response* (Oxford: Dictum press, 2021), pp. 83-89.

the second half of the eighteenth century have together led to a radical shift in what Trueman calls the 'social imaginary'—that is, the way most people understand the world and how to behave within it.[1064]

These developments have been as follows:

First, the secularisation of Western society and the consequent loss of the sense of the world as God's creation means that there has been a shift in people's views of the world from *mimesis* (from the Greek for 'imitation') to *poesis* (meaning 'creating). As Trueman explains:

A *mimetic* view regards the world as having a given order and a given meaning and thus sees human beings as required to discover that meaning and conform themselves to it. *Poiesis*, by way of contrast, sees the world as so much raw material out of which meaning and purpose can be created by the individual.[1065]

Secondly, there has been the related loss of the idea of 'sacred order'. In Western culture today most people no longer believe that there is fixed moral order which has been established by God and which all human beings therefore need to respect.

Thirdly, as a result, Western culture lacks an agreed basis for ethics. So, as Alasdair MacIntyre has argued, the basis of ethical decision-making has, by default, become mere emotivism—that is, ethics based on personal feeling and preference.[1066]

Fourthly, there has also been a change in the way in which most people view the purpose of human existence—the good to which human beings should aspire. What has emerged is what Charles Taylor calls a 'culture of authenticity'. This is an understanding of life that says

---

[1064] Carl Trueman, *The Rise and Triumph of the Modern Self* (Wheaton: Crossway, 2020), pp.36-37.
[1065] Trueman p.39.
[1066] Alasdair MacIntyre, *After Virtue* (London: Duckworth, 1983).

...that each of us has his/her own way of realizing our humanity, and that it is important to find and live out one's own way—as against surrendering to conformity with a model imposed on us from outside, by society, or by the previous generation, or religious or political authority.'[1067]

Fifthly, there has been the development of what Philip Rieff calls the 'therapeutic society'—a society in which social institutions are viewed as being set up to foster the individual's sense of psychological well-being as they live out their unique authentic existence.[1068]

Sixthly, since the work of Sigmund Freud, it has come to be widely believed that 'humans, from infancy onward, are at core sexual beings. It is our sexual desires that are ultimately decisive for who we are.'[1069] The acceptance of Freud's ideas has been facilitated by the huge growth in pornography but also the many developments in modern medicine which make the results of sexual activity less serious by separating sex from childbirth and by providing more effective treatment for sexually-transmitted diseases.

Finally, the work of Neo-Marxist scholars such as Wilhelm Reich and Herbert Marcuse has led to the idea that the traditional view of the family (consisting of a married couple and their children), together with the traditional sexual morality linked to this, are inherently oppressive and need to be overthrown.

Imaginary identity and subjective experience

As Trueman argues, the result of these seven developments has been to create a 'social imaginary' that is based on *poiesis* rather than *mimesis*: we live in a world of our creating. In such a world the idea of being a woman trapped in a man's body begins to make sense. On the one hand, there is no fixed order of things, and no fixed pattern for

---

[1067] Charles Taylor, *A Secular Age* (Cambridge Ma and London: Belknapp Press, 2007), p.475.
[1068] See Philip Rieff, *The Triumph of the Therapeutic* (Chicago: Chicago University Press, 1966).
[1069] Trueman, p.27.

human existence or behaviour; thus there is no yardstick against which one can measure whether the idea is wrong. On the other, it becomes perfectly natural for an individual to say something such as:

'The purpose of my existence is to live as authentically as possible in accordance with what I perceive to be my true self. If this then involves seeing myself as a woman, even though I have a man's body, then that is what I should do.

Furthermore, society should support me in so doing because only then will I achieve psychological well-being. Thinking otherwise is immoral because it involves damaging my psychological well-being through a refusal to give recognition to who I believe myself to be.'

The same factors create a social imaginary in which the acceptance of same-sex relationships and the claim to a gay or lesbian identity also makes sense. Again, there is no fixed order of things and no fixed pattern for human behaviour, and thus no yardstick against which one can say same-sex relationships are wrong. And so, the individual may often justify an action as follows:

'The purpose of my existence is to live as authentically as possible in accordance with what I perceive to be my true self. If this involves having sex with someone of my own sex, then that is what I should do. In addition, because, as Freud has taught us, sexual desire is at the core of human identity, my desire for sex with someone of my own sex defines who I am. I *am* gay or lesbian.'

As Trueman goes on to say, within this worldview:

'...mere tolerance of homosexuality is bound to become unacceptable. The issue is not one of simply decriminalizing behaviour; that would certainly mean that homosexual acts were tolerated by society, but the acts are only part of the overall problem. The real issue is one of recognition, of recognizing the legitimacy of who the person thinks he actually is. This requires more than mere tolerance, it requires equality before the law and recognition by the law and in society. And that means that those who refuse to grant such recognition will be the ones who find themselves on the wrong side of both the law and emerging social attitudes.

The person who objects to homosexual practice is, in contemporary society, actually objecting to homosexual identity. And the refusal by any individual to recognize an identity that society at large recognizes as legitimate is a moral offense, not simply a matter of indifference.'[1070]

This is why LGBTQI+ campaigners react so strongly against the idea that those Christians who object to same-sex sexual relationships can speak of 'hating the sin but loving the sinner'. Within a post-Freudian worldview sexual identity and sexual behaviour cannot be separated. Hence to hate the sin is also to hate the sinner.

An additional but related aspect of modern Western culture is the central place given to personal experience. If there is no fixed moral order, how should individuals decide how they should live? The answer increasingly is that they should simply 'try it and see'. In other words, as they proceed through life they should decide, on the basis of their personal experience, what pattern of life, and what pattern of sexual identity and activity, gives them that sense of psychological well-being which is the proper goal of life.

As Trueman points out,[1071] this idea of experience as normative can be found in one of the seminal works of modern Western thought, Jean-Jacques Rousseau *Confessions*.[1072] Life, according to Rousseau, should be lived on the basis of reflecting on one's experience. This approach stands in contrast to the earlier *Confessions* of Augustine.[1073] For Augustine what is normative is not his experiences, but the teaching of Scripture, since it is only through the witness of Scripture that he is able to make sense of his experiences.

[1070] Trueman, pp.68-69.
[1071] Trueman, chapter 3.
[1072] Jean-Jacques Rousseau, *Confessions* (Oxford: OUP, 2008).
[1073] Augustine, *The Confessions* (Oxford: OUP, 2008).

What all this means is that Western society has now reached a place where human beings are playing the role of their own creator, constructing identities for themselves, and testing everything at the solitary bar of their own subjective experience. I am who I think I am on the basis of my unique experience and everybody else must accept this fact.

Western secular ideology from a Christian perspective

From a Christian perspective there are three fundamental problems with the Western secular ideology described by Trueman.

The first problem is that it is idolatrous. It is idolatrous because it puts human beings in the place of the creator God. It falsely claims that it is we and not God who create who we are and who determine how we should live. It is also idolatrous because it sees the highest human good as being not to love and serve God, but to love and serve our own subjective desires, particularly our desire for sexual fulfilment.

The second problem is that it insists that everybody has to accept the claims I make about my own identity. This idea is problematic because it assumes that I can never be mistaken about who I am. However, the fact that humans can be (and frequently are) mistaken means that it actually makes perfectly good sense for someone who has, or thinks they have, better information about who I am than I have, to refuse to accept my account of myself.

This further means that there is nothing wrong in principle with Christians believing that those who identify as gay, or lesbian were not created to find their fulfilment in sexual relations with those of the same-sex, or with Christians declining to accept that someone who is biologically male is actually female, or vice-versa.

The third problem is that it mistakenly contrasts obedience to God's will as revealed in Scripture and the Christian tradition with the exercise of human freedom. As Richard Bauckham explains:

The crux is the question of obedience to God's will. Is this a kind of heteronomy (subjection to another) that contradicts human autonomy (self-determination)? Many modern people think so. But, properly understood, obedience to God transcends this contradiction. When I love God and freely make God's will my own, I am not forfeiting my freedom but fulfilling it. God's will is not the will of another in any ordinary sense. It is the moral truth of all reality. To conform ourselves freely to that truth is also to conform to the inner law of our own created being. To learn obedience to God involves, of course, a long and painful struggle, as it did for Jesus (Hebrews 5:8), who exercised his freedom as Son never more fully that in his acceptance off his Father's will in Gethsemane (Mark 14:36). But it is a journey into the fullest freedom: the goal of our salvation in which theonomy (obedience to God's will) and autonomy will fully coincide. That is why the Anglican collect for peace says that 'to serve you is perfect freedom.'

Once again, the key is love. The limit constituted by God's will is not a restriction on our freedom when we accept it by loving God by freely embracing God's will, by making God's will our own. We transcended the limit by accepting it. In this way we fulfil through love of God the freedom we receive from God through God's love for us.[1074]

Two further challenges

The fundamental challenge that the existence of this ideology poses for the Church in the Western World, is that it means that the Church now exists in a society in which the majority of people view the world through the lens of an aggressive and all-pervasive ideology that is problematic for the three reasons just described. Like the Church of the first three centuries, or the Church in Eastern Europe during the Communist era, the Church in the Western World, including the Church of England, has to be willing to be counter cultural by maintaining and proclaiming Christian truth in a world that is dominated by lies.[1075] The challenge for bishops is how to lead the Church in doing this.

[1074] Richard Bauckham, *God and the Crisis of Freedom* (Louisville: Westminster John Knox Press, 2002), pp. 46-47.
[1075] For this point see Rod Dreher, *Live not by lies – A manual for Christian Dissenters* (New York: Sentinel, 2020).

This challenge is made more difficult by the fact that the influence of the ideology that has just been described has resulted in two further challenges to the Christian Church in the Western World (including the Church of England), one external and one internal.

Being the bad guys

The external challenge has two elements to it. The first element is that for very many in the Western world the incompatibility between traditional Christian theology and sexual ethics and the modern belief in self-creation and sexual freedom means that Christians are now the 'bad guys.'

To quote Stewart McAlpine:

Only a few generations ago, Christianity was the good guy, the solution to what was bad. Rather than being on the wrong side of the law, we were the law. Christian morality was assumed and passed mainly unchallenged. The cultural, legal and political power structures affirmed Christians. Then something changed. Over the course of the twentieth century, we became just one of the guys: one option among many -a voice to be considered but not to be followed unquestioningly. If Christianity worked for you, fine; if it didn't work for me, also fine.

Most of us think we still live in that world. Most Christian books, sermons and podcasts assume that we do. In many ways, we've only just worked out how to live well as one of the guys.

But the problem is that that's not where we are now. The tide has shifted further. Christianity is no longer an option; it's a problem. The cultural, political and legal guns that Christianity once held are now trained on us -and it's happened quickly. The number of those professing faith has fallen dramatically. The number of those who reject the faith they held until their late teens has risen dramatically. The seat at the cultural table that we assumed was ours for keeps is increasingly being given to others. We're on the wrong side of history, the wrong side of so many issues and conversations. If this were a Western, we would be the guys wearing the black hats whose appearance is accompanied by the foreboding soundtrack. It's come as a surprise, we're not sure how it happened, we don't like it and we don't feel we deserve it - but we are the bad guys now. [1076]

The perception that Christians are the bad guys and that their sexual ethics are morally unacceptable has been reinforced in recent years by the revelation of cases of sexual abuse in numerous churches, such as the sexual abuse perpetrated by Bishop Peter Ball noted earlier in this study. The existence of such abuse is seen as somehow discrediting further Christian ethical teaching even though the abuse in question happened precisely because the abusers deliberately disregarded Christian sexual ethics in the way they behaved.

Because Christians are now the bad guys, and because people need protection from the bad guys, the second element of the external challenge is that Christians are now increasingly facing not only widespread social disapproval, but the threat of legal sanctions against what have hitherto been viewed as perfectly normal forms of religious activity.

For example, as George Hobson writes:

Critics of homosexual practice and the gay lifestyle, even when they are welcoming of gays and eager to help those who wish to change their lifestyle, are labelled 'homophobic' and are subject to the severest condemnation by those who see themselves as morally enlightened. On account of the politicization of this issue through pressure from the powerful Gay Lobby and its political supporters, it will soon become a criminal offence to offer such criticism, and Christian organizations such as churches or Christian schools that cleave to traditional biblically based ethical doctrine and practice will

---

[1076] Stewart McAlpine, *Being the Bay Guys – How to live for Jesus in a world that says you shouldn't* (Epsom: The Good Book Company 2021), kindle edition pp.2-3

come under attack in the courts and even find their leaders being dragged off to jail. [1077]

Although Hobson is writing specifically about the response to criticism of homosexual practice, the same sort of response is also now made to those who are critical of the practice of gender transition. They too now face severe moral condemnation as transphobic and the threat of legal sanctions.

This two-part external challenge creates two problems for the Church. First, the perception of Christians as the 'bad guys' makes it more difficult for the Christian message to get a hearing. After all, who wants to listen to what the bad guys have to say? If Christians are 'homophobes' and 'transphobes' then the rest of what they have to say can simply be dismissed. Secondly, the perception that Christians are 'bad guys' and the threat of legal action against those who espouse traditional Christian doctrine and practice will inhibit the Church's work in that it will lead people to refuse to publish Christian material, lead to Christians having restricted access to the media, and mean that organisations will refuse to let Christians use their venues for meetings. In addition, it will potentially mean Christians having to choose between disobeying God or suffering punishment for breaking the law, neither of which are desirable.

Rejecting a theology of unconditional affirmation and cheap grace

[1077] George Hobson, The Episcopal Church, Homosexuality and the Context of Technology, (Eugene: Pickwick Publications, 2013), kindle edition, Loc.3114-3124. The trial of a Christian MP and a Lutheran bishop in Finland for publishing material expressing a traditional Christian sexual ethic ('Trial of Räsänen and Pohjola completed: decision comes at the end of March') https://evangelicalfocus.com/europe/15454/trial-of-rasanen-and-pohjola-completed-decision-comes-at-the-end-of-march) and the calls in the UK for a ban on 'conversion therapy' that would effectively outlaw many forms of Christian ministry including simply praying with people (see 'Let us pray' at https://letuspray.uk/) are evidence of the truth of Hobson's statement.

The internal challenge to the Church is posed by a new form of theology that first became prevalent in North America but has now spread across the Western world. As Philip Turner explains in his essay 'ECUSA's God and the Idols of Liberal Protestantism,' this theology begins with the belief that:

...the incarnation is to be understood (in an almost exhaustive sense) as a manifestation of divine love. From this starting point, several conclusions are drawn. The first is that God is love pure and simple. Thus, one is to see in Christ's death no judgement upon the human condition. Rather, one is to see an affirmation of creation and the persons we are. The great news of the Christian gospel is this. God wants us to love one another, and such love requires of us both acceptance and affirmation of the other. From this point we can derive yet another, accepting love requires a form of justice that is inclusive of all people, particularly those who in some way have been marginalized by oppressive social practice. The mission of the church is therefore to see that those who have been rejected are included and that justice as inclusion defines public policy.[1078]

As the title of Turner's essays reveals, in these words he is describing what he calls the 'working theology' of The Episcopal Church in the United States. However, as previously noted, this theology has spread across the Western world, and it has now firmly taken root in the Church of England. Thus, the mantra of the need for 'inclusion' which has spread across the Church of England in recent years reflects the influence of the sort of theology summarised by Turner.

It is not difficult to see the connection between this kind of theology and the prevailing cultural ethos of diversity, equality and inclusion which has resulted from the developments in Western culture described by Trueman. According to the diversity, equality and inclusion ethos, everyone is to be accepted and affirmed on their own

[1078] Philip Turner, 'ECUSA's God and the Idols of Liberal Protestantism' in Ephraim Radner and Philip Turner, *The Fate of Communion* (Grand Rapids and Cambridge: Eerdmans, 2006, p.249).

terms, particularly the members of hitherto marginalized sexual minorities. In similar fashion, in the theology described by Turner everyone is to be accepted and affirmed by those in Church because everyone is unconditionally affirmed and accepted by God.

Furthermore, just as in wider society acceptance and affirmation are seen as requiring the social inclusion of the members of sexual minorities on their own terms as a matter of justice, so within the Church (including in the Church of England) it is increasingly being argued that justice demands that members of sexual minorities are likewise fully accepted on their own terms, which in turn means that LGBT people should be able to serve in all forms of ministry and that churches should be willing to celebrate same-sex marriages.

For example, the 'The Change We Want to See' section of the website of the LGBT pressure group One Body One Faith declares:

- we want the Christian churches to be places where all people, particularly those who identify as gay, lesbian, bisexual or transgender, are welcomed and affirmed, not just tolerated.

- we want church communities to be places where people are safe to explore questions of sexuality, faith and spirituality in ways which are intelligent, respectful and compassionate, where we can reach different conclusions without hurting one another.

- we want gay, lesbian, bisexual, and transgender people to be treated the same way as our straight and cisgendered siblings, in our lives, our relationships and our ministry.

- we want to be able to celebrate our marriages in our places of worship, so that we can acknowledge God as the source of the love between and within us.

- we want our families to feel welcome in our churches, throughout their journey of life and faith, and especially when they are feeling vulnerable or confused or facing times of transition and change.

- we want to be able to offer our gifts in all forms of ministry, on the same terms as our brothers and sisters, and not to have to choose between our calling to serve God, and our loving relationships.[1079]

From this viewpoint it is not enough for churches to say that LGBT people are welcome to attend. To be properly inclusive churches must also fully accept their relationships (hence allowing same-sex marriages) and their gender identities and cease to place any restrictions on the ministries they are allowed to exercise.

From an orthodox Christian perspective, the underlying theology of unqualified divine love and affirmation on which this challenge is based is heretical for two reasons.

It is heretical because it claims that Christ's death involved no judgement on the human condition. This is heretical because if ask If we ask why Christ had to die our death on the cross in order that we might be saved the answer Paul gives us in Romans 6: 6-7 is that:

We know that our old self was crucified with him that the sinful body might be destroyed and we might no longer be enslaved to sin. For he who has died is freed from sin.

What he is saying in these verses is that our fallen nature was slain in the death of Christ in order that we might have liberation from the domination by sin which our old nature ('our old self') necessarily entails. Christ's death was thus *both* an act of God's judgement *and* an act of God's love. The cross was an act of God's judgement in that on the cross the death penalty was carried out on us as sinners. Our sinful existence ('the sinful body') has no right to exist before God and it was therefore ended. It was at the same time an act of love since the

[1079] One Body One Faith, 'The Change We Went to See' at
https://www.onebodyonefaith.org.uk/about-us/the-change-we-want-to-see/

purpose of this judgement was to destroy our enslavement to sin in order that we might become free to be the people God intends us to be.

It is also heretical because it teaches what Dietrich Bonhoeffer famously labelled 'cheap grace', that is 'grace without repentance.'[1080] It affirms God's love for us, but it is silent about our need to respond to that love in repentance.

As Hobson explains, the issue is that:

God in Christ is turned towards us, yes: but we as sinners living in a fallen world are by nature turned in on ourselves and away from him, and we cannot authentically go toward him unless we first turn round, or change course, which is what repentance means. [1081]

As he goes on to say:

In order to receive the gift of forgiveness of sins, the promised gift of the Holy Spirit, and the gift of eternal life won for us by the atoning passion of Jesus Christ, we must repent and believe, and this will involve going in the opposite direction from the self-focused one we were travelling in before. the Bible calls this 'metanoia.' it is a matter of conversion. Jesus becomes our Lord and Master instead of our own ego. The way we experience this turning away from self and towards God will vary greatly from person to person, but it must happen if we want to be incorporated genuinely into the 'new creation' that the authentic Church, as a corporate society, is, and that each believer, as a member by faith of this corporate society, is (Galatians 6:15; 2 Corinthians 5:17; Ephesians 4:24). [1082]

The truth that Christ's death was an act of judgement and the requirement for repentance go together because the character of repentance is to turn away from those things belonging to our sinful

[1080] Dietrich Bonhoeffer, *The Cost of Discipleship* (London: SCM, 1959) p. 35.
[1081] Hobson, Loc.2933.
[1082] Hobson, Loc. 2946-2965.

state which were put to death when Christ died on the cross. That is why the Christian life has traditionally been seen in terms of mortification and vivification, mortification involving the rejection of the old way of life which was put to death when Christ died for us, and vivification involving the entering into the new way of life that Christ died to make possible.

Furthermore, just as it is heretical to say that God simply loves and affirms us without acknowledging the reality of God's judgement and the need for repentance, so also it is heretical to say that the role of the Church is simply to accept and affirm people. This is because the Church is called to preach 'repentance and the forgiveness of sins' (Luke 24:47). That is to say, the Church must make clear to people the truth which we have just been outlining, namely that receiving the forgiveness of sins that Christ offers involves people being willing, in the power given to them by God through the Holy Spirit, to turn away from that sinful form of existence from which Christ died to set them free.

We can see Paul making just this point clear to the Christians in Galatia in Galatians 5:16-24:

But I say, walk by the Spirit, and do not gratify the desires of the flesh. For the desires of the flesh are against the Spirit, and the desires of the Spirit are against the flesh; for these are opposed to each other, to prevent you from doing what you would. But if you are led by the Spirit you are not under the law. Now the works of the flesh are plain: fornication, impurity, licentiousness, idolatry, sorcery, enmity, strife, jealousy, anger, selfishness, dissension, party spirit, envy, drunkenness, carousing, and the like. I warn you, as I warned you before, that those who do such things shall not inherit the kingdom of God. But the fruit of the Spirit is love, joy, peace, patience, kindness, goodness, faithfulness, gentleness, self-control; against such there is no law. And those who belong to Christ Jesus have crucified the flesh with its passions and desires.

Finally, as has already been indicated in chapter 15, it would be heretical for a church to do what LGBT pressure groups such as One

753

Body One Church demand, which is to accept and affirm LGBT people without requiring them to repent of same-sex sexual relationships or the assumption of a gender identity that does not reflect the sexual identity given to them by God. Rather than being an act of justice this would be an act of double *injustice*, injustice against God, by telling people that they do not have to live in the way God created them to live, and injustice against the people concerned who would be left living in this way with the risk of being cut off from God and all good for ever.

To understand why this is so we must begin by recognising that when God created human beings in his image and likeness, he created them to be male or female. In the words of Genesis 1:27: 'So God created man in his own image, in the image of God he created him; male and female he created them.' This teaching is reiterated by Jesus in Matthew 19:4: 'Have you not read that he who made them from the beginning made them male and female.'

There is a very small percentage of people, some 0.018% of live births (approximately 1:500), who are genuinely 'intersex' in the sense that they combine both male and female elements in their physiology. However, the existence of such people still points to the fundamentally dimorphic, male or female, nature of human sexuality. Where they are able to reproduce, and that is often not the case, they do so either as male or female. Their condition is a developmental disorder rather than the existence of a third type of human being and is the exception that proves the rule.

Because this is the case, except in these highly exceptional and biologically distinct cases, believing rightly in 'God the Father who hath made me and all the world' in the words of the Prayer Book Catechism, means accepting with gratitude that I am the particular male or female human being that God has created me to be and living accordingly.

As Oliver O'Donovan writes in his book *Begotten or Made?*:

When God made mankind male and female, to exist alongside each other and for each other, he gave a form that human sexuality should take and a good to which it should aspire. None of us can, or should, regard our difficulties with that form, or with achieving that good, as the norm of what our sexuality is to be. None of us should see our sexuality as mere self-expression, and forget that we can express ourselves sexually only because we participate in this generic form and aspire to this generic good. We do not have to make a sexual form, or posit a sexual good. We have to exist as well as we can within that sexual form, and in relation to that sexual good, which has been given to us because it has been given to humankind.[1083]

This means that it is not legitimate either to deny the God-given form by rejecting the division of humanity into male and female, or to deny the particular version of that form that God has given to us by making us either male or female, something that is determined not by our feelings (as many today would claim), but by our biology. As we have noted before, 'my body is me' and this means that 'my biology is me.'

However difficult the form that God has given us may be for us to accept, to deny it would be sinful because it would involve refusing to say to God 'thy will be done' by refusing to love the self who God has made us to be.

Refusing in this way to say to God 'thy will be done,' in either our thinking or our behaviour, is a very serious matter because it brings with it the inescapable risk of eternal separation from God. As C S Lewis writes in his book *The Great Divorce*, there is an inescapable binary choice facing all human beings. 'There are only two kinds of people in the end: those who say to God, 'Thy will be done,' and those to whom God says, in the end, 'Thy will be done.'' [1084]

Lewis' point is that God has given human beings freedom to shape their own destinies. We can choose to say to God 'thy will be done' and

---

[1083] Oliver O'Donovan, *Begotten or Made?* (Oxford: OUP, 1984), pp. 28-29.
[1084] C S Lewis, *The Great Divorce* (Glasgow: Fontana, 1972), pp. 66-67.

be happy with God for ever in the world to come, or we can choose to turn our back on God. If we do this God will respect our decision, but the inevitable consequence will be that in the world to come we will be cut off from God and all good for ever. The fundamental problem with both gender transition and same-sex relationships is that they do involve a rejection, in both theory and practice, of the sexual identity which we have been given by God and thus a failure to say to God 'thy will be done.'

Gender transition

In the case of gender transition, the issue is people who are suffering from a deep discomfort with their sexual identity (the condition known as 'gender dysphoria') refusing to accept the sexual identity of their body as given and seeking some to inhabit some other form of sexual identity instead. By doing this they act in a way that is incompatible with the biblical teaching that we should live in accordance with the sexual identity that God has given to us by the creation of the particular bodies that we possess.

This teaching can be found in Deuteronomy 22:5 which prohibits cross-dressing on the grounds that, as Peter Harland puts it: 'to dress after the manner of the opposite sex was to infringe the normal order of creation which divided humanity into male and female.'[1085] It can also be found in 1 Corinthians 11:2-16 where St Paul tells the Corinthians that men should follow the dress and hair codes which proclaim them to be male and women the codes which proclaim them to be female because, in the words of Tom Wright in his commentary on this verse: 'God's creation needs humans to be fully, gloriously and truly human, which means fully and truly male and female'.[1086]

Such teaching does not mean that Christians should uncritically embrace the gender stereotypes of any given society. What it does mean is that we should glorify God through our bodies by living in a

---

[1085] P.J. Harland 'Menswear and Womenswear: A Study of Deuteronomy 22:5,' (*Expository Times,* 110, No.3, 1988), p.76.
[1086] Tom Wright, *Paul for Everyone – I Corinthians* (London: SPCK, 2003), p.143

way that proclaims to our society the truth of our creation by God as male or female. We should be saying through our bodies, God has made me male, or God has made me female.

Engaging in gender transition is incompatible with this calling because it necessarily involves refusing to accept and live out the truth of the male or female identity that God the creator has given to us, by deliberately adopting instead an artificially created alternate identity instead. To acknowledge this point is not to minimise the acute distress experienced by people with gender dysphoria. It is, rather, to give a theological account of what using gender transition to relieve this distress entails.

The argument is often made that people who engage in gender transition cannot be said to be sinning since they are not deliberately choosing to go against God's will. They see the identity they are seeking to live out as their true God given identity, their 'authentic self,' and they simply desire to live according to this true identity.

This argument is true as an account of how the people involved view their situation. However, two further points need to be noted.

First, we have to distinguish between how an individual subjectively views their identity and what is objectively true. To be male or female is a matter of biology, it is a matter of the body someone has been given by God and for which and in which they are called to glorify him, and this truth is unaffected by how someone views him or herself. This means that someone who is biologically male or female, and who rejects this identity, is in fact rejecting the sex that God has given them, regardless of how they themselves view the matter.

Secondly, the fact that people with gender dysphoria have a distorted view of their situation which they then make the basis of sinful actions is not in fact something which makes them unique. As a result of the Fall human beings have lost the ability to always see things as they truly are (see Romans 1:21). Acts of sin (of whatever kind) occur when a distorted view of reality resulting from the Fall leads to wrong desires which in turn give birth to wrong actions. As Augustine argues in Book XIV of The City of God, 'our will is for our welfare' and this results in acts of sin because, misled in our thinking as a result of the Fall, 'we commit sin to promote our welfare.'[1087] This is what is involved in gender transition just as in all other forms of sin. Eve wanted the apple because she thought it would be for her good. People desire gender transition for the same reason.

Same-sex relationships

In the case of same-sex relationships the rejection of sexual identity, and hence the rejection of the body, may appear to be less obvious, but it still exists. The point is that same-sex relationships involve either a man refusing to accept that as a man he was created by God to have sex with a woman: or a woman refusing to accept that as woman she was created to have sex with a man.

This does not, of course, mean that to be a man or a woman one has to have sex with a member of the opposite sex. Christ and John the Baptist were no less male and no less fully human for being celibate. What it does mean is that a man was created to have sex with a woman rather than a man (and vice versa). To be a man is to be one who is potentially husband-to-a-wife, father-to- a-child and vice versa. To engage in same-sex sexual activity is to reject this God given truth about human sexual identity. It is very similar to gender transition in that it rejects a core aspect of the duty to conform our lifestyle and behaviour to the form of embodiment that God has given us.

As O'Donovan writes, human beings are:

...clearly ordered at the biological level towards heterosexual union as the human mode of procreation. It is not possible to negotiate this fact about our common humanity; it can only be either welcomed or resented.[1088]

[1087] Augustine, *The City of God*, Book XIV.4, text in David Knowles (ed), Augustine, City of God (Harmondsworth: Penguin 1972), p. 553

[1088] Oliver O'Donovan, *Transsexualism – Issues and Argument* (Cambridge: Grove Books, 2007), p.6.

To engage in same-sex activity is sinful because it involves translating resentment against the way we have been made by God into a form of activity which actively goes against the way God has made us to be. It involves saying 'I will live the way I want to live regardless of the way God made me.' This may not be what people consciously think they are doing, but it is what they are doing in practice.

This is the point that underlies the prohibition of sexual relationships between men in Leviticus 18:22 and 20:13. Like all the other sexual prohibitions in these two chapters, the prohibition of men having sex with other men reflects the teaching contained in Genesis 1 and 2 about how God created the world. According to this teaching, God created human beings as male and female, with men designed to have sexual relations with women within marriage and vice versa. Gay sex is an 'abomination' in Leviticus because it involves a rejection by an individual of this key aspect of the created order.

This is also the point that Paul is making when he describes same-sex relationships as 'unnatural' (*para phusin*) in Romans 1:27. In line with other Jewish thinkers of his time, Paul thinks they are unnatural because they violate the heterosexual form of sexual activity God has created men and women to engage in (as shown by the way their bodies are constructed).

For Paul same-sex sexual activity is thus a rejection of human createdness which parallels, and points to, the rejection of the creator through idolatry. That is why he cites it as the first example of the consequences of idolatry in human behaviour. As Tom Wright puts it 'the fact that such clear distortions of the creator's male-plus-female intention occur in the world indicates that the human race as a whole as a whole is guilty of a character-twisting idolatry'.[1089] Rejecting the creator and rejecting our createdness go together.

[1089] Tom Wright, *Paul for Everyone, Romans, Part 1: Chapters 1-8* (London: SPCK, 2004), pp.22-23. For a detailed exploration of Paul's teaching in Romans 1 see

Same-sex marriages are a further development of the basic error involved in all same-sex relationships. In terms of Christian theology, they too involve a failure to conform our sexual relationships to our God given embodiment. Marriage as created by God is a sexual relationship between two people of the opposite sex (Genesis 2:18-24). It follows that two men cannot enter into marriage with each other, and neither can two women. Same-sex marriages involve a denial of this truth.

What all this means is that same-sex relationships (including same-sex marriages) and gender transition both involve a rejection of the necessary implications of the first article of the Creed. People may still sincerely believe in 'God the Father Almighty, Maker of heaven and earth,' but they refuse to truly accept, or live out, this belief in so far as it relates to the existence of the particular men and women whom God has created.

As Martin Luther explains in his *Small Catechism*, the answer to the question of what it means to confess 'I believe in God, the Father almighty, Maker of heaven and earth' is 'I believe that God has created me and all that exists; that he has given me and still sustains my body and soul, all my limbs and senses, my reason and all the faculties of my mind'. In other words, the Christian belief in God the creator is not just a vague deistic belief that God is the ultimate source of all that is, but also the very specific belief testified to in Psalm 139 that God made me as the particular combination of body and soul that I am. Both same-sex relationships and gender transition involve in different ways a rejection of that basic truth. They thus involve, ultimately, a failure to say to God 'thy will be done' and to glorify God in the body by living according to this truth, and this, as previously noted, carries the risk of eternal damnation. That is why Paul warns the Corinthians in 1 Corinthians 6:10 that those who persist in same-sex sexual activity 'will not inherit the kingdom of God.'

Robert Gagnon, *The Bible and Homosexual Practice* (Nashville: Abingdon Press, 2001), pp. 229-302.

Because this is the case, from an orthodox Christian perspective any church which supports same-sex relationships or gender transition is a church which is in serious error in its teaching and practice. It is giving support to forms of behaviour which involve serious moral error because they involve people departing from the way God created them to live. To put it simply, it is a church which does not love people enough to seek to prevent them from living in ways that are contrary to way God made them to live.

Love does not mean simply affirming whatever choices people wish to make. It means seeking their ultimate good by helping them to understand what the right choices are and then choose them. A church which gives support to same-sex relationships or gender transition is failing to do this.

C.   Back to the future - meeting the challenges of our day

Why the early Church triumphed

As has already been noted, the Church today is back in the situation it was in the early centuries. Then too it faced a society marked by an idolatrous world view and a lax view of sexual ethics, in which Christians were widely regarded as the 'bad guys' and in which faithful Christians faced legal penalties including, on occasion, the death penalty.

The good news is that the Church of the early centuries eventually triumphed. In spite of the opposition it faced, the Church thrived and grew, with scholars estimating that it grew by about 40% a decade up to the end of the 4th century. Contrary to what has often been suggested, it did not triumph because it was recognised by Constantine. It was already triumphing by the time Constantine recognised it.

If we ask why the Early Church triumphed in this way the fundamental theological answer is, of course, that God made it happen. However, as the *Westminster Confession* reminds us, in his providential work in the world 'God maketh use of means'[1090] to carry out his purposes and in the case of the Early Church the 'means' that God used was a church that had seven key characteristics.

First, *it was a church that had a clear structure of theological authority.* The ultimate authority was the Scriptures, but alongside the Scriptures there was the 'rule of faith' (the precursor of the Creeds) that summarised the key teaching of the Scriptures and provided a framework for interpreting them correctly. In addition, as we have, seen it had in the bishops a set of people whose primary responsibility it was to teach the Scriptures, as interpreted according to the rule of faith, and to make sure that other members of the clergy did the same.

Secondly, *it was a church that sought to make sure that the teaching of the Church was not contaminated by heresy.* From the earliest time of which we have record the Church sought to prevent heresy being taught and the faithful from believing it. Whereas today we tend to see the structural unity of the Church as more important that combatting heresy, in the Early Church it was the other way round. Both the writers of the New Testament and later orthodox Fathers such as Athanasius were prepared to divide the visible Church rather than let heresy prevail.

Thirdly, *it was a church that kept eternity in view.* The early Christians from the New Testament onwards believed that all human beings would be resurrected to a new form of bodily existence at the end of time, but the almost universal consensus was that there would be an eternal divide between those who would enjoy this new form of existence with God forever in heaven, and those who would suffer eternal punishment forever in hell.

Fourthly, *it was a church that was religiously exclusive.* The early Christians believed, as their Jewish forebears had done, that there was only one true God, who for them was the Triune God who had become incarnate in Christ, and that to worship any other god was idolatry.

[1090] *The Westminster Confession* V.II in Leith p. 200.

This meant as Larry Hurtado puts it, that Christianity was the 'destroyer of the gods.'[1091] In the words of Lee Gatiss:

Every convert to Christianity was a loss to the pagan world. The old gods were destroyed as Christianity advanced, which was not true when people simply switched allegiance from one pagan god or goddess to another, in a pluralistic culture that was happy with huge diversity.[1092]

Fifthly, *it was an evangelistic church*. Because it was religiously exclusive and believed that the only way to guarantee an eternity spent in heaven rather than hell was through faith in Christ, the early Christians sought to convert everyone they could (which was not something pagan religions sought to do). Furthermore, it was the ordinary Christians who did most of the evangelizing. In the words of Kenneth Latourette:

...the chief agent in the expansion of Christianity appears not to have been those who made it a profession or made it a major part of their occupation, but mean and women who carried on their livelihood in some purely secular manner and spoke of their faith to those they met in a natural fashion.[1093]

In addition, as well as being an evangelistic church it was also an apologetic church in the sense that it was a church that took seriously the need to engage in apologetics aimed at showing (a) why Christians were not the 'bad guys' and (b) why Christianity was the true religion while paganism and Judaism were not.

Sixthly, *it was a church that cared for those in need*, both inside and outside the Christian community. They gave alms to the poor and

---

[1091] Larry Hurtado, *Destroyer of the gods – Early Christian distinctiveness in the Roman world* (Waco: Baylor University Press, 2016).

[1092] Lee Gatiss (ed), *Gospel flourishing in a time of confusion* (Watford: Church Society, 2019), p. 71.

[1093] Kenneth Latourette, *A History of the Expansion of Christianity, vol.1* (New York: Harper & Brothers, 1937), p.116

cared for the sick and when the plague came and those who could fled the Christians stayed and cared for the sick and dying, even at the cost of their own lives. In the words of Paul Johnson, they created 'a miniature welfare state in a society which for the most part lacked social services.'[1094]

This kind of loving action gave credibility to Christian teaching and made such an impact that the apostate Emperor Julian exhorted pagan priests to follow their example because it was the 'moral character, even if pretended' of the Christian that led people to desert the pagan gods.

Seventhly, *it was a church that welcomed everybody, but made very high demands on believers.* The early Christians welcomed people from both sexes, all nations and all social classes (see Galatians 3:28), but unlike the members of other religious groups in the Roman Empire 'believing in Christ came with an ethical claim over every second of your day or night and a set of orthodox doctrinal beliefs.' [1095] Furthermore, if a Christian departed from orthodox belief or right ethical behaviour (which included an absolute restriction of sexual intercourse to heterosexual marriage) they would, as we have seen, be disciplined and only restored to full communion if they repented of their wrongdoing.

In addition, although it was not the case that all (or most) early Christians faced persecution or were martyred, it was expected that being a Christian meant standing firm in the face of persecution when it did come and, if necessary, choosing death rather than apostasy.

What is also worth noting is that not only was this the kind of church that triumphed in the face of the challenges of the early centuries, but it also this kind of church that has been successful in spreading the Christian faith successfully in every generation since, and it is still this kind of church that is growing today in places such as Southeast Asia,

---

[1094] Paul Johnson, *A history of Christianity* (New York: Athanaeum, 1976), p.75.
[1095] Gatiss, p.72.

Sub-Saharan Africa and South America.

In terms of the Church of England, it is worth noting that the last time the Church of England saw significant growth was in the immediate post war period, and this was period which was marked by a renewed commitment within the Church both to traditional Christian orthodoxy, and to evangelism in the wake of the 1945 report *Towards the Conversion of England*.[1096] By contrast, it was when the Church of England began to lose its grip on orthodox theology and ethics in the 1960s, and began to emphasise social and political action at the expense of evangelism, that the Church of England began to enter into its present period of decline.[1097]

The message seems clear. We know the kind of church God wills to use fulfil the great commission. Given that is the case, the message to the bishops of the Church of England seems equally clear. If they want the Church of England to endure and triumph in the face of the contemporary challenges we have just looked at, then then they need to do what they can to see that the Church of England is this kind of church.

The agenda for bishops today and in the future
The question that then arises is what can bishops do to see that the Church of England is this kind of church?

The first answer to this question is that the proposals that have been leaked to the press for a reordering of the episcopate involving 'non territorial missionary bishops' and 'non diocesan episcopal roles to speak into particular issues' and giving suffragan bishops a 'territorial focus' [1098] are ecclesiologically problematic, unnecessary and irrelevant.

[1096] The Archbishops' Commission on Evangelism, *Towards the Conversion of England* (London: Press and Publications Board of the Church Assembly, 1945)
[1097] See Adrian Hastings, *A History of Christianity in England 1920-1985* (London: Fount 1987), parts V and VI.
[1098] See Madeleine Davies, 'Radical Reform ahead if top-level plan adopted', *Church Times,* 11 February 2002, pp.2-3.

They are ecclesiologically problematic because, as we have seen, from New Testament times onwards the God given role of bishops has been to exercise the oversight of the clergy and laity in a particular geographical area. For example, James was made Bishop of Jerusalem (not Bishop for Jewish believers) and Titus was made Bishop of Crete (not Bishop for the Pauline mission).

Obviously, bishops retain their orders and are still therefore bishops if they retire from this role and move on to do something else. Thus, Michael Marshall was still a bishop when he headed up the national Springboard initiative with Michael Green and Tom Wright was still a bishop when he returned to academia. A bishop without a specific territorial responsibility is therefore not an impossibility.

However, what it is not right to do is to deliberately create a form of episcopacy that has no responsibility for shepherding the flock in a particular area. Some Orthodox churches have done this, but they have not been right to do so because doing this means giving someone the title 'bishop' without giving them the episcopal responsibility that properly goes with it. Furthermore, this idea also clearly goes against Canons C17, 18 and 20 which, as we have seen describe the role of bishops in specifically diocesan terms.

They are unnecessary as far as suffragan bishops are concerned because all suffragan bishops already have a 'territorial focus' in that they are the suffragan bishops of a particular diocese. The PEVs are often seen as an exception to this rule, but in fact, as we have seen, they are suffragans of the dioceses of Canterbury, York and London who operate in other dioceses with permission as suffragans of the diocesan bishops in those dioceses. If what the leaked paper really means is that all suffragans should be area bishops, this would be problematic for dioceses such as Rochester or Bristol where an area scheme would not be appropriate.

They are irrelevant because there is no evidence that the present arrangements for bishops in the Church of England prevent them from acting as 'good-enough' bishops and there is equally no evidence that playing around with episcopacy in the way proposed is necessary to enable bishops to help the Church of England to become the kind of church God wills to use to fulfil the Great Commission in today's world.

The second answer is that there is clear action that bishops can take individually and collectively as those with episcopal jurisdiction to help the Church of England become this kind of church.

First, in the face of the idolatry of modern Western secular thought, the beliefs help by members of non-Christian religions and the heresy of unconditional divine acceptance and affirmation the has come to infect much of the Western Church, the bishops need to teach clearly and with conviction the truth about who God is and what he has done, the truth summarised in the Catechism in the *Book of Common Prayer* and expounded by Luther in his *Small Catechism* of 1529.

In the former we read:

Catechist. Rehearse the Articles of thy Belief.

Answer: I believe in God the Father Almighty, Maker of heaven and earth:

And in Jesus Christ his only Son our Lord, Who was conceived by the Holy Ghost, Born of the Virgin Mary, Suffered under Pontius Pilate, Was crucified, dead, and buried: He descended into hell; The third day he rose again from the dead; He ascended into heaven, And sitteth at the right hand of God the Father Almighty; From thence he shall come to judge the quick and the dead.

I believe in the Holy Ghost; The holy Catholick Church; The Communion of Saints; The Forgiveness of sins; The Resurrection of the body, And the life everlasting. Amen.

Question. What dost thou chiefly learn in these Articles of thy Belief?

Answer. First, I learn to believe in God the Father, who hath made me, and all the world.

Secondly, in God the Son, who hath redeemed me, and all mankind.

Thirdly, in God the Holy Ghost, who sanctifieth me, and all the elect people of God.

In the latter we read:

The First Article

I believe in God the Father Almighty, Maker of heaven and earth.

What does this mean?

I believe that God has made me and all creatures; that He has given me my body and soul, eyes, ears and all my members, my reason and all my senses, and still preserves them; that He richly and daily provides me with food and clothing, home and family, property and goods, and all that I need to support this body and life; that He protects me from all danger, guards and keeps me from all evil; and all this purely out of fatherly, divine goodness and mercy, without any merit or worthiness in me; for all which I am in duty bound to thank and praise, to serve and obey Him. This is most certainly true.

The Second Article

I believe in Jesus Christ, His only Son our Lord; Who was conceived by the Holy Spirit, born of the virgin Mary, suffered under Pontius Pilate, was crucified, died and was buried. He descended into hell; the third day He rose again from the dead; He ascended into heaven and is seated at the right hand of God the Father almighty; from there He shall come to judge the living and the dead.

What does this mean?

I believe that Jesus Christ is true God, begotten of the Father from eternity, and also true man, born of the virgin Mary; and that He is my Lord, Who has redeemed me, a lost and condemned creature, purchased and won me from all sins, from death and from the power of the devil; not with gold or silver, but with His holy, precious blood, and with His innocent suffering and death; in order that I might be His own, live under Him in His kingdom, and serve Him in everlasting righteousness, innocence and blessedness; even as He is risen from the dead, lives and reigns to all eternity. This is most certainly true.

The Third Article

I believe in the Holy Spirit, the holy Christian Church, the communion of saints, the forgiveness of sins, the resurrection of the body, and the life everlasting. Amen. What does this mean?

What does this mean?

I believe that I cannot by my own reason or strength believe in Jesus Christ, my Lord, or come to Him; but the Holy Ghost has called me by the Gospel, enlightened me with His gifts, sanctified and kept me in the true faith; just as He calls, gathers, enlightens and sanctifies the whole Christian Church on earth and keeps it with Jesus Christ in the one true faith. In this Christian Church He daily and richly forgives me and all believers all our sins; and at the last day He will raise up me and all the dead, and will grant me and all believers in Christ eternal life. This is most certainly true.[1099]

Those in the Church of England need to know and hold to these basic Christian truths and share them with the others, and so the bishops, as those called to be the primary teachers of the Church, need to be constantly teaching them. It is important that bishops comment on the issues of the day both inside and outside the Church, but the most important thing they are called to do is to instruct the faithful in the fundamental truths concerning God's identity and his mighty acts of creation, redemption and sanctification. History shows that when the faithful are confident about these truths then the Church will flourish.

Secondly, in view of the fact that many people both in the world and in the Church are focused on the life of this present world, and those who do believe in life after death increasingly assume that it will involve the same outcome for everyone, bishops need to teach clearly and

[1099] Martin Luther, *The Small Catechism,* text at The Evangelical Lutheran Synod, https://els.org/beliefs/luthers-small-catechism/part-2-the-apostles-creed/.

with conviction the meaning of Christian belief in 'the life everlasting.' In the words of the seventeenth century bishop John Pearson, they need to declare:

I do fully and freely assent unto this as a most necessary and infallible truth, that the unjust after their resurrection and condemnation shall be tormented for their sins in hell, and shall so be continued in torments for ever, so as neither the justice of God shall ever cease to inflict them, nor the persons of the wicked cease to subsist and suffer them; and that the just after their resurrection and absolution shall as the blessed of the Father obtain the inheritance, and as the servants of God enter into their masters joy, freed from all possibility of death sin and sorrow, filled with all conceivable and inconceivable fulness of happiness, confirmed in an absolute security of an eternal enjoyment and so shall they continue with God and with the Lamb for ever more.[1100]

In today's world Christians care often shy about mentioning hell, believing that they will be seen as cruel and heartless if they teach about its reality. However, if hell is real, then what is in fact cruel and heartless is not to warn people about its existence so that they may do what is necessary to avoid it.

Likewise, as Lewis comments:

We are very shy nowadays or even mentioning heaven. We are afraid of the jeer about 'pie in the sky,' and of being told that we are trying to 'escape' from the duty of making a happy world here and now into dreams of a happy world elsewhere. But either there is 'pie in the sky' or there is not. If there is not, then Christianity is false, for this doctrine is woven into its whole fabric. If there is, then this truth, like any other, must be faced, whether it is useful at political meetings or no. Again, we are afraid that heaven is a bribe and that if we make it our goal we shall no longer be disinterested. It is not so. Heaven offers

---

[1100] John Pearson, *An Exposition of the Creed* (London: George Bell, 1902), p.600-601.

nothing that a mercenary soul can desire. It is safe to tell the pure in heart that they shall see God, for only the pure in heart want to. There are rewards that do not sully motives. A man's love for a woman is not mercenary because he wants to marry her, nor his love for poetry mercenary because he wants to read it, nor his love of exercise less disinterested because he wants to run and leap and walk. Love, by definition, seeks to enjoy its object.[1101]

People both inside and outside the Church need to know the truth that 'here we have no lasting city, but we seek the city which is to come' (Hebrews 13:14) so that they me live rightly in the light of it and so the bishops need to be clearly and constantly teaching it to them.

Thirdly, the bishops need to teach clearly and with conviction that the only guaranteed way to enjoy a blessed eternity is through faith in Jesus Christ. This is because, as Article XVIII puts it:

They also are to be had accursed that presume to say that every man shall be saved by the law or sect which he professeth, so that he be diligent to frame his life according to that law and the light of nature. For Holy Scripture doth set out to us only the name of Jesus Christ, whereby men must be saved.

In the words of Bishop Harold Browne in his commentary on this article, what it warns against is that:

...latitudinarianism, which makes all creeds and all communions alike, saying that all men may be saved by their own sect, so they shape their lives according to it, and according to the law of nature. The ground, on which it protests against this view of matters, is that the Scriptures set forth no other name but Christ's whereby we may be saved. The opinion here condemned therefore, is not a charitable hope, that persons, who have never heard of Christ, or who have been bred in ignorance or error, may not be inevitably excluded from the benefit of His atonement; but that cold indifference to faith and truth, which

---

[1101] C S Lewis, *The Problem of Pain* (Glasgow: Fount, 1978), pp.132-133.

would rest satisfied and leave them in their errors, instead of striving to bring them to faith in Christ and to His Body the Church, to which alone the promises of the Gospel are made, and to which, by actual revelation God's mercies are annexed.[1102]

Because the sort of latitudinarianism to which Browne refers is common in both the world and the Church today, bishops need to bear clear witness to the biblical exclusivism of historic Christianity declaring clearly and with conviction '...there is salvation in no one else, for there is no other name under heaven given among men by which we must be saved' (Acts 4:12).

Fourthly, because the only guarantee of salvation is through faith in Christ, bishops must be striving to bring people to faith in him. As leaders of mission, they must be evangelists themselves and must also teach and equip the clergy and laity to be evangelists as well.

In their teaching they must explain clearly both the nature and aim of evangelism.

In the words of *Towards the Conversion of England*, they must explain that:

To evangelise is so to present Christ Jesus in the power of the Holy Spirit, that men shall come to put their trust in God through Him, to accept him as their Saviour, and to serve Him as their King in the fellowship of His Church. [1103]

They must also explain, (a) that the aim of evangelism:

...is Conversion. Conversion is the reorientation of life from self to God through Christ Jesus. Conversion may be sudden: a revolutionary experience, like a revealing flash of lightning, which enables the convert to commemorate a spiritual birthday. Or conversion may be

---

[1102] Harold Browne, *An Exposition of the Thirty Nine Articles* (London: John W Parker, 1847), p440.
[1103] *Towards the Conversion of England*, p. 1.

gradual: an evolutionary development like the dawn of day, or the miracle of the harvest field [Mark 4:26-29]. But whether sudden or gradual, it is the birth right of every child of God to be converted, or (in St. Pauls' phrase) to 'be *alive* unto God in Christ Jesus our Lord' [Romans 6:11]. Short of this there is no stopping place for the evangelist, no sure resting place for the convert.[1104]

(b) that conversion generally involves: 'two stages which, though logically successive, are generally intertwined in practice. The first or preliminary stage consists in arousing the interest of those to whom the message is being delivered - meeting their objections and his little difficulty is, and showing how the gospel finds men just where they are, satisfying their deepest needs. The other stage is the actual bringing the convert to the point of decision - that personal abandonment to the divine will in purpose which is involved with the acceptance of Christ Jesus saviour and king. This is primarily a matter of the individual will. While, therefore, all evangelism is in essence a personal ministry, this is more markedly so in the second stage of evangelism. For the affecting of a conversion under the operation of the Holy Spirit, the direct and immediate contact of a person with a person almost always seems to be called for.' [1105]

Fifthly, bishops must teach and practice care for those in need both inside and outside the Church. Such care is required as obedience to the command to 'love your neighbour as yourself (Leviticus 19:18, Luke 10:25-27), but also as a necessary accompaniment to evangelism.

This is because, while the verbal proclamation and defence of the intellectual truth of the Christian faith are a necessary part of evangelism, they are not necessarily the best place to start. In the post-modern consumer society we now inhabit, claims to be declaring the truth about the human condition are regarded with widespread

---

[1104] *Towards the Conversion of England*, p.36.
[1105] *Towards the Conversion of England*, pp.37-38.

suspicion in the same way that we regard with suspicion the claims made by advertisers and other people who are trying to 'sell' us things.

As Graham Tomlin argues in his book *The Provocative Church,*[1106] what this means is that people will only take Christian truth claims seriously and therefore be open to start on the path to conversion if these truth claims can be seen to be embodied in a plausible fashion in the life of the Christian community. To put it another way, non-Christian will only take the Christian message seriously if Christians don't just 'talk the talk' but also 'walk the walk.'

In addition, Christians who 'walk the walk' are the best antidote to the claim that Christians are the 'bad guys.' People will find implausible to believe that Christians are truly the bad guys if their practical care for those in need shows otherwise.

However, bishops must explain that walking the walk is not a substitute for 'talking the talk.' Christians still need to explain to non-Christians that they are caring for others not because they are naturally nice people but because they have met the one true God in Jesus Christ and have found the fulness of life he promised (John 10:10) in living in obedience to his commands. Tomlin's argument is that Christian care for those in need will provoke people to ask questions (hence the title of his book) and that will give the opportunity to talk to people about the nature and truth of the Christian message.

Sixthly, bishops must teach that while all types of people are to be welcomed into the Church, this does not mean that all types of behaviour are to be accepted within the Church. This is something that the Church has never believed from New Testament times onwards. On the contrary, it has always been held that there is a God given pattern of right behaviour to which Christians must adhere. Christians are called to God-determined rather than self-determined people and

---

[1106] Graham Tomlin, *The Provocative Church* (London: SPCK, 2002).

that means living in a particular way. We can see this for example in the exhortations contained in Paul's letters. Thus, Paul tells the Ephesian Christians in Ephesians 5:1-20:

Therefore be imitators of God, as beloved children. And walk in love, as Christ loved us and gave himself up for us, a fragrant offering and sacrifice to God.

But fornication and all impurity or covetousness must not even be named among you, as is fitting among saints. Let there be no filthiness, nor silly talk, nor levity, which are not fitting; but instead let there be thanksgiving. Be sure of this, that no fornicator or impure man, or one who is covetous (that is, an idolater), has any inheritance in the kingdom of Christ and of God. Let no one deceive you with empty words, for it is because of these things that the wrath of God comes upon the sons of disobedience. Therefore do not associate with them, for once you were darkness, but now you are light in the Lord; walk as children of light (for the fruit of light is found in all that is good and right and true), and try to learn what is pleasing to the Lord. Take no part in the unfruitful works of darkness, but instead expose them. For it is a shame even to speak of the things that they do in secret; but when anything is exposed by the light it becomes visible, for anything that becomes visible is light. Therefore it is said,

'Awake, O sleeper, and arise from the dead,

and Christ shall give you light.'

Look carefully then how you walk, not as unwise men but as wise, making the most of the time, because the days are evil. Therefore do not be foolish, but understand what the will of the Lord is. And do not get drunk with wine, for that is debauchery; but be filled with the Spirit, addressing one another in psalms and hymns and spiritual songs, singing and making melody to the Lord with all your heart, always and for everything giving thanks in the name of our Lord Jesus Christ to God the Father.

As Paul's words make clear, adhering to the Christian ethic in obedience to God involves doing (or not doing) many different things, but as we have seen during this study, part of what it involves is living as the man or woman God created us to be rather than choosing our own sexual identity and only engaging in sexual intercourse within its God-given setting of heterosexual marriage.

This in turn means that bishops need to teach, over against the prevailing ethos of Western society, and even at the price of being labelled transphobes and homophobes, that gender transition and same-sex relationships are not acceptable forms of Christian behaviour. Transgender people and those in same-sex relationships must be unconditionally welcomed into the Church just like anyone else, but the Christian community needs to encourage them, as part of submission to the kingship of Christ, to live according to their biological sex and abstain from same-sex sexual activity.

Seventhly, bishops need to take seriously their calling to 'banish and drive away all erroneous and strange doctrine contrary to God's word; and both privately and openly to call upon and encourage others to do the same' and also to 'correct and punish' those who are 'unquiet, disobedient and criminous.' For the sake of the spiritual health of the flock and the integrity of its witness to the watching world, bishops need to refute heretical ideas, and use their powers of jurisdiction to discipline both those who teach heresy and those who encourage or practice ungodly form of behaviour. As we have seen in the course of this study, this is what bishops have been called to do since apostolic times and what they still need to do today.

Finally, bishops, as the senior presbyters within the Church, need to select, train, and appoint other presbyters, deacons, and lay ministers of various kinds to work with them to carry out the tasks just outlined. As we have seen, this is what Timothy and Titus were instructed to do, and it is what bishops still need to do today. A bishop, however godly and however talented, cannot transform a diocese on their own, but they can do it if they have godly ministers working with them.

What bishops need to do after *Living in Love and Faith*

In the very near future the bishops of the Church of England will have to decide what action to take following the *Living in Love and Faith* process.

The basic answer is clear, what the bishops ought to do is to affirm orthodox Christian teaching on sexual identity and practice by commending to the Church of England something along the lines of the *Nashville Statement on Human Sexuality* set out below:

Preamble

Evangelical Christians at the dawn of the twenty-first century find themselves living in a period of historic transition. As Western culture has become increasingly post-Christian, it has embarked upon a massive revision of what it means to be a human being. By and large the spirit of our age no longer discerns or delights in the beauty of God's design for human life. Many deny that God created human beings for his glory, and that his good purposes for us include our personal and physical design as male and female. It is common to think that human identity as male and female is not part of God's beautiful plan, but is, rather, an expression of an individual's autonomous preferences. The pathway to full and lasting joy through God's good design for his creatures is thus replaced by the path of shortsighted alternatives that, sooner or later, ruin human life and dishonor God.

This secular spirit of our age presents a great challenge to the Christian church. Will the church of the Lord Jesus Christ lose her biblical conviction, clarity, and courage, and blend into the spirit of the age? Or will she hold fast to the word of life, draw courage from Jesus, and unashamedly proclaim his way as the way of life? Will she maintain her clear, counter-cultural witness to a world that seems bent on ruin?

We are persuaded that faithfulness in our generation means declaring once again the true story of the world and of our place in it— particularly as male and female. Christian Scripture teaches that there is but one God who alone is Creator and Lord of all. To him alone, every person owes gladhearted thanksgiving, heart-felt praise, and total allegiance. This is the path not only of glorifying God, but of knowing ourselves. To forget our Creator is to forget who we are, for he made us for himself. And we cannot know ourselves truly without truly knowing him who made us. We did not make ourselves. We are not our own. Our true identity, as male and female persons, is given by God. It is not only foolish, but hopeless, to try to make ourselves what God did not create us to be.

We believe that God's design for his creation and his way of salvation serve to bring him the greatest glory and bring us the greatest good. God's good plan provides us with the greatest freedom. Jesus said he came that we might have life and have it in overflowing measure. He is for us and not against us. Therefore, in the hope of serving Christ's church and witnessing publicly to the good purposes of God for human sexuality revealed in Christian Scripture, we offer the following affirmations and denials.

Article 1

WE AFFIRM that God has designed marriage to be a covenantal, sexual, procreative, lifelong union of one man and one woman, as husband and wife, and is meant to signify the covenant love between Christ and his bride the church.

WE DENY that God has designed marriage to be a homosexual, polygamous, or polyamorous relationship. We also deny that marriage is a mere human contract rather than a covenant made before God.

Article 2

WE AFFIRM that God's revealed will for all people is chastity outside of marriage and fidelity within marriage.

WE DENY that any affections, desires, or commitments ever justify sexual intercourse before or outside marriage; nor do they justify any form of sexual immorality.

Article 3

WE AFFIRM that God created Adam and Eve, the first human beings, in his own image, equal before God as persons, and distinct as male and female.

WE DENY that the divinely ordained differences between male and female render them unequal in dignity or worth.

Article 4

WE AFFIRM that divinely ordained differences between male and female reflect God's original creation design and are meant for human good and human flourishing.

WE DENY that such differences are a result of the Fall or are a tragedy to be overcome.

Article 5

WE AFFIRM that the differences between male and female reproductive structures are integral to God's design for self-conception as male or female.

WE DENY that physical anomalies or psychological conditions nullify the God-appointed link between biological sex and self-conception as male or female.

Article 6

WE AFFIRM that those born with a physical disorder of sex development are created in the image of God and have dignity and worth equal to all other image-bearers. They are acknowledged by our Lord Jesus in his words about 'eunuchs who were born that way from their mother's womb.' With all others they are welcome as faithful followers of Jesus Christ and should embrace their biological sex insofar as it may be known.

WE DENY that ambiguities related to a person's biological sex render one incapable of living a fruitful life in joyful obedience to Christ.

Article 7

WE AFFIRM that self-conception as male or female should be defined by God's holy purposes in creation and redemption as revealed in Scripture.

WE DENY that adopting a homosexual or transgender self-conception is consistent with God's holy purposes in creation and redemption.

Article 8

WE AFFIRM that people who experience sexual attraction for the same sex may live a rich and fruitful life pleasing to God through faith in Jesus Christ, as they, like all Christians, walk in purity of life.

WE DENY that sexual attraction for the same sex is part of the natural goodness of God's original creation, or that it puts a person outside the hope of the gospel.

Article 9

WE AFFIRM that sin distorts sexual desires by directing them away from the marriage covenant and toward sexual immorality— a distortion that includes both heterosexual and homosexual immorality.

WE DENY that an enduring pattern of desire for sexual immorality justifies sexually immoral behavior.

Article 10

WE AFFIRM that it is sinful to approve of homosexual immorality or transgenderism and that such approval constitutes an essential departure from Christian faithfulness and witness.

WE DENY that the approval of homosexual immorality or transgenderism is a matter of moral indifference about which otherwise faithful Christians should agree to disagree.

Article 11

WE AFFIRM our duty to speak the truth in love at all times, including when we speak to or about one another as male or female.

WE DENY any obligation to speak in such ways that dishonor God's design of his image bearers as male and female.

Article 12

WE AFFIRM that the grace of God in Christ gives both merciful pardon and transforming power, and that this pardon and power enable a follower of Jesus to put to death sinful desires and to walk in a manner worthy of the Lord.

WE DENY that the grace of God in Christ is insufficient to forgive all sexual sins and to give power for holiness to every believer who feels drawn into sexual sin.

Article 13

WE AFFIRM that the grace of God in Christ enables sinners to forsake transgender self-conception and by divine forbearance to accept the God-ordained link between one's biological sex and one's self-conception as male or female.

WE DENY that the grace of God in Christ sanctions self-conceptions that are at odds with God's revealed will.

Article 14

WE AFFIRM that Christ Jesus has come into the world to save sinners and that through Christ's death and resurrection forgiveness of sins and eternal life are available to every person who repents of sin and trusts in Christ alone as Savior, Lord, and supreme treasure.

WE DENY that the Lord's arm is too short to save or that any sinner is beyond his reach.[1107]

In addition, the bishops also ought to propose a revision of the Church of England's current discipline so that services to mark gender transition are no longer permitted, so that those who have undergone gender transition are not permitted to be ordained, and so that lay

[1107] *The Nashville Statement* at https://cbmw.org/nashville-statement/

ministers as well as ordained ministers are expected to abstain from both gender-transition and same-sex relationships.

Moving in this direction would bring about howls of protest from both inside and outside the Church of England, but the bishops should ignore this and act in this way anyway, simply because it is the right thing to do.

It is, however, sadly possible that the majority of the bishops, with the support of the General Synod, will eventually seek to move the Church of England in the same sort of liberal direction already taken by The Episcopal Church, the Anglican Church in Canada, the Scottish Episcopal Church and the Church in Wales.

If this happens what should orthodox bishops do? The answer depends on exactly what is proposed.

If what is proposed is the establishment of a 'pastoral accommodation' allowing clergy to bless same-sex relationships and civil same-sex marriages on a permissive basis, then orthodox bishops will need to work to establish the right for bishops not allow such blessings in their dioceses and for a system of delegated episcopal oversight to be created which would allow clergy and parishes who did not want to allow such blessings to come under the jurisdiction of a bishop who took the same position (with reciprocal arrangements for liberal parishes whose bishop did not give permission for such blessings to take place).

If what is proposed is a change to Canon B.30 which would change the Church of England's definition of marriage and allow same-sex marriages to take place, then orthodox bishops will need to work to establish a third province for orthodox Anglicans within the Church of England, alongside the existing provinces of Canterbury and York. This province, which parishes would be able to opt into by means of a vote by their Parochial Church Councils, would have its own bishops, its own convocation, and its own code of Canon law, and as a result it would be able to give robust long-term protection to clergy and parishes who wish to adhere to traditional Church of England teaching and practice and provide a base from which the re-evangelization of the rest of the Church of England and the English nation might take place in God's good time. [1108]

If they are not able to bring either of the two previous options to pass, then orthodox bishops. like other orthodox clergy and laity, should be prepared to consider leaving the Church of England and forming a new orthodox Anglican province outside the Church of England along the lines of ACNA in North America, which would provide a home for orthodox Anglicans in England, Wales and Scotland. [1109]

The formation of this new province would mean establishing parallel episcopal jurisdictions in these three countries. As we saw in chapter 12, such parallel jurisdictions should ideally not exist, but they are legitimate when a church and/or bishop in a particular place departs from Christian orthodoxy in matters of belief or conduct to such a serious extent that faithful Christians have no alternative but to separate themselves from that church or that bishop. In this situation it will be necessary to create a new church with its own bishops and hence to create a new parallel episcopal jurisdiction.

This is exactly the situation which the proposed new province in England, Wales and Scotland would be designed to meet. The Church in Wales and the Scottish Episcopal Church and their bishops have already accepted same-sex marriages and in the situation envisaged the Church of England and the majority of its bishops would have done the same. Creating a parallel jurisdiction would thus be the right thing to do.

Bishops in this new province would have legitimate episcopal jurisdictions in the Church in England, and would thus be the heirs of James, Ignatius, Athanasius, Augustine, and Cranmer, even if they no longer possessed episcopal jurisdiction in the Church of England.

[1108] For a detailed study of these two options see Martin Davie and Stephen Hofmeyr, *Visibly Different* (London: CEEC 2002), Chs.6-7.
[1109] Hopefully, the Free Church of England and the Anglican Mission in England would agree to become part of this new province.

What we have to pray for, of course, is that none of the options just described will prove necessary, but that the bishops as a whole will act as the shepherds they are call to be by protecting those in the Church of England from the influence of the modern Western ideology of self-determination and the ungodly views of sexual identity and sexual behaviour that flow from it.

To this end we should pray constantly for all the bishops of the Church of England, using the prayer for a new bishop in the 1662 *Ordinal*:

Almighty God and most merciful Father, who of thine infinite goodness hast given thine only and dearly beloved Son Jesus Christ, to be our Redeemer and the Author of everlasting life; who, after that he had made perfect our redemption by his death, and was ascended into heaven, poured down his gifts abundantly upon men, making some Apostles, some Prophets, some Evangelists, some Pastors and Doctors, to the edifying and making perfect his Church: Grant, we beseech thee, to these thy servants such grace, that they may evermore be ready to spread abroad thy Gospel, the glad tidings of reconciliation with thee; and use the authority given them, not to destruction, but to salvation; not to hurt, but to help: so that as wise and faithful servants, giving to thy family their portion in due season, they may at last be received into everlasting joy; through Jesus Christ our Lord, who with thee and the Holy Ghost liveth and reigneth, one God, world without end. Amen.

Appendix I
The process for permitting women to become bishops in the Church of England

1. The legislative process

As noted in chapter 5, women were ordained as deaconesses in the Church of England from 1924, as deacons from 1987 and as priests from 1994.

Once women had been ordained to the priesthood and began to occupy senior posts within the Church of England, such as archdeacons and deans, the issue of the ordination of women to the episcopate inevitably began to be raised and in July 2000 General Synod passed a motion from the Archdeacon of Tonbridge, Judith Rose:

That this Synod ask the House of Bishops to initiate further theological study on the episcopate, focussing on the issues that need to be addressed in preparation for the debate on women in the episcopate in the Church of England, and to make a progress report on this study to Synod in the next two years.

The working party set up in response to this motion produced the 'Rochester' report. *Women Bishops in the Church of England?* in 2004. In February 2005 Synod voted to 'take note' of this report and in July of that year it then voted to 'set in train the process for removing the legal obstacles to the ordination of women to the episcopate.'

Work on this process then followed in five stages:

Stage 1 July 2005-July 2006 - a report from a group led by the Bishop of Guildford, and then a further report by the Bishops of Guildford and Gloucester, set out the options for achieving the ordination of women as bishops.

Stage 2, July 2006-February 2009 - General Synod passed a motion in July 2006 declaring 'That this Synod welcome and affirm the view of the majority of the House of Bishops that admitting women to the episcopate in the Church of England is consonant with the faith of the Church as the Church of England has received it and would be a proper development in proclaiming afresh in this generation the grace and truth of Christ' and a legislative drafting group led by the Bishop of Manchester produced draft legislation for the ordination of women as bishops, together with an illustrative code of practice covering the arrangements for those unable to accept the ministry of female bishops.

Stage 3: February 2009-July 2010 a revision committee, led again by the Bishop of Manchester, produced a revised version of this legislation which was endorsed by General Synod with only minor amendments.

A compromise plan put forward by the Archbishops of Canterbury and York (involving the creation of a mechanism providing for 'co-ordinate jurisdiction' in parishes unable to accept the ministry of a female bishop so that a male bishop would fulfil episcopal functions for those parishes) was endorsed by the House of Bishops and the House of Laity but narrowly failed (90 votes against to 85 in favour) in the House of Clergy.

Stage 4: July 2010-November 2012 – the draft measure agreed by General Synod was approved by 42 of the 44 dioceses through votes in their diocesan synods, but an amendment by the House of Bishops, offering further concessions to opponents, meant that many proponents of the measure would have reluctantly voted it down, and the synod at York in July 2012 adjourned the decision to a later synod.

On 20 November 2012, the General Synod failed to pass the proposed legislation for the ordination of women as bishops. The measure was lost after narrowly failing to achieve the two-thirds majority required in the House of Laity (132 for and 74 against) after being passed by the House of Bishops and the House of Clergy.

Stage 5: November 2012 – November 2014

At its meeting on 7 February 2013, the House of Bishops decided that eight senior women clergy, elected regionally, would participate in all meetings of the house until such time as there were six women who were bishops sitting as of right.

In May 2013 the House of Bishops expressed its commitment 'to publishing new ways forward to enable women to become bishops' and in July 2013, General Synod agreed to reintroduce legislation in November.

The new draft legislation was considered by General Synod in November 2013 and February 2014 and after receiving approval in all the diocesan synods that were able to meet within the necessary time frame (43 of 44) the measure to introduce women bishops passed all three houses of General Synod on 14 July 2014, achieving the two-thirds majority required in all three. It gained the necessary parliamentary approvals and royal assent in the subsequent months and was given final approval by the General Synod on 17 November 2014.

Alongside the measure Synod also gave its approval to 'Five guiding principles' drawn up by the House of Bishops to which all prospective ordinands now have to agree. These principles are:

1. Now that legislation has been passed to enable women to become bishops the Church of England is fully and unequivocally committed to all orders of ministry being open equally to all, without reference to gender, and holds that those whom it has duly ordained and appointed to office are true and lawful holders of the office which they occupy and thus deserve due respect and canonical obedience;

2. Anyone who ministers within the Church of England must be prepared to acknowledge that the Church of England has reached a clear decision on the matter;

3. Since it continues to share the historic episcopate with other Churches, including the Roman Catholic Church, the Orthodox

Church and those provinces of the Anglican Communion which continue to ordain only men as priests or bishops, the Church of England acknowledges that its own clear decision on ministry and gender is set within a broader process of discernment within the Anglican Communion and the whole Church of God;

4. Since those within the Church of England who, on grounds of theological conviction, are unable to receive the ministry of women bishops or priests continue to be within the spectrum of teaching and tradition of the Anglican Communion, the Church of England remains committed to enabling them to flourish within its life and structures; and

5. Pastoral and sacramental provision for the minority within the Church of England will be made without specifying a limit of time and in a way that maintains the highest possible degree of communion and contributes to mutual flourishing across the whole Church of England. [1110]

2. Two key point about the process

Two key points about the process to permit women to become bishops in the Church of England need to be noted.

The first is that the final stage of the decision-making process took place under acute political pressure both from supporters of women bishops in the Church of England and from Parliament. Under the rules of the General Synod once legislation has been rejected by a session of General Synod, the proposal cannot be considered again during the life of that Synod. This means that once the draft measure to allow women bishops had been defeated in November 2012, the proposal to allow women to be bishops should not have been re-introduced until November 2015 at the earliest.

[1110] The five guiding principles at
https://www.churchofengland.org/sites/default/files/2017-10/the_five_guiding_principles.pdf.

However, it was made clear that Parliament expected faster action and the leaders of the Church of England promised that such action would be forthcoming. To quote the *Guardian's* article on the subject:

David Cameron has urged the Church of England to 'get on with it' and reverse its decision to reject female bishops.

The prime minister told MPs that the church needed 'to get with the programme', adding: 'You do have to respect the individual institutions and the way they work, while giving them a sharp prod.'

Later the PM's spokesman said Cameron could not understand why the review of the decision should take years, as the Church of England has said.

His remarks made at prime minister's question time are the clearest sign yet that he does not want to leave the issue alone, even if he is not going to change the law to make the church subject to the European court of human rights.

Cameron said he was 'very sad' about the result. 'On a personal basis I'm a strong supporter of women bishops. I'm very sad about the way the vote went yesterday and I'm particularly sad for the archbishop of Canterbury, Rowan Williams, because I know he saw this as a major campaign that he wanted to achieve at the end of his excellent tenure of that office. I think it's important for the Church of England to be a modern church in touch with society as it is today and this was a key step it needed to take.'

The Speaker, John Bercow, also urged backbenchers to see if they could ask the equalities minister, Maria Miller, to come to the Commons and make a statement, so giving MPs an opportunity to express their dismay at the decision of the church. The prime minister's spokesman added that it was right for parliament to express a view.

Rowan Williams earlier told the General Synod that the Church of England had 'a lot of explaining to do' after its rejection of legislation that would have allowed women to become bishops.

In a strongly worded speech on Wednesday, Williams warned that the failure of the vote in the house of laity on Tuesday had made the church's governing body appear 'wilfully blind' to the priorities of secular society.

'We have – to put it very bluntly – a lot of explaining to do,' he said. 'Whatever the motivations for voting yesterday ... the fact remains that a great deal of this discussion is not intelligible to our wider society. Worse than that, it seems as if we are wilfully blind to some of the trends and priorities of that wider society.'

Justin Welby, the bishop of Durham, who succeeds Williams as archbishop next year, has insisted that women will eventually be ordained as bishops despite the change being voted down.

He said the General Synod had 'overwhelmingly' backed the idea, although it did not receive the two-thirds majority needed among lay members.

Welby said he agreed with comments by the archbishop of York, John Sentamu. 'Sentamu has said there will be women bishops and I agree with him,' he told the Press Association.

'The church has voted overwhelmingly in favour of the principle. It is a question of finding a way that there is a real consensus that this is the right way forward.[1111]

In the face of this pressure General Synod agreed to go against its normal rules and allowed the matter to come back to Synod in November 2013. The question that must be asked is whether Synod should have allowed itself to be swayed by political and social pressure in the way that it was, or whether it should have stuck to its guns and followed the normal synodical process.

[1111] David Cameron: 'Church of England should 'get on with it' on female bishops,' *The Guardian*, 21 November 2012.

The fear with regard to what happens after LLF is that the bishops and the synod will give in to political and social pressure in a similar way. They will bow to what parliament and the wider culture seem to require.

The second point is that although the process produced a mechanism for introducing women bishops it never provided a rationale for introducing women bishops. General Synod agreed with the House of Bishops in 2006 that having women bishops would be a 'proper development' but it was not explained either at the time or subsequently why this was the case.

Chapter 8 of the Rochester Report notes:

At the end of the discussion of the development of doctrine in chapter three of this report...it was suggested that a permissible development is one that:

Is Biblically based in the sense that it:

- Has explicit or implicit support in specific biblical texts.

- Enables us to make coherent sense of the overall biblical picture

- Takes the logic of the biblical material and applies it in a new cultural and historical context.

Takes Tradition seriously in the sense that it:

- Shows understanding of what the traditions of the Church (as manifested in the totality of its life) have been concerning a particular matter.

- Shows that it has understood the reason(s) for the existence these traditions.

- Builds on the Church's existing traditions rather than simply rejecting them.

Takes reason seriously in that it:

- Can be shown in a rational and coherent fashion that such a development is rooted in Scripture and tradition in the ways outlined above.

- Such a development will enable the Church to respond creatively and persuasively to the issues raised by contemporary culture and contemporary Christian experience.

What has become clear from the material considered by the Working Party and surveyed in this report is that there is a fundamental difference of opinion on all these three aspects of a permissible development.

Scripture

Those who argue for the status quo contend that the present position in which women cannot be bishops is biblically based in that it is supported by the practice of the New Testament Church and is the explicit teaching found in texts such as 1 Cor 11.2-16;14: 33-38 and 1 Tim 2.9-15. They also maintain that it best conforms to the overall biblical picture of the relationship between men and women ordained by God (described as the principle of 'headship' by Conservative Evangelicals). As they see it, the way to apply the biblical material in today's context is to find appropriate ministries for women that give scope to women's talents and abilities while respecting the traditional, biblical ordering of the Church.

Those who hold that women should be bishops are equally clear that their position is biblically based because it reflects the way in which, according to the New Testament, women played an equal role alongside men in leading the early Church and the teaching about the fundamental equality of women and men contained in Gal 3:28. It also best conforms to the biblical picture of an original equality between men and women disrupted by sin but restored through the saving work of Christ. As they see it, the way to apply the biblical material in today's context is to open up all ministries equally to both women and men.

Tradition

Those who argue for the status quo hold that their position is the one that best respects tradition as it reflects the consistent pattern of Christian belief and practice maintained down the centuries under the guidance of the Holy Spirit in almost all parts of the Church. In their view, a decision to ordain women as bishops would not be evolution but revolution, the repudiation of the considered mind of God's people over the past two millennia and the mind of most of the Church of Christ in the present day. It would call into question the claim of the Church of England that its form of ministry is a sign and instrument of the Catholicity and Apostolicity of the one Church of God across space and time.

Those who hold that women should be bishops see their position as consonant with tradition, not only because they think that there is evidence for the presence of women in the ministry of the Church in the early centuries, but, more fundamentally, because they think that the development of tradition on this matter has been skewed by the effects of a patriarchal culture that has prevented the Church from fully reflecting the egalitarian approach of the Bible itself. In our day, the Church has the possibility of a true development of tradition in this area, a development that will retain the Catholic three-fold order of ministry as a sign and instrument of Catholicity and Apostolicity, but will allow it to be a more faithful representation of the biblical revelation by being opened up to women as well as men.

Reason

Those who argue for the status quo see their position as supported by reason. They hold that it can be rationally shown that their position is the one that has the support of Scripture and tradition and is the one that will be most beneficial to the Church of England. Not only will it preserve the Church of England's theological integrity, but it will also preserve internal and ecumenical unity, and giving space for the agreed process of open reception of the ordination of women as priests to take place. As they see it, the Church of England can best address the questions about the relations of men and women raised by contemporary culture by remaining faithful in this way to the biblical teaching about equality of status but diversity of role.

Conversely, those who favour the ordination of women as bishops also see their position as having the support of reason. For the reasons outlined above they believe that their position is demanded by Scripture and consonant with attentiveness to Tradition. As they see it, the Church of England has already accepted the principle that women should be ordained alongside men and the ordination of women as priests has been widely accepted. The time is therefore right to take the next logical step, which is to open the episcopate up to women as well. This will benefit the Church of England because of the distinctive gifts that women will bring to episcopal ministry, and it will enhance its mission by showing the wider world that it is serious about its message concerning the equality of men and women before God. [1112]

Those who wrote the Rochester report intended that there should be a proper debate about these contrasting viewpoints within the Church of England so that whatever decision the Church of England eventually made would have a proper and agreed theological basis.

However, this never happened. At no point in the process did the Church of England agree why having women bishops would be a permissible development on the basis of Scripture, tradition, and reason, or explain why the objections to this development on these grounds were unfounded.

This has left the Church of England in a deeply unsatisfactory situation. The Church of England as a whole, and the House of Bishops as guardians of its doctrine, have a responsibility to be as theologically certain as they can be that the decisions made by the Church of

---

[1112] The House of Bishops Working Party on Women in the Episcopate, *Women Bishops in the Church of England?* (London: Church House Publishing, 2004), pp. 230-232.

England are the right ones. In the case of the process for introducing women bishops, this responsibility was not properly discharged.

If someone asks why the Church of England agrees that it is theologically permissible to have women bishops all that can be said is that a majority of the House of Bishops said this was the case and a sufficient majority in General Synod agreed with them.

This does not mean that it is wrong for women to be bishops, but what it does mean is that we do not know why the Church of England thinks that it is right. This absence of theological justification for having women bishops is wrong in principle (since the Church of England should know why it believes that what it has done is right in the eyes of God) and it is deeply unfair to women bishops themselves, who should be able to say why the Church of England believes that their ministry is theologically legitimate.

There also has to be a serious concern that the Church of England will handle the post LLF process in the same way that it handled the introduction of women bishops, by seeking to find ways in which those with different views can live with the blessing of same-sex relationships or the introduction of same-sex marriages, while avoiding the central issue of whether these would be theologically legitimate developments in the first place. The current Church of England mantra about 'good disagreement' adds to this concern since it focuses on the need to live well with disagreement rather than deciding whether the matter concerned is one on which disagreement is tolerable.

Appendix 2
Meeting objections to the appointment of bishops by the Queen [1113]

In line with the legislation passed during the reign of Henry VIII as part of the breach with Rome, all bishops of the Church of England are today appointed by the Queen, who acts on the advice of the Prime Minister.

This method of appointment is often objected to on the grounds that 'the Church should appoint its own bishops.'

This objection comes in two parts. The first part is an objection in principle to a bishop not being chosen by the Church itself. The second part is an objection to the fact that the Queen acts on the advice of the Prime Minister who may not be a member of the Church of England or even a Christian. As has been noted, the role of the Prime Minister in the appointment of bishops is currently under review, but at the moment he or she still has a necessary part to play in the appointment process.

In response to the first part of the objection the point that needs to be made is that in reality all bishops are chosen by the Church.

A name is submitted to the Queen (who is in any case the senior lay member of the Church of England) by a diocesan bishop (in the case of suffragan bishops) or by the Crown Nominations Commission (in the case of diocesan bishops or archbishops). On the advice of the Prime Minister, the Queen, exercising her God given responsibility for the well-being of the Church and the nation, either accepts the name offered to her or asks the Church to provide another name for consideration. In the case of archbishops and diocesan bishops the

---

[1113] The material in this appendix is adapted from Martin Davie, *A Guide to the Church of England* (London and New York: Mowbray, 2008), pp. 70-71.

successful candidate is then formally elected, in accordance with ancient tradition, by the Dean and Chapter of the diocesan cathedral.

Also in accordance with ancient tradition, election is then followed by confirmation of election. As the 2001 Church of England report *Working with the Spirit: Choosing diocesan bishops* explains:

In the Church of England, the election of a diocesan bishop is confirmed by the archbishop of the province (or by his vicar-general acting on his behalf) and the election of an archbishop by a commission consisting of the senior bishops of the province and the archbishop of the other province. It is the confirmation of the election which actually makes the candidate bishop of the diocese and commits to him 'the care, government and administration of the Spirituals of the said Bishopric.' [1114]

The purpose of the confirmation of election is to confirm that the wider Church is content that a fit and proper person has been elected as a bishop or archbishop, and what we see in the process as a whole is different branches of the Church of England each exercising their proper responsibility to ensure that a suitable person is appointed.

In response to the second part of the objection the point that needs to be made is that it is constitutionally necessary for the Prime Minister to be involved in the process because in this, as in other matters, the Queen has to act with the advice and consent of her ministers. If the Prime Minister had complete freedom of choice in the name to be recommended to the Queen then his or her own religious beliefs (or lack of them) might be an issue, but as the names recommended by the Prime Minister are those the Church itself has already judged to be fit to be bishops there can be no question of the Prime Minister imposing on the Church someone whom the Church considers to be unsuitable.

In addition, because a diocesan bishop is someone who is going to play an important role in the life of the nation, and is potentially going to be

[1114] *Working with the Spirit: Choosing Diocesan bishops* (London: Church House Publishing, 2001), p.81.

a member of the House of Lords, the Prime Minister has a legitimate political interest in seeing that someone suitable is appointed just as he or she has a legitimate political interest in other senior public appointments.

To sum up, what takes place when a bishop is appointed is a process in which the Church, the Queen (herself a part of the Church) and the Prime Minister all have their own proper role to play in order to ensure that a suitable person is chosen to exercise episcopal ministry in the life of the Church and of the nation as whole.

Furthermore, while the election of a diocesan bishop and the consecration of new bishops are normally formalities in the sense that when candidates have been nominated by the Queen then the election and/or consecration then automatically follows, in the event of a totally unsuitable person being nominated the Dean and Chapter could refuse to elect, those involved could refuse to ratify an election, and bishops could refuse to consecrate. The church can thus, *in extremis* act to block a royal episcopal appointment.

The theological justification for the Queen's involvement in the life of the Church, of which appointing bishops is a part, is helpfully set out by Hooker who writes:

A gross error it is, to think that regal power ought to serve for the good of the body, and not of the soul; for men's temporal peace, and not for their eternal safety: as if God had ordained kings for no other end and purpose but only to fat up men like hogs, and to see that they have their mast. Indeed, to lead men unto salvation by the hand of secret, invisible and ghostly regiment, or by the external administration of things belonging unto priestly order, (such as the word and sacraments are,) this is denied unto Christian kings: no cause in the world to think them uncapable of supreme authority in the outward government which disposeth the affairs of religion so far as the same are disposable by human authority, and to think them uncapable thereof, only for that the said religion is everlastingly beneficial to them that faithfully continue in it. [1115]

The point Hooker is making makes is that human beings have souls as well as bodies. They are not purely material beings that can find their true end in life if their material needs are taken care of. They are also spiritual beings who can only find their true fulfilment in a right relationship with God. As the person with responsibility for the welfare of his or her subjects, it is consequently the Queen's role to see that the Church as an institution is in a state in which it can perform its spiritual tasks properly so that this right relationship with God is made possible.

Appointing bishops is part of performing this role in accordance with the oath made by the Queen at her coronation:

Archbishop. Will you to the utmost of your power maintain the Laws of God and the true profession of the Gospel? Will you to the utmost of your power maintain in the United Kingdom the Protestant Reformed Religion established by law? Will you maintain and preserve inviolably the settlement of the Church of England, and the doctrine, worship, discipline, and government thereof, as by law established in England? And will you preserve unto the Bishops and Clergy of England, and to the Churches there committed to their charge, all such rights and privileges, as by law do or shall appertain to them or any of them?

Queen. All this I promise to do.[1116]

[1115] Hooker, Book VIII.iii.3, p. 511.
[1116] The Queen's Coronation Oath, 1953 at https://www.royal.uk/coronation-oath-2-June-1953.

Bibliography

Primary Sources

An Admonition to Parliament, in W H Frere and C E Douglas eds, *Protestant Manifestoes* (London: SPCK, 1907).

The Alternative Service Book, (London: SPCK, 1980).

An Anglican-Methodist Covenant (Peterborough and London: Methodist Publishing House/Church House Publishing, 2001).

Anglican Moravian Conversations (London: Council for Christian Unity, 1996).

Anglican-Roman Catholic International Commission, *The Final Report* (London: SPCK, 1982).

Anselm, *Proslogion*, in *Anselm of Canterbury – The Major Works* (Oxford: OUP, 1998).

Ambrose, *On the Duties of the Clergy* in *The Nicene and Post Nicene Fathers*, 2nd series, vol. X (Edinburgh and Grand Rapids: T&T Clark/Eerdmans, 1997).

Ambrosiaster, *Comm. In Eph.* in Kenneth Kirk et al. *The Apostolic Ministry* (London: Hodder and Stoughton, 1947).

Ambrosiaster, *Comm. In 1 Tim.iii.10*, in Kirk.

*Apostolicity and Succession (*London: Church House Publishing, 1994).

Thomas Aquinas, *Commentary on the Letters of Saint Paul to the Philippians, Colossians, Timothy, Titus and Philemon* (Lander, Wyoming: The Aquinas Institute, 2012).

The Archbishops' Commission on Evangelism, *Towards the Conversion of England* (London: The Press and Publications Board of the Church Assembly, 1945).

The Archbishops' Group on the Episcopate, *Episcopal Ministry* (London: Church House Publishing, 1990).

Athanasius, *Defence against the Arians* in *The Nicene and Post-Nicene Fathers*, 2nd series vol. IV (Edinburgh and Grands Rapids: T&T Clark/Eerdmans, 1998).

Augustine, *Ad Catholicos Fratres Liber Unos*, in Lee Gatiss (ed) *Fight Valiantly!* (Watford: Church Society, 2019).

Augustine, *City of God* (Harmondsworth: Penguin, 1972).

Augustine, *The Confessions* (Oxford: OUP, 2008).

Augustine, *Contra Julianum Pelagianum* in E Giles, *Documents Illustrating Papal Authority* (London: SPCK: 1952).

Augustine, *De Baptismo contra Donatistas*, in Giles.

Augustine, *Enarratio in Psalmum* LVI in Giles.

Augustine, *Letter LXXXII* in *The Nicene and Post-Nicene Fathers,* vol. I, (Edinburgh and Grand Rapids: T&T Clark/Eerdmans, 1994).

Augustine, *Sermon 339* in Edmund Hill, *Augustine, Sermons III/9 (306-340A) on the Saints* (Hyde Park: New City Press, 1994).

Augustine, *Sermon 149* in Giles.

Augustine, *Sermon 295 in Giles.*

Augustine, *Sermon 340* in Hill.

Augustine, *Sermon 340 A* in Hill.

Paul Avis, *Becoming a Bishop* (London: Bloomsbury/T&T Clark, 2015).

John Ayre (ed.), *The Catechism of Thomas Becon* (Cambridge: CUP, 1844).

John Ayre (ed.), *The Early Works of Thomas Becon* (Cambridge: CUP, 1843).

John Ayre (ed.) *The Works of John Jewel,* vol. 1, (Cambridge: CUP/Parker Society, 1848).

John Ayre (ed.), *The Works of John Whitgift D.D. – The second portion* (Cambridge: CUP, 1842).

Ernest Barnes, *The Rise of Christianity* (London: Longmans, Green and Co, 1947).

Richard Bauckham, *God and the Crisis of Freedom* (Louisville: Westminster John Knox Press, 2002).

Basil of Caesarea, *Letter LIV,* in The Nicene and Post Nicene Fathers 2nd Series, Vol. VII (Edinburgh and Grand Rapids, T&T Clark/Eerdmans, 1996).

Bede, *A History of the English Church and People* (Harmondsworth: Penguin, 1968).

Bede, *The Exposition of the Apocalypse* (Downers Grove: IVP, 2011).

Thomas Bilson, *The Perpetual Government of Christ's Church* (Oxford: OUP, 1842).

The Book of Concord, 'A Treatise on the Power and Primacy of the Pope' at http://bookofconcord.org/treatise.php.

Dietrich Bonhoeffer, *The Cost of Discipleship* (London: SCM, 1959).

John Bramhall, *Protestants' Ordination defended*, in John Bramhall, Works, Vol. V (Oxford John Parker, 1845).

Gerald Bray, *Documents of the English Reformation* (Cambridge: James Clarke, 1994).

Colin Buchanan, Eric Mascall, J I Packer, and Graham Leonard, *Growing into Union* (London: SPCK, 1970).

Called to Witness and Service (London: Church House Publishing, 1999).

John Calvin, *Institutes of the Christian Religion* (Grand Rapids: W B Eerdmans, 1975).

David Cameron: 'Church of England should 'get on with it' on female bishops,' *The Guardian*, 21 November 2012.

The Canons of the Church of England, 8ed (London: Church House Publishing, 2022).

Canons of the Council of Antioch in *Nicene and Post Nicene Fathers* 2nd series, vol. XIV (Edinburgh and Grand Rapids: T&T Clark/Eerdmans, 1997).

Canons of the First Council of Constantinople in *Nicene and Post Nicene Fathers* 2nd series vol XIV.

Canons of the Council of Laodicea in *The Nicene and Post Nicene Fathers,* 2nd Series, vol. XIV.

Canons of the Council of Neo Caesarea, in *The Nicene and Post Nicene Fathers,* 2nd Series, vol. XIV.

The Canons of the Council of Nicaea in *The Nicene and Post-Nicene Fathers,* 2nd series, vol. XIV.

Canons of the Council of Serdica in *Council of Serdica (344)* at https://newadvent.org/fathers/3815.htm

Samuel Carr (ed.), *The Early Writings of John Hooper* (Cambridge: CUP, 1843).

Catechism of the Catholic Church (London: Geoffrey Chapman, 1994).

The Catechism of the Council of Trent at http://catholicapologetics.info/thechurc/catechism/Holy7Sacraments-Orders.shtml

Henry Christmas (ed.) *Nicholas Ridley - Works* (Cambridge Parker Society/CUP, 1843).

John Chrysostom, *Hom. In Tim.* in Kenneth Kirk et al. *The Apostolic Ministry* (London: Hodder and Stoughton, 1947).

John Chrysostom, *Hom. In Phil. i.1* in Kirk.

John Chrysostom, *On the Christian Priesthood,* trans Philip Schaff and William Stephens, (New York: Christian Literature Company, 1889).

Clement of Alexandria, *The Stromata, or Miscellanies* in *The Ante-Nicene Fathers*, vol. II (Edinburgh and Grand Rapids: T&T Clark/Eerdmans, 2001).

Clement of Alexandria, *The Instructor* in *The Ante-Nicene Fathers*, vol II.

Clement of Alexandria, *Who is the rich man that shall be saved?* in *The Ante-Nicene Fathers*, vol. II.

1 Clement in J B Lightfoot, J R Harmer and Michael Holmes, *The Apostolic Fathers*, 2ed (Leicester: Apollos, 1990).

The Clergy Discipline Measure 2003 as amended at https://www.churchofengland.org/sites/default/files/2017-10/cdm-2003-as-amended-by-scdm-jan-2017-as- published_0.pdf.

The *Clergy Discipline Rules 2005* at https://www.churchofengland.org/sites/default/files/2021-07/C%20D%20Rules%20%282021%29.pd.

Roger Coleman (ed.), *Resolutions of the twelve Lambeth Conferences, 1867 -1988* (Toronto: Anglican Book Centre, 1992).

Common Worship Ordination Services, 'introduction by the House of Bishops' at https://www.churchofengland.org/prayer-and-worship/worship-texts-and-resources/common-worship/ministry/common-worship-ordination.

Constitution of the General Synod at http://peterowen.org.uk/articles/gs-constitution.html.

Constitutions and Canons Ecclesiastical 1604 at https://www.anglican.net/doctrines/1604-canon-law/.

George Corrie (ed.), *Hugh Latimer, Sermons and Remains* (Cambridge: CUP, 1844).

George Corrie (ed.), *Sermons of Hugh Latimer* (Cambridge: CUP, 1844) .

Council of Carthage, *Letter to Celestine*, in E Giles *Documents Illustrating Papal Authority* (London: SPCK: 1952).

Council of Chalcedon, Canon 28, in B J Kidd, *The Roman Primacy to 461*, (London: SPCK, 1936).

Council of Chalcedon, Fourth Session, in in E Giles *Documents Illustrating Papal Authority* (London: SPCK: 1952).

Council of Chalcedon, *Letter to Leo I*, in Giles.

Council of Ephesus, *Letter to the Emperors Theodosius and Valentinian* in Giles *Documents Illustrating Papal Authority* (London: SPCK: 1952).

Council of Ephesus, *Letter to Celestine* in Giles.

Council of Ephesus, Third Session in Giles.

Council of Rome in E Giles, *Documents Illustrating Papal Authority* (London: SPCK: 1952).

Cyprian, *Epistle V* in *The Ante-Nicene Fathers*, vol. V (Edinburgh and Grand Rapids: Eerdmans, 1995).

Cyprian *Epistle XXVI* in *The Ante-Nicene Fathers*, vol. V.

Cyprian *Epistle, XL* in *The Ante-Nicene Fathers*, vol. V.

Cyprian *Epistle XLI* in *The Ante-Nicene Fathers*, vol. V.

Cyprian, *Epistle LVII.* in *The Ante-Nicene Fathers*, vol. V.

Cyprian, *Epistle LXIV* in *The Ante-Nicene Fathers*, vol. V.

Cyprian, *Epistle LXVI* in *The Ante-Nicene Fathers*, vol. V.

Cyprian *Epistle LXVII* in *The Ante-Nicene Fathers*, vol. V.

Cyprian *Epistle LXVIII* in *The Ante-Nicene Fathers*, vol. V.

Cyprian *Epistle LXX* in *The Ante-Nicene Fathers*, vol. V.

Cyprian *Epistle LXXVI* in *The Ante-Nicene Fathers*, vol. V.

Cyprian, *On the Unity of the Church*, in *The Ante-Nicene Fathers*, vol. V.

Martin Davie and Stephen Hofmeyr, *Visibly Different* (London: CEEC 2002).

Madeleine Davies, 'Radical Reform ahead if top-level plan adopted', *Church Times,* 11 February 2022.

Decree of the Council of Ephesus against Nestorius in *Nicene and Post Nicene Fathers*, vol. XIV. (Edinburgh and Grand Rapids: T&T Clark/Eerdmans, 1997).

The Dioceses, Pastoral and Mission Measure 2007 at https://www.legislation.gov.uk/ukcm/2007/1/contents .

Dionysius of Corinth, *Letter to Soter*, in E Giles, *Documents Illustrating Papal Authority* (London: SPCK: 1952).

Doctrine in the Church of England (London: SPCK, 1982).

Dogmatic Constitution on the Church in Walter Abbott (ed), *The Documents of Vatican II* (London: Geoffrey Chapman, 1967).

George D'Oyly, *A Letter to the Ecclesiastical Commissioners of England on the subject of reviving the institution of Suffragan Bishops* (London: Rivington, 1843).

Rod Dreher, *Live not by lies – A manual for Christian Dissenters* (New York: Sentinel, 2020).

The Ecclesiastical Jurisdiction Measure 1963 at https://www.legislation.gov.uk/ukcm/1963/1/contents.

Bart Ehrman, *The Apostolic Fathers,* Volume I (Cambridge: Harvard University. 2003), *Epistle of Clement to James* in *The Ante-Nicene Fathers*, vol. I (Edinburgh and Grand Rapids: T&T Clark/Eerdmans, 1995).

Eusebius, *Ecclesiastical History* (Cambridge and London: Harvard University Press, 1980).

Epiphanius of Salamis *The Panarion* in Philip Amidon, *The Panarion of St. Epiphanius, Bishop of Salamis* (Oxford University Press, New York, 1990)

First Dogmatic Constitution on the Church in Philip Schaff, *Creeds of Christendom* at https://ccel.org/schaff/creeds2.v.ii.i.html.

The five guiding principles at https://www.churchofengland.org/ sites/default/files/2017-10/the_five_guiding_principles.pdf.

The Form of Presbyterial Church Government at www.reformed.org/documents/wcf_standards/index.html?mainframe=/documents/ wcf_standards/p395-form_presby_gov.html.

Margaret Gibson, *The Didascalia Apostolorum in English* (London: C J Clay, 1903).

Lee Gatiss (ed.), *Gospel flourishing in a time of confusion* (Watford: Church Society, 2019).

Gildas, *Liber Querulus de excidio Britanniae* (A Public Domain Book: Kindle).

Charles Gore, *The Church and the Ministry*, revd. ed, (London: SPCK, 1936).

Gregory the Great, *The Book of Pastoral Rule* in The *Nicene and Post Nicene Fathers*, 2nd series, vol. XII (Edinburgh and Grand Rapids: T&T Clark/Eerdmans, 1997).

Gregory the Great, *Letters, Book 5*, in *The Nicene and Post Nicene Fathers*, 2nd series, vol. XII.

Gregory Nazianzen *Oration II* in *The Nicene and Post Nicene Fathers*, 2nd series, vol VII (Edinburgh and Grand Rapids: T&T Clark/Eerdmans, 1996*).*

Gregory Nazianzen, *Oration XXI* in *The Nicene and Post Nicene Fathers*, 2nd series, vol VII.

Gregory Nazianzen, *Oration XVIII* in *The Nicene and Post Nicene Fathers*, 2nd series, vol VII.

Gregory Nazianzen, *Oration XLIII* in *The Nicene and Post Nicene Fathers*, 2nd series, vol VII.

Gregory Nazianzen, *To Cledonius the Priest against Apolinarius* in *The Nicene and Post Nicene Fathers*, 2nd series vol. VII.

Growing Together in Unity and Mission (London: SPCK, 2006).

Joseph Hall, *Episcopacy by divine right asserted* (London: 1640).

P.J. Harland 'Menswear and Womenswear: A Study of Deuteronomy 22:5,' (*Expository Times*, 110, No.3, 1988), pp.73-76.

Arthur Headlam, *The Doctrine of the Church and Christian Reunion* (London: John Murray, 1920).

Hilary of Poitiers, *Tract XIV*, Ps 8.

Christopher Hill and Edward Yarnold (eds.) *Anglicans and Roman Catholics: The Search for Unity* (London: SPCK/CTS, 1994).

Hippolytus, *The Apostolic Tradition of Hippolytus of Rome* at www.bombaxo.com/hippolytus.html.

'The same Hippolytus on the Seventy Apostles' in *The Ante -Nicene Fathers*, vol. V (Edinburgh/Grand Rapids: T&T Clark/Eerdmans, 1995).

George Hobson, *The Episcopal Church, Homosexuality and the Context of Technology* (Eugene: Pickwick Publications, 2013).

The Homilies, Ian Robinson (ed.) (Bishopstone: Brynmill/Preservation Press, 2006).

The First Book of Homilies, Lee Gatiss (ed.) (Watford: Church Society, 2021).

Richard Hooker, *The Laws of Ecclesiastical Polity* (Oxford: OUP, 1841).

House of Bishops' Declaration on the Ministry of Bishops and Priests (GS Misc 1077) at https://www.churchofengland.org/sites/default/
files/2017-11/GS%20Misc%201077%20House%20of%20Bishops%
20Declaration%20on%20the%20Ministry%20of%20Bishops%20and%20Priests
%20-%20Guidance%20note%20from%20the%20House.pdf

The House of Bishops, *Living thankfully before God: Living fairly before each other* (London: The Archbishops' Council, 2010).

The House of Bishops, *The Nature of Christian Belief* (London: Church House Publishing, 1986).

The House of Bishops Working Party on Women in the Episcopate, *Women Bishops in the Church of England?* (London: Church House Publishing, 2004).

Ignatius of Antioch, *To the Ephesians* in J B Lightfoot, J R Harmer and Michael Holmes, *The Apostolic Fathers*, 2ed (Leicester: Apollos, 1990).

Ignatius of Antioch *To the Magnesians* in Lightfoot, Harmer and Holmes.

Ignatius of Antioch, *To the Philadelphians*, in Lightfoot, Harmer and Holmes.

Ignatius of Antioch *To Polycarp*, in Lightfoot, Harmer and Holmes.

Ignatius of Antioch, *To the Romans* in Lightfoot, Harmer and Holmes.

Ignatius of Antioch, *To the Symrnaeans* in Lightfoot, Harmer and Holmes.

Ignatius of Antioch, *To the Trallians* in Lightfoot, Harmer and Holmes.

Michael Ingham, 'Statement by Bishop Michael Ingham following the vote on motion 7' at https://www.anglican.ca/news/statement-by-bishop-michael-ingham-following-the-vote-on-motion-7/3005742/.

Innocent I, *Epistle 29 to the Council of Carthage*, in E Giles, *Documents Illustrating Papal Authority* (London: SPCK: 1952).

Innocent I, *Epistle 30 to the Council of Mileve*, in Giles.

Irenaeus of Lyons, *Against Heresies* in *The Ante-Nicene Fathers*, vol.I (Edinburgh and Grand Rapids: T&T Clark/Eerdmans, 1995).

Irenaeus of Lyons, *Letter to Florinus* in Eusebius, *Ecclesiastical History* (Cambridge and London: Harvard University Press, 1980).

Jerome, *Comm. in Tit.* I 6-7 in Kenneth Kirk et al. *The Apostolic Ministry* (London: Hodder and Stoughton, 1947).

Jerome, *Letter CXLVI to Evangelus* in *The Nicene and Post-Nicene Fathers*, 2nd series, vol. VI (Edinburgh and Grand Rapids: T&T Clark/Eerdmans, 1996).

Jerome, *Lives of Illustrious Men* in *The Nicene and Post Nicene Fathers*, 2nd series, vol. III (Edinburgh and Grand Rapids: T&T Clark/Eerdmans, 1996).

Philip Krey, *Nicholas of Lyra's Apocalypse Commentary* (Kalamazoo: Western Michigan University Press, 1997).

Thomas Lathbury, *A history of the convocation of the Church of England: from the earliest period to the year 1742* (London: J. Leslie, 1853).

Thomas Lathbury, *A letter respectfully addressed to the Right Hon. Sir Robert Peel, Bart., First Lord of the Treasury, on the Restoration of Suffragan Bishops* (London: John W. Parker, 1844).

Leo I, Epistle XIV.11, in John Kelly, *Early Christian Doctrines*, 4ed (London: A&C Black, 1980).

C S Lewis, *The Great Divorce* (Glasgow: Fontana, 1972).

Living in Love and Faith (London: Church House Publishing. 2020).

The Lollard Conclusions of 1394 in in H Gee and W R Hardy (eds) *Documents illustrative of the History of the English Church* (London: Macmillan 1896).

Martin Luther 'Preface to Jerome Letter 146' in *Works Vol.60* (St. Louis: Concordia, 2011).

Martin Luther, 'That a Christian assembly or congregation has the right and power to judge all teaching and to call, appoint and dismiss teachers, established by Scripture' (LW 39) in in Lee Gatiss (ed) *Fight Valiantly!* (Watford: Church Society, 2019).

Martin Luther, *The Small Catechism* at The Evangelical Lutheran Synod, https://els.org/beliefs/luthers-small-catechism/part-2-the-apostles-creed/.

Alasdair MacIntyre, *After Virtue* (London: Duckworth, 1983).

The Malta Report, 1968, paragraphs 17-20 at https://www.anglicancommunion.org/media/105272/the_malta_report.pdf

'Marks of Mission' at https://www.anglicancommunion.org/mission/marks-of-mission.aspx

The Martyrdom of Polycarp in J B Lightfoot, J R Harmer and Michael Holmes, *The Apostolic Fathers*, 2ed (Leicester: Apollos, 1990).

The Muratorian Canon at http://www.bible-researcher.com/muratorian.html

The Nashville Statement at https://cbmw.org/nashville-statement/.

Michael-Nazir Ali, 'Towards a theology of choosing bishops' in *Working with the Spirit: choosing diocesan bishops* (London: Church House Publishing, 2001).

Lesslie Newbigin, *The Gospel in a Pluralist Society* (London: SPCK, 1999).

John Newman, *The Restoration of Suffragan Bishops Recommended* (London: Rivington, 1835).

Oliver O'Donovan, *Begotten or Made?* (Oxford: OUP, 1984).

Oliver O'Donovan, *Transsexualism – Issues and Argument* (Cambridge: Grove Books, 2007).

One Body One Faith, 'The Change We Went to See' at https://www.onebodyonefaith.org.uk/about-us/the- change-we-want-to-see/.

'The Order for Morning Prayer' in *The Book of Common Prayer* (Cambridge: CUP, N.D.)

'The Order of Confirmation' in *The Book of Common Prayer.*

Ordinance for the abolishing of Archbishops and Bishops at https://www.british-history.ac.uk/no-series/acts-ordinances-interregnum/.

John Overall, *Convocation Book* at https://www.anglican.net/works/john-overall-convocation-book-1606-government-of-catholic-church-kingdoms-of-the-world/#p3-15.

J I Packer, *Taking God Seriously* (Wheaton, Crossway, 2013).

J I Packer, 'Why I Walked - Sometimes loving a denomination requires you to fight' at https://www.gafcon.org/sites/gafcon.org/files/resources/files/why_i_walked_by_ji_packer.pdf.

Papias, *Fragment X,* in *The Ante-Nicene Fathers,* vol. I (Edinburgh and Grand Rapids: T&T Clark/Eerdmans, 1996).

Polycarp. *The Letter of Polycarp to the Philippians* in J B Lightfoot, J R Harmer and Michael Holmes, *The Apostolic Fathers,* 2ed (Leicester: Apollos, 1990).

Richard Price and Michael Gaddis, *The Acts of the Council of Chalcedon* (Liverpool: Liverpool University Press, 2007).

The Principles of Canon Law Common to the Churches of the Anglican Communion (London: The Anglican Communion office, 2008).

The Queen's Coronation Oath, 1953 at https://www.royal.uk/coronation-oath-2-june-1953.

Michael Ramsey, *The Christian Priest Today* (London: SPCK, 1985).

Michael Ramsey, *The Gospel and the Catholic Church,* 2ed (London: SPCK, 1990).

The Porvoo Common Statement (London: Council for Christian Unity, 1993).

Reformatio Legum Ecclesiasticarum, in Gerald Bray (ed), *Tudor Church Reform* (Woodbridge: Boydell Press/Church of England Record Society, 2005).

Report of the Lambeth Conference of 1930 (London: SPCK, 1930).

Philip Rieff, *The Triumph of the Therapeutic* (Chicago: Chicago University Press, 1966).

John Robinson, *Honest to God* (London: SCM, 1963).

'The Root and Branch Petition (1640)' in H Gee and W R Hardy (eds) *Documents illustrative of the History of the English Church* (London: Macmillan 1896).

Jean-Jacques Rousseau, *Confessions* (Oxford: OUP, 2008).

J. C Ryle, *Charges and Addresses* (Hope Mills: Heritage Bible Foundation, 2011).

James Scholefield (ed), *The Works of James Pilkington* (Cambridge: CUP, 1842).

'The Second London Confession' in William Lumpkin, *Baptist Confessions of Faith* (Valley Forge: Judson Press, 1969).

The Shepherd of Hermas in J B Lightfoot, J R Harmer and Michael Holmes, *The Apostolic Fathers*, 2ed (Leicester: Apollos, 1990).

Siricus, *Epistle 1* in E Giles, *Documents Illustrating Papal Authority* (London: SPCK: 1952).

The Six Lambeth Conferences 1867-1920 (London: SPCK 1920).

Socrates *Ecclesiastical History* in *The Nicene and Post-Nicene Fathers* 2nd series, vol. II (Edinburgh and Grand Rapids, T&T Clark Eerdmans, 1997).

Sozomen, *Ecclesiastical History* in *The Nicene and Post-Nicene Fathers* 2nd series, vol. II (Edinburgh and Grand Rapids, T&T Clark Eerdmans, 1997).

Maxwell Staniforth, *Early Christian Writings* (Harmondsworth: Penguin, 1978).

Suffragan Bishops (The Church of England: GS Misc 733, 2001).

The Suffragan Bishops Act 1534 at https://www.legislation.gov.uk/aep/Hen8/26/14/contents.

The Suffragan Nominations Act at http://www.legislation.gov.uk/ukpga/Vict/51-52/56.

Stephen Sykes, 'A Theology of Episcopacy' in *Resourcing Bishops* (London: Church House Publishing, 2001).

Charles Taylor, *A Secular Age* (Cambridge Ma and London: Belknapp Press, 2007).

Jeremy Taylor, *Of the sacred order and offices of episcopacy* (London: Richard Royston, 1647), p.12, text at https://quod.lib.umich.edu/e/eebo/A64057.0001.001/1:1?rgn=div1;view=fulltext.

Tertullian, *Against Marcion* in *The Ante-Nicene Fathers*, vol. III (Edinburgh and Grand Rapids: T&T Clark/Eerdmans, 1997).

Tertullian, *An Answer to the Jews* in *The Ante- Nicene Fathers,* vol III (Edinburgh/Grand Rapids: T&T Clark/Eerdmans, 1997).

Tertullian, *On Baptism* in *The Ante-Nicene Fathers*, vol. III.

Tertullian, *On Modesty* in *The Ante-Nicene Fathers* vol. IV (Edinburgh and Grand Rapids: T&T Clark/Eerdmans, 1994).

Tertullian, *On Prescription Against Heretics* in *The Ante-Nicene Fathers*, vol. III.

Theodore of Mopsuestia, *Exp. In 1 Tim.* in Kenneth Kirk et al. *The Apostolic Ministry* (London: Hodder and Stoughton, 1947).

Theodoret, *Ecclesiastical History*, in *The Nicene and Post-Nicene Fathers* 2nd series, vol. III (Edinburgh and Grand Rapids, T&T Clark Eerdmans, 1996).

Graham Tomlin, *The Provocative Church* (London: SPCK, 2002).

Carl Trueman, *The Rise and Triumph of the Modern Self* (Wheaton: Crossway, 2020).

Philip Turner, 'ECUSA's God and the Idols of Liberal Protestantism' in Ephraim Radner and Philip Turner, *The Fate of Communion* (Grand Rapids and Cambridge: Eerdmans, 2006).

Twelfth Ecumenical Council: Lateran IV 1215 at https://sourcebooks.fordham.edu/basis/lateran4.asp.

James Ussher, *The Original of Bishops and Metropolitans* in Richard Snoddy (ed), *James Ussher and A Reformed Episcopal Church* (Lincoln: The Davenant Press, 2018).

Zeger Van-Espen, *Dissertatio de Misero Statu Ecclesiae Ultrajectinae* in F W Puller, *Orders and Jurisdiction* (London: Longmans, Green and Co, 1925).

Horace Walpole, *The Letters of Horace Walpole*, vol.4, https://www.gutenberg.org/cache/epub/4919/pg4919.html

Henry Walter (ed.), *Tyndale - Doctrinal Treatises* (Cambridge: Parker Society/CUP, 1848).

John Webster, *Holy Scripture* (Cambridge: CUP, 2009).

The Westminster Confession in J H Leith, *Creeds of the Churches*, revd. ed (Oxford: Basil Blackwell, 1973).

World Council of Churches, *Baptism, Eucharist and Ministry* (Geneva: World Council of Churches, 1982).

World Council of Churches, *New Delhi Statement* at https://www.oikoumene. org/resources/documents/new-delhi-statement-on-unity).

Working with the Spirit: Choosing Diocesan bishops (London: Church House Publishing, 2001).

N T Wright, *Scripture and the Authority of God* (London: SPCK, 2006).

Zosimus, *Historia Nova* in John Morris, *The Age of Arthur* (London: Phoenix, 1973).

Secondary Sources

Nicholas Adams, 'Pelagianism: Can people be saved by their own efforts?' in Ben Quash and Michael Ward (eds), *Heresies and How to Avoid Them* (London: SPCK, 2007).

James Anderson, *The Epistle of James* (Grand Rapids: Eerdmans, 1976).

J P Audet, *La Didache: Instructions des Apotres* (Paris: Gabalda, 1958).

Paul Avis, *Reshaping Ecumenical Theology* (London and New York, T&T Clark, 2010).

Sabine Baring-Gould, *The Church Revival* (London: Methuen, 1914).

Steven Bassett, 'Church and diocese in the West Midlands; the transition from Romano-British to Anglo-Saxon control' in John Blair and Richard Sharpe (eds), *Pastoral Care Before the Parish* (Leicester: Continuum, 1992), pp.13-40.

Richard Bauckham, 'James and the Gentiles (Acts 15:13-21) in Ben Witherington III (ed), *History, Literature and Society in the Book of Acts* (Cambridge: CUP, 1996).

Richard Bauckham, *Jesus and the Eyewitnesses: The Gospels as Eyewitness* Testimony, 2ed (Grand Rapids: Eerdmans, 2017).

W. Bauer, F. W. Gingrich and F. Danker, *A Greek-English Lexicon of the New Testament and other Early Christian Literature* (Chicago & London: Chicago UP 1979).

BBC *'Exposed: The Church's Darkest Secret'* , parts 1 and 2 on You Tube at https://www.youtube.com/watch?v=bNep7fCaj2g and https://www.youtube.com/watch?v=adoDCbr5_SA

Christopher Beeley, *Leading God's People* (Grand Rapids: Eerdmans, 2012).

Roger Beckwith, *Elders in Every City* (Carlisle: Paternoster Press, 2003).

William Beveridge, *Ecclesia Anglicana, Ecclesia Catholica* (Oxford: OUP, 1846).

Joseph Bingham, *Origines Ecclesiasticae*, (London: William Straker, 1843).

Dietrich Bonhoeffer, *The Cost of Discipleship* (London: SCM, 1959).

Paul Bradshaw, *The Anglican Ordinal: its history and development from the Reformation to the Present Day* (London: SPCK 1971).

Gerald Bray, *The Faith We Confess* (London: Latimer Trust, 2009) .

Allen Brent, *Ignatius of Antioch; A Martyr Bishop and the Origins of Episcopacy* (London: T&T Clark, 2009).

Raymond Brown and John Meier, *Antioch and Rome – New Testament Cradles of Catholic Christianity* (New York and Mahwah: Paulist Press, 1983).

E. Harold Browne, *An Exposition of the Thirty-Nine Articles*, 5ed (London: John W Parker and Son, 1840).

F. F. Bruce, *The Acts of Apostles*, 3ed (Grand Rapids and Leicester: Eerdmans/Apollos, 1990).

John Burgon *The Last Twelve Verses of the Gospel according to S. Mark* (Oxford: OUP, 1871).

John Burgon, *Lives of Twelve Good Men* (London: John Murray, 1891).

Gilbert Burnet, *An Exposition of the XXXIX Articles of the Church of England* (Oxford: Clarendon Press, 1819).

Arthur Burns, *The Diocesan Revival in the Church of England, c.1800-1870* (Oxford: Clarendon Press, 1999).

L A S Butler 'Suffragan Bishops in the Medieval Diocese of York,' *Northern History*, Vol. LXVIII, December 2000.

Fergus Butler-Gallie, *A Field Guide to the English Clergy* (London: Oneworld Publications, 2018).

George Caird, *The Revelation of St John the Divine* (London: A&C Black, 2ed, 1984).

John Calvin, *The Acts of the Apostles 1-13* (Edinburgh and London; Oliver & Boyd, 1965).

John Calvin, *The Complete Bible Commentary Collection of John Calvin.*

James Cartwright, *The Church of St James. The primitive Hebrew Christian Church of Jerusalem: its history, character and constitution* (Miami: Hard Press, 2017.

Owen Chadwick, *Michael Ramsey- A life* (London: SCM, 1998).

Frederick Chase, *Confirmation in the Apostolic Age* (London: Macmillan, 1909).

Bruce Chilton and Jacob Neusner, *The Brother of Jesus - James the Just and His Mission* (Louisville: Westminster John Knox Press: 2004).

John Collins, *Deacons and the Church: Making Connections between Old and New*, (Harrisburg: Morehouse Publishing, 2003).

John Collins, *Diakonia: Re- interpreting the Ancient Sources,* (Oxford: OUP, 1990).

Patrick Collinson, "Elizabeth I (1533–1603)", Oxford Dictionary of National Biography, Oxford University

Press, 2004; online edn, January 2012, doi:10.1093/ref:odnb/8636.

Patrick Collinson, *The Elizabethan Puritan Movement* (Oxford: OUP, 1998).

Andrew Damick, *Bearing God* (Chesterton: Ancient Faith Publishing, 2017).

Peter Davids, *Commentary on James* (Grand Rapids: Eerdmans, 1982).

Martin Davie, *A Guide to the Church of England* (London and New York: Mowbray, 2008).

Martin Davie, *The Athanasian Creed* (London: Latimer Trust, 2019).

Martin Davie, *The Gospel and the Anglican Tradition* (Malton: Gilead Books, 2018).

Gregory Dix, 'The Ministry in the Early Church' in Kenneth Kirk et al, *The Apostolic Ministry* (London: Hodder & Stoughton, 1947).

Eamon Duffy, *Saints and Sinners: A History of the Popes* (New Haven and London, Yale University Press, 2014).

James Dunn, *Unity and Diversity in the New Testament* (London: SCM, 1977).

George Edmundson, *The Church in Rome in the First Century* (London: Longmans, 1913).

David Edwards, *Christian England* (London: Fount, 1989).

W. R. Farmer, *The Last Twelve verses of Mark* (Cambridge: CUP, 1974).

Gordon Fee, *1 and 2 Timothy, Titus* (Exeter and Peabody: Paternoster Press/ Hendrickson), 1988).

Dick France, *Timothy, Titus and Hebrews* (Oxford: BRF, 2001).

Robert Gagnon, *The Bible and Homosexual Practice* (Nashville: Abingdon Press, 2001).

Jean Gaudemet, 'Chorepiscopus' in Andre Vauchez (ed), *Encyclopedia of the Middle Ages (London: Routledge, 2000).*

Moira Gibb, *An Abuse of Faith,* at: https://gallery.mailchimp.com/ 50eac70851c7245ce1ce00c45/files/28fa6c7e-0bf4-476b-ba2d- 81d2c85503c3/Report_of_the_Peter_Ball_Review_21.06.17.pdf

William Gibson, *James II and the Trial of the Seven Bishops* (Basingstoke: Palgrave Macmillan, 2009).

Kevin Giles, *Patterns of Ministry among the First Christians* (Melbourne, Collins, Dove, 1980).

Paula Gooder, *Diakonia in the New Testament: A Dialogue with John Collins,* p.10 at https://www.researchgate.net/publication/233653611_Diakonia_in_the _New_Testament_A_Dialogue_with_John_N_Collins.

David Gooding, *True to the Faith: A Fresh Commentary on the Acts of the Apostles* (London: Hodder and Stoughton 1990).

Charles Gore, *Roman Catholic Claims,* 3ed (London: Rivingtons, 1890).

W H Griffith Thomas, *The Catholic Faith* (London: Church Book Room Press, 1960).

W H Griffith Thomas, The Principles of Theology, 4ed (London: Church Book Room Press, 1951).

Donald Guthrie, *Galatians* (Grand Rapids & London: Eerdmans/Marshall, Morgan & Scott, 1973).

Donald Guthrie, *New Testament Introduction,* (Leicester, Inter Varsity Press, 1970).

Adolph von Harnack, *Der Brief des britischen Konigs Lucius an den Papst Eleutherus,* Sitzungsberichte der Koniglich Preussichen Akademie der Wissenschaften, 1904.

T. Harvey 'Presbyterianism' in Martin Davie, Tim Grass et al (eds.), *New Dictionary of Theology Historical and Systematic* (London & Downers Grove: Inter Varsity Press, 2016).

Adrian Hastings, *A History of Christianity in England 1920-1985* (London: Fount 1987).

Stanley Hauerwas, *Matthew* (London: SCM,2006).

Colin Hemer, *The Book of Acts in the setting of Hellenistic History* (Tubingen: Mohr, 1989), I H Marshall, (Luke: Historian and Theologian, Exeter: Paternoster Press, 1970).

David Holloway, *Episcopal Oversight – A Case for Reform (*Oxford: Latimer House, 1994).

Bengt Holmberg, *Paul and Power: The Structure of Authority in the Primitive Church as reflected in the Pauline Epistles* (Philadelphia: Fortress Press, 1980).

P E Hughes, *The Second Epistle to the Corinthians* (Grand Rapids: Eerdmans, 1992).

Larry Hurtado, *Destroyer of the gods* (Waco: Baylor University Press, 2016).

William Jacob, *The Making of the Anglican Church Worldwide* (London: SPCK, 1997).

Joachim Jeremias, *The Parables of Jesus* (London: SCM, 1994).

Paul Johnson, *A history of Christianity* (New York: Athanaeum, 1976).

Cheslyn Jones, Geoffrey Wainwright and Edward Yarnold (eds), *The Study of Liturgy* (London: SPCK, 1985).

'Jurisdiction' in *The New Oxford Dictionary of English* (Oxford: OUP, 1998).

John Kelly, *Early Christian Doctrines*, 5ed (London: A&C Black, 1980).

John Kelly, *The Pastoral Epistles* (London: A&C Black, 1986).

Eric Kemp 'Bishops and Presbyters at Alexandria, *'Journal of Ecclesiastical History*, Vol 6, Issue 2, October 1955, pp.125-142.

William Kerr, *A Handbook on the Papacy* (London: Marshall, Morgan and Scott, 1950).

David J Knight, *King Lucius of Britain* (Stroud: The History Press, 2012).

Richard and Catherine Kroeger, *I suffer not a woman (*Grand Rapids: Baker 1992).

Michael Kruger, *Canon Revisited* (Wheaton: Crossway, 2012).

Colin Kruse, 'Ministry,' in Gerald Hawthorne, Ralph Martin and Daniel Reid (eds), *Dictionary of Paul and his Letters* (Downers Grove & Leicester: Inter-Varsity Press, 1993).

Kenneth Latourette, *A History of the Expansion of Christianity, vol.1* (New York: Harper & Brothers, 1937).

Sandra Laville, 'Former bishop admits sexually abusing young men,' The Guardian, 8 September 2015.

J H Leith (ed.) Creeds of the Churches, revd ed (Oxford: Blackwells, 1973).

Peter Leithart, *The Gospel of Matthew Through New Eyes – Volume Two Jesus as Israel* (West Monroe: Athanasius Press, 2018).

Peter Leithart, *Revelation 1-11 (*London/New York: T&T Clark, 2018).

J B Lightfoot, *The Epistle of St. Paul to the Galatians* (Grand Rapids: Zondervan, 1966).

J B Lightfoot, *St Paul's Epistle to the Philippians*, 4ed (London & New York: Macmillan, 1891).

Iain MacKenzie, *Irenaeus' Demonstration of the Apostolic Preaching* (Aldershot: Ashgate, 2002).

Thomas Manson, *The Church's Ministry* (London: Hodder and Stoughton, 1948).

Joseph Mayor, *The Epistle of St. James*, 2ed, London: Macmillan, 1897).

Douglas Moo, *James* (Leicester & Grand Rapids: Inter-Varsity Press/Eerdmans, 2000).

Leon Morris, *Revelation* (Leicester: Inter-Varsity Press, 1983).

Robert Mounce, *The Book of Revelation* (Grand Rapids/Cambridge: Eerdmans revd. ed, 1998).

Stephen Neill, *Anglicanism*, 4ed (London: Mowbray, 1977).

Oliver O' Donovan, *On the Thirty Nine Articles* (Exeter: Paternoster Press, 1986).

Thomas Oden, *First and Second Timothy and Titus* (Louisville: John Knox Press, 1989).

Roger Olson, *The Story of Christian Theology* (Leicester: Apollos, 1999).

Michael Ovey, *Your will be done – Exploring eternal subordination, divine monarchy and divine humility* (London: Latimer Trust, 2016).

Ian Paul, *Revelation* (London/Downers Grove: Inter-Varsity Press, 2018).

David Petts, *Christianity in Roman Britain* (Stroud: Tempus publishing, 2003).

Colin Podmore, *Aspects of Anglican Identity* (London: CHP, 2005).

Colin Podmore, 'The choosing of bishops in the Early Church and the Church of England' in *Working with the Spirit: choosing diocesan bishops* (London: Church House Publishing 2001).

F W Puller, *Orders and Jurisdiction* (London: Longman, Green and Co, 1925).

Michael Ramsey, *Images Old and New* (London: SPCK, 1963).

Alan Richardson, *An Introduction to the Theology of the New Testament* (London: SCM, 1982).

Alan Richardson, *Creeds in the Making* (London: SCM, 1982).

Armitage Robinson, *William of Malmesbury 'On the Antiquity of Glastonbury,'* at https://en.wikisource.org/wiki/Somerset_Historical_Essays/William_of_Malmesbury_%27On_the_Antiquity_of_Glastonbury%27.

John Robinson and David Edwards (eds) *The Honest to God Debate* (London: SCM 2012).

George Salmon, *The Infallibility of the Church* (London: John Murray 1914).

David Scaer, *James the Apostle of Faith* (Eugene, Wipf and Stock, 1994).

Thomas Scott, *Commentary on the whole Bible,* vol.III (London: Jordan and Maxwell, 1803).

David M Smith, 'Suffragan Bishops in the Medieval Diocese of Lincoln,' *Lincolnshire History and Archaeology,* Vo.17, 1982.

Charles Smyth, *Cyril Foster Garbett, Archbishop of York* (London: Hodder and Stoughton 1959).

John Stott, *The Epistles of John* (Leicester and Grand Rapids: IVP/Eerdmans, 1988).

John Stott, *The Message of 1 Timothy and Titus* (Nottingham: Inter-Varsity Press, 1996).

John Stott, *The Message of 2 Timothy* (Leicester: IVP. 1973).

John Stott, 'The New Testament Concept of Episkope,' in R.P. Johnston (ed), *Bishops in the Church* (London: Church Book Room Press, 1966).

John Strype, *Memorials of Archbishop Cranmer,* Bk II, Ch.4 cited in Edgar Gibson, *The Thirty Nine Articles of the Church of England* (London: Methuen, 1902).

William Telfer, 'Episcopal succession in Egypt,' *Journal of Ecclesiastical History,* Vol. 1 Issue 3, January 1952, pp.1-13.

William Temple, *Readings in St. John's Gospel* (London: Macmillan, 1947).

Gerd Theissen, *The Social Setting of Early Christianity* (Edinburgh: T&T Clark, 1982).

A H Thompson, 'Ecclesiastical History,' in Kenneth Kirk (ed), *The Study of Theology* (London: Hodder and Stoughton, 1939).

Richard Trench, *Commentary on the Epistles to the Seven Churches in Asia* (New York: Charles Scribner, 1863).

Gregory Vall, *Learning Christ – Ignatius of Antioch and the Mystery of Redemption* (Washington DC: The Catholic University of America Press, 2013).

Zeger Van-Espen, *Dissertatio de Misero Statu Ecclesiae Ultrajectinae* in *Supplementum Ad varias Collectiones Operum* (Brussels: 1768)

Andrew Walls, 'Deacon,' in J D Douglas (ed), *The New Bible Dictionary* (Leicester: Inter-Varsity Press, 1962).

J W C Wand, *The High Church Schism* (London: Faith Press, 1951).

Daniel Waterland, *A Critical History of the Athanasian Creed* (London: Forgotten Books, 2015).

David Wenham, *The Parables of Jesus* (London: Hodder and Stoughton, 1989).

Michael Wilcock, *The Message of Revelation* (Leicester: Inter-Varsity Press, 1975).

Peter Williams, *Can we trust the Gospels?* (Wheaton: Crossway, 2018).

David Winter (ed), *Matthew Henry's Commentary, Acts to Revelation* (London: Hodder and Stoughton, 1975).

Theodore Wirgman, *The Doctrine of Confirmation* (London: Longman, Greem and Co, 1902).

Tom Wright, *Acts for Everyone, Part1* (London: SPCK, 2008).

Tom Wright, *Paul for Everyone – I Corinthians* (London: SPCK, 2003).

Tom Wright, *Paul for Everyone, The Pastoral Epistles 1 and 2 Timothy and Titus* (London: SPCK, 2003).

Tom Wright, *Paul for Everyone – The Prison Letters, Ephesians, Philippians, Colossians and Philemon* (London: SPCK, 2002).

Tom Wright, *Paul for Everyone, Romans, Part 1: Chapters 1-8* (London: SPCK, 2004).

Subject index

Page numbers with 'n' refer to a footnote. For example, 180n319 means footnote 319 on page 180. Numbers with 'app' indicate pages in the appendices.

Printed in Great Britain
by Amazon

86906541R10475